# Introduction to
# ECONOMICS

ENGLAND:        BUTTERWORTH & CO. (PUBLISHERS) LTD.
                LONDON: 88 Kingsway, W.C.2

AUSTRALIA:      BUTTERWORTH & CO. (AUSTRALIA) LTD.
                SYDNEY: 20 Loftus Street
                MELBOURNE: 430 Bourke Street
                BRISBANE: 240 Queen Street

CANADA:         BUTTERWORTH & CO. (CANADA) LTD.
                TORONTO: 1367 Danforth Avenue

NEW ZEALAND:    BUTTERWORTH & CO. (NEW ZEALAND) LTD.
                WELLINGTON: 49/51 Ballance Street
                AUCKLAND: 35 High Street

SOUTH AFRICA:   BUTTERWORTH & CO. (SOUTH AFRICA) LTD.
                DURBAN: 33/35 Beach Grove

U.S.A.          BUTTERWORTH INC.
                WASHINGTON D.C.: 7300 Pearl Street, 20014

# Introduction to
# ECONOMICS

*By*

ALEC CAIRNCROSS

*FOURTH EDITION*

LONDON
BUTTERWORTHS
1966

To
The Cambridge Economists
of all countries

# PREFACE TO THE THIRD EDITION

The writer of a textbook submits himself voluntarily to the punishment of Sisyphus: the labours of one edition are no sooner ended than time begins to undo them and preparations for the next must be faced. Reviewers, readers, and publishers form a solid pressure group, listing errors that need correction, passages that need re-writing, improvements that need to be made. The grateful author, conscious of his shortcomings, willingly consents to try again to master them and produce the perfect textbook.

But alas! the task becomes more forbidding each time it is attempted. One's colleagues write more and more books and there are more and more colleagues to write them. The enthusiasm which an author brings to the study of learned monographs at 25 has begun to flag at 50. The theories that seemed so simple that even beginners might understand them come to need more and more qualification and—what is worse—the theories, with all their qualifications, appear to throw a less vivid light on the problems of the real world.

Even when courage revives it is not easy to find the sticking-point. Will a little patching do or must one screw oneself up to start all over again? How much of the old text, composed in the thirties, is fit for human consumption in the sixties?

As a young man of 25 I could cheerfully put on the armour of older authorities and brave my readers with a borrowed omniscience. I was up-to-date because fresh from Cambridge, full of the confident over-simplifications that beginners need in order to excite them, and under little temptation to obtrude my own ideas for the simple reason that I had few to offer. I also enjoyed the advantage that I was not quite sure whether I had mastered the more difficult concepts and took special pains to resolve my doubts in the passages where those concepts were introduced. This very lack of facility in economic theory, by predisposing me against obscurity of argument, may have been instrumental in winning me the goodwill of readers who were similarly afflicted. I remember with gratitude encounters in this country and abroad—often in the most surprising places—with readers who appeared to bear me no grudge after struggling through an earlier edition of this book.

I doubt whether, now that I lack some of the advantages which I then enjoyed, I could face the writing of an entirely new elementary textbook. These things are for the young or the retired. Even if I could, the end-product would be very unlikely to suit the beginner: it would take too much for granted and strain too ardently after originality. The only practicable course open to me was to make extensive revisions of the more obsolescent chapters; and although this is not the book that I should write if I were starting afresh, it is probably better adapted to its purpose than the textbook that would have emerged after complete re-modelling.

Most economists would agree that the central theme of a newly-written textbook should be growth and development. But this is a theme that can be handled in various ways: one can, for example, study development at the level of the household, or of the firm, or of the economy as a whole, or of entire societies. I have elected to start from development of the individual business unit. This form of development is familiar to most readers; not so familiar that, as with development at the level of the household, analysis would seem platitudinous or paradoxical; nor so unfamiliar that, as with development at the level of the economy, analysis would be too complex for the beginner (and by no means only the beginner). The individual business is the natural unit to start from since it is within the individual business (and household) that most of the changes occur which add up to economic development in the larger sense. Concentration at the outset on the business unit has also the merit that it forces on the reader's attention the inter-connection between economic, administrative and technological problems—an interconnection of which other approaches make him too little aware. Finally—not to conceal the most important reason —this method of treatment happens to be the one originally adopted. I am advised that it meets the convenience of beginners; and to refrain from changing it, by a happy coincidence of wants, meets the convenience of the author.

In keeping the form, I have by no means, however, adhered to the substance. About half of Part I is new and there are extensive changes in Part II which now includes an introductory chapter on economic growth and development. Part V has been almost entirely re-written and I have also revised a good deal of Part VI. On the other hand, the middle parts on value and distribution, with the exception of Chapter 21, are largely intact. I am not at all sure what theory of distribution should be put in place of the one on which my generation was reared; and if the theory of value has advanced perceptibly over the past decade, I am not aware of any changes that those advances call for in an introductory textbook.

In deciding what revisions to make, I have profited greatly from discussions with Mr. D. J. Robertson, and am indebted to him also for comments on drafts of the early chapters. I have also had the advantage of comments from Mr. M. Gaskin on the chapters on Money and Employment. Mr. A. I. MacBean has helped me with a number of calculations and in the preparation of the index. I should also like to acknowledge the efforts of Miss Alison Lee to rescue my MSS from its native illegibility. Finally, my thanks are due to those readers who have been good enough to draw my attention to errors and misprints in the second edition.

GLASGOW
18 *May*, 1960.                                                          A.C.

# PREFACE TO THE FOURTH EDITION

I have taken advantage of the need for a new edition to make a number of changes and bring the figures up-to-date. Chapters 31 and 32 in the Third Edition have been recast so as to form Part VI and Chapters 33–35 have also been re-arranged and revised. Apart from this, the main changes are in Chapter 30 and the Appendix to Chapter 25. Minor changes will be found in some of the earlier chapters, notably Chapters 5 and 14. I have added a note on sources of current statistics.

LONDON
*March*, 1966.                                                          A.C.

# CONTENTS

# LIST OF TABLES

# LIST OF DIAGRAMS

# PART I—INTRODUCTORY

CHAPTER 1

# WHAT ECONOMICS IS ABOUT

Economics is not a subject that can be learned, like mathematics, as a series of propositions that follow from one another with the neatness of a Chinese box. It is much more like medicine, compounded of imperfect knowledge, worldly wisdom, obscure jargon and scientific analysis. The student of medicine learns many things about the human body that are meant to improve his powers of diagnosis; but he can make mistakes, and his patients can disagree with him, sometimes quite violently. The student of economics is in much the same position. He learns a great deal about the economy of his country and of other countries. But since he is studying things with which everybody is familiar, such as production, trade, and income, and his conclusions about these things do not usually rest on an infallible logic beyond the comprehension of the ordinary man, he is wise to get used to the idea, right at the beginning, that there is room for disagreement in economic diagnosis and that people will disagree with him.

To make matters worse, when he passes from diagnosis to treatment, he finds an uncomfortable gap between the two. It is one thing to analyse what is going on in some branch of the national economy but quite a different thing to prescribe treatment, or in other words recommend the policy that ought to be adopted. There is very rarely one single treatment appropriate to an economic disease and the ultimate selection may have to be guided by entirely non-economic considerations. An economist may be confident, for example, that he knows what is causing inflation and yet feel that this does not entitle him to say what, if anything, should be done to stop it. Some economists go so far as to argue that policy is not their affair and that they should content themselves with outlining the probable consequences of particular policies without coming down in favour of any of them. Even if this seems overscrupulous, it is right to remember that, in matters of policy, economic and non-economic considerations may have to be weighed against one another and that, in such matters, there is no single answer. In this, economics differs from the physical sciences,

I

where every difference of opinion can be put to the test of fact and, if the facts are known, resolved at once. Differences of opinion in the social sciences are not just differences about facts but may be differences about values. Everyone is entitled to his own view as to what matters most, and need not accept the pronouncements of experts if these pronouncements rest on a private conception of social priorities which he does not share.

All this is very confusing to a beginner who comes to economics in the hope of finding certainty. It is bad enough not to be quite sure what the subject is all about, or what the word "economic" means, but completely devastating to be told at the outset that there is no simple body of doctrine to be mastered and that, whatever an economist says, somebody is pretty sure to disagree. It might seem a waste of time to study anything so apparently inconclusive; but nobody gives up studying medicine because doctors disagree. Economics may be unlike many of the physical sciences which have an appeal for the man who likes one answer to every question; but it is in the same boat as most other subjects that deal with human behaviour and are unable to reduce it to the kind of inexorable scientific laws that govern the behaviour of atoms.

How can one learn a subject that seems to have no beginning and no end? By reading systematically through a textbook? Perhaps; although it is not uncommon for the dawn of understanding to come a great deal later. Learning economics is not unlike learning to talk. A child listens and makes noises and after a good deal of gibberish, begins to talk intelligibly; a student of economics does much the same and takes about the same length of time to master the vocabulary. There is usually no fixed sequence in which the different parts of the subject are grasped; an understanding of each part is necessary to an understanding of the others, so that the student has to go over the ground two or three times rather fast before he can see the interconnection of ideas. Wherever he begins, he must make the round and come back again to where he started; he must not assume that he can understand everything completely as he goes along.

Strictly speaking, therefore, what the beginner needs is something to serve as a cocktail: in which as in one of Shaw's Prefaces, everything is a little mixed and shaken together so as to leave behind a blurred but exhilarating vision and a growing appetite. Once he has tossed down an intoxicating dose or two, he is in a position to address himself more systematically to the solid fare of a textbook. Of course, this is not what happens. The beginner is too anxious to get to the meat of the subject, and with a proper sense of economy is shocked that anyone should expect him to buy, read, *and preferably forget* a book claiming to introduce him to an important intellectual discipline. The writer of a textbook, for his part, can no more bear than the Ancient Mariner to let his audience go before unfolding all he has to say with due solemnity.

## Plan of the book

The textbook writer must, however, begin somewhere and must at least appear to obey some logic in the order in which he moves forward. Here he comes up against a difficulty to which the reader should be privy. He can start by looking at the problems of the economy as a whole and encourage the reader to put himself in the position of the Chancellor of the Exchequer, faced with conflicting advice as to how to improve the standard of living, deal with a crisis in the balance of payments, prevent unemployment, stop prices rising, and so on; or he can start with more familiar, everyday matters, such as the things that shape the decisions of an individual business man about what to produce, what to charge for his product, when to instal new machinery and so on. Some readers fancy themselves as Chancellor and everybody would like to know more about how the country is run, so that many economists plump for the first alternative and call Part I of their textbook "Macro-economics" (or the analysis of the economy in the large). Other readers find "Macro-economics" hard going because it has never occurred to them to think of national income, capital formation and a whole lot of other abstractions that lie at the heart of this part of economic theory. They prefer to be introduced to these abstractions more gently and only after they have accustomed themselves to the more elementary level of discussion with which they meet in "Micro-economics" (or the analysis of the behaviour of individual consumers and producers).

In this book, the second, less exciting approach is adopted. The reader is given a brief glimpse of the higher peaks that lie ahead of him before being led off in Part II for a spell on the foothills of economic theory; most of this Part is devoted to an analysis of the forces governing production in the individual business, taking for granted the existence of a market. In Part III production is looked at in terms of the way it responds to market forces, the connection between these forces and the wants of consumers, and the mechanism by which, in the economic system we know, the pattern of production is made to match the pattern of consumers' wants. Part IV analyses the influence of market forces on the productive resources at the disposal of society, their allocation between different uses, the incentives they are offered and the rewards they obtain. Then in Part V comes an introduction to macro-economic problems, concentrating on fluctuations in economic activity and the forces causing them; this Part also deals with the role of banks and other financial institutions. Finally, Part VI discusses problems of international trade and payments and Part VII the general objectives of economic policy and the ways in which the state can contribute towards the achievement of those objectives.

### Treatment of subject-matter

So much for the plan of the book. But there is a further decision that the writer has to make at the outset: how is he to treat the questions that arise at each stage? He can try, for example, to be as general as possible and abstract from the detail of individual instances, the circumstances of this industry or that, the peculiarities of his own country and generation; the more he does this, the more he is carried towards exposition in terms of mathematical models, with a limited group of variables, each denoted by a mathematical symbol, to represent the significant factors at work. This involves a highly theoretical approach to economics and like all pure theory, it has the merit of training the student to frame questions and to frame them very precisely. But it is not a very satisfactory approach for the beginner unless he is both a skilled mathematician and has a wide knowledge of the facts of economic life. It is usually much more attractive to him if he can be given doses of theory rather sparingly while he familiarises himself with the practices of economic institutions. Many textbooks, therefore, swing to the opposite extreme and become little more than a descriptive analysis of particular institutions or, at best, of a particular economy. Even so, they cannot avoid abstraction, since without abstraction categories vanish and thought itself becomes impossible. But they do not oblige the student to adopt a radical attitude and ask himself what would happen under quite different institutions or in a quite different economy. He learns enough to make sense of what is going on here and now but without gaining much insight into what is transitory and what is part of the permanent make-up of economic life.

There are other possibilities. One is to lay emphasis on the historical development of economic variables: to explain what the historical experience has been in dealing with the problems that exercise us today, how magnitudes have altered, institutions have grown, attitudes have been modified. This can be a rather fruitless or even dangerous approach, since what has happened cannot tell us what to do. But it does help to convey a firmer grasp of the limits of effective action. The early economists thought well of the historical treatment of economic problems because it was their ambition to discover the laws of motion of society just as Newtonian physics studied the laws of motion in the natural world. It came into disrepute in the later nineteenth century when too much was claimed for it. Now it is making a come-back because economists have resumed their interest in the transformation and development of economies through successive stages of growth and because, simultaneously, they have begun to examine much more precise quantitative records of the economic growth of nations and to reach more confident conclusions from those records.

The textbooks of the future will certainly require to draw heavily on all this new knowledge and discuss the morphology of economic growth. Indeed, the time will come when it will be no more reasonable to cover the whole field of economics in a single volume than it would be to cover the whole of medicine. Different branches of the subject are already beginning to hive off so that even professional economists cannot pretend to be expert in all of them. Yet this increasing specialisation must remain limited, like all specialisation, by the market for which it caters. Economists may enjoy themselves writing for one another but if they think that their conclusions are of any practical value they must be prepared to explain and defend them to non-specialists in language free from jargon and technical shorthand. For nearly all that matters in economics, this is still possible; the important things that the specialists argue about can generally be translated, with some effort, into first-year stuff.

In this book little use is made of mathematical economics and there are few references to the growing science of econometrics which tries to fill the "empty boxes" of economic concepts like "elasticity of demand" by reducing the available statistics to mathematical formulae. The level of abstraction is comparatively modest; but no textbook can equip the student to handle economic problems if it does not teach him to use the normal tools of analysis in every economist's tool-kit. He cannot avoid grappling with concepts like "marginal cost", "the multiplier", or "gross national product", however little they convey to him on first acquaintance. All that can be done to help him find a way through the intellectual bog is to throw him plenty of illustrations and let him hang on to those until he is safely over. It helps some students, too—though not all— to have a point elaborated in a statistical table or in a diagram.

There is unfortunately little room in which to give an adequate historical slant to the problems under discussion. There is much to be said for starting off with an account of the rise of industrial society from the eighteenth century onwards and the controversies by which this rise was attended; for such an account, however, the student must look elsewhere. Some attempt is made throughout to give a sense of historical perspective but it is only in some of the later chapters that this becomes the dominant preoccupation.

## What is economics about?

Now let us turn back to the beginning and ask what economics is about. This is a natural question to put; but the beginner will get little satisfaction from the answers that economists usually give. Some economists give a precise definition which usually conveys nothing at all to the newcomer to the subject and is thought too narrow or too misleading by the average professional. The best course is to accept that economics is what economists write about and then look to see what they do write about by studying the table of contents of some textbooks. For example, it is obviously about money, banking and international trade; about wages and profits; about production, consumption and the standard of living; and so on. An alternative course is to look at the examination papers that first-year students of economics are invited to answer. For anyone wanting to find out what professional economists think their subject is about, there is no surer method than looking through the examination questions that they put.

A definition in terms of illustrations is never very satisfactory to the logical student. He wants to know what are the central problems of economics in the way that health and disease are the central problems of medicine. He is not particularly interested in exact definitions—after all, who would undertake to define health or disease with any precision?—but would like some working rule that tells him when he is well within or well outside the boundaries of the subject.

There are plenty of working rules. Alfred Marshall, the great Victorian economist, said that economics was about "man in the ordinary business of life"; not about all aspects of human behaviour, but about man as buyer and seller, producer and consumer, saver and investor, employer and worker. This definition has the advantage of stressing that economics is a social science, concerned with social problems. A definition which may give the beginner a more useful clue to the scope of the subject is that economics studies the part played by money in human affairs. It is about the getting and spending of money; how men earn a living and what sort of living they earn; how money affects their way of life and their outlook on life.

If we pursue this definition we find that economics is really not so much about money as about some things which are implied in the use of money. Three of these—exchange, scarcity and choice—are of special importance. Let us take them in turn.

## 1 Exchange

Money implies exchange. It is in fact the medium of exchange. In a primitive community, where exchanges are rare, we can dispense with money and resort to direct barter. Money is unnecessary so long as we are at the stage of trying to satisfy all our wants by our own efforts, growing our own wheat, milling our own flour, baking our own bread, and only now and again exchanging, say, wheat for a ploughshare or a calf for a millstone. But immediately we begin to specialise, and cease to produce goods for our own use, money becomes indispensable if exchanges are to take place smoothly. Exchange becomes triangular—we convert goods into money and money into other goods, instead of simply bartering goods for goods. If exchanges did not take place in this apparently circuitous way, no one who specialised in making bricks or bowler hats would relish a morning's shopping. The grocer might have no use for bricks; and match-sellers would hesitate to accept the hundreth part of a bowler hat. A walletful of money goes so much further than other walletfulls!

Nowadays, therefore, exchange rarely takes the form of direct barter. Instead, we do business with money. We buy what we want with money, sell for money, fix prices in terms of money, are paid our wages, salaries, or dividends in money, save money, and measure our wealth in money. But the problems which present themselves to us in terms of money are similar to the problems raised by direct barter. There is a surface difference between money-exchange and barter-exchange, but little difference in principle. Economics, therefore, does not limit itself only to money-problems but studies exchange-problems of all kinds. It is in fact, about exchange rather than about money, for exchange underlies the use of money.

**Exchange implies interdependence**—When we exchange, we have stopped being self-sufficing and have become dependent on those from whom we buy and to whom we sell. Our fortunes are linked with theirs. If they are poor or unemployed then we are likely to be in danger of poverty and unemployment ourselves. Famine and flood in one part of the world can create scarcity and distress thousands of miles away by cutting off supplies of foodstuffs and raw materials. We are all within the circle of exchange. Yet this interdependence rarely occurs to us: it is so easy to overlook the implications of exchange. Consider, for example, some everyday event like the purchase of a packet of cigarettes. I take from my pocket a small piece of metal—probably Mexican silver alloyed with Canadian nickel—and offer it to a total stranger who accepts it with alacrity. In exchange I receive a cardboard packet whose contents are the product of workers from all over the globe—Norwegian lumbermen, Turkish peasants, Malayan tin-miners, American inventors. I draw also on the services of British workers scattered over the country. But about all these workers, through whose efforts I am able to smoke my cigarettes, I am ignorant. Their creed, their way of living, their income, the colour of their skin, do not interest me. I can drive my bargain with them without even knowing that they exist. The cash-nexus that binds us is the loosest of bonds. If leaves me free to pursue my own interest, undeterred by any sense of moral obligation to other workers as fellow-citizens. They satisfy my wants and earn the means of satisfying theirs. And that, to most of us, might seem to be the end of the matter.

But *not* to the economist. It is precisely these exchange-bargains which he sets out to investigate. Why, he asks, do people exchange at all? What advantage does society reap from leaving people free to satisfy their wants by exchange? When is exchange fair and when unfair? Is it in the social interest that exchanges dictated by mutual self-interest should be left unregulated by the State? Or, if regulation is desirable, on what principles should the State intervene?

## 2 Scarcity

The use of money implies scarcity. Money itself must be scarce or it will cease to be used. If the supply of money is increased without limit it will soon lose value and in the end no one will accept it. Whatever passes as money, therefore, must necessarily be scarce. So also—and this is the important point must be the things that money will buy. We only exchange one scarce thing for another. We do not pay for air and earth and water unless somehow they are stinted just as the supply of money is stinted.

The fact of scarcity makes it necessary for us to economise, i.e., to make the most of what we have. We have constantly to be counting the cost, weighing up alternatives, and going without one thing so as to be able to buy more of another. Nominally it is money that we economise, for what we have to decide is whether to spend money on this or on that. What we are really doing, however, is to economise the things that money will buy. We try to buy, with our limited income, the collection of goods and services which gives us most satisfaction. We are faced with the fact that these goods and services are scarce, and we have to accommodate this scarcity as best we can to our wants and needs. Similarly, in earning money we have to husband our scarce time and energy in order to obtain as large a return as possible (in money *or* in amenities and personal satisfaction) for our efforts. On some men, of course, the pressure of scarcity and want bears harder than on others. On the millionaire, for example, the pressure is negligible; he can almost always neglect considerations of cost. But for others the necessity of making ends meet enforces constant self-denial.

**The economic problem**—What is true of each of us is true also of society as a whole. There is an economic problem of making the *social* income go as far as possible. The goods produced in any country are limited in amount and insufficient to maintain a standard of more than moderate comfort. There are very few things that can be provided free of charge, even in a rich country like Britain. We can make as much use as we like of public libraries and roads. But we cannot help ourselves to books and motor-cars, much less to food and clothing. The more of one thing is offered to us, the less can we have of other things. We cannot have more of *all* simultaneously. If A is free, B will be all the dearer. The provision of free motor-cars, for example, would lead to an expansion of the automobile industry and the transference to it of engineers, materials, and machinery from other industries. Motor-cars would be more abundant; but other things would be scarcer. Only if we set a very high value on motor-cars (like the value which we set on education and on health services) will we be prepared to face the cost of offering them free.

This need to balance value against cost is forced on every country by the insatiability of human wants and the scarcity of productive resources. It has to be decided what commodities, and how much of each should be produced; and the decision must rest, explicitly, upon estimates of cost and value. What costs a great deal and is of comparatively little value will not be produced at all; what is valued highly and costs little to produce will be provided first and in ample quantities; what happens with the large range of intermediate commodities will depend on the type of economic system and the way in which values and costs are measured.

It is as a result of our efforts to deal with scarcity (i.e., to economise) that exchange arises. We try to ration our limited means among the innumerable wants that compete for satisfaction and find that we can make our limited means go further by striking bargains with our neighbours. We give what we have in relative abundance—muscle or brain, professional knowledge or organising ability—for what is comparatively scarce, what we could not do, or could not afford to do, ourselves. We sell our time and energies and spend our earnings on what others have laboured to produce. In doing so, we are offering the goods or services in which our talents show to greatest advantage (or least disadvantage) for the goods or services which others are specially fitted to produce.[1] We are supplementing our deficiencies—our imperfect versatility, for instance—out of the proficiencies of others. Not only are we able to draw on the skill of others—skill which we may not possess at all—but we are also able to give our whole energies to a single task—one to which, either through practice or natural bent, we are far more fitted than those who engage in it only intermittently. By exchanging, we are making our efforts go further towards meeting our wants. We are reducing the pressure of scarcity and achieving economy. Exchanges arise, therefore, in order to alleviate scarcity, and scarcity is necessarily implicit in exchange.

## 3 Choice
The use of money also implies choice. We have to choose between the many

---

[1] This must not be taken to mean that everyone is engaged in just that occupation for which he is ideally suited—that would obviously be nonsense. What is meant is that people tend to specialise, *so far as their limited opportunities permit*, in the occupations which give fullest scope to their peculiar gifts and inclinations.

claims on our purse when we spend money, and between the many uses to which we might put our time and energy in earning it. We cannot spend the same evening in the cinema and in the theatre. We must choose one form of entertainment or the other. We may have to choose, also, between spending an extra shilling or so on a seat and spending the same shilling later on cigarettes.

Our choice, of course, is not always made rationally. That is, we do not always weigh up carefully the possible ways in which we might spend our money. We are much more lighthearted and irrational in buying sweets, for example, than we are in renting a house. We buy, very often, impulsively or through habit or force of example. Or we may buy because our "sales resistance" has crumpled at the sounding of some advertiser's trumpet. It is irrational to pay more than is necessary for a thing; and yet hardly a day passes but we buy goods without asking their price, or cannot be bothered to look for cheaper brands. We do not take the trouble to find out where prices are lowest; or we take excessive trouble to save a trifling sum, like the wealthy man who walks to save a penny fare. We do not budget for so much on clothes, so much on amusements, so much on food, so much on our savings account, and so on, but spend haphazard so long as the money lasts. Or at least that is what large numbers of us do. Perhaps, however, the careful housewife—and the tradition amongst economists is to think of housewives as the persons who hold the purse-strings— is more rational in her buying. The economic woman may be less of an abstraction than the economic man!

The way in which we make a choice is of great importance to the economist. For he cannot tell how much weight to place on the preferences expressed in the spending and earning of money until he knows how far these preferences are *rational* (i.e., self-consistent and giving due weight to all the facts). If, for instance, people persist in buying an expensive brand of cigarette it is important to know whether they buy it out of a liking for that particular brand or because they are ignorant of cheaper brands with the same flavour or because of snob-appeal in the advertisements. Until the psychology of cigarette-smokers is explained to us, we cannot say whether the production and the sale of these high-priced cigarettes involve a social waste. If smokers are rational there *may* still be a waste (for instance, the price may be kept high by a monopoly). But if they are irrational, there is certainly a waste; they are paying more than the cost of other cigarettes that would afford equal satisfaction.

In economics we begin by assuming that choice is rational. The so-called "economic man" is simply one who is completely "rational" in satisfying his wants, and pays no regard to the interests of others. It is, of course, an abstraction from the facts to assume that men are self-interested and rational. But to make this kind of abstraction is the only satisfactory procedure open to us.

If we assume that people are self-interested and rational, we can predict how they will behave given a certain monetary inducement, and we can work out an analysis of action and reaction. For instance, if similar goods are on sale at different prices, or similar jobs advertised at different rates of pay, we know that men will, other things being equal, purchase the cheaper goods, and apply for the better-paid job. If we could not make such generalisations if men were quite irrational, then we should never "get anywhere" in economics. So we begin by assuming that choice is deliberate and rational, without, however, overlooking the part played by impulse, custom, and inertia. Later, we may study the psychology of choice more closely; analysing what shapes our expectations and desires, and sifting what is basic in our wants from what is superficial or conventional. But to begin with, we ignore these difficulties, take people's desires for granted, and assume that choice is rational.

In the economic system as we know it in Great Britain, choice rests largely with the individual. His preferences go to determine what is to be produced and what is not. Every penny spent on A is a vote in favour of the production of A; every refusal to buy B is a vote against the production of B. The free choice of individual consumers between the goods competing on the market helps to determine what industries can carry on at a profit. The industries that cannot show a profit are not carried on at all. Those that show excessive profits attract competition and expand until people's wants—as indicated by the price which they are prepared to pay—are more adequately met. That is, if competition is possible and effective. But if some commodity is monopolised, consumers may be powerless to get what they want (and will pay for) in the proper quantity. They show their readiness to cast votes for more of the commodity by offering high prices for it. But the election is disregarded. No one is willing to stand against the monopolist. So he is able to preserve an excessive scarcity by keeping people out of his line of business. He makes things scarcer than people want them to be and earns high profits by doing so.

Thus a country like ours does not deliberately decide what industries fit best with its advantages and needs and on what scale they should be carried on. The decisions that might otherwise rest with a central planning authority take shape instead in the market. One industry expands and another contracts as consumers alter their preferences and purchases. The scarce productive resources of the community are not rationed between the different industries by some Planning Commission. They flow into the channels lubricated by the expenditure of consumers.

But is it desirable that the individual should retain so much freedom of choice? What if consumers are irrational or incapable of judging between competing goods? Would it be better to appoint a State Planning Commission with power to decide what kind of goods should be produced and what kind of jobs workers should be encouraged to take up? Should each man's daily rations be assigned to him as the average man's daily work is at present? With whom should choice rest, and through what agencies is it best exercised? Here is another batch of problems for the economist.

## A more precise definition of economics

We have seen that the use of money implies exchange, scarcity and choice, and that it is these things rather than money itself which are the starting-point of economics. Hence it is necessary to recast our preliminary definition of economics as the study of the part played by money in human affairs. We must find a more precise definition which goes to the roots of the matter. But which root? Some economists stress exchange, and others scarcity and choice. It might seem from what we have said that the act of exchanging is simply a way of overcoming scarcity and that it is therefore scarcity and its consequences that is the point of departure of economics. But it is possible to imagine circumstances in which scarcity exists and choice is free and yet there are no problems requiring analysis by an economist. Suppose, for example, that we lived in a Robinson Crusoe type of society in which everyone supplied his own requirements and was too busy "cultivating his garden" to exchange anything with his neighbours: or that society was organised on a Christmas Presents principle, every man working and giving away what he made, and living on the gifts that he received from others. Would these systems give rise to any specifically economic problems? The obvious answer is, no. There might be muddle and waste and bad accounting. But the problems of an exchange-system—for instance, those connected with tariffs, unemployment, taxation, and so on—would have no existence.

In the Christmas Presents society, choice is, so to speak, vicarious. People have to content themselves with whatever others provide for them, and are free to devote their time to their private hobbies, unharassed by the problem of making ends meet. There is no economic problem. Robinson Crusoe raises more difficult issues. Although he cannot exchange, he can exercise choice in conditions of scarcity. He illustrates how people set about satisfying their wants when exchange is impossible, and the study of his problems may be a useful preliminary to the study of exchange itself. But on his success in achieving economy, the economist, as economist, has little comment to offer. It may take an accountant or a philosopher to tell us when a man is getting the most out of his income, or making the most of his time. But it does not take an economist—who may be no more economical in this sense than other people. His job is to study economising once it takes on a *social* aspect: that is, once our attempts to economise impinge on the attempts made by other people. In our private lives we economise many things—words, patience, golf-clubs, and so on—that have no place in economics, because our acts of economy have no social repercussions. The problems of economy that face us are not always problems in economics.

Any definition of economics must allow for this social aspect of the subject and should not be couched exclusively in terms of scarcity and choice between alternatives. A possible definition would be: *Economics is a social science studying how people attempt to accommodate scarcity to their wants and how these attempts interact through exchange.*

## Economics and other subjects

A precise definition like this immediately suggests that there is a clear line of division between economics and allied subjects. This is not so. Economics overlaps with many other subjects which study our wants and their satisfaction —psychology, ethics, advertising, and so on. The connection betweeen these subjects may be illustrated from an example—cigarette-smoking again.

**Ethics**—Let us start with ethics. Suppose that I want to smoke a cigarette in defiance of my parents' wishes or in a crowded railway compartment. I may pause to ask whether it is right for me to smoke. This is a question for ethics, which discusses the moral aspect of wants. If, however, I ask whether the whole practice of cigarette-smoking is wrong I raise an economic as well as an ethical problem. I cannot decide whether smoking is good or bad until I know a good deal about the *consequences* of smoking, and to obtain this knowledge I may have to consult an economist. I may be afraid to condemn smoking because, for example, if everyone gave up smoking, there might be a big increase in unemployment. An economist would be able to assist me in judging what stress to lay on this danger.

Not only do ethical problems lead on to economic problems: the reverse is also true. It is hard to keep a discussion of any economic problem free from moral judgments of right and wrong. If I ask whether cigarettes sell for more than they cost to produce, and why that should be, I am sticking to "pure" economics. But immediately I ask whether it is *fair* to charge such high prices, or whether it is *right* for girls to be paid such low wages for drudgery in a cigarette factory while the managing director earns perhaps ten times as much, or whether it is *in the public interest* to admit Virginian and Empire tobacco to the British market on the same terms—in fact, if I ask any of the questions I am likely to ask—I cannot be answered to my satisfaction unless I make plain what

I consider "fair", or "right," or "in the public interest": that is, unless I lay down definite principles of fairness and justice. In the problems of the real world, moral and economic issues are hopelessly tangled up. We can unravel the threads calling this moral, and that economic. But in the answer to the problem, they must be woven together. However reluctant economists may be to introduce the brittle thread of ethics (so often snapped by disagreement) into their analysis, they cannot offer the guidance which is so urgently sought of them unless they do. They can explain how the economic system works without putting the mantle of philosophy over the rather drab working clothes of economic science. But they cannot say how the system can be made to work *better*. They can offer light, but not fruit; and it is fruit for which most people turn to economics. Immediately the economist does venture to offer counsel—as is expected of him—he appears in the rôle of sheep in wolf's clothing, economist turned philosopher. That is a rôle which he must play consciously—not sheepishly, as if there were no wolf's clothing there!—if his conclusions are to command attention and respect.

**Politics**—The same difficulty of demarcating the province of the economist is also raised by politics. Again there is apparently a clear line of division in subject-matter while in practice the line is often difficult to draw. Politics studies our wants, not for goods and services, but for things like equality, justice, and order. These are wants which are satisfied, not by reducing the pressure of scarcity, but by making people behave in certain ways. If we want order, for example, we want power to impose standards of conduct on our fellows; we do not allow people to behave as they choose, but pass laws denying some rights and upholding others. Thus if smoking were forbidden by law, the justification of this provision would be a matter for the political philosopher. He might try to discover, for instance, whether, if the principle involved were extended to parallel situations, its acceptance would be likely to command general approval. Quite possibly he would find it hard to decide without some knowledge of economics. This would be even more essential if a proposal was made to tax smoking severely without prohibiting it. If, finally, the Chancellor of the Exchequer wanted advice about proposals to raise the duty on tobacco and to grant a subsidy to tobacco-growing he would be likely to consult an economist rather than a political philosopher. In giving advice, the economist would again be filling a dual rôle, for the questions put to him would raise issues in politics as well as in economics.

How far-reaching this overlapping of economic and political problems might become can readily be appreciated if we suppose that the onus of deciding what commodities to produce, and how much of each, came to rest entirely with Parliament. The consumer would cease to vote for this industry or that by spending money on its products and would vote instead for the candidate who promised him more guns or butter or whatever he happened to want most. The elector would replace the consumer. A system of rationing would be in general use and exchange would continue only on a limited scale. Economic and political issues would be almost indistinguishable.

**Psychology and technology**—The relationship of economics to the other subjects studying human wants is simpler to explain. If we ask, for example, why people want to smoke, we shall have to go to psychology, and probably also to history and physiology, for an answer. If we ask how cigarettes are produced, we shall be forced to study the technique by which tobacco is grown, blended, and packed, the technique of engineering, the technique of paper making, the technique of printing, and so on indefinitely through the whole range of science. In economics we begin by taking wants and technique for granted and do not inquire either how the want arises or how it can be satisfied. Our questions are in terms of cost and value, not of motive or technique. But it is impossible to ignore either of these. Take motives, for example. The broad assumptions on which economics is built up are essentially assumptions about motives, and these assumptions may, if we neglect psychology, lose touch with the facts. We cannot lightly assume, for instance, that the general desire of business men is to maximise their profits and that this desire does not conflict seriously with more ultimate desires like those for power or social distinction or for creative activity and a rôle in life. A business may stop short of its most profitable size or expand beyond it because the owner does not think exclusively in terms of maximising his profits. The more complex men's motives are, the more does a knowledge of psychology become indispensable to the economist. Similarly with technique. There may be nothing in the description of, say, a coal mine to call forth the special talents of the economist. But if he takes the trouble to see a mine at first hand he may cease to make foolish statements that bring his profession into disrepute. That is, he should know what he is talking about. Before discussing speculation, for example, he should know something of stock and commodity exchanges; before discussing the price of cloth, he should be familiar with the chain of processes that lie between the growing of raw cotton and the finishing and dyeing of cotton fabrics. He should know how things work.

## Why economists disagree

The close connection between economics, ethics, and politics—and we shall meet with plenty of examples later—makes it easy to understand why economists disagree. They are likely to disagree whenever they do not share the same political sympathies, the same conception of social justice, or the same intuition of what is practicable. The more the problem admits of scientific treatment, the more do economists approach to unanimity. But even in purely technical problems, into which ethics and politics do not enter, there is plenty of disagreement.

## The value of economic studies

For some people, the value of economics lies in disciplining them in sustained thinking about social problems. The student who is accustomed to a slipshod dogmatism, and is unaccustomed to tracing the consequences of admitted facts through chains of reasoning, stands to gain enormously from the discipline which the study of economics imposes on him. He comes to see what it is that he is assuming and becomes alive to the wider implications of those assumptions. He is forced to state his argument quite unambiguously, so that verbal mis-understandings are cleared away. He learns to be more impartial and look at all sides of the question; to generalise properly by distinguishing what is relevant from what is irrelevant; and to pay more attention to the average, inconspicuous case (as revealed, for instance, by statistics) and less to the few striking instances under his nose. For others, the value of economics lies mainly in shaking them out of an unreasonable complacency in their political philo-sophy. They may be all for changes in the wage-system or in the money-system which are either demonstrably impracticable, or practicable only if accom-panied by further changes in which they are not prepared to acquiesce. Or they may be for no changes at all, without having weighed the case for and against. They may be roused to think for themselves on encountering the wide range of points of view which economists express, and accept less readily the dogma and propaganda purveyed so liberally by all the agencies which control public opinion.

Above all, economics is of value in allowing us to judge and frame policies in the light of full knowledge of how the economic system works. Everyone, willy-nilly, is an economist, for everyone has his view of how economic forces work, and what, if anything, should be done to control them. We all at some time or another maintain that workers should be paid a "living" wage, or that there is a deficiency of purchasing power, or that rents are too high, or some such proposition. These are propositions which one must be an economist of sorts to debate. But, of course, "economists of sorts" are not trained economists. The trained economist discusses propositions of this kind with the help of a whole apparatus of thought—what is called "economic theory"—which has the same advantage over untrained common sense that medical science has over popular medicine: with this reservation—that the ordinary man has a much sturdier disbelief in the pretensions of economists than in the pretensions of doctors. He makes no claim to understand or dispense with the higher calculus; but economic theory, chiefly because of an exaggerated impression of the failure of economists to agree, is all too frequently dispensed with. The result is that elementary misconceptions flourish everywhere: in the conduct of business, in moral judgments, and in public policy. Economics is to these misconceptions what chemistry is to alchemy, or astronomy to astrology. It does not furnish a panacea or a creed. But it does serve the negative purpose of discrediting the crank and the charlatan; and it inculcates a technique of thinking without which a sound judgment of affairs is hard to come by.

One final point. It must not be supposed that economists are blind to everything but economy and efficiency. They may, privately, have a great liking for uneconomical and inefficient ways of doing things. But they assume that most people would prefer to work less hard or in more congenial occupations if they suffered no loss of income in doing so; that is, they assume that an economy of human effort is, in present circumstances, desirable, and that if there is some more efficient way by which the work of the world could be done, then it would be a pity not to try to discover it. They are interested mainly in *money*-incomes and *money*-costs—in making money-incomes high and money-costs low. But they do not suppose that every rise in incomes and every cheapening of goods and services is an advance in human welfare. For they know that the things that money will buy are not what men most desire; and that cheapness in money-costs may conceal dearness in flesh and blood, in social amenities, in human needs and enthusiasms.

Economists, then, do not regard money and the things that money will buy with a special veneration. But they know more vividly than others, how enormously monetary considerations influence human conduct. They know that those who affect to despise money are generally well provided with it. They know that men tend to believe what it is in their interest to believe and that men's interests are inseparably linked with their bread and butter and the way it is earned. They know how unemployment and poverty can change men's minds as well as their bodies: how the course of our lives depends on the income and occupation of our parents: how the desire for power and mastery can be turned to acquisitiveness and greed. Knowing these things, economists are in no danger of underrating the economic factor in human affairs. But they can also avoid exaggeration. They have learnt something of the plasticity of human motives and ambitions and know that the hope of gain and the fear of unemployment have not always been the main incentives (and will not always be the most effective ones) for contriving that the work of society is done. Money and jobs are not the only human obsessions. It happens that the rôle which a man plays in life has come to depend more and more on the economic function which he performs and the social standing which his income obtains for him. But the time may come when prestige attaches to other and more important things than a man's income or his job, when the tiresome necessity of earning a livelihood has become less pressing, and qualities of spirit have come into their own.

CHAPTER 2

# THE CENTRAL PROBLEMS OF ECONOMICS

Imagine that you decide to open a shop and have a limited amount of capital to enable you to do so. You would have many things to decide, some of them personal and of no special interest to the economist, but many of them typical of the decisions that economists study.

(i) First of all, you would have a settle *what* you proposed to stock and sell. If you decided, for example, to become a grocer you would have to limit the range of groceries you stocked, if only because of limitations of space, and you would have to decide *how much* of each item you wanted to stock. From time to time, you might change your mind if the turnover did not match your expectations, and at the end of a year or two, the stock would perhaps be quite different from what it was at the beginning.

(ii) You would also have to make up your mind what group of customers you were aiming to supply—*for whom* you were providing shopping facilities. Would you select your stock, arrange your window display, and offer credit terms with an eye on well-to-do customers or would you aim at a mass market that was much more sensitive to the price of your goods?

(iii) Next, you would have to decide *how* you proposed to carry on the business: whether, for example, to make it a self-service shop or one in which you served your customers from behind the counter; how much use to make of credit; what deliveries you were prepared to make to customers' homes; and so on.

(iv) You would have to make a further decision as to *where* to site your shop, and whether it might be useful to open a branch in some other locality. You might want to be near the centre of town or prefer to pick a suburban area where you saw a better chance of a growing custom.

(v) At some stage, you would be faced with opportunities of expansion: *how rapidly* would you want to grow and what risks would you be prepared to run in order to speed up the process? How, for example, would you obtain the necessary finance—out of your own profits or by borrowing elsewhere? Would you be prepared to buy out a competitor or build new branches or enlarge your existing shop?

(vi) There would also be considerable fluctuations in your turnover, sometimes because of seasonal factors, sometimes for other reasons. How would you try to cope with these fluctuations and *how would you secure a steadier turnover*?

## Micro-economic decisions

The economist is interested in how you would make these decisions, not because he wants to help you to make them wisely—although his training and knowledge may be of some service if he offers you advice—but because he wants to examine the social implications of your behaviour. What he asks himself is whether if everybody is free to open a shop, the shopping facilities that will then come into existence will give the consumer what he wants without using up resources of man-power and capital that would be better employed in some other way. Might there not be too many shops, or excessive distributive margins, or shops of the "wrong" kind, in the "wrong" places? Would shopping facilities adapt themselves quickly enough to changing techniques of distribution, changing social habits, the growth of new towns and new suburbs? Would it be better if the freedom of decision of individual shop-keepers were limited by laws and by-laws or if the government itself entered the field and began to build and operate certain types of shop?

Before he can attempt to answer any of these questions, the economist has to think, not of policy recommendations, but of what actually happens. He has to make an intensive study of the way in which competition works. What leads to the opening of more shops? What is it that determines the success of one kind of shop and the failure of another? Why are small shops able to compete effectively against larger shops and chains of shops? What governs the retail margin that shops are able to charge? It is only when questions of this kind have been answered, that it is possible to reach conclusions about the advantages or failings of competition in distribution.

Shopkeeping is only one activity among many. Unless he is making a special study of it, the economist is not interested in shopkeeping as such. He is looking for general principles applicable to a wide range of activities and he cannot take it for granted that shopkeeping is typical. So although he may cite it by way of illustration, he has also to look at other activities, such as manufacturing, or agriculture, or teaching, to see whether different principles apply there.

## Macro-economic decisions

When he is talking about the decisions made in an individual business the economist is in the realm of micro-economics. But there are also macro-economic decisions that are essentially similar and have to be taken about the economic system as a whole. This does not mean that they are taken consciously by one person or group of persons; they may be settled by the movement of events or represent the outcome of all the decisions taken by individual producers and consumers in relation to their own affairs. Whether taken consciously or not, decisions have to be arrived at in every economic system about the aggregate production of the community that are parallel to the decisions made by the individual shopkeeper about the services he provides. This will be more apparent if we run over the decisions listed above.

### (i) Allocation of resources

First, what is to be produced? In every society, whether it be Russia or the United States, Italy or Melanesia, it is necessary to decide *what* commodities, and *how much* of each, to produce. The way in which the decision is taken and the kind of people who take it, are, of course, very different in different countries. The responsibility may rest with the government, operating through a bureaucracy, and planning the level of production in each industry; or it may be left to market forces and the free choice of consumers and producers; or the matter may be settled largely by social custom in communities where there is no central government and nothing corresponding very closely with the economist's conception of a free market. In practice, governments normally take some responsibility, but make use of market forces, these forces in turn operating within a framework of social custom. The difference between economic systems is largely one of degree—the degree to which governments override the forces of the market, and the degree to which these forces are shackled by custom and tradition. In the modern world, every system is a mixed system, whether it is Capitalist or Communist, industrial or pre-industrial, and the mechanism by which the pattern of production is ultimately determined is a highly complex one.

The study of this mechanism occupies an important part of economic theory. In particular, it is not easy without the help of economic theory to understand how market forces operate. It would seem easy for the government to make a set of clear-cut decisions about the use of productive resources, in the same way as an army commander issues a set of instructions to his troops in order to give effect to a plan of campaign, or a works manager establishes a production programme and makes arrangements to carry it out. But these analogies, except perhaps in war-time, are misleading. The aim of production is not to win a battle but to satisfy consumers' wants; the government cannot dragoon consumers into wanting what it says they are to be allowed, or compel workers into exerting themselves in the job which it says they must do. There can be no simple strategy that resolves the problems set by scarcity of resources so long as consumers are not all alike in their wants and it is these multifarious wants to which production must be geared. The less the government is prepared to use compulsion, the more it must make use of some indicators of consumer demand; and no one has yet devised indicators that successfully replace the operations of the market, in which the free choice of consumers registers itself in the purchase of one commodity and the rejection of another, while the free choice of producers helps to set the terms on which both commodities are offered for sale.

The government may, of course, refuse to accept market indicators as final and may bring into play its powers of compulsion. A well-known Soviet economist, Professor Ostrovityanov, contesting the heresies of his Polish colleagues, put the orthodox Marxist view of the matter in these terms: "the idea is widespread among foreign (sc. Polish) economists . . . that output should be regulated by the free fluctuation of market prices . . . under the influence of supply and demand. Such ideas involve the unleashing of elemental forces and would cause anarchy in production, contradicting the very essence of the socialist planned economy."[1] But even in the U.S.S.R. market forces do exert great influence on the planning of production. Similarly in capitalist countries there never has been a time when governments completely abstained from regulating production (for example, by protecting or subsidising particular industries) and they have shown increasing unwillingness to allow market forces undisputed sway. In war-time, indeed, the capitalist system in countries like the United Kingdom came to have a close family resemblance, in respect of production planning at least, to the system that has evolved in communist countries.

Experience in war-time showed how little understood by "capitalist" business men were the forces of the market that are supposed to govern the allocation of resources under the capitalist system. If a business man moved from the running of a large firm to the central control of an important raw material, he was liable to take it for granted that when the material became scarce it should at once be rationed. It hardly occurred to him that it might be better to let it become dearer, with a view to enforcing economy on consumers and inducing a larger supply from producers. His attitude, that is, was that of someone accustomed to obtain results within an existing organisation by direct action rather than that of a believer in the free play of market forces. He would have been hard put to it to explain why one "treatment" should be right in war-time and the other in peace-time. But it is precisely because the answer to conundrums

---

[1] Quoted by A. Nove, "The Problem of 'Success Indicators' in Soviet Industry", *Economica*, February, 1958, p. 12.

like this is not obvious that economists have given so much thought to the way in which supply and demand operate.

**The theory of value**—The branch of economic theory in which issues of this kind are discussed is often referred to as the theory of value, but it could equally well be called the theory of cost or the theory of output. It deals with the allocation of resources between different uses (and so with output); and with economy in the use of resources (and so with the value of output in relation to its cost in input). The theory may either be formulated in terms of production or in terms of price and cost, depending largely on whether the point of view adopted is that of the producer or the consumer. In this book the theory is approached through the discussion in Part II of how individual producers behave, and developed at a more abstract level in terms of prices and costs in Part III.

It must not be imagined that in the theory of value or any other part of economic theory, economists have discovered a touchstone for the ideal or optimum combination of goods that a community with given resources should produce. What should be produced depends upon what people want, and what people want is not just a bundle of goods on sale in the shops but something that satisfies much deeper urges than can be satisfied by the spending of money. So far as the issue is whether one bundle is nearer than another to what people want, economists can usefully comment on the tests by which this might be decided and on the situations in which reliance on market forces alone would be unwise. They can have a more positive rôle in analysing what would be likely to happen if something were done (e.g., by the government) to interfere with the workings of the market; *if* a commodity were rationed; *if* output were to be cut down; *if* the price were to be put up; and so on. In other words, they are particularly concerned with *changes* in the use of resources, including those changes that represent a deliberate attempt to control and regulate market forces.

### (ii) The distribution of income

The second question in our list was: *for whom*? The same question arises in relation to total output: whose wants is production intended to satisfy? When we talk about the consumer exercising his free choice we have to recognise that this freedom is limited by the purchasing power at his disposal and that in this sense a rich man has more freedom and can exercise a bigger pull on production than a poor man. When we look back to the first question, therefore, we may feel a little doubtful whether it is right to take consumer demand as the inevitable starting-point in the planning of production. Is it as important to produce the luxuries that a rich man wants to buy as to produce the food and clothing of which the poor are unable to buy enough?

A rich man may say that what he spends is his own money and that he has earned it. But this is not an argument that the Chancellor accepts in levying taxes: what we earn we owe to the favourable conditions in which we live far more than to any personal exertions, and our right to retain and spend our income rests, not on those exertions, but on the advantages to society of the institution of private property.[1] If we can be forced to part with some of our income in taxation, we can also be denied the right to purchase some commodities or more than a fixed amount of some of them. In a famine no one supposes that food should be reserved for the highest bidders; and in war-time and other emergencies, production is not allowed to respond freely to effective demand. Even in normal circumstances, the fact that purchasing power is unequally distributed between different consumers may be a compelling reason for penalising or limiting some forms of production and encouraging or subsidising others. It may be thought desirable, for example, to build more houses and offer some of them at less than an economic rent to poorer tenants in order to prevent the next generation from being brought up in hopelessly overcrowded conditions.

If a country goes too far in suppressing the advantages of a larger income, it runs the risk of endangering its production plans. These plans may rest on the offer of differential rewards to particular groups of workers or high returns to investment in risky enterprises; and if higher purchasing power is never allowed to be reflected in higher consumption of so-called luxuries, it is likely to lose its appeal and result in apathy, immobility and lack of enterprise. Production and the sharing out of what is produced are not two completely separate problems since the one reacts on the other. The share that anyone gets affects his output; and at the same time if it is desired to produce more of one set of things and less of another those who produce the first set are likely to obtain a bigger share of total output and those who produce the second set are likely to have their share reduced. "To each according to his needs, from each according to his abilities" is all very well as a slogan but what each man gets affects what each man gives.

The economist is no more entitled to say what is the ideal distribution of

---

[1] "The organiser of industry who thinks that he has 'made' himself and his business has found a whole social system ready to his hand in his skilled workers, machinery, a market, peace and order—a vast apparatus and a pervasive atmosphere, the joint creation of millions of men and scores of generations. Take away the whole social factor and we have not Robinson Crusoe, with his salvage from the wreck and his acquired knowledge, but the naked savage living on roots, berries and vermin." (L. T. Hobhouse, *The Elements of Social Justice*, pp. 162–63; quoted by Paul Samuelson, *Economics* (1st edition) p. 484n.)

income than he is to say what is the ideal pattern of production; indeed, he can probably contribute less to the discussion of this issue since he cannot so readily work out tests on plausible assumptions. His contribution is again likely to be one of explaining the effect of market forces on the distribution of income and the probable consequences of interfering with these forces. The actual distribution of income in any country obviously depends on a great many other factors: force, fraud, luck, taxation, the laws governing inheritance, social mobility, and the importance attached to wealth, all play a part varying with the institutions, attitudes, and values of the community. It would be impossible to generalise all these influences into a simple set of propositions; and the economist does not pretend to anything so ambitious. His humbler, and more fruitful, task is to try to foresee the less obvious consequences of trying to *change* the distribution of income.

In carrying out this task, the economist makes use of what he has already established in the theory of value. He is able to do this because he first resolves income into its component elements of wages, rent, interest and profit and then goes on to develop a theory of wages, a theory of rent, and a theory of interest and profit. Each of these things is, from one point of view, a price and subject to the same kind of influences as govern the price of a commodity. The more stress is laid on these influences, the more value and distribution can be made to form complementary parts of a single theory embracing both the value of outputs (the price of goods and services) and the cost of inputs (wages, rent, interest and expected profit). Indeed, if the theory of value itself is to be meaningful and useful, it can hardly limit itself to one set of prices—the prices of outputs—and take for granted the other—the prices of inputs—since the two sets of prices interact on one another. Whether the economist is right to treat a theory of wages, rent, interest and profit as if it added up to a theory of the distribution of income is rather more doubtful.

### (iii) The technique of production

Even if we know what has to be produced and for whom, we still have to decide *how*. There are many different ways of producing a single commodity such as a dress and a choice has to be made between the alternative techniques. This choice cannot itself be dictated by technical considerations but depends upon economic factors.

Suppose, for example, that in a planned economy the output of power ten years hence has been laid down in the plan. There are alternative forms of power: electricity, coal, coal gas, natural gas and oil may all be used. The choice between them is not automatic but depends, in part at least, on their cost. The plan must therefore rest on some view of the relative cost of each form of power in ten years' time. Even if a separate figure for electric power is written into the plan on some more or less arbitrary assumptions, someone must still decide in what proportion the expansion in generating facilities should take the form of nuclear reactors, coal-burning power stations and hydro-electric installations. This, too, may be settled arbitrarily; but even when it comes to building a thermal power station it is necessary to decide what sort of machinery to install; and the manufacturer of machinery in turn has to decide what technique to use in order to produce it.

Each of these decisions is important if productive resources are not to be used wastefully. If a country has a large supply of skilled labour, for example, the decisions taken should clearly be biased so as to encourage the use of skilled labour; if it is short of capital, the decisions should be biased in the direction of economy in the use of capital. How this can best be achieved is a matter explored in economic theory.

### (iv) International trade and the location of economic activity

This line of thought leads economists into international comparisons and the factors governing trade between countries. If some countries are plentifully endowed with resources that are scarce in other countries there is room for specialisation between them and for an exchange of products that each can produce most cheaply. International trade offers opportunities of economy and it is necessary to reflect on the extent to which advantage should be taken of those opportunities. There are also problems arising out of the movement of labour and capital from one country to another and the causes and consequences of such a movement.

The theory of international trade, in which these questions are considered, is not altogether the counterpart of the theory that discusses *where* production should be located (which was the fourth of the problems facing our shopkeeper) although it does try to explain what causes an industry to be concentrated in one country or type of country rather than another. The more exact counterpart is the theory of location which deals with the geographical dispersion of economic activity, and of particular activities, within a country. Wherever geographical factors enter, however, there are common elements of principle: an explanation of the factors governing the location of industry in Scotland, for example, leads on to an explanation of the trade between Scotland and England and may easily lead on to an explanation of the trade between the United Kingdom and the rest of the world.

### (v) Economic growth

All of the issues discussed so far relate to the allocation of resources at a point in time and to the distribution of the final output between different commodities, different consumers and different places. But there is a further set of questions that emerge whenever we look at the development of production over time. What makes production grow? How can it be made to *grow more rapidly*? Why is the rate of growth faster in some countries than in others? These questions were very much in the minds of some of the earliest economists and after a period of comparative neglect have returned to the forefront of economic discussion. They are not questions that can be answered by the exercise of simple logic, but involve reflection on the facts of growth, which are not altogether easy to establish. They may not even admit of a set of systematic answers that can be dignified by the name of theory. On the other hand, they are questions of very great practical importance and lie nearer to the preoccupations of the average speculative citizen than do most questions of price theory.

Take, for example, one issue in the theory of economic growth. Is it necessarily cumulative? If one man, or firm, or country gets a jump ahead of others does the gap widen progressively? If not, how is it possible to narrow it? We are told that it is easier to make the second million than the second thousand; does this mean that income must come to be more and more unequally distributed unless the balance is tilted the other way by taxation? A firm making large profits can afford to instal the latest machinery while less profitable concerns may have to make do with what they have; must each industry, therefore, pass under the control of a progressively small number of firms? Productivity in the United States is higher than in other countries; does this confer on the United States a cumulative advantage in her foreign trade, and are other countries doomed to lag further and further behind her?

### (vi) Economic fluctuations

While growth may be the main subject of debate today, it was instability that pre-occupied the economists of a generation ago when unemployment was the greatest social scourge apart from war itself. Fluctuations in economic activity still occur even if they do not assume such terrifying proportions as in the slump of the nineteen thirties. What causes them and what keeps them in check? How can production be made to *grow more steadily*? This is one more of the central problems of economics and one on which economists can claim to have thrown a flood of light.

We shall come to each of these problems as we proceed: they have been cited at this early stage so that the reader may have some idea where he is going. He will find little in the early chapters about the larger, macro-economic issues discussed in the last few pages; but when he does reach them, he will be in a better position to comprehend them from having grappled with the simpler micro-economic issues facing the individual firm or industry. It is to these issues that we turn in Part II.

In the next two chapters we discuss what production and trade involve and the productive resources that are available for employment. In Part II we begin with the growth of production and the factors contributing to it, laying special emphasis on technical progress and specialisation. We then turn to localisation of industry and the growth of production in particular areas. The following chapters deal with various aspects of industrial growth such as the place of large and small firms, industrial finance, and monopolistic influences.

# CHAPTER 3

# PRODUCTION, CONSUMPTION AND TRADE

Whatever economics is about, it is certainly about economic activities and the main forms of economic activity are production and trade. Everybody thinks he knows what these terms mean but there are in fact many ambiguities in their normal use which it is important to clear up at the outset.

## Production

It is common, for example, for the word "production," and still more the word "productive," to be used rather narrowly. Some people think of productive work as work done on the factory floor or on the farm, usually involving manual effort and leading to the creation of some physical product like a piece of cloth or a crop of wheat. It is quite common for the office staff to be described as "unproductive workers" and for other occupations of which people disapprove—the work of bookmakers, entertainers, soldiers, and so on—to be dismissed in the same way. In the U.S.S.R., economic theorists exclude from production all services that yield nothing tangible and they measure the growth of production by an index composed entirely of physical products like coal and steel. Many of those who make comparisons between the U.S.S.R. and other countries use this index and implicitly accept it as a satisfactory measure of economic growth. Nor are the Soviet economists without some claim to orthodoxy because they derive their practice from the usage of the classical economists including Karl Marx and Adam Smith. In *The Wealth of Nations*, the foundation stone of modern economics, Adam Smith rejected as unproductive "some of the gravest and most important, and some of the most frivolous professions: churchmen, lawyers, physicians, men of letters of all kinds; players, buffoons, musicians, opera-singers, opera-dancers, etc." on the grounds that "the work of all of them perishes in the very instant of its production."

## Consumption

This view of the matter might be justifiable if the sole object of production were the accumulation of reproducible wealth: the creation and enlargement of the means of production. But production is not something undertaken for its own sake or in order to increase production later on. Its prime purpose is to meet the wants of consumers; the test of what is and what is not productive is the contribution that is made to the satisfaction of those wants. Consumers don't want steel; they want the things into which steel is fashioned. In a sense, they don't even want these things; they want to *use* them, to enjoy the *services* they provide.

This may seem like a quibble. What is the difference between wanting a motor-car and wanting the use of a motor-car, especially when most people want the motor-car for their own exclusive use? But that the distinction is a real one becomes clear if we ask ourselves how it is possible to consume a motor-car year by year over its life. It does not disappear and, if well maintained, may not even deteriorate perceptibly. It is just as likely to be scrapped because it is out-of-date as because it no longer functions. We do not consume it by using it up in any physical way; we exhaust its utility, employing its services in a steady flow over its useful life until these services cease to satisfy us.

## Utility

Now if, with this in mind, we look at production, the apparently solid distinction between productive and unproductive activities in terms of the creation of material goods, crumbles away. People do not so much make goods as make them more serviceable. They create, not material objects, but utility. When for example, a man makes a pair of boots, he rearranges pieces of leather from a *form* in which they are not wanted into a form in which they are wanted. When someone transports the boots from factory to warehouse, he is taking them from a *place* where they are not wanted to a place where they are wanted. When someone stores the boots in his warehouse, he is holding them over from a *time* when retailers do not want them to a time when they do. There is no essential difference between these activities. They all create utility, either of form, place, or time, and so improve the facilities for the satisfaction of our wants; that is, they are all productive.

In the same way, if we look at different occupations, there is no difference in principle between manual and other kinds of work: between the making of a violin and the playing of it in a concert-hall. It can be argued that we are more dependent for the bare necessities of life on farm labourers and bricklayers than on shopkeepers, cinema stars and university professors. But such an argument makes very little sense as soon as we reflect that we enjoy a high standard of living precisely because it is not made up exclusively of the bare necessities of life and that nothing would lower it again so effectively as to require everyone to turn farm labourer or bricklayer.

Production, to sum up, is simply the creation of utility: that is, of the power to satisfy human wants. Consumption is the using up of utility when we come to satisfy our wants. When we produce goods, we build up a store of wealth upon which we can draw. But, strictly speaking, we do not produce or consume goods at all. We render and are rendered services, some of which are consumed on the spot, while others are stored in bread and butter, collars and ties, ships, houses, and so on, and are used up in periods varying from a few minutes to hundreds of years. Our efforts are productive if they are of service to some one. If they are not, then we may fairly call them unproductive.

## Unpaid services

The economist usually narrows his study of production to that part of it which involves the making of goods for sale or the rendering of paid services. It is important to remember, however, that a great deal of productive effort goes on without payment: for example, within the household or in primitive communities where the circulation of money plays a very restricted part in the organisation of production. It has been estimated that if one were to put a market value on the unpaid services of housewives, they would be equivalent, in the United States, to as much as one-quarter of the entire national income.[1] In subsistence economies, where the market is narrow and specialisation limited, little money changes hands and yet the community makes a living by the same kind of exertions as would yield a substantial money income if trade with other areas were feasible. In the transition from a subsistence to a market economy, therefore, production in the narrow sense of actual sales increases more rapidly than production in the broad sense of total output, and the usual statistical measures of growth (in terms of the money income) exaggerate the improvement occurring in the standard of living. In the same way, comparisons between production in an industrial country like the United Kingdom and in a pre-industrial country like China exaggerate the gap between the two if they are made on the basis of monetary transactions. Estimates made by Professor Kuznets show that an apparent ratio of 12:1 between income per head in the U.S.A. and in China in the years 1931–36, on a basis which is supposed already to take account of the greater reliance on subsistence production in China, differences in the cost of living, and so on, falls to a ratio of 7:1 or less if the full implications of the differences in economic structure are worked out.[2]

Apart from unpaid services there is another set of economic activities which the economist usually excludes from his reckoning but which we all know to be important. In an industrial community we may not spend much of our

---

[1] S. Kuznets, *Economic Change* (London, 1954), p. 195.
[2] S. Kuznets, *op. cit.*, p. 189.

time in selling what we produce, especially if we can turn over our output to be marketed by others; but we inevitably spend a considerable time, as consumers, in buying. This represents an expenditure of effort not very different from the effort of production, although we may derive positive enjoyment from it just as we may derive enjoyment from our work. If we were completely logical we should deduct from the value of production some allowance for the trouble consumers have to go to in purchasing what is produced. Even if we think that this would be going too far, we should at least refrain from dismissing as unproductive efforts to save consumers trouble by incurring high selling costs through delivery services, advertising, etc. While these may be wasteful they may also be as valuable to consumers as costs incurred inside a factory.

## Trade

It is axiomatic that if goods are made for sale there must be trade; production in the economist's sense cannot take place in the absence of trade. The connection between the two is extremely close not only in logic but as a matter of historical experience. It is arguable that the growth of trade is a necessary preliminary to the growth of industry and that it is usually the expansion of markets that provides the main impulse to industrial development.[1] The process is one that can be observed at work in under-developed economies that are still acquiring commercial experience and have hardly yet begun to dabble in manufacturing. Speaking of West Africa Professor Bauer points out how trade

"promotes the growth of resources. . . . It widens markets and thus promotes specialisation and increases production, both of export crops and of produce for local consumption. It serves to bring new commodities to the notice and within the reach of actual or potential producers of cash crops, making it worth their while to produce for sale, and, at the same time, providing a market for these products. This process encourages production and the extension of capacity, more especially the extension of acreage under

---

[1] Compare, for example, Paul Mantoux, *The Industrial Revolution in the Eighteenth Century* (London, 1927) p. 93 (quoted by Youngson, *Possibilities of Economic Progress*, (Cambridge, 1959) p. 111): "Sometimes the advancement of industry, by forcing trade to find new outlets, enlarges and multiplies commercial relations. Sometimes, on the other hand, fresh wants, created by the extension of a commercial market, stimulate industrial enterprise. Nowadays the first case is the more usual. . . . But is not this . . . one of the newest and most original features in the modern factory system? The fact that it is able to anticipate demand, to modify, or even sometimes to create it, is due to its extraordinary adaptability and to the rapid and incessant improvements in its technical equipment. . . . This was not the case with the old industry. Limited both by the slowness of technical improvement, and by the difficulty of communication, production was forcibly confined to the known wants of its habitual market. To manufacture for a clientèle of unknown and distant possible consumers would have been considered an act of madness. In short, industry had to be regulated by the condition of trade connections. . . . In those days progress in industry was almost impossible unless it was preceded by some commercial development."

cash crops. . . . The accumulation of capital and its productive employment are stimulated. . . . Trade also brings into prominence and influence a type of trader-entrepreneur accustomed to the ways of an exchange-economy, notably the habitual and systematic use of money."[1]

## The structure of production

It may convey a more concrete idea of the make-up of economic activity if we show how the total labour force is employed in a country such as Great Britain.

DIAGRAM I

DISTRIBUTION OF WORKING POPULATION IN GREAT BRITAIN, JUNE, 1964

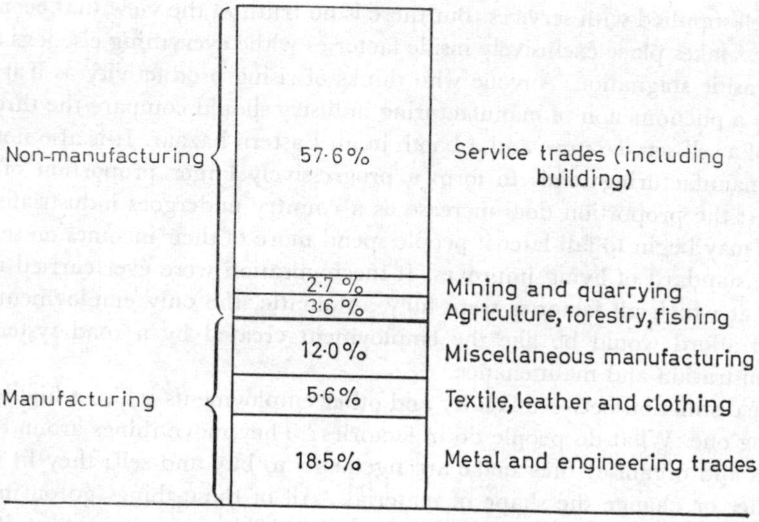

| Non-manufacturing | 57·6% | Service trades (including building) |
| | 2·7% | Mining and quarrying |
| | 3·6% | Agriculture, forestry, fishing |
| Manufacturing | 12·0% | Miscellaneous manufacturing |
| | 5·6% | Textile, leather and clothing |
| | 18·5% | Metal and engineering trades |

Source: Monthly Digest of Statistics

Not much more than one-third of the working population is engaged in industrial employment, and of this group about half are in the metal and engineering trades. What is sometimes described as "primary" production accounts for less than 4 per cent., or just over 6 per cent. if the extractive industries are included. Services of all kinds (for example, transport, distribution, entertainment, public administration, and professional services) occupy a little over half the working population (see Diagram 1).

---

[1] P. T. Bauer, *West African Trade*, (Cambridge, 1954) pp. 28–29.

B

Since Britain is a large exporter of manufactures these figures do not err on the side of belittling the place of industry in the economic structure. In other industrial countries less dependent on foreign markets employment in manufacturing is sometimes a much lower proportion of the total; in the United States, for example, the proportion is about one in four. It is a great mistake, therefore, to think of the factory or the farm as the typical productive unit; a shop, a government office, or a bus depot is just as typical. Even the common notion that industry lies at the centre of a kind of solar system while all other forms of economic activity are held in place like planets by the gravitational pull of industry is difficult to justify. There is some truth in the view that the *location* of factories has a strategic influence on the *location* of service trades, although the line of causation is often the other way round, factories going to the places that are well supplied with services. But there is no truth in the view that economic progress takes place exclusively inside factories while everything else jogs along in parasitic stagnation. Anyone who thinks of rising productivity as if it were purely a phenomenon of manufacturing industry should compare the throughputs of a self-service store and a booth in an Eastern bazaar. It is also not true that manufacturing tends to form a progressively larger proportion of total output; the proportion does increase as a country undergoes industrialisation but it may begin to fall later if people spend more of their incomes on services as the standard of living improves. If mechanisation were ever carried to the point at which all factories were fully automatic, the only employment they would afford would be like the employment created by a road system—in administration and maintenance.

The distinction between factory and other employments is also a highly misleading one. What do people do in factories? They move things around; they design and organise; they make arrangements to buy and sell; they fit things together or change the shape of materials. All of these things go on in non-industrial jobs. Transport, for example, is one of the most important of non-industrial employments; but there are probably more people whose occupation is to move or transport goods inside factories than are employed in transporting goods outside factories. A great deal of the freight moved on the railways consists of coal; when we see this taking place we easily forget the immense amount of movement taking place below ground, the thousands of miles of rail laid underground, and the one miner in five who, in British mines, is employed in haulage. Similarly, what do people do on farms? In a non-industrial country the mass of the population may appear to be employed in agriculture when half their time is really being taken up with buying, selling and transporting, and they may spend only a few weeks each year at work in the fields.

## Business units

Production is organised in units that vary widely in size and complexity. The simplest type of unit is the *establishment*, which is the work-place of a single worker or a group of workers under common direction. A costermonger's barrow is an establishment; so is a shop, garage or hospital. In manufacturing industry the usual establishment is a factory; but some manufacturing establishments—for example, in the clothing trades—are private houses where the only machinery is a handloom or a sewing machine or there may be no more than a pair of knitting needles. A single factory may also house several establishments: under the "room and power" system, a number of small textile spinners may divide one floor of a factory without so much as a partition between their spinning frames, and pay rent individually to the factory-owner. There is an American factory making nuts and bolts that has let space to a cooperage undertaking from which it buys wooden containers for its products. A large American warehouse has gone so far as to form a separate company to acquire and maintain the fork-lift trucks that are used in the warehouse: so that there are two establishments in common ownership within the one building.

An establishment may be the sole place of business of a firm; but many firms own and operate several branches, so that there are fewer firms than establishments. The *firm* is treated in economics as the unit of control, in which decisions are taken about what is to be produced and how it is to be produced. It is the firm that hires labour and land, borrows or invests the necessary capital, purchases raw materials, organises the process of manufacture, and markets the finished product. A firm may be a one-man show, like a taxi-driver; or a small unincorporated business, like a shopkeeper; or a partnership, like a firm of accountants; or a private company, owned by up to fifty different people; or a public company whose shares are dealt in on the stock exchange; or a public corporation running an entire industry, like the National Coal Board. Whatever its size and form of organisation, it is a decision-taking unit, and anyone studying production and the behaviour of producers has to start from the firm.

When we say that the firm is a decision-taking unit, we imply that each firm takes decisions independently of other firms (although not without being influenced by their actions). This is not an altogether realistic assumption since there are often links between one firm and another in the form of understandings, interlocking directorates, memberships of employers' associations, and so on; this may make it difficult to say where one firm stops and another begins. An even closer association arises when one firm holds a block of another firm's shares; a quite limited holding may give the first firm effective control over the second, and if the holding exceeds 50 per cent. the two firms are best regarded as parts of a single business unit. A *business unit* consists of a group of firms under a single control, although there may be minority holdings in any member of the group.

An *industry* consists of a number of competing firms or business units. The firms may be producing the same commodity (e.g., fish), or working on the same material (e.g., brass), or using the same process (e.g., building). There are thus three quite different bases on which we may group firms together into industries. Naturally this leads to difficulties of classification. Shipbuilding, for example, will be included in the steel industry if we use *materials*, and with building if we use *processes*, as a basis of classification. In practice, we rank shipbuilding as a separate industry, partly because it is big enough to justify the title, partly because its *product* is one in which many firms specialise. The crucial test is the way in which competition is delimited; and it is clear that shipbuilding firms are in active competition with one another, but are isolated from the competition of other firms which use steel or which are engaged in building.

It is exceptional to find all the firms in an industry confining themselves to the same range of products or processes or materials. Firms do not specialise along similar lines, but often compete in several different industries at the same time. A shipbuilding firm, for example, may engage in coal-mining and steel-making. Railways may own hotels, golfcourses, and Atlantic liners. It is in a few industries only that firms confine themselves within the boundaries of their trade and are completely segregated from other industries. Again, even when the limits of an industry are clearly defined, there may be little in common between two firms within it. The Leyland Motor Company, which manufactures commercial vehicles, no more competes with Rolls Royce than British European Airways competes with the Raleigh Cycle Company. Each firm within an industry has its own peculiar style or quality of product, or its own peculiar methods of manufacture, or uses its own peculiar materials. Sometimes these peculiarities are comparatively trifling (e.g., in cotton spinning), but in most industries they are of considerable and increasing importance. They make it very difficult to draw a clear line of division between firms which are in direct competition with one another (e.g., two coal-mining firms in adjacent areas), and firms between which competition is rather remote (e.g., a coal-mining firm and an oil company). At best, the classification of firms into industries is a rough one.

## The public sector

In conditions of private interprise, most firms are privately owned and managed. Some undertakings, however, have to be run by the State; the Armed

Forces are an obvious example. The range of activities conducted by the State varies from country to country and in most countries has been greatly extended over the past generation. As matters stand in Great Britain, the public sector— that is, those economic activities that are conducted by the State or by agencies of the State—includes the nationalised industries, such as coal-mining; public corporations, like the B.B.C.; local government undertakings, for example, municipal transport; the public social services, including education, the National Health Service, unemployment insurance, old age pensions, etc.; the work of the Civil Service, both national and local, and of the Armed Forces; and a large number of miscellaneous activities. Nearly one worker in four is directly employed by the State in one capacity or another; and of the total national income, over one-third is paid in one form or another to the State.

In these circumstances, it would be misleading to study the workings of the economic system as if it responded exclusively to the operations of private firms. In the past, however, it is on the private sector that the attention of economists has been concentrated. Even now, it is difficult to avoid giving disproportionate attention to the private sector, because the activities of the State have not been submitted to the same kind of systematic analysis as has the working of a system of private enterprise.

There is a sharp antithesis in the principles governing the public and the private sector, wherever the former involves the provision of services free of charge (e.g., education, medical treatment, etc.), or the employment of workers on tasks that yield no product measurable in terms of money (e.g., most of the Civil Service). There is nothing unique about such services. They are the same in principle as services provided within the family; but they differ fundamentally from the services provided by private industry.

No such antithesis arises, however, where the State is running an industry on commercial lines. An employee of the National Coal Board (which is a nationalised undertaking) might find that the British Petroleum Company (in which the State has a large interest) or Imperial Chemical Industries Limited (which is a private concern) came to decisions in much the same way about much the same things, were run with just as much regard for the public interest, and experienced much the same kind of muddles.

**The market**

A private firm—and this applies equally to a nationalised undertaking— requires to strike a bargain both with the factors of production which it employs and with the purchasers of its products. For example, it has to bargain with labour about the wages which it will pay, and with its customers about the price which it will charge. These bargains are driven in what is called "the market." The market, it should be clearly understood, is not a place—although bargains are still driven about wages at hiring fairs, and about prices on wheat, metal, and other exchanges. The market, in economics, is simply the network of dealings in any factor or product between buyers and sellers. These dealings may be regular and organised, or they may, as in the market in second-hand violins, be spasmodic and unsystematic.

It is round the market in this sense that the economic system under private enterprise revolves. Production is ruled by market requirements: if goods cannot be sold in the market they will cease to be produced. Men's incomes are governed by what "the market" will offer for their services and for the hire of their capital. The vast impersonal force of the market shapes the environment in which we earn our livelihood: we are free only within limits set by the market. At times, when we are in the grip of unemployment, the limits seem narrow and irksome; at other times, when we draw on the bounty of distant lands for the everyday necessities of life, the limits seem singularly wide and generous. It is the business of the economist to throw light on these limits and to suggest how they may be thrust further back by a proper organisation of our resources.

CHAPTER 4

# THE FACTORS OF PRODUCTION

Productive resources are usually classified by economists under three broad headings into labour, land and capital. The first of these represents human resources; the second, natural resources; and the third, man-made resources.

## Factors as physical things

All three factors have a physical existence: they are tangible resources capable of employment for different purposes (or of being left unemployed). The labour force is made up of men and women working either on their own account or for pay; the stock of capital includes the physical assets that have been built up by human effort and thrift in the past—house-property, factories, power stations, railways, machines and so on; land consists of the free gifts of nature which are in human ownership and under human control, such as mineral deposits, forests, and agricultural land. It is not always easy to distinguish man-made from natural resources and for some purposes it is preferable to group them together as the external facilities which assist labour in production.

In any productive activity it is necessary to combine all three factors since land and capital can produce nothing unaided by labour—even if it is only the labour of reaping—and labour can produce nothing without some capital—even if it is only the capital out of which it maintains itself. There is no necessity, however, to combine the factors of production in a fixed way or for fixed purposes; and the business of organising production, whether in a single establishment or in the whole economy, is largely one of deciding how to combine the factors and to what use to put them. This is a much more complicated business than it sounds since the units that have to be combined are not standard, homogeneous specimens of each factor, each interchangeable with every other unit of the same factor, but individual men and women, individual machines, or individual bits of land. It may suit the economist to adopt a Caesar-like division of the factors into three; but this should not conceal the infinite variety of each factor and the vastness of the jig-saw puzzle into which they are fitted.

## Factors as services

It is possible to think of the factors of production in a quite different way: not as physical units but as services or as the sources of productive power. Knowledge, skill, organisation, enterprise, and thrift, for example, have been among the most powerful factors in raising productivity and might accordingly be ranked as factors of production. But while this usage would direct our attention to some of the keys to economic progress, the traditional classification seems preferable. We already take account of thrift when we include capital, since thrift is of no service unless it leads to an addition to the stock of capital. The first three items in the list are all attributes of labour: every worker possesses some knowledge, skill and organising ability and it is, indeed, these things, the fruit of intelligence and judgment, that distinguish the human factor.

This is a proposition, which, however evident, is inconsistent with any attempt to identify labour with manual labour and the toil and exertion that manual labour frequently involves. Toil and exertion are far more characteristic of machinery, which can work on unremittingly for twenty-four hours a day. Even in agricultural communities it is horses and oxen, and not human brawn, that supply most of the necessary power. Work that does not call for the exercise of intelligence, and is purely mechanical, can (as the word "mechanical" implies) be taken over by machinery. It may happen of course, that the machinery is costly to make and operate, or that muscle-power is abundant and cheap, so that men continue to be used for what is literally inhuman work. But the more machinery is improved, and the scarcer brawn becomes relatively to skill and judgment, the more will toil-saving inventions be introduced. Muscle-power and machinery are in direct competition with one another and the one can replace the other. But the work of the human mind cannot be replaced. There are devices which, as we shall see, make a little intelligence and judgment go a long way in modern industry. But there are none which eliminate them completely from business any more than from the rest of life.

In saying all this, we are not assuming that the introduction of machinery is an unqualified good, or that it makes work somehow more "human." A man's muscles and imagination, to which machinery frequently gives little scope, are as much a part of him as his intelligence and nerves. When the machine sets the tempo and not the worker, there can be little opportunity for initiative and craftsmanship; and these are things the value of which is not exhausted within working hours. They enrich a man's personality in all his doings, and personality is a far more important product of industry than the goods and services which it is the humble duty of economists to discuss.

If it is judgment rather than toil that is labour's main characteristic, we can draw no sharp line of distinction between the labour of, say, a 'bus driver and the labour of the director of an omnibus company. There may not be the same technique of judgment in both jobs. The problems of negotiating a street corner are very different from the problems of negotiating for the purchase of a fleet of new 'buses. But both require intelligence and judgment. If the skills differ, the ingredients do not. For there can be just as much purposive control, planning, and adaptation of means to ends in driving a 'bus as in managing a company.

It is not for this reason that there is no need to single out organisation as a separate factor of production. There may be a number of people who call themselves managers or organisers and have rather more organising ability or rather more scope for organising than other workers have. But they are not a class apart. It may not be everyone who organises *men* in industry, with power to give orders under threat of dismissal. But everyone, be he office boy, labourer, foreman, or works manager, has to organise either men or things. Moreover each worker—and not simply the general manager—will be paid more if his work involves the responsibility of organising. The greater the skill and judgment he has to show, the more he can expect to earn. Some people draw higher incomes than others for their organising; but everyone who is not doing completely mechanical work draws *some* income for what is really organising.

### Enterprise as a factor

It is rather more difficult to decide how to treat enterprise. It is clearly not a factor of production in the sense in which labour, land and capital are factors: it is not part of available resources. Yet when we look at the customary classification of the rewards of the factors of production we find a fourfold division into wages, rent, interest and profit and it is natural to expect a parallel and fourfold division of factors. Since profit can be regarded as a reward for enterprise, or successful risk-taking, there is something to be said for elevating enterprise to the apparent vacancy among the factors of production. This has, however, two important drawbacks, the second of which is decisive.

First of all, it is a mistake to associate enterprise with a single factor, capital, since capital is not the only factor that is exposed to risks and is paid for its enterprise. Labour runs risks too: risks, for example, of unemployment, slow promotion or physical injury. The steeplejack and the coalminer may not risk any capital; but they risk their lives. There are risky occupations as well as risky undertakings; and part of the wages paid in these occupations might be classed as a return for enterprise, in just the same way as part of the return to investors in risky undertakings is classed as a return for enterprise. The peculiarity of capital—and this is the second and decisive point—is that it has usually a riskless alternative, since it is possible to lend one's capital with the virtual certainty that the money will be repaid. Pure interest is, in fact, interest on a debt that is free from any risk of default, and as soon as such a risk enters, the return on capital contains an element of profit as well as interest. This means that we ought to look on interest and profit as a joint return on capital with the element of profit increasing the greater the risk that the capital may be lost, and the element of interest representing the risk-free return that the capital could earn if transferred to some completely safe investment.

### Financial assets as a factor

From this point of view, if we feel obliged to add a fourth factor of production, the strongest candidate is money and the whole range of *financial assets* in which we can invest our money: deposits with building societies, insurance policies, government bonds, mortgages, stock exchange securities and so on. These assets take the form of debts or titles to property rather than property itself. For the most part, they yield interest without any significant element of profit; but where the investor is more venturesome and buys shares on the stock exchange he expects to share in the profits of the company in which he has invested.

It is not immediately obvious how the pieces of paper which we call financial assets contribute to the productive process; it certainly cannot be assumed that the issue of more paper, whether in the form of money or securities, will enhance productivity or swell the national income. For present purposes, however, it is sufficient that many of the most important decisions that producers have to take are financial decisions involving the borrowing of money or the purchase or sale of stock exchange securities. Transactions in financial assets have a place in economic organisation that can be as important as the place of transactions in physical assets.

### LABOUR

Labour as a factor of production usually means the "labour force," the group of workers who are either already in employment or are available for employment, given the opportunity. The use of the phrase "man-power" conveys the same general idea of the human resources available to the economy. The size of the labour force is not fixed, nor is its effectiveness in producing goods and services; it obviously grows as population grows and improves in productive power with education and training.

## (a) Population

The size of the labour force is not a simple function of population. A varying proportion of the population is either too old or too young to work or is engaged in household and other duties and does not seek paid employment. In the United Kingdom, for example, the proportion of the population aged 15–64 increased from 59 per cent. in 1871 to over 69 per cent. in 1939 and has since fallen to about 65 per cent. This means that the population of working age has fluctuated in relation to the population lying outside the age-groups from which most of the labour force is drawn. An important influence on the proportion of working age is the trend in the birth rate, which fell from about 35 per 1,000 in the 1870's to about 15 per 1,000 in the 1930's; this has resulted in a large reduction in the proportion of children in the population. Another important influence is the increase in expectation of life: in 1870 an Englishman had an expectation of life at birth of 40 years compared with over 66 years today, and this increase in longevity has gradually raised the proportion of older people in the population. Emigration and immigration can also bring about important changes in age-distribution since migrants usually include an abnormal proportion of men and women of working age: when emigration from Britain was at its peak something like half the migrants were aged 20–35 and this outflow tended to lower the relative size of the working population.

In under-developed countries where the working life is comparatively short, these considerations can be of special importance. An extension in the expectation of life from 30 to 45 may almost double the effective working life provided it results from a decline in the mortality of adults; and if it is accompanied by greater freedom from sickness and disease, the impact on the effective labour force will be still more pronounced. On the other hand, an increase in the expectation of life from 65 to 75 reflecting a fall in mortality at advanced ages will be unlikely to have any marked effect on the size of the working population. In practice, the experience of under-developed and industrial countries is not in such sharp contrast. Medical science has done very little for many years to increase the expectation of life at ages above 55–60, while an extension of the average working life continues to swell the labour force in industrial countries; at the same time, the greatest triumphs in public health in under-developed countries have been in reducing the high mortality of babies and children and the immediate effect of this has been to raise rather than lower the proportion of dependants to the working population.

**Working habits**—The size of the labour force is also affected by changes in working habits. During the second World War, for example, the working population of Great Britain (including the Armed Forces and those who were registered as unemployed) grew from 19·8 million in 1939 to 22·3 million in 1943, most of the increase being due to the absorption into paid employment of over 2 million more women who were previously engaged in household duties. Similarly, between 1948 and 1957 a further 1·4 million workers were added to the British labour force, at a time when the population of working age showed little change, through the entry (or re-entry) into the labour market of married women and the postponement of their retirement from industry of large numbers of older workers. Both of these changes took place at a time when there was an acute shortage of labour and opportunities of employment were ample; if it became much harder to find a job, changes in the reverse direction might occur, older workers retiring earlier and married women withdrawing from the labour market.

**Working hours**—Another change that lends elasticity to the supply of labour is in working hours. In the nineteenth century, working hours were generally over 60 a week and often 66 or more. They fell progressively to 54 in 1913 and by 1939 were normally 48 or less. During the war, although no extension took place in the nominal length of the working week, the hours actually worked increased substantially because of overtime and the practice of regular overtime working continued once the war was over. A further nominal contraction in hours to 40 in the post-war period has been consistent with the maintenance in most industries of hours of work (including overtime) not very different for the average worker from those of pre-war years. On the other hand, paid holidays have become increasingly common and the length of the holiday period has grown, so that man-hours worked per annum have diminished slightly.

All of these influences on man-power are in the long run subordinate to population growth. The importance of population growth is particularly obvious when it is rapid or when it is taking place in countries suffering from over-population; but even when population is stationary it is still necessary to explain why it is stationary and when there is no evidence of over-population it is still necessary to enquire how one can judge whether a country is over-populated or not. This is a highly controversial area of discussion and one in which some of the generalisations that were once fashionable have since been discredited. But it is not possible to disregard the problems that are raised by population growth or to treat it as something unaffected by the operation of economic forces; the interaction of demographic and economic forces is undeniable, and the influence of population growth on economic development is highly important.

**The Malthusian theory**—All subsequent thinking about population growth has been greatly influenced by the views put forward by the Rev. T. R. Malthus in his "Essay on Population," the first edition of which appeared in 1798. This was the first scientific attempt to explain how changes in population came about; and although some of his fears and forecasts have since proved mistaken, the situation which he was analysing is not without its modern counterparts. Malthus was writing at a time when the growth of population, hitherto relatively slow, had suddenly accelerated, largely because improvements in personal hygiene, the growth of medical science, and probably also better nourishment, combined to lower the death-rate. This was not quite how it looked to Malthus who was more inclined to stress the influence of earlier marriages and a higher birth-rate. From his point of view the important issue was how the balance between births and deaths was preserved and how it would be re-established if, as a result of a divergence between the two, population started to grow or decline.

With the help of later research, we can see this issue in clearer perspective than Malthus because we are more conscious than he could have been of the astonishing contrast between the historical record over the span of human history up to the eighteenth century and in the ensuing period. The record of earlier centuries is one of remarkable stability. World population is estimated to have doubled between the beginning of the Christian era and the middle of the seventeenth century: this represents a rate of increase of no more than 5 per cent. per century. The estimates are highly speculative and the rate of growth varied from country to country and from century to century. Nevertheless, the presumption of comparative stability is a very strong one as can be readily demonstrated by projecting backwards the rates of growth of 10–20 per cent. per decade experienced in most western countries over the past century.[1] Any divergence between birth- and death-rates must have been, throughout the ages, either almost insignificant or random and the conditions of life such as to perpetuate stability of population. In most countries birth- and death-rates probably varied little until recent times: both were very high by the standards of modern industrialised countries and the expectation of life was comparatively low. Literally half the children died in infancy and those who survived to maturity had to face the risks of disease, famine and war.

**Positive checks**—These were Malthus' three "positive checks" to population growth, their effect being to maintain the death-rate. They were reinforced by "preventive checks" operating to keep down the birth-rate:

---

[1] A rate of increase of 10 per cent. per decade is sufficient to multiply a population nearly sevenfold in two centuries, by a factor of 45 in four centuries; and by a factor of 13,500 in a thousand years.

postponement of marriage to later ages when fertility is lower, and deliberate birth-control after marriage. The essence of Malthus' argument was that if population growth was not checked by a low birth-rate it would be checked, sooner or later, by a high death-rate brought about by disease, famine and war. These positive checks would come into play because of the failure of the means of subsistence to grow at the same rate as population; only if mankind chose to make use of the preventive checks and regulated its numbers could pressure on the means of subsistence be kept at bay.

Malthus' analysis was well-timed because the traditional balance between births and deaths had clearly been disturbed and no one could foresee how it would be restored. Some people blamed the Poor Laws for the disturbance and argued that they both removed barriers to early marriage and provided inducements to have more children; to anyone holding these views, Malthus' arguments were highly congenial since they pointed to calamities in store and implied that a change in policy would restore the *status quo*. It is very doubtful whether the Poor Laws did have the effects alleged; people who showed no concern over the fertility of the poor when their children died may simply have become more censorious when the children lived, and found plenty of examples of reckless marriages "on the dole" to lend plausibility to their strictures. What is certain is that by far the more important element in the general acceleration of population growth in the eighteenth century was a sharp fall in the death rate.

**The fall in fertility**—This was followed, after an interval, by a drop in the birth-rate, beginning, in Britain, in the 1870's. There is evidence that the decline in fertility, as measured by births per married woman in the fertile age-group, had already turned downwards in the fifties; and in the United States, where the birth-rate in the eighteenth century was much higher than in Britain (over 50 per 1,000 or an average of 8 children per marriage), the decline started much earlier.[1] The decline in the birth-rate continued until the nineteen thirties, when it reached 15 per 1,000 in Britain and was for some years below 20 per 1,000 in the United States. At those levels, less than half what had been customary in earlier centuries it looked as if equilibrium had been restored between birth- and death-rates, and there was even talk of a declining population in Britain and other countries within a decade or two. However, the long-continued fall in the birth-rate not only came to an end but recovered a little while the death-rate continued its downward trend.

---

[1] W. H. Grabill, C. V. Kiser, and P. K. Whelpton, *The Fertility of American Women* (New York, 1958), pp. 5, 17.

The lag of the birth-rate behind the death-rate caused population to increase: in the two centuries between 1750 and 1950 the population of Britain multiplied nearly sevenfold and throughout almost the entire period grew at a fairly steady rate of about 10 per cent. per decade. In other countries an even faster rate of growth was recorded: in North America, for example, population grew from about 1 million in 1750 to 165 million in 1950, and in Latin America from about 10 million to 162 million. These rates of growth were due quite as much to immigration from Europe as to an excess of births over deaths. The United States alone received over 30 million immigrants in the sixty years before 1930.

TABLE I

ESTIMATES OF WORLD POPULATION BY REGIONS, 1650-1950

| Year | Millions | | | | | | |
|------|---------------------------|-------------------|------------------|---------|------|--------|----------------|
|      | Europe (incl. U.S.S.R.) | North America | Latin America | Oceania | Asia | Africa | World Total |
| 1650 | 1   | 1   | 7   | 2  | 260  | 100 | 470  |
| 1750 | 145 | 1   | 10  | 2  | 435  | 100 | 693  |
| 1850 | 275 | 25  | 33  | 2  | 655  | 100 | 1090 |
| 1950 | 595 | 165 | 162 | 13 | 1270 | 200 | 2405 |

Source: Rounded from estimates quoted from W. F. Willcox and the United Nations in S. Kuznets, "Population, Income and Capital," in Economic Progress (ed. L. Dupriez, Louvain, 1955).

The pattern of births that has emerged throws some light upon the forces that have caused the reduction in the birth-rate. There are now comparatively few large families of six or more children and fewer also of the childless and single-child families that were so common thirty years ago. A contraction in the number of large families has continued in Britain all through the past twenty years whether the birth-rate was falling or rising. In the United States, three "completed" families in five consist of two, three, or four children whereas families of this size were outnumbered in the twenties by "completed" families with one or no children. These facts demonstrate the importance in relation to current trends in the birth-rate of family planning and of the fashionable view of the optimum size of family. But what makes the fashion change? Here is a question that would require a book to itself: we should have to consider the influence on family life of an industrial and urban society, the emancipation of women, the mechanisation of the home, the re-direction of acquisitive impulses, and a variety of other circumstances, the relative importance of which varies from one society to another.

Whatever the mechanism by which birth- and death-rates have been brought nearer together, it has not been the mechanism that Malthus feared. There has been no increasing pressure of population in industrial countries, no fall in living standards or return to the previous conditions of disease and under-nourishment. On the contrary, if changes in the standard of living have formed part of the mechanism, it has been through their effect on the birth-rate rather than on the death-rate: the effort to maintain or improve their standard of living has made many families regard children as directly competitive with higher consumption and contributed in this way to the fall in the birth-rate. It is also difficult to maintain that the increase in population over the past two hundred years has simply diluted gains in productivity that would other-wise have been shared among fewer people. Part of the tremendous expansion in production that has taken place is directly attributable to the growth in the scale on which the economy functions and the increase in population has made an important contribution to this growth in the scale of operations.

When one looks at what is happening outside the industrial countries, how-ever, Malthus' fears seem more justified. The improvement in public health through the elimination of malaria and other disease by the systematic appli-cation of medical knowledge has had an immediate effect on death-rates far beyond anything previously recorded. There are some countries like Ceylon where the death-rate has been reduced by over 50 per cent. in less than ten years; in a wide group of under-developed countries the death-rate has fallen within a short period from 20–25 per 1,000 to 10 per 1,000 or less—rates which obviously cannot be maintained unless everybody lives to over 100. This sharp fall in death-rates has not been accompanied by any parallel reduction in birth-rates and in many parts of the world these remain at levels of 40 or even 50 per 1,000 of the population. There is not, as yet, any convincing proof that birth-rates will follow death-rates down, as happened in western countries in the course of industrialisation. Meanwhile population is growing very fast— sometimes at rates of 3 per cent. per annum—under the impulse of medical rather than economic improvements, so that, while man-power is abundant, other resources in land and capital are lagging behind. It may be possible to enlarge the resource-base more rapidly in such countries, and to find new jobs and more food for the extra population. But even this will not restore equilibrium unless there is a change in attitudes towards fertility since unless at some point birth-rates start to fall the pressure of population is bound eventually to make itself felt.

Some economists faced with this dilemma, argue that if only there is a special effort to make output rise faster than numbers, the resulting improvement in the standard of living will operate as it has done in the past to make people more inclined to limit the size of their family. If the effort fails, people will have no higher standards at which to aim and will continue to reproduce themselves on a scale that will doom even their existing standard of living. Either the standard of living improves and the pace of population growth slackens or the standard deteriorates and population growth does not slacken. The change for the better or for the worse is cumulative since any slackening in population growth reinforces the improvement in the standard of living. This is an ingenious and plausible view, quite different from Malthus', but it rests on a hypothesis that is as yet unproven. We cannot assume that fertility is governed in all continents by the forces that have governed it in Europe and North America; different societies entertain quite different ideas about masculinity, the importance of male heirs, the balance of power between husband and wife, and so on. It is also very much of an over-simplification to treat the fall in the birth-rate in Europe and North America as the direct outcome of an improvement in living standards; the mere fact that birth-rates have not fallen continuously but have recovered from their lowest levels during a period of great prosperity should be sufficient to suggest the complexity of motives affecting birth-rates.

**Migration**—If we turn from birth- and death-rates to migration from one country to another, we need have less hesitation in looking first to economic forces for an explanation. The large-scale inter-continental movements of population in the nineteenth century were dominated by hopes of economic advancement, although fears of racial or political persecution and the desire for a freer life also played their part. The largest movement, that to North America, brought over one million emigrants a year across the Atlantic in the first decade of this century. South America received fewer immigrants, but they formed a higher proportion of the population affected; in the Argentine, for example, the ratio of immigrants to the native-born population reached 30 per cent. in 1914.[1] In South-east Asia also, international migration was at its peak in the years before the first World War and some 8 million Chinese, for example, were living abroad, chiefly in Malaya, Siam, Formosa and the East Indies.

Within countries, the movement of population has been on an even larger scale. In Western Europe, millions left the countryside for the towns during the nineteenth century and this process of urbanisation still continues; in the U.S.S.R., for example, the urban population grew from less than 30 million

---

[1] W. Ashworth, *A Short History of the International Economy*, p. 178.

(within the present boundaries) in 1926 to 100 million in 1959, while the rural population has dropped from about 135 million to 109 million over the same period. In some countries a further shift has taken place into regions previously under-populated and little developed, In the United States, one-third of the population now lives west of the Mississippi where a century or so ago most of the area was thought to be a desert; in the U.S.S.R., over 30 per cent. of the population lives east of the Urals in an area once thought to be equally inhospitable, and the proportion is increasing rapidly.[1]

**Influences on labour supply**—We have now identified a number of factors influencing the size and growth of the labour force in particular countries or places. It remains to put these various influences in perspective by indicating the order of magnitude of the changes they may produce.

First of all, the ratio of the labour force to total population usually remains fairly stable because some of the factors influencing it offset one another.[2] For example, the tendencies to longer schooling and to earlier retirement are offset by the tendency for married women to take paid employment. In the United Kingdom the labour force has varied over the past eighty years between 68 and 73 per cent. of the population of working age and the proportion has never changed in any decade by more than 4 per cent. in either direction. Between one year and another, changes in working hours can be of much more importance; even over longer periods such as a decade they are capable of outweighing all other influences on the effective labour force. In the nineteen twenties, for example, hours of labour were 12–15 per cent. less in Western Europe than they had been in 1913. The fall was a discontinuous one, never since repeated on such a scale; but taking it as an example of what can happen in a decade, it represents a more rapid change than any that has taken place in the British labour force through population growth over a similar period.

Population growth itself, as we have seen, may reach 3 or even 4 per cent. per annum through natural increase alone. Although it would be foolish to speak of a normal rate of increase, past experience suggests that such rates are exceptional and that it is more common for growth through natural increase to be limited to 1–2 per cent. per annum. There have been times when immigration had contributed on a similar scale to the growth of population and when emigration has removed over 1 per cent. of a country's population annually: annual immigration into Canada, for example, averaged 5 per cent.

---

[1] "Comparisons of the United States and Soviet Economies" (Joint Economic Committee, Congress of the United States, 1959), Part I, p. 61.

[2] A. Maddison, "Economic Growth in Western Europe, 1870–1957," *Quarterly Review of the Banca Nazionale del Lavoro*, March 1959, p. 8,

of the population in the years immediately before the first World War; on the other hand, emigration removed at least 1 per cent. of the Irish population in nearly every year from 1846 until the end of the nineteenth century. But these are highly unusual rates of migration and the only movements on a similar scale in recent years have been the inflow of Jewish refugees and migrants into Israel and the expulsions of population from central European countries that took place during and after the war. If we are looking to the future and not the past, we are probably safe in treating the balance between births and deaths as the principal determinant of long-term changes in the size of a country's labour force.

### (b) Education and training

The human resources of any community are obviously not a matter of numbers alone; they vary with the capabilities of the working population and these capabilities can be improved by education and training. The importance of education lies partly in making the population literate and partly in making it more open-minded and capable of evolving or profiting from new ideas. Without literacy, the spread of knowledge is slow and many of the clerical, accounting and other tasks that occupy a large proportion of the labour force in an industrial country cannot be performed. The more advantage is taken of technological progress, the higher the level of education required, not only in the technologists themselves but also in those who employ them, or form their staff, or have business dealings of any kind with them. More important still for the mass of the population is the training and experience which it brings to its work. The complex tasks of modern industry frequently require relatively little formal education, but they presuppose a skill and competence that rest on thorough familiarity with the quirks and snags of the job, and on a social background in which there is both the incentive and the opportunity to pick up the necessary knowledge. All this may seem platitudinous in a country like Great Britain; but in a pre-industrial country with a low standard of living and a high rate of illiteracy, the problem of enlarging the experience and raising the level of skill of the working population is overwhelming.

### (c) Labour organisation

Labour differs from the other two factors of production in the simple fact of its humanity. It is not a mere instrument of production but the mass of citizens engaged in their daily work. These are the same citizens who, in a different capacity, elect the government of their country and enjoy democratic rights to pronounce on the laws which they are expected to obey. They are, therefore, in a position to change the institutional framework within which they work and to lay down conditions that all employers (whether private firms or public corporations) must observe. As workers, they also show ordinary human reactions both towards one another and towards their employers. They are afraid of redundancy and unemployment; anxious to strengthen their bargaining power and improve their working conditions; jealous of any privileges they enjoy; proud of their skill; sensitive to encouragement and approval; moved by the desire to stand well with their fellows. How they exert themselves depends on many complex factors as well as on the pay they receive: on the interest they take in their work, the notions of social justice they entertain, the accepted norms of effort, the need to maintain solidarity with other workers.

It is not possible, therefore, to treat labour as a mere aggregation of units or to confine an analysis of the supply of labour to the responses that follow changes in population or in pay. It is necessary also to take account of the influences governing industrial relations within the individual establishment and in the economy at large. It is also necessary to take account of the influence of workers' organisations—for example, of shop stewards and trade unions—because these organisations (and the corresponding organisations of employers) not only affect the terms on which labour is employed but help to shape industrial relations and are the agencies through which the pressures on both sides of the labour market tend to make themselves felt.

## LAND

Land as a factor of production has lost much of its former importance. In the days before the Industrial Revolution, perhaps two-thirds of the workers of Britain were employed in agriculture, against a mere twentieth at present. The owners of agricultural land drew in rent over a fifth of the total income of the country, whereas nowadays the proportion is barely one per cent. A corresponding change has come over economic theory. The discussions of rent which fill the pages of Adam Smith and John Stuart Mill have dwindled sadly in the modern textbook.

What resources do we include in land? Generally speaking, all the free gifts of nature which yield an income: agricultural and building land, mines, fisheries, etc. We do not include sunshine, rain, and other natural agents, which assist in production, since these are not in anyone's ownership and control. They are resources over which we have no power of disposal, and which, therefore, we cannot economise.

### Characteristics of land
  (i) Fixity of supply—The characteristic of land on which economists have

laid most emphasis is the fixity of its supply. Coastal erosion and flooding may reduce somewhat the land surface of the globe, while slight additions may be made through exploration, discovery, or the building of dykes. But, broadly speaking, and with the possible exception of mineral deposits, no great change in the supply is likely to take place. If, however, we are thinking of fertile, cultivable, land this is much less true. Erosion, for instance, can lay waste millions of acres of arable land. Continuous cropping, neglect, incompetence, or ignorance can all reduce the fertility of the surface soil. On the other hand, fertility can be increased by laying out capital on land improvement. Reclamation, drainage, manuring, irrigation—even afforestation—can make available a larger supply of cultivable land. Rich crops of cotton can be grown on land where sagebrush and cactus were once hard put to it to survive. It might seem, therefore, that to say that our land resources are fixed in supply is exaggerating a little. Fertility can be used up and it can be increased. There are no "original and indestructible powers of the soil," or if there are, it is impossible to disentangle them from the powers which capital expenditure on land improvement has created.

From this it is an easy step to the conclusion that there is no fundamental difference between land and capital, and that there is no need to classify them as separate factors of production. Land, it is sometimes argued, is simply a piece of property with a very long life, and of a sort not easily added to. There is no need to separate it too rigidly from other pieces of property by pretending that it can never wear out and never be added to. Its supply is not rigidly fixed, but it takes an unusually long time for an increase or decrease to take place.

All this is true if by land we mean cultivable land, or simply fertility. But when a farmer uses land (and still more when a builder does) he has the use not only of the powers of the soil (indestructible or not) but also of a given area which enjoys an annuity of air, sunshine and rain and is in his exclusive occupation. Fertility can be changed by the farmer, but climate and situation cannot. We can improve site-values, but we cannot multiply the sites themselves. As for mineral deposits, it is quite plain that we can do nothing to increase the supply, although we can do a great deal to make the supply more accessible (e.g., by prospecting, sinking shafts, building railways, etc.).

Thus in land as we find it there are two elements which in practice can rarely be separated, but in theory always. One is variable and the product of human effort, and one is constant and the free gift of nature. It is the constant element— the advantages of climate, aspect, situation, etc., that come from the exclusive ownership and use of a site or of mineral deposits—which constitutes land.

It is this theoretical distinction that has led economists to treat land as a separate factor of production. But even if the distinction had never been drawn, it would almost have been necessary to invest some imaginary factor to take the place of land—a factor which, like land, would have been fixed in supply. In economics, we frequently have to distinguish between resources which are strictly limited in supply over the interval of time under discussion (e.g., machinery and plant), and resources which can readily be varied (e.g., semi-finished goods, labour, etc.). The first set of resources raises problems very similar to those raised by the use of land, and it is useful to be able to apply the theory that has already been worked out in connection with land.

To take a simple example. An important corollary of the fact that land is fixed in supply is that the owners of land are in a position of monopoly. They have exclusive use of resources without which our most urgent wants cannot be met. If those wants become more urgent (for instance, because population increases and more people have to be fed), no new land resources can be created to supplement the old, and landowners are put in a position to hold society up to ransom by charging higher rents. They profit, not because they have performed some additional service to the community, but because they happen to own resources which have become scarcer relatively to the community's need of them. They will continue to profit because the scarcity of land cannot be relieved by setting men to work to make more of it.

All this is true, not just of land, but of anything that is fixed in supply. If, for instance, there is a sudden, but sustained, demand for steel from the ship-building or automobile or armament industries, it will be impossible to expand the capacity of the steel industry for some time. Until new furnaces and rolling-mills come into production, the owners of the existing steel plants are in the same position of advantage as landowners faced with a rising demand for land. They may raise their price to the higher level which the market will bear, and reap an extra profit without extra effort. But theirs is not a continuing advantage, for the scarcity of steel can be overcome. After a time, high profits will encourage the construction of new steel-making plant, which will enter into competition with the old and bring down prices and profits. In the long run, the supply of plant can always be increased: high profits therefore, tend to be self-extinguishing. But even in the long run, the supply of land cannot be increased: high rents, therefore, may continue indefinitely.

**(ii) No cost of production**—A second characteristic of land is that it has no cost of production. No one paid a penny to have it created, and it costs no one a penny in actual outlay to allow it to be used. It is already in existence and awaiting employment. In this it differs from both labour and capital. Labour has to be reared—a troublesome and costly business—and does not offer itself for employment without a struggle; there are sacrifices to be borne by the parents of a worker in bringing him up and by the worker himself in seeking employment rather than yielding to the attractions of leisure. Similarly, capital has to be built up out of savings—which for most people means a sacrifice of present enjoyment. It is not, like land, indestructible, and can be used up and not replaced if the return to investment is not satisfactory. Thus while the provision of labour and capital is costly—in the sense that it puts us to some sacrifice either of leisure or of present enjoyment—there is no cost, no sacrifice of some desirable alternative, in providing land. The land is there for the owner to make the best of it, but labour and capital are not "there." How much of them exists depends largely on what they are paid, not on nature's bounty. We are not committed to saving some given sum, or working for so many weeks, or days, or hours at some fixed speed, irrespective of the efforts and sacrifices involved. We count the cost of working and saving. But the productive power of land is not of our making and puts us to no cost. If we choose to improve this productive power by sinking capital in land, then such man-made fertility has, of course, a cost of production. But naturally fertility and the advantages of climate and situation possessed by any particular piece of land have no cost of production.

From this it follows that an increase in land values must represent an increase in the wealth of individual landowners without the performance of any equivalent service on their part, unless the rise is due to the sinking of capital in improvements. On the other hand, a fall in land values represents a windfall loss to landowners with no offsetting gain. Generally, with an increasing population, we expect to see land values moving upwards. In nineteenth century Britain, however, land values remained remarkably steady (taking agricultural land only). This must be set down to the opening up of vast tracts of land in America and elsewhere, and the consequent damping down of the pressure on British land. The land of the New World came into competition with the land of the Old, drawing off large numbers of emigrants, and sending back supplies of foodstuffs which, instead of becoming increasingly dear, became increasingly cheap. Nevertheless the fear remained that the needs of an increasing population would eventually force up land values and deposit an "unearned increment" in the lap of British landlords. As for *urban* land values, they rose steadily as the towns grew in size, and there was never any doubt that the fortunate owners of sites in and around the towns were enjoying a substantial "unearned increment."

The fact that it costs nothing to supply land (as contrasted with the cost of labouring or saving) leads to a second important conclusion. For if it costs nothing to supply land, nothing is gained by making no use of it. Hence if the choice lies between letting land for an almost nominal rent and not letting it at all, it will pay to let it. The rent will be fixed by what the market will bear, not by cost, for the reason that there is no cost. It will always pay to obtain from land whatever income it will bring in, over and above the expense of farming it. Where land is not used for any purpose whatever, it is presumably because it is too inferior in fertility or in situation to yield a surplus above the cost of farming it.[1]

This reasoning can be extended to any productive agent where nothing is gained by failure to make use of it. A piece of machinery, for example, may depreciate no more rapidly when in use than when idle. If so, the real cost of using it (the sacrifice to which its owner is put) is nil, and it will pay to keep it in use so long as operating costs are covered. It is true that, unlike a piece of land, the machine cost something to produce, that the owner has hopes of recovering this "sunk" cost, and that, if he does not, he will be unlikely to replace the machine when it wears out. But his past hopes and present chances are two different things. The cost of producing the machine has little connection with the cost of using it. The first was incurred long ago, and in economics one of the most important principles is that "bygones are forever bygones." The second is the cost of efforts and sacrifices which people are induced to make *now*; and the use of the machine involves no sacrifice whatever. The cost of using it is nil. We have here one more example of the analogy drawn above between land and durable capital.

(iii) **Heterogeneity**—A third characteristic of land is its heterogeneity. No two pieces of land are exactly alike in fertility or in situation. Some are highly fertile and situated near large urban markets, while some are on mountain tops and miles from anywhere. It is possible to arrange each piece of ground (or each deposit of minerals or each fishery) in descending order of value, ranging from those which it would pay to use in almost any circumstances to those which are unlikely ever to be used at all. We might have Manhattan Island at one end of the list and the South Pole at the other. A line can be drawn somewhere on the list between pieces of land which repay cultivation and those which do not; between pieces which are worth building on and pieces which are not; between deposits which can profitably be mined and deposits which can not; and between fisheries which it does and does not pay to exploit. This line is generally referred to as *the margin*. Land for which there is no remunerative use of any kind is called "sub-marginal"; land which it is just worth while

---

[1] In the real world, where agricultural land depreciates when not in use (e.g., because it becomes overgrown with weeds) the reasoning given above is reinforced. It is doubly important to find a user for land if capital is lost as well as no rent earned when the land lies idle.

to cultivate is said to be "on the margin of cultivation"; and land which yields a substantial surplus above farming costs is described as "intra-marginal." The margin, or line of division, is not, of course, fixed. It is pushed outwards, so as to include land that was formerly sub-marginal, if, for example, population increases and the demand for foodstuffs becomes more pressing. Or if, to take the opposite case, population falls, or people eat less food, or larger crops can be grown on the existing area under cultivation, the margin will press inwards and more land will pass into the sub-marginal, unused class. Similarly with mining. A fall in mining costs, for example, will bring pits which were previously uneconomic above the margin, while a rise in costs will force some pits over the margin into idleness, because mining operations have ceased to be worth while on the thinnest seams, or leanest ores, or deepest deposits, or in the most gaseous or flooded pits.

The margin of cultivation divides land which yields a surplus over costs of cultivation in any use (no matter what), from land which cannot be made to yield a surplus in any use whatever. A second kind of margin, the margin of transference, divides land which it pays to use for one purpose (e.g., dairy-farming) from land which it pays to use for another (e.g., cattle-rearing). We can range land used for dairying and cattle-rearing in order of what one may call "relative suitablity" for dairying, at current prices of milk and store cattle and at current levels of farming costs. There will be some land (e.g., rich pasture or land near the towns) for which dairying can easily outbid cattle-rearing. There will also be some land (e.g., hill-grazings and land in rather inaccessible places) where the advantage clearly lies with cattle-rearing. Land intermediate between these types can be allotted with more difficulty, and may pass from one use to the other, crossing and re-crossing the margin of transference, as milk prices rise or fall relatively to cattle prices. Land near to the margin of transference may be relatively well-suited to both dairying and cattle-rearing (and pay a high rent), or relatively ill-suited (and pay a low rent). The main point is that the pull on both sides, whether strong or weak, is roughly equal. If the pull of one side is strengthened (e.g., by a rise in the price of milk) more land is transferred across the margin, and a new margin, at which the pull on both sides balance again, comes into existence.

The third characteristic of land is one shared in by all the factors. The conception of the margin, which derives from this characteristic, can be applied, therefore, to labour and capital as well as to land. If pieces of land are different from one another, so are workers and their tools. If there are marginal tracts of sheep-land, there are also marginal shepherds and marginal sheep. There is no conception in modern economics of which such extensive use is made, or which is so fundamental to an understanding of the subject, as the conception of the margin. We shall meet with it in many forms from now on.

## The law of diminishing returns

Reflection on the characteristics of land gave us, about 150 years ago, one of the most famous of economic laws—the law of diminishing returns:

*Successive applications of labour and capital to a given area of land must ultimately, other things remaining the same, yield a less than proportionate increase in produce.*

This "law" is simply a generalisation based on experience. If the law were not true, if by doubling his outlay an labour and capital a farmer could double his produce, every farmer could save nearly the whole of his rent by giving up all but a small piece of his land and concentrating all his labour and capital upon that piece. Instead of spending £10 on each of 50 acres, he could multiply his outlay fifty-fold on a single acre and still grow as much as before. Similarly there would be no point in having large herds of cattle if every addition to the feeding stuffs increased the weight of the cattle at a steady rate, without limit. A single bullock would supply the nation. But the bullock, in point of fact, responds with constant or increasing returns only if he has been half-starved, and with rapidly diminishing returns if he has not.

A farmer may, *for a time*, work under increasing returns (that is, additions to his outlay on labour and capital may yield a *more* than proportionate increase in produce). It may happen for example, that he spreads his work over so large an area that he would gain by concentrating his labour and capital on a smaller space. This may be the result of bad organisation; he may, for example, be sowing so lightly that his crops are smothered by weeds. But it may also in the short run be due to the inability of the farmer either to use less land or more capital. His land may, for example, be understocked, in the sense that if he could raise the necessary capital he could feed a larger herd of cattle and obtain a larger return per pound of capital invested. In the same circumstances it would pay the farmer to use less land (and so save rent) but the terms of his lease may make this (for the time being) impossible.

Other things, too, must remain the same. The return to labour and capital per acre of land may be raised and the law of diminishing returns suspended if some new discovery makes land more fertile, or if, because farmers are better trained or more skilled, they are able to put capital to a better use than their less efficient predecessors. Fertilisers can treble the weight of wheat crops: new brands of sugar can yield six times as much as the old: new feeding stuffs can fatten cattle to weights undreamt of 200 years ago. But once a discovery has been made the law reasserts itself. At Rothamsted wheat was grown on five plots, one receiving mineral manure alone and each of the others various "doses" of nitrogen. One dose of nitrogen increased the yield by 10·3 bushels, a double dose by 19·4 bushels, three doses by 21·3 bushels and four doses by 21·8 bushels. The successive increments of nitrogen therefore conformed to the law of diminishing returns by yielding diminishing increments of product.

Many of these propositions can be more readily understood with the help of a diagram. In Diagram 2, units of labour and capital applied to, let us say, an acre of land are plotted on the X axis and the increments in product yielded by each successive unit of labour and capital are plotted along the Y axis. The

DIAGRAM 2

THE LAW OF DIMINISHING RETURNS

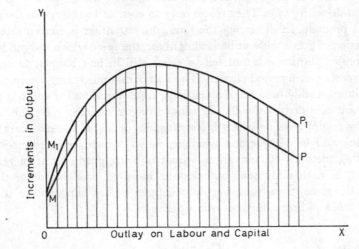

total crop is represented by the sum of the increments, i.e., by the total area under the curve MP. At first, there are likely to be increasing returns: if twice as much labour and capital is used, the crop will more than double. Later, there will be decreasing returns: the increments (represented by strips of constant width) will become smaller and smaller. If an improved type of fertiliser comes on the market, the productivity of the soil will be increased, and the curve of productivity will rise from the position MP to the position $M_1P_1$. If labour and capital become scarcer and costlier, the distance along the X axis which we will move for each £1 spent will shorten (i.e., the strips will be narrower) and the same crop will now cost more to grow. It will be observed that the diagram shows actual quantities of product and not the cash value of these yields.

A tendency to decreasing returns is generally associated with a tendency to increasing cost. If equal applications of labour and capital yield diminishing increments of product, then each successive increment will be increasingly costly. The fifth pound's worth of fertiliser may add two bushels to the yield of an acre of wheat while the tenth pound's worth adds only one bushel. The cost of an extra bushel, therefore, will rise from 10/- to £1 as cultivation becomes more intensive. In other words, the greater the quantity of foodstuffs which we try to raise on a given area of land, the more costly will these foodstuffs be. It is this conclusion, so enormously important to a country with a rapidly increasing population, that has made the law of diminishing returns so celebrated.

For a clear understanding of the laws of diminishing returns and increasing cost, it is essential to keep two points in mind. First, the laws have nothing whatever to do with *profits*. They relate only to cost, or to returns in the sense of physical product. In discussing the laws, our attention is concentrated on the production of goods without bothering about the price which the goods will fetch. Secondly, the laws do not tell us what will in fact happen to costs if output increases over a period of years. The cost of manufacturing a commodity may be falling steadily because of inventions, discoveries, and so on. But these influences are excluded by the clause "other things remaining the same." The fact that the cost of growing wheat *is becoming* less, or *will be* less ten years from now, is irrelevant to the question whether, under present circumstances and using existing methods of cultivation, wheat is being produced at increasing cost or not. If each additional bushel costs more to produce, other things remaining the same, then, whatever does happen or has happened in wheat-farming, the law of increasing cost is in operation.

## CAPITAL

When we speak of our capital we include two different things: our property (i.e., our goods and chattels and any business property we own) and our financial assets (including cash in hand and titles to wealth such as stocks and shares). Let us take these in turn.

### Physical assets

Property or physical capital consists of a stock of assets possessing a money value. In the narrow sense of trade capital, it includes only assets in the hands of producers; in the broad sense, it becomes co-extensive with social wealth, and includes assets in the hands of consumers (dwelling-houses, motor-cars, etc.) or belonging to the community.

Trade capital consists of the fixed instruments of production (buildings, ships, machinery, etc), goods in process, and stocks of finished goods. The last two items are classed together as working capital, while the first is called fixed capital. The line of division is easily drawn, since fixed capital is not used up in a single use, whereas working capital is.

Social capital is something rather broader. It includes not only trade capital, but also non-commercial assets that possess a money value. These are productive resources equally with trade capital, since they have been accumulated with a view to satisfying human wants. We cannot, for example, rule out house-property from capital; for it is just as indispensable to meeting some of our wants as are railway carriages or blast furnaces to meeting others. Nor can we draw a satisfactory line of division between houses let to tenants, and bringing in an income of profit to their owner, and houses retained by landlords for their own use and supplying them with shelter which would otherwise have to be bought.

The distinction between social capital and wealth is one of stand-point. Capital is an agent in *production*: it represents resources that can be used in the future. Wealth is a fund upon which we can draw in *consumption*: it represents stored up facilities for the satisfaction of future wants. But what are "resources" to the producer are "facilities" to the consumer. No one distinguishes as a private citizen between his capital and his wealth, except when speaking of his stock-in-trade (i.e., of trade capital). For society as a whole, the same identity exists so long as we think consistently of wealth and capital in real terms as a stock of assets, and ignore debts altogether.

Arguments about physical capital very often assume that it consists mainly of machinery used in factories. This assumption is, however, quite false. There is usually far more capital sunk in a country's house-property than in all the machinery used in its factories and mines. It is in buildings (including factory buildings, shops, etc.), in transport (roads, railways, ships, etc.), and in public utilities (gas, water, electricity, harbours and docks, etc.) that by far the largest proportion of a country's capital is invested.

## Financial assets

**(a) Money**—So accustomed are we to include money in our capital that we do not always distinguish carefully between money and capital. The terms, in everyday speech, are used interchangeably. For instance, we speak of a millionaire "leaving a great deal of money." No doubt, by *our* standards, he did leave a fair amount of cash to his heirs. But his legacies probably consisted in the main of valuable property (ships, factories, rubber plantations, etc.) or of stocks and shares and other titles to wealth. Capital can always be given a money-valuation. But there is a difference between reckoning capital in terms of money, and using the terms "capital" (or "wealth") and "money" to mean the same thing.

When we seek to increase our capital, we do so firstly by adding to our stock of money. Normally it is money that we save and money that we borrow. Often, therefore, we talk loosely of wanting more money when what we really want is more capital. We want more money, not simply for ourselves, but, in our patriotic moods, for the whole country. We believe—quite mistakenly—that what is true for each of us must be true for all taken together, and that everyone would be better off if there were more money in the country. If there were more *capital* in the country, there would be a real gain to the community. But an increase in the stock of money would not, of itself, increase the stock of capital one iota. An increase in the supply of money—as David Hume argued two centuries ago—simply makes money less scarce and, therefore, less valuable. As the increased supply circulates, prices are driven up and money loses purchasing power. To be at pains to increase the supply of money (at any rate in good times) is rather like forcing food on a thin man who is already well-fed. Instead of making him fatter, you simply ruin his digestion.

The fact is that *any* stock of money will do to let the business of the world be transacted if prices and incomes are in line with the existing supply. An increase in the total stock is of service to the community only in special circumstances, whereas an increase in a person's stock of money is of service to him at any time. Money is capital to a person because it represents liquid resources which he can turn into concrete capital whenever he chooses. Money is not capital from the social point of view because society cannot use it to increase its stock of concrete capital, any more than Robinson Crusoe could have done so. Unlike a person, society cannot dispose of its money because there is no one to whom the money could be disposed of. A single country, however, can dispose of its gold holdings (and sometimes of part of its currency) to other countries, and might fairly treat its gold reserve as capital.

The confusion of money with capital and wealth might seem too crude to have played much part in history. But when we study the history of trade policy, we find that for centuries statesmen defended a policy of tariffs and trade restriction by arguments build on this confusion. They passed laws prohibiting the export of good English money under penalty of death. They took measures (such as tariffs on imports, and bounties on exports) to preserve a favourable balance of trade with foreign countries, and to force them to pay in treasure for the balance of their purchases. They believed, with Thomas Mun —an economist of the seventeenth century—that "the ordinary means to increase our wealth and treasure is by foreign trade, wherein we must ever observe this rule: to sell more to strangers yearly than we consume of theirs in value." This balance of trade doctrine chimed with the intense nationalism of the period—as it does still—and issued in beggar-my-neighbour policies which were designed to increase our stock of the precious metals and deprive other countries of theirs.

We have seen that money is not a factor of production in the sense that it forms part of our productive resources. And yet it is clear that money is constantly being converted into the concrete capital which does form part of our resources, and that concrete capital is always convertible and is constantly being converted into money. A manufacturer borrows money with which to build his factory (i.e., he converts money into concrete-capital). A shopkeeper tries to sell his stock as fast as he can for money, with which he then buys more stock (i.e., he turns concrete-capital into money and back again). A great many decisions about capital, therefore (e.g., whether we will add to it, whether we will hold it in a liquid form, and so on), are to all appearances decisions about money. In fact, however, they are really decisions about how we will use our real resources. Our decisions to save and invest money are decisions about how much concrete capital there is to be, and what form it is to take. So long as we hold money, we can dictate whether resources will be used to meet our immediate wants (e.g., by spending the money on opera-seats) or whether they will be used in order to make an addition to our stock of capital assets (e.g., by investing the money in a new house). We have "free" capital at our disposal. Once invested, however, capital ceases to be "free." It is sunk in a real asset like a house, and can only be "recovered" (i.e., our money—or "free" capital with its power of disposal over liquid resources) as the asset wears out and the funds set aside annually to cover depreciation mount up to the sum needed in order to replace it.

To make all this clearer, let us see in more detail what is happening beneath the veil of money when we decide to save. First of all, we refrain from spending money on services (e.g., on tram fares, cinema tickets, etc.) or on goods for immediate consumption (food, clothing, etc.)—that is, on what are called "consumption goods." This means that we refrain from buying the services of those who make these goods. If we cut out buying chocolate, we deprive of a job the men, machines, and land which formerly supplied our want for chocolate. The first effect of saving, therefore, is to cause unemployment. Or, if as much chocolate as before is produced, stocks of unsold chocolate will accumulate, or will be disposed of only at unremunerative prices which impoverish the producer; neither of these things can go on indefinitely.

If, however, our savings are borrowed and expended on capital extensions, the borrower draws into employment men, machines, and land, paying out of our savings for the building of "capital goods" (factories, machinery, houses, etc.). Thus a boom in the capital goods industries accompanies and balances a slump in the consumption goods industries. Saving throws butchers and bakers and chocolate-makers out of work; investment creates employment for bricklayers, riveters, engineers, etc. The savers accumulate claims to the services of the factors of production; the borrowers exercise these claims. The transfer of money from savers to borrowers is a transfer of claims on productive resources. Moreover if the claims are not exercised *pari passu* with their accumulation, the savings have been wasted. The whole purpose of saving is to release productive resources from the task of meeting our day-to-day wants in order to undertake the more important task of enlarging our stock of capital equipment. To save is to spare productive power; and if that productive power is not utilised when the saving is done, it does not survive to be utilised later. Saving, as Sir Dennis Robertson put it, is the one thing that cannot be saved. There is no sense in sparing what no one proposes to use.

If, therefore, there is a hitch in the conversion of savings into concrete capital, or if productive resources cannot be easily switched from the consumption goods industries to the capital goods industries—and these are big "ifs," as we shall see when we come to discuss unemployment—saving has failed (in part at least) in its purpose. Instead of enriching the community by permitting works of enduring value to be set in hand, it will impoverish all those whose jobs it was to provide for the savers. The goods that are saved are not produced—there is no market for them; and no goods are produced in their place.

It is not just when savings are running to waste that the goods "saved" are not produced. As we have seen, what is saved is ultimately productive power, which is diverted from making the goods formerly bought by the savers to making capital goods for the borrowers. As savings increase, a change comes over the organisation of the labour force, so that more men are employed in the capital goods industries and fewer in the consumption goods industries. *Current* saving permits an addition to be made to concrete capital. Hence men work on new factories, new roads, new ships, new machines, etc. *Past* saving has accumulated a huge stock of concrete capital, which has constantly to be repaired and replaced. Hence new factories and roads and ships are needed because the old ones are wearing out; while an increasing number of men are engaged as engineers, plumbers, masons, roadmenders, etc., in maintaining the existing stock in working order. Production becomes more "roundabout." Instead of setting about making goods directly, men are called upon more and more to make goods to make the goods, or even to make goods to make the goods which make the goods—and so on, much as in the House that Jack Built.

**(b) Securities**—When money is lent, the burden of finding an outlet for savings in productive enterprise is transferred to the borrower. It is he who builds and owns the real asset that is added to our stock of capital. The lender retains only an expression of debt, a title to wealth, from which he expects to derive an income. Debentures or bonds, for example, will be added to his capital, while the companies to which he has lent build new factories or install more machinery. If we are thinking of capital as a factor of production we should include the machinery and the factories and exclude the bonds. But if we are thinking of capital, as we often do, as anything that yields us an income, debts will interest us just as much as real capital. If it were true that capital always yielded an income because it was a productive agent, then it would be easy to reconcile the two points of view. The income yielded by debts would be exactly equal to the productivity of the corresponding assets, and it would make little difference whether we regarded capital as income-yielding or as income-creating. But, in fact, debts are often unchanged when the value of the assets changes, or when the assets (like the munitions on which a large part of the National Debt was expended) have been blown to smithereens.

What applies to bonds applies also to other titles to wealth. The buyer of shares in a public company, for example, becomes one of the owners of the company and of its assets and expects his investments to yield him an income. He retains a piece of paper in the form of a share certificate, and the expectation of dividends. Corresponding to the paper and the expectation is the property of the company, which may or may not yield a profit and allow dividends to be paid.

## The Factors of Production and Productivity

When production increases, it may be because of an increase in the quantity of productive resources employed or because of an increase in their productivity: that is, in output per unit of labour, land and capital. It makes a great difference which is the cause of the growth in production, since on this depends whether the increased output has to be shared between a constant or a larger number of units of the factors of production. If there is no improvement in productivity, the only ways in which the standard of living of the population can be raised are through the provision of fuller employment for the available man-power or through an expansion in the supply of the other two factors of production, land and capital. Indeed, if man-power outstrips these two factors, for example because of population growth, the effect may be a fall in output per head and so in the standard of living because some of the additional man-power may be left unemployed or because the failure of land and capital to increase proportionately brings into play the law of diminishing returns: land and capital may operate as bottlenecks as the economy expands. The more common situation is one in which capital grows faster than man-power but

C

land remains relatively fixed. This might produce a gradual improvement in production per head, especially if capital could be used as a substitute for land (for example, through the use of fertilisers); but it could not bring about the rapid improvement that has in fact occurred over the past century or two. For an explanation of this improvement, we must look to the influences governing productivity, and particularly to the effects of scientific and technical progress.

In this chapter, it has been the supply of the factors of production that we have discussed, not their productivity. In the next few chapters we shall take the supply of the factors for granted and look at some of the influences on the efficiency with which they are used. We can observe those influences most clearly in the individual units, or firms, in which production is carried on; it is to the ways in which production is organised in such units that we now turn.

# PART II—INDUSTRIAL ORGANISATION

## CHAPTER 5

# GROWTH, TRANSFORMATION AND DEVELOPMENT

It would be possible to analyse the organisation of industry in purely static terms as if the object of industrial activity were to organise a constant stock of resources so as to satisfy fixed wants by unchanging methods. Such an analysis would obviously be a travesty in any modern economy where resources, wants and methods of production are always changing and where the facts of economic growth and development dominate the environment within which production is carried on. Before we embark on a discussion of industrial organisation, therefore, we must sketch, however briefly, the more important of those facts and the more obvious of their implications.

In a growing economy a great many things increase simultaneously. There is usually more labour, more capital, more trade, a higher standard of living, and so on. These purely quantitative changes we may call *growth*. Everything does not—indeed, could not—increase equally, so that different parts of the economy show different rates of expansion and some parts may even have to contract. The structure of the economy has thus constantly to be adapted in order to restore balance between the different elements in it. This process of structural adjustment we may call *transformation*. In addition, the process of growth gives rise to new situations of a different kind: new attitudes emerge, new techniques are discovered and new institutions are organised. These are changes in the things that shape economic activity; they are reflected in the economic magnitudes that register growth but they are themselves essentially qualitative. We shall refer to these elements of novelty as *development*.

## I  GROWTH

We may begin by indicating the changes in some of the more important magnitudes to which we have just referred, leaving aside, until we come to the discussion on development, the causes of those changes.

(i) First of all, total output grows progressively except in periods of intense slump. This expansion in output brings with it a parallel expansion in incomes and purchasing power, since the more a country produces the richer it is, and there is a corresponding growth in the size of the market.

(ii) Secondly, the increase in production is usually accompanied by, and is partly due to, an increase in population, so that output per head rises more slowly than total production. In some countries the increase in production may be exceeded by the growth of population so that output per head actually falls. (See (vi) below).

(iii) The increase in production usually requires a more or less proportionate increase in the stock of capital. The accumulation of the additional capital is itself facilitated by the growth of production, especially if production outdistances population and so leaves a larger surplus from which savings can be made.

(iv) There is in most countries a steady improvement in productivity, i.e., in the efficiency with which productive resources are used. This improvement, together with the growth of capital, is the source of a rise in output per head. It is not easy to measure the change in productivity but the growth of output per man-hour serves as a rough guide. Strictly speaking, this measures the gain in productivity only in relation to the input of labour, without reference to the input of capital. If capital keeps pace with production, the change in output per man-hour exaggerates the rate of improvement in productivity per unit of labour and capital, but it serves as an accurate index both of the direction in which productivity is moving and of any acceleration that is taking place in the movement of productivity.

(v) The growth in productivity, measured in this way, normally yields a rather slower increase in output per head, a contraction in hours of work absorbing some of the gains from higher productivity. This increase in output per head brings with it an equal increase in income per head since, as we shall see,[1] output and income are really the same thing seen from two different angles. Income per head is the index used by economists to measure changes in the standard of living (although they recognise that it is not always a trustworthy index and never a complete one).[2] Rising productivity and a rising standard of living, therefore, go together.

---

[1] Below, pp. 356, *et seq.*

[2] There are special circumstances such as war-time when a large increase in output per head may be absorbed by the State without any improvement in the standard of living. There are also major changes in conditions of life which may not show up either in total production or in income per head. For example, hours of work in Britain have contracted by about one-third over the past century; working conditions are very much better; people are healthier and have a far greater chance of surviving to old age. The improvement in health and education, in security

(vi) Although growth is normally accompanied by higher productivity, there is nothing automatic about the association between the two. It would be possible for labour and capital to grow in such a way that each new factory duplicated existing ones, leaving output per head and per man-hour unaffected. The growth of population might also bring the law of diminishing returns into play by producing a growing shortage of land and natural resources. This would cause output per head to *fall* in some of the principal economic activities such as agriculture and would pull against the effect of technical progress and other factors operating to raise productivity.

The magnitude of some of the changes in production over the past century is illustrated in Table 2, on page 70. This summarises recent calculations of the growth in total production,[1] production per head and production per man-hour in a number of countries since 1870. The estimates are given in the form of indices, using as a base the year 1913, which comes roughly halfway through the period 1870–1960. The changes that have occurred are measured first in relation to the magnitudes applicable to 1913 and then, in the lower half of the table, as average annual rates of change over the periods 1870–1913, 1913–50 and 1950–60. The latter period is added to indicate how more recent experience compares with experience over the two longer intervals of time before and after 1913.

The increase in production per head has generally been less rapid than in total production or in output per man-hour; it has been outstripped by the first because of the simultaneous growth in population and by the second mainly because of the contraction in hours worked. In all the six countries shown, production has at least doubled since 1913; in the United States it has multiplied twenty-three times and in Sweden over ten times since 1870. The rate of increase has shown wide variations from country to country and in recent years has varied between an average of 2·6 per cent. per annum in the United Kingdom and 7·6 per cent. per annum in Western Germany. The growth in output per head has been greatest in Sweden: it is now nearly six times as large as in 1870. Production per man-hour in Sweden is nine times as great as in 1870. Other countries, while showing rather lower rates of improvement, also record striking advances. Moreover, the growth in productivity was particularly rapid

---

from misfortune and in access to common enjoyments, is not adequately measured by the income expended on the social services that provide them. On the other hand, part of the rise in income per head might be regarded as offsetting some of the inconveniences of modern industrial life—smoke, noise, strain, fatiguing journeys to work, and so on—if these inconveniences were thought to be peculiar to the present day.

[1] The measure of total production used in Table 2 is gross national product. For an explanation of this concept, see below, p. 366.

TABLE 2

THE GROWTH OF PRODUCTION, 1870–1960

| Growth in Production (1913 = 100) | | | | | | | |
|---|---|---|---|---|---|---|---|
| | | U.S. | U.K. | Germany (Fed. Rep.) | France | Italy | Sweden |
| Total production | 1870 | 17 | 39 | 30 | 51 | 55 | 29 |
| | 1913 | 100 | 100 | 100 | 100 | 100 | 100 |
| | 1960 | 403 | 244 | 327 | 200 | 288 | 311 |
| Production per head | 1870 | 45 | 63 | 51 | 55 | 71 | 39 |
| | 1913 | 100 | 100 | 100 | 100 | 100 | 100 |
| | 1960 | 217 | 193 | 208 | 216 | 229 | 224 |
| Production per man-hour | 1870 | 37 | 52 | 42 | 46 | 59 | 32 |
| | 1913 | 100 | 100 | 100 | 100 | 100 | 100 |
| | 1960 | 305 | 231 | 250 | 264 | 298 | 290 |

| Growth rates per cent. per annum | | | | | | | |
|---|---|---|---|---|---|---|---|
| Total production | 1870–1913 | 4·3 | 2·2 | 2·9 | 1·6 | 1·4 | 3·0 |
| | 1913–1950 | 2·9 | 1·7 | 1·2 | 0·7 | 1·3 | 2·2 |
| | 1950–1960 | 3·2 | 2·6 | 7·6 | 4·4 | 5·9 | 3·3 |
| Production per man-hour | 1870–1913 | 2·4 | 1·5 | 2·1 | 1·8 | 1·2 | 2·7 |
| | 1913–1950 | 2·4 | 1·7 | 0·9 | 1·6 | 1·9 | 2·0 |
| | 1950–1960 | 2·4 | 2·0 | 6·0 | 3·9 | 4·1 | 3·5 |

*Source:* A. Maddison, *Economic Growth in the West* (The Twentieth Century Fund, New York, 1964).

in the fifties; it was 2 per cent. per annum or more in all six countries included and exceeded the secular average by a comfortable margin in all except the U.S. It needs no great command of arithmetic to demonstrate what a transformation in living standards would accompany the prolongation of such rates of improvement over several decades; if production per head grows at 3 per cent. per annum, it doubles every 23 years.

## 2  TRANSFORMATION: CHANGES IN THE PATTERN OF ECONOMIC ACTIVITY

These rapid rates of growth are accompanied by large changes in the composition of final output and in the distribution of man-power and other resources between different industries and areas. Some of these changes are predictable and reflect the shift in spending patterns as people become better off. For example, there is a well-known generalisation, known as Engel's Law, that the proportion of income spent on food tends to decline as income grows: a poor man is obliged to spend a great deal of his income on food, while a rich man, although spending a larger absolute amount on food, will devote a higher proportion of his income to other things. One implication of this Law is that, as *per capita* incomes rise, the industry which supplies us with food (i.e.

agriculture) will tend to occupy a relatively smaller place in the economy. On the other hand, there are various services (e.g. professional services) on which a community spends a higher proportion of its income as it grows richer, and these services, therefore, tend to occupy an expanding proportion of the labour force.

DIAGRAM 3

INDUSTRIAL STRUCTURE OF THE LABOUR FORCE IN RELATION TO INCOME
PER HEAD

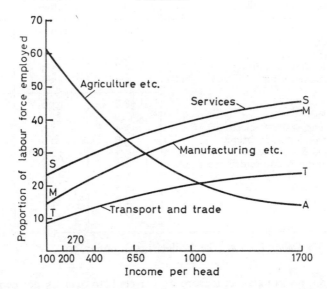

These tendencies can be illustrated from calculations made by Professor Simon Kuznets. In making these calculations, Kuznets divided the labour force (excluding unpaid family labour) into three main industrial groups in each of 38 countries, the groups consisting of agriculture, forestry and fishing (A sector); mining, manufacturing and construction (M sector); and all other activities and services (S sector). He then grouped the 38 countries in terms of production per head and worked out the relative size of the A, M and S sectors in each of seven groups of countries with average *per capita* incomes ranging from about 100 dollars in the poorest group up to 1700 dollars in the richest. The A sector employed a much larger slice of the labour force in the poorest than in the richest group of countries, the variation being between 61 per cent. at the one end and 14 per cent. at the other. On the other hand, the M sector expanded from 15 per cent. of the labour force in the poorest group to over 40 per cent.

TABLE 3

WORKING POPULATION OF SCOTLAND BY INDUSTRIAL GROUP, 1851–1951

| Percentage of total working population employed in: | 1851 | 1901 | 1951 |
|---|---|---|---|
| | | Percentage | |
| Agriculture, forestry and fishing .. | 27·4 | 12·5 | 7·3 |
| Mining and quarrying .. .. .. | 3·8 | 6·7 | 4·4 |
| Manufacturing .. .. .. .. | 38·8 | 34·6 | 36·0 |
| Services trades (incl. building) .. .. | 30·0 | 46·2 | 52·3 |
| | 100·0 | 100·0 | 100·0 |
| Manufacturing groups: | | | |
| Metal trades .. .. .. .. | 4·8 | 11·1 | 16·3 |
| Textiles, leather & clothing .. .. | 28·8 | 15·7 | 8·0 |
| Other manufacturing .. .. .. | 5·2 | 7·8 | 11·7 |
| | 38·8 | 34·6 | 36·0 |
| Service trades: | | | |
| Building, gas, water & electricity .. | 5·3 | 7·5 | 7·7 |
| Transport & communications .. | 3·8 | 8·6 | 8·4 |
| Distribution & commerce .. .. | 5·3 | 12·4 | 14·7 |
| Public administration & defence .. | 1·3 | 1·5 | 6·4 |
| Professional services .. .. .. | 2·2 | 3·3 | 7·1 |
| Domestic service .. .. .. | 9·3 | 8·7 | 2·3 |
| Other services .. .. .. .. | 2·8 | 4·2 | 5·7 |
| | 30·0 | 46·2 | 52·3 |

Source: *The Scottish Economy* (Cambridge, 1954), pp. 77, 79.

in the richest, and the S sector from 24 per cent. to over 45 per cent. Further sub-division of the S (or services) sector showed that the expansion was largely confined to two groups, one of which was transport and communications and the other, trade and finance. These two together accounted for only 8 per cent. of the labour force in the poorest countries and for 24 per cent in the richest.[1]

These figures and Diagram 3, which is based on Professor Kuznets' data, illustrate the structural adjustments between different sectors of an economy to which economic growth gives rise. They bring out the dynamic character of specialisation and the need confronting every economy to adapt itself not only to its failures but also to its successes. Man-power and other resources must be ready to abandon one specialised pursuit in favour of another; and the more rapidly the economy grows the more pressing is this necessity.

[1] S. Kuznets, *Six Lectures on Economic Growth* (Free Press of Glencoe, Illinois, 1959).

## Another illustration

The same conclusions can be reached from figures for a single industrial country showing long-term changes in the distribution of its man-power. In Table 3 are shown the changes that took place in the half-centuries on either side of 1901 in the working population of Scotland. Agriculture contracted and the service trades expanded, while the manufacturing sector, at first sight, employed a comparatively static proportion of the working population. On closer inspection, however, even this sector underwent a great transformation, for while the textile, leather and clothing trades employed 29 per cent of total man-power in 1851, they employed no more than 8 per cent in 1951, and their rate of contraction over the century was very little different from the rate of contraction of Scottish agriculture. Similarly, although the service trades as a group were an expanding sector of the labour market, domestic service, which had been the largest single element in the total for the group in 1851, contracted sharply in the last two decades and had become a relatively small element in the total in 1951.

### 3   DEVELOPMENT

Development is a more complicated business than growth and transformation. It overflows beyond the purely economic aspects of life and may alter radically the whole structure of society from the family at one end to the functions of the State at the other. The kind of economic development that has taken place since the industrial revolution has transformed work and leisure, changed the balance of political power, overthrown class relationships, introduced new educational needs and opportunities, and modified religious convictions and behaviour. Nor should one think of it as a once-for-all affair that gradually peters out; on the contrary, the pace of development is probably at least as rapid, even in the most "advanced" countries, as in any previous period.

## Techniques, attitudes and institutions develop

For present purposes, we must confine ourselves to a single aspect of development—its contribution to growth and particularly to the growth of productivity. From this point of view, development embraces the three broad elements which we referred to earlier as techniques, attitudes and institutions. These three elements interact with each other and with the growth of productive resources to produce growth. Apart from any advantages that flow from the sheer size of an economy and hence can be derived from a multiplication of the factors of production, and apart also from the discovery of fresh resources

C*

not hitherto charted, it is through development and development alone that productivity improves.[1]

## Development *is* innovation

This may seem a bold statement if the full compass of what is included in development is not understood. For development takes in all forms of innovation: in technology, in personal conduct, in methods of organisation, in laws and customs. It may be development in one country if the laws are enforced; in another, if cows cease to be sacred; in a third, if a man can make more money than his neighbours without having his house burned down or suffering other mischief. In an industrial country, it is natural to lay stress on advances in science and technology and on innovations in methods of production as the principal source of rising productivity. But even in such countries attitudes may be hostile to new techniques and unresponsive to financial incentives; business may be looked upon as rather degrading; and existing institutions—for example, company legislation or the machinery for financing new enterprises —may not be adapted to the needs of a developing economy. In pre-industrial countries, the need for social change to accompany technical change stands out far more clearly: in those countries attitudes and institutions lag quite as much as technology behind the practice of industrial countries, and the problem is not so much one of growth within an existing framework as of the replacement of one civilisation by another.

## How techniques, attitudes and institutions interact

The various elements that constitute development interact with one another and with the growth of productive resources. We can see this best in an underdeveloped country or by looking at the process of development in Western Europe over the past two or three centuries. A more experimental and secular temper in the population makes it possible for knowledge to grow more systematically, to acquire the force and universality of science and to issue in a cumulative and self-sustaining process of industrial innovation. The new methods and machines react on popular attitudes, creating new habits, new wants and new expectations; people become more willing to contemplate improvements, more perceptive of opportunities of improvement and more ready to take advantage of those opportunities. At the same time, the spread of new ideas and new attitudes, and the upheavals associated with industrialisation and the growth of modern technology, work a revolution in social, political

---

[1] This proposition does not apply rigorously to a single country since any one country may benefit from changes taking place abroad.

and economic institutions. New forms of organisation have to be devised—the joint stock company, for example—and their introduction, like the introduction of newly invented machines, opens up fresh possibilities of growth. All of these changes may be accelerated by a simultaneous, and partly independent, expansion in productive resources through geographical and geological discovery, population growth and the accumulation of capital assets.

## Capital accumulation and growth

The interconnection between the different elements is often overlooked when economists dwell on some one factor as the prime source of economic growth. They may, for example, lay stress on the accumulation of capital as indispensable to higher levels of output and productivity. It is true that in the early stages of industrialisation there is frequently an acute shortage of physical assets to provide a framework for subsequent growth. Such towns as there are may be small and poorly equipped to serve as centres for marketing and distribution; factory production may be almost unknown; there may be few sources of electric power and no adequate transport system. In such circumstances, capital can be a bottleneck and the growth of capital may permit a much improved organisation of resources. In industrial countries too, more capital is usually required in order to take advantage of new processes and to produce new products, so that the forward movement of the economy pivots on the continuous accumulation of capital assets embodying the latest advances in technique.

The accumulation of capital, however, is not something completely autonomous and divorced from other social and economic forces. It involves an effort of saving and saving reflects an attitude towards the future.[1] This attitude is itself something that has to be developed: it depends upon social institutions—the assurance that property rights will be respected, the convenience with which savings can be invested, the emergence of intermediaries like banks and insurance companies—and it depends also upon the opportunities that exist for fruitful investment. In a society governed by custom and routine the need for savings and the incentive to save are alike reduced; but where innovation is rapid both are powerfully reinforced.

---

[1] Cf. S. H. Frankel, *The Economic Impact on Under-developed Societies* (Oxford 1953). "The great growth of capital in the eighteenth and nineteenth centuries in Europe was due . . . to the emergence of new types of social activity. 'Saving' was not a mechanical act but the result of new attitudes in social behaviour. To repair and maintain; to think of to-morrow not only of to-day; to educate and train one's children; to prepare oneself for new activities; to acquire new skills; to search out new contacts; to widen the horizon of individual experience; to invent, to improve, to question the 'dead hand of custom', and the heritage of the past—in all these . . . lay the causes of capital accumulation." (pp. 69–70).

**What produces innovation?**

The process of innovation lies at the heart of economic development. But it is, as we have seen, a highly complex process. It rests first and foremost on the growth of knowledge and experience. The most important asset of any community it its intellectual, not its physical capital: not only the knowledge which it already possesses and the less communicable experience which it has built up, but the capacity to add to them both and to put them to use in commerce and industry, and the willingness to be guided by knowledge and experience rather than by dogma and received opinion. It is this intellectual capital that allows the community to discard old ideas and frame or learn new ones, and to profit from that substitution of new processes and products for old which issues in higher productivity and which we call technical progress.

The growth of knowledge, once scientific habits of mind take root, follows an inner logic of its own. But the application of scientific knowledge, and the direction taken by scientific research, are no more independent of social factors than is capital accumulation. Both respond to commercial incentives. Scientists and technologists may pursue truth for its own sake; but the firms who employ them or make use of their results do so in the expectation that they will profit by doing so. Spurred on by competition, each firm is constantly reviewing the techniques which it uses so as to take advantage of new knowledge and, by superseding one process or method of production by a better one, reduce its costs and raise its productivity. When it makes an innovation in technique, it rarely takes over a ready-made invention, conceived and developed outside competitive industry by some individual scientist. There is usually a long and expensive process to be gone through before a novel idea, wherever originating, emerges as a working model and a still longer and more expensive process before the working model is translated into large-scale production. At each stage, money has to be provided and the readiness with which this is done will depend not only on the prospects of mastering the technical snags and producing an acceptable design but even more on the market possibilities for the finished product.

**Innovation and technical progress**

Technical progress should not be thought of in terms of the discontinuous introduction of major inventions, important though these may be. It consists, rather, in a continuous search for improvements in existing materials, machines and methods of production, a simultaneous scrutiny of market opportunities in the hope of devising new products or changes in existing products more to the liking of consumers, and, in addition, a combing through of the ideas flowing from scientific research in order to adapt these ideas to commercial applications. The pace of technical progress is faster the more rapidly knowledge spreads and is applied; and this brings us back once again to the social factors governing the numbers, alertness, power, and commercial ability of those who see advantage in innovation.

### The expansion of overseas markets

If we look back on the steady and continuous growth in production since the industrial revolution, and leave aside the part played by the increase in population, technical progress and the accumulation of capital are bound to strike us as two of the dominant forces at work. But there was a third: the expansion of overseas markets. This was not independent of the other two, for it was largely made possible by the railway and the steamship on the one hand and by the investment of large amounts of capital abroad on the other. The settlement of countries overseas and the expansion in markets that went with it did, however, permit the industrial countries of Europe to re-deploy their resources and profit from a division of labour with other countries. A market grew up in Europe (and especially in Great Britain) for the foodstuffs and raw materials produced overseas and the newer primary producers were able to accelerate their development by specialising on exports to that market. In return, they imported manufactures and capital equipment from specialist producers in Europe. This trade not only expanded the scale on which industrial products were made in European factories, with all the attendant benefits of large-scale operation, but enabled a country like Britain to give up producing some of its foodstuffs at high cost and transfer agricultural workers to industrial occupations in which they could earn substantially higher wages. The growth of overseas markets contributed in this way to the more productive employment of Britain's man-power; it brought into play that process of transformation which we saw earlier to be a normal concomitant of a rise in the standard of living.

### Trade, specialisation and development

There are other circumstances in which the expansion of markets may play a similar role. For example, the emergence of a subsistence economy, isolated from markets, into a money economy, growing cash crops and exchanging them for imported manufactures, makes for an expansion of production and a higher return to the factors of production. It can also be the first step in the economic development of a backward country: the growth of trade and the specialisation that goes with it is an indispensable preliminary to the operation of other factors for higher productivity. Robinson Crusoe could add to his resources and income by making for himself new bits of equipment and so accumulating capital; he could raise his productivity by acquiring new skills, finding better ways of organising his time, and inventing new tools. But if he had a market for his output he would be able to make progress much more rapidly since he would acquire many things that he either could not make for himself or could make only with great difficulty. The development of a system of trading relationships in a money economy may thus be an important element in economic growth.

We may think of this element as production for a market, or as exchange and trade, or as specialisation, because all three are facets of the same thing. When we exchange, we inevitably specialise. We limit the range of things we do and enlarge the range of things we consume; we give up variety in our work for the sake of variety when we come to spend the proceeds. The usual form of exchange is working for money in a specialised occupation, the money entitling us to the products of other specialists. The more of our time we give to working for money rather than to producing things for ourselves, the more we must specialise in making the products which we trade and the more dependent we are on a market for our services.

Once a money economy has emerged and full advantage has been taken of opportunities of trade, the growth of markets continues to be an important influence on production. But at this stage it is no longer an entirely new institution—production for a market—that is in course of development and exercising the stimulus to growth which, as we have seen, new institutions can exert. An expansion of markets, once trading relationships have been established, may be no more than the reflection of an expansion in output due to other factors, such as technical progress and capital accumulation. The more a country produces, the higher is its income and the wider the market confronting individual producers. This widening of the market may afford opportunities of specialising in different directions or to a greater degree; but it no longer makes the difference between an economy in which specialisation is governed by market forces and one in which it is not.

Since specialisation is the subject of the next two chapters, it is important to see how it bears on the present topic. In a sense, the growth of specialisation is no more than a particular example of institutional development. But it is also something much more, since it is the basis of exchange and therefore of the economic activity which it is the business of economists to analyse. The various elements in economic development that we have been discussing would all be robbed of much of their importance but for extensive specialisation. Take, for example, the introduction of rail transport which revolutionised production in the nineteenth century. Railways required a great deal of capital for their construction and the steam locomotive represented a major advance in technique.

But the capital could never have been raised had there been no specialists in finance—promoters, bankers, issuing houses, etc.—to investigate, and to obtain support for, business propositions which might be made to yield a profit. Similarly, the steam engine could never have led to the railway had there been no division of labour between engine-drivers, engine-makers, guards, porters, signalmen, and so on.

We shall be discussing specialisation mainly in the context of industrial organisation. But industry, as we have seen, employs only a limited proportion of the man-power of a country and specialisation is not confined to industrial occupations. It is just as important to economic development that men should specialise in non-industrial as in industrial pursuits. The fact that economists fasten attention on industry by confining their analysis almost exclusively to industrial problems and illustrating their argument with industrial examples, justifies the reader in assuming that industrial problems have a special import-ance and in suspecting, quite rightly, that economists are more familiar with industry than with other sectors of the economy or find industry an easier sub-ject for generalisation. But it does not justify him in thinking of the economic system as bounded by industry and of production as equivalent to manufac-turing.

## Specialisation in the firm and the industry

This sketch of the growth and transformation of production, and the ways in which economic development takes place, is on a wider canvas than the chapters which follow. In those chapters, instead of an aerial survey of the broad forces governing production and productivity, we take a worm's eye view of the operation of those forces within the individual firm and industry. We begin with specialisation in its most elementary form as division of labour and look at some of its more obvious advantages and disadvantages. We then turn to specialisation by geographical area and the gravitation of different industries to one area rather than another; this part of the discussion is confined to localisation within a country and does not extend to international division of labour, a subject reserved for treatment in Chapter 31. The following chapters deal mainly with the ways in which productive resources are organised within individual firms: the balance that is struck between large firms and small; the need for specialist financial institutions if capital is to be found for large-scale production; the danger of monopoly if a single firm is able to achieve a dominant position in the market.

Although the object of this Part is to explain the organisation of industry as it exists rather than the way it changes over time, it is not possible to understand the problems of a firm or industry without some glimpse of the forces of dynamic change operating on it from outside and inside. A firm's markets change as the economy expands and the expansion of the economy is no more than the sum of the expansions that individual firms achieve. It is within firms that productive assets are accumulated and technical innovations are made. If economies grow and develop so also do firms and industries; and in judging whether they are efficiently organised we cannot do so in purely static terms. We must look not only to the way in which they use resources at a point in time but also to the scope which they offer for growth and development in the future.

# CHAPTER 6

# SPECIALISATION: DIVISION OF LABOUR

Specialisation and exchange are opposite sides of the same penny: without specialisation there could be no exchange, no trade, and no production for a market. Every economic system, therefore, rests on specialisation. Without it, we should return to a subsistence economy and to the low and precarious standard of living typical of such economies.

It was Adam Smith who first analysed the contribution made by specialisation to industrial efficiency. First of all, no two persons have exactly similar gifts. A professor may be a poor hand at cookery, and his cook be incapable of lecturing coherently. It will be an advantage if each concentrates upon what he can do best. Even if the professor is an excellent cook it will still be an advantage (since professors are more difficult to replace than cooks) if the professor refrains from taking up cookery.[1] The *special* gifts (and not just *any* natural gift) of each man are given the greatest possible scope when he specialises so as to devote the whole of his time to the occupation for which he is best suited. The labourer can make full use of strength and endurance, the skilled artisan of manual dexterity, and the company director of good judgment and organising ability. At the same time, those who lack the skill or physique necessary for some kinds of work are able to concentrate on other tasks in which their deficiencies are less of a handicap. Jobs in which a healthy or talented man would be wasted can be left to cripples and dunderheads. But specialisation is never perfect: there are plenty of square pegs in round holes. People may misjudge the aptitudes which they possess or which their job requires. Or they may be prevented by ignorance or bad organisation or lack of opportunity from finding work which makes full use of their natural bent. It is true that the force of

---

[1] There may be special circumstances, however, which make it worth his while to give at least some of his time to cookery: e.g., in self-defence, because the only cooks whom he can find are a menace to his digestion; or to indulge a passion for cooking; or to profit from a rise in the social importance of cooks and a general detestation of professors. There is a parallel between these cases and protectionist arguments in favour of limiting *international* division of labour.

competition will reduce the number of misplaced specialists by penalising them for their "error." People who mistake their vocation generally earn less than they might. But it would often be much simpler to offer a little good advice ("vocational guidance"), or free education, or more efficient labour management, rather than depend on the workings of competition to make people gravitate to suitable jobs.

Specialisation not only frees men to follow their natural bent. It *develops* skill in the specialist. Even if all men were alike, they would acquire, by constant practice, a knack of doing their specialised jobs. "The division of labour," as Adam Smith put it, "by reducing every man's business to some one simple operation, and by making this operation the sole employment of his life, necessarily increases very much the dexterity of the workman." Movements which at first are performed slowly and with difficulty are relegated, in William James' phrase, "to the effortless custody of automatism," and becomes rapid and precise. A trained typist will work much faster and with far less effort than an amateur who types only occasionally. Practice also familiarises a worker with the difficulties of his job, so that, for example, he can cope quickly with breakdowns and take steps to avoid them. Improvements, too, may occur to him. As he performs the same tasks day after day, he may see some method of simplifying the machinery or making it more nearly automatic.

Next there is a saving of time. In switching from one job to another, workers have to put away one set of tools and materials and assemble another. Very often they have to re-set their machinery—for instance, to spin a different count of yarn, or weave a different cloth, or roll a different section, in a steel rolling-mill. More time is wasted in warming to the new job. In the change-over, a man "commonly saunters a little. . . . When he first begins the new work he is seldom very keen and hearty: his mind, as they say, does not go to it, and for some time he rather trifles than applies to good purpose."[1] In unspecialised work, not only time but equipment is wasted. A man can only engage in a large number of tasks if he owns a correspondingly large number of tools, or if he runs the risk of being unable to borrow some tools when he wants them. When work is specialised, however, each worker is able to put his tools to constant use, and needs a much smaller supply of them.

Finally, specialisation makes possible a great extension in the use of machinery. Any manufacturing process can be split up into a number of distinct operations. "There are about ninety operations in making a pair of shoes, a hundred and fifty in making a man's coat, and thirteen in making a strip of steel into a spring leaf for an automobile spring."[2] Of these operations some are

---

[1] Adam Smith, *Wealth of Nations*, Book I, Chapter I.
[2] S. H. Slichter: *Modern Economic Society*, p. 93.

simple and regular, involving only the automatic repetition of identical move-ments. These can be taken over by machinery. Other operations require adjustment and control by a human agent. So long as these cannot be dispensed with, mechanisation can never be complete. In the making of electric lamps, for example, the wire may be drawn, the glass blown, and the lamps sealed mechanically, but the building, feeding, re-setting, and repairing of the machin-ery, and the collection and assembly of the parts, require constant control by a worker whose movements are never *exactly* repetitive.

Now if every stage of manufacture from start to finish were in the hands of the same worker, it would be very difficult to disentangle the mechanical operations and turn them over to a machine. For the machinery necessary for a single stage in manufacture is very often much too expensive to be worth introducing unless it is kept in constant use, and it is likely to be capable of handling an output far greater than a single worker could cope with. If, how-ever, each worker makes himself responsible for one or two operations only in the manufacture of a product, each stage of manufacture can be kept in gear with the succeeding stages, and if there is a wide enough market for the finished product, no opportunity of mechanising any operation need be missed. If a machine at one stage can handle a thousand times as much as the machine at the next, we need simply use the two machines in the ratio of a thousand to one, and adjust the number of workers at each stage correspondingly.

Thus the introduction of expensive machinery is generally worth while only if men will give their whole time to feeding it and tending it, and give up working on other products, and even at other stages of manufacture. The use of machinery, in other words, dictates a comparatively narrow type of specialisa-tion. From the simple division of labour where each man confines himself to the making of a single product from start to finish (specialisation by *product*), we pass to a more minute division of labour where the worker is responsible for one stage only in the process of manufacture (specialisation by *process*). The range of the worker's task is narrowed and standardised to suit the needs of the machine, while his share of the finished product becomes more and more difficult to identify. He may be tightening a succession of bolts with an electric wrench, watching for dents on tin cans as they pass before him on a moving belt, or assembling the same component part on one wireless set after another. There may be nothing that he can point to as his handiwork, or only some standard part, interchangeable with the product of thousands of other men.

## MACHINERY AND EFFICIENCY

Although machinery goes hand in hand with specialisation, the two things are obviously quite distinct, and each makes a separate contribution to industrial efficiency. The special contribution made by machinery can be summed up as precision and power.

**Precision**—The products of the machine, like its movements, are identical (or nearly so). Thus all the economies of standardisation are opened up whenever mechanical production becomes possible. In the days of James Watt and Adam Smith, "screw threads were in the main cut by hand by chipping and filling, every screw was different from every other, nuts and bolts had to be paired by specific fitting, and replacement in the ordinary sense was impossible."[1] Nowadays watch-screws weighing nine thousand to the ounce can be turned out at a vast rate and are indistinguishable under a microscope. The parts of a motor engine are accurate to within one-thirtieth the thickness of a human hair. Thus they can be made and tested in different departments (or in different factories), and can be assembled without waste to make engines whose reliability is known in advance. The parts are interchangeable, and as they can be kept in stock everywhere (or obtained quickly from the manufacturer) repair and replacement are cheap and easy. Expensive journeys are saved, since orders can be given from samples. An enormous amount of uncertainty is taken out of business: the product of the machine inherits the precision of the machine and maintains a common standard of performance on which the purchaser can depend. Above all, machinery can raise the productivity of unskilled labour enormously by putting at its command a precision unattainable by even the most skilled of workers.

**Power**—Secondly, machinery harnesses natural forces to produce power immensely greater than the muscle power of men or animals. In the Industrial Revolution it was water power that was harnessed. A water-wheel, driven by the current of a stream, provided the motive power for the whole factory. Later, steam power was introduced, at first to economise water by pumping it back after use into the reservoir above the wheel, and shortly afterwards to replace water power altogether. This was done by means of the steam engine which generated power from coal and started a new revolution in manufacturing and transport. Later still, the power to drive machinery was supplied by electricity generated from water, coal, and oil.

The power harnessed by machinery can take over tasks that exhaust the worker and shorten his life. Before the invention of the steam plane, for example, a carpenter employed to smooth floor boards was often an old man at forty. He

---

[1] *Factors in Industrial and Commercial Efficiency* (H.M.S.O., 1927), p. 273.

soon contracted heart disease and did not last "in his utmost vigour above eight years."[1] The work of the nineteenth century navvy was tiring in the extreme. But the operator of a mechanical scoop, moving a huge load of earth a great distance every minute, can do the work of hundreds of navvies without feeling exhausted at the end of the day. The machinery, moreover, is tireless. It represents power on tap. In many kinds of plant it can be left to work on, practically untended, provided material is supplied at certain intervals, and the product taken away when finished. A whole chain of operations, in many of which human muscles count for nothing, can be delivered over to machinery to be carried through with almost infallible regularity and exactitude.

Finally, the force supplied by machinery enables us to do what would otherwise be beyond our powers. We can build and operate motors, steamships, and aeroplanes; we can roll steel and crush rock; we can use electric vacuum-cleaners, refrigerators, central-heating, air-conditioning, and so on: all of which would be impossible without the assistance of machinery.

## The dangers of specialisation

We have concentrated up till now on the advantages of specialisation and machinery. Industrial efficiency is improved, unskilled labour used to better purpose, and more goods or more leisure made available to society. Against these benefits, however, must be set many serious drawbacks. Some of these are due purely to specialisation, and others mainly to the introduction of machinery.

First of all, workers may specialise too narrowly. A change of occupation is often a form of relaxation. It frees the mind from boredom and strain by introducing variety into work. It is also a form of insurance against unemployment, since the worker can turn from one occupation to the other when it suits him. Above all, it broadens a man's character and outlook. Set a man a wide variety of tasks and he has a chance to develop initiative, judgment, and resource. Narrow his tasks, and you may narrow the man. The more specialisation limits the scope of a man's work, the greater the risk that it will stifle something in his character. Industry not only provides for men: it also *produces* men. And the great danger in excessive specialisation is that it tends to be far more successful in providing for men than in producing men of the right sort.

Secondly, from the social point of view, specialisation loosens the ties by which the community is bound together. Specialists have their peculiar background. They live in a world of their own, cut off from other specialists by their training, their habits, and above all by their interests. There is thus a constant danger of sectionalism: the specialists entrench themselves in organised groups

---

[1] Adam Smith, *Wealth of Nations*, Book I, Chapter VIII.

in defence of their interests, and often in disregard of the interests of the community. Against this sectionalism, unity of culture is the only prophylactic. But in a society of specialists, where men's ideas are often unintelligible to one another, their tastes incongruent, and their moral standards uncertain, such unity is hard to achieve. For a common culture in which all can share, there must be a common framework of reference and common preoccupations. But when specialisation is pushed too far, the common framework tends to be destroyed, and the common preoccupations to be overlaid by other, more specialised, interests.

Thirdly, those who specialise in making a single product or in doing a single job run great risks. They depend on their fellows to buy their goods and services and to sell them in return the products which they lack. They hope to be able to win a livelihood by exchanging the goods which they can produce and do not want for the goods which they do want and which others can produce. If exchanges can be made quickly and readily, well and good. But exchange is often costly, or slow and unreliable. The parties may live at great distances from one another, or much time may be taken up in striking a bargain, or there may be no regular dealings, so that it is not easy to find a buyer or a seller at short notice.

These risks and difficulties are multiplied enormously when production is undertaken in advance of demand, and when the circle of exchange widens to include specialists in every country in the world. When the village tailor makes shirts to order for his neighbours he runs little risk. But when a number of textile workers, most of them strangers to one another, co-operate to make a shirt in Lancashire in the faith that someone in Australia will want a shirt of just that size, pattern, and colour, and that his path and the path of the shirt will cross when he is in the right frame of mind to buy the shirt, the risks of the textile workers are obvious. They are not, perhaps, so enormous as they seem, for men are creatures of habit, and their wants do not change so rapidly that they cannot be predicted with fair confidence a few months ahead—even from a distance of several thousand miles. Nor are the risks as great as they would be in the absence of rapid transport (by steamship) and modern methods of communication (by cable and wireless). The steamship cuts down the time which it takes for the shirts to reach Australia, while cable and wireless services put Lancashire and Australia in close touch with one another, so that news is available in one country shortly after it is known in the other. This saving in time reduces the period over which forecasts must be made, and so makes it possible to foresee market requirements with greater accuracy and more certainty. But when all allowance is made, risks remain enormous. For the worker, no less than for the capitalist, there is no assured market. His specialised gifts are not certain of constant employment; his specialised job is not certain to yield him a steady wage; his chances of turning his hand to some other job are not certain to remain good. He is at the mercy of a future which he cannot foresee.

Even if a worker is consistently reasonable in his judgment of the risks which he runs in specialising, the unforeseen may occur and all the risks of specialisation will come home to roost with him in poor wages and unemployment. But he is not likely to judge reasonably. He will be tempted to over-specialise by ignorance of the risks involved, or by over-confidence in his ability to retain a well-paid, specialised job, or because he knows that, when unemployed, he can still draw unemployment benefit. Nor will he have the opportunity, if he decides that specialisation is risky, of showing a preference for a wider range of tasks than he combines in his daily work. He has, at best, a limited choice of jobs, all of them, with few exceptions, highly specialised, and it will be hard for him to find the right niche in an industrial system catering so exclusively for specialists. It is not on the preferences of workers and on their judgments of future prospects that the degree to which they specialise mainly depends, but on the decisions of their employers and on force of circumstances.

The work of specialists, then, is co-ordinated through exchange. Exchange brings with it risks which ought to limit specialisation, but which, through ignorance or over-confidence on the part of the specialists, or because of their powerlessness as wage-earners, do not in fact limit specialisation as much as they should. Men are taught a single trade when they could, with advantage, learn two. They are kept constantly to a single department when they could, with advantage, be moved from one department to another. And they are put to a few tasks, when they could, with advantage, undertake more varied work.

Co-ordination takes place not only through exchange, but also within each firm. Thus a specialist, when he is not his own master, is at the mercy, not only of market forces, but also of the whims of his employer. He has to work to orders under a discipline imposed from above. Since the introduction of machinery, this discipline has become far more rigid and irksome.[1] Each worker, whatever his temperament, must adjust his speed of working to the pace set

---

[1] "The Industrial Revolution added discipline, and the discipline of a power driven by a competition that seemed as inhuman as the machines that thundered in factory and shed. The workman was summoned by the factory bell; his daily life was arranged by factory hours; he worked under an overseer imposing a method and precision for which the overseer had in turn to answer to some higher authority; if he broke one of the long series of minute regulations he was fined, and behind all this scheme of supervision and control there loomed the great impersonal system. . . . No economist of the day . . . ever allowed for the strain and violence that a man suffered in his feelings when he passed from a life in which he could smoke or eat, or dig or sleep as he pleased, to one in which somebody turned the key on him, and for fourteen hours he had not even the right to whistle." J. L. and B. Hammond, *The Town Labourer*, pp. 31–3.

for him by the machinery or by his mates. If he is a slow worker, the strain of speeding-up will tell on his nerves; if he is a fast worker, he will be annoyed and bored because he is constantly being held up and finds it impossible to work steadily.

### Machinery and working conditions

To the drawbacks of specialisation we must add the drawbacks of machinery. We have to put up with working conditions that are noisy, dangerous, and unhealthy. We have to allow the pollution of the atmosphere with smoke and fumes from lorries and engines, factory chimneys and power stations. We have to crowd workers together in the vicinity of factories, surrounded by din, dirt, and dinginess. Above all, machinery very often makes work highly monotonous or drives men out of work altogether.

We must be careful, however, not to exaggerate. It is commonly believed, for example, that the agricultural worker's job is far less monotonous than the factory-worker's. This is an attractive belief—particularly to the intellectual, with his horror of machine-tending and his love of country life. But it is a belief, which, if we may take both sets of workers at their word, is not always justified. Much agricultural work, such as ploughing and milking, can be extremely dull[1]; on the other hand, factory work, with some striking exceptions, can be comparatively pleasant, especially when it means company and conversation. The operations of the cotton-weavers are often contrasted unfavourably with those of the old hand-loom weaver. But they are less laborious, less monotonous, call for more judgment, and are immensely more productive than his. "I loved the mills," said an unemployed weaver to Mr. Oakeshott, during an investigation at Blackburn. "I loved the company and the people and everything about them. The mill was home to me. I'd do anything in the world if I could get back to them."[2] Thousands of other workers, less outspoken, feel much the same of jobs which, to the outsider, seem dull and monotonous.

### Machinery and unemployment

Machinery creates unemployment; but it also creates employment. Labour is required for the building and installation of machinery, and to keep it in operation and repair. Presumably, too, the cost of producing the machine-made goods is reduced, and with it the price. Thus consumers are able to buy more of the machine-made goods, and more men are needed to produce them. Or

---

[1] Cf. Disraeli: "There is no nation in the world that leads so monotonous a life as the Irish, because their only occupation is the cultivation of the soil before them. These men are discontented because they are not amused."

[2] *Men Without Work* (Cambridge, 1938), p. 151.

if consumers prefer to buy some other kind of goods with the purchasing power which is released when prices fall, their expenditure will create openings for employment elsewhere. It will only be if the men whose jobs are taken over by machinery cannot, or will not, move to some other occupation that they will be permanently displaced.

This reasoning is confirmed by observation. Machinery has been introduced on an enormous scale in the last century and a half but the number of men in employment has increased five-fold. The industries which, before the war, had the lowest unemployment percentages were often those, like motor-car production, radio manufacture, etc., which made the greatest use of machinery, while most of the industries in which unemployment was concentrated—for instance, shipbuilding and the textile trades—were depressed mainly because of a deficiency of demand, not because they had been adopting more mechanical methods of production.

As a rule, the workers who are displaced by machinery are absorbed within the firm which employs them. Of those who are not absorbed, a large proportion find work again within a short time. The unsuccessful remainder, who, in time of rapid technical change, may be fairly numerous, are left in chronic unemployment. But such "technological" unemployment is rarely more than a small fraction of total unemployment.

### Automation

These conclusions are not affected by the more recent changes in industrial technique which are summed up in the word "automation." This one word does duty for a wide variety of methods of production ranging from the use of automatic transfer machines in the motor-car industry to the extensive use of instruments which allows the operations of a large modern chemical plant to be controlled by a handful of men. The limiting case is the automatic factory in which, once the machinery is set in motion, the raw material is processed and delivered in finished form without being touched by hand. It might seem that developments of this kind introduce an entirely new element into industry and must inevitably create widespread redundancy of labour. It is true that they carry the process of mechanisation one stage further and that they dispense with the labour formerly required to tend individual machines and move materials from one machine to the next; for this reason, they economise unskilled and semi-skilled labour. But automatic transfer machines merely allow a sequence of operations to be performed on a single machine and are no more revolutionary in their implications than the introduction of the line conveyor which fixes the sequence of operations and allows them to be performed with less effort. Nor is modern instrumentation altogether novel except when it reaches the point where an entire plant is designed round the instrument panel from which it is controlled. Even automatic factories have to be built and maintained, the equipment has to be set and serviced, the operations of the factories have to be planned, and their products have to be marketed. There is no question, therefore, of complete displacement of labour and every likelihood of greater demands on skilled staff. Like other labour-saving improvement in technique, automation may lead to redundancy and create difficult problems of re-absorbing the displaced workers elsewhere; it may, therefore, give rise to social distress and injure particular groups of workers. With reasonable mobility and willingness to change jobs and a little forethought by employers, however, re-absorption is usually possible, and it often takes place within the business where automation is introduced.

It is easy to idealise the past and pick on machinery as the cause of an imaginary fall from grace. But if we do justice to the immense improvement which machinery has made possible in health, education, and security, and in the working and living conditions of the mass of the people, we can be in no doubt of the great contribution to human welfare that we owe to machinery.

# CHAPTER 7

# SPECIALISATION: LOCALISATION OF INDUSTRY

Districts, like persons, specialise. There is a geographical division of labour which leads each city, county and country to abandon some lines of production and extend others beyond local requirements. Each area restricts the range of its products, because such specialisation enables it to obtain other products more cheaply by importing them. Through trade with its neighbours, the area is able to export what it has in comparative abundance in return for what it has in comparative scarcity.

Geographical specialisation can be looked at from two different angles. We may ask: Why does a given area carry on some industries and not others? Or we may ask: Why is a given industry carried on in some areas and not in others? Economists have built up the theory of international trade—to which we will come by and by—in answer to the first question, and the theory of the location of industry in answer to the second. In the study of international trade, our attention is generally focused on the struggle which goes on between industries *inside* a country (or region) for the use of the scarce resources available there. We see how some industries survive while others are crowded out, and how the volume of industry expands if labour and capital are attracted to the country, and contracts if they flow abroad. In the study of localisation, we start from the competition *between* regions for a given industry, or for industry as a whole, and discuss why one region can pull harder than another. These two lines of thought do not conflict with, but supplement one another.

### The Clyde shipbuilding industry

Suppose, for example, that we ask why some industry—say shipbuilding—has become localised on the Clyde. We have really two questions to answer, not one. First, why the Clyde rather than some other *place*—the Thames or the Severn? Second, why shipbuilding rather than some other *industry*—steel or textiles? We have to show, not only that there is a pull on shipbuilding to the Clyde, but that the pull is *relatively* greater than the pull on other industries.

That the Clyde has natural advantages in shipbuilding is obvious enough. The ship-yards are within a few miles of plate-mills, and coal mines, and can obtain boilers, pump-feeding plant, deck and steering gear, fans and ventilating equipment, scientific instruments, and almost everything that is necessary in the fitting out of ships, from firms that have grown up with the industry along the banks of the Clyde. Skilled labour in abundance is available both in ship-building itself and in the subsidiary industries. Close contact can be maintained with the shipping companies which have their headquarters in Glasgow, so that the ultimate owners of many of the ships are able to exercise supervision over the building of them. Thus transport, labour, and administrative costs can all be kept low. It was these low costs which brought the industry to the Clyde and which kept it there.

But if the Clyde is suited to shipbuilding, it is suited to other industries as well. Shipbuilding, after all, is a parvenu among Clyde industries. A century ago, the textile industries were by far the most important in the Clyde valley; at that time the metal industries were already forging ahead; and not long after, shipbuilding took the lead. This transformation was not due to any change in the natural advantages of the district. The Clyde was, and remained, as well suited to cotton manufacture as Lancashire. There was an excellent port, an abundance of coal for the generation of power, an atmosphere of unquestionable humidity, and plenty of pure water for bleaching. The district was also well suited to the manufacture of steel and steel products. The coal measures lay next rich deposits of ore, and when these were worked out, pig iron and scrap could be imported cheaply by sea. The textile industries had trained up in the manu-facture and repair of machinery a supply of skilled engineers on whose services the rising metal industries could draw. Finally, the nearness of Glasgow meant not only a local market for ship-plates, but also low freights on exports of steel to foreign countries. Yet both of these industries, without by any means dis-appearing, lost ground to shipbuilding. The Clyde ceased to rival Lancashire as a textile centre, and offered little or no competition to South Wales and the North-East Coast in the manufacture of tinplates, structural steel, and other steel products.

Thus it is not enough to explain the triumph of one industry over others, in a district like the Clyde, in terms of some natural advantage. A district may be well suited to a wide variety of trades, and yet concentrate on a few, just as a person with great natural gifts may develop only those in which he is most outstanding. Specialisation is not on the basis of absolute, but of *comparative* (i.e., relative) advantage. The Clyde came to have a comparative advantage in shipbuilding when iron (and later, steel) displaced timber in the construction of the hull. This comparative advantage enabled the industry to attract labour from its rivals by offering wages higher than they could afford for comparable work: to attract capital away from them by offering higher profits: and to outbid them for the command of sites along the Clyde.

## The weight of inertia

If we were to try to discover, not why the shipbuilding industry grew on the Clyde but why it is still there, our explanation might have to be in different terms. It is no longer true that the industry is out-bidding other industries for labour in a rapidly expanding industrial area; on the other hand, shipbuilding remains the largest industrial employer and the Clyde has maintained itself as a leading shipbuilding centre. It is likely that this is due, not to the original advantages that it enjoyed, but to the advantages that it has acquired as a result of building ships of all kinds, and the facilities that have come into existence over the past century: the specialised equipment that the yards possess; the highly skilled labour that they can recruit; the knowledge of shipowners' requirements accumulated by their staffs; the ancillary services available in the area. Some of these advantages are shared by other local industries and lend them a similar weight of inertia. The fact that the area has experience of a wide range of industries makes it easier for existing industries to carry on successfully and is an incentive to new industries to locate themselves there.

## The forces governing location

If we turn from shipbuilding and try to generalise the forces tending to bring an industry to a given area, we can adopt one of two courses. We can either follow the line of thought that we have been pursuing and think of the advantages offered by the area or we can start from the other end and ask what elements in the costs incurred by the industry would be affected by the choice of location. In the discussion which follows (pp. 95–102), the first course has been adopted; but we must first emphasise that the various advantages that an area can offer will only cause an industry to choose that location if they translate themselves into cost differentials in favour of the area.

Among those differentials it is usual to lay particular stress on two: transport costs and labour costs. If it makes a great deal of difference where an industry is located, it is usually because transport or labour costs could be materially reduced by the choice of one location rather than another. The influence of transport costs is discussed below (pp. 96–98) in relation to the convenience of an area as a point of assembly for raw materials or for the distribution of finished goods to their principal markets. The greater that convenience, the less the cost per unit of product of transporting materials from their source of supply or of shipping finished goods to their market. The direct importance of transport costs is often exaggerated, particularly in relation to consumer goods: the cost of delivery of such goods to their market is often less than 1 per cent. of the net selling price. Their importance is more apparent in the heavy industries and in industries that reduce their raw material to a less bulky or more easily transported form; but even in those industries, raw materials have been exerting a diminishing influence over the past generation.[1]

The direct influence of transport costs may also be reinforced or even over-shadowed by the indirect influence of the factor of distance. This operates within individual firms against a dispersal of activities over different parts of the country. For example, it may deter the management from opening branch factories rather than extending the parent factory, or from separating the main factory from the sales organisation, on the score of the greater difficulty of supervising and co-ordinating dispersed activities. On the other hand, if markets are dispersed, the management may be willing to consider decentralisation to local units in order to save transport costs. This and other problems involved in the balancing of large-scale production in a central location against smaller-scale dispersal to branch factories are further discussed below (p. 102–3) and in Chapter 9.

The influence of labour costs on the location of industry within a country is generally limited. It might seem unlikely, unless the country is large, that there should be wide differences in rates of pay or in labour efficiency between different areas. But surprisingly large differences in earnings do persist even when trade union rates are negotiated on a country-wide basis; and it remains easier to find labour of the right type or with the right skills for a particular industry in one part of the country rather than another. The difference in labour costs can be such as to give a decisive locational advantage to an area; if wages are much below wages elsewhere, without any offsetting difference in labour efficiency, this may cause an industry to concentrate its expansion in the area, as happened between the wars in the American cotton industry. At other times, there may be a continuing lack of balance between the opportunities of employment open to men and women, and a chronic surplus of one or the other. In the coalfields and engineering towns, for example, there is normally a marked preponderance of jobs for men and a corresponding surplus

---

[1] See below p. 96. A good example is provided by the oil industry: "Forty years ago, only 30 per cent. of the crude oil was refined into a saleable product, kerosene, and so locating refineries on the oil fields saved large costs of transporting the 70 per cent. of crude oil destined to become waste product. At the present time, 90 per cent. of the crude oil is converted into saleable products, so that the advantages of locating refineries on the oilfields have been considerably reduced." (R. S. Edwards and H. Townsend, *Business Enterprise*, p. 146, citing J. D. Butler, "The Influence of Economic Factors on the Location of Oil Refineries," *Journal of Industrial Economics*, July 1953.)

of women seeking work. This leads to a migration of women to other areas; but it also gives rise to an inward movement of industries employing women, in order to take advantage of the surplus. Again, if there is a labour shortage in some parts of the country and unemployment in others, there is a strong locational pull towards the areas of unemployment, particularly if government policy is concentrated on eliminating any remaining pockets of unemployment.

We may now return to the first approach to location in terms of the advantages offered by different areas.

### 1   Natural Advantages

First, there are the natural advantages of the area. These include its amenities—its possession of suitable sites and a suitable climate. Thus the flat, sunny country of East Anglia is far better suited than the wet glens of the Highlands to wheat-growing. Colour-printing is easier in a dry, and cotton-spinning in a damp, climate. And so on. The natural advantages of an area include also its access to sources of power and to raw materials and markets; these determine the savings in power and transport costs that it can offer.

(a) **Power costs**—Before the eighteenth century, power-driven machinery was rarely used, and cheap power was not an important localising force. With the introduction of the water-wheel, factories—and especially cotton-mills—came to be built upon the banks of rivers with a good natural fall. Such rivers were most plentiful in the hilly parts of the country (i.e., in the north and west), and industries using water-power, therefore, tended to become localised there. A great impetus was given to this movement when steam came into use as the chief source of power, for coal, from which steam was generated, was located in the districts in the north and west to which the textile industries were already gravitating. Of course, coal might have been brought by rail to the older centres of industry, but as it was expensive to transport, and none of its weight passed into the finished product, manufacturing costs were lower in the mining areas. As coal was used also as a fuel, as a reducing agent (in the metal industries), and as a raw material (in the chemical industries), the pull of the coal-belts was tremendous, and a whole network of industries grew up, attracting labour and capital from all over the country. There are signs that this process is now being reversed. The development of new sources of power—particularly oil and electricity—has greatly weakened the dependence of industry on coal, and is bringing about a redistribution of industry in favour of the large urban market (e.g., London), and at the expense of the mining districts (e.g., South Wales). The new factories which have sprung up around London in the last thirty years make use of electrical rather than steam power, and although they pay over 60 per cent. more for electricity than factories in Yorkshire, their bill for power and fuel is usually less than 5 per cent. of total costs—too small to be a decisive factor in location.

In the heavier industries, in which steam power and coal continue to be important elements in costs, the use of coal has been economised by great advances in furnace technique (e.g., in steel-making, in the generation of electricity, etc.), and the pull of raw materials and of the market has been strengthened relatively to the pull of coal. This has been illustrated very strikingly by the migration of the steel industry to the ore deposits away from the coalfields where it has traditionally been located. In pre-war years the old-established areas of South Wales, Scotland, and the North-East Coast lost ground steadily, while the Lincolnshire ores attracted to Scunthorpe, Corby, and Redbourn steel plants engaged in the manufacture of sheets (Lysaght's), tubes (Stewart and Lloyd's), steel billets (Richard Thomas'), steel forgings and castings (Firth and Brown's), and other steel products. The migration of the industry was not due *solely* to changes in technique favouring location at the ore-fields. The expanding markets for steel products were in the Midlands and South (e.g., in the motor and building industries), while the contracting markets (either abroad, or in shipbuilding) were those upon which the older areas were most dependent. It should be added, too, that the original location of the steel industry was due in part to the presence, in close conjunction to the coal seams, of rich ores which have since been worked out. In the United States, the parallel migration of the steel industry down to the Great Lakes, and away from the Pittsburgh area, had a similar origin. The industry moved towards the ores of Michigan and Minnesota, and followed the market for steel products westwards.

(b) **Transport costs**—Nearness to an industry's markets and its sources of raw materials very often pull in opposite directions, so that the advantages of one have to be weighed against the advantages of the other. Where there is great loss of weight in manufacture, or where the raw material is very bulky and the finished product compact and easily transported, production will be carried on near the source of supply of the raw material. Thus, the crushing and concentration of ores is normally undertaken at the minehead, even when smelting or refining is carried on elsewhere. The pulping of wood, the pressing of grapes and apples, and the distillation of oil from coal are examples of the same tendency. If, however, the finished product is bulky, and loss of weight negligible, it will be the large markets which exert the biggest pull. The making of bricks, bread, bottles, and other bulky goods is generally carried on all over the country near each important market.[1] Tinplate manufacture is more highly localised than any other industry; but the making of tins, cans, and household utensils from tinplate is widely diffused, because it is much cheaper to transport a box of plates than a pile of tins of various shapes and sizes. Similarly, the assembly of motor-car parts is carried on in many countries in which the manufacture of these parts is uneconomical. The market has succeeded in attracting the later stages of manufacture because the final product is costlier to transport than the parts.

Where several raw materials are combined in a single product, and their combined pull is strong (because of loss of weight or bulk) in relation to the pull of the market, the final location of the industry will represent the resultant of the pulls exerted by the various materials and will be such as to keep transport costs at a minimum.[2] The importance of each constituent in relation to others will depend upon what weight of it is used per unit of the final product.[3] If it is a weight-losing material, its pull, relatively to that of *other materials*, will not be any the greater; but of course the pull of all raw materials *vis-à-vis* the *market* will be strengthened. The steel industry has moved away from the coalfields, not because coal loses less weight in the smelting of iron ore, but because less coal has to be moved per ton of ore.

When the raw materials used include some that are available everywhere (e.g., water, sand, clay, etc.), industry is attracted towards the market. For if these materials are incorporated in the final product at the point of sale instead of elsewhere, the cost of transporting them is saved. Brewing, brick-making, and, above all, the manufacture of aerated waters, illustrate the working of this tendency.

When several markets have to be supplied, the location of the industry will again represent a compromise between conflicting pulls. A large market like London, with enormous spending power per square mile of area (high "market density"), will pull a great deal harder than a country town or rural district. It will do so for two reasons: first, because production near a large market saves the cost of transport on goods sold locally, and these form a high proportion of output; and second, because large-scale production at a low cost is easier when market density is high. We have seen already that the pull of London and the South-East has been growing because of the rise of new forms of power less highly localised than coal, and of new products less dependent upon localised materials. We have now to add that the increased importance

---

[1] Nevertheless bread-making is being increasingly centralised, and bricks have been carried from as far north as Lairg in Sutherland to the London market.

[2] Other things (e.g., labour costs) being equal.

[3] And also, of course, on the distance it has to be carried.

D

of large-scale production and the greater ease and comparative cheapness of transport have tended to concentrate industry near the chief markets, and especially London, since the outlying markets can be supplied more cheaply from a single point of manufacture.


## 2  ACQUIRED ADVANTAGES

The natural advantages of an area in any given industry are generally reinforced by acquired advantages. Transport facilities are provided or improved. Roads, railways, docks and harbours are built. Commercial services of all kinds—banking, warehousing, accounting, and so on—become available. Labour becomes familiar with the technique of the industry, and a high standard of workmanship is developed. Manufacturers are able to discuss problems of mutual interest, and in this way, or because of the appearance of trade and technical journals, improvements and inventions are stimulated. The district acquires a prestige which binds customers to it. An organised market for the product or for materials comes into existence. Subsidiary industries spring up in the neighbourhood, supplying accessories and parts, or making use of by-products.

**(a) Vertical disintegration**—At this stage a change comes over the type of specialisation practised: as the industry obtains a firmer footing and grows in size, the process of manufacture often begins to "disintegrate," the separate stages as they split off being taken over by a specialist firm or industry. The supply of machinery and material, the utilisation of by-products, the organisation of traffic and marketing may be undertaken by such specialist firms. Cotton firms, for example, no longer make their own machinery but buy it from engineering firms. Motor manufacturers buy in radiators, carburettors, electric equipment, chassis-frames, and other parts from specialists who can produce very cheaply by supplying several firms at once. Shipbuilding yards assemble the products of dozens of industries. Similarly in building it is usual in large contracts for the steelwork, masonry, plumbing, air-conditioning, furnishing, and so on, to be contracted out to firms specialising in a single branch of the industry.

**(b) Lateral disintegration**—In a localised industry, "disintegration" by *product* is also frequent. That is, neighbouring towns (or firms) specialise in supplying different markets, or use similar materials to make different products. In the West Riding of Yorkshire, for example, Bradford specialises in worsteds, Dewsbury in "heavy" woollen cloths, Huddersfield in fine woollen cloths, and the Colne Valley in tweeds. In Lancashire, the cotton industry is even more highly specialised, the south concentrating on spinning and the north and east on weaving, while towns inside these areas specialise within narrow limits in the counts of yarn which they spin or the fabrics which they weave.

There is no *necessary* connection between the industrial disintegration which we have been discussing and the concentration of an industry in a given area. The first involves further specialisation on the part of firms and industries, the second, further specialisation on the part of geographical areas. In the world as we find it, however, both types of specialisation very often occur together; and it is easy to see that, so long as the firms in a given industry are isolated from one another instead of being localised in a single district, they will be forced to do many things for themselves rather inefficiently, and will have to do without services which a specialist could supply to a localised industry. *One* cause of disintegration (but not the only one) is clearly localisation. The more firms of the same type settle in the same locality, the more they tend to specialise and diverge from one another.[1]

Acquired advantages not only strengthen the pull on an industry to a given area, but help to keep the industry there when the natural advantages of the area have ceased to exist. There is no obvious reason why lace-making should be carried on in Nottingham or boot-making in Leicester except that both towns have acquired a long experience in their staple trades. A group of inter-dependent industries is even harder to unscramble; for even when one of the group might profitably start again elsewhere it may be so knit together with surrounding industries that a change in location would be extremely costly. Changes in location, therefore, generally come about less through deliberate transference than through the rise of firms in a new area and the decline of firms in the old.

### 3   COMPARATIVE ADVANTAGES

A clear superiority over other areas in natural or acquired advantages will not by itself attract an industry to a given location. Other industries may enjoy an even greater advantage in the same location; and this comparative advantage will allow them to compete successfully for the limited resources available in the area. In due course, if the area has such all-round advantages, there will be an influx of resources—including more workers—and a wider range of industries may be built up as the area prospers and grows. But at any one time

---

[1] Industrial change may be in the direction of integration rather than disintegration. For a discussion of various forms of industrial integration, see below, pp. 178–84.

the extent to which an industry locates itself in a given area will depend upon the competition for labour, land and capital within the area; and an industry will locate itself more readily in the area if it is not faced with a scarcity of productive resources due to the competition of other industries.

The competition between one industry and another that goes on within any given region can be observed also within smaller areas. Inside each town, for example, there is competition for sites. Some industries will pay high ground rents so as to be near to their workers, or to docks, warehouses and railway stations. Other industries, which have more difficulty in economising ground space and need ample room for expansion, may prefer to move to the outskirts where ground rents will be much lower. The clothing and milling trades are examples of the first tendency, motor-car and wireless manufacture of the second. The rough pattern into which the industries of a district sort themselves is in constant change as one industry yields space to others. One firm may vacate a site because the ground rent has become higher than it can afford: another firm may take over the site in order to extend its premises and retain a central location. There is a steady centrifugal pressure by which commerce squeezes industry from the inner parts of a town. The older factories near the centre are forced to re-locate themselves as hostels, offices, warehouses and shops creep outwards. The factories near the city boundaries may have to move farther out as the suburbs become built up.

### 4   CUMULATIVE ADVANTAGES

Once a great locational change is in progress and industry is on the move, the change will gain momentum from sympathetic movements of labour. There will be not only a re-shuffling of industries inside each area, but also a series of expansions and contractions of whole areas, in the sense that more labour will be put at the disposal of industries in expanding areas, and withdrawn from industries in contracting areas. This movement of resources will give the expanding areas a cumulative advantage, for it will both keep down some of the costs of firms trying to establish themselves there, and at the same time bring them a new local market when the immigrant workers begin to spend their wages. The contracting areas on the other hand will suffer from a cumulative disadvantage for they lose a customer in every migrant, and every customer lost may mean still another migrant.

### The degree of localisation

The more these advantages are monopolised in any industry by a small number of areas, the more highly localised will the industry be. At one extreme, we have the mining of gilsonite (which takes place only in Utah) or nickel (which comes almost exclusively from Sudbury, Ontario); at the other, services of all kinds (of shopkeepers, policemen, postmen, lawyers, 'bus drivers, etc.) which, being in demand everywhere and impossible to store, must be rendered everywhere.

## The degree of diversification

The more outstanding are the advantages of a single industry or small group of industries, over other industries in any area, the narrower will be the range of industries in that area. In other words, industry will be highly diversified where the available resources, either in raw materials or in skill and experience, are varied, or when varied tastes and a wide market can be supplied; and it will be highly specialised when only a limited range of resources can be exploited, and when tastes are standardised and narrow. Chile, for example, cannot readily turn from guano to other lines of production, and the American prairies have little alternative to wheat-growing. But in Britain industry is amazingly diversi-fied, not only because of her own varied resources—her coal and iron, her vast capital, long experience, and abundant skill—but also because her manufac-turing centres, being within a short distance of the big ports, have easy access to the materials and markets of every other seaboard.

## Depressed areas

When the degree of diversification in an area is low, it risks all the disadvan-tages of excessive specialisation. If the main industry is depressed, the depression is communicated to the industries supplying local needs. There may be no other major industry to fall back on, and the difficulties of making a switch will then be enormously increased, since it is far harder to build up new in-dustries than to build on old ones. Continued depression in the main industry will bring into existence a problem of long-term unemployment, especially amongst the older workers who can neither pick up a new technique nor move far afield in search of jobs. The younger workers may find employment in other areas, but their removal will unbalance industry more than ever. The social life of the community will suffer through the loss of many of its natural leaders, and through the chronic unemployment of a large fraction of its mem-bers. Unless invigorated from without, the whole community may throw up the sponge and wait apathetically for better things. In short, the problem of de-pressed areas comes into existence: the problem, that is, of persistent unemploy-ment concentrated in pockets up and down the country. It is a problem which cannot altogether be got rid of so long as areas specialise at all. But it might be made a less serious problem if governments were to promote the diversification of industry in depressed areas, and indeed in any area too narrowly dependent upon a staple trade with an uncertain future.

## The dynamics of location

It is one thing to try to explain the existing locational pattern: it is quite another to explain why individual firms pick on particular locations. The location of an industry might be rational even if the choice of location made by each firm in it was almost entirely haphazard.[1] Firms that made a bad choice would die off; firms that made a good choice would flourish and expand, until the industry was concentrated in the localities that they had selected. There is plenty of evidence that few firms engage in elaborate calculations before deciding where to go: particularly small firms—and most firms start small. There is also evidence that few firms ever want to move from their existing site so long as there is room for expansion, and that if they are obliged to move they like to stay in or near their home town.

When a firm decides to move to a new factory or to open a branch elsewhere, it may consider all the factors that we have already enumerated: the availability and cost of power; the convenience of the site in relation to raw materials on the one hand and markets on the other; the adequacy of local transport facilities and commercial services; the ease with which it can hire labour with the necessary experience, skill and drive; the competition it may have to face for the resources it requires; the momentum of expansion in the area to which it proposes to move. But it will also be influenced—and perhaps decisively—by other considerations, many of them arising out of the additional burden that such a move imposes on its limited managerial resources.

First of all, most firms do not have an unlimited amount of time and money to spend in looking for a suitable location. A management that is planning an expansion is probably already under some pressure to meet existing orders and may be unable to release staff to make a full investigation. If it makes use of the services of a consultant, it has still to find time to set out its problem and

---

[1] "Mr. Ford started to manufacture motor cars in Detroit because it was his home town. Sir William Morris (later Lord Nuffield) chose Cowley because the school in which his father was educated happened to be for sale. Neither of these excellent motives can be regarded as promising certain success to those who imitate them. . . . Mr. Ford and Sir William Morris either by acumen or by chance discovered places of production with great natural advantages." E. A. G. Robinson, *Structure of Competitive Industry*, p. 152.

"Why is our glass industry concentrated in St. Helens? Because the great-great-grandfather of the present chairman was apprenticed to a doctor in St. Helens and in due time practised there, because his sons were brought up there, because they put some money into a glass works, the technical manager of which had to withdraw. This explains how they got in but not how they survived. Their survival was due to the general suitability of the area—the proximity of the port of Liverpool, coal, excellent sand (with low iron oxide content) and alkali close by." R. S. Edwards and H. Townsend, *Business Enterprise* (London, 1958), p. 158.

check the advice which it ultimately receives. It may confine itself, therefore, to a rather cursory inspection of a limited number of sites in the more obvious localities with the necessary physical characteristics. Secondly, the additional managerial effort involved in planning, building and operating a new factory will dispose an expanding firm to select a location that makes this effort less formidable. It will be disinclined to move to a remote site or one with which communications are difficult; it will avoid a location that lacks subcontracting facilities and specialist services, so that it is forced to extend its own responsibilities to tool-making, die-casting, and so on; it will, for the same reason, prefer to go where it can be sure of a regular supply of components, made to its specifications by local firms; it is likely also to try to confine the new factory to the manufacture of relatively simple products, requiring relatively little supervision and managerial effort. Finally, the need to transfer or recruit staff to manage the new factory will bias the firm in favour of locations which its staff will find attractive as places in which to live, because this will ease the task of managerial reinforcement. It will show a similar preference for locations which enlarge the knowledge and experience of its staff and improve their usefulness as managers. If the location is one in which the staff will be brought into frequent contact with new ideas, the latest scientific knowledge, and lively and stimulating associates, this will add greatly to its attractiveness, particularly in industries in which expansion is rapid and the shortage of capable managers is correspondingly acute.

### The State and location

In post-war years a large number of new factories have been built in the areas of Great Britain that are remote from London—what before the War were called the Depressed Areas, but are now described as Development Areas. The location of these factories is generally assumed to reflect government pressure and government planning and there is no doubt that by control over factory-building, the offer of financial assistance, and in other ways, the influence of the government was powerfully exerted in favour of location in the Development Areas. It is arguable, however, that the shortage of labour elsewhere was at least as effective in inducing firms to choose new (and often less convenient) locations. The experience of wartime, when an acute shortage of labour developed in London and the Midlands while there was still a surplus in the outlying regions, demonstrated clearly the inertia of the existing geographical pattern of industry and the resistance to dispersion in response to any force less compelling than lack of man-power.

It is obviously desirable that an industry should be located where it can be carried on efficiently and at low cost. If it is located in some other area, the higher level of costs will mean a waste of resources and a loss of social product. On the other hand, it is also desirable that there should be a sufficient concentration of industry in each area to employ all the available labour. If industry moves from one locality to another, the first community may decay while the other prospers; no new industry may grow up to take the place of the old, so that chronic local unemployment results. There will then be a waste of resources that falls not on private firms in the shape of higher costs but on society in the shape of a bill for maintaining the unemployed, or, if they are successful in finding jobs elsewhere, in empty schools and dwelling-houses, and in local services that are no longer fully used.

There may thus be a conflict between the private and the social interest. If work is always brought to the worker, industrial efficiency may suffer; if the worker has to move in search of work he may remain unemployed or there may be a loss of social capital when he moves. The acuteness of the conflict depends upon the industry and upon the community. In some communities the social capital is hardly worth preserving and the chances of new industries succeeding are too faint. There are mining valleys, difficult of access, where the houses are old and the amenities poor; rather than rehabilitate these it would be better to provide more housing elsewhere. In some industries one location may be about as good as another; leather handbags, radio valves and typewriters may be examples. A push towards a depressed area would reduce unemployment there, and might put fresh life into the area, as well as providing a second line of defence at a later date against renewed depression in the older industries in the area. The more industries can be shown to be "footloose," and oriented neither towards markets nor towards raw materials, the greater the ease with which they can be induced to move to new locations if public policy so requires, and the stronger the case for taking the work to the worker. If in addition most firms choose a new location rather haphazardly it is much easier to get them to change their mind and, if denied location in one area, to be content with location in another.

The State can bring influence to bear on the location of industry in a variety of ways. It can offer a good information service to assist firms in their search for a suitable locality and a suitable site. It can grant loans on favourable terms, offer exemption from taxes, build factories for rent at cheap rates, and contribute to the cost of training schemes, provided firms will go to selected areas. It can encourage the setting up of factory estates in those areas and subsidise improvements in the transport system and other facilities. It can arrange to issue building licences more freely than in other areas. It can instruct government departments to try to place more contracts with firms in the depressed areas. It can steer to those areas foreign firms wishing to set up branches in the country. The cumulative effect of measures such as these can be great, particularly when many firms are seeking to expand.

Yet it is pressure confined almost entirely to manufacturing industry; and in Great Britain manufacturing industry accounts for only about one-third of total employment. It is true that manufacturing industry is generally the magnet attracting transport, distributive and other services, and that as one industry grows it tends to attract others to the same locality. But there are other magnets: a convalescent hospital, a prison, the offices of a football pool, an insurance company or a government department—to take a few examples—can exert a locational pull just as strong and independent as the pull of industry. Even within manufacturing industry there are large sections—for example, in steel, wool-combing, heavy chemicals, and so on—where normal locational forces are too strong and the effective choice of locations is extremely limited. For these and other reasons, the amount of employment provided in the factories built in any one year in the Development Areas has been small in relation to the fluctuations in unemployment in those areas that occurred in pre-war years. Control over the location of new factories is no guarantee against severe localised unemployment; it does, however, make for a steady reduction in such unemployment when it might otherwise be steadily increasing.

D*

# CHAPTER 8

# LARGE-SCALE PRODUCTION

Specialisation, as Adam Smith pointed out, is limited by the size of the market. In a narrow market (e.g., in an isolated village), a worker must be able to turn his hand to many different jobs. The demand for his services in any one of these jobs will not be sufficient to keep him continuously occupied in it. In the same way, it will be impossible to use expensive machinery if it has to stand idle for long periods; or to introduce the elaborate organisation—in management, costing, research, marketing, and so on—which is indispensable in a modern business of any size. Production must be on a large scale before full use can be made either of machinery or of specialists and specialised departments. This is true of the establishment (e.g., a single factory), of the firm (which may own several factories), of the industry (which consists of a number of competing firms), and of industry as a whole. As each of these expands in size, new opportunities of specialisation, new types of machinery, and new kinds of organisation make it possible to achieve economies which were impossible so long as production was on a smaller scale.

The economies of large-scale production—called for short "economies of scale"—may be either "internal" or "external."

*Internal economies* are those which are open to a single factory or a single firm independently of the action of other firms. They result from an increase in the scale of output of the firm, and cannot be achieved unless output increases. They are not the result of inventions of any kind, but are due to the use of known methods of production which a small firm does not find worth while. They are also not to be confused with any bargaining or monopoly advantages which large firms may acquire. These advantages may swell the profits of large firms and incite small firms to grow bigger; but they do not (except indirectly) make large firms more *efficient* than small ones.

*External economies* are those which are shared in by a number of firms or industries when the scale of production in any industry or group of industries increases. They are not monopolised by a single firm when it grows in size, but are conferred on it when some *other* firms grow larger. Whenever an increase in the output of one firm has a favourable reaction on the efficiency of other firms, either in the same industry or in other industries, these firms enjoy the benefit of external economies.

## EXTERNAL ECONOMIES

The chief types of external economies have already been illustrated in our discussion of localisation.[1] There are:—

### 1   Economies of concentration

When a number of firms settle in a single neighbourhood they enable each other to derive mutual advantages through the training of skilled workmen, the provision of better transport facilities, the stimulation of improvements, and so on. Each employer has less difficulty in finding the kind of labour he wants, and can make use of special services—e.g., in merchanting his goods— which would not be available to scattered firms. In a country which has not yet been industrialised, economies of concentration can be of special importance. Each new firm and each new industry attracted to the country help to build up a machine-sense, and a common stock of knowledge and experience on which each succeeding manufacturer can draw.

### 2   Economies of information

In a large industry it becomes worth while to issue trade and technical publications to which everyone has access. Manufacturers are thus saved much independent research which, in a smaller industry, they might be forced to undertake for themselves. It becomes possible also to set up research associations which will carry out research work on behalf of individual firms and publish the results for any firm to use. Economies of information are clearly of much more importance when applied to industry in general than when confined to a single industry. Cheap newspapers and information bureaux, an efficient weather-forecasting service, adequate provision for research, and so on, are of enormous advantage to industry as a whole, but far too much for a single industry to provide unaided. Thus it very often falls to the government to bear the cost of information and research services, the benefits of which are shared throughout industry.

---

[1] See pp. 98-9.

## 3 Economies of disintegration

The growth of an industry may foster the splitting off of some process which can be carried on more efficiently by a specialist firm or industry. On this further specialisation nothing need be added to what has been said above.[1] The economies which the specialists firms enjoy are internal economies and will be discussed presently.

What are external economies at one moment may be internal economies the next, if several firms unite with one another. To a village butcher, killing a few cattle a week, half of the animal is waste. But if the village grows into a thickly-populated urban district, with a large number of slaughterhouses, each of the local butchers will be able to dispose of this "waste" at a good price. Specialist firms will "make combs, buttons, knife and cane handles from the horns and hoofs; glue from parts of the bones and cartilage; pipe stems, chessmen, dice, artificial teeth, crochet needles or electrical bushings from the bones; pharmaceutical supplies from the glands, artists' brushes from the soft hair in the interior of the ears."[2] The butchers will benefit from external economies. But exactly the same economies might be enjoyed if the butchers were to amalgamate with the specialist firms to form a large meat-packing concern. The economies which, in the British livestock industry, are still largely external to the slaughterhouses could be made internal by the adoption of the methods of the Chicago packers.

External economies, therefore, are not different in kind from internal: what are external, and what are internal, economies depend simply upon what operations it is profitable to combine under a single management. In the steel industry, for example, external economies are likely to be of less importance than in the textile industries, because the processes of manufacture must be integrated in the interests of conservation of heat in steel-making, but may be separated in the interests of efficient management in the manufacture of textiles.

### INTERNAL ECONOMIES

Internal economies can be grouped together under five headings: technical, managerial, commercial, financial, and risk-spreading.

### 1 Technical economies

Technical economies affect the size of the single establishment, rather than of the firm, which may own and operate several different establishments. An

---

[1] See pp. 98–9.
[2] S. H. Slichter, *Modern Economic Society*, p. 126.

establishment may be anything between an ice-cream barrow and Ford's Rouge Plant at Detroit, covering over a thousand acres and employing 100,000 workers. In industries where technical economies of scale are great, the size of the typical establishment will tend to be correspondingly great; while in industries where size is of little technical advantage, and the methods of large plants can be easily duplicated on a smaller scale, the typical establishment will tend to remain small. In gold-mining, tinplate manufacture, and the generation of hydro-electric power, the large plant uses methods of far greater efficiency than are open to smaller units; in those industries, therefore, large plants are the rule. In agriculture, on the other hand, it often makes little difference whether a farm is large or small. The same farming methods may be used whether the dairy herd is one of thirty or three hundred and whether the sheep flock is numbered in hundreds or in thousands. If, therefore, we find many large dairy herds and sheep flocks, it will probably be because farmers are trying to take advantage of economies of scale which are not purely technical. It is only in arable farming that farm machinery (e.g., the combine-harvester) gives the large unit a marked advantage in technique over the small.

Technical economies are of three kinds:—

(a) **Economies of superior technique**—Many types of machinery cannot be reproduced at all on a smaller scale, so that a small plant is driven either to install machinery which it cannot keep in continuous use, or to put up with less efficient machinery of a different type. A large motor-works can use giant presses, which turn out all-steel tops, body-panels, and fenders in one piece, while in small factories a whole series of operations, more laborious and less mechanical, is necessary.[1] Only a large tinplate works can make use of continuous strip rolling. Tabulating and calculating machines are economical in a large office, but uneconomical in a small one. A rotary printing press, linotype machines, and so on, are indispensable to most daily newspapers, but not to a small jobbing printer. Electrically-driven overhead cranes are in use in large engineering works and not in small. There are, in fact, few industries without some striking differences in technique between large and small establishments. The small establishments generally make more use of small machines worked by hand-power, while the large establishments make more extensive use of large machines worked by steam or electricity. From a technical point of view, these modern sources of power are superior and this superiority is communicated to large units of plant.

---

1 That is, so long as there are no specialist firms from which the small factories can buy pressed steel parts.

**(b) Economies of increased dimensions**—Even when a machine can be duplicated on a smaller scale, there is often a purely mechanical advantage in using large machines. There is an economy, for example, when size diminishes losses by friction, or evaporation, or cooling. The carrying capacity of a ship increases in proportion to the cube of its dimensions; the resistance to its motion increases, roughly speaking, in proportion to the square of its dimensions. The power required to drive a given weight through the water is less, therefore, in a large than in a small ship. Again, if we double the dimensions of a water tank by building one twice as long, twice as broad, and twice as high, it will hold eight times as much water as before. But the walls of the tank will have increased only four times in area, and since the loss of heat by radiation depends upon the area of the walls, and not upon the volume of water in the tank, the rate at which the water will cool will be greatly reduced. A large boiler, therefore, will be more efficient than a small one. Similarly, a large furnace has great advantages over a small one. These advantages are of special importance in the chemical and metal industries where there is great scope for the conservation of heat through an increase in the scale of plant.

There is a further economy in the use of large machines. In spite of their greater output, they can generally be operated by a team no larger than is required for a much smaller machine of the same type. Whatever the size of a rolling-mill, a steam shovel, a locomotive or a concentrator, the number of men required is much the same. "To turn a valve, to operate a switch, or to watch a gauge is no more arduous, though much more responsible, labour for a super-power station than for a tiny plant."[1]

Not only is the large machine cheaper to operate. It is also relatively cheaper to construct. An electric motor developing 20 h.p. does not require twice the material of a 10-h.p. motor, and takes little more labour to assemble. A double-decker bus is not twice as costly as a single-decker; the bodywork may be no stouter, and the engine, apart from a difference in horse-power, identical. In the building of a ship, a furnace, a factory, a telephone system, or a broadcasting station—to say nothing of the manufacture of pails and post-card albums—the size of the unit can generally be doubled without a doubling of labour and material costs.

It must not be supposed, however, that large mechanical units are *necessarily* more efficient than small ones; much depends upon what particular dimensions are increased, or what difficulties the increase in size is intended to overcome. The farmer who, impressed by the economies of increased dimensions, was silly enough to double the length, breadth, and depth of his plough, found that

---

[1] E. A. G. Robinson, *Structure of Competitive Industry*, p. 32.

it needed not one but forty horses—with a large gang of men in attendance—to drag it through the earth.[1] When a ship is very big, the resistance to its motion is greatly increased by skin friction, and size becomes a handicap. The large unit, too, may forfeit its advantages if there is no labour capable of handling it properly, or no raw materials of the quality required.

(c) **Economies of linked processes**—The operations of a single large machine are not likely to be the only ones undertaken in an establishment. There will be other operations, linked with those which the machine performs; and the more processes are linked together the larger, inevitably, will be the establishment. We must include amongst economies of scale, therefore, any economies resulting from this linking of processes.

The linking of processes in a single plant leads to many economies. There is generally a saving in time and a saving in transport costs, since two departments of the same factory are closer together than two separate factories. It is mainly for this reason that the editing and the printing of newspapers are generally carried on in the same building, and that most factories have their own repair, testing, and box-making departments. In coal-mining, the washing and screening of the coal takes place at the pit-head, partly because, since coals of different grades are sold in different markets, a saving in transport costs is effected. In short, wherever a process would normally be localised in the vicinity of the raw materials, there is a strong tendency for it to be carried on within the establishment where the materials are prepared.

There is a saving, too, in fuel and power wherever the physical conjunction of two processes makes for the conservation of heat. The most striking example is that of steel-making. In an integrated plant, the pig-iron is taken to the steel furnaces in a molten condition, and the steel ingots, once they have solidified and have been re-heated in the soaking pits, can be rolled and re-rolled without being allowed to cool. The hot gases from the coke ovens and blast furnaces are used to heat the steel furnaces and soaking pits, and to generate the electricity which works the rolls in the rolling mills and the blowers in the blast furnaces. Thus the consumption of coal per ton of finished steel can be reduced from the 1913 average of over three tons to not much over one ton in a modern plant.

The linking of different stages of manufacture is obviously not governed exclusively by technical considerations. It may be no more than the most convenient and profitable path along which a business can expand. Even when technical considerations are uppermost, they are often coupled with other

---

[1] J. M. Clark, *Economics of Overhead Costs*, p. 116.

motives such as the avoidance of uncertainty. A factory may decide to make rather than buy supplies of materials and components because it wants to be sure of obtaining what it needs at the right time, in the right quantities, and of the right quality. Any irregularity in the flow, or any failure to meet specifications in quality or design, will aggravate the managerial problem of organising production efficiently and lead to higher costs. For reasons of this kind, an engineering factory will usually make its own screw nails and so remove any danger of unpunctual supply. Similarly, textile firms may spin their own yarn in order to be able to vary their material to suit the fabrics which they hope to market. Or, where a firm has a reputation for a highly individual product, it is likely to insist on supervision and control, often in its own premises, at each stage of manufacture.

Once several processes are linked within the same plant, it becomes necessary to *balance* them against one another. If the plant is to operate with maximum efficiency, the scale on which each process is conducted must not only exhaust the economies possible at that stage, but must be adapted to the demands of the succeeding stage. One machine, when working to capacity, may be able to handle 100 units of output; the capacity of a second machine may be 250 units, of a third 300, and of a fourth 2,000. If each of these machines is to be kept in gear with the others, it will be necessary to use more than one model of each machine, and to produce more than 2,000 units of output. The ideal solution would be to scale up output to 6,000 units (i.e., the L.C.M. of the capacity outputs of each machine) and use 60 machines of the first type, 24 of the second, 20 of the third, and 3 of the fourth. In the real world, however, capacity outputs do not fit together so neatly as in this example, and the L.C.M. would often be impossibly high. Some possible economies, therefore, have to be sacrificed by overdriving one machine and running another below capacity. On the other hand, the risk of disorganisation through breakdowns—especially at bottlenecks like our fourth machine—will tend to push normal output beyond the L.C.M., since the operation of a second unit will act as a safeguard against complete stoppage all along the line. Similarly, if routine repairs (e.g., the re-lining of blast furnaces) can be carried out only when a large unit of plant stands idle, several units of the same type will usually be operated together.

Technical factors set a lower, not an upper limit, to the most efficient scale of operations: they create economies, never diseconomies. In any given state of technique, there comes a level of output beyond which no further reduction in costs can be obtained through the technical economies that size permits. But equally, there is no reason to expect a deterioration in technical efficiency with further growth since the most efficient units of plant can be duplicated and multiplied. If, therefore, there are other savings to be made—in management, in finance, in marketing, and so on—there is no reason why technique should set limits to expansion. We must look in other directions for obstacles to growth.

## 2 Managerial economies

Managerial economies may be effected either by increasing the size of an establishment or by grouping a number of establishments under one management. Both methods of expansion create opportunities for increased specialisation. These opportunities are not confined to the managing staff but extend to the entire labour force. Workers can be kept fully employed on a narrower range of tasks. In a small garage, a man may be a mechanic, taxi-driver and petrol attendant. In a small office—e.g., in accountancy, banking or law— a clerk has generally more varied duties than in a large one. But it is mainly at the managerial level that specialisation is carried further. This specialisation is twofold:—

(a) **Delegation of detail**—In a small business, the owner spends much of his time going to and fro in his shirt sleeves, superintending and assisting with the work of his factory. He has probably a thorough grasp of every side of the business and a strong hold on the loyalty of his workers. He may enjoy being worker, foreman, and manager combined, and have no wish to change. But if he is an able organiser, he will produce at lower cost—and incidentally make a larger profit—by expanding his business and delegating routine and details to subordinates. This will leave him free to concentrate on the more difficult work of organisation. He will have time to make a full study of special problems, keep abreast of changes in technique, make influential "contacts," and form a plan of campaign on the basis of adequate information. But all this will only be possible in a large business, where his time is not taken up with what a lower-paid worker could do equally well, and where his powers of foresight, initiative, and judgment are spread over the maximum volume of output to which they will stretch. Mr. Ford and Lord Nuffield would have been wasted on a poultry-farm or the local cinema; they might even have failed disastrously. But they were far from being wasted on the Ford and Morris Motor Companies, where their organising ability was given full scope, and could be paid for handsomely with advantage to the companies.

(b) **Functional specialisation**—Division of labour can also take place, so to speak, horizontally. The work of management is split up through the creation of separate departments, each of which is put in charge of an expert administrator. One specialist becomes responsible for the organisation of production, one for sales, one for transport, still another for the maintenance of machinery and buildings. There will be other departments engaged in costing and estimating, research, the hiring of workers, the purchase of materials, the preparation of new designs, the keeping of accounts, the arranging of finance, and so on. Each large department may be further sub-divided and its duties distributed between a large number of specialists. The sales department, for instance, has not only to make and enter up sales satisfactorily; it has also to keep customers in good humour, find out where sales resistance is weak, guess what people will want to buy, and persuade them to buy it. In a small business, these are minor duties which the owner-manager must take in his stride; the average farmer, for instance, does not lose much sleep over them. But in a large modern business nothing short of the appointment of a public relations officer, and the setting up of market research and advertising departments, will get them done.

The same division of functions takes place on the board of directors. The job of the directors is to guide the general policy of the business, much as Cabinet Ministers are supposed to govern the policy of government departments, without undertaking the detailed work of administration. One director may make himself responsible for finance, another for marketing, and a third for engineering problems. Thus the board of directors may be turned into an all-star team, in which are knit together widely different talents and experience. Each of the directors will have his blind spot; and, if he were in complete control, might soon turn upside down the organisation of departments unfamiliar to him. But in a large business, with any luck, he can be suitably chastened and chained. There will be enough to keep him busy in Department A, for which he has a flair, and no need to let him loose on Department B, in which he is a comparative duffer.

The appointment of specialists and the setting up of specialised departments, is economical only in a large business. A research chemist, an accountant, or a works manager may draw a salary which would make him much too expensive for a small concern and yet prove cheap at the price in a large one. A large business can afford a separate staffing department which will test applicants for vacancies, arrange for their training and assign them to posts for which they are suited.[1] Similarly with research: a small firm cannot possibly spend large sums on a research laboratory, but a large one may spend several million pounds a year. The American Telephone and Telegraph Company "has several thousand people at its headquarters and laboratories who do nothing

---

[1] The small business, however, may be more successful in recruitment of new workers because the employer can pick recruits to suit his own requirements, see to their training, and detect misfits earlier than would be possible in a larger firm.

but make new inventions and develop new methods of operation."[1] But as this company spends over £100,000,000 a year on extensions and improvements alone, its research budget is a trifle in comparison with the economies to which the research may lead. The expenditure on research by a large British company like Imperial Chemical Industries is just as enormous in comparison with what smaller companies can afford and just as insignificant a fraction of the company's total budget. The full benefits of a research, or any similar, department can be enjoyed only by very large enterprises.

## 3 Marketing economies

Economies in the purchase of materials and sale of goods may be just as important as economies in manufacture. In the eastern counties of England, for example, a pre-war inquiry showed that smallholders were paying 10 per cent. more for their feedingstuffs and 20 per cent. more for their fertilisers than "large-scale" (300 to 500 acres) farmers. Smallholders were also in receipt of lower prices for their grain.[2]

In other industries the possibility of making substantial economies in buying and selling is equally great. Raw materials may come to 50 per cent. or more of the cost of an article. Nearly 40 per cent. of the cost of a newspaper, 60 per cent. of the cost of bread, and 75 per cent. of the cost of cotton yarn goes on raw materials. Selling costs may reach even higher proportions. The cost of labour and materials in patent medicines is generally negligible in comparison with the price. Half of the price of milk goes to meet the cost of the distributor. In furniture, jewellery, and luxury goods of all kinds, a distributor's margin of 50 per cent. and upwards is common. Clearly, a slight saving in the cost of distribution may be more valuable than a substantial cut in manufacturing costs. What we have to decide, however, is not whether there is room for economy, but whether there are more opportunities to make such economies in a large than in a small business.

First of all, the large buyer is able to obtain preferential treatment. He is quoted the lowest prices and offered discounts and rebates. He can obtain freight concessions from railway and road transport companies, liberal credit from the banks, and prompt delivery, careful attention, and special facilities from manufacturers. Even when others go short of materials, he is still able to obtain them. This preferential treatment is often the fruit of bargaining strength. Prices must be "cut to the bone" because the large buyer might enter into

---

[1] S. H. Slichter, *Modern Economic Society*, p. 13.
[2] A. W. M. Kitchin, "Smallholdings and the agricultural structure," *Economic Journal*, 1934, p. 668.

competition with the firms from which he buys. Thus Ford's are said to be able to buy steel sheets below the normal market price, partly because they operate steel furnaces as a yardstick with which to measure costs.[1] In the same way, firms which might run their own fleet of motor vans and lorries are in a strong position to demand freight concessions. Or if the market is narrow, and the large buyer has few important competitors, he will be able to bring pressure on the firms which supply him by threatening to withdraw his custom and influence.

The bargaining advantages of large businesses make them profitable. But they do not make them *efficient*. A big firm may put money in its pocket by using its bargaining strength to beat down the price of materials. But it does so only at the expense of some other firm. The mere transfer of profit from one firm to another works no more improvement from the social point of view than the operations of gamblers or pickpockets. It is not a true economy at all. Similarly a big firm may find itself in a position of monopoly and mark up the price of its products, or sell an inferior quality at the old price. Here, too, there is no economy but only the exploitation of a monopoly advantage. Preferential treatment to large-scale buyers is a sign of economy in marketing only when it is offered by the seller in consequence of a reduction in his costs.

Such a reduction will normally take place when a large order enables plant to be run to capacity and without constant adjustment and frequent spoilage. A truckload will not cost twice as much to transport as two half-filled trucks. Steel sections rolled to one specification will cost less than an assortment of sections of the same weight, since the work will not be held up by the need to change the rolls. A large order which gives a factory steady work for six months is obviously more satisfactory than a series of small orders which provide work intermittently. In these and similar cases, better terms can be quoted for large orders than for small, and the firms which are big enough to place large orders make corresponding savings.

A reduction in costs also takes place because large orders enable the sales staff to be used to capacity. If customers double their orders it will not be necessary to double the sales staff. A traveller for one variety of tinned foods can book an order for fifty-seven with little extra trouble. There is more here than a saving in time. A manufacturer who has built up a reputation, or a distributor who has a good clientele, for the sale of one product, can sell others on the footing of his reputation or connection. If motorists buy your tyres they may buy your golf-balls, too. Every commodity which a firm sells is an advertisement for every other which it is trying to market. Manufacturers, therefore, may be

---

[1] And also as a safeguard against failure of supplies (e.g., because of a strike).

induced to expand their business by taking up new lines, and so using their sales organisation and their sales advantages to the full. At the same time, they will have a further motive for offering better terms to firms placing large orders, and these firms, in their turn, will be tempted to expand.

The large firm, then, enjoys preferential treatment, partly because of the economies of large orders. It also enjoys other advantages in marketing. It can employ expert buyers, skilled in the selection and blending of materials. It can submit its materials to strict tests, grading them so that the final product is of uniform quality, and reducing the risk of waste from faulty materials. It can generally bide its time in buying and selling, and refrain from making purchases or sales when the market is unfavourable.[1] Its customers will have the advantage of a better service of repairs and replacements than those who have bought from smaller firms. In making their purchases, they will have a wider range of choice, out of a greater variety of stocks, and will frequently be able to obtain immediate delivery from stock of goods which a smaller firm would require time to manufacture.

## 4  Financial economies

The large firm has also many financial advantages. It has a wider reputation and more influence amongst those who have money to lend or invest. It can borrow from bankers upon better security and raise capital more readily through the issue of shares and debentures than a small firm. There is a wide and regular market for these shares, so that shareholders can realise their capital without any of the trouble to which they would be put in a small private concern. Thus the cost of obtaining credit or of raising fresh capital is lower for a large than for a small firm.

This difference in the cost of borrowing might seem to be proof of a bargaining advantage rather than of true economy. For a large business to be granted easy credit because it has several bankers on its board of directors is graft and not economy. For a shareholder to invest in a company whose shares are quoted in the financial pages of the newspapers rather than in one of which he has never heard, does not mean that the first company will make better use of his money than the second. We do not look on a company which hires its labour very cheaply as an efficient company (although it may be); why then should a company hiring its capital cheaply be given that title?

---

[1] On the other hand, it must often make contracts for large quantities so as to allow of steady production. These large orders, placed openly, may force up the price against the company—all the more if the number of producers who can guarantee delivery is no more than two or three. A small competitor is in a much better position to "shop around" the market, obtaining secret concessions from the published price and buying odd lots when the opportunity offers. For an example from the glucose trade, see A. S. Dewing, *Financing of Public Corporations*, p. 760.

All this is true. But it is incontestable also that the lending of money in large quantities, like the bulk purchase of materials, is less costly than the lending of money in small quantities. A system of large-scale production allows capital to be raised with more convenience to the lender than a system where production is in the hands of a large number of small firms. This convenience to the lender—for instance, the greater ease with which he can recover his capital— is an economy of scale exactly like the convenience of supplying a large order rather than a series of small ones.

## 5    Risk-bearing economies

Large firms are often less exposed to risk than small ones. First of all, they are able to eliminate risks by grouping them. We can often predict what will happen *on the average* with fair certainty when the *individual* items defy prediction altogether. Thus we can say with some confidence that 5,000 people will commit suicide in Britain next year, but we cannot possibly say who they will be. Similarly with births and deaths, motor accidents, burglaries, fires, and all the contingencies against which we can insure. The larger the number of instances, the less the risk of errors in judgment. In a large business, therefore, where the same operation is more often repeated than in a small one, uncertainty can be reduced. "To the owner of a cow the loss at calving time is uncertain, while to the owner of a great herd this loss appears as a regular percentage that can be computed and allowed for . . . Again, in a small refinery the possibility of over-doing a batch of oil or sugar may be a source of serious uncertainty, while in a large refinery the law of the average prevails."[1]

The grouping of risks is of particular importance in finance. A large bank or insurance company, for example, tends to be more stable than a small one because it is less likely to be overwhelmed by a purely local catastrophe. The collective investments of a large bank are far more secure than the investments of each of the branches. Similarly the insurance benefits payable by a large company vary less from year to year and can be more accurately foreseen than the benefits payable by a small company. Through their greater stability, large financial enterprises are able to command the confidence both of their customers and of their investors. Thus they are in a position to quote attractive terms for their services and to raise their capital comparatively cheaply.

When similar risks are grouped, the law of averages applies and uncertainty is reduced. When dissimilar risks are grouped, the advantage is less definite, but far from negligible. The spreading of risks is, indeed, one of the main preoccupations of modern industry. Firms may seek to spread their risks by diversi-

---

[1] E. A. Ross, *Uncertainty as a Factor in Production*, quoted in C. O. Hardy, *Risk and Risk-bearing*, p. 19.

fying their output, or markets, or sources of supply, or processes of manufacture. Such diversification makes the firm less vulnerable to sudden changes and allows it to remain a going concern where smaller, less diversified, concerns would be forced to give up business.

**(a) Diversification of output**—Where a firm is likely to be injured by a decline in the demand for its product, it will be likely to look round for other products which can be easily manufactured simultaneously with the first. In this way, it may be able to level out a slump in one product against a boom in another. Or if something happens to interrupt the manufacture of one, it will still be possible to carry on with the manufacture of the others. One of the main reasons why mixed farming has such a hold on British agriculture, for example, is that it is unusual for all branches of farming to be equally depressed, so that the farmer who is selling several different products can make ends meet by setting the profits from one against the losses on the others. If the depression lasts a long time—as agricultural depressions do—he can cut down the production of his biggest losers and switch to the more profitable branches of farming (e.g., from stock-raising to dairy-farming, or from wheat-growing to barley and oats).[1] Similarly one may find a fish-and-chip shop selling ice-cream, or a refrigerating plant dovetailed with a skating rink. One firm will manufacture mustard and barley water; another, electric equipment and wireless sets. The more fickle the demand, either from one season to another, or from year to year the stronger will be the tendency to spread risks and steady production by diversifying output.

**(b) Diversification of markets**—Even when only one product is manufactured, increased sales, if there are to be a larger number of markets than before, may reduce the danger of fluctuations in demand. The sale of electricity for all purposes is less variable than the sale to industrial consumers only; the total sale to domestic consumers is more stable than the sale for heating, lighting, or cooking only. It pays distributors, therefore, to develop the domestic market; or, if they already supply electricity for lighting, to encourage consumers to use electric radiators, refrigerators, and cookers—to say nothing of radios, razors, and hair-wavers, all of which are, or should be, used at different times of day, and sum up to give a comparatively stable demand. In the same way, a railway which is largely dependent upon mineral traffic may find it worth while to develop suburban passenger transport. A firm which sells a new product in a

---

[1] There are also many technical advantages (e.g., the elimination of bare fallows by an alternation of fouling and cleaning crops, and the more even distribution of labour requirements throughout the year).

local market may seek to make the demand broader and steadier by advertising it on a national scale.

**(c) Diversification of sources of supply and, (d) of processes of manufacture**—Here the same principle applies. Large firms may be better able to maintain output when some particular source of raw materials is cut off (e.g., by a strike), or when some particular process of manufacture becomes uneconomical or impossible. If, for instance, they use steam power as well as electricity bought from a central distributing agency (the "grid"), a failure in the supply of electricity, or a rise in the price of coal will not hold up production altogether. A large business is likely to draw its supplies of raw materials from a wider area than a small one, and will be less exposed, therefore, to the danger of having its supplies cut off altogether.

It may seem strange to think of the spreading of risk as an economy; but if we mean by economy, "making the best use of resources, including human judgment," the term is quite properly applied to the spreading of risks that are known to be great. A firm which goes on producing regardless of risks may turn out goods at very low cost for a time, but if it is left high and dry by a change which might have been foreseen, and which other firms foresaw, its costs in the long run will work out above, and not below, theirs. For it will have sunk capital in an organisation which is put out of action by a change which might reasonably have been predicted. It will have led resources, to put it vulgarly, up the garden path, and committed them to uses in which they are of little further value. It would have been more *economical* to spread risks at the start by sacrificing some of the advantages of specialisation for the safeguards of diversification.[1]

Risk-spreading economies only make for large-scale production if they do not greatly complicate the business of managements. But this complication is hard to avoid when products, processes, and markets are diversified.[2] Risk-spreading and managerial economies, therefore, very often pull against one another. Sometimes the net result is in favour of large firms; when, for example, two products with different seasonal peaks can be dovetailed under one management. At other times the spreading of risks can be accomplished only in comparatively small firms. A mixed farm, for instance, requires far more

---

[1] This line of argument must not, of course, be pushed too far. There are limits to the advantages of spreading risks. What these are depends upon what view it is "reasonable" to take of the future, and how strongly one may "reasonably" hold that view.

[2] "The more restricted the variety of the processes undertaken by a single business, . . . the simpler is the task of direction. The more simple the work of direction, the larger is the volume of output which can be efficiently controlled by a single mind. And the larger the volume of output the greater is the scope for the major economies of modern techniques." F. Lavington, "Technical Influences on Vertical Integration," *Economica*, 1927, pp. 27–8.

supervision than a wheat farm in the prairies, and is much smaller, in spite of the larger number of things which it produces.[1]

Risk-spreading and technical economies are also in conflict with one another. A firm cannot obtain the full benefit of the technical advantages of large-scale production unless it sinks a great deal of capital in machinery and plant. If the plant can be run to capacity, so that it produces steadily on the scale for which it was designed, technical economies can be exploited up to the hilt. But if there is a risk of discontinuous operation, small firms using less expensive machinery, or less elaborately organised, may come into their own. In the steel industry, for example, it is very often the relatively small plants which survive an industrial depression most successfully. They are inferior, from the technical point of view, to large integrated plants designed to handle enormous outputs. But they have the advantage of lower standing charges on their machinery and plant, and have less difficulty, therefore, in making enough profit on a low output to cover these charges. They can also make savings more readily on operating costs if output has to be reduced below capacity. In a large integrated plant, there is a nice balance between the blast furnaces and coking plant, the steel furnaces and the rolling mill. But this balance is completely upset if the plant has to be run below the level of output for which it was designed. The heat supplied by the coking plant, or consumed in the soaking pit, cannot be halved to match a halving in the output of steel. If blast furnace gas is used to generate electricity, it will be impossible to damp down the furnaces and keep the rolling-mill in operation. The team of men who work the plant at full capacity will be almost as large as the team required for an output 20 per cent. lower. In a small firm operating costs are more flexible. A firm owning no blast furnaces, for example, will find it easier to substitute scrap for pig-iron in its steel furnaces whenever scrap is comparatively cheap. It will also be more adaptable to quick *changes* in output. The costs of damping down and relighting furnaces, or of stopping and starting again in any other part of the works, are high in a large plant, where regular operation at a constant level of output is indispensable to efficiency. In a small steelworks changes in output are less disorganising and can be made at less cost. Thus the risk of change, like the risk of operating below capacity, tends to halt the growth of the firm below the technical optimum.

The spreading of risks through an increase in sales will normally also reduce marketing costs. This double economy in marketing and risk-spreading is always a temptation to firms to put new products on the market, especially when they have their own sales organisation. A familiar example is the farmer

---

[1] Smaller, judged by the total value of what it produces, and not simply in point of area.

who takes to raising chickens as a side-line and sells the eggs from his milk-cart. But risk-spreading, as we have seen, does not always make for an increase in output and sales. In mixed farming and steel-making, for example, risks are on the side of the small firm. Some marketing economies may have to be sacrificed, therefore, to permit of the spreading of risks by the small farm and steelworks. The large wheat farmer who changes over to mixed farming will find that his marketing costs have risen.

### The Logic of Large-Scale Production

Many of these economies of large-scale production are illustrations of three general principles which have been named by Professor Sargant Florence the principle of multiples, the principle of bulk transactions and the principle of massed (or pooled) reserves.[1] The first of these we encountered in discussing the economies of linked processes and the consequent need to balance the outputs of specialised machines at their lowest common multiple if the machines are to work to full capacity. The same principle underlies the employment of specialists and the full utilisation of managerial ability.[2] Sometimes it is referred to as the principle of indivisibility since it rests on the impossibility of reproducing a machine on a smaller scale. The second principle underlines most of the marketing and financial economies that have been described: a large order or a large loan may involve no more trouble than a small one. But the principle also embraces what we have called "economies of increased dimensions" which derive from having a big unit with the same mechanical properties as a smaller one. The same locomotive may either draw more trucks or bigger trucks: in either event the unit cost of transport will be reduced. The third principle, which is the most difficult to understand, can be regarded as the basis of what we have described as "risk-bearing economies." Professor Sargant Florence illustrates it in relation to the holding of stocks and shows that, with a large turnover, it is not necessary to increase stocks proportionately. One of the principal functions of stocks is to meet aberrations in demand but the greater the number of individual orders, "the more likely are deviations to cancel out and to leave the actual average results nearer to the expected results."[3] Thus the size of the stock held in reserve need not increase

---

[1] P. S. Florence, *The Logic of British and American Industry*, pp. 50–52.

[2] Cf. Florence, *op. cit.*, p. 52: "Any given specialisation of equipment or men involves for balanced production a large scale of operation or production; but conversely it is only a large scale of operation or production that admits of specialisation with all its well-known economic advantages. It is only large-scale production that will justify a special research organisation, intensive costing, or the working up of by-products able to occupy researchers, cost accountants or by-product plant profitably for their full time."

[3] Florence, *op. cit.*, p. 51.

proportionately to output if orders are more numerous and the cost of holding stocks is correspondingly reduced.

### Is size ever a handicap?

The economies of scale which we have described relate to particular commodities: the bigger the output, the greater the efficiency with which a single commodity can be produced. Economies of scale, and the consequent savings in costs, may be reaped at the level of a single plant, or in a group of plants owned by a single firm or, if they are external economies, they may involve a whole industry. Some external economies may be obtainable only when the total scale of output—not the output of a single commodity—is large either in relation to a particular area or over the whole economy. Indeed, they may, like some economies of information, be world-wide and dependent on the size of world markets rather than of the national market. At whatever level they are enjoyed, they are reflected in increased productivity, so that, as the market becomes larger and specialisation can be carried further, costs of production fall.

We may reasonably ask, however, whether costs always fall with size or whether there may not be some countervailing tendency for size to become a handicap. This is a question that economists have usually discussed in relation to individual firms and commodities. It is not without interest, however, in relation to industrial areas as well, since size may begin to bring congestion and each newcomer may create inconvenience instead of adding to the facilities enjoyed by established firms. The reason why economists have concentrated on firms and commodities is that they have found difficulty in explaining why, if costs fall continuously with output, one firm should not succeed in capturing the entire market. If the odds are so heavily on the large firm by virtue of its size, how do small firms manage to carry on?

This is a question to which we shall turn in the next chapter. Three explanations have been put forward, one in terms of the difficulty of efficient management in large firms, one in terms of market limitations and one in terms of the risk of loss from larger outputs. We shall deal here only with the first.

### The optimum firm

The implication of this explanation is that, once a firm's production exceeds a certain volume it begins to encounter increasing difficulty in co-ordinating its activities and managerial *dis*economies creep in. These *dis*economies are sufficient to offset any remaining technical or other economies of scale so that eventually higher outputs involve it in higher unit costs. On this showing, there would be some optimum scale of production at which costs were at a minimum.

Firms producing on a scale smaller than this (i.e., of less than optimum size) would be incurring higher costs, e.g., by sacrificing the use of expensive machinery without any compensating advantage. Firms of more than optimum size would also be incurring higher costs, e.g., because the organisation was cumbersome and beyond the powers of its directors to manage properly.

A further implication would be that any concentration of production in a single firm, or in a nationalised industry, would run the risk of losing some of the advantages of large-scale production because of the comparative inefficiency of management in a very large productive unit. The maximum economy would be obtained by dispersing the total output over several firms of optimum size; and this would be true independently of any further gains that might result from the competition of those firms with one another.

Now there is no doubt that this line of explanation is in keeping with a great deal of everyday experience. It is common ground that the larger the firm, the more complicated, as a rule, are the problems of management. These problems manifest themselves in the difficulty of ensuring proper co-ordination between different departments and different people and in the need to devolve more authority on subordinates. It is harder to maintain speed of decision when there are more people to be consulted and harder to prevent misunderstandings as the chain of command lengthens.

### The need for delegation

First of all, there is a limit to what one man can take in, reflect upon and decide about. It is impossible to supervise the work of more than a small group of immediate subordinates if only because it takes time to discuss matters with them and time is the scarcest commodity of which a top manager disposes. The more matters arise for decision, therefore, the more necessary it becomes to share or delegate authority. But this raises a fresh set of problems. Those who share authority, like the members of a Cabinet, must have confidence in one another's capabilities, good sense and above all loyalty. They must be willing to accept the decisions of their colleagues within the area of competence allotted to each and abide by the collective decision in all matters referred upwards for a joint review. Any reservations on this score are bound to lead to vacillation and delay, give rise to personal conflict and rivalry, and take from the efficiency of the whole organisation.

### Difficulties of delegation

Similar difficulties accompany the delegation of authority to subordinates: with this addition, that it may be more difficult to retain the loyalty of an able subordinate precisely because he may dislike being in a subordinate position.

Moreover, the more complex the problems that create the need to delegate, the more awkward is the task of co-ordination. If every man's duties are precisely defined, he may show an excess of zeal not to usurp those duties and shirk responsibility for a decision. If his duties are not precisely defined, he may get to cross-purposes with his colleagues, indulge in empire-building, fail to maintain liaison with other departments, or just slack. If delegation is on a hierarchical basis, each man down the line taking responsibility for every aspect of the work of his department, from buying materials to training staff, there will be little scope for the specialists on each of these aspects. If it is on a functional basis, there is likely to be friction between the heads of the specialist departments: high specialisation, in management as in everything else, means a looseness of contact between the specialists—between the sales manager and the works manager, the chief engineer and the head of the research department, the materials controller and the finance director—and these loose contacts can breed oversights, misunderstandings and demarcation disputes. Even when a staff is attached to a hierarchical line of command—in the line-and-staff system of organisation—so as to feed in expert advice to each departmental head and undertake research, prepare plans or check results on his behalf, there are still a number of inherent weaknesses in a large organisation: a tendency to red tape; a decline in the sense of urgency; failure in communications, both in the flow of information to those who need it and between those who are in charge of the organisation and those whose work is being organised.

All this may be true; but it does not justify us in holding that firms become progressively less efficient the larger they grow, or that large firms are unable to survive competition with smaller firms because they have passed some managerial optimum. On the contrary, the biggest firms seem to be successfully maintaining their place in the economy and to be growing still bigger.[1] As a firm grows, it develops a new administrative structure appropriate to its size; this takes time and the fact that it takes time means that there is a limit to the *rate* at which a firm can grow without loss of efficiency.[2] It is quite possible also that the effort of growth may prove too much for a firm that has to make a rather large jump in size and that, before it has reorganised its administrative structure satisfactorily, it will make heavy losses and be wound up. There is

---

[1] Between 1949 and 1955 the profits of the hundred largest British companies increased from 25·2 per cent. to 31·5 per cent. of all industrial profits. In the years 1949–53 only two British companies with net assets of over £1m. were liquidated (out of a total existing in 1948 of 764); a further 21 were taken over by other companies (but all or nearly all were making profits) and 4 went out of business for other reasons. See S. J. Prais, "Size, Growth and Concentration" in *Studies in Company Finance*, ed. B. Tew and R. F. Henderson (Cambridge, 1959), pp. 108, *et seq.*

[2] For a fuller discussion see E. T. Penrose, *The Theory of the Growth of the Firm* (Oxford, 1959), pp. 18 *et seq.*

no need to swing to the opposite extreme and suggest that large firms are immune from disaster. But, given time, they should be able to decentralise their organisation sufficiently to permit of efficient operation.[1]

## Financial groups

A large firm may push decentralisation to the point at which it consists of a group of separately organised businesses, enjoying almost complete automony. General Motors Corporation, for example, allows individual units in its system to compete with one another and seeks "to make each separate unit self-contained, complete with all the functions essential to its full development."[2] The companies in the Vickers group "operate themselves very largely. Vickers Limited itself is a holding company, holding in almost all cases a 100 per cent. holding. It acts as the financial controller, and indeed the banker, in regard to all the financial requirements of the companies."[3] Where companies are so loosely associated in a single group, bound together by financial control rather than as parts of a single administrative structure, it is difficult to see how size can prevent any real handicap on the score of managerial inefficiency. Yet as Mrs. Penrose has pointed out, the tendency for the biggest firms to move in this direction is already perceptible. "As an industrial firm becomes larger and larger, and its operations become progressively more decentralised with the lines of authority becoming more tenuous, permitting greater autonomy in the constituent parts, is it not possible that the firm will increasingly acquire the characteristics of a financial holding company, lose those of an industrial firm, and finally become virtually indistinguishable from an investment trust? And if this does happen, can we safely assume that the principles that govern the growth of an industrial firm are equally applicable when the organisation is metamorphosed into an essentially financial firm?"[4]

## Is there an optimum size of firm?

These questions point to one of the weaknesses in the concept of the optimum size of firm. The concept makes sense only if it is applied to a group of firms

---

[1] Cf. P. S. Florence, *op. cit.*, p. 64, "The contention here is not that large organisations will inevitably be more efficient than small; but simply that it is *not* inevitable that larger organisations will eventually fail because of management. Corporate management may become *more* efficient with size owing to specialisation of member managers, or if it becomes less efficient, its deficiency may in effect be counter-balanced by other factors. Sometimes admittedly there will be no counter-balance. Some firms fail with size because of management, if the immediate jump in size which they attempt is too great; or if the management is incapable of adapting its structure, or (and this is important for whole industries) if each unit transaction which management tries to undertake requires close attention to detail and quick adjustment to uncertain circumstances."

[2] Annual Report, 1942, quoted by E. T. Penrose, *op. cit.*, p. 175n.

[3] Evidence before the Committee on the Working of the Monetary System, Q11303.

[4] E. T. Penrose, *op. cit.*, p. 19.

making similar products, i.e. to an industry. But large firms rarely confine themselves to a single industry. A large firm may be a comparatively small producer of wooden furniture. Its efficiency as a producer of wooden furniture will be related, not just to its output of this one product but to the total scale of its operations as well. If we try to apply the concept of the optimum, therefore, we have first to decide whether it is wooden furniture and the scale on which it is being produced, or the actual firm, and the scale of its operations, that we have in mind. The firm may be a highly efficient producer of a wide variety of products, including wooden furniture, and may limit its production of the latter because it prefers to concentrate its resources in other directions. The scale of its production of furniture is low; but this is no proof that there would be little economy in large-scale production within a single firm of a different type. On the other hand, the total scale of production is high; but this is equally no proof that large firms, by virtue of their size, are particularly suited to the industry of furniture-making.

While we can analyse the economies that result from larger outputs of individual commodities, and the economies that result from the larger scale of operations of an individual firm, it is confusing to tie together the two types of economy as if all firms produced only a single commodity. Once we start comparing, not some idealised group of firms of varying size all producing the same article, but the large and small firms of real life, we have to take account of the changes in product-mix, and the simultaneous changes in administrative structure that go with size. This makes it very difficult to compare like with like and measure efficiency against some identifiable optimum; the only satisfactory basis of comparison is cost of production or power to survive in free competition with other firms.

The structure of industry is highly complex, with different products integrated with one another in different firms and a fairly wide scatter in the scale on which they produce any one commodity. There may be an "optimum" social output of the commodity: beyond a certain volume it may become increasingly difficult, without some rise in cost, to produce more of it. There may also be an optimum distribution of this output between different firms and a *minimum* scale of production below which efficiency is demonstrably sacrificed. There may, finally, be some weaknesses of organisation to which large firms are more prone than small. But we cannot usefully talk of an optimum size of *firm* so long as firms of different sizes do different things and do them in different ways with a different administrative structure.

### Influence of the industrial environment

Similarly, we cannot look at a firm in isolation from its industrial environment.

Firms exist in association and in competition with other firms; they are linked organically with one another.[1] Their growth is conditioned by the play of opportunity on a given endowment of managerial ability, financial strength, and so on, just as the growth of organisms is conditioned by the play of environment on a given hereditary endowment. Firms grow by grafting and proliferation rather than as homogeneous units with which new units of the same kind are geared mechanically.

A firm, therefore, must be looked at against a background of market conditions from which we cannot abstract. Its costs depend not simply on how it does things (that is, on what is happening inside the firm), but also on what it has to do, and what it has to do depends upon the industrial environment. If the environment changes, the optimum changes, and the growth of the firm of itself may be sufficient to alter the environment.

If, for example, the growth of a firm reduces the competition to which it is exposed this may automatically ease the task of management: industrial combination might create an environment favourable to the operation of larger units than could survive intense competition—"favourable" in the sense of making for lower costs, not just of making for higher profits. Many of the risks which keep the optimum firm comparatively small are themselves the product of competition. The individual producer must adapt his plans to the plans of his competitors without knowledge of their intentions. He is in the dark about the new models and new products which they mean to bring out, the output which they propose to market, and the methods by which they hope to market that output. Thus he is kept busy meeting their competition, retaliating in kind for invasions of his market, scheming to steal a march on them by some new agreement with distributors or some new advertising campaign, giving uncertainty for uncertainty. If all this competitive effort were inevitable, the optimum firm would remain small, since a large firm would lack the adaptability and thrustfulness necessary in a highly competitive market. But competitive secrecy and uncertainty are by no means inevitable. A monopoly gets rid of both. So also would nationalisation—the formation of a State monopoly.

Competitive pressure may also induce a firm to make a wide variety of

---

[1] Compare A. N. Whitehead, *Science and the Modern World*, p. 238.
"The trees in a Brazilian forest depend upon the association of various species of organisms, each of which is mutually dependent on the other species. A single tree by itself is dependent upon all the adverse chances of shifting circumstances. The wind stunts it: the variations in temperature check its foliage: the rains denude its soil: its leaves are blown away and are lost for the purpose of fertilisation. . . . But in nature the normal way in which trees flourish is by their association in a forest. Each tree may lose something of its individual perfection of growth, but they mutually assist each other in preserving the conditions for survival. The soil is preserved and shaded; and the microbes necessary for its fertility are neither scorched, nor frozen, nor washed away. . . . A species of microbes which kills the forest, also exterminates itself."

products, and this variety, by complicating the problem of management, tends to limit the growth of the firm. In a monopoly, however, it would be possible to carry specialisation a good deal further, and to concentrate particular products on particular units. Similarly, although it tends to change the temper of management and create a more elaborate hierarchy than private enterprise, nationalisation is capable of yielding important economies without the dangers to the public interest that a private monopoly would involve.

We cannot assume, therefore, that there is necessarily a loss in efficiency if an industry is taken over by a monopoly or if it is nationalised by the State; and this is true even in industries in which the typical productive unit is relatively small.

CHAPTER 9

# SMALL-SCALE PRODUCTION

In the last chapter our attention was concentrated on the advantages of large-scale production, while the forces making for small-scale production were touched on very briefly. In this chapter we shall look at the other side of the picture and try to discover why small-scale production still holds its own.

The overwhelming majority of business units are extremely small; many are one-man businesses and many more employ only a handful of workers. There are, for example, about half a million shopkeepers and 300,000 farmers, while the total number of persons engaged in shopkeeping and farming is well under four million. In the building industry at least 1 man in 10 works on his own account or as employer. In the professions, in road transport, and in a wide range of service trades from laundries to bookmaking, the small firm predominates. Even in manufacturing industry the number of really large firms is tiny. In 1935 there were only 100 firms in British industry employing over 5,000 workers and about 1,000 firms employing over 1,000 workers. The smaller firms, however, did not account for more than a limited proportion of the employment and output in the industries covered (which included public utility companies and building firms as well as mining and manufacturing). There were about an equal number of workers in firms employing over 1,000 workers and in firms employing between 100 and 1,000 workers, and workers in each of these two groups considerably outnumbered those in the smaller firms employing less than 100 workers.

No comparable figures are available for post-war years as returns are now made by establishment rather than by firm. But there is no evidence of any marked change in the balance between small and large units. As will be seen from Table 4, which relates exclusively to the factory trades, there are about 1,000 establishments employing over 1,000 workers, and these establishments account for about 30 per cent of all manufacturing employment; the 13,800 establishments employing between 100 and 1,000 workers account for 45 per cent. of total manufacturing employment; and the remaining 25 per cent. is accounted for by the large number of small establishments, nearly all of them separate enterprises, that employ less than 100 workers.

TABLE 4

SIZE OF ESTABLISHMENT IN MANUFACTURING INDUSTRY IN THE UNITED KINGDOM IN 1954[1]

| Average number employed | Number of establishments | Number of persons employed (thousands) | Proportion of total employment (per cent.) | Proportion of net output (per cent.) |
|---|---|---|---|---|
| 11 − 24 | 16832 | 275 | 3·6 | 3·1 |
| 25 − 49 | 14726 | 518 | 6·8 | 5·8 |
| 50 − 99 | 10826 | 760 | 10·0 | 8·9 |
| 100 − 199 | 7162 | 1001 | 13·2 | 12·1 |
| 200 − 499 | 5076 | 1553 | 20·4 | 19·9 |
| 500 − 999 | 1534 | 1048 | 13·7 | 14·4 |
| 1000 − 4999 | 982 | 1844 | 24·2 | 27·1 |
| 5000 − 9999 | 59 | 405 | 5·3 | 5·6 |
| 10,000 & over | 13 | 227 | 2·9 | 3·0 |
| Total | 57210 | 7631 | 100·0 | 100·0 |

[1] Excluding establishments employing an average of less than 10. There were about 80,000 such establishments with a total employment of some 400,000.

*Source:* Census of Production for 1954.

These figures understate the degree of concentration in the larger units since one firm may own several establishments and several firms may be controlled by a single business unit. Moreover, while they show the position for the whole of manufacturing industry, they do not show the wide variation that exists between one industry and another. There are literally scores of commodities— mustard, safety matches and cotton thread are familiar examples—produced exclusively or almost exclusively by one or two big firms. Taking as a measure of the degree of concentration, the proportion of total employment in the three largest concerns, Evely and Little have arrived at the results shown in Table 5. These results, which relate to 1951, are not very different from those reached earlier by Leak and Maizels for 1935.

The figures in Table 5 are for 220 separate trades grouped by industry, employment in the three largest units in each trade being aggregated and compared with total employment in the group of trades classified as an industry.

TABLE 5

CONCENTRATION OF EMPLOYMENT IN THREE LARGEST BUSINESS UNITS, 1951

| Industry group | Number of trades covered | Employment in trades covered (thousands) | Aggregate of employment three largest units in each trade (thousands) | Degree of concentration (per cent.) |
|---|---|---|---|---|
| Chemicals and allied trades | 16 | 336 | 170 | 51 |
| Electrical engineering and electrical goods .. .. | 8 | 341 | 164 | 48 |
| Vehicles .. .. .. | 8 | 444 | 182 | 41 |
| Iron and steel and non-ferrous metals .. .. | 15 | 512 | 200 | 39 |
| Drink and tobacco .. | 7 | 172 | 62 | 36 |
| Mining and quarrying .. | 21 | 312 | 109 | 35 |
| Non-electrical engineering | 20 | 755 | 236 | 31 |
| Food .. .. .. | 18 | 454 | 136 | 30 |
| Other metal industries .. | 27 | 403 | 117 | 29 |
| Other textiles .. .. | 18 | 360 | 99 | 27 |
| Paper and printing .. | 10 | 422 | 88 | 21 |
| Cotton .. .. .. | 3 | 246 | 52 | 21 |
| Other manufacturing and service trades .. .. | 23 | 539 | 105 | 20 |
| Woollen and worsted .. | 6 | 164 | 30 | 18 |
| Clothing and footwear .. | 17 | 477 | 66 | 14 |
| Building, contracting and civil engineering .. | 3 | 433 | 54 | 12 |
| Total .. .. .. | 220 | 6369 | 1868 | 29 |

Source: Evely and Little, Concentration in British Industry, p. 62.

The degree of concentration in large units varies greatly from industry to industry; it is high in the chemical, metal and engineering group and low in the building and clothing industries. On the average, about three out of every ten workers in the 220 trades covered were in one of the three largest business units in their trade.

In spite of this concentration in large units, the fact remains that there are small firms in most trades and that in some trades it is the large firm that is rare. How are we to account for this, in view of the economies to which large-scale production leads?

(i) In some industries, the answer is a straightforward one: it is the absence of any major economies of scale. There may be little scope, for example, for highly capital-intensive techniques and no close links between succeeding stages of manufacture. Technical economies may be realisable in a comparatively small plant and there may be no strong motives to combine different plants under a single control. Thus a small café does not suffer from the handicaps of a small aircraft firm.

(ii) A second reason is that the process of growth takes time. This is true partly because of imperfections in competition that give shelter to an existing concern and allow it to carry on in spite of comparative inefficiency; and partly because a large firm cannot grow without a great deal of effort, involving planned additions to its resources and their re-organisation in a new administrative framework. Thus many small firms are able to survive for a time because the bigger firms suffer from indigestion if they try to gobble them up too quickly.

(iii) The fact that it takes time for big firms to expand helps the small firms in another way. Since the economy as a whole is growing, new opportunities of expansion are for ever being created and these opportunities are open to the small as well as to the larger firms. If the opportunities increase faster than the large firms are able to seize them, and if there is no special difficulty in entering the trade, there is obviously room for small firms to grow both in size and numbers even if they are unable to match the large firms in productive efficiency.[1]

(iv) A fourth explanation is that there are always plenty of people ready to start a new business, many of whom must ultimately fail. Small firms are constantly being launched as new enterprises since it is usual in business, as in human existence, to start small and grow. These new enterprises show a high "infant mortality" and may be operated for years at a loss before being finally wound up. The eventual failures—and, of course, the eventual successes—swell the number of small firms at any point in time.[2]

(v) Large firms that want to avoid being labelled monopolists may tolerate or even encourage smaller competitors. Similarly, orders may be placed regularly with high cost small firms in order to keep them in business as an insurance against complete dependence on a single large supplier.

---

[1] Cf. E. T. Penrose, *op. cit.*, pp. 222–23, "The productive opportunities of small firms are thus composed of those interstices left open by the large firms which the small firms see and believe they can take advantage of. If enough small firms judge their prospects reasonably correctly and act accordingly, then the rate of growth of the economy will exceed the rate of growth of the large firms. And if the existing small firms are unable or unwilling to fill all the interstices, there will be scope for the successful creation of new firms."

[2] For example, American studies show that 1 or 2 retailers out of 10 go out of business within the first year of operation and that in some cities less than half the manufacturing firms last as long as four years (P. S. Florence, *op. cit.*, p. 53). The death-rate appears to fall rapidly with size (*ibid.*, p. 66).

(vi) In addition to these reasons, there are the various obstacles to growth to which we referred in the previous chapter: managerial obstacles, market obstacles and financial obstacles.[1] Managerial obstacles have already been discussed and they are also implicit in the second and third of the reasons given above, which lay emphasis on the effort of growing rather than on the additional managerial burdens that larger size may bring with it. We shall deal briefly with these burdens before turning to marketing and financial obstacles to growth.

### 1   MANAGERIAL OBSTACLES

First of all, the range and complexity of the problems of management are greater in large than in small firms. In any industry, therefore, where there is need of constant supervision and rapid decision—where each firm must use a great deal of management, or "decision-taking," per unit of product—small firms will predominate. Their advantages lie in the absence of divided responsibility, in the attention which they can give to detail, and in their ability to cater exactly for the wants of their customers. In retail shopkeeping, in farming, and in trades where the influence of fashion is great, or a very high quality of product is demanded, the small firm has no difficulty in holding its ground. But in trades that can be reduced largely to routine—the railways, the post office, etc.—or in which the range of problems is narrow—in cotton-spinning as compared with cotton-weaving,[2] or in the worsted as compared with the woollen trades[3]—the advantage lies with the larger firm.

Given the range of problems in an industry, the large firm may be assisted by the development of new forms of organisation and new methods of business management. The rise of cost accounting, for example, makes it easier to cope with the problem of tracing waste, and allows comparisons to be drawn between the efficiency of different departments and factories. The joint-stock system provides the large firm with facilities for raising enormous amounts of capital, and smooths the path of able men as they try to expand their business to the limits of their organising ability. The spread of education and the growth of business morality makes it easier to delegate tasks to subordinates. Thus in industries where advantage can be taken of cost accounting, scientific management, up-to-date office equipment, and so on, even complex problems can be handled satisfactorily.

---

[1] Above, p. 123.
[2] Cotton yarns are spun by standard methods to standard specifications; in weaving, on the other hand, the mills generally produce a fairly wide range of product, differing in quality and pattern.
[3] The woollen trades call for much more skill in blending from a great variety of raw materials.

The managerial obstacle to growth is, in the last resort, a personal one. There is a limit to the range and complexity of the problems which a business man, however able and however ably served, can tackle satisfactory. The burden of detail becomes enormous, particularly in a business made up of scattered plants faced with their own special problems. If there is little devolution of responsibility to departmental and branch managers, they are deprived of initiative and degenerate into mere cogs in the machine. If, on the other hand, responsibility is delegated, subordinates of outstanding ability must be appointed and must be handsomely paid. These subordinates may, and frequently do, launch out on their own in competition with their former employers. The zeal and energy which they then show for their own interests may be out of all proportion to their previous efforts on behalf of their employers, for as salaried officers they have much less at stake, and are much less inclined to make sacrifices. From a mixture of motives—from a love of independence and uncertainty, from pride or ambition, or the urge to create[1]—men may prefer to run a small business of their own rather than act as subordinates at a higher rate of pay. Their workers, too, may prefer to remain with an employer who knows their habits and history rather than move to a larger business where there can be no personal contact between employers and employed.

Some small firms are simply the large firms of tomorrow: not very many, because there are few large firms at any time. But in some of the newer industries, where a balance between large and small firms has not yet been struck, a rapidly expanding market often carries some of the small firms along with it, until what was initially the province of a host of small firms, many of them new, becomes dominated by the larger survivors.

There are other small firms that would be quite capable of expanding if the management showed more enterprise. These firms may not be organised to take full advantage of the opportunities open to them; they may be family businesses, content to jog along with a steady turnover, lacking the managerial resources to plan for expansion, and more afraid of prejudicing existing profits than attracted by the chance of doubling them.

From the point of view of management, therefore, small firms may survive, for one of three reasons. They may be large firms in the making; they may be capably managed by men who are indifferent to the possibilities of growth; or they may be managed by men who lack the judgment, experience, and organising ability needed in order to manage a large firm. Similarly, large businesses may be dwindling because of incompetent management; or they may

---

[1] One motive of some importance is the desire of the owner to leave to his son an occupation as head of his business and not just the capital which could be realised by selling out.

be growing because of the enterprise of the management; or they may be changing little in size and be managed with more than average competence.

## 2   MARKET OBSTACLES

Where the market is too narrow to permit of large-scale manufacture, the firm necessarily remains small. A firm might reduce its costs by doubling its output, but if the firm could not dispose of the extra output, there would be no sense in producing it. It is only when the market is big enough that no economies of scale need to be sacrificed and firms can expand freely in size.

The market may be limited in various ways.

**(a) Geographical**—First, it may be limited by distance, as, for example, the market of the local baker is limited. Rather than incur high transport costs (including waste in transit) by supplying distant customers, firms may prefer to produce on a small scale for local needs only. Whenever firms are distributing their products over a thinly-populated district, expansion will involve heavy outlays on marketing to set against any savings in the cost of manufacture, and the firms will remain small. This is true also of sources of supply. If the raw materials of an industry are widely scattered, and are expensive to assemble at a central site, production will tend to be carried on in scattered factories drawing on local supplies. The milling of timber, grain, and minerals illustrates this tendency, while the furniture trade and the light castings industry illustrate the first.

The obstacle of high transport costs is all the greater when markets and sources of supply are not only diffused but also overlap. If production is carried on by small firms up and down the country, the cost of assembling and radiating supplies is greatly reduced, and since producers and consumers remain in close contact with one another, there is no need for a long chain of middlemen. In dairying, for example, there is an obvious advantage in having villages and small towns supplied with milk straight from the farm. But if the areas of production and consumption lie some distance apart, so that there is a bottle-neck through which supplies must flow on their way to market, it will be easy for large firms, located at the bottle-necks, to drive small firms, situated on each side, out of business. This point can be illustrated from the livestock industry. In countries and regions which export a large proportion of their meat (e.g. Argentine, New Zealand, or Scotland), the points of export are bottle-necks through which the meat must pass. Thus the cattle can be assembled for slaughter in large meat-packing establishments. In a country like England, however, where both the market and the cattle are spread all over the country, the slaughterhouses are much smaller in size, since the cost of assembling the cattle for slaughter and radiating the meat to local butchers from a centralised slaughterhouse would be very high. In the United States the importance of the export market has declined, and with it the importance of Chicago and the large packers. The expansion of the home market has led to a decentralisation of the industry in smaller plants set up in the leading cattle districts.

Thus the obstacle of distance is strengthened by an increased overlapping of the areas of production and consumption. It is strengthened also by a rise in transport costs and by a reduction in the density of the market or of sources of supply. The trend, however, is generally towards *lower* transport costs and *increased* density. We find bread-making, for example, concentrated increasingly in bakeries in the towns as a result of improved methods of distribution. An area whose bread used to be made in bakeries scattered through villages and suburbs is now supplied by a few large bakers. A further example is provided by the brewing industry, where the substitution of canned for bottled beer, by reducing transport costs, operates in favour of the large firm. Similarly a fall in coal freights, or in the cost of transmitting electricity, may lead to the erection of larger power stations. An increase in the consumption of electricity within a given area (i.e., an increase in the density of demand) will have the same effect.

Distance, in other words, provides the small firm with a sheltered zone which other firms can with difficulty penetrate. Each small firm, supplying a local market, is partially insulated from competition, but if it tries to push its way into more distant markets, it meets with keener and keener competition round the fringe of invasion.[1] This market resistance to expansion checks the growth of firms to their optimum size. The check will be greater the higher the cost of transport, the more scattered the market and the sources of raw materials, and the more they overlap.

(b) **Psychological**—This line of reasoning can be extended from geographical to any other limitation of the market. Each firm, as we shall see, is normally marketing products which differ slightly from the products of its competitors. In the shoe trade, for example, no two firms cater for exactly the same shape of feet, specialise in exactly the same range of sizes, use leather of

---

[1] For example, a steel company operating a comparatively small plant in Texas had a virtual monopoly of the semi-fabricated steel business in the surrounding territory, being protected by high freight rates from competition from steel-makers in other states. When the size of the plant was doubled in 1926 it became necessary to extend sales into more distant markets, previously supplied by other steelworks. The cost of delivery was greater, while selling prices were held down by competition. In spite, therefore, of an improvement in the efficiency of the plant, the margin of profit disappeared and the company failed at the beginning of 1929. (A. S. Dewing, *Financial Policy of Corporations*, p. 724n.)

E*

exactly the same quality, or market their shoes in exactly the same pattern and style, with exactly the same guarantees and advertisements. Each firm has a clientele of its own, just like the bakers in adjoining villages. The market is broken up, not only by distance, but by the tastes, habits, and prejudices of consumers. Miss A insists on clogs, Miss B on brogues, so they buy from different firms. Mr. Broadfoot finds comfort in the shoes of Messrs. C; Mr. Narrowfoot will buy from no one but Messrs. D. One firm supplies Lady Snooty, another Mrs. Bourgeois, a third John Hiker, a fourth baby Jones, and so on. The market for each firm is limited by the requirements of the customers who are within its "sphere of influence." There is thus a market resistance to expansion which can be overcome only by finding new buyers or by invading the market of other firms. This puts the firm to the expense either of special concessions to its customers, or of an advertising campaign, or of the manufacture of new brands of product. It has to attract new customers by reducing its price, or by selling a better quality of product, or by persuading people that its products are "superior," or by doing something equally costly. These costs of growth, like high transport costs in a scattered market, shelter the small firm by penalising invasion of its market. The more varied the attachments which consumers form (the less the density of demand), and the less responsive they are to efforts to change their attachments (e.g., by advertisement, or by concessions in service, quality, or price), the more difficult will it be to dislodge small firms from their hold on the market.[1] It is only when consumers are indifferent from whom they buy, and what brands they buy—or when they actually have a preference for dealings with large firms—that the market ceases to be a major obstacle to expansion.

### Branch factories

The market obstacle can, however, be circumvented in two ways: by setting up branch factories, or by manufacturing a wide range of products or brands of the same product. The setting up of branch factories is a way of circumventing the geographical limitation of the market; the manufacture of a wide range of products is a way of circumventing the psychological limitation. Neither of these "dodges" is altogether satisfactory.

Branch factories under a central management can supply the adjacent territory without incurring the high transport costs and other marketing expenses of a single large establishment. They can specialise in the articles, brands, and sizes required locally, and supply orders promptly from a stock

---

[1] A familiar example is retailing, where small shops have an intimate knowledge of the requirements of their customers, and can bind them by the use of credit even when large firms are charging much lower prices.

which is small in comparison with the stock carried by independent units. Each branch can participate in the technical improvements made by the others, and can detect and eliminate waste by comparing its accounts regularly with theirs. Risks are spread, since a period of bad trade in one district can be set against a period of good trade in another, while if production is held up at one plant by fire or strike, customers can still be supplied from other plants. These and similar advantages make for the combination of scattered plants in a single firm when the individual plants are prevented from growing by market limitations.

Distance, however, sets a limit to the combination of plants just as it does to the size of the individual plant. The more scattered the units and the poorer the system of communication between them, the more insuperable are the difficulties of efficient supervision by the central office. If local circumstances differ greatly, responsible and expensive district managers must be appointed. Each plant must be given more latitude, and this makes it all the harder for the central office to keep them in step with one another, and frame a suitable policy. In short, branch factories sooner or later bump up against the managerial obstacle to expansion.

### The range of products

The same obstacle, as we have seen, checks the multiplication of products, patterns, styles, etc., within a single plant. It is only through the sacrifice of great economies in management (and also in technique) that firms can overcome the market obstacle to expansion by extending their range of product.[1] The work of management becomes more complicated, and at the same time the technique appropriate to the large-scale manufacture of a single product or style of product has to be abandoned. More than this, multiplication of products very often fails in its object. For if every firm adopts the same expedient and tries to supply the whole gamut of varieties sold by its competitors, it will end by producing everything on a small scale and selling in a market which has shrunk because of the universal rise in costs of production. The public will be offered a wide variety of styles, but it will be denied the benefits of large-scale production, for each firm will manufacture much the same varieties as its

---

[1] How great these economies can be may be illustrated from the experience of the Jantzen Knitting Mills which originally turned out sweaters, coats, caps, stockings and many other varieties of knitwear. Some of these products were eliminated until finally in 1926 it was decided to concentrate entirely on swimming suits of only one quality and to make these on a large scale. "Prior to the simplification programme, an operator sewing a special seam turned out nine seams per hour. Under simplification, by means of special machines and specialisation on this one operation, she produced with no greater effort 45 of these seams per hour. . . . Supervision was made simpler, with the result that foremen and superintendents found time for more work of a constructive nature." Robbins and Holts, *Industrial Mamagement*, p. 58, quoted by P. S. Florence, *Logic of Industrial Organisation*, p. 28.

competitors, instead of specialising on a limited range of styles and turning them out on a large scale. Sometimes the economy of concentrating on a few special lines is small and confined to the time saved in re-setting machinery. But more often the failure of firms to specialise more narrowly causes waste from the social point of view, while market resistances to growth simply increase *pari passu* with the variety of output of the typical firm.

It is impossible, for example, to doubt the wastefulness of selling (in the United States) 10,000 brands of wheat flour, 4,500 brands of canned corn, 1,000 brands each of canned peaches and salmon, 500 brands of mustard and 300 brands of pineapple.[1] In Britain, articles in common use—e.g., electric switches, paper bags, envelopes, labels and string—are sold in an equally bewildering array of brands, patterns, sizes, and colours. A single firm, manufacturing one article in a dozen different sizes, shapes, and colours will turn out no less than 1,728 varieties. If there are twenty other firms, each using slightly different specifications, the number of varieties may be over 30,000. If, finally, each of these firms is simultaneously turning out some ten or a dozen quite different products, the waste and confusion can readily be imagined. Nor is this an impossibly extravagant picture. The engineering trades, for example, include a "very large number of relatively small firms . . . each with a separate organisation, separate establishment charges, separate buying and selling arrangements, and each producing a multiplicity of articles. Some of them seemed to take a special pride in the number of things which they turned out . . . The result of many firms being employed upon producing a large number of articles in common use is . . . confusion in the types of articles produced, so that no two manufacturers seem intentionally to produce the same article. Each one claims some special merit of his own."[2]

Apart altogether from the social waste involved, the production of a whole range of styles, while it may be forced—or appear to be forced—on each manufacturer by the action of his competitors, does not free a firm from the limitations of its market. The pressure to expand may be diffused over a wider area; but so, too, is the resistance to expansion. If one firm markets a new variety of product, other firms tend to follow suit. Even if they do not, they can threaten retaliation in other ways. Suppose, for example, that the new variety sells well. Then unless new layers of demand are tapped, sales will be mainly at the expense of the old varieties, and competing firms will find themselves in difficulties. They must either reconcile themselves to reduced sales or fight to retain their "share" of the market. Very likely, they will fight—for instance, by

---

[1] S. H. Slichter, *op. cit.*, p. 553.

[2] Quoted from the *Report of the Board of Trade Engineering Trades Committee*, (1916–17) by P. S. Florence, *The Logic of British and American Industry* (London, 1953), p. 81.

cutting prices, or by spending more on advertising. The firm which took the initiative will then lose some of its original gains. So long as the threat of retaliation has to be faced, therefore, the marketing of new varieties of product is not greatly successful in overcoming market resistance to growth.

There is a market resistance to expansion on the side of supply as well as on the side of demand. A firm—or more frequently an industry—may find it difficult to obtain adequate supplies of one or more of the factors of production—adequate, that is, for optimum production. Labour, land, materials, or money-capital may be scarce, so that larger supplies can be obtained only at increasingly higher rates of pay. A rise in output will then bring about a rise in costs. Rather than incur such additional cost, firms may be content to remain small.

### 3   FINANCIAL OBSTACLES

An important reason for the survival of small firms is the difficulty of procuring sufficient capital. A small firm seeking to expand has generally to finance extensions of plant out of profits, or out of the personal savings of its owners and their friends. It is usually ignorant in matters of finance and unfamiliar with institutions other than the joint-stock banks from which it might borrow. If it does try to borrow, it has a difficult job of interesting possible lenders who know little or nothing of its affairs or the capabilities of its management, cannot judge how well it would use the capital and want to be sure of getting back what they lend whenever they need the money. The security that it can offer is limited, and it has usually to meet more than usually rigorous tests of creditworthiness. The more the owner borrows, the more he puts at hazard the entire future of the business, not merely the loss of some of its capital; if the investment which he makes turns out badly, he may be unable to meet his debts and be forced into a bankruptcy that slower growth would have avoided. If, instead of seeking a loan he were prepared to sell a share in the business, he might attract capital more readily; but this is a price that few owners with good prospects of expansion willingly pay. The very single-mindedness by which they thrive makes them reluctant to share control or run any risk of having to surrender it. Thus even when additional capital could be found, the owner may not know where to go for it, may not be able to offer adequate security or may not be willing to accept the conditions on which it would be provided.

These obstacles are greatest where it is long-term capital that is required. Medium-term capital can be obtained for some purposes on hire-purchase without the need to pledge anything except the specific assets acquired. This is an expensive form of credit, but highly convenient from the point of view of the small producer; he is not troubled with elaborate enquiries from the lender and his credit in other directions remains undiminished. For short-term credit he can draw on the banks or, with less difficulty, on trade credit from suppliers. The cost of trade credit, in terms of interest charges (and possibly also in loss of freedom to buy elsewhere) can, however, be very high and such credit does not provide a very reliable foundation for long-term expansion.

Finance is a more important limiting factor in private than in public companies. Once a firm is sufficiently large to be floated on the Stock Exchange it is likely to find the task of raising additional capital a great deal easier. As a public company with its shares quoted on the Stock Exchange it can make an issue of capital to its own shareholders or to the investing public, using the machinery of the new issue market. The rise of the joint stock system has thus removed some of the more important financial obstacles to growth. How it has done this, and how far it has been successful, will be discussed in the next chapter.

There remains one group of forces which we may call "desire for competitive strength." These forces occasionally limit the growth of firms, but more usually encourage firms to combine so as to increase their bargaining power or in order to establish a monopoly position. This group of forces will be left over for analysis in Chapter 11.

# CHAPTER 10

# THE FINANCE OF LARGE-SCALE PRODUCTION

Before the industrial revolution, the representative firm was tiny by modern standards, and was owned and managed by one man or by a partnership. The chief industries were carried on on a small scale in the fields or in the cottages, rather than on a large scale in factory and mine. It was only in foreign trade that there was much scope for the large firm. It was in foreign trade, therefore, that the need for large-scale borrowing first made itself felt; and it was in foreign trade that modern methods of finance (e.g., through the joint-stock company) were first evolved.

The channels into which savings could flow, or through which they could be borrowed, were narrow. The landowners and the merchants had almost a monopoly of capital and used it on their land and property or in their businesses without much recourse to borrowing. There was little scope for expansion and little incentive, therefore, to accumulate capital or to borrow it. Improvements to property, social display, and mere extravagance swallowed up what the capitalists of later centuries, putting money before magnificence, would have sunk in stocks and shares, or factory buildings and plant. It was not until later, when the agricultural revolution began to create opportunities for investment, that thrift acquired its attraction and its virtue. Nevertheless, even in those days, there were a few spectacular investments which strained the fortunes of the wealthiest landowners. At the beginning of the seventeenth century the Earl of Bedford spent over £100,000 on the draining of the fens, and in the following century the Duke of Bridgewater managed to raise more than twice as much for his canals by cutting down his personal expenses to £400 a year and borrowing from his own tenants to pay wages.

The inventions of the eighteenth and nineteenth centuries, and above all the coming of the railway, increased enormously the scale to which a business could profitably grow. But large-scale production without borrowed capital was impossible. The immense sums required exceeded the fortune of even the richest capitalist. Nor was the alternative method of raising capital through partnerships at all suitable. Partnerships are possible only between persons who have complete confidence in one another, since agreements made by any one partner are binding on the partnership. Each partner, moreover, is liable without limit for the entire debts of the partnership, however small the stake which he has in it. If one partner wishes to withdraw, or dies, it becomes necessary for the surviving partners either to buy him out—perhaps at great trouble to themselves—or find a purchaser who is acceptable to everyone. These difficulties—the moral and financial risks of partnership and the danger of unexpected withdrawals—multiply rapidly as the number of partners, or the capital which they have to put up, increases. It is impracticable either to raise small sums from a large number of partners, or large sums from a small number. It is necessary, therefore, to find some device by which persons can provide the capital required by a large business without running the risks to which partners are exposed. The limited joint-stock company is just such a device.

## Public companies

A joint-stock company, or business corporation as it is called in America, is a body corporate with a common seal, carrying on business under the management of a board of directors and owned by a group of shareholders. After registration, the company enjoys certain privileges which enable it to overcome the legal obstacles to growth that beset the one-man firm and the partnership. First, the moral risk is removed. A shareholder, unlike a partner, cannot bind the company by his acts. The decisions which bind the company are taken by his representatives, the directors, or by the officials appointed by them. So long, therefore, as shareholders have confidence in their directors, they have little need of confidence in one another. Partners require to be in daily contact with one another. But shareholders can sleep soundly in complete ignorance of the identity, and hence also of the honesty, ability and intentions of their fellow-shareholders. Secondly, in a limited company, the financial risk is greatly reduced. Before 1855, when limited liability was introduced, shareholders were regarded by the law as partners, pledging the whole of their property against any debts incurred by the company. If the company failed, therefore, the shareholders might be ruined.[1] In 1855, however, it became legal to limit liability to the nominal value of the shares, so that, as a rule, the maximum loss which a shareholder stands to make is represented by the capital which he has actually invested. Finally, withdrawals cease to be

---

[1] The failure of the City of Glasgow Bank in 1878, for example, ruined thousands of small shareholders, who had to pay £2,750 in cash for each £100 of their shares.

troublesome. Shareholders are at liberty to sell out whenever they choose, and can do so without disturbance to the work of the company. There is an organised market (the Stock Exchange) in which shares are readily negotiable, so that there is usually no difficulty in finding a buyer.

The joint-stock company makes it possible to tap the savings of a large number of people, without requiring them to take part in the management of the company. These people provide the capital of the company and receive in return stocks, shares, debentures, etc., entitling them to an income in the form of dividends on their stocks and shares or interest on their debentures. The terms on which the capital is supplied differ for different classes of shareholder. There are differences in income-rights, in the risks which shareholders run, and in the power of control which they can exercise. The least definite rights to participate in the profits of the company, the greatest risks, and the greatest powers of control are those attaching to ordinary shares. At the other extreme are debentures, which are loans to the company, not shares in it. They carry a fixed rate of interest, comparatively little risk, and no power whatever over the company so long as interest is paid regularly and the rights of debenture-holders are not threatened. Between these limits, as a kind of compromise, stand the preference shares.

## Shares and shareholders

In theory, control of a company normally rests with the ordinary share-holders. They elect—or perhaps one should say approve—the directors, and can, by exercising their voting rights, supersede the retiring directors until, after a period of years, a completely new board has been appointed. The ordinary shareholders rank last in their claims on the property of the company, and participate in the profits only after other shareholders have received their share. Thus they bear the heaviest risks. Preference shareholders normally have voting powers only when it is proposed to alter their rights, or to wind-up the company, or when their dividends are in arrears. They are paid, not a fluctuating dividend, but a fixed rate of, say 6 per cent. This dividend is not exceeded when the company is making large profits, however high the dividend earned by ordinary shareholders. It may not be paid at all, if the company is in difficulties and failing to earn a large enough profit. The dividends paid to preference shareholders necessarily vary less than the dividends on ordinary shares, and the risks run are correspondingly less. They are less also because preference shares usually rank ahead of ordinary shares if the company fails and its assets have to be liquidated. This difference in risk corresponds to some extent with the difference in voting power and control between the two types of share.

The capital of a company is not provided solely by its shareholders. Borrowings are made through the sale of bonds or debentures, and this borrowed capital goes to supplement the share capital. Debenture-holders are not, like shareholders, proprietors of the company. They are creditors with no voice in the management and policy so long as they receive interest on their bonds. The debentures which they hold are generally repayable after a stated term of years at a fixed price, and form a first charge on the assets of the company.

### Private companies

When the capital required does not exceed about £250,000 it is generally more economical to raise capital privately, rather than by public subscription. A private company can be formed enjoying many of the advantages of public joint-stock companies, including limited liability. Private companies need not publish their accounts; they cannot have more than fifty shareholders; and the transfer of their shares is restricted. They can be converted into public companies if they want to raise additional capital by inviting the public to buy their shares or if the owners are obliged to realise their capital, for example because of heavy estate duties. The smaller firms in British industry are mainly private companies; they are ten times as numerous as public companies but, being much smaller on the average, they control only half as much capital.

### The capital market

The complex of arrangements by which new capital can be raised is called the capital market. This is not the same as the Stock Exchange, which exists to facilitate the exchange of existing stocks, shares and debentures between one investor and another; it refers rather to fresh borrowing and lending, either by a new issue on the Stock Exchange or by transactions outside the Stock Exchange altogether. The public joint-stock company may make an issue of shares or debentures for public subscription, or it may prefer to make an issue privately to existing shareholders. In a private company the capital is normally provided by the owners or by their friends and business associates. In all companies, an important source of new capital is profit and the reserves accumulated out of past profits: most successful companies rely heavily on self-financing of this kind as a means of expanding their activities. There are also various financial intermediaries—insurance companies and investment trusts, for example, to which a company may turn for additional capital. Working capital, to finance stocks and work in progress, is normally raised on short term from the banks in the form of bank advances. The State may also lend a hand and set up new financial institutions to remedy real or supposed deficiencies in the capital market.

## Investment and risk

The joint-stock system, then, increases the supply of capital at the disposal of a single business, and so removes one of the chief obstacles in the way of large-scale production. But large-scale production requires that capital shall be available not only in large amounts, but for long periods, and for risky undertakings. Large businesses almost invariably use much fixed capital. This capital is, so to speak, highly specialised—that is, sunk in forms from which it will not be recovered for many years (ploughs as compared with seed), or in forms with a very limited number of uses (battleships as compared with crude steel). The longer the life of the fixed assets (the building and plant), the longer the period for which investors must part with their capital; and the more highly specialised are the fixed assets (either because they are durable or because they are not adaptable) the greater will be the risks which investors run. It may prove impossible to make regular use (or indeed *any* use) of the fixed capital over the period of its life; or it may yield a return lower than was expected; or it may yield a return which, while up to expectations, is less than might have been obtained by holding the capital in a more liquid, less specialised form and taking advantage of a change in circumstances favourable to some other line of investment. Whatever the *result* of sinking capital in fixed assets, the uncertainty is great; and the large firm, with the bulk of its assets fixed and specialised, has given an unusually high quota of hostages to fortune and has given them irrevocably for an unusually long time.

Add to this the risks of producing in advance of demand. Any large business —and many small ones too—supplies a market remote in time and space— a market whose requirements cannot be accurately foreseen. The wants of this market lie in the future and at a distance, but production must be undertaken here and now. The whole organisation of the business, and not just its fixed capital, is built and operated in ignorance and uncertainty of the future demand. The owners must adventure their capital over the period of production and bear the risk of loss through error or misfortune.

There are thus two difficulties which the joint-stock system has to overcome. The first arises from the desire of the investor for liquidity. He wishes to be able to recover his capital quickly and without loss; but it has been sunk in durable plant, and can be recovered (in depreciation allowances) only over the life of the plant. How can the needs of the investor be met? The answer is that although the asset is illiquid, the investor's shares are not. There is a market in which they can be sold at any time (but not necessarily at their purchase price) —the Stock Exchange. The function of the Stock Exchange is to make stocks and shares easily marketable. If there were no Stock Exchange, shareholders who wished to sell out would be in the same position as holders of a mortgage, or of shares in the village gasworks. They would be put to the trouble of advertising, or of negotiations with a lawyer, before they were able to find a purchaser. Even when a purchaser had been found, he might offer no more than a knockdown price. So long as the market for shares was so poorly organised, people would be reluctant to lock up their money in stocks and shares. The Stock Exchange, by improving the marketability of shares, correspondingly encourages investment in them. Since dealings are regular, the investor in a large company can sell at a moment's notice at a price which is uniform throughout the market. Since dealings take place over a wide area on local exchanges connected with one another by telephone and cable, very large blocks of shares can be sold without greatly depressing their price. Thus the market price of shares, in normal circumstances, is steadier as well as more uniform when dealings are organised than when they are not.

The second difficulty to be overcome is the disinclination of investors to expose their capital to risk of loss. This disinclination is reduced by a fourfold specialisation in risk-bearing.

First, there is a specialisation between directors and shareholders. Many owners of capital show little aptitude or inclination for the work of managing a business, while many capable business men have little or no capital. The joint-stock company, in divorcing ownership from management, simultaneously unites management with capital. Capital and business ability are brought together, and the resources subscribed by shareholders are put at the disposal of directors who are presumed to possess good judgment and organising ability. The union of capital and business ability renders a double service. On the one hand, more money is saved because acceptable channels of investment have been created; and, on the other hand, the limits within which business men are able to exercise their judgment are expanded. There is more capital available, and more of it is loaned to, or invested in, large businesses.

Secondly, the practice of issuing different kinds of shares caters for the different dispositions to take risks of different classes of shareholders. There is a specialisation in risk-bearing, not only between directors and shareholders, but also between debenture-holders and shareholders, and between preference, ordinary and deferred ordinary shareholders. This grading of bonds and shares according to the risks which the owners run allows the enterprise of investors to be harnessed more effectively in support of risky undertakings. The supply of risk-bearing, as it is sometimes put, is increased.

Thirdly, the participation of a large number of shareholders in each company limits and diffuses the risks which they run. A man with a total capital of £10,000 may scruple to sink three-quarters of it in a partnership with a dozen others. He may hesitate even more to invest the same sum in a company over which he has no control. But if, instead of being one of twelve, he is one of a hundred or two, and is asked to put up, not £7,500, but a few hundred pounds only, he will have much less hesitation. If he chooses, he can invest in a large corporation like the American Telephone and Telegraph Company with over half a million investors—more investors, indeed, than employees. He can then invest the rest of his capital in other businesses and spread his risks over a large number of shareholdings. His risks will be still further reduced by the limitation of his liability in each investment to the value of his shares. The shareholder, therefore, can limit his risks in three ways; by limiting his stake in each investment, by investing in a number of different companies, and by enjoying the protection of limited liability. This limitation of risk will once again make it easier for large or risky undertakings to raise capital.

Finally, there are various financial intermediaries which are enabled by the joint-stock system to borrow small amounts on good security and lend large amounts where the return is comparatively uncertain. The deposits of the joint-stock banks, for example, consist very largely of small sums, withdrawable at short notice. The assets, on the other hand, include advances, for periods up to six months or a year, of very large amounts, and blocks of Government bonds, not redeemable for several years, running into hundreds of millions of pounds. The banks' depositors lend their money in complete safety and without trouble; the deposits are lent by the banks after a great deal of trouble to discover which firms can offer satisfactory security, and not all of the loans are recovered in full.

Insurance companies and building societies perform similar functions. They receive a large proportion of the current savings of the public, the insurance companies in premiums on life assurance, and the building societies in repayments of principal on mortgages, or in deposits or from shareholders. These savings, when pooled together in this way, can be lent for longer periods, or in larger amounts, or to riskier undertakings, than when they were in the hands of individual savers.[1]

Another important agency in achieving these results is the investment trust. An investment trust aims at spreading the risks of its shareholders by distributing its assets over a large number of different shares—either in different companies or in the same industry and area, or, more commonly, in different companies scattered throughout the whole range of industry and over the whole area of the globe. The purchase of shares in an investment trust, therefore, allows a small capitalist to take an interest in a large number of enterprises

---

[1] Building societies usually lend most or all of their money to private house-owners but may also finance property development (including commercial and office property).

exposed to a variety of risks, instead of linking his fortunes too closely with the one or two companies only in which he could otherwise afford to take shares.

These investment intermediaries, with the exception of the banks, either did not exist or were of negligible importance less than a hundred years ago. By 1959, the combined assets of the joint-stock banks, savings banks, building societies, insurance companies, and investment trusts amounted to over £20,000 millions. The current savings made through investment intermediaries, including the huge sums put to reserve every year by joint-stock companies of all kinds, form a high proportion of the total annual savings of the country.

### Diffusion of ownership

Stock Exchange securities are owned by three broad groups: by private persons, by investment intermediaries, and by companies as part of their reserves. Of these groups, the first is still the most important. The last, unless acquiring a business investment in a subsidiary or allied company, is likely to confine itself to gilt-edged securities. An increasing proportion of industrial securities is held by investment intermediaries; their holdings of ordinary shares (or common stocks, as they are called in America) now amount to about 30 per cent. of the total in the United States. In Britain the division into private and institutional holdings is complicated by the existence of "nominee accounts" registered by banks and stockbrokers and made up of large numbers of individual holdings, most of them private. About one in six of the 250,000 equity shareholdings in the twelve leading British steel companies is a nominee account; nearly one-quarter of the nominal value of the equity capital is held by insurance companies and pension funds, the proportion varying widely from one steel company to another; and private individuals own between 23 and 68 per cent. of the shares, mostly in holdings of under 500 shares. In six of the twelve companies the number of shareholders exceeds the number of employees.[1]

While steel cannot be taken as a typical industry, the diffusion of ownership to which these figures testify is characteristic of the larger British and American companies. In 30 large British companies in 1941 there was an average of over 27,000 shareholders, nearly all of them with less than 1,000 shares; only 1,000 shareholders held over 1,000 shares; and the largest 132 shareholders held 36 per cent. of the total shares while the other 99.5 per cent. held only 64 per cent. Similarly, in American business corporations with assets over $1m. in 1937–39

---

1 "Who Owns the Steel Industry?" *The Times*, 10 April 1959.

the average shareholding was 7,350, reaching an average of over ten times that figure for corporations with assets of $500m.; shareholders with less than 1,000 shares formed 97·5 per cent. or more of the voting "electorate" but in no size-group of corporation held more than half the shares.[1]

The number of shareholders is very often comparable with the number of employees[2] so that the average stake of a shareholder in any one company is roughly equivalent to the amount of capital employed per worker in the company. This diffusion of ownership makes it easier to mobilise the necessary capital; but it also makes it difficult, if not impossible, for shareholders to assume the full responsibilities of ownership. They are, in the nature of things, absentees, and their interest in their property rarely extends beyond the return they can obtain from it.

## Speculation

The owners of a company are not only absentees; they do not even remain the same absentees. They buy and sell again, not because death and necessity part them from their capital, but because they see a chance of a speculative profit. Their interest may be confined to the capital appreciation which they expect from a rise in the price of their shares over the next few days or weeks.[3] At this stage, they have ceased to be property-owners with a stake in the company and entitled to the same rights as other property-owners, and have become speculators pure and simple.

Now speculation is inseparable from all investment; every owner of capital must "take a chance" in whatever form he holds his capital. Risk is universal. Speculation, too, may be of immense advantage to society. Every pioneer of a new process "speculates" his capital on its success. Every storer of wheat who buys the surplus of a bumper year speculates on a short supply in the succeeding years. Thus skilful speculation can work improvement in our use of scarce resources, or reduce the risks (e.g., of famine) to which their scarcity exposes us. The speculator is not just a gambler, but a specialist in risk-bearing, who, if he bears necessary risks wisely, saves us from those who are more imprudent, or less capable (through ignorance, or lack of capital, or excess of caution) of bearing the risks which they run. But the risks must be unavoidable, not the product of bad organisation or a desire to encourage gambling; and the speculators must be well-informed and sound in judgment, not acting on

---

[1] P. S. Florence, *op. cit.*, pp. 183–84, quoting H. Parkinson, *Ownership of Industry* and T.N.E.C. Monograph 30.

[2] P. S. Florence, *op. cit.*, p. 179.

[3] The turnover in the shareholders of a company is comparable with the turnover in the labour force. In the United States over a quarter of the shares in the larger companies were sold in 1939 and 1940 (P. S. Florence, *op. cit.*, p. 181).

"inside" information which others do not share, nor seeking to spread rumours and false impressions, nor backed by such weight of capital that they can corner the market and reap monopoly profits.

How far are these conditions satisfied on the Stock Exchange? That the Stock Exchange is intended to reduce unavoidable risks we have already seen.[1] It makes it less risky to lock up money for long periods, and thus increases the flow of capital into productive investment. But there are also risks on the Stock Exchange which are, so to speak, fictitious. The operations of the "bears," who speculate for a fall in prices, are designed to alarm the public and create a sense of risk of which the "bears" can take advantage; the operations of the "bulls," who speculate for a rise in prices, are designed to make risks appear less than they really are, with equal advantage to the speculators. Thus even if professional speculators, or those whose interest is predominantly speculative, were exceptionally judicious and capable of keeping market prices in correspondence with the real risks, they are not free to do so. It does not pay to steady market prices when by unsteadying them there is a better chance of profit. The real risks become overlaid by the fictitious risks, and wisdom dictates a forecast, not of what prices should be, but of what, given the psychology of the market, prices will be.

It is sometimes suggested that Stock Exchange speculation is pure gambling. But gambling only makes money change hands; speculation makes not only money but also stock change hands, and reacts on prices. When money changes hands, only the gainer and loser (and their dependants) are affected. But when the price of stocks and shares moves up or down, there is a long chain of repercussions on economic life. The investment of capital, the cost of living, the amount of unemployment, are all tied up with stock prices. Capital flows into those trades whose shares speculators are prepared to buy, and out of those trades whose shares speculators are pressing to sell. Men's jobs, too, depend upon the course of speculation. Where capital cannot be raised, men cannot find employment, and the ease with which capital can be raised depends not only on the real prospect of return on it, but also on the mood of speculators.

## Concentration of power

The joint-stock company was originally a democratic organisation. In intention it is a democracy of capitalists, entrusting their surplus funds to a cabinet of their own choosing, and retaining an active interest in the use to which their capital is put. In practice, it has come to be the means by which financial and industrial power is concentrated in the hands of a small number

---

[1] See above, p. 147.

of persons who are only vaguely and on rare occasions responsible to their shareholders.

This concentration of power is not the product of a simultaneous concentration of wealth; capital is not less, but more, equally diffused. Power has been concentrated because the bonds between ownership and control have been loosened. It is not necessary to own the entire capital of a company in order to control it. It is enough to have "a controlling interest." This may be secured through ownership of a bare 51 per cent. of the ordinary shares of the company. If, for example, capital is raised through the issue of debentures, preferred stock, and ordinary shares each to the value of a million pounds, the comparatively modest investment of £500,100 in ordinary shares will carry with it control of the company's £3,000,000. Generally, however, a controlling interest can be purchased much more cheaply. The policy of the company can be dominated by a strong minority, holding perhaps no more than 10 to 20 per cent. of the voting shares, so long as there is no rival minority of equal or greater strength, and so long as the management is not antagonistic. The larger the number of shareholders, and the more diffused the shares of the company amongst them, the harder does it become to take concerted action to dislodge a powerful minority from control.

Many companies have reached such a size that control either by a majority or by a strong minority is impossible. The largest single interest may amount to no more than a fraction of 1 per cent. of the company's capital. In such companies, and in those where there is in fact no large and organised minority group, control normally rests with the management. The directors can remain quietly in power, procuring their own reappointment by the use of proxies.[1] Shareholders who attack the management are put to the expense of preparing and issuing circulars, and run the risk of depreciating the value of their shares by criticism damaging to the company's reputation. Thus even large shareholders, rather than fight a policy which they consider unfair and unwise, may prefer to take the easier course of selling out at a sacrifice price. The meetings of the company where shareholders are supposed to assert their authority are either deserted,[2] or, when a fruitless struggle for power is on, bear gardens.

There are, in addition, various legal devices by which control can be concentrated. Of these the most striking is known as "pyramiding." One company may obtain a controlling interest in another, which in turn has a

---

[1] Shareholders have the option of voting in person, or refraining from voting, or signing a proxy transferring their vote to a nominee of the management. Most shareholders cannot attend company meetings—if they did they could not be accommodated.

[2] For example, at the meeting in 1919 when the Standard Oil Company of New Jersey decided to issue $100 millions of preferred stock, a single shareholder was present. (Slichter, *op. cit.*, p. 160.)

controlling interest in a third—and so on through a long chain of companies. The first, and some of the intermediate companies, will generally be holding companies, not engaged in production, but holding the securities of other companies, collecting the dividends on these securities, and in a position to govern the policy of the subsidiary companies. At the base of the pyramid will be a number of large operating companies, while at the apex will be a comparatively small holding company, dominated by a single interest. Complete control over the entire property of the companies grouped together in the pyramid rests with the holding company at the top and with the persons controlling it. The use of debentures, preferred stock, non-voting and weighted shares extends the area of the pyramid. We reach a position in which an investment of less than twenty million dollars was sufficient to secure control over eight Class I American railways with combined assets of over two billion dollars.[1]

Concentration of control has gone furthest in the United States. Of the 200 largest companies (other than banking companies) in that country, two-thirds were controlled in pre-war years by the management or by legal devices like pyramiding and the issue of voting trust certificates, and this group of companies owned four-fifths of the combined wealth of the 200 companies.[2]

A study by Professor Sargant Florence of the 92 British industrial and commercial companies with a capital of £3m. or more in 1951 showed that 16 had a single shareholder with 20 per cent. or more of the voting power.[3] There were a further 8 companies in which the directors held at least 12 per cent. of the ordinary shares. In these 24 companies—roughly one in four of the total—it seems reasonable to conclude that control rests with the larger shareholders, including shareholders who are also directors. In some of the other large companies Professor Florence found that a small group of shareholders, not necessarily forming a coherent body ready to take joint action, held a sizeable portion of the shares. On the average, the 20 largest shareholders commanded 22 per cent of the votes attaching to ordinary shares. This suggests that although the management is likely to be free, within wide limits, to control the policy of the bigger companies, this is by no means always so, and that large shareholders can still exercise considerable influence.

## Division of interests

The policy of any firm reflects a compromise between the various controlling interests. There are divisions of interest between large shareholders and small,

---

[1] In the Van Sweringen system—which later collapsed. See Berle and Means, *The Modern Corporation and Private Property*, p. 73.

[2] Berle and Means, *op. cit.*, p. 94.

[3] P. S. Florence, "A New Inquiry into Ordinary Share Ownership." *The Times*, 11 and 12 August 1959.

between the owners and the management, between holders of shares and holders of debentures. How these divisions are reconciled depends upon the legal rights which each group possesses, and on the pressure which they can bring to bear on the company.

The large shareholders, for example, may seek to manipulate prices so as to increase the profits of some other company in which they have a still larger interest. The smaller their holding, the greater the temptation. They may exploit the company by selling materials to it at exorbitant prices or by forming a selling agency which draws handsome commissions for marketing the company's products. They may buy up or build small plants and re-sell them to the company at a profit. They can obtain inside information and use it in Stock Exchange speculation. If they control several companies, they can make their speculations doubly profitable by switching business from one company to another so as to mislead investors. There is no end to the ways in which those in control can, if they are so minded, exploit those who are not. The more diffused the capital of the company, the more helpless is the small shareholder.

Conflicts may also arise between the owners and the management. The officers of the company may reinvest profits in other companies so as to increase their own power, and without consulting the interests of their shareholders. Or they may offer higher wages to their workers, or better service to their customers, out of pride in their company—a pride which the shareholders, if they share it, may not wish to see indulged quite so generously.

Similarly, there is a division of interest between the different classes of investor in the company. The ordinary shareholder will support a riskier policy than is to the advantage of the holders of preference shares and debentures. For whereas these investors if things turn out well, gain nothing, and if things turn out badly may lose their capital, the ordinary shareholders stand to gain a great deal, and, if they lose, can throw part of the burden of loss on the other groups. If, for example, a company is in danger of bankruptcy, the ordinary shareholders may be willing to run it at a loss, by allowing plant to depreciate without adequate expenditure on upkeep and renewal. By such a policy the ordinary shareholders can lose nothing, and have hopes of tiding over a bad period until there is again a chance of making a good profit. But the debenture-holders see the fixed assets, which are the security for their loan to the company, depreciating steadily. Their interests are threatened, and their trustees may be forced to take action.

## The joint-stock company and the control of industry

The joint-stock company was one of the great social inventions of the nineteenth century. In a comparatively short time, it has come to be the predominant form of industrial organisation in private enterprise economies and the prototype of the public corporation in mixed economies. The 2,500 largest companies, raising their capital by public subscription, employ nearly half the workers in British manufacturing industry and earn about two-thirds of the total industrial profits; most of the remainder is accounted for by private companies. Outside the field of industry and public utilities, the company form of organisation is less prevalent; in farming, in many of the service trades and to a smaller extent in distribution, the unincorporated business remains typical.

Like all thriving institutions, the joint-stock company shows great flexibility. Its primary purpose is to allow large capital funds to be put at the disposal of a single enterprise; in doing so it allows numerous enterprises to be linked together in a wide variety of ways. At the same time, it is a form of industrial government raising issues of social policy as well as of economic efficiency. It exercises authority over large groups of workers and controls the use of large blocks of the community's resources. In a democratic community it is a matter of some importance, therefore, who is in control of the larger companies and whether the joint-stock company is an efficient instrument for promoting the welfare of the community.

Control within a joint-stock company does not assume any standard pattern: the locus of control is often obscure and varies from company to company, but is rarely shared effectively among the body of shareholders. There is a divorce between ownership and control, between risk-bearing (which is inseparable from ownership) and risk-taking (which is the prerogative of control). Sometimes the divorce is absolute and no shareholder can hope to have any perceptible influence on the company's policy; sometimes it is far from absolute and the principal shareholders, even when in possession of only a minority of the shares, retain powers of control or at least of veto. When the government of the company is unmistakably in the hands of the management, there is still room for doubt as to the distribution of authority between the different elements in the management. The directors may have only nominal control; the Chairman, the Managing Director, or some Executive Committee may be more influential than the Board as a whole or any group of executive officers of the company. The directors, if they do exercise joint control, are subject to pressure from the government, from public opinion, and from their employees as well as from their shareholders; they may also find their powers restricted, when they wish to use them, by the need to conciliate others, the limitations of their own knowledge and time, and the inevitable delegation of authority to subordinates. Whatever the formal position, it is no easier to locate the effective voice in the government of a company than in the government of a country.

The use of the powers which the sheer size of the largest companies confers on them raises equally wide issues. There are, for example, the attendant dangers of monopoly either in the purchase of materials and components or in the sale of products. The large company may block, by unfair means, the efforts of smaller competitors to enter its markets. It may use its financial strength to drive them out of business or buy them up for the sake of a quiet life. It may gain a stranglehold on patents which it denies to other firms and does not use or carry further itself.

Against these and other dangers the state may take action by anti-monopoly legislation, not aimed specifically at public companies. It may reinforce this by company legislation, laying down conditions that all public companies have to satisfy, such as the publication of consolidated accounts. It may buy or acquire some of the shares of the larger companies or take them over and run them as public corporations. We shall discuss possible courses of action in Chapter 36. In the meantime we must look in more detail at the way in which the larger companies grow and consider how far the enlargement of their powers involved in the process of growth may be justified by the economies of scale that they are enabled to enjoy.

# CHAPTER 11

# THE GROWTH OF BUSINESS UNITS

We saw in Chapter 5 that production in most industrial countries has been growing at a rapid rate. There has been a parallel growth in the size of the business unit; the typical factory produces a larger output than fifty years ago and the number of factories under the control of a typical business unit has grown. These are changes in absolute size; what of the relative share of large and small firms? Have the large firms grown faster than the small or is the concentration of production in large units tending to diminish?

This is not a question to which we can return a firm answer. But in spite of mergers, take-over bids, and the prominence that is given to bigness in industry and commerce, there appears to be no unmistakable trend towards concentration in the larger units either in the United States or in the United Kingdom. What evidence there is suggests that, over the past fifty years, there has probably been comparatively little change.[1]

Although large firms as a group may have maintained their share of total production, this does not mean that *the same large firms* occupy the position in the market that they held fifty years ago. The identity of the firms in any size-group is constantly changing and the biggest firms in the sixties are not the firms that were biggest at the beginning of the century; one need only think of the oil companies to recognise the truth of this. When the size of the average business unit grows, therefore, there is no uniform expansion that affects each existing firm in roughly the same way. What happens is that firms grow at a wide scatter of rates, unrelated in any definite way to their initial size; some fail to grow at all and shrink in size; some are absorbed by their competitors; and some go bankrupt, give up business or are wound up.

## Motives and methods

A firm may seek to expand from two fairly distinct motives. It may be attracted

---

[1] For the U.S.A., see M. A. Adelman. "The Measurement of Industrial Concentration," *Review of Economics and Statistics*, November 1951; for the U.K., see Evely and Little, *op. cit.*

by the prospect of lower costs of production (resulting from economies of scale), or by the prospect of higher prices (resulting from a bargaining advantage or the winning of a position of monopoly). At the same time a firm may seek to expand along either of two paths. It may extend its own plant and fight for a larger share of the market; or it may try to buy out, or combine with, other firms which have their own plant and organisation. Between the two motives to growth and the two methods by which growth takes place there is no necessary connection. It is true that the monopoly motive is generally most prominent when a firm grows by combination, while the economy motive is generally the dominant one in growth by extension. But the difference is one of degree, not of kind. Firms may and do combine in order to reduce their costs; they may and do extend their plant so as to entrench themselves more firmly in a position of monopoly. Growth towards a larger and more efficient scale of operations or towards monopoly may take place along either route.

Whichever method of expansion is adopted, both motives are commonly present. Monopoly gains are always an incentive to expansion; savings in costs can often be made simultaneously, so that the first motive is reinforced by the second. But sometimes the two come into conflict. For example, it may happen that expansion along one route is accompanied by lower costs, and along another by higher prices. A firm may hesitate between setting up small high-cost branch factories in outlying districts where competitors are at a disadvantage, and building extensions at low cost to its main plant alongside its chief competitors. Or it may have to choose between extending its plant and buying out some of its competitors. Plant extension may improve efficiency greatly, but it will also intensify competition and probably force down prices. Expansion by purchase, on the other hand, while it may be relatively costly and give rise to technical and managerial difficulties, is likely to strengthen the firm's hold on the market and maintain prices or even allow them to be increased. The extra expense of amalgamation must then be weighed against the higher prices and larger receipts which are in prospect. The two motives to expansion, becoming tangled up with alternative methods of expansion, come into conflict with one another.

When such a conflict arises, the social interest is comparatively clear. The monopoly motive is, in general, anti-social; while the economy motive is, in general, in the public interest. So long, therefore, as we can readily distinguish between expansion aiming at monopoly and expansion aiming at economy, we can, by legislating against monopolistic expansion, allow firms to grow in size only when such growth is unmistakably in the public interest. But in practice the two motives to expansion generally reinforce one another rather than conflict with one another, and the public interest, therefore, is by no means obvious.

The greater the economies of scale, the more closely do efficiency and size coincide, until to have more than a single firm is to invite waste of resources and uneconomic methods of production. Efficiency and monopoly become inseparably linked, and we have to lump what we dislike for the sake of what we like. Alternatively, we have to resort to State control or State ownership, rather than leave in private hands powers which may be used against the common good.

The difficulty of disentangling the two motives has increased steadily with the constant improvement in industrial technique and business administration. So long as large scale production offered only modest economies, the distinction between the two motives coincided broadly with the distinction between the two methods of expansion. The growth of independent concerns could be taken as a sign of superior efficiency from which the public would benefit in lower prices. Combination, on the other hand, was a device for getting prices up, not—except as an afterthought—for re-organising production so as to get costs down. It was rarely a means of stepping up the size of the business unit in order to gain the benefits of large-scale production, but very often a short cut to monopoly. There was room for several competing firms and monopoly had to be reached at a bound or not at all. Broadly speaking, therefore, attempts at monopoly could be blocked by legislation against combination.

**Local monopolies**

Where the market was limited or scattered, however, there were local monopolies in the growth of which combination had played no part. Of these monopolies the local chemist's shop or the municipal gasworks were typical. These monopolies, free from the "taint" of combination, were regarded as natural and advantageous. It was obviously stupid to have two chemists' shops or town gasworks, for the sake of competition, when one would do perfectly well. Competition involved wasteful overlapping of effort and duplication of capital. Now what applies to local monopolies in a limited market applies also to national monopolies when large-scale production is impossible for lack of a sufficiently wide market. It is wasteful to build two continuous strip tinplate mills when one is big enough to supply the whole market. But if tinplate is made by a large number of firms it may be necessary for them to combine before the way is clear for a single large mill. Combination then brings economies as well as monopoly, and can no longer be singled out as *the* anti-social method of expansion.

It was from the railway that this lesson was first learnt. A railway system could not expand competitively, by building a line parallel to other lines, without great waste of capital. After the early years, the only rational method of expansion was by combination. But combination spelt monopoly, and no monopoly was more feared. The obvious advantages of a unified railway system had thus to battle against the Victorian horror of monopoly. A truce might have been called through nationalisation—and this was in fact contemplated in the first railway bills—but private enterprise was held in too great veneration. In the end, safeguards against the abuse of monopoly power were worked out, and combination was allowed to proceed.

The lessons learnt from railway expansion have since been extended to many other industries. Monopoly is the price we have to pay for efficiency, if size and efficiency go together. From the social point of view, monopoly, redeemed by economies of scale and regulated by the State, becomes almost respectable; and a reflected respectability falls on combination, in which the motive of economy now mingles with the desire for monopoly. We cannot so easily single out combination for attack when its results cease to be wholly bad, and when exactly the same results might be achieved by the spontaneous growth of a large firm.[1]

The more highly we rate the virtues of size, the better will we think of combination. *Either* method of growth will be more likely to win approval. But combination will be doubly attractive. For when firms are already large, it is difficult and costly to oust them from the market by competition, and comparatively easy and cheap to amalgamate. Especially if the market is narrow, shrinking or uncertain, and if the firms in the field are operating large amounts of durable, fixed capital, nothing short of combination will allow firms to grow. The alternative is to build and battle—to duplicate the plant of competitors, and try to annihilate them in a long-drawn-out cut-throat struggle. Thus as the minimum scale of efficient production keeps growing, and puts a steady pressure on firms to expand in order to keep pace, it is to combination rather than to plant extension that industry turns increasingly.

## Motives to Growth

### (a) The economies motive

The first motive to expansion—the prospect of reductions in cost because of economies of scale—has already been discussed. These economies, however,

---

[1] Professor Jewkes, in a review of British monopoly policy in the post-war period, warns us against assuming too readily that size and efficiency necessarily go together in industries that are dominated by a large firm or group of large firms. "In the ten reports in which the (Monopolies and Restrictive Practices) Commission has provided evidence of the relative costs and profits of different sized firms, there is only one, that relating to electronic valves and cathode ray tubes, where it was found that the largest producer showed the lowest costs. In other cases there seems to have been no evidence that size and efficiency moved together." ("British Monopoly Policy, 1944–56," *Journal of Law and Economics*, Vol. 1, 1958, p. 18.)

F

were looked at from the point of view, not of *growth* but of *size*. The angle from which they were approached was not the actual processes by which firms expand, but the comparative efficiency of large and small firms. But expansion is often arrested because the attraction of economies of scale is offset by obstacles to growth. Two obstacles—one marketing, one financial—are outstanding.

The obstacle of a limited market has already been touched on. It is difficult for a small firm to grow if it supplies a scattered market, or if it has to make its way against firms which have already a firm grip on the market—firms, for example, which have won the goodwill of dealers and consumers over a long period of years, or which can afford an expensive advertising campaign if their market is invaded, or which can bring pressure on dealers to boycott new competitors. This market resistance to growth is enormously stronger when a firm has to expand discontinuously, jumping from a size at which it can supply a local market to a size at which it has to fight for a national market. The risk of failure may deter many firms from sacrificing a comfortable profit to a fifty-fifty chance of death or glory.

Secondly, there is a financial obstacle. A severe setback in trade, against which every firm must guard, puts a very heavy strain on young and small firms, since they have limited access to credit facilities, and no large reserves on which to fall back if they are in temporary difficulties. Firms hesitate, therefore, to push on with schemes for expansion until they have firmly established their financial strength. This hesitation holds up the growth of the firm even when substantial economies are in prospect.

### (b) The monopoly motive

The second motive—the prospect of monopoly gains—has been identified up till now with profiteering—the charging of excessive prices. We have had in mind the pure monopolist, undiluted by any kind of altruism or by fear of retaliation by other firms. Such a monopolist, with exclusive power over the supply of a commodity, is able to make increased profits, not by rendering some special service or by producing more efficiently, but by selling less and charging more. He can force consumers to put money in his pockets, not because he gives them more, but because he gives them less. He simply exploits scarcity.

But monopoly power is generally sought from other motives than the desire to profiteer. First of all, the removal of the threat of competition may, on occasion, make possible genuine economies. When there are two or three firms in a market, each is "kept guessing" by the manoeuvres of its competitors, and may spend more time and money in trying to defeat these manoeuvres than in improving the services which it offers to the public. Each firm tries to keep in step with the others in public (e.g., by charging the same price), and to steal a march on them in private (e.g., by offering "backhanders," or discounts, or special terms of credit, or supplementary services). Sometimes the public gains from such competition in low prices and better quality, but occasionally it finds itself denied what it wants—a reduction in prices—and offered services it could well do without. At the same time, the competing firms are often forced by ignorance of their rivals' intentions into short-sighted policies from which the whole industry must ultimately suffer. They may each install more plant when prices are high, and then have to cope with the losses in which they are involved by the over-capacity of the industry. A single firm, with a secure hold on the market, is in a better position to take the long view; freed from the uncertainties of the competitive struggle, it can concentrate on making better and cheaper goods.

Against these economies of unity and stability must be set the temptation to slackness and apathy. There is no need to be enterprising and efficient when a comfortable profit can be made from a cautious dependence on routine. The stronger the monopoly, the less does it need to set its standard of performance against the standard of potential rivals. A firm whose control over any market is constantly challenged by other firms of equal strength must base its control on low costs. It may find competition a nuisance, but it is forced by the "nuisance" to cater for its customers' wants with reasonable efficiency. Remove the nuisance and the spur of competition goes too. A very healthy baby, whose loss would be much lamented, may be lost sight of when the bath water of competition is poured away.

Secondly, firms may unite to form a monopoly in self-defence. They may be afraid of the entry into the market of a new competitor and hope to keep him out by presenting a united front. Two newspapers, for example, may meet a threat to start a third newspaper by amalgamating; in so doing, they take the risk of a fall in profits in order to escape the risk of an even greater fall if the threat to start a third newspaper is carried out. The defensive motive is specially prominent when the market is invaded by a large firm situated in some other part of the country or abroad. Two of the largest British companies—the Imperial Tobacco Company and Imperial Chemical Industries Ltd.—were originally defensive combinations which aimed at meeting American and German trusts on an equal footing.

Self-defence may prompt other kinds of expansion. A firm which has to buy components from a monopoly may begin to manufacture them so as to reap a profit made, partly at its expense, by the monopoly. Sometimes the motive for this extension of scope is not so much self-defence against other monopolies as bargaining strength against competitors. For example, a firm which sells to shops and merchant houses which handle the products of other firms may extend its marketing organisation so as to push its own sales. It must, like many firms in the clothing, boot, chocolate and druggist trades, open its own shops. Or, as in the electrical and engineering trades, it may have its offices or agencies in all the chief cities, abroad as well as at home. In the marketing of tea, petrol, etc., firms very often distribute direct to the retailer, partly from a desire to attach him to their interests.[1]

Bargaining strength shades into the power to bully other firms. A large enterprise or combine with monopoly powers enjoys comparative immunity from retaliation and can, therefore, take unfair advantage of its business neighbours. It can cancel its orders with far less hesitation than a smaller firm, especially if it is not only a large buyer but the sole, or almost the sole, buyer in the market. It can allow delays in delivery or make delivery of inferior goods. It can threaten to cut off supplies from its customers and force them to give up buying from a potential rival. It may even squeeze out these rivals altogether by organising a boycott, or by bringing pressure to bear on the firms which supply them with raw materials, or on the banks which supply them with credit.[2] Thus the bullying of other firms develops into the exclusion of other firms from the market. Although not protected from competition by its superior efficiency, or by laws granting powers of monopoly, a firm obtains a hold on the market which it is almost impossible to challenge. In theory, any firm is free to compete; in practice, no firm will take the risk. Competition will be particularly difficult if the technical optimum is large or if the market is narrow. A new firm will hesitate to set up in opposition to established concerns if it can get a footing only by sinking an enormous amount of capital in plant, or in building up a connection. If there is only a limited market, it will be necessary to capture a share from a firm or firms which are already strongly entrenched. The new firm will have to face the task of attracting customers who are tied by inertia, ignorance, or fear to the monopoly. It has to offer not simply a better or cheaper article, but an article so much better or cheaper, or one so effectively advertised that the interest of the monopolist's customers is aroused. It has to make it worth while for these customers to risk the loss of patronage or supplies from the monopolist. It has to hang on through any price-war or boycott which the monopolist may initiate in an effort to smash competition. And all the time the monopolist may be trying to absorb his competitor, or to make terms which divide the market

---

[1] The same purpose may be served, *without* expansion of the sales organisation, by the grant of an exclusive agency to a single retailer in each district.

[2] Some of these practices, and others such as exclusive dealing agreements, tying contracts, and deferred rebates, may be forbidden by law. For a discussion of the law governing restrictive practices see below, pp. 171-72.

and restore conditions of monopoly in each part of it.[1] Even when a new firm succeeds in invading a market which is monopolised by a large firm, the net change from the point of view of the consumer may in the long run be precisely nil.[2] The form of monopoly disappears, but the substance remains.

## Monopoly and freedom of entry

The exclusion of competitors from the market is the very essence of monopoly. Whatever form the monopoly motive assumes, the desire to impede entry into the market is always present. If there is unified control there *can* be no other firms in the market; self-defence is simply defence of a market against invasion by another firm; fighting strength is nothing but power to keep out other firms; even bargaining strength, in the last resort, is based on the threat to exclude some firm from a privileged market or to enter a market previously monopolised. It is this exclusion of competitors which makes profiteering possible. But the danger of profiteering is not always equally formidable. The economies of unified control may even bring prices down; increased bargaining strength over other firms may simply produce a fresh division of the spoils, not higher prices to the consumer. It is only when firms combine for the sole purpose of raising prices, without making any attempt to change or co-ordinate their methods of production, that profiteering pure and simple takes place.[3] But unless the firms continue to be separately managed and merely agree to raise prices in concert, such outright profiteering is generally diluted by economies both of scale and of unified control, and by the desire to build up a strong combine by stabilising rather than raising prices.

## Monopoly power and competitive strength

Monopoly power and competitive strength are the same thing looked at from different angles. Both are the product of expansion when expansion loosens the foothold of other firms in the market and makes the entry of new firms into the market more difficult. Strength, whether for bargaining, fighting or throttling, can be used, and is used, to put up prices against the consumer

---

[1] For example, the Monopolies and Restrictive Practices Commission reported it as the "consistent policy, wherever possible" of the British Oxygen Company "to take over or buy out other producers of oxygen and dissolved acetylene" and that it had done this "primarily, though not solely, in order to extend and preserve its own monopoly in the supply of these gases." (*Report on the Supply of Certain Industrial and Medical Gases* (H.M.S.O., 1956, para. 250).

[2] Indeed, prices may *rise*. The volume of business will be divided, so that the large firm will have to produce on a smaller scale, probably at higher cost. If neither firm sees any possibility of driving out the other, a policy of live and let live may be adopted with prices adjusted to the higher level of costs.

[3] A sudden increase in demand (e.g., in war time) allows independent and competing firms to profiteer in exactly the same way.

and to push down prices against the supplier of raw materials. It permits increased profits to be made without any improvement in efficiency. The desire for strength or monopoly, while not identical with the desire to profiteer, very often goes with it.

The desire for competitive strength has another side to it—it represents, in Professor Macgregor's words,[1] a "revulsion against risk." There is the risk of wide fluctuations in prices, outputs and profits when firms with heavy overhead costs (e.g., railways, steamships, etc.) compete in a limited market. There is the risk of failure of supplies or of markets when either comes under the control of a monopoly. There is the risk, too, of recurrent disorganisation of the market by in-and-out firms; these may be of the type which periodically dump a temporary surplus and then retire within their protected market; or they may be floated without adequate knowledge and backing, and meet disaster after a short-lived and ill-advised competition with established concerns. To protect themselves against these and similar risks, firms may seek strength through combination or expansion. No question of profiteering need arise; a reduction in any of these risks is, *so far as it goes*, a gain to society. But the question of profiteering does in fact constantly arise; it is hard to reduce the risk of excessive competition (the first risk cited above), or of intermittent competition (the third risk), without simultaneously raising barriers against competition of any kind. Society gets rid of undesirable competition, but only by sacrificing the main safeguard against the abuse of monopoly power. Once again, strength acquired for one purpose may be used for another; escape from risk may lead straight to profiteering.

The monopoly motive to combination is held in check by various forces of which the chief are public opinion and potential competition. Public opinion makes itself felt through the boycotting of the monopolist's products, or through anti-trust legislation designed to prevent (or at least to obstruct) monopolistic combination. Potential competition is an even more powerful check. If prices are put too high, consumers may turn from the products of the monopolist to substitutes of various kinds. New firms may begin production; old firms in foreign countries or in other lines of business may enter the market; satisfactory substitutes may be devised or may be already on sale. The wider the range of substitutes, actual or potential, the less is the power of the monopolist to charge extortionate prices and the less powerful, therefore, is the incentive to form a combine in the hope of making monopoly profits. If, for example, it is easy for new firms to get a footing in a market, a monopoly will always have the threat of competition hanging over it, and will only be able to maintain its position

---

[1] D. H. Macgregor, "The Rationalisation of Industry," *Economic Journal*, 1927.

by superior efficiency. On the other hand, if new firms cannot possibly compete (e.g., become the monopoly holds important patents), it is comparatively safe to charge high prices and draw an inflated profit in "comfortable somnolence."[1] In most trades new firms find themselves in an intermediate position—faced with great, but not overwhelming, difficulties in trying to establish themselves. These difficulties,[2] which are constantly increasing, provide monopolies with a margin when they fix their prices. They can make their prices a little, but not too, excessive.[3]

Until the first world war the threat of new competition was particularly powerful in Great Britain. The natural resources of the country were plentiful, scattered and difficult to monopolise, so that new firms could not readily be deprived of supplies. Foreign producers were within easy reach of the British market, and there were no tariff barriers to keep them out; British producers, therefore, had to face the competition of imports, and so long as this was so, they could not easily exploit the home market. It was impossible also for one firm to obtain exclusive use of the means of transport, or to secure special treatment from the railways (like some of the American trusts); goods could be shipped cheaply by land or by water, and as distances were very short the cost of transport was rarely a large or strategically important item. With the adoption of a high tariff policy one of these safeguards against monopoly has gone. At the same time the growing importance of large-scale production strengthens the established firm. To found a small firm is easy, but to found a large firm in a market which is no longer expanding rapidly is a very risky undertaking. The hold of the established firm over the channels of distribution is also becoming steadily tighter, and the task of the new and growing firm correspondingly stiffer. Finally, the State, instead of obstructing, was before the war compelling combination and brought into existence a host of monopolistic organisations in agriculture and fishing, coal, steel, cotton and other industries. During the war the convenience of dealing with a few large units, or with trade associations, told in the same direction.

### (c) The power motive

The desire for size and strength may have its origin in a striving after power rather than after profit. Thus, in addition to the two motives to expansion which have so far been discussed, a third—the desire for economic power for its own sake—very often enters. A business is an instrument both for the making

---

[1] Report of the Committee on Trusts, p. 24.
[2] For examples, see above p. 164.
[3] In comparison, that is, with the price which would satisfy a new firm if it could take over the monopolist's business.

of profits and for the winning of personal power and a place in the sun. Its growth is governed, therefore, almost as much by the pride and ambition of its owners or managers as by the prospect of savings in costs or monopoly gains. Control of a large business is flattering to a man's sense of importance; he has scope for his energies, and freedom to plan and speculate and build after his own heart. His work is stimulating, because responsible and creative. It carries with it power and leadership over large numbers of workers; the excitement of a game; the satisfaction of a role in life; a sense of real achievement; the prospect of founding an industrial dynasty. These are incentives to which even the salaried administrators of joint-stock companies respond. Their eagerness to extend the operations of their company is shown both by the large sums which they put to reserve instead of distributing in dividends, and by the frequency with which they overreach themselves in trying to absorb other companies. The motive to expansion either out of undistributed profits or through amalgamation is very often power rather than prudence or profit.

Economic power carries with it independence. But love of independence by itself is an obstacle to growth. In a limited market, if one business is to expand, others must be pushed towards bankruptcy or must combine with the first. But if independence is highly valued, each firm may prefer to hang on stubbornly in spite of low profits rather than merge with an expanding competitor. Those who put independence before profit probably outweigh those who are willing to sacrifice profit to ambition, and on balance, therefore, the desire for economic power prevents rather than promotes industrial combination and the growth of the firm.

### (d) The financial motive

When a firm expands by combining with other firms there is a profit to be made by *effecting* the combination quite distinct from the profits of the combination *once effected*. Hope of making a profit of the first kind is still another motive of expansion. How does such a profit arise?

Industrial combination is generally financed through the raising of capital on the Stock Exchange. There may either be a "take-over" bid, (i.e., an offer by one of the parties to the merger to the shareholders in the other), or a promoter may arrange the amalgamation on his own initiative and make a Stock Exchange flotation of shares in the merger. The second method, which used to be the more common, leaves the promoter with a profit if he is able to acquire the companies on better terms than those on which he can induce the public to subscribe. No one, not even the promoter, can predict accurately what the gains from combination will be. But it is possible to make great play with the various economies of large-scale production that may result, the reputation and business connections that have been built up by the undertakings which are being merged, the extensive and growing market which they serve, and so on. The earning power of the combination can then be capitalised generously so as to set a value on the assets in excess of their cost to the promoter, and investors, if in the right mood, will buy the shares.

### (e) Other motives

To these four motives to expansion might be added others of less importance. For example, a company may be forced to expand in order to comply with changes in the law. It may require either to add a new department or extend an old one or combine with some other firm. An Act requiring the compulsory pasteurisation of milk would be likely to affect dairymen in one or other of these ways. Again, there is sometimes what might be called a "fiscal" motive, when the exemption of a company's undistributed profits from tax puts a premium on expansion.[1] The shareholder has the alternative of seeing £1 put to reserve or receiving, say, 15s. in dividend and investing it in some other company. Naturally he will be inclined to plump for the first alternative and approve—if his approval is sought—the building up of reserves for use in making extensions of plant or in buying up other companies. On the other hand, if profits put to reserve are subject to tax, an obstacle to expansion is created. The young and efficient firm which depends on high profits to provide capital for growth takes longer to overhaul the established firm which has already more capital than it can use.[2]

### METHODS OF GROWTH

A firm may grow either by extending its plant or by combining with other firms. The first method involves an expansion in the capacity not only of the firm, but also of the whole industry; the second method produces a change in the pattern of ownership and control of the industry, but not in its capacity. Of the two, the second is much the more complex; combination covers a wide variety of methods of growth.

When we speak of two firms combining we generally think of two quite independent units coming under the same management. But how many firms

---

[1] Such exemption does not exist in Great Britain, but the proposal for exemption has often been made. Limitation of dividends, whether statutory or voluntary, tends to operate in the same way.

[2] In some industries, however, a premium on expansion may persist even when all profits are subject to tax. Various outlays which help the business to expand can be charged, by judicious accountancy, to "income account" (i.e., treated like other items of ordinary expenditure), and so escape tax, although the company benefits from such outlays in exactly the same way as from profits put to reserve. For example, no tax is paid on advertising outlay, but advertising helps to build up an important asset in the form of "goodwill."

F*

nowadays are "quite independent"? The management of one firm nearly always has a finger in the pie of other firms. Perhaps the directors have seats on the boards of other companies; or influential shareholders are equally influential shareholders in other companies; or friends and relatives of the directors, the shareholders or the staff hold positions of responsibility in other companies. Every company has personal links with others and these links limit its independence. The management is forced to show regard for interests outside the firm, and that regard may undergo little change once the forms of combination have been gone through. The same staff, the same shareholders, the same directors—even the same *policy*—may remain after "combination." What is generally called "combination," in short, may be no more than a tightening of the links between two firms with common interests—more a gesture of recognition of mutual dependence than a destruction of independence.

### Restrictive practices

A firm's independence or freedom of action may be limited not only by personal links, but also by trade etiquette or by understandings with other firms. In the eighteenth century, Adam Smith observed that "people of the same trade seldom meet together even for merriment and diversion but the conversation ends in a conspiracy against the public, or in some contrivance to raise prices." Nowadays "conspiracies against the public" are as common as ever. In a large number of markets the prices to be charged and the areas to be supplied by each competitor are settled by gentlemen's agreements and informal understandings. In these understandings trade associations play an important part. By bringing business men into close personal contact, or by promoting the exchange of information on methods of cost accounting in use, prices charged, output, costs and so on, trade associations create an atmosphere of co-operation favourable, first to policies of "live and let live," and later to joint action to maintain prices and restrict output. The information collected and exchanged provides a basis for a common policy and suggests the need for one. Very often, however, such a policy is narrowly conceived in terms of monopoly at its worst. It is designed to put an end to price-cutting and protect profits on invested capital. It does this, but only at the price of perpetuating inefficiency. There is neither the comprehensive planning and general overhauling of technical methods that might be expected to result from outright combination, nor the weeding out of inefficient firms and inefficient methods that might be expected to result from competition *à outrance*.[1] Instead, pressure

---

[1] Competition does not always make for the survival of the efficient firm. The old and well-established (but inefficient) firm may ride the storm of trade depression more successfully than the young and efficient (but poorly connected) firm.

is put equally on efficient and inefficient firms; the efficient firms are clamped down within their existing markets while the inefficient firms survive freely in theirs.

Understandings do not amount to combination in the narrow sense. But they represent a sacrifice of independence and a limitation of competition which are comparable in their effects with actual combination. Combination in the sense of concentration of control is a matter of degree rather than of kind, and understandings between competitors carry us a stage nearer to full concentration.

The next stage is a formal agreement to limit competition, for example by fixing minimum prices or introducing quotas on output. Such agreements were common in Britain before the war although, as contracts in restraint of trade, they were generally not enforceable at law. At that time, when most industries had a great deal of unused capacity and low prices might have ruined firms that had good long-term prospects, public opinion was sympathetic to restrictive agreements and the government itself encouraged, or even compelled, a number of industries to form marketing boards, centralised selling agencies and other price-fixing organisations, similar to the cartels described below. Since the war, with trade extremely active and prices rising continuously, there has been a change in the attitude of the public and of the government and new legislation has been introduced against restrictive practices.

The Monopolies and Restrictive Practices Acts of 1948 and 1953 brought into existence a Commission—now the Monopolies Commission—to which the government could refer for investigation any industry in which restrictive practices were suspected on the part of a firm or group of firms producing one-third of the total output. This Commission had no powers enabling it to require firms to desist from restrictive practices. Its functions were primarily fact-finding; but it could also report that certain practices were contrary to the public interest, and as the law laid down no criteria by which to judge the public interest, the reports of the Commission built up a kind of case-law on which later legislation could be drafted. Such legislation was introduced in the Restrictive Trade Practices Act of 1956, which required a wide range of agreements to be officially registered and set up a Restrictive Practices Court with power to decide whether the restrictive clauses in those agreements are in the public interest.[1] The most important features of this legislation are that it places on those who enter into a restrictive agreement the onus of establishing, to the satisfaction of the Court, that it is in the public interest—not merely unlikely to be damaging, but of positive value to the public—and that, since each decision

---

[1] For a full account of this legislation, see S. R. Dennison, "The British Restrictive Trade Practices Act of 1956," *Journal of Law and Economics*, Vol. II, October 1959.

of the Court operates as a precedent with all the force of law, a few decisions are sufficient to put an end to a very large number of agreements. The Monopolies Commission remains in being to report on individual firms with monopoly powers but no longer investigates agreements between firms. Neither the Restrictive Practices Court nor the Monopolies Commission have powers to investigate the activities of trade unions, nationalised industries or statutory bodies.

British legislation is directed much more strongly against *agreements* than against *mergers* and in this respect is in contrast with American legislation. The chief preoccupation of American policy is with the danger of market control by a small group of large producers—what economists describe as oligopoly[1]— while the emphasis in Britain has been more on the danger of restrictive agreements between producers. American legislation has not prevented the emergence of very large firms nor a degree of industrial concentration at least as marked as in Britain. On the other hand, it is doubtful whether British legislation has yet succeeded in promoting as keen price-competition as exists in the United States. In both countries, the legislation has exercised great influence without fully accomplishing its declared purpose.

Whatever the present position, most British industries have had experience of price-fixing agreements at one time or another. The usual arrangement is to fix minimum prices so as to prevent price-cutting. But whenever the temptation to price-cutting is great (e.g., under the stress of trade depression), the agreement tends to be evaded or openly violated. It can also be evaded by the offer of high discounts or of special concessions such as a low price for articles which do not come under the agreement.

### Sharing the market

Price agreements frequently lead to agreements to share the market. Shipping conferences, for example (i.e., associations of steamship lines), not only agree to charge similar rates of freight but also arrange for the division of traffic by limiting each line to a certain number of sailings or to certain ports of sailing. When competition is by tender, arrangements may be made to share the market through an association which decides who is to make the lowest tender and take the contract. The other members either do not tender at all or put in higher tenders as a blind. Sometimes sharing the market is combined with a pooling arrangement. To take shipping again, part of the freight on some cargo—say, tea from Calcutta—may be pooled and divided into an agreed ratio between the conference lines engaged in the trade. Some of the lines trading

---

[1] See below, p. 247.

from Calcutta may carry little or no tea, but will nevertheless participate in the pool. An alternative arrangement is for each line to be allotted an agreed proportion of the traffic and to pay a fine into the pool on cargoes in excess of this proportion, or draw from the pool to compensate for any deficiency.

Agreements to fix prices or to share the market are very often combined with agreements to limit output. Indeed, prices cannot be kept up in the face of falling demand *unless* producers cut down their output and offer a smaller quantity of goods for sale; if producers continue to press supplies on the market, prices *must* fall below the "fixed" minimum, or the supplies will remain unsold. Similarly, sharing the market means that firms bind themselves to limit output to the needs of their own (reserved) market or to some fixed proportion of total trade. Restriction of output is implied, therefore, in agreements to share the market or to refrain from price-cutting; the responsibility of limiting its output falls on each firm individually. Sometimes, however, associations are formed to organise restriction of output for the industry as a whole. When an industry is depressed, for example, each firm may agree to work only a proportion of its plant. Or the aggregate output to be produced may be fixed by a central body and divided up between the members of the association in proportion to their output in the past. Each firm is allotted a quota. If this quota is exceeded, a fine must be paid into a pool in proportion to the excess; while, if a firm fails to reach its quota, a payment is made to it out of the pool. When this pooling system is not in operation, it is generally possible for producers to expand output beyond the limit set by their quota by purchasing the unworked quota of other producers. Later, when quotas are under revision, these purchases of quota can be used as a lever to procure a higher share of output under the new agreement.

One of the most obvious effects of quota arrangements of this kind is that the high-cost members of the association tend to be sheltered from competition while the more efficient, low-cost members can expand only with difficulty. They have to pay fines or buy quota so as to qualify for larger quotas when revision takes place, usually on the basis of past outputs. Their share of the market is not completely frozen; but the changes that would be brought about by free competition are slowed down and the public is denied opportunities of making purchases at lower prices.

## Cartels

Associations which not only fix prices or allot quotas, but also undertake the business of marketing, are called cartels.[1] A cartel acts as a selling agency on

---

[1] The term is frequently applied to some of the looser types of association described above. In the strict sense, however, a cartel means primarily a selling agency with monopoly powers acting on behalf of independent producers.

behalf of its members, distributing orders between them in accordance with some agreed formula, and not interfering in any way with their internal management. The functions of producing and of marketing are separated, production being carried on by independent units under semi-competitive conditions, while all sales are made through the agency of a monopoly. The profits, or losses, of the sales monopoly are pooled and shared between the members in proportion to output. Sales in special markets (e.g., abroad) may be made at prices varying with the keenness of the competition that has to be met. Prices in the home market, for example, may be kept up while sales at cut-throat prices are made with a view to driving out competitors in some foreign market. Or a special levy per unit of output may be made on each firm so as to subsidise exports.

### Trusts

The cartel, and the looser types of association which have been described so far, all stop short of actual combination. In this they differ from those financial groups which Americans call "trusts." A trust is simply a large firm formed by consolidation of independent companies, or a group of associated companies under the control of a single interest, the firm or group of firms being large and strong enough to exercise powers of monopoly. Trustification may take place in a variety of ways—by "take-over" bids, by acquisition of a controlling interest, by the formation of a holding company, and so on. The biggest of the British trusts—Imperial Chemical Industries—was formed by the issue of shares in exchange for those of four large companies, each of which was in a strong position in one branch or other of the chemical industry. Another example of a British trust is Unilever, which grew by absorption of competitors until it was producing 75 per cent. of the soap made in Britain. The subsidiary companies in a trust of this size generally retain a good deal of independence, and only the broad lines of policy—especially investment policy—are dictated to them.

When obstacles to centralisation exist, trusts and cartels may differ little in their results, however much they differ in form. Each of them becomes simply a means of combining bigness in marketing (for the sake of economies of large-scale marketing or, more probably, for the sake of monopoly and competitive strength) with smallness in producing (for the sake of efficient management). When the obstacles to centralisation are removed a real difference emerges between the trust and the cartel. The cartel is then a prop for units which are uneconomically small; trustification, on the other hand, may be used to bring units together so as to allow them to operate with greater efficiency within a single administrative structure. Like the cartel, the trust can integrate the price policy of the units, enforcing uniform prices; unlike the cartel, it can also integrate their methods of production, suppressing inefficiency, specialising plants to particular products or markets, standardising varieties of product, and using wide powers of co-ordination over the whole field of production, research, marketing, and so on.

Combination, then, ranges from loose agreements at one end to outright amalgamation at the other. At each stage, control over price and over methods of production becomes more and more concentrated. First the monopoly powers of the combine are consolidated through more stringent agreements between the members; then the unit of management is expanded through the trustification of the members. Which method of combination is selected depends upon the advantages and costs of bringing about concentration of control.

## Advantages of mergers

Let us take the advantages (to the combine, not necessarily to the public) first. Full concentration (e.g., in the trust) is to be preferred whenever economies of scale are in prospect. Management of large-scale units, for example, may have become easier, or technical changes may be making for expansion in the size of the business unit. Mere understandings and agreements generally do little to adapt industry to these changes, but tend rather to hold them up. Secondly, where the interests of producers differ widely, it may be hard to arrive at agreement between them short of amalgamation. Even if a looser agreement is possible, it may have to be too vague or too exposed to the risk of disloyalty to be of value.[1] Consolidation in a trust, however, will ensure unity of control and a common policy. The vested interests which block the concentration of production in the most efficient plants will find the ground cut from under their feet, and at the same time each plant can be forced to charge a uniform scale of prices. Thirdly, full concentration may be the most effective method of suppressing competition. So long as firms are linked loosely together by agreements or understandings, they may find it harder to take concerted action against a new competitor than a large trust. Fourthly, it is generally easier for a trust than for a cartel to raise new capital when an industry needs to be re-equipped and re-organised. The new capital may be raised from the public when the trust is formed, or may be supplied by firms with surplus

---

[1] Compare, for example, the following comment on the working of the Coal Mines Act, 1930: "Collieries with newly opened seams have bitterly resisted the regulations which have prevented them from expanding. The exporting colliery has demanded prices that would enable it to meet foreign competition, prices which would be unprofitably low for the inland colliery. One district has insisted upon uniform prices at the point of consumption; another has declared for uniform prices at the pit-head. The mechanised mine with heavy fixed costs has desired low minimum prices and continuous operations; others have preferred high prices and part-time operations. These are but a few of the many questions that have continuously threatened to disrupt the industry." (A. F. Lucas, *Industrial Reconstruction and the Control of Competition*, p. 100.)

reserves when they are merged with firms in financial difficulties. Finally, the law generally puts more obstacles in the way of the cartel and agreements "in restraint of trade" than in the way of outright combination to form a trust.

## Limitations of mergers

Most of these advantages must be qualified, however. First of all, the economies of scale which can reasonably be expected from consolidation are often grossly exaggerated. It is too often assumed that the profits of a trust cannot be less than the joint profits of the firms out of which it was formed. It has repeatedly happened, however, that earnings after consolidation have worked out far below previous earnings, in spite of the trust's monopoly advantages and in spite of the optimistic forecasts of promoters.[1] Secondly, it is not to be supposed that disunity dissolves into unity whenever the wand of consolidation is waved. Sectional interests persist inside the trust, pushing the claims of one plant against another just as they might in a cartel, but generally with less vehemence and certainly with less power to threaten mischief. Thirdly, the strength of a trust is not necessarily greater than that of a cartel. A trust rarely controls the whole industry, whereas cartels very often do. The looser form of combination is the more elastic and comprehensive, and elasticity and comprehensiveness are often more essential to strength than unity. The monopoly of the salt trust—the Salt Union—was twice broken by new competition, but re-established successfully when it formed a cartel with its chief competitors. Finally, legal obstacles to trustification are sometimes at least as overwhelming as legal obstacles to other methods of combination. For the Big Five in banking to combine without Parliamentary approval and encouragement would be impossible. But they are free to make agreements fixing minimum rates of interest on loans.

These qualifications are reinforced by the comparative costliness of forming a trust. There are, first, the costs of arranging the merger itself. These include not only lawyers' fees and bankers' commissions, but also the financial profits of the promoters. They include, too, excessive payments made to manufacturers for their plant—the cost, for example, of old and inefficient plants which are bought up only to be closed down almost at once; and the cost of firms which earn little or no profit for the trust, but which hold out successfully for exorbitant compensation because they have a high "nuisance value"—power, if left outside, to make things awkward for the trust. Secondly, there are the costs of meeting new competition attracted by the formation of the trust.[2] Manufac-

---

[1] Cf. Dewing, *Corporate Promotions and Re-organisations*, p. 547.

[2] Such competition will be impossible if the trust has a monopoly of some essential raw material a stranglehold on the channels of distribution, or legal protection through legal patents or franchises. In all other circumstances, competition will be possible, but not necessarily easy (see above, pp. 163-4).

turers who have sold their out-of-date plants to the trust may invest their money in new factories, modern in design and the last word in efficiency. They can draw on long experience in choosing a site and machinery for their plant, and on thorough familiarity with trade conditions and the special wants of influential customers in managing their business.[1] Thus they are formidable competitors of the trust—so much so that an undertaking not to compete for a period of years is often asked for from producers when they are bought out. Other, less experienced, competitors may be attracted by the high profits which the promoters of the trust anticipate.[2] And there will also be strong competition from firms not absorbed by the trust—all the stronger because the burden of regulating output and stabilising prices will fall heavily upon the trust. To get rid of all this competition, trusts are often forced to expand, buying up one after another of their competitors at great cost, but without putting an end to new competition. Alternatively, they have to abandon hope of exploiting their monopoly and concentrate their energies on securing the economies which size brings within their reach.[3]

In comparison with the cost of forming a trust, a cartel is inexpensive to organise and the cost of framing an agreement between trade competitors is negligible. A cartel, it is true, may be embarrassed by new competition much as a trust is, and may be forced to make terms (e.g., the grant of a large quota to new competitors) which are just as costly as purchase at an exorbitant price. But this new competition is not brought into play more or less automatically through the formation of the cartel; there is no displacement of managerial talent and capital, less publicity, and less need to shoulder the burdens of other producers by allowing them to share in the advantages of a stable market. The new competition which a cartel has to face is the penalty either of inefficiency or of exorbitance.

The view which producers (or promoters) take of these advantages and costs determines how far combination will go and what form it will assume. If the advantages are great (e.g., if important economies are likely to result) and if the costs are low (e.g., if producers are willing to surrender their independence cheaply) amalgamation will proceed rapidly. If the advantages are limited and if the cost of outright combination is high, then resort may be had to some other form of combination more in keeping with the special advantages hoped for, and the special obstacles met with. A wide variety of methods of

---

[1] Cf. Dewing, *op. cit.*, p. 564.

[2] It may even happen that business men have factories put up for the express purpose of inducing trusts to buy them out. In the early history of American railways, for example, branch lines were sometimes built and offered for sale to the main line company on exorbitant terms.

[3] In the end, this may put the trust's monopoly far more securely beyond challenge than any patched-up combination.

combination may be considered, some concentrating control over price, some concentrating control over production also. One method of combination may be found which sets up a pattern of control superior to the existing pattern.[1] If the cost of changing from one to the other is not excessive, it will be adopted. It is this change in the pattern of control that we mean by combination.

## DIRECTION OF GROWTH

The growth of a firm, as we have seen may take place by either of two methods —plant extension or combination. Cutting across this division is another, based on the *direction* of growth. When a firm increases the size of its establishment, or combines with neighbouring establishments of the same type, it may continue to make the same products by the same processes on the same site. Generally, however, the growth of a firm, whether it takes place by plant extension or by combination, involves changes in the site or in the scope of the firm's operations. The term "integration" is applied to changes which add new products and processes and the term "disintegration" to changes in the direction of fewer products and processes. The use of a larger number of sites, when the firm builds or buys factories in other parts of the country, is called "diffusion"; and the enlargement of one establishment accompanied by the closing down of establishments in other parts of the country is called "concentration."[2]

A firm may grow, therefore, along one of several routes. It may grow *horizontally* by combining with firms which make similar products; *vertically* by undertaking processes of manufacture in continuance of those which it already performs; *laterally* by extending the list of products which it turns out; *territorially* by operating over a wider area. But growth is rarely one-dimensional— it takes place, as a rule, along several of these routes simultaneously. A firm which sets up a branch factory, for example, grows horizontally if the new factory produces goods similar to those manufactured in the main establishment; vertically, if the new factory runs a repair department and the main establishment does not; laterally, if the range of products is slightly different; and territorially, if the branch factory is at a distance from the main establishment. Thus the pattern of growth is often woven from different types of integration. Sometimes it is woven, not from integration alone, but from integration mixed with

---

[1] The superiority may arise from a concentration of control over the amount marketed and the price charged, or from a concentration of control over methods of production, or from a blend of concentration of the one with dispersion of the other.

[2] Changes in the direction of more or fewer sites might be called territorial integration and disintegration respectively, so as to preserve the parallel with changes by product or process see above, p. 98). Unfortunately these labels have come to be applied the other way round, territorial integration, for example, meaning concentration on a *smaller* number of sites. To avoid confusion, therefore, the terms "concentration" and "diffusion" have been used in the text.

disintegration. A firm may decide, for example, to increase the scale of output of standard lines (horizontal integration) and cease production of special lines (lateral disintegration). Or it may decide to abandon some processes of manufacture (vertical disintegration) so as to specialise on a larger scale on the remainder (horizontal integration). Or again, it may add a new stage of production at one plant (vertical integration) and close down a similar plant elsewhere (concentration plus horizontal disintegration).

(a) Horizontal integration—Horizontal integration leaves the range of a firm's activities unchanged. It may take the form of an extension of plant and an accompanying increase in output without change of product or process; or, alternatively, it may consist of the combination of firms making similar products. For example, an iron-smelting company may build more blast furnaces or combine with another iron-smelting company.

The normal method of growth is horizontal. The firm which is successful in one line of business naturally seeks to extend that line. The firm which is anxious to protect itself against price-cutting and loss of business tries to combine with other firms in its own trade. It is not only that business men like to stick to a trade with which they are familiar. Both the economies motive and the monopoly motive press far more powerfully horizontally than in any other direction. If a firm grows by widening the range of its operations rather than by simple expansion of output, economies of scale must as a rule be sacrificed. Similarly, a combine of miscellaneous firms generally lacks the strength of a combine of similar firms.

(b) Vertical integration—Vertical integration is the union of a sequence of processes formerly carried on by separate firms. Three different varieties of vertical integration can be distinguished. First, an extension of the process of manufacture, backwards towards the raw materials or forwards towards the market. For instance, a steel firm may take over the previous stage of production and build its own blast furnaces, or combine with a company which is engaged in the production of pig-iron ("backward integration"); or it may continue processes already performed and build rolling mills or amalgamate with the firms which buy its steel ("forward integration"). Secondly, auxiliary goods and services required in the manufacture of a firm's main products may be provided within the firm instead of purchased from outside. For example, the firm may undertake its own repairs, generate its own power, or make its own tools or designs. Third, the special service of marketing may be taken over by the firm.

The motives to vertical integration differ with the type. The motive to forward integration, for example, is generally to find a market; the motive to backward integration is to secure sources of raw materials. Forward integration is not uncommon in times of depression, when firms are anxious to push the sale of their product and so reap the economies of operating at full capacity. Backward integration is to be expected mainly in times of boom when there is a danger of a shortage of raw materials. Thus a steel firm might buy over a ship-building yard when trade is bad, and blast furnaces when trade is good. Since combinations of all kinds are easiest to carry through in times of boom—the financial motive being very strong at such times—the antithesis is never quite so sharp as this. But there is a *relative* preponderance of forward over backward integration in times of depression, and of backward over forward integration in times of boom.[1] Similarly, the assumption of marketing functions is generally prompted by the desire for bargaining strength,[2] whereas the motive to provide auxiliary services within the firm is more often to be found in the technical economies of linked processes.[3]

Of the economies of scale to which vertical integration leads, two only are of much importance. The first—economies of linked processes—have been particularly striking in the steel and chemical industries, where it is essential to conserve heat by having each process in close conjunction with the succeeding one. In other industries, it is economical to link auxiliary services with the main process or processes (e.g., the making of machines, the generation of electricity, etc.). Generally speaking, however, it tends to be more economical to split up processes than to link them, since splitting (disintegration) allows specialist firms to carry on each process on a large scale. It is to the other set of economies—economies due to the spreading or avoidance of risk—that we have to look for the main force working against disintegration and in favour of integration.

The chief risk against which vertical integration safeguards a firm is failure of supplies. A firm which is unable to count on regular and punctual delivery of raw materials runs the risk of being constantly held up by lack of supplies. It can protect itself against this risk by holding large reserves of stocks, but this

---

[1] Whether combination is forward or backward must be judged from the position of the dominant partner.

[2] See above, pp. 115-6 The technical difficulties involved in integration of production with marketing are very great, unless the retailer handles only a narrow range of goods. The manufacturer of shovels, for example, will have no wish to retail them if he has to handle simultaneously everything from hot-water fittings to hearthrugs and even goats (cf. H. Smith, *Retail Distribution*, p. 94n.). Nor will the perplexities of drapers who sell cat's meat and ladies' underwear in Bethnal Green (*ibid.*) appeal to the textile manufacturers of Lancashire. Even when retailing is highly specialised (e.g., in shoes, oil products, motor-cars, etc.), it is rarely possible for the producer to defend his entry into retailing on grounds of efficiency. The real motive is generally the bargaining advantage which he obtains by building up a special market for his goods.

[3] See above, pp. 111-2.

procedure is both costly (since there are storage and interest charges to be met), and risky (since the price of stocks may fluctuate enormously). The firm may be forced, therefore, to secure direct control over the supply of its raw materials through vertical integration. Again, a firm may make its own materials in order to be certain that they are of good and uniform quality. Or it may do so because of the risk that supplies will be unprocurable before its physical plant has had time to wear out, or before a full return has been obtained on the cost of building up the business organisation and sales connections. Or a firm may undertake the manufacture of its materials as a precaution against a rise in their price, or against the danger that they may come under the control of a combine, and be monopolised. Vertical combination, in fact, is very often a counterstroke to horizontal combination.

A vertical integrated firm enjoys various other advantages. It can effect economies of unified control of the succeeding stages of production. If each stage is in separate ownership, the chain of independent firms may hang back from innovations which are in the common interest of the group, but from which the innovator derives little advantage. The design, quality and, above all, the durability which one firm looks for in its components may be unattractive from the point of view of the firm supplying them. Integration enables the conflicting interests of the various stages of production to be reconciled; each firm's special knowledge, and the profits which result from its use, can be pooled in the combine and new processes of common advantage can be introduced. Moreover, a policy which keeps each stage of production in step with the one before and the one after can be formulated. In the cotton industry, where there is little vertical integration, a change in demand must be transmitted gradually along the chain of independent firms, each of which, reacting in ignorance of what is happening further along the chain, easily misinterprets market tendencies and makes an excessive adjustment to the change in demand. In motor-car production, on the other hand, each department is synchronised with the others, from the purchase of raw materials to the marketing of the finished product, and adjustment to reports by retail agents of a change in demand can be made quickly all along the line. Integration introduces more comprehensive planning.

Vertical integration is often a method of extending monopoly from one stage of production to another. In many industries there is some bottleneck, control of which carries with it control over the whole industry. Strategic importance may attach, for example, to mineral deposits, or to transport facilities, or to the channels of distribution. If any of these come to be monopolised, the monopolist can bring pressure to bear on producers at other stages, and can enter into competition with them so as to extend its monopoly advantage. The

Standard Oil companies, for example, used to have a monopoly of pipe-lines for the transportation of crude oil from some of the American oilfields. Their refineries were given an advantage over independent refineries by charging the latter high transportation rates and by imposing onerous shipping requirements such as high minimum shipments of oil. The companies' advantage in refining was reinforced by their monopoly of the tank-wagon wholesale delivery of oil—a service which was on too large a scale to be readily undertaken by a rival company and which other companies were not free to use. Similarly, the ownership of refrigerator cars, and stockyards, by the large American meat-packers helped to preserve them from competition in the main business of meat-packing.

The trend towards vertical integration is much less powerful than the trend towards horizontal integration. It is obstructed by lack of familiarity with the technique of other stages of production and by lack of capital with which to finance vertical expansion.[1] Above all, it is obstructed by the forces which make for the specialisation of firms on a narrow range of processes. Disintegration goes on side by side with integration as one industrial process after another reaches the scale at which it can be turned over to specialist firms. The mediaeval scribe is displaced by firms of publishers, printers, paper makers, machine makers, and a host of others.[2] The livestock industry breaks up into cattle breeding, cattle rearing, cattle fattening and the preparation of feeding-stuffs with all its ramifications. Even in the steel industry, tube making, heavy forging, the manufacture of stainless steel, and many other branches still resist integration.

(c) **Lateral integration**—Lateral integration is the turning out of additional products or styles of product. When, for example, a railway runs refreshment rooms, hotels, steamships, and so on, it is providing services which are connected *laterally* with rail transport; whereas, if it builds its own locomotives it is expanding *vertically*, since locomotives are essential to rail transport, while refreshment rooms, fortunately, are not. In this example, lateral extension is undertaken in order to supply markets with which a connection has already been built up—railway passengers need refreshment, hotel accommodation, etc., and it is convenient and economical to have them provided by the railway. In addition, there is a spreading of risk, especially if a *competitive* service like road transport is integrated; total receipts from all the company's activities

---

[1] Cf. Marshall, *Industry and Trade*, p. 216: "A firm with limited capital can seldom undertake considerable vertical expansions with success; for such expansions are not easily made by gradual steps. On the other hand, a business may proceed gradually and tentatively when extending its operations horizontally in the same stage." (Quoted by Marquand, *Dynamics of Industrial Combination*, p. 44.)

[2] Cf. Allyn Young, "Increasing Returns and Economic Progress," *Economic Journal*, 1928.

will be more stable than receipts from rail transport alone.[1] The use of the same raw material in a variety of products, or the fact that the same technical problems are involved, may also lead to vertical integration. A firm which produces motor-cars, for example, may branch into aeroplane manufacture. Again, firms frequently take up the manufacture of new products which have been discovered by their research department or which have been brought to them by inventors unable to obtain a backing elsewhere. Sometimes a new department or branch factory is added, but more commonly a subsidiary company is formed to manufacture the new product. Lateral integration is also a line of retreat or of advance when competitive pressure changes. If, for instance, competition develops in the poorer qualities of a product a firm is likely to fall back on the special qualities in which its reputation and connections help to insulate it from competition; in falling back, it is likely to look for new styles and brands which will compensate for its loss of trade in standard lines. A firm which is expanding may vary its output for similar reasons; once it begins to bump up against the limits of its market it may find it easier to make headway by branching out into new lines rather than by pushing on with the old ones.

Except in industries where the products are highly standardised, lateral growth is almost as common as horizontal. Indeed, if we put aside combination and the setting up of branch factories (both of which are predominantly horizontal), and think in terms of the establishment only, we shall probably find that change from one line of production to another plays at least as large a part in growth as horizontal expansion and contraction. This does not mean, however, that firms are tending to make a wider variety of products. Firms switch from one line to another, but do not necessarily add new lines to old.

**(d) Territorial integration**—The growth of the firm is frequently accompanied by geographical diffusion—the planting of branches over a wider area, or union with firms in other parts of the country. In some industries, indeed, diffusion and growth are almost indistinguishable. Chain stores, railways, electric supply companies, and other firms engaged in transport and distribution, find extension over a wider area much the easiest path of growth. In other industries diffusion is less attractive. The tremendous reduction in transport costs which has taken place over the last century has made it possible to

---

[1] Integration of competitive services also introduces the monopoly motive, since control (or suppression) of substitutes is the basis of monopoly power. Railways may engage in road transport in order to protect themselves against competition from independent road transport companies. Lateral integration may also be a method, not of defending but of exploiting a monopoly advantage. A firm with a monopoly of one important product may put pressure on dealers to handle its entire line of products ("full-line forcing") by threatening to deprive them of its monopolised product. By extending its line of products, it can take full advantage of its bargaining strength.

concentrate industry in large central units which supply an area formerly served by a multitude of small local firms. The economies of large-scale production are often more than enough to compensate for the extra cost of drawing on a large area of supply, or of radiating output over a wide market. The big firm on a central site can do things more cheaply, in spite of the handicap of a bigger outlay on transport, than small local producers scattered through each village. A familiar illustration is the decline of farm butter- and cheese-making and the concentration of dairying in creameries.

The battle between economies of scale and market resistances,[1] therefore, has gone heavily in favour of economies of scale, and by implication, it would seem, in favour of centralised production also. But the implication is incorrect. The improvement in transport and communications has made possible not only large-scale production on a central site, but also the union of scattered plants under the same management. The railway, the Post Office, and the telephone, make it easy for a firm to manage plants hundreds of miles apart—a feat which would have been almost impossible two hundred years ago. Thus where the main economies of scale are not *technical*, and can be realised in a comparatively small plant, the firm tends to grow by diffusion, not by concentration. Again, if there are strong forces making for lateral or vertical integration, and there is a locational pull on the integrated products or stages of production towards different districts, firms will be forced to operate branch factories in each of these districts. If a firm which manufactures rubber tyres wishes to own rubber plantations and textile mills it will probably have to go to Malaya for the first and to Lancashire for the second. Similarly, it will be unlikely to carry on the production of golf balls or rubber cushions in the districts in which its tyre factory is located.

### GROWTH AND PUBLIC POLICY

The discussion of industrial organisation in this and the preceding chapters has been primarily descriptive and analytic. The aim of these chapters has been to convey some understanding of the forces at work rather than to draw conclusions as to the way in which those forces can or should be controlled by public policy. But enough has been said to show that some form of control is necessary. Without control, industry may evolve monopolistic forms of organisation that pursue the interests of their owners to the detriment of the public interest, or it may leave in being a number of highly competitive units that maintain their independence only at the sacrifice of other social interests.

---

[1] See above, p. 136.

Those interests are primarily twofold:

(a) the production of goods and services at the lowest possible real cost; and
(b) the progressive reduction of real costs through improvements in methods of business organisation, techniques of production, quality of product, and so on.

There is a general presumption that those objects are most likely to be secured where consumers are free to choose between the alternatives open to them and producers are free to enter a market and offer wider alternatives or better terms; this is a presumption in favour of competition. This presumption is reinforced by the social importance of freedom of choice and the injustice that attends the exercise of monopoly power. On the other hand, there is a presumption in favour of large-scale production when this makes for efficiency; it may be better to have a narrower range of alternatives if they are also cheaper. This is a presumption which may justify some degree of monopoly, though not necessarily the uncontrolled exercise of monopoly powers. This presumption in turn is reinforced by the practical importance of assuring some private advantage, however temporary, to those who make improvements; patent legislation, for example, recognises the need to introduce what Mr. Downie called an element of "grit" into the competitive process.[1] In addition, competition, like monopoly, has an unhealthy aspect when pushed too far and can deflect effort into a search for short-term gains at the expense of long-term development.

These conflicting presumptions cannot be reconciled in some simple formula for the organisation of industry. In one industry, free competition may yield the best results; in another, a large producer held in check by potential rather than actual competition; in another, a public corporation exercising a statutory monopoly. Each industry must be looked at in relation to the techniques it uses and the market it supplies before any worth-while judgment can be formed as to how its organisation might be improved.

We shall be discussing the control of industry more fully in Chapter 36. In the meantime we must turn to consider competition and monopoly from the angle, not of industrial organisation, but of supply and demand and the price-mechanism by which they are adjusted to one another.

---

[1] "There must be some, so to speak, grit in the system which prevents any advance of one firm from being immediately imitated with full effectiveness by all the other firms in the industry." (J. Downie, "How should we control monopoly?" *Economic Journal*, Vol. LXVI, December 1956, p. 575.)

CHAPTER 12

# THE EXISTING ORDER: A PRELIMINARY SURVEY

We speak of a capitalist "system." But is there a system at all? Are there no constant gluts and shortages to prove that too much of this and too little of that have been produced? Or recurrent unemployment to prove that some resources are often not used at all? There is no comprehensive scheme by which, for example, the citizens of London are fed, clothed, and housed. No one arranges for the supply from day to day of the exact number of gallons of milk, or loaves of bread, or pounds of sausages which are daily consumed. Probably no one knows. No one arranges that the most important industries will be guaranteed the resources they need. We are free to go on producing what no one wants or what is over-abundant, however pressing the need for our services in some other job. No one arranges that sheep will provide mutton and wool in just the combination that satisfies the demand for each. Farmers can choose their own breed of sheep in complete ignorance of what other farmers are doing, where their mutton goes to, or who is clothed in the wool.

So much freedom of choice, combined with so much ignorance, might seem sure to lead to chaos. Yet the citizens of London are fed, the most important industries do not disappear, and wool and mutton find buyers without too much difficulty. Resources are mobilised to meet our wants with *some* appearance of order. Is there, then, some "invisible hand" steering resources into the right channels just as large-scale planning might do? Is there, after all, a system?

We must be careful, first of all, not to under-rate the amount of planning which is undertaken by individual firms. Each firm has to decide what articles to produce, where to produce them, how much of each to produce, and what methods of production to employ. A large firm, like Imperial Chemical Industries, is faced with broad questions of policy that are not very different, even in scale, from the problems that a State Planning Authority would have to solve. In smaller firms planning is narrower in scope. But there is a daily task of organisation, of planning what is to be done, and giving instructions who is to do it. This planning of details can be undertaken by firms which have little knowledge of what is going on elsewhere. It is often unsatisfactory because there is no one whose business it is to co-ordinate the plans of the individual firms. But the work of organisation undertaken inside each firm, however unsatisfactory at times, does represent a contribution to planning which would have to be made somehow if comprehensive planning were introduced.

Secondly, we must remember that consumers do their planning too. Each consumer plans his own expenditure, buying first what he most requires and spending what is left of his income to satisfy his wants in decreasing order of urgency. If what he wants greatly is scarce, he offers a high price and so induces someone to supply him with it. On the other hand, he penalises any one who persists in trying to market too much of a commodity (in relation to the supply of other commodities) by paying only a low price for it. Now prices govern profits, and the prospect of profit shapes the plans of producers, drawing them into industries where they are good, and drawing them out of industries where they are poor. At the same time, the tendency for consumers to buy in the cheapest markets, and for the factors of production to sell their services where the highest price is offered, drives high-cost producers to the wall and reinforces the motives of the survivors to use the most efficient methods of production. Those who charge high prices cannot find a market: those who pay low wages cannot find employees. The staying-power of a firm or industry—in the absence of State interference—depends upon its ability to show a profit; and this profit—if competition is working freely—is a sign that consumers have a more urgent demand for the product of the firm or industry than for the amount of any other commodity that could be produced at equal cost.

Not only, therefore, is there a *system* of rewards and punishments—the spur of profit and the penalty of loss—knitting together the plans of consumers and producers; it might also seem as if the system were an *ideal* one—that the incentive of private profit works to secure just those results which are most in the public interest, and that large-scale planning, or indeed government intervention of any kind, is superfluous. It was this rosy view of the workings of supply and demand that crystallised in the doctrine of *laissez-faire*. In the twentieth century, with its experience of the hard facts of unemployment, poverty, monopoly, and a hundred other evils, supply and demand and *laissez-faire* are fallen idols. Private profit and social advantage do not coincide. The system is far from ideal: but the main point, for the present, is that there *is* some system and not just chaos.

### The price mechanism

The system that has just been described is generally referred to as "the price-mechanism": that is, the mechanism by which prices adjust themselves to the pressure of demand and supply and in their turn operate to keep demand and supply in balance. It is a mechanism resulting from the free association of consumers and producers in a market, each side concluding such bargains as it finds satisfactory at the ruling price. The price-mechanism is the product of a "market economy" in which consumers and producers exercise freedom of choice within the market, buying or not buying, selling or not selling, hiring or firing as suits their interests best. The more perfectly the market operates, the more each individual buyer and seller is powerless to alter the terms on which he can buy and sell or the less room there is for monopolistic pressure or for what Adam Smith called "the higgling of the market." The interests of buyers and sellers do not need to be reconciled by consultation, negotiation and awards; everyone has to accept the market price. This price faithfully reflects any change in the requirements of consumers or any change in the obstacles to supplying them, putting simultaneous pressure on the whole body of producers and consumers to modify their plans and their behaviour in the direction appropriate to the new degree of scarcity and abundance.

## Capitalism

A great many phrases have been used above almost as interchangeable expressions: "capitalism," "*laissez-faire*" "private enterprise," "market economy," "price-mechanism." But these are not all by any means the same. *Laissez-faire* was a slogan meaning "Remove the shackles!" and summarised an economic philosophy; it dates from a period well after the main features of modern capitalism had already taken shape. Private enterprise is a convenient description of one feature of capitalism and the market economy of another; but it would be possible to have a great deal of private enterprise without rights of property or an organised market, and the market could still function in a socialist state. As for the price-mechanism, it could fit into different types of economic system. There are many socialists who not only accept the theoretical virtues of the price-mechanism but claim that without socialism it cannot function to the best advantage; in their view socialism would be a way of really giving effect to the rules of perfect competition instead of pretending that those rules are already in force under capitalism.

Capitalism embraces both the price-mechanism and a particular set of institutions governing the ownership and control of property (for example, inheritance). If the institutions were different (if, for example, all property reverted at death to the State), the price-mechanism might function as before but capitalism as an economic system would undergo a change. A panegyric of the price-mechanism, therefore, is not a sound defence of capitalism or *laissez-faire* since it sets on one side the social context (poverty and inequality, for example) in which the price-mechanism operates.

The two main features of capitalism are the private ownership of property and freedom of enterprise. In capitalist society men have the right to accumulate property without limit for their exclusive use, and the right to dispose of it as they choose so long as they keep within the law. They have also the right to lend their capital or adventure it in any business, subject to such restrictions as the State imposes. These are not absolute rights; they rest upon the law, altering when the law alters. The State can impose death duties, set a maximum to the property that can be owned by one man, lay down the terms on which money can be lent or invested, and so on. Rights of property and freedom of enterprise can be made to wither away until capitalism is no longer recognisable as such.

In the capitalist system as it exists at present these two features are associated with others; above all, with class divisions. The ownership and control of property is heavily concentrated in the hands of a comparatively small class of persons; on the other hand, the mass of the population owns little or no property and depends for its income on working for a weekly wage. There are also other classes to some extent intermediate between these two: for example, there are many thousands of independent workers and employers of labour, most of them drawing their income mainly from their own exertions rather than from any property they own; a large number of salaried workers, some earning less than the average wage-earner, some more than the average employer; and a class of small rentiers and property-owners living mainly or exclusively on income from property, supplemented perhaps by pensions. The class divisions, moreover, are not absolute, as many people in the course of their lives move from one group to another, and as some people may be in more than one group at any one time: property-owners may draw a salary and wage-earners own some property. While there is no clear line of division, however, between the various classes, there is no blinking the fact that for some people income comes mainly from work while for others an important, sometimes a major, contribution comes from property.

## The price-mechanism under capitalism

In the next few chapters the working of the price-mechanism in a capitalist economy is analysed in some detail: not as it has been functioning, particulary in the recent past, but as it would function if State interference and (initially at all events) monopoly could be disregarded. These are rather large abstractions, and it is desirable to dwell on them at the outset.

The importance of monopolistic influences has already been stressed. To abstract from these influences might seem to imply a misrepresentation of the way in which capitalism works and an identification of it with free and effective competition. Obviously there is no such identity. Competition may operate more strongly under capitalism than under any other system of society. But even under capitalism competition is limited by elements of monopoly that can be very powerful. Conversely, if capitalism were to be replaced by some other economic system, competition in one form or another would continue. Because of the dominant role of competition in the capitalist system, however, an understanding of the system presupposes an understanding of the tendencies of competition; and these tendencies can be more readily grasped if they are assumed to work themselves out in abstraction from any elements of monopoly. This is generally expressed by saying that it is necessary to begin by assuming "perfect" competition—a technical term meaning that no individual producer or consumer has any control over market prices. By starting from the extreme of "perfect" competition, we can go on to study the ways in which competition is limited in the real world; whereas if we drop the thread of "perfect" competition we shall find it hard to disentangle the workings of competition and monopoly.[1]

## Government control

Unrestricted private enterprise, too, is something of an abstraction. It does not, and in a sense, never has existed. Society—whether capitalist or not—has always exercised some control over industry and over the freedom of action of producers and consumers. Even in the heyday of private enterprise there was a section of public opinion that disliked competition or innovation as such and a much larger section of the public that was actively hostile to particular manifestations of enterprise: the introduction of labour-saving machinery, dumping, the free sale of spirits, the employment of child labour, etc. As for the government, it was far from pursuing a consistently *laissez-faire* policy towards industry: hours of labour, payment of wages in kind, conditions of work, joint-stock companies, and trade unions all gave rise to important regulatory enactments. The railways were controlled almost from the beginning and if they were not nationalised it was not from any doctrinaire aversion to nationalisation. The State was expected to hold the ring in industry and commerce, to lay down the rules of the game, and if necessary, to join in it.

Since Victorian times a whole range of devices has been developed for bringing pressure on business men to conform to the wishes of the government.

---

[1] When economists believe that competition is, *in fact*, not far from perfect—once a fairly common belief—their theories can easily be interpreted as a complicated apology for the existing social system. We must be on our guard against being taken in by our own simplifying assumpions.

The State can exhort or cajole; it can work up a campaign; it can tax or subsidise; it can use statutory controls (for example, over raw materials); it can compel by edict or veto; it can even send round the secret police. The extent to which the State intervenes, and the methods of control practised, vary with the political system. But they also vary under the same political system: so much so that some re-christening seems desirable. No single phrase like capitalism can hope to cover every type of economy on this side of the iron curtain from Turkey to Tahiti; or from one Queen Elizabeth to the next. One economy shades into another, while the conventional labels conjure up false antitheses or conceal genuine differences. The ghost of Marx might find it as hard to recognise Communism in Soviet Russia as the ghost of John Stuart Mill to recognise Capitalism in Britain or (for that matter) the United States.

The controls exercised by the State tend to dampen the normal competitive reactions of industry. If a product becomes scarce, the  overnment may control the price so that it does not become dear: the competitive incentive to produce more and relieve the scarcity is then weakened and may disappear. If the product does become dear, producers may be unable to expand for lack of the necessary licences. If, to take the opposite case, there is overproduction and some firms cannot sell enough to cover their costs, the government may come to their rescue with a subsidy or by restricting imports from abroad, so that the contraction to be expected under free competition does not take place.

The reactions of consumers are also dampened. If scarcity is not allowed to lead to higher prices the incentive to economise is weakened and the scarcity may grow instead of being abated. The price of British motor-cars has never been fixed by the government; but the price policy of car manufacturers in the conditions of post-war years illustrates what happens when prices are fixed below the level that consumers are willing to pay. Orders accumulated, became duplicated as motorists placed orders with one manufacturer after another, until, as the queue grew, a speculative demand entered to take advantage of the difference between the controlled price and the price that those in the queue were willing to pay. In such conditions, a black market is soon in full swing. It becomes very difficult to tell what the real shortage of motor-cars is, the orders on the books of manufacturers being a misleading guide. Whatever the shortage, it is aggravated by the absence of a rise in price of new cars and the lack of incentive to make do with existing cars.

Price-control is often supplemented by rationing. This gets rid of the queue by converting one kind of shortage into another. Instead of allowing those at the front of the queue to be served first, rationing spreads the shortage over the body of consumers in order to guarantee everyone a minimum. This is fair enough as a war-time measure to deal with a physical shortage of essential goods; but it is not so easy to justify as a long-term measure, and even in war-time rationing is generally confined to a limited number of items—foodstuffs, clothing, sweets, petrol, etc.

The significance of consumer rationing in the present argument is that it represents one form of limitation to the freedom of response of the price-mechanism. If goods become scarce, the State may prefer to ration them rather than allow supply and demand to have free play. It will then become quite false to argue that scarcity drives up prices until the high prices choke off demand. The choking off will be done as a matter of policy by the government without any change in prices.

Thus the rewards and punishments by which the plans of producers and consumers are co-ordinated do not always arise from the operation of ordinary market forces; other incentives and other compulsions have been superimposed by the State. Market prices reflect government controls as well as the scarcity or abundance that the market would reveal in their absence. The influence of the government on prices, when its revenue is about one-third of the national income, would in any event be enormous; but it is greater than it would be if it acted merely as a large buyer or a large seller because it sets out deliberately to control the workings of the price-mechanism. Few prices of any importance are nowadays unaffected by its decisions. Either it exerts its influence by direct controls over production, consumption or price or through taxes, levies, duties, subsidiaries, grants, etc.

This influence, however, exerted, is set on one side in the following chapters. In any realistic account of the economic system it cannot be neglected; but the effects of intervention can best be gauged in relation to the results of non-intervention. We must start from supply and demand, and the workings of the price-mechanism, if we are to see in what respects those workings are defective and require to be controlled and in what respects government control is unnecessary, dangerous or harmful.

# CHAPTER 13

# THE PRICE MECHANISM

## The function of prices

An understanding of the mechanism by which supply and demand are balanced is fundamental in every branch of economic theory. This mechanism is generally referred to as "the price mechanism" or "pricing"; for it is about prices that supply and demand pivot. If supply increases, while demand remains constant, prices will fall; if demand increases, while supply remains constant, prices will rise. These movements in prices tend to restore the balance between supply and demand. If there is an excess of supply over demand, or of demand over supply, prices tend to move so as to wipe out the excess and bring supply and demand back into line with one another. It is this sensitiveness of prices that enables them to knit together the plans of producers and consumers. They can choke off an over-supply by falling below cost of production to levels unprofitable to producers; and they can choke off an excessive demand by rising to levels at which consumers do not think it worth while to buy.

In balancing supply and demand, prices perform an important social function. On one side, they reflect our "values," our estimates of how much things are worth; on the other, they reflect the scarcity of things, and the cost of making them available to consumers. They preserve a balance between value and cost. But the balance may not be struck in the best possible way. Prices may reflect our wants imperfectly (for example, because of ignorance); and they may get out of line with costs (for example, because of monopoly). Market prices, that is, may diverge from those ideal prices which would accurately reflect our wants and the cost of meeting them. For some commodities the price will be too high and for others too low.

From a slightly different angle, the function of price is to ration a limited supply of goods amongst consumers. The highest bidders, for whom the goods have great utility, are able to buy what they want so intensely, while those who think the price too high are forced to content themselves with other goods which they consider a better bargain. Similarly the price paid for land, labour and capital rations the limited supply of productive resources between competing industries. Those industries which can offer the highest prices for the factors of production are able to commandeer supplies; while industries which find these prices (rent, wages or interest) too high to yield a profit are forced to contract, surrendering the resources in their employment to better-placed industries whose goods are in more urgent demand. Prices serve to distribute goods and resources to the points at which they are scarcest in relation to the wants of consumers. Accurate pricing is the essence of economy.

But pricing is not in fact accurate. Goods fall to those who are prepared to pay the highest prices; but high prices mean less to a rich man than to a poor man, so that those who buy goods are not necessarily those for whom the goods have most utility. A poor man might be willing to make great sacrifices for the sake of a visit to London, a motor-car, a university education for his son, and so on; a rich man might attach comparatively little value to any of these things. But he might pay for them none the less, while the poor man found them beyond his means. Similarly, if consumers are hasty or ill-informed in making purchases, the goods which are produced will not be those which are of most value in meeting their wants. Finally, the output of some goods may be unduly limited through monopolistic control. Pricing, therefore, may fall short of the ideal. Too much of one commodity, too little of another, may be produced. Of our limited productive resources an excessive share may be put at the disposal of one industry and a deficient share left for another.

### The theory of price or value

We are faced, therefore, with two distinct sets of problems. First, we have to analyse how pricing does in fact work; and, second, we have to analyse how, ideally, it ought to work in the best interests of society. The first problem is one of explaining how the prices of different commodities come to be what they are. We have to ask questions like: why can we buy several tons of coal for the price of a fur coat? Why are some prices above, and some below, cost of production?

The second problem discussed in the theory of price, or value, is that of what prices should be. This problem may be approached from two different angles: the angle of the just price and the angle of ideal output. We may ask: on what principles are we to decide when a given price is just and when extortionate? Or we may ask: on what principles of price-fixing will we secure an optimum allocation of productive resources between alternative uses? In short: how ought we to value the products of one industry as compared with the products of another?

It should be observed that the second problem lends itself to scientific treatment much less readily than the first. When an economist discusses how prices *are* determined in the real world, he will be wrong only if his reasoning is faulty, or if his pronouncements are based on inadequate or inaccurate observation. But when he discusses how prices *should* be fixed, or what principles *should* govern the allocation of resources between industries, he may find himself in disagreement with his colleagues, however careful and competent he is. For he will be raising questions of social justice on which no economist can claim to speak with authority.

## The importance of social institutions

It is essential to study how prices are, or should be, fixed against the background of a given organisation of society, in a given context of social institutions. We can assume institutions broadly similar to those with which we are familiar —private property, inequality of income, a wage- and money-system, recurrent unemployment, joint-stock enterprise, and so on—or institutions widely different from our own: the institutions, for example, of a South Sea island or a world of monopolies. It is natural, in a discussion of price-determination, to assume the institutions of a capitalist economy, since the questions posed and answered would otherwise have little relevance to the society in which we live. This is not to say, however, that a discussion of the forces determining prices in other types of society is superfluous or uninteresting. Such studies might be of great assistance in enabling a decision to be made on the merits of alternative sets of institutions. An understanding of the way in which prices are arrived at in a prisoners-of-war camp, or of the methods by which prices are regulated in Soviet Russia, for example, may make it easier to judge what changes are practicable under capitalism.

If we are discussing how prices *should* be fixed, an institutional background is equally necessary. Prices which are fair in a society governed in one way may not be fair in a society governed in another. For instance, it may be fair in a society of teetotallers to charge high prices for wines and spirits to a small minority of hardened drinkers; while in a society of hardened drinkers such prices might rightly be considered outrageous. In a land of slum-dwellers it may be fair to make house rents specially low to facilitate slum clearance; whereas low house rents might not be at all fair in a country free from slums. Where women workers are mainly engaged in earning pin-money it may be fair to pay them less than men for work of equal value; whereas "equal pay for equal work" might be the proper maxim where men and women were equally dependent on wage-earnings for their livelihood.

This point is of particular importance when we are discussing the justice of price discrimination—that is, of charging different prices to different groups of consumers for the same service. Suppose, for instance, that some consumers are rich and some are poor, and that the distribution of income is universally admitted to be unfair. Then it may be right to charge rich customers higher prices than poor consumers. Arrangements may be made for selling potatoes, or milk, or wireless sets, or cinema tickets to the poor below the current market price. But if people's money incomes were admittedly fair, or approximately fair, such arrangements might properly be condemned. Similarly, discrimination might be introduced with a view to assisting unemployed or disabled persons when in different circumstances the right course would be to increase the incomes of these persons. Fairness and expediency cannot easily be disentangled, and expediency turns very much on the social background against which price-fixing takes place.

### Price and value

The theory of prices is sometimes spoken of as the theory of value.[1] This alternative title is intended to make it clear that it is exchange values, or *relative* prices, that are under discussion. Suppose, for example, that pears cost 3d., plums 1½d., and apples 1d. Then the exchange value of pears is two plums or three apples each. Suppose now that money loses half its purchasing power and that the price of pears goes up to 6d., of plums to 3d., and of apples to 2d. The exchange value of pears in terms of plums, apples and other commodities is unaltered. All that has changed is the value of money in terms of commodities. Thus a rise in the price of plums may reflect a change in their value relatively to other commodities or relatively to money. The theory of prices, therefore, is faced not with one problem but with two. It must explain what causes a change in relative prices or exchange values; and it must explain what causes a change in the value of money. The first problem is dealt with in the theory of value, the second in the theory of money.[2]

Early theories of value were theories of what governs prices *in the long run.*

---

[1] At least five different meanings of the term "value" can be distinguished: moral good, aesthetic merit, utility, exchange-value, and ideal exchange-value. When we say, for example, that we "value" freedom, we are using value in the moral sense. We think that freedom is something to which men are morally entitled, something that they should have; we are certainly not thinking in terms of supply and demand. Again, if we set a high "value" on Shakespeare's plays or Beethoven's music our judgment is an aesthetic one. If we speak of water as being "valuable," we mean that it answers to some well-known human needs, not that it fetches a high price; we are thinking of its utility. The "value" of a house may refer to its selling or exchange-value or to the price which some imaginary purchaser might or should be willing to pay for it (for instance, we speak of house-property fetching less than its "value"). In economics "value" is sometimes used to mean exchange-value, and sometimes to mean utility, or "value-in-use."

[2] A strict separation of the two problems is not possible. A change in relative prices, for example, may be sufficient to precipitate a change in the value of money; and a change in the value of money is invariably accompanied by changes in relative prices. In elementary economics, however, it is legitimate to assume that the two problems can be disentangled: otherwise no progress towards understanding either is ever likely to be made.

Day-to-day fluctuations in price—fluctuations in "the temporary or market value" of commodity—were put down to "the higgling of the market," or dismissed with a vague reference to supply and demand. Analysis was confined to "normal" or "natural" values—that is, to the long-run trend of prices, about which day-to-day fluctuations take place.

### The labour theory of value

Most early theories were variants of the labour theory of value. According to this theory the "natural" value of a commodity depends on the amount of labour embodied in it—on "the toil and trouble" bestowed on its production. The value of all commodities, it was argued, is reckoned in terms of money. Since the value of money is constantly changing, however, money cannot be the ultimate standard of value. But there must be *some* ultimate and invariable standard, some circumstance common to all commodities, by which exchange values are determined. Now we know that labour is needed in the production of almost everything of value, and that commodities "are counted dear or cheap according as they can be had with much or little labour." The effort expended in an hour's labour, moreover, will always produce the same quality of goods; labour is a reliable measuring rod, whereas money is not. Finally, it is clear that in a primitive community with little capital, exchange values will correspond fairly closely with the amount of labour embodied in each commodity. The laws of nature, which were supposed to apply in such a community, were often appealed to as a standard in the eighteenth century, and coloured much of the political and economic theory of the period. It seems to be in accordance with these natural laws that prices should correspond to the cost, in human effort, of producing commodities.

The most striking deficiency of this theory is that it neglects the influence of *demand* on value. It is obvious that commodities acquire value just as much because they satisfy our wants (i.e., possess utility) as because they cost some effort to produce (i.e., embody labour). But while it is easy to see the relationship between effort and value it is not easy to see the exact connection between utility and value. The things that have most utility (e.g., water) are often the least valuable; while the things that are of doubtful utility (e.g., diamonds) are often of most value. It was this puzzling "paradox of value" that led Adam Smith and other economists to give up the attempt to relate utility to value and to fall back instead on labour.

The second main deficiency is that the theory gives only a partial explanation of the influence on value of *supply*. It is plain that, of a number of things in equally urgent demand, those are most valuable that are most limited in supply (i.e., that are scarcest). But it is not so plain that those things are scarcest, and consequently most valuable, that require most labour to produce. *One* reason why things are scarce and valuable is that human labour is needed in order to produce them. But there are other reasons. There is, for example, the initial scarcity of land and raw materials with which labour co-operates. If a ton of tobacco sells for more than a ton of wheat, the explanation may lie just as much in the comparative scarcity of land suitable for tobacco-growing as in the comparative laboriousness of tobacco-growing. Another factor governing the relative supply of commodities, and hence their exchange values, is the scarcity of capital. Dress-making, for example, uses far more labour in proportion to capital than electricity-making. If capital becomes more abundant, therefore, it is reasonable to expect a fall in the value of electricity in comparison with the value of gowns, even though no change takes place in the labour required to make a gown or a unit of electricity. Finally, it is often the commodities that take the largest number of labour-hours to produce, or call for the most intense effort, that are cheapest. The products of the navvy fetch far less than the products of the lawyer from the point of view either of duration or intensity of toil. The reason is that navvies are abundant while lawyers are scarce. In short, it is not labour, but scarcity—or supply, which is just scarcity the other way round—that governs value—jointly, of course, with demand. Labour—toil or effort—is one thing among several that helps to moderate scarcity and so to create value.

Sometimes the labour theory of value is supported by an appeal to justice and the rights of man. It is suggested (for example, in the Marxian version of the theory) that labour alone creates value, and that, if market values are in excess of wage costs, then the labourer is being exploited and is receiving less than the value of his product. The surplus of rent, interest and profit falls to the capitalist class, not in return for any service which they perform, but because they happen to be the owners of the instruments of production. This is not so much a theory of value (i.e., of relative prices) as a theory of distribution (i.e., of the earnings of the factors of production). It is unnecessary, therefore, to discuss it in detail at this stage. The assumption in the theory that labour alone creates value is false, even if "labour" is interpreted broadly to include skill and judgment. The activities of saving and risk-taking, for example, can be just as productive as labouring; they are almost as essential to the creating of value.

### The cost of production theory

A more modern version of the labour theory is that prices are governed, in the long run, and in the absence of monopoly, by the cost of production. This seems plausible enough, and is in harmony with much that goes on in the business world. Nevertheless the theory breaks down, and for much the same reasons as the labour theory breaks down. First, it neglects the influence of demand. We have already seen that costs of production generally vary with the scale of output—that is, that there is no single cost of production for each commodity irrespective of the amount of it that is being produced. Now this amount is presumably equal to the amount that consumers want to buy, i.e., to the *demand* for the commodity. Until we know what the demand is, therefore, we do not know the scale of output of the commodity, and we also do not know its cost of production. But if we do not know the cost of production until we know the demand, it is useless to tell us that price is governed by cost. Demand (or utility) and supply (or cost) are like the two blades of a pair of scissors (to use Marshall's metaphor)—it is as idle to argue that one or other governs prices as to argue that it is this blade or that that does the cutting.

Secondly, the theory is emasculated by the qualifications "in the absence of monopoly" and "in the long run." In modern business, it is monopoly that is the rule, free competition the exception. There are elements of monopoly in every trade, and it is these elements of monopoly that raise the most difficult problems in economic analysis. Such an analysis cannot proceed solely in terms of cost production; there is nothing to compel a monopolist to fix his prices at or near to cost of production. We must bring in demand if we are to develop a theory of prices under monopoly. Similarly, it is not denied that prices may be above or below cost in the short run; the theory refers only to what takes place in the long run, given time for changes to work themselves out. But the short run is much more interesting than the long run; as Lord Keynes once reminded us, in the long run we are all dead. And we cannot say how far above cost, or how far below, prices will range in the short run until we have made a study of demand.

Thirdly, the theory gives only an incomplete account of the influence of supply. Cost of production seems simple and unambiguous enough. But in fact there are few phrases in economics so hard to interpret. Firms vary enormously in efficiency: some go on producing, year after year, at high cost, while others have costs consistently lower. In which firms are we to measure cost of production? Or again, when a firm produces several different commodities in the same building, how are we to distribute the overhead costs of the building between each of the different commodities? If sheep *will* persist in providing us with mutton and wool simultaneously, how are we to distinguish the cost of wool from the cost of mutton? To these questions, the cost of production theory returns no answer.

The deficiencies of the cost of production theory will become clearer when the modern "marginal" theory of value had been explained. Before we turn to this theory, however, we must clear away some of the confusion that clings to the terms "supply" and "demand."

# CHAPTER 14

# SUPPLY AND DEMAND

The price of an article depends upon two distinct sets of forces, generally referred to as supply and demand. "Supply" means the quantity offered for sale by producers and, "demand" the quantity that consumers are willing to buy. Thus the "supply" of coal does not mean the amount of coal lying underground waiting to be mined (except, of course, in other contexts); it means the amount of coal which coal-owners are willing to put on the market at various prices. Similarly, the "demand" for coal does not mean the amount of coal which people need, or would like to have, but the *effective* demand, the amount which people are willing to buy at various prices. It should be observed that we cannot speak of demand, or of supply without specifying some price. There is, for example, no such thing as *the* demand for coal. People will buy more coal when it is cheap than when it is dear. Similarly with supply. Coal-owners will be more willing to mine and sell coal when the price is high than when it is low.

Thus demand and supply vary with price. But they also vary with other things —for instance, with people's tastes, or the standard of living, or the state of technical knowledge. The changes that take place in demand and supply in response to changes in these other things (what are called "demand *conditions*" and "supply *conditions*") differ, however, from the changes that take place in response to changes in price. Demand conditions and supply conditions are generally independent of one another whereas price affects demand and supply simultaneously. A change in the technique of coal-mining will affect the supply of coal, for instance by lowering the cost of mining it, but it will be unlikely to react directly on the demand for coal. A change in the price of coal, on the other hand, will affect both the supply of coal and the demand for it.

The fact that supply and demand both respond to changes in price means that supply and demand can be balanced if an appropriate price is charged. The higher the price, the more will be supplied and the less demanded; the lower the price, the less will be supplied and the more demanded. Any gap between supply and demand can be closed, therefore, by raising or lowering the

200

price. If coal-owners offer for sale more than the market will absorb at the current price, the price of coal will be forced down until the surplus disappears, either through consumers buying more or because coal-owners reduce their output. Similarly if consumers insist on having more coal, it will be through the offer of higher prices that they induce coal-owners to undertake the mining of an increased supply. Given the state of demand (demand conditions) and the state of supply (supply conditions) there will be one price (the equilibrium price) at which demand and supply can be made to balance in the sense that every buyer is able to obtain as much as he wants and every seller to sell as much as he wants at the current price, and competition will drive the price to the balancing point.

### Supply and demand curves

Thus, on the one hand, supply and demand depend upon, and vary with, price; and, on the other, price depends upon, and varies with supply and demand.

TABLE 6

DEMAND AND SUPPLY SCHEDULES FOR ORANGES

| Price of oranges | Number of oranges consumers would buy ("demand schedule") | Number of oranges offered for sale ("supply schedule") |
|:---:|:---:|:---:|
| Pence | Millions | Millions |
| 1 | 8,000 | — |
| 2 | 4,000 | — |
| 3 | 2,000 | 400 |
| 4 | 1,000 | 1,000 |
| 5 | 500 | 3,000 |
| 6 | 200 | 5,000 |
| 7 | 50 | 6,000 |
| 8 | 10 | 6,500 |

The inter-relationship between supply, demand and price can be illustrated by drawing a supply curve and a demand curve. These curves show how much of a commodity will be offered for sale at any given price, and how much of it consumers will be likely to buy at any given price. The supply curve will normally be sloping upwards from left to right, and the demand curve will slope downwards from left to right. Where the two curves intersect, demand and supply will be equal. The price at which this equality is achieved is known as the equilibrium price.

G*

Suppose, for instance, that we are discussing the price of oranges. We can draw up schedules like those in Table 6 to show how many oranges will be offered for sale, and how many will be bought, at any given price. As the price of oranges goes up, the number offered for sale goes up too; at first, very rapidly, because it will pay to stop growing other kinds of fruit and grow oranges instead; later,

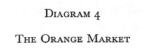

DIAGRAM 4

THE ORANGE MARKET

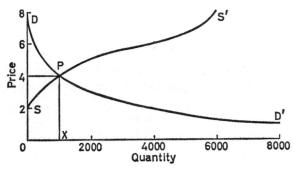

increasingly slowly, because there is a limit to the area on the surface of the earth where oranges can be grown. On the other hand, as the price goes up, the number of oranges bought begins to fall off. Some people will give up eating oranges because they cannot afford them; nearly everybody will buy fewer oranges and spend their money on other things that have not risen in price— apples, for example; the manufacturers of orange juice will restrict their purchases.

The schedules of supply and demand given in Table 6, when plotted on a graph (Diagram 4), gives us the supply curve and demand curve for oranges. SS′ (the supply curve) illustrates the changes in supply that are likely to result from a variation in the price of oranges, and DD′ (the demand curve) the changes in demand. The curves intersect at P and the equilibrium price PX is, therefore, 4d. This will be the price ruling in the market under the conditions assumed in Table 6. For 4d. is the only price which balances demand and supply. At any price higher than 4d. there is always an excess of oranges which can find a market only when they are offered for sale below the current price. At any price lower than 4d. there will always be a shortage of oranges and buyers will make higher offers in order to obtain supplies. A low or high price at one point in the market will communicate itself—on the assumptions that we are making—to all other points in the market. Thus if dealings begin at some price other than 4d., they may be expected to oscillate for a time round 4d. until it is clear that at this price a sufficient number of buyers will be forthcoming to take the whole supply of oranges off the market and that the requirements of buyers can be met in full. The price of 4d. will then become the uniform price throughout the market and there will be no unsatisfied buyers and no unsatisfied sellers.[1]

## Changes in demand and supply

A change in price will come about whenever there is a change either in demand or in supply. Suppose, for example, that the public develops a liking for orange juice and is ready to buy more oranges than before at any given price.

DIAGRAM 5

AN INCREASE IN THE DEMAND FOR ORANGES

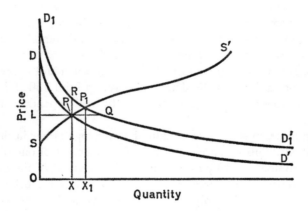

This will be represented by a movement of the demand curve to the right. Consumers will be willing to buy LQ, not LP, at the market price PX and correspondingly larger quantities at any other price. At first, however, the quantity on sale will be unchanged and the price will be forced up steeply to RX. Once producers are able to respond to this rise in price, supplies will begin to increase and the price will fall to the point at which the new demand curve

---

[1] This is not intended as a realistic description of how prices are fixed in a market like Covent Garden. The market spoken of above is not a place but a network of dealings (see above, p. 38).

$D_1D'_1$ intersects the supply curve SS', that is, to $P_1X_1$. This will be the new equilibrium price.

When a change takes place on the side of supply, for example because orange trees yielding a bigger crop are discovered, it will be the supply curve that is displaced: in the example given, it will move to the right because larger quantities will be put on the market at any given price. A new and lower price will then be established at which consumers make larger purchases than before.

We must carefully distinguish between an increase in demand or in supply represented by a movement of the whole curve and an increase represented by a movement *along* the curve. Only the first kind of increase can initiate a change in price; the second is a reaction to a change in price and cannot be the cause of it. A change in demand in response to a change in price is not an independent change in the state of demand but simply the reflection of some antecedent change in the state of supply. If we fail to grasp this distinction we are apt to get in a muddle. We may argue, for example, that an increase in demand will push up the price but that at the higher price demand will fall off, so that the price will come down again, until we don't quite know whether the price will be higher or lower than before. This kind of muddle is particularly common when people start discussing the effects of a tax on a commodity. A flat tax or import duty of, say, 1d. per orange will raise the supply curve by the same amount throughout its length and make it cut the demand curve nearer the origin; the demand, but not the demand curve, will fall and the equilibrium price will rise. How much the price will rise by will depend on the shape of the two curves.

Changes in price, in short, are initiated by a change either in demand or in supply conditions. This is represented by a displacement of one of the curves, which, unless compensated by an offsetting displacement of the other (a very unlikely occurrence) must force the price to a new equilibrium level. Put differently, if demand and supply are tending to get out of line with one another, they can be kept in line by an appropriate change in price. In the last resort it will be price that preserves equilibrium.

### Elasticity

In order to understand how price balances supply and demand, we must study in more detail how each of these responds to small changes in price. The rate of response is measured by what is called "elasticity." The elasticity of demand for a commodity is the rate at which the quantity bought changes as the price changes, other things remaining the same. The elasticity of supply of a commodity is the rate at which the quantity offered for sale changes as the price changes.

These definitions are easier to understand in terms of the simple formulae:

$$\text{Elasticity of demand} = \frac{\text{Percentage change in quantity bought}}{\text{Percentage change in price}}$$

$$\text{Elasticity of supply} = \frac{\text{Percentage change in quantity offered}}{\text{Percentage change in price}}$$

In the schedules given in Table 6, for example, the elasticity of demand, when the price of oranges is 4d., lies between $\frac{5}{10}/\frac{1}{4}$ (i.e., 2) and $\frac{1}{1}/\frac{1}{4}$ (i.e., 4) according as we are considering an increase or a decrease in price. If we could consider infinitely small changes in price and quantity, the elasticity of demand would be the same whether we measured it in terms of a rise or a fall in price; but all that we can say from studying the schedule is that at the equilibrium price it lies somewhere between 2 and 4. The elasticity of demand is not the same at all points on the demand curve; when the price is 2d., for example, the elasticity lies between 1 and 2, and when the price is 6d. the elasticity of demand lies between $4\frac{1}{2}$ and 9. In this particular example, the elasticity of demand is greater than 1 at all prices above 1d. and increases as the price goes up; but it is easy to construct examples in which elasticity is less than 1, or in which elasticity falls with a rise in price. If it were true that people bought just as much salt at 8d. as at 1d. the elasticity of demand would not only be less than 1; it would be zero. If the only consumers of oranges left in the market when oranges rose above 8d. were so well-to-do that they would go on buying almost as many at 9d. or 10d., then the elasticity of demand would change abruptly at 8d. and the demand would suddenly become relatively inelastic.

The elasticity of demand measures the ease with which people can put up with a small reduction in their consumption of a commodity, or alternatively the ease with which they can be induced, by a reduction in price, to consume a little more of it. If people buy the same amount of a commodity irrespective of the price, i.e., if they cannot do without *any* of the amount which they are buying then demand is absolutely inelastic (elasticity is equal to zero). If people cease to buy the commodity altogether when it rises slightly in price, then demand is perfectly elastic (elasticity is equal to infinity). These are the outer limits. Within these limits we can distinguish between demands that change more rapidly, and demands that change less rapidly than price. Just on the dividing line, a given change in price will lead to an exactly proportionate change in the quantity bought; elasticity of demand is then equal to unity. On one side of the line, elasticity will be greater, and, on the other side, less than unity. When elasticity is greater than unity—that is, when a given change in price leads to a more than proportionate change in demand—we say that demand is *elastic*. When elasticity is less than unity—that is, when a given change in price leads to a less than proportionate change in demand—we say that demand is *inelastic*. It will be observed that elasticity is a matter of degree and that, even when demand is inelastic, there are still some elements of elasticity.

The three limiting cases can be represented graphically as follows:—

DIAGRAM 6

LIMITING CASES OF ELASTICITY ON DEMAND

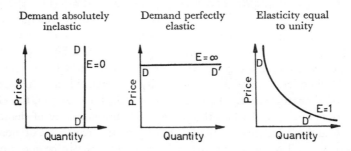

In the borderline case where demand is neither "elastic" nor "inelastic" but is equal to unity, the outlay of consumers will be constant as prices change, and the demand curve will take the form of a rectangular hyperbola. In this case, since by hypothesis the changes in price and in quantity bought are inversely proportional, the multiple of price and quantity (i.e., the amount spent) must be constant. Consumers will buy less of the article as its price rises but will pay more per unit of it and the rise in price will be exactly balanced by the increase in purchases, so that consumers spend the same amount of money as before. This allows us to formulate an alternative test of elasticity of demand: whether people spend more or less on an article as its price rises. If they spend more, demand is inelastic; if less, demand is elastic.

Suppose, for example, that we divide the demand for oranges, expressed in the schedule in Table 6, into three elements, and distinguish the demands of working-class consumers, middle-class consumers and well-to-do consumers. The result might be something like that shown in Table 7.

Working-class consumers have a consistently elastic demand; they spend less money on oranges with each increase in price. Middle-class consumers have an inelastic demand up to 3d. but an elastic demand at higher prices. The well-to-do have an extremely inelastic demand at low prices; they are prepared to spend more than three times as much on oranges at 4d. each than at 1d. each (although they get fewer oranges for their money). They have then a fairly elastic demand as the price rises to 7d.; and thereafter their demand begins to be inelastic again.

TABLE 7

THE DEMAND FOR ORANGES

| Price of Oranges | Number of oranges that would be bought by: | | | |
|---|---|---|---|---|
| | Total | Working-class | Middle-class | Well-to-do |
| Pence | Millions | | | |
| 1 | 8,000 | 6,500 | 1,250 | 250 |
| 2 | 4,000 | 2,750 | 1,000 | 250 |
| 3 | 2,000 | 1,000 | 750 | 250 |
| 4 | 1,000 | 300 | 500 | 200 |
| 5 | 500 | 150 | 250 | 100 |
| 6 | 200 | 50 | 125 | 25 |
| 7 | 50 | — | 40 | 10 |
| 8 | 10 | — | — | 10 |

| Price of Oranges | Amount spent on oranges by: | | | |
|---|---|---|---|---|
| | Total | Working-class | Middle-class | Well-to-do |
| Pence | Million pence | | | |
| 1 | 8,000 | 6,500 | 1,250 | 250 |
| 2 | 8,000 | 5,500 | 2,000 | 500 |
| 3 | 6,000 | 3,000 | 2,250 | 750 |
| 4 | 4,000 | 1,200 | 2,000 | 800 |
| 5 | 2,500 | 750 | 1,250 | 500 |
| 6 | 1,200 | 300 | 750 | 150 |
| 7 | 350 | — | 280 | 70 |
| 8 | 80 | — | — | 80 |

## The measurement of elasticity

The example given above is a hypothetical one. But economists have been able to make rough estimates of the actual elasticity of demand for some commodities by drawing up what is called a "statistical" demand curve. In its simplest form, this consists of a number of points plotted on a graph from observed prices and sales in past years. The graph (Diagram 7) shows how sales of potatoes in the United Kingdom varied in relation to their price in each of a number of pre-war years, each cross representing one particular year. The points lie roughly along a curve: and from the shape of the curve the elasticity of demand for potatoes can be calculated. The curve indicates that a rise in price by 1·5 per cent. reduces consumption by about 1 per cent.: that is, that the elasticity of demand for potatoes is about 0·7.[1]

DIAGRAM 7

STATISTICAL DEMAND CURVE FOR POTATOES

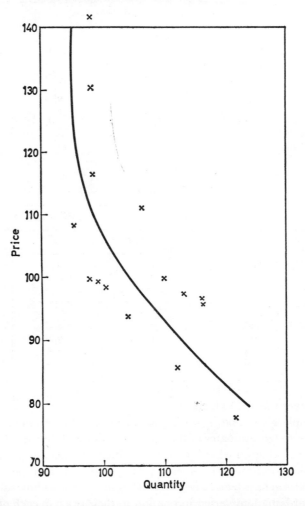

1 These estimates and the data from which Diagram 6 is constructed are taken from an article by Prof. K. S. Lomax on "The Demand for Potatoes" in *The Manchester School*, May 1950.

## Elasticity of demand and substitution

The elasticity of demand for a commodity depends mainly on the range of available substitutes. The better the substitutes available, the more elastic will be the demand for the commodity. If motor-cars became dearer, the demand may not fall off very much, because people do not consider bicycles and buses very good substitutes for motor-cars. But if the price of Austin motor-cars goes up and there is a very similar model on sale (e.g., the Morris), demand will be transferred to the cheaper model and the sales of Austins will fall heavily; that is, demand will be elastic. In the same way, the demand for tea will be less elastic than the demand for a particular brand of tea, because brands of tea are better substitutes for one another than cocoa, coffee, etc., are for tea. If there are absolutely perfect substitutes on sale (e.g., wheat of the same grade sold by different farmers), then the demand will be perfectly elastic; no one will be able to raise his price above the price paid to his competitors without losing his entire market.

The possibilities of substitution will be greater when there is a wide range of uses to which the commodity can be put. Electricity, for instance, is used for heating and lighting, for the supply of power, and so on. Hence it can be substituted for coal, candles, gas, petrol, wireless batteries, etc., whenever it becomes cheaper. As electricity falls in price in relation to other things, people find it worth while to reduce their expenditure on a great many different things and transfer this expenditure to electricity. Thus the demand for electricity is fairly elastic.

On the other hand, the demand for wheat is highly inelastic. Most people put wheat to a single use (i.e., they eat it), so that when wheat falls in price, they can only increase their purchases of wheat if they elect to eat more of it. This generally means a change of diet which is not very acceptable. So far, however, as wheat is used for other purposes (e.g., as a feeding-stuff) and so far as people are prepared to switch to wheat from potatoes, rye, oats, rice, and other substitutes whenever wheat is relatively cheap, the demand will retain some elements of elasticity.

Again, the demand for necessities is generally much less elastic than the demand for luxuries. The demand for potatoes, for instance, is far more inelastic than the demand for oranges. For necessities like salt or sewing thread, on which we spend a very small fraction of our income, demand will be particularly inelastic, since a rise of perhaps 50 per cent. in price may mean no more than a few pence on our annual outlay. Similarly, rich people have a less elastic demand than poor people. The poor man has constantly to be considering how he can spend his income to best advantage and is sensitive to changes in price; while the rich man, faced with a rise in price, may not bother to look for a substitute.

The demand for pineapple will be far less elastic in Park Avenue than in China town.

Elasticity arises in two different ways. Existing consumers will tend to buy more as prices fall, and new consumers will be tempted to make purchases. Sometimes, of course, only one source of elasticity is present. Practically everyone is already buying potatoes; new consumers cannot be found. On the other hand, it is rarely possible to persuade people to buy two copies of the same book; new consumers have to be found. Generally speaking, elasticity arises less through increased purchases by existing consumers than through the tapping of successive layers of demand from *potential* consumers as prices are brought down.[1]

## Practical importance of elasticity

The conception of elasticity is of great practical importance. Suppose that the railways are thinking of increasing fares. One of the first questions that they will have to reflect on is: how much traffic will be lost? How many passengers will give up travelling by train and travel by some other means or not travel at all? This is the same question in another form as: how elastic is the demand for rail travel? Similarly, if the government is thinking of putting a higher duty on tobacco it will have to form some idea of the impact on smoking habits, of the rate at which the demand for cigarettes and tobacco will fall off as the price goes up: that is, of the elasticity of demand. Manufacturers trying to work out the best price for a new line in stockings or hot-water bottles are faced with the same problem and will require to form some estimate of the elasticity of demand. They may not think in the precise terms in which elasticity has been formulated by economists. But there is no reason to suppose that their judgment is any the better for neglecting (or avoiding) the economist's formulation.

## Elasticity of supply

The elasticity of supply of a commodity measures the ease with which producers can meet a small rise or fall in price by increasing or reducing supplies.

---

[1] Elasticity of demand, as discussed above, is sometimes called "price-elasticity" to distinguish it from "income-elasticity." This measures the responsiveness of demand to a change in income. As people become better off, their consumption of some commodities grows much more rapidly than others: for example, they spend a smaller proportion of their income on food and a larger proportion on recreation and entertainments. This means that they have a low income-elasticity of demand for food and a high income-elasticity of demand for recreation. Just as the conception of price-elasticity is of great importance in analysing fluctuations in prices, the conception of income-elasticity is useful in analysing fluctuations in income. It is also valuable in a study of the dynamics of prices in explaining the tendency of some prices to rise relatively to others with increasing prosperity.

Supply is said to be elastic or inelastic according as a change in price causes a more than proportionate or less than proportionate change in supply.

The elasticity of supply depends upon the range of alternatives open to the producer. If, for example, he is selling in several different markets his goods are likely to be in elastic supply to any one market; a fall in prices in that market will induce him to sell his goods elsewhere. Again, if he is producing several different goods, and can switch fairly easily from one to another, then each of his products will be in elastic supply. Or if the alternative of closing down his works and going out of business altogether will not involve him in heavy loss, then again supply is likely to be elastic. Finally, supply will be elastic if each producer's employees can readily obtain employment in other industries, if the materials which they use have alternative markets, and if their equipment is readily convertible to other uses. The more attractive these alternatives, the less will be the incentive to continue in the industry when prices fall, and the greater, therefore, will be the contraction in output and in supply.

With supply as with demand, elasticity arises in two ways: through a change in the output of existing producers and through a change in the number of producers. A full discussion of these changes must be postponed until later.[1]

### Elasticity and time

The response of consumers and producers to a change in price is generally spread over a period of time; some reactions are immediate and some delayed. If, for example, the price of cameras goes up, firms that are already making cameras may produce more and some firms outside the industry may decide to start producing cameras. But the new firms will take a little time before they can put cameras on the market; and the output of the industry as a whole may be limited by some common bottleneck such as optical glass, so that no expansion beyond a certain point can take place until the firms making optical glass have expanded their capacity, trained additional labour, etc. There will be a succession of adjustments as time goes on, all making for a higher level of output at some stage. The elasticity of supply, therefore, will grow with the passage of time. So also will the elasticity of demand. In the short run consumers may have no alternative but to pay higher prices; but in the long run the range of alternatives widens and substitution becomes easier. If railways freight charges go up, there may be no immediate reduction in traffic; but a great many businesses will make enquiries about alternative forms of transport and some will place orders for lorries or make trial shipments by water. The

---

[1] See Chapter 16.

result will be a gradual transfer of freight away from the railways, the elasticity of demand increasing progressively.[1]

## Fluctuations in prices

Elasticity, whether of demand or of supply, makes for stability of prices. The price of a commodity like wheat, which is in inelastic demand, will have to fall drastically if a surplus has to be absorbed; whereas a comparatively slight reduction in price will be sufficient to secure the absorption of a surplus of oranges, which are in elastic demand. The more elastic the demand, the more stable the price. Similarly the price of commodities like rubber, which are in inelastic supply, will fluctuate more than the price of commodities like motorcars, which are in elastic supply. The more elastic the supply, the more stable the price. Where demand and supply are very elastic—i.e., highly sensitive to changes in price—it will require no great change in price to keep them in step with one another. Prices will fluctuate more widely if either demand or supply is highly variable. The supply of strawberries varies enormously between December and June, and between one year and another, and this causes wide fluctuations in the price of strawberries. The demand for seaside holiday accommodation varies from one season of the year to another, and resorts that are crowded one year may have plenty of room in later years; these fluctuations in demand are reflected in fluctuations in hotel and boarding house charges. When a commodity is both in highly inelastic demand and subject to wide variations in supply, the range of price fluctuations may be enormous. The farm price of potatoes, for example, may be £5 a ton one year and £30 a ton the next because large fluctuations in the crop encounter a highly inelastic demand.

Fluctuations in price are much more pronounced in agriculture and mining than in industry. Staple raw materials and foodstuffs such as wool, rubber, tin, wheat, sugar, coffee, and so on, undergo the most astonishing changes in price in a matter of months, while many manufactured goods are sold at the same price year in, year out, and many others change in price only at rare intervals and by comparatively short hops. This difference arises largely because the supply of agricultural and mining products is highly inelastic, so that it is not easy to match a change in demand by a corresponding change in supply, while the supply of manufactured goods is highly elastic and can be easily expanded or contracted in step with demand. One consequence of the difference is that the incomes of agricultural communities fluctuate more widely than the incomes of industrial communities. On the other hand, since the elasticity of supply in industry is only achieved by cutting down output and discharging workers when demand

---

[1] See also Chapter 19 for a fuller discussion of the influence of time on elasticity.

falls off, the comparative steadiness of prices in industrial communities is bought at the cost of relative unsteadiness of employment.

It may happen that a general fall in agricultural prices actually brings about an *increase* in agricultural output. The fall in prices cuts farmers' incomes; farmers may try to make up for the cost by extra effort; if they do, they will grow more farm produce and when the larger supply comes on the market it will drive prices still lower. The same kind of thing can happen in coalmining; a shortage of coal tends to drive up prices and enables coalminers to press successfully for higher wages; the higher wages may make the miners disinclined to work so hard, since they will be able to earn as much as before in a shorter time; and, if this is the predominant reaction, the shortage of coal will be intensified, not reduced. These are, however, unusual and abnormal cases, just as it would be abnormal for a fall in price to make demand fall off.

### Elasticity in conditions of instability

The abnormal cases that have just been cited have much in common with another set of "perverse" reactions to a change in price: those set in motion by a general inflation or deflation. If the general level of economic activity and the general level of prices are unstable, then it becomes impossible to treat each change in the price of a single commodity as an isolated phenomenon: producers and consumers will regard it as a symptom of a general trend and will base their response to it on their conception of the trend. Consumers will make purchases not because the price is what it is but because it is expected to go higher. A cut in prices may make consumers stop buying in the expectation of a further fall. The fear of general inflation may cause a run on the commodities most likely to become scarce or to increase sharply in price (for example, durable consumers' goods), while fears of deflation may make some commodities unsaleable and leave the demand for others (perishable goods, for example) unaffected. In conditions of instability and uncertainty of this kind, it is not possible to talk in terms of elasticity in the ordinary sense. The conception of elasticity presupposes a definite change in price without any *arrière-pensées* about further changes or about the whole conjuncture of events.

### Difficulties in the construction of demand and supply curves

The drawing of demand and supply curves is not always such a simple matter as the discussion so far might imply.[1] How, for example, can we draw a demand curve for motor-cars? What price are we to plot against the number of motor-cars being sold to the public? Should it be the price of Austins or Rolls Royces,

---

[1] The assumptions underlying the drawing of demand and supply curves will be examined in more detail below (Chapter 16).

of 10 h.p. or 90 h.p. cars, of second-hand cars "in working order," or brand-new models fitted with the latest gadgets? Or if we try to calculate an average price for the whole group, how are we to average a fall in the price of some models against a rise in the price of others if the sales of each model do not respond equally to a given change in price? These practical difficulties make it impossible to represent the state of demand for motor-cars with complete accuracy in a demand curve. A demand curve is intended to represent the demand for something uniform—for a commodity: but motor-cars are a group of commodities rather than a commodity. Inside the group are cars which, from the point of view of producer or consumer, are about as far removed from one another as a power-house is from a television set. Other "commodities" are just as heterogeneous. It is rare for the products of a large number of firms to be exactly alike, and it is correspondingly rare, therefore, for a demand curve to be possible that represents demand conditions exactly.

A supply curve may raise even greater difficulties. The curve is intended to show how much will be offered for sale at the market price. But what if there is no market price and each manufacturer can charge what he likes? Ford's do not first enquire after the price which their cars are fetching and then decide how many to sell. They try to make a market at a price which they fix themselves. They are willing to sell at that price far more cars than they are able to dispose of in practice; and if sales begin to increase, they are just as likely to lower as to raise the price of their cars. A supply curve of Ford motor-cars, therefore, cannot possibly be drawn.[1] It is also impossible to draw a supply curve of motor-cars in general. If we cannot tell how many cars a particular firm will offer for sale at any given price, we cannot tell how many cars will be offered for sale by the whole industry. The fact is that the drawing of a supply curve presupposes keen competition between a large number of firms, each taking the market price for granted and with no power to control it. There must be no trace of monopoly in the market—not even such limited monopoly as arises when firms make goods differing ever so slightly from the products of their competitors.

The apparatus of demand and supply curves must always be used guardedly. It suggests to many people a permanency in the state of demand and supply which is not in keeping with the facts: both demand and supply are in a constant state of flux. It suggests, too, that it is price, and price only, that keeps demand and supply in line with one another—that price-competition is the only

---

[1] It is, of course, quite possible to draw a cost curve of Ford motor-cars. But a cost curve and a supply curve are two quite different things. The first relates to the firm; it is a curve of costs (i.e., of the expense to which a firm is put in order to produce a given output). The second relates to the industry; it is a curve of supply prices (i.e., of prices, expectation of which will induce sellers to put a given quantity of their product on the market).

kind of competition. For many things, this is plainly not so. But, however one may question the legitimacy of drawing curves, they are an indispensable first step on the way to clear thinking about prices. The ladder may be rickety, and we may have to kick it out of the way later, but without it we will never reach the heights from which its shakiness becomes apparent.

# CHAPTER 15

# DEMAND

Prices are governed by supply and demand: that is, by cost on the one hand and utility on the other. The influence of cost on price is obvious enough, but not the influence of utility. What possible connection is there between the utility of water or of diamonds and their price? An answer to this question was put forward round about 1870 by three economists, each working independently of the others: Jevons in England, Walras in Switzerland, and Menger in Austria. The answer was based on a psychological generalisation—the Law of Diminishing Utility—on a new and very important conception—that of the margin—and finally on a logical distinction—the distinction between Total and Marginal Utility.

## The law of diminishing utility

The value which we set on a commodity—its utility—depends upon how much we already have of it. The more we have, the less importance we attach to a further addition to our consumption. If, for example, we have been smoking twenty cigarettes a day, we do not appreciate the offer of a free cigarette nearly so much as we should if our consumption had for some reason fallen to one cigarette a day. The utility of an additional cigarette, and hence (since cigarettes are all alike) of cigarettes in general, is less when we are smoking twenty cigarettes a day than when we are forced to content ourselves with one.

## The margin

Suppose now that cigarettes cost 3d. each. We are then faced with the problem, how many cigarettes to buy. We must weigh the satisfaction which we get from smoking cigarettes against the satisfaction which we might get by spending our money on other things. Each additional cigarette that we buy will have less and less utility, while each additional 3d. spent on cigarettes can be spared only at greater and greater sacrifice of other things. Ultimately our consumption of cigarettes must reach the point at which we are in doubt whether it is worth while to spend 3d. on another cigarette. We are then on the *margin of consumption* and the last cigarette which we think it just worth while to buy is the *marginal* cigarette. The margin is to be thought of as a boundary cutting off purchases which are worth while from purchases which are not. Some purchases will be well inside the boundary: we should never think of doing without at least one loaf of bread every week. Other purchases will be just as clearly beyond the boundary: we should never think it worth while to buy a hundred loaves of bread every week. On or near the boundary will be the purchases about which we hesitate—the fifth loaf of bread, the fourth packet of cigarettes, and so on. These are our marginal purchases.

The margin which bounds our consumption of any commodity is not fixed. A fall in the price of cigarettes will push the margin outwards towards purchases which were previously not worth while, but which become worth while at the lower level of prices. We may reject the twentieth cigarette as not worth 3d. and count the thirtieth cigarette well worth 2d. The margin is drawn tightly or loosely according as things are dear or cheap; it is a boundary that shifts to and fro as prices move up or down.

## Marginal utility and total utility

The total utility of a commodity is the utility of the whole amount which we are consuming at any given time; the marginal utility is the utility of the marginal unit—the unit which we think is least worth while to consume. The total utility will naturally increase with every addition to our consumption—unless we have already so much that further additions are a positive nuisance. The marginal utility will fall as our consumption increases since we shall be adding units which, in accordance with the law of diminishing utility, we appreciate less and less; as the margin of consumption is pushed outwards, utility at the margin, or marginal utility, falls. The total utility of a commodity measures the strength of our demand for the whole supply of it, the marginal utility measures the intensity with which we want a little more of it.

## The paradox of value explained

Let us apply this distinction to water and diamonds.

The total utility of water is infinite: it would be impossible to give up using water altogether. But the marginal utility of water is negligible: we are put to no great inconvenience by having to do without a single pailful of it; and if we were given an *extra* pailful after using as much water as we required, it would clearly have no utility whatsoever. On the other hand, if everyone had to do without diamonds, there would be no great hardship; the total utility of diamonds is small in comparison with the total utility of water. The utility of a single diamond is, however, quite appreciable. Diamonds are so scarce that one more or less can make a considerable difference to our enjoyment of life. It is for this reason that diamonds are extremely valuable while water is free. The intensity with which people want one more gallon of water bears no comparison with the intensity with which they want one more diamond.

## Marginal utility and price

The idea of marginal utility gives us the clue to the connection between utility and price. We find, in fact, that the price of any commodity is governed, on the side of demand, by its utility at the margin of consumption, i.e., by its marginal utility. Suppose, for example, that we are trying to decide how many cigarettes to smoke per week. The larger the number of cigarettes that we smoke, the less is the marginal utility of cigarettes, and the less, therefore, is the value that we set on an extra cigarette. But we cannot set one value on the last cigarette and a different value on the others. They are physically indistinguishable, and so of equal utility: and each costs exactly the same as the others. The price that we are prepared to pay for cigarettes, therefore, must be equal to the price of the last or *marginal* cigarette which we think it just worth while to buy. Now the price of the marginal cigarette is exactly balanced in our minds against its utility. The price of cigarettes in general must also be balanced, therefore, by the utility of the marginal cigarette. So we reach the important conclusion that the amount of any commodity which is purchased at a given price will tend to be such as to make the marginal utility of the commodity to each purchaser equal to its price. Demand operates so as to make marginal utility and price equal to one another.[1]

## Marginal uses

Cigarettes, from which the marginal principle has so far been illustrated, have normally only one use. Most commodities, however, have several different uses which can often be arranged in order of importance. If there is only a limited supply of the commodity, this supply will be reserved for the more important uses; as the commodity becomes more and more abundant, the less important uses will be provided for one by one. With any given supply, or at any given price, there will be some uses to which it is just worth while to put the commodity: these will be marginal uses. Suppose, for example, that the amount of water is so reduced that we need to economise it and are willing to pay a price for more. For the sake of concreteness, suppose that we are living in one of those primitive villages where the number of wells is small and the

---

[1] This reasoning assumes that the market price is fixed and that consumers have no bargaining power. The price of cigarettes will cease to be equal to their marginal utility if the purchase of an additional cigarette affects the terms on which the remainder can be purchased.

women draw water all day until at night the wells are dry. A shrinkage in the water supply will cause the margin of uses to which water is put to contract. First of all, people will be forced to give up using water for some comparatively unimportant purposes, e.g., washing floors. If more wells cease to give water, they may require to give up washing clothes and dishes, then faces and hands. Later they may have to ration drinking water. As the margin of uses to which water is put contracts, the utility of water in its marginal use mounts higher and higher. We are put to a greater and greater sacrifice by having to do without water first for one purpose, then for another. Conversely, the more water we have, the more trivial the uses to which we can afford to put it, and the less the price which we will be prepared to pay for more of it.

The utility of a commodity in that use which is just marginal tends, like marginal utility, to be equal to price. If the margin of consumption coincides with one particular use for the commodity, then utility in the marginal use is simply a special case of marginal utility. The price will be just sufficiently low to make this marginal use worth while, but sufficiently high to rule out uses of less importance to us. A fall in prices will cause the margin of uses to be pushed outwards; a rise in prices will make it press inwards again. Generally when a commodity becomes more plentiful, it is not only the margin of uses, but also the margin of consumption *in each use* that is pushed outwards. The margin is a boundary cutting each line of advance in consumption and not just a limiting point along one line. At all points on the boundary a marginal extension has a utility less than the price of the commodity, while a marginal contraction results in a sacrifice in utility greater than the price of the commodity. The margin is drawn round those units of the commodity which— whatever the use to which they are put—it is just worth while to buy.

## Marginal purchasers

Just as there are marginal purchases, so there are marginal purchasers. A book, for example, will find some buyers at 15s., a larger number at 10s., and a still larger number at 5s. At any given price, there will be some people who find the book just within their means. These are the marginal purchasers— people who are on the margin of doubt whether they should buy the book or spend the money on something else.

## Consumer's surplus or rent

The fact that some purchasers are marginal while others are not, means that intra-marginal purchasers enjoy a surplus or rent. A consumer who would be willing to pay 15s. for a book, will be 10s. in pocket if he finds that the market price is only 5s. In the same way, the fact that some purchasers are marginal while others are not, means that consumers enjoy a surplus on intra-marginal purchases. The marginal cigarette may be just worth 3d., but all the other cigarettes which we buy must, by the law of diminishing utility, be worth more. All cigarettes sell at the same price. If the marginal cigarette is just worth while, therefore, the other cigarettes must be more than worth while. They yield a surplus above their cost to their purchasers. Suppose, for example, that we have to choose between going without cigarettes altogether and paying a larger sum for our present consumption. Within limits, we should generally be willing to pay the larger sum. The difference between what we do pay and the maximum amount that we should be prepared to pay is our consumer's surplus on cigarettes.

### The practical importance of the margin

There is an old saying:—"Take care of the pence and the pounds will look after themselves." This is simply a vivid application of the marginal principle. Proper attention to the margin will help consumers to get the most out of their limited income. Suppose, for example, that a housewife takes with her to the fruit market a basket and a purse, meaning to empty her purse and fill her basket with fruit. How should she set about buying the best selection of fruit? Clearly, she must arrange her purchases so that she will not be better off if she spends more on one kind of fruit and less on another. This condition will be satisfied if the last pennyworth of oranges has the same utility as the last pennyworth of apples, bananas, and other fruits. Each addition to her consumption of oranges reduces the marginal utility of oranges and raises the marginal utility of other fruits since she has less money left over to spend on them. Her demand for oranges becomes less intense, while her demand for other fruit becomes more intense. At the margin where these two intensities just balance, the last penny which she spends on oranges has the same utility as the last penny spent on other fruits; she would be worse off by spending more on oranges and less on other fruits, or vice versa. Her money is spent to the best advantage (in the sense that her wants are most adequately satisfied) if she succeeds in equalising the marginal utility of money in each of its uses.

### The theoretical importance of the margin

Analysis in terms of margins has the great merit that it fixes attention on the behaviour of buyers who are in doubt whether to buy a *little* more or a *little* less. Now it is the decisions of thesepersons that have most in fluence on the amount bought and so on prices. Those to whom "price is no consideration," or who buy without inquiring what things cost are not the "key" buyers. They affect prices in the sense that if they did not buy, total demand would be less, and prices therefore, would be different; but they do not affect prices by boycotting what is dear and lining up where things are cheap. Their weight is thrown neither on the side of dearness nor of cheapness. It is to those who consider carefully what they can afford, who always ask the price, and constantly readjust their budget to stretch it to its furthest limits—to those, in other words, who, for whatever reasons, have an elastic demand—that we must look to keep down prices. Theirs are the marginal purchases which would cease to be made if prices rose. And it is at the margin that pressure on exchange values is exerted.

## The margin, elasticity, and substitution

The idea of the margin is closely related to an earlier conception—that of elasticity. It is at the margin, and only at the margin, that there is elasticity. It is marginal purchases that are discontinued, and marginal purchasers who cease to buy when prices rise. The more purchases and purchasers are marginal or near-marginal, the greater will be the elasticity of demand. The two ideas, indeed, are held together as in a vice by a third idea— substitution. Elasticity, as we have seen, depends largely on the range of substitutes; and all substitution is essentially marginal. Substitution takes place at the margin of consumption; as prices move up or down we try to substitute a little of one commodity for a little of another. The more successful we are, the more elastic is demand and the more readily does the margin shift in response to a change in price.

## The law of diminishing utility again

The ease with which the margin can be shifted depends upon the rate at which marginal utility is diminished. So we have come round again to the law from which we started—the law of diminishing (marginal) utility. This is the fundamental law of demand and merits more attention, therefore, than we have given to it so far.

Stated formally the law is that, other things remaining the same, an increase in a person's rate of consumption of a commodity reduces the intensity with which further increments are demanded—that is, reduces the utility of the commodity at the margin. This is a law of almost universal application. It can be applied not only to things like bread and butter, railway journeys, men's hats, and so on, but also to the lectures of economists, the speeches of politicians, and even the number of suspects in detective stories. There are, however, some important limitations to the law. First, other things must remain the same. Suppose, for example, that a man is drinking beer. Then if each successive half-pint is to have less and less utility he must drink his beer, the same brand of beer, in the same public-house, with the same cronies, and the same landlord to judge his sobriety. He is not allowed to go wandering about enjoying a continual change of *milieu*. Secondly, we must not be trying to make a collection of something. If our beer drinker gets it into his head that he must complete a tour of the local public-houses, then the law of *increasing* utility will apply, for each successive drink will bring him nearer to his goal. Thirdly, our income, or at least our consumption of *other* commodities must remain constant. The marginal utility of beer depends upon how much wine we can afford. Similarly, the marginal utility of bread would increase if we could no longer afford to buy scones, teabread, and other wheaten foodstuffs; the marginal utility of a visit to the cinema would be much higher if we could not afford a television set, or fuel and light for our living-room. Finally, we must not develop a craving. A man who takes to drinking beer may find his thirst growing by what it feeds on, so that the more he drinks the more he wants to drink. Here again we have increasing, instead of diminishing, utility; although since the man is no longer the same, so to speak, after drinking as he was before, it is a little difficult to decide for *whom* beer has increasing utility—the novice who took to drink or the drunkard with the craving for it.

## Other laws of demand

The psychology of desire is too complicated to be embraced within a single law. Of all aspects of human desire, satiability and love of variety are most relevant to economics; and both these aspects are expressed in the law of diminishing utility. But the law takes no account of other aspects of desire—the part played by impulse, for example. Again, it concerns only the form and not the content of our wants: in a full study of demand we should require to analyse the things that shape each of our wants and purchases—our love of power, our desire for a role in life, our fear of boredom or of social disapproval, the necessity to keep up with the Joneses, and so on. But an attempt to consider these motives and to reduce them to general laws of demand would take us much too far afield.

### AN ALTERNATIVE VERSION

The theory of marginal utility, even when it is stated in a simplified form, is difficult for students to understand. The word "utility" leads to constant confusion. First of all, "utility" is used in economics to mean "desiredness" or "strength of demand." But it is associated in people's minds with "usefulness" and "desirability." The result is that "utility" can be used to muddle up economic and ethical considerations. This was repeatedly done by Jevons, Edgeworth and others, and is still being done by professional economists. Students are to be excused, therefore, if they fall into a confusion which besets even the most wary. Secondly, the theory of marginal utility was worked out at a time when most economists were utilitarians[1] (hence the muddle of economics with ethics) and believed that utility was something quantitative. They spoke of a quantity of utility as they might have spoken of a pound of cheese. But it would be as reasonable to speak of a quantity of temperature. The fact is that we can only measure the intensity of one demand in terms of the intensity of another, and that, behind the screen of "utility," is exactly what the theory does—or should do.

If we remove the screen, what kind of theory are we left with? In its essentials the new theory is very much like the old. But it lays emphasis on the word "preference" instead of on the word "utility." Where we talked of "marginal utility" we now talk of "marginal preference."

### The margin: preferences

When we value an article we do so only in relation to the alternatives open to us—in relation, for example, to the available substitutes. Our values are the expression of a preference. Now these preferences may be absolute. We may detest cocoa and adore tea. If asked to choose between the two we may always plump for tea. This rules out one possible alternative to tea and narrows the field of choice. But there are still plenty of other alternatives where, just because our means are limited in comparison with our wants, we *cannot* have absolute preferences. We are forced to balance tea against these alternatives and to *modify* our preferences if the alternatives become less attractive or more attractive because of a rise or a fall in their price. Suppose that we group these alternatives together and call them, for short, "coffee." It may happen that if tea costs thrice as much as coffee, we give up drinking tea, while if coffee costs twice as much as tea, we give up drinking coffee. Within this range of prices we will probably drink both tea and coffee, but will vary the proportion in which we drink them so as to take advantage of changes in the relative price of tea and coffee. We may find it possible to draw up a schedule showing the various combinations in which, if our income remains fixed, we will drink tea and coffee at different price-ratios. The schedule may be something like the table on page 224.

This schedule illustrates three points. First, that we give up coffee for tea, the dearer coffee becomes in relation to tea. A change in price leads us to substitute the one for the other. Second, that the number of cups of coffee that we

---

[1] I.e., they measured the goodness of an action by its utility.

are willing to sacrifice for the sake of *one more* cup of tea decreases the more cups of tea we drink. Rather than do without our first three cups of tea, for instance,

| Price of tea / Price of coffee | Cups of tea | Cups of coffee |
|:---:|:---:|:---:|
| 3·0 | 0 | 50 |
| 2·5 | 3 | 41 |
| 2·0 | 5 | 37 |
| 1·5 | 9 | 30 |
| 1·25 | 14 | 23 |
| 1·0 | 21 | 15 |
| 0·75 | 35 | 3 |
| 0·5 | 40 | 0 |

we are prepared to give up 50—41 = 9 cups of coffee. Each cup of tea, to begin with, is worth three cups of coffee to us. But when we are already drinking 14 cups of tea, we are prepared to sacrifice no more than eight cups of coffee for seven more cups of tea—that is, a cup of coffee and a cup of tea are of much the same value to us. Thus we find it progressively harder to substitute a little more tea for a little less coffee, the more tea and the less coffee we are drinking already. Our preference for tea over coffee, *at the margin* where we have to balance a little more of one against a little less of the other, falls steadily. Given the amounts of tea and coffee that we are drinking, this "marginal preference" can be measured by the ratio in which we are prepared to sacrifice a small quantity of coffee for the sake of a little more tea. In the two examples given above, our marginal preference is approximately 3 and 1. Clearly our marginal preference is not the same thing as our general or total preference; just as marginal utility is not the same thing as total utility. We may prefer tea to coffee in the sense that we should prefer to do without coffee altogether rather than do without tea altogether. But we may simultaneously value an occasional cup of coffee twice as highly as our usual cup of tea. If a cup of coffee were to cost twice as much as a cup of tea, our general preference for tea would not necessarily prevent us from buying coffee now and again.

A third point illustrated by the schedule is that the relative price of tea and coffee and our marginal preference for one in terms of the other tend to equality with one another. When the price of tea is three times the price of coffee we should be prepared to sacrifice 9 cups of coffee for 3 cups of tea; when tea costs half as much as coffee, we should only be prepared to sacrifice 3 cups of coffee for 5 cups of tea. In other words as relative prices fall from 3·0 to 0·5, marginal preference falls from 3·0 to 0·6. The coincidence is not exact, but this is because the schedule is not sufficiently detailed, so that marginal preference has to be measured by taking comparatively large variations in our consumption of tea and coffee, instead of the small (really infinitesimal) variations assumed in pure theory. Why relative prices and marginal preference should tend to equality is not difficult to understand. Marginal preference measures the terms on which we are prepared to sacrifice a little of one commodity in order to obtain a little more of another. Relative prices measures the terms on which we *can obtain* (by exchange) a little more of one commodity by parting with a little of another. If the two are not equal, therefore—if our marginal preferences are out of line with relative prices—we must be overlooking an opportunity of gain. If, for example, a cigar can be had for the price of 10 cigarettes, and we count the satisfaction of one more cigar equal to the sacrifice of 12 cigarettes (i.e., if relative prices are in the ratio of 10 : 1, and our marginal preference is 12 : 1), then the purchase of another cigar in place of 10 cigarettes leaves us two cigarettes to the good. We will switch, therefore, from cigarettes to cigars until our marginal preference is brought into line with their relative price—until, in fact, we are indifferent whether or not we use the price of a cigar to buy cigarettes.

We modify our preferences, then, so as to bring them into line with prices. But this is only part of the truth. Prices are themselves pulled into line with our marginal preferences. Demand, as we saw above, not only responds to changes in price but helps to determine price. An increased supply of mutton, for example, will find a market only at a price which is low enough to encourage the substitution of mutton for other commodities (e.g., beef)—at a price, in other words, which is in keeping with people's preferences for mutton as compared with beef (and other alternatives) at the margin of choice. If marginal preferences are inelastic, then the fall in mutton prices will be heavy. But if marginal preferences are elastic (i.e., if a small change in relative prices is sufficient to cause a large switch-over in consumption) then the extra supply of mutton on the market will be absorbed without any drastic cut in prices.

Now marginal preferences will obviously be elastic if there are plenty of satisfactory substitutes. We will have no strong preference for a commodity if a wide range of alternatives is available, and we will be able to extend or contract our consumption of it whenever one of these alternatives becomes slightly dearer or slightly cheaper. The elasticity of our marginal preferences, therefore, just like the elasticity of demand, as defined above, depends upon the range of available substitutes. This is not surprising for elasticity of demand is just an example of elasticity of preference—the example *par excellence*. Suppose, for example, that we are measuring the elasticity of demand for butter. What

H

are we really doing is to weigh up our preference for a little more butter against the sacrifice of a little more money and to find out how elastic this preference is as the price of butter in terms of money changes. Money sums up all the alternatives to butter and not just a few, like margarine or jam. It stands for all the substitutes that we might buy if butter were to become dearer. Just as money is the common denominator of exchange, so elasticity of demand is the common denominator of elasticities of preference. We can convert all exchange values into money values; and in the same way we can convert our preference for one commodity as compared with another into our preference for each as compared with money.

If one price is high and another low, therefore, the conclusion to be drawn is, not that we prefer the first commodity to the second, but that we prefer *a little more* of the first to a *little more* of the second. The value that we set on commodities is governed by our preferences at the margin of choice, i.e., by our marginal preferences. If these preferences are inelastic, so that only a small proportion of our purchases are marginal, then comparatively small changes in supply will cause very large changes in prices. If, however, our preferences are elastic, so that a large proportion of our purchases are marginal, prices will be comparatively stable. The stability of prices depends upon the ease with which we can vary our demand to meet a change in the pressure of supply. It is at the margin that this change in pressure must be studied. The pressure of demand on prices depends upon our marginal preferences; the pressure of supply, as we shall see in the next chapter, depends upon marginal costs.

# CHAPTER 16

# SUPPLY: COST AND PRICE

In the last chapter we saw how the price of a commodity is governed on the side of demand, by the value that consumers set on marginal units of it. We have now to see that, on the side of supply, the price of a commodity is governed by the cost of producing marginal units of it. Just as we tried to go behind the demand curve in order to study the preferences of consumers, so we must now try to go behind the supply curve to the costs of producers. We shall find that the link between cost of production and price is much more complicated than the link between utility, or preference, and price. Cost of production is not nearly so simple a conception as it seems.

Cost controls supply in two ways. It controls the volume of output which each firm finds it profitable to produce, and it controls the number of firms that can carry on at a profit. If the cost of producing a commodity rises, other things remaining the same, the supply will contract for a double reason—first, because each firm will cease to manufacture units of output that no longer pay their way; and, second, because some firms will find it necessary, or advantageous, to abandon production of the commodity altogether. The rise in costs will press on supply at the margin—on units of output which it was just worth while for each firm to produce, and on firms which found it just worth while to carry on production of the commodity. Other (intra-marginal) units of output will continue to be supplied, and other (intra-marginal) firms will continue in business at the higher level of costs.

## Marginal cost

Thus it is marginal, rather than average, cost that controls supply. Marginal cost is the net cost of a marginal addition to output. This addition may be made either within the individual firm or through the entry of a new firm into the market. Marginal cost, therefore, can be used in two quite distinct senses. It can be used to mean the cost to any one firm of increasing its output by a single unit. Or it can mean average cost of production in that particular firm which just finds it worth while to continue production. Marginal cost in the first sense may be quite different from marginal cost in the second sense.

It might be supposed that just as price tends to be equal to marginal utility so price would tend to be equal to marginal cost (in one or other of the above senses). This supposition would be correct if it were possible to make assumptions about supply parallel to the assumptions that were made implicitly in our study of demand. We assumed a state of competition between consumers in which each bought only a small quantity of the total supply, had regard solely to his own interest, and had no power to influence prices. Consumers, that is, were supposed to take prices for granted, and to be able to buy as much as they wanted of any commodity at the ruling market price. These assumptions, which are not altogether unrealistic when applied to demand, are generally quite inappropriate when applied to supply. One producer very often sells a substantial proportion of the total supply; his competition with other firms may be limited by understandings or agreements; and his powers over prices may be far from negligible. Producers, that is, are rarely able to take prices for granted and sell as much as they please at the ruling price. They have to regulate their output so as to keep from forcing down prices and spoiling their market. Similarly, a new firm may be unable to find a market without incurring special selling costs (e.g., by advertising). It has to build up a connection and "make a market" for itself, instead of simply offering its goods for sale at current prices.

In the special circumstances in which competition between producers is similar to the competition which we supposed to exist between consumers, price and marginal cost (in both senses) will be equal. In those circumstances, competition will be "perfect," that is, no single consumer or producer will control a sufficiently large proportion of purchases or sales, or enjoy sufficient "pull" with his suppliers or customers, to be able to influence the market price. In all other circumstances, whether there is a monopoly in the ordinary sense or monopolistic competition of one kind or another, price will be above marginal cost. A clear understanding of these propositions is extremely important.

## Cost under perfect competition in the individual firm

We may begin by analysing the way in which cost and price are likely to be related, in conditions of perfect competition, within an individual firm. Let us assume that the firm is making a single commodity only and that, since it is by hypothesis able to sell as much as it can produce at the market price, it does not resort to advertising or any kind of sales pressure. These assumptions (which are obviously unrealistic) rule out a number of complications for which provision can be made later.

The Scribblo Propelling Pencil Company, Ltd.—to take a concrete example—is one of a large number of pencil manufacturers in keen competition with one another and the public likes its pencils as well as any. The price of pencils is 4d. and the company is wrestling with the problem: how many pencils should it produce and sell in order to maximise its profits. It calls for a report from its accountants and they, after delving into all the facts and figures and throwing in a few guesses here and there to supplement the facts, submit the following table:—

TABLE 8

COST OF PRODUCTION OF SCRIBBLO PENCILS

| Output (million pencils) | Fixed Cost (million pence) | Variable Cost (million pence) | Total Cost (million pence) | Average Cost (pence) | Marginal Cost (pence) |
|---|---|---|---|---|---|
| 0 | 6·0 | 0·0 | 6·0 | ∞ | |
| | | | | | 3·5 |
| 1 | 6·0 | 3·5 | 9·5 | 9·5 | |
| | | | | | 3·1 |
| 2 | 6·0 | 6·6 | 12·6 | 6·3 | |
| | | | | | 2·9 |
| 3 | 6·0 | 9·5 | 15·5 | 5·1 | |
| | | | | | 2·8 |
| 4 | 6·0 | 12·3 | 18·3 | 4·6 | |
| | | | | | 3·0 |
| 5 | 6·0 | 15·3 | 21·3 | 4·3 | |
| | | | | | 3·2 |
| 6 | 6·0 | 18·5 | 24·5 | 4·1 | |
| | | | | | 3·5 |
| 7 | 6·0 | 22·0 | 28·0 | 4·0 | |
| | | | | | 4·0 |
| 8 | 6·0 | 26·0 | 32·0 | 4·0 | |
| | | | | | 4·7 |
| 9 | 6·0 | 30·7 | 36·7 | 4·1 | |
| | | | | | 5·6 |
| 10 | 6·0 | 36·3 | 42·3 | 4·2 | |
| | | | | | 6·6 |
| 11 | 6·0 | 42·9 | 48·9 | 4·4 | |

The accountants have divided Scribblo's costs into two elements: one, representing "overheads," is fixed and does not vary with output; the other, representing the cost of labour, materials, and so on, increases as output increases. If the total cost at each successive level of output is averaged over the total output, it falls at first because of the element of fixed costs, which drags down the average. At a later stage, average cost begins to increase, for example because Scribblo's are working to capacity and having to pay overtime rates of pay.[1]

### Diagram 8
#### The Cost of Production of Pencils

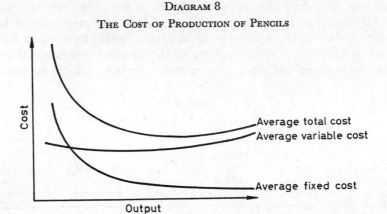

The relation between fixed, variable and total costs is illustrated in Diagram 8. Fixed costs per unit of output take the shape of a rectangular hyperbola; variable costs per unit of output fall gently until capacity is approached and then begin to rise; total costs per unit of output (i.e., average costs) fall steeply at first but eventually begin to increase.

### Marginal and average cost

Marginal cost of production is shown in the last column of Table 8. Marginal cost is the net cost of a marginal addition to output. To be more precise, it is the increment in aggregate costs when output is increased by one unit; or alternatively, it is the expense that could be avoided by reducing output by one unit.[2] The column headed "Marginal Cost," therefore, is derived from the

---

[1] Even if Scribblo's were a new firm and had not yet installed its plant, its costs would show the same kind of variations. At first it would enjoy the benefit of economies of large-scale production and the larger the scale of production on which it decided, the lower would be its costs. There would come a point, however, at which a larger scale of production meant higher costs, either because the business was too large for efficient management or because output began to press on the supply of some scarce factor of production. If more workers were needed, for example, it might be necessary to offer higher wages so as to attract them from other districts and other trades, or alternatively to take on workers of less than average skill. For a fuller discussion, see Chapter 18.

[2] These two things are not necessarily identical. As a rule the difference will be insignificant. But if, before output can be increased further, a change has to be made in the organisation of the firm, or in the layout of the plant, or in the machinery in use, there will be a discontinuous change in costs at that level of output. The net cost of an extra unit of output may then be much higher than the savings resulting from a cut in output by one unit. An additional complication is introduced by the time factor since the savings that result from a fall in output for a few weeks are very different from the savings that could be made if the reduction in output were for an indefinite period.

column headed "Total Cost" by taking the increment in total costs as output rises from one level to the next. Strictly speaking, it should be calculated on the basis of infinitely small variations in output; but for practical purposes we can take the extra cost of producing one million pencils more, and divide the result by one million in order to obtain the marginal cost of a pencil at the level of output assumed. Marginal cost, as appears from Diagram 9, is at first below

DIAGRAM 9

AVERAGE COST, MARGINAL COST AND PRICE OF PENCILS

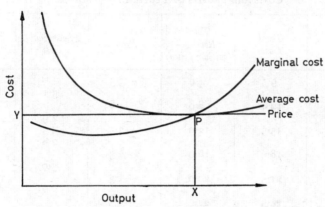

average cost. The main reason for this is that marginal cost includes no element of fixed cost whereas average cost does. Even if fixed cost is left out of account, however, marginal cost will be below average *variable* cost so long as both are falling: the greater economy of making one more unit has a proportionately smaller impact on average than on marginal cost since it has to be averaged over the whole output. Eventually, marginal cost begins to rise; but so long as it remains below average cost (i.e., so long as each additional unit costs less than the average) average cost continues to fall. When marginal cost exceeds average cost (i.e., when each additional unit costs more than the average) average cost rises too. When marginal cost is exactly equal to average cost, average cost is neither rising nor falling but is at the turning point where it touches bottom. Thus the marginal cost curve in Diagram 9 intersects the average cost curve at its minimum point.

## Marginal cost and price

Now the interesting thing is that this is also the point at which Scribblo's will make their maximum profit. Profit will be at a maximum if price and marginal cost are equal. If the price were above marginal cost, it would be possible to make an additional profit by putting on the market pencils that would add more to total sales proceeds than to total costs. If the price were below marginal cost, some units of output would not be paying their way; by ceasing to produce them Scribblo's could reduce their costs faster than their revenue. It is easy to test this by hypothetical examples. It emerges also from Table 9, although in a rather curious way:—

TABLE 9

COSTS AND PROFITS OF PENCIL MANUFACTURE

| Output (million pencils) | Total Cost | Total Revenue (million pence) | Profit | Marginal Cost | Price |
|---|---|---|---|---|---|
| 1 | 9·5 | 4·0 | —5·5 | | 4 |
| | | | | 3·1 | |
| 2 | 12·6 | 8·0 | —4·6 | | 4 |
| | | | | 2·9 | |
| 3 | 15·5 | 12·0 | —3·5 | | 4 |
| | | | | 2·8 | |
| 4 | 18·3 | 16·0 | —2·3 | | 4 |
| | | | | 3·0 | |
| 5 | 21·3 | 20·0 | —1·3 | | 4 |
| | | | | 3·2 | |
| 6 | 24·5 | 24·0 | —0·5 | | 4 |
| | | | | 3·5 | |
| 7 | 28·0 | 28·0 | — | | 4 |
| | | | | 4·0 | |
| 8 | 32·0 | 32·0 | — | | 4 |
| | | | | 4·7 | |
| 9 | 36·7 | 36·0 | —0·7 | | 4 |
| | | | | 5·6 | |
| 10 | 42·3 | 40·0 | —2·3 | | 4 |

If the price of pencils is 4d., Scribblo's can just cover their costs when they are producing between 7 and 8 million pencils but with any larger or any smaller production they will make a loss. At this level of output, price, marginal cost and average cost are all equal; Scribblo's costs are at a minimum; and they are maximising their profits.

## Average cost and price

Is this a coincidence? Does it mean that Scribblo's will close their doors and wait until their accountants come back with a new set of curves that obey a different geometry? Not a bit of it. The situation results directly from the assumption of perfect competition. For this implies that if pencil manufacturers make more than what we may call a "competitive" or "normal" profit, more firms will start to manufacture pencils and by their competition force down prices and profits to a "normal" level. This so-called "normal" profit is really part of cost of production since it is the minimum return that would induce Scribblo's (or a similar firm) to undertake the production of pencils. If the accountants have done their work correctly, therefore, the average cost of production already includes an indispensable provision for "normal" profits. Average cost in this sense may be equal to price, and under perfect competition it cannot remain for any length of time below price, except in firms with some outstanding advantage over their competitors. But if price and average cost are equal and at the same time price and marginal cost are equal, average and marginal cost must also be equal and this condition is fulfilled only when average cost is at a minimum.

This rather involved reasoning and the conclusion to which it leads help to explain why economists are inclined to use perfect competition as a yardstick and to regard its outcome as an economic ideal. If perfect competition forces firms to produce at minimum cost and with no more than a "normal" profit, it is certainly a highly desirable state of affairs; and even it it is impossible to create conditions of perfect competition it may be possible to borrow some of the rules that apply under perfect competition and try to make use of those rules in running a nationalised industry or in fixing prices.

## Monopoly costs and prices

Let us now abandon the assumption of perfect competition and go to the other extreme. Suppose that Scribblo's produce a unique kind of pencil and that they have no competitors. This will mean that there is no established market price that they can take as given. They will have to decide both how much to produce and how much to change; in addition to drawing a cost curve they will have to draw a demand curve. Under perfect competition the demand curve for Scribblo's output (whatever the shape of the demand curve for pencils in general) is perfectly elastic; it is represented in Diagram 9 by a horizontal straight line drawn through the price. Under monopoly the demand curve will be like the demand curve for any commodity, falling from left to right.

Let us assume that their costs are as before and that the demand schedule for their pencils is as given in Table 10. The demand schedule shows an inelastic demand for Scribblo pencils up to 6d. and an elastic demand at higher prices. If Scribblo's wanted to get the maximum *revenue* from the sale of their pencils they would charge 6d. But it is the excess of revenue over costs that they want to maximise, and this maximum is reached when the price is somewhat between 7d. and 8d.

H*

If it were possible to consider smaller variations in price we could narrow down the difference until it was negligible and so arrive at *the* price yielding maximum profit to the monopolist.

TABLE 10

DEMAND FOR SCRIBBLO PENCILS

| Quantity (millions) | Price (pence) | Total Revenue (million pence) | Marginal Revenue (pence) |
|---|---|---|---|
| | | | 12 |
| 1 | 12 | 12 | |
| | | | 8 |
| 2 | 10 | 20 | |
| | | | 7 |
| 3 | 9 | 27 | |
| | | | 5 |
| 4 | 8 | 32 | |
| | | | 3 |
| 5 | 7 | 35 | |
| | | | 1 |
| 6 | 6 | 36 | |
| | | | —1 |
| 7 | 5 | 35 | |
| | | | —3 |
| 8 | 4 | 32 | |
| | | | —5 |
| 9 | 3 | 27 | |
| | | | —7 |
| 10 | 2 | 20 | |
| | | | —9 |
| 11 | 1 | 11 | |

## Price and marginal revenue

Under perfect competition the position of maximum profit is one in which price and marginal cost are equal; under monopoly it is one in which marginal revenue and marginal cost are equal. Marginal revenue is the net revenue obtained from the sale of a marginal addition to output: it is the increment in aggregate receipts when one more unit is sold or the reduction in aggregate receipts when one unit less is sold. If Scribblo's (or any other firm) are producing on the scale of output at which their profits are maximised, an increase or decrease in output by one unit must leave profits lower than before. In other words, a marginal addition to output will increase aggregate costs by more than it increases aggregate revenue, while a marginal reduction in output will save less in cost than it sacrifices in revenue. Marginal cost cannot be above marginal revenue unless at least one unit of output is not paying its way; nor can it be below marginal revenue or there will be an extra profit to be made by making and selling at least one more unit of output. Marginal cost and marginal revenue must, therefore, be equal when profits are a maximum.

TABLE 11

COSTS AND PRICES OF SCRIBBLO PENCILS

| Price (pence) | Total Revenue (million pence) | Total Costs (million pence) | Surplus of Revenue over Cost (million pence) | Marginal Revenue (pence) | Marginal Cost (pence) |
|---|---|---|---|---|---|
| 12 | 12 | 9·5 | 2·5 | 12 | 3·5 |
| 10 | 20 | 12·6 | 7·4 | 8 | 3·1 |
| 9 | 27 | 15·5 | 11·5 | 7 | 2·9 |
| 8 | | | | | |
| | 32 | 18·3 | 13·7 | 5 | 2·8 |
| 7 | 35 | 21·3 | 13·7 | 3 | 3·0 |
| 6 | 36 | 24·5 | 11·5 | 1 | 3·2 |
| 5 | 35 | 28·0 | 7·0 | —1 | 3·5 |
| 4 | 32 | 32·0 | — | —3 | 4·0 |
| 3 | 27 | 36·7 | —9·7 | —5 | 4·7 |

The relationships between marginal and average cost, and marginal and revenue average (i.e., price) are illustrated in Diagram 10. The demand curve slopes down steeply and the marginal revenue curve even more steeply, cutting the X axis at the point where elasticity becomes more than unity.[1] The cost curves are the same as in Diagram 9. The surplus of revenue over costs is represented by a rectangle which has a maximum area in the position PQRS. This is the position in which marginal revenue is equal to marginal cost. Average cost is higher, and price higher still.

In Diagram 10 the curve of marginal revenue is consistently below the demand curve; marginal revenue is lower than price. The reason for this is that any attempt to increase the sale of pencils involves a reduction in price and this reduction applies to all pencils, not just to those which are bought because of

[1] As elasticity and slope are often confused it should be observed that in Diagram 10 the demand curve has a constant slope throughout almost all its length while demand changes from being inelastic to being elastic. The slope measures the ratio of an absolute change in demand to an absolute change in price; elasticity measures the ratio of two *percentages* changes.

the cut in price. The pencils previously disposed of at the higher price bring in less revenue than before, and this loss of revenue has to be deducted from the price of the additional pencils that are sold before we arrive at the net increase

DIAGRAM 10

PRICE UNDER MONOPOLY

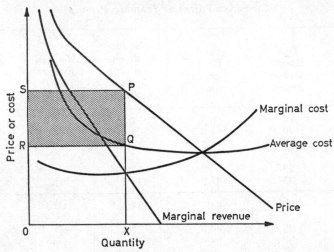

in total revenue, or marginal revenue. Marginal revenue, that is, must fall short of price by an amount equal to the concession that has to be made to existing buyers to extend sales. This concession is great if demand is inelastic and small if demand is elastic.[1]

---

[1] If the demand curve is represented by $P = f(X)$, then marginal revenue is equal to

$$\frac{d\,(PX)}{dX}$$

$$= P + X \frac{dP}{dX}$$

$$= P \left( 1 + \frac{X}{P} \cdot \frac{dP}{dX} \right)$$

But elasticity of demand $\qquad = -\frac{P}{X} \cdot \frac{dX}{dP}$

Hence marginal revenue $\qquad = P - \frac{P}{E}$

and the excess of price over marginal revenue will be the greater, at a given level of price and output, the less is the elasticity of demand.

## Perfect competition as a limiting case

When competition is perfect, the difference between marginal revenue and price disappears. Increased sales can be made without any need to cut the price and so make a concession from which existing buyers gain. The demand for Scribblo pencils, under perfect competition, is perfectly elastic and the demand curve and marginal revenue curve coincide in a horizontal straight line drawn through the market price. The rule that marginal revenue and marginal cost are equal when firms are earning their maximum profit will still hold: but since price and marginal revenue will, for once, be equal, price and marginal cost will also be equal—as we discovered earlier. Perfect competition is thus a limiting case to which the more general rule still applies.

## A measure of monopoly

We can, indeed, take the ratio of price to marginal revenue as an index of the degree of monopoly or competition in any market. The nearer the two approach equality with one another, the more nearly "perfect" is competition and the less power of monopoly does a firm enjoy. The ratio of the two is governed by the elasticity of demand for the product of the firm.[1] Elasticity in turn is governed by the range of available substitutes. But these substitutes are simply the most closely competing products. So we arrive at the conclusion that the ratio of price to marginal revenue is a measure of the force of competition.

But this ratio, if the firm is maximising its profits, will be the same as the ratio of price to marginal cost. Apart from the introduction of the word "marginal," this is not a very novel conclusion. We all think of a monopolist as someone who can charge more than the cost of production for his goods. What the argument of this chapter shows is that the more a firm is able to use monopoly power in fixing its price, the higher, in general, will the price be in relation to (marginal) cost; and conversely, the more competition approaches "perfection," the narrower will be the divergence between price and (marginal) cost.

## Price and average cost in a competitive industry

Up till now the discussion has been focused on the individual firm with occasional glances at the industry as a whole. But since output can vary either because of changes within existing firms or because of the entry of new firms into the industry there is a second type of marginal addition to output to be considered and a second meaning to be attached to marginal cost. There are

---

[1] Notice that we are talking about the demand for the product of a *firm*, not, as in Chapter 14, about the demand for a *commodity* (i.e., the product of an industry or group of firms competing with one another). For example, we are discussing the demand for Scribblo pencils, not for pencils in general.

marginal *firms*; and marginal cost may be used to mean the average cost of production in a marginal firm.

An industry is generally made up of firms varying widely in profitability. Some firms earn high profits because of the superior judgment or organising ability of the management, others because their plant is well laid out and up to date, others because they have access to a large market or to cheap raw materials, and others again because of the skill or energy of the workers whom they employ. On the other hand, some firms earn comparatively low profits because they lack these advantages. In coal-mining, for example, there is a wide range of profits between one pit and another according to the depth of the coal seams from the surface; the thickness of the seams; the chemical composition of the coal; the presence or absence of water or gas; and a hundred other factors. Some pits rarely make losses while others rarely make profits.

The firms in the industry which we take to be marginal are those which, over a period of years, earn a profit just sufficient to induce them to remain in the industry. This minimum profit—which may be high or low—is really an element in the costs of these firms. A firm which has no prospect of earning a reasonable profit will ultimately close down, just as a man who sees no prospect of earning a wage commensurate with his abilities will ultimately seek employment elsewhere; the firm will have failed to cover its total costs.

Thus a marginal firm is one whose average costs (including "normal" profits in the sense of the minimum profit discussed above) are just covered by price. If the price falls, marginal producers will be squeezed out and a new group of firms will find themselves on the margin of production. If the price rises, the margin will be pushed back as more firms find it worth while to come into the industry. The pressure of a change in demand and in price will cause the margin of production to shift inwards to firms whose costs are lower or outwards to include firms with higher costs of production. At a given level of demand the price will tend to equality with the average cost of production of the marginal producer. Other firms, in receipt of the same price, and producing at lower cost, will be able to earn a surplus profit—a profit higher than would suffice to keep them in the industry.

At any given moment, of course, price may fall below marginal cost. It is only over a period of years, averaging profits against losses, that the marginal producer will look for a certain minimum balance of profit. This makes it difficult and sometimes impossible to identify the marginal firms in an industry. We cannot always pick on the firms which are making the smallest profits or the biggest losses, for the firms which are making losses now may survive to make large profits in the future. They may, for example, be young and growing firms which have not yet solved their problems of organisation and marketing, but are on the way to a solution. Even if they are firms which are certain to go out of business sooner or later, we may still hesitate to call them marginal firms. We may know that at current prices there will be a constant succession of firms which will take their place with no more success—that it is a normal feature of the industry, in fact, that there should be some firms in it which cannot show a profit at all, even in good times. Such firms are not marginal, but sub-marginal; their costs are higher than the costs of marginal firms, and will not be covered by price, even in the long run.

It must not be supposed that marginal firms are necessarily the least efficient firms. It may happen, for example, that some firms are efficient in manufacturing a number of different lines of product and that they are ready to abandon any one line whenever it is less remunerative than the others. A farmer may grow wheat, barley and potatoes at low cost and yet be a marginal wheat farmer because the profit which he makes from his wheat is barely enough to keep him from giving up wheat-growing in favour of barley- or potato-growing. He is on the margin of transference between wheat and other agricultural products.

Price, then, tends to be equal to the average cost of marginal producers and to exceed the average cost of other producers in proportion to any special advantages which they enjoy.

**Price and average cost under monopoly**

It might be thought that all this ceases to apply when we are dealing with a firm in a position of monopoly. So long as the monopoly lasts there can be no newcomers, and the only limit to the monopolist's profit is set by the elasticity of demand for his goods and the pressure of public opinion. In practice, however, so absolute a monopoly is rare. New firms could and would compete if the price were sufficiently attractive. But they are generally under a handicap of some kind in entering the monopolist's market—for example, they might have to go to a great deal of expense in developing a substitute and to more expense in advertising it. There is, so to speak, a cost of entry into the market and within the limits of this cost, the monopolist can raise his price without fear of competition. Looked at in this way, most monopolists are in the same position as other firms. They have potential competitors who can be regarded as marginal; and the monopoly price cannot be raised above the expected average cost of those competitors including the cost of overcoming any handicap or restriction on entry into the monopolist's market.

Although the tendency of monopoly is to raise prices above costs, this does not imply that prices under monopoly must be higher than under competition. The costs of the monopolist may be so far below the costs of the competing firms which might replace him that his price also is lower than theirs would be.

In short, the tendency of competition is to reduce prices to equality with cost—with the marginal cost of each firm, and with the average cost of a marginal firm. The tendency of monopoly is to raise prices above cost and profits above normal. In the modern world we generally meet with a mixture of competition and monopoly. There are substitutes, but not perfect substitutes, for each firm's products, and there is generally a threat of competition from newcomers.

### The logic and the facts: full-cost pricing

Many business men, comparing the logic of the foregoing argument with their everyday experience, would be inclined to dismiss the argument as academic. Few of them have heard either of marginal cost or of marginal revenue. Only a proportion of them have the costing machinery necessary for the estimation of average, still fewer for the estimation of marginal cost. Even if costing were in universal use, it would in many industries be extremely difficult to apply it to the estimation of marginal cost, while marginal revenue must almost always be a matter of guesswork. In many industries the usual procedure is to fix a price on the basis of average direct costs in labour and materials plus an allowance for overheads. This allowance is worked out so as to cover average fixed costs, not at the capacity level of output at which the plant was designed to operate, but at a rather lower level (say 80 per cent. of capacity) which takes into account fluctuations in activity and is treated as normal or standard for the purpose of costing. Sometimes the procedure is less elaborate: retail prices, for example, are often arrived at by adding a customary percentage margin to the wholesale price, irrespective of actual selling costs; and in manufacturing industry, firms may use a similar method, adding a uniform percentage mark-up above direct costs for a wide variety of products without any accurate assessment of the fixed costs attributable to each.

Both of those procedures are usually referred to as "full-cost pricing" and they are frequently cited as evidence of the disdain with which economists treat the elementary facts of business life. The economist on the other hand is sceptical about the "facts" because they carry the logical implication that the business man, almost as a matter of principle, charges less than he might. The way to make as big a profit as possible is to charge, not on the basis of cost, but what the market will bear; this means varying the price with *demand* on the one hand and *marginal* cost on the other, not deliberately ignoring both. How are we to reconcile the logic and the apparent facts?

(i) Businesses may be reluctant to vary traditional margins because they are influenced by long-term considerations. They may fear the entry of new competitors that would result from exploiting an active market and feel that it would do none of the existing firms in the market any good to cut margins below the long-term norm in the middle of a slump. On this interpretation, margins and mark-ups are based, not on the costs of existing firms, but on the long-run costs of potential entrants.

(ii) Margins do in fact vary. Firms are prepared to discriminate (which is inconsistent with full-cost pricing), to shade their prices in order to get a contract or meet competition, to throw a large share of fixed costs onto items in which competition is relatively feeble, and so on. Even when they work out their standard costs, they have to take account of demand factors in deciding what level of output to treat as normal, and after establishing the "full cost" of their product, they may and do decide from time to time to charge less for it.

(iii) Not only do margins vary, but costs vary. If prices are fixed on a cost basis, how can firms with different costs end by charging the same price? Yet in competitive markets, this is what happens.

(iv) The use of a fixed margin is not inconsistent with maximising profits if it saves a great deal of trouble. In a firm turning out a large number of different products for a variety of constantly changing markets it would be a very formidable undertaking to work out a price appropriate to each transaction on anything except a simple and uniform basis. Pricing would be a very arbitrary affair if, for everything that was sold, a guess had to be made as to the maximum that could safely be charged; there could be no standard price-list, no guarantee that the same price would always be charged for the same commodity. It might be wiser to make prices some multiple of direct costs, varying the multiplier to suit general market conditions.

(v) Marginal and average cost in some industries lie close together. This is so, for example, in an industry like motor-car manufacture where a large proportion of unit cost is represented by bought-in materials and components while fixed costs, although large in the absolute, are relatively small as a proportion of unit cost. Marginal cost, moreover, is often almost constant between, say, 70 per cent. and 100 per cent. of capacity. In these circumstances, it would require a large change in demand to make prices alter perceptibly whether they were based on marginal or "full" cost; and the price changed on the one basis would be fairly close to the price charged on the other.

These considerations suggest that the business man may not be so illogical nor the economist so inobservant after all. The behaviour of prices and costs differs from one market to another, and what is true in one market is not true in another. It would be a mistake, therefore, to think that the few simple propositions to which this chapter has been devoted provide an adequate clue to the complexities of cost and market structure throughout industry; but they take us a little way along the road.

# CHAPTER 17

# MONOPOLY AND COMPETITION

The average man draws a sharp distinction between monopoly and competition. Under monopoly, he thinks, someone has complete, or at least substantial, control over the whole supply of a commodity; whereas under competition the commodity is supplied by several independent firms. This distinction is satisfactory only if we can draw a hard and fast line between one commodity and another. A monopolist, we say, is selling something different from other people. But how different? Must the difference be as great as that between milk and tea, or can it be as small as that between milk from one farm and milk from another, or between one brand of tea and another? Are we to call Bovril and Oxo and Camp Coffee commodities and their manufacturers monopolists? If a single firm supplies us with 8 h.p. motor-cars while other firms confine themselves to higher-powered cars, is the first firm a monopolist? The more we reflect, the more we are driven to conclude that practically every firm is in some sense a monopolist. Everywhere in business, firms are selling a product which is differentiated in style, brand, quality, package, size, etc., from the products of other firms. Each firm constantly lays stress on the uniqueness of *its* product, insisting that it is not only better but different from other products. Even where no obvious physical difference exists, firms try by advertisement to create the conviction that there is a real difference. They try also by the offer of special services to make it more convenient for customers to deal with them rather than with competitors. In a wide variety of ways, firms seek to insulate themselves from competition by creating a special market in which their goods are preferred to others. They are able to bind customers to themselves in such a way that they will neither lose all their custom if they change a price appreciably higher than elsewhere, nor gain a very large number of new customers by charging a price appreciably lower. Their discretion in fixing prices is generally limited, and prices tend to be in broad correspondence with prices in other parts of the market. But the fact that firms have any power at all over prices is proof that they have acquired powers of monopoly within their special market.

The fact is that we never find monopoly undiluted by competition, and very rarely find competition undiluted by monopoly. In most lines of business there is a blend of competition and monopoly in which one or the other may preponderate. The difference between monopoly and competition is one of degree, not of kind.

### Elements of competition under monopoly

Competition is fundamentally the offer of a substitute; monopoly is fundamentally the absence of substitutes. But there can never be an entire absence of substitutes. So long as our purchasing power is limited, everything on which we might be induced to spend our money is in a sense a substitute for everything else that we buy. If any one commodity becomes more expensive we can always give up using it and substitute some other commodity. We may continue to satisfy the same want if there are close substitutes (e.g., margarine for butter), or we may be driven to satisfy some quite different want so that the substitution becomes very roundabout (e.g., we may buy a book instead of going to the cinema). What we obviously cannot do is to go on buying a constant amount of any one commodity, however high its price.

Even if competition within an industry is suppressed, therefore, the monopolised product has still to face the competition of other industries. Indeed, such competition as survives nowadays is more and more between industries and less and less between firms within an industry. As monopoly grows, prices are arrived at through bargains between organised industries, and the common interests of the firms in each industry come into open conflict with the interests of the allied firms in other industries. A particularly striking example of the change in the arena of competition from the firm to the industry was provided by those pre-war joint advertising campaigns in which one industry appealed to us to Eat More Fruit, a second to Eat More Bread, a third to Eat More Fish, a fourth to Eat More Margarine, and a fifth to Eat More Butter—invitations which were obviously competitive, since the more heartily we fell in with one the less our ability (in appetite and in purse) to fall in with the others.

The competition with which a monopolist is faced comes not only from other products already on the market but also from *potential* substitutes that might be made available to consumers if prices were to rise. High prices may drive consumers to devise new substitutes for the monopolised goods or tempt new firms to enter into competition with the monopolist. Such potential competition will tend to keep prices down, since the monopolist will have no wish to invite it and will have no confidence in his ability to meet it if he has lost the goodwill of his customers by overcharging.

The power of monopolists over prices, therefore, is limited by the competition of substitutes, actual or potential—in other words, by the elasticity of demand for the monopolist's product. The more elastic the demand, the more closely will price and (marginal) cost approximate to one another. The less elastic the demand, the greater will be the power of the monopolist, and the more excessive the price which he is able to charge. So we return to the conclusions reached in Chapter 16. Every producer is more or less of a monopolist; and every producer will maximise his profits by equating marginal revenue and marginal cost. The more of a monopolist he is, the less elastic will be the demand for his produce; the greater, therefore, will be the ratio of price to marginal revenue; and the greater, finally, will be the ratio of price to marginal cost.

## Perfect competition

Perfect monopoly—unlimited control over the market price of a commodity—does not exist; perfect competition—competition purged of every element of monopoly—is rare, but it can exist. For competition in a commodity to be perfect, each individual buyer and seller of the commodity must regard the market price as entirely beyond his control. Buyers will have no incentive to restrict their purchases for the sake of driving down the price; sellers will have no incentive to restrict output or withhold supplies for the sake of maintaining or raising the price. Each buyer or seller will form his own judgment of the probable course of prices and will treat the price which he anticipates as unaffected by his individual purchases or sales.

Perfect competition on the side of buyers is common enough. The average housewife, competing with millions of other housewives, could not conceivably, by the impact of her purchases, budge the price of staple commodities. On the side of supply, examples of perfect competition are much harder to find. Wheat is one: the wheat farmer in the Middle West is hardly likely to hesitate about growing a few bushels more or less for fear of upsetting prices in the Chicago wheatpit. Gold is another example: the goldminer is unlikely to be afraid of spoiling his market by despatching an extra ounce or two of gold to London. Even in wheat and gold, however, competition is not altogether perfect. The price of wheat is greatly influenced by the operations of wheat pools, storage schemes, and so on, all of which introduce elements of monopoly into the market. The price of gold depends mainly on the willingness of a single buyer, the Federal Reserve Board to go on paying $35 an ounce to have gold dug up, and several million dollars to have it buried again. Thus it is only from the point of view of the individual farm or mine that competition in wheat and gold is perfect.

When there is perfect competition, price ceases to be above marginal cost. Each firm can sell freely as much as it chooses without fear of spoiling its market;

it can treat the demand for its product as perfectly elastic. If the firm tries to increase its sales, the additional supply put on the market is negligible in comparison with the total supply, and the fall in price, therefore, is so small that it does not enter into the firm's calculations. Price and marginal revenue are then necessarily equal, since each additional unit sold adds its full price to the total revenue of the firm; and if the firm is successful in equating marginal revenue and marginal cost, so as to maximise its profits, price and marginal cost must also be equal.

Perfect competition can be regarded, therefore, as the limiting case of imperfect or monopolistic competition. The more nearly competitive conditions approach "perfection," the closer to unity will be the ratio of price to marginal cost: the greater the deviation towards monopoly the further will price rise above marginal cost. How do these deviations arise?

### Elements of monopoly

Perfect competition pre-supposes two conditions; a large number of competing sellers and a perfect market. The first condition is easy enough to understand, but the second is less obvious. A perfect market is one in which buyers have no preferences as between the different units of the commodity offered for sale, sellers are quite indifferent to whom they sell, and both buyers and sellers have full knowledge of prices in other parts of the market. If markets were perfect, each firm would have to face the competition of products which were not only physically interchangeable with its own but which were considered by consumers to be perfect substitutes in every way. No firm would be able to charge more than the market price without losing the whole of its custom to its competitors, while no firm could charge less than the market price, since if it were to quote lower prices than its competitors, consumers would at once transfer their custom to it and other firms would be forced to come into line. There not only would be but *could* be only one price throughout the market.

The markets of the real world are rarely perfect. Firms seek to shelter themselves from competition by creating or supplying a special market in which they enjoy the goodwill of their customers. The existence of goodwill, however, is incompatible with the requirements of a perfect market since it rests on consumers' preferences for the goods of a particular seller. The number of firms competing with one another is also, as a rule, limited. If competition is restricted to a small number of firms the situation is described technically as oligopoly, just as when there is a single seller it is described as monopoly. The normal situation in business is one of market imperfection combined with oligopoly. In motor-car manufacturing, for example, the Big Five produce nearly all the smaller cars but do not make exactly the same model of car.

Even in the textile industry, where the number of firms is legion, it will often be found that a particular product like bath towels or West of England woollen flannel comes mainly from a small group of firms, each with its own specialities.

Although market imperfection and oligopoly are generally combined, they are analytically distinct.

**1   Oligopoly**—If there are only a few firms competing in a perfect market, and there are no understandings or agreements between them, we have a situation of pure oligopoly. Each firm, therefore, will have an interest in restricting production for fear of forcing down prices; or alternatively, each firm will have an interest in refraining from cutting prices, for fear other firms retaliate. Village butchers, for example, may keep up the retail price of mutton while the wholesale price is falling; each knows that if he takes the lead the others will follow suit, leaving profits lower all round.

Oligopoly is rarely "pure"; it is nearly always combined with market imperfection. When there are no more than two or three competitors they have their own special market and are in keen competition only for "marginal" customers. The village butchers, for example, have each their own clientele, which may melt away gradually if it suspects overcharging but normally provides a firm nucleus for the butcher's business every week. Frequently oligopoly is combined with specialisation within the market: if there are only two firms, for example, one may sell goods of high quality while the other sells standardised goods of lower quality.

**2   Market imperfection**—There are a number of reasons why markets are imperfect. First of all, there are imperfections due to ignorance. Buyers and sellers may be ill-informed about the terms on which dealings are proceeding elsewhere. Consumers, for example, generally know the price charged in a limited range of shops only, and buy from their regular suppliers without troubling to obtain other quotations. In the same way, they may go on buying a familiar brand in ignorance of cheaper substitutes on the market. Secondly, there are preferences due to the different suitability of competing goods for the purposes of different buyers. Each seller will try to cater for the special requirements of a given group of buyers, offering them goods of a quality, style, colour, etc., nearer to their taste than the goods offered by his competitors. Or he will try to carve out a special market by providing additional services—regular delivery, long credit, free insurance, gift coupons, etc. Some of his customers—those who are farthest away, or whose preferences are least satisfactorily met—will remain, so to speak, on the fringe. They will be marginal, in the sense that they can be most readily detached by competitors. Other customers—nearer geographically or in taste—will be firmer in their allegiance, and will desert to rival sellers only if the incentive is a strong one. Finally, the market may be imperfect because of preferences which do not originate in real differences between the products of each seller but in fancied differences or in habit. If I buy from Blank instead of from Blink, I may do so, not because experience has shown me that Blank's cigarettes, or petrol, or pills, are better than Blink's but from sheer force of habit, or because, after reading the advertisements, I am biased in favour of Blank's, or because, without making a thorough test, I believe that Blank's goods are better suited to my purposes. I may also buy from Blank because he is a friend of mine, or because he buys from me, or because he went to the same school or goes to the same church. Blank has my goodwill, and I am part of his special market.

## Prices and cost under imperfect competition

Under imperfect competition the price will be above the marginal cost of production. How much higher will depend upon the market situation. If there is a monopoly in the ordinary sense, the products of the monopolist will be sharply differentiated from those of other firms, and the monopolist, by reducing his price slightly will be able to draw custom from a wide field. No other firms will be likely to feel the loss of custom sufficiently to be obliged to retaliate. We can then apply the ideas of marginal cost and marginal revenue in order to determined what price will yield maximum profits. Price will be above marginal cost and the ratio of the two will be governed by the elasticity of demand for the firm's product.

The same formula will cover a situation in which there are many firms competing in an imperfect market so that one firm can extend its sales by cutting its price, but can extend them only to a limited extent and without having to reckon on retaliation by any of its competitors. If, however, there is oligopoly the formula will be far more difficult to apply. The competing firms will not be able, like the monopolist, to draw a tentative demand curve for their output, showing what will happen to sales at any given price. Each firm will be aware that if it cuts its price it will have to face retaliation; and it will have to puzzle out what will happen to its sales on various assumptions about their behaviour. This it can only do successfully if it has a shrewd understanding of the psychology of its competitors or long experience of their normal reactions. The oligopolist will have his eye as much on his competitors as on his customers and will be guided by his impression of *their* costs as much as by his knowledge of his own. He cannot calculate his marginal revenue nor the elasticity of demand for his products until he has estimated how large an increase in sales will follow a given cut in prices; and if he is uncertain about the train of events that will follow a cut in prices (e.g., whether or not there will be retaliation by other firms) then he cannot estimate precisely how sales will respond. He can, indeed he *must*, form some sort of judgment, but his judgment will be subject to a wide margin of error.

It is possible to construct elaborate theories of price determination under oligopoly on particular hypotheses as to the dominant frame of mind of the competing firms. These theories may assume various levels of sophistication and aggressiveness and provide for any number of competitors from two upwards. But they tend to degenerate into exercises in mathematics and to become as involved as a pure theory of diplomacy, covering peace, war, and all degrees of coldness in a cold war. They have, therefore, no place in this book.

### Price-competition and service-competition

When competition becomes imperfect, price ceases to be the sole consideration of consumers. A slight reduction in price by one seller, instead of drawing custom from all over the market, may pass completely unnoticed. A large reduction in price will certainly bring new customers; but if they come in large numbers from the clientele of rival firms, the reduction in prices is likely to spread throughout the market until most of the new customers are tempted back to their original suppliers. Price as an instrument of competition, therefore, becomes either increasingly ineffective or increasingly unpopular. It is condemned as foolish if it is unsuccessful, and as cut-throat competition if it is successful. This is the point of view of business: the public, which enjoys the benefit of lower prices is not likely to feel itself injured. If no one took the lead in cutting prices how should we ever get things more cheaply, and how would inefficient firms ever be made to give way to their more efficient competitors?

The decline of competition in price has diverted competition into other channels. Price-cuts by a single firm may be contrary to trade etiquette, but other devices for attracting custom are still sanctioned: advertising, improvements in quality or in service, the offer of a wider variety of goods and so on. All these devices have this in common: that they represent an actual outlay with a view to increasing sales, whereas the device of lowering prices represents a sacrifice in *revenue* with the same end in view. When competition reduces prices, the gain to consumers is unmistakable: they save money which they would otherwise have had to spend. But when competition improves quality and makes services more lavish, the gain is more debatable; consumers get more for their money, but they might get still more if they could have the old quality and service at a lower price and were free to spend the difference in price on other articles of more utility. To the man who can barely afford a third-class fare in a Transatlantic liner, the competition which drives each steamship company to offer him a fast trip and the best of food is of less service than the competition which would bring down the fare.

## Selling costs

We considered in Chapter 16 a firm which was free to vary the price which it charged and the amount which it produced. We reached the conclusion that the firm would try to equate marginal cost and marginal revenue. But we took no account of a third variable in the policy of the firm—selling costs. Selling costs include all expenditure designed to create, increase or maintain the demand for a firm's products. Advertising expenditure is the most obvious example, but improvements in quality, special services, etc., have exactly the same effect. They modify the preferences of consumers by making the firm's products, in appearance or in fact, better suited to consumers' requirements, and so increase the firm's sales just as advertising does. It is often very difficult in practice to distinguish between production costs and selling costs unless a firm is making a standard product that cannot be easily modified; the cost of making more units of the article gets tangled up with the cost of adapting it to suit new groups of consumer, or of advertising more widely, or of holding stocks in new markets. In principle, however, the distinction is clear; production costs have no influence on demand whereas selling costs are incurred *in order to* influence demand.

The existence of selling costs forces us to modify, but not to abandon, the marginal theory. The firm will push its sales costs, just as it pushes its production costs, up to the margin at which the last £1 spent on advertising, or on free gift schemes, or on any other kind of sales pressure, just repays itself by yielding a net increase of £1 in revenue (*net*, that is, after deducting the cost of producing the extra goods which are sold). Marginal sales cost, in other words, will tend to equal revenue from the last unit of sales outlay, just as marginal production cost tends to equal revenue from the last unit produced. With this reservation: that whereas the revenue from the last unit produced can occasionally be estimated with some confidence, the revenue from the last unit of sales outlay is almost altogether beyond human conjecture. Who can predict what £1,000 spent on advertising will yield?

We have seen that there are two margins—one of quantity produced, one of selling outlay. Two, however, is a gross understatement: there is a whole series of margins, cutting all the paths of policy open to the firm. The firm may consider, for example, a slight change in quality, or in finish, or in packaging, or in style. A change in any of these will involve an increase in outlay and in receipts, and the firm will move along the path of change until it reaches the margin at which a further move will add more to outlay than to receipts. *Any marginal increase in outlay will, if maximum profits are being earned, involve a barely equal increase in receipts, and marginal cost and associated marginal revenue will tend *everywhere* to equality.*[1]

## Conclusion as to price under imperfect competition

Under perfect competition price and marginal cost will tend to be equal, but where there are elements of monopoly, firms will be afraid to spoil their market and will limit their output so that prices remain above marginal cost. This fear of spoiling the market will arise if the market is imperfect or if the number of competing firms is small. Market imperfection gives each firm an incentive to limit output to the requirements of its special market, while competition between a limited number of independent firms gives each an incentive to restrict output for fear of provoking retaliation.[2]

## Profits under imperfect competition

Under perfect competition the number of competing firms is large and, quite apart from this, new firms can enter the industry freely; there will also, as we have seen, be some high-cost firms on the margin of production, and some firms with slightly higher costs, just beyond the margin, ready to enter the industry whenever prices rise. But what if potential competitors are under a handicap, so that they are attracted into the industry only when prices are considerably above marginal cost? Marginal producers will then be making abnormal profits, while new firms that might produce at less cost and still make

---

[1] It will not be true, of course, that *any* slight increase in costs should lead to an equal increase in receipts. The increase in costs must be such that *the best possible use* is made of the money in the direction in which it is expended. There may be a variety of changes in style which could be made at a cost. A large number will clearly not be worth while: some will be worth considering: and a true marginal change will be one which just barely pays for itself.

[2] The phrase "spoiling the market" is applied above to a reduction in price which either provokes retaliation or is shared equally by established customers (who are willing to pay a higher price). The phrase can, however, be used in other senses. It can be applied, for example, to reductions in price which:

(a) by creating an expectation of a further fall, cause demand to fall off instead of stimulating it;
(b) stimulate sales at the expense of sales at a later date. Consumers or dealers may store their purchases and refrain from buying when prices go up again;
(c) accustom the public to cheapness in price or quality and create opposition to any subsequent attempt to raise prices. What was intended as a temporary reduction in price may easily become a permanent one.

It is clear that the forces making against price-cuts are even stronger than might appear from the text. Yet price-cuts do occur. The reader will find it instructive to find reasons why this should be so.

satisfactory profits will be debarred from competing. New firms will have to meet costs of entry as well as costs of production, while established firms, protected from competition, will have no costs of entry and will reap correspondingly high profits. These excessive profits, since they result from impediments to competition, are essentially monopoly profits.

### Restrictions to entry

What are these impediments to competition? Sometimes they are due to legal restrictions. The Elizabethan monopolists, for example, were able to buy complete immunity from competition by a cash payment to the Crown. The holder of a patent enjoys a statutory monopoly for sixteen years. The Traffic Commissioners can limit the number of licences issued to public service vehicles as they think fit, and can block competition from new transport companies very effectively. Some industries are nationalised and protected by the State in one way or another from competition.

When legal restraints are absolute, so that there is full private monopoly, prices might seem free to rise without limit. In fact, however, there is a double check. The monopolist will not wish to lose his monopoly by too obvious abuse of his powers; what the law has given, the law, under pressure of public opinion, can take back. Secondly, excessive prices will lose not only goodwill but customers; there is a limit to what people will pay, as well as to what they will tolerate. The more elastic the demand, the sooner will this limit be reached, and the greater, therefore, will be the resistance to a rise in prices.

Legal restrictions make costs of entry infinite. So also does complete monopoly of raw materials; the International Nickel Company, for example, has no need to fear competition from other nickel producers in fixing prices. But when the monopoly of raw materials is a local one only (e.g., the Aluminium Company's monopoly of bauxite deposits in the United States) then costs of entry become finite and measurable. They will, in fact, be equal to the cost of transport of alternative supplies from the nearest available point. Potential competitors are handicapped by distance from the local monopolist's market so that, if their costs are equal to the monopolist's and there are no economies of large-scale production, the monopolist can safely augment his price by the cost of transport from the nearest alternative source of supply. He will then make a surplus profit on each unit of output equal to this addition to his price. The surplus (or monopoly) profit will be equal to the cost of entry into his market or—what comes to the same—to the gap between price and the average cost of a marginal supplier.

Limitation of entry may also arise when existing firms have exclusive control over the channels of distribution. They may be able, for example, to black-list new firms and cut them off from the normal retail outlets. The mere fact, too, that existing firms have already built up a business connection gives them a strategic advantage over new firms, and may enable them to smother competitors who, although more efficient, have difficulty in gaining a foothold in the market. This strategic advantage will be particularly great where heavy capital outlay either on advertising or on fixed plant is necessary before production can be started. The newcomer must plunge boldly in instead of feeling his way. Hence he will run a heavy risk of failure without the chance to cut his losses. If the market is narrow he will have to face the additional risk of bringing down prices to levels unattractive to himself and unprofitable also to his competitors. One village cinema, for example, may find it easy to make a large profit. But a second cinema may introduce overcapacity and leave neither cinema with a satisfactory profit. Thus a firm which has the advantage of priority in a narrow market—particularly in industries using large amounts of fixed capital, like the steel or the railway industry—may continue to earn profits higher than a new firm of equal efficiency would consider adequate. There may be an appearance of free competition. But costs of entry, due to the narrowness of the market, the initial risks on a heavy capital investment in face of competition, and the hold of the established concern both on supplies of labour and materials and on the market, will combine to shelter the existing firm from competition and protect it in the enjoyment of a monopoly profit.

## Conclusions as to profits under imperfect competition

The fact that there is imperfect competition does not necessarily mean that more than normal profits are being made. The level of profit depends upon whether there are restrictions on entry into the industry, even if those restrictions rest only on the narrowness of the market. It is quite conceivable that although every firm exercises some degree of monopoly power, in the sense that it has some control over its price, it earns no more in profit than it would in conditions of perfect competition. Monopoly in the first sense is far more pervasive than most people think; but in the second sense it is a great deal more rare. Price may be above marginal cost in the vast majority of firms; but it is rarely above, or appreciably above, the average cost of a marginal firm.

What this means is that the chief waste resulting from imperfect competition is not the waste of profiteering but the waste of an inefficient use of resources. Under imperfect competition, firms produce on a scale of output below the level at which their costs would reach a minimum; to produce a given output more *firms* are needed than would suffice if competition were perfect. Each firm may earn no more than a normal profit, but the industry as a whole produces at higher cost. It is for this reason that some economists would be disposed to welcome a *reduction* in the number of firms in certain industries even though this is a step towards monopoly in the ordinary sense of the term. More competition might merely *raise* costs; the best may be the enemy of the good.

# CHAPTER 18

# SUPPLY: COST IN RELATION TO OUTPUT

The fact that cost of production varies with output is constantly overlooked. People speak of *the* cost of production of an article as though there were only one cost, irrespective of the *amount* of the article produced. But it is well known that in some industries (e.g., the motor industry) costs fall when a substantial increase in output takes place, while in other industries (e.g., wheat farming) costs rise when output is increased. Why is this?

The reason why costs may fall as an industry grows bigger has already been explained. If the industry is to expand, either the constituent firms must produce on a larger scale or new firms must grow up alongside the old. The first method of expansion may very well result in internal economies, the second in external economies. Economies of either type will reduce the average cost of production.

The reason why costs may rise is more obscure. The cost of any article *within each firm* may ultimately begin to rise as output expands. But this does not mean that sooner or later additional supplies of the commodity will only be available at increasing cost. For if all firms are alike and there is perfect competition, an unlimited number of new firms, of the same size and efficiency, will be ready to enter the industry and provide, at constant cost, for any increase in demand, however great.

In the last chapter we saw that firms are not, in fact, alike and that freedom of entry into an industry is generally limited. Here we have two possible explanations of rising costs. As an industry expands it attracts new firms which have either progressively higher costs of production or progressively greater difficulty in gaining a foothold. The second explanation, which will not be pursued here, turns on an increasing degree of monopoly; the first, which is by far the more important, turns on the scarcity and heterogeneity of productive resources.

The first explanation has so far been expressed in terms of firms; when prices rise, and the margin of production is thrust back, the new firms entering the industry are less favourably situated than the old. But it is not really the new *firms* that are more costly; it is the new *factors of production* attracted into the industry. If the cost of coal rises when the output is increased, it may be because sub-marginal coal deposits have to be mined, or because the new seams are worked by less experienced miners, or because the new pits are less ably managed. It makes no difference which factor is responsible for the rise in costs, and it makes no difference whether that factor is employed by new or by existing firms. The important point is that an *industry* can obtain command over additional labour, land, raw materials, managerial ability, etc., only by the offer of increasingly generous terms; by drawing in units of lower efficiency or with a higher supply price.

The industry must either use resources that were formerly left out of employment altogether, or bid against other industries for resources in their employment. Farmers, for example, can grow more wheat either on sub-marginal land or on land which would otherwise have been sown to oats or barley. Motor manufacturers can obtain more steel either by inducing the steel industry to bring more furnaces into production or by leaving less steel for shipbuilding, tinplate manufacture, etc. Expansion, in short, means the use of a larger share of the limited supply of productive resources, and these resources will be released by other industries only when they find themselves unable to bid high enough to retain them. Additional resources, therefore, can be commandeered by an expanding industry only at increasing cost.

### The meaning of cost

This line of reasoning leads us to a new view of cost. The cost of producing any commodity is fundamentally the cost of *detaining* productive resources so as to make their services available to the industry producing the commodity *rather than* to some other industry. Now the cost of detaining resources is equal to the value of these resources for other purposes, plus the cost of transferring them from their existing employment to the most attractive alternative employment.[1] Cost, in other words, measures the pull of competing attractions. If the cost of any factor is not covered, that factor will move to some other industry, and the value of what it could produce in that industry is its cost in its present use. Cost, therefore, must always be considered in terms of alternatives. Cost measures what we could produce instead—what we forgo by using productive resources for one purpose rather than for another. Alternatively, it measures what we could save by not using the resources at all. If, for example,

---

[1] It may happen that other industries are paying resources less than their full value, so that the force of attraction is diminished. For the sake of simplicity, this possibility is ignored.

labour were employed for seven hours a day instead of eight, there would be a fall in the output of goods and services, but labour would enjoy more leisure and would be relieved from disagreeable duties. The sacrifice of leisure and the additional irksomeness involved in working for eight hours measure the cost of the additional goods produced in the final hour.

An illustration may help to make this view of cost clearer. When I give a friend the use of my car for the day "at cost," how is he to decide how much to pay me? If he consults my garageman he may be told that £1 is a fair amount, since the garageman calculates that he could not afford to keep cars for hire for less than this. My friend may then point out that I already own the car, that I have to provide garage accommodation for it anyhow, and that if he had not borrowed it, it would not have been used at all. Provided the car is returned undamaged, I am no worse off by letting my friend have it free. The cost, therefore, is nil, because the *alternative* of letting the car stand idle would be just as expensive.

## Cost and rent

It must not be supposed that every unit of resources is paid no more than its cost. It is, in fact, only the marginal units which earn just enough to keep them from moving to some other industry. Other units, which have a greater bias towards their present employment, will earn a surplus above their "transfer cost." This surplus, which is exactly similar to the surplus earned by intra-marginal firms, is called "rent." Thus the earnings of any unit of resources are made up of two parts—"transfer cost" and "rent." The "rent" element in earnings will be high, where a factor is specially proficient in its present use, or suited to it temperamentally, or disinclined to move elsewhere. The idea of rent is one to which we will return in later chapters.

## Scarcity, heterogeneity, mobility

We have seen that rising costs originate in the scarcity and heterogeneity of the factors of production. The tendency for costs to rise in any industry is the more pronounced the scarcer are the factors which it employs (i.e., the larger the proportion of the total stock engaged in the industry) and the more heterogeneous these factors are (i.e., the poorer the substitutes on which it can draw). In an industry like building, which employs a very large proportion of the bricklayers, masons, slaters, etc., in the country, there is a strong tendency towards rising costs; whereas in radio manufacture, which employs a comparatively small proportion of electricians, the tendency towards rising costs is almost negligible. Similarly, since the difficulty of finding more land suited to wheat-growing is greater than the difficulty of finding more land suited to dairy-farming, the cost of wheat tends to rise more steeply than the cost of milk. There is a third factor on which the tendency to rising costs depends—the mobility of productive resources. The greater the ease with which the factors of production can move from one industry to another, the less rapidly will costs rise. If, for example, labour is highly adaptable, or if most industries use a somewhat similar technique, then the cost of expanding any one industry will be much less than it would be if every worker were given a long and narrow training which fitted him for one job and one job only.

### Relative scarcity

When an industry expands it may be specially difficult to obtain an adequate supply of some one factor. If no increase is possible, and there are no substitutes for the factor, the industry will be unable to expand further. But if there is some alternative technique which eliminates—in part or altogether—the use of the scarce factor, then expansion will be able to proceed at (presumably) rather higher cost. Resort to such alternative techniques, in order to meet a relative scarcity of some one factor, takes place every day. The problems raised by these changes in technique call for special consideration.

We start from two sets of facts—that great changes take place from time to time in the scarcity of one factor of production in relation to the others, and that corresponding changes take place in the use made of that factor relatively to the other. In some ages and countries labour is abundant and capital is scarce; methods of production, therefore, are such as to economise capital and use plenty of labour. In other ages and countries it is capital which is abundant and labour which has to be economised. The same services are rendered by combining the factors of production in very different proportions. Harvesting in China, where capital is scarce, is done with the scythe; in Canada, where labour is scarce, it is done with the combine harvester. In passenger transport there are endless possibilities of variation—from the labour-consuming rickshaw to the capital-consuming Transatlantic liner. The motor omnibus, the taxi, the railway sleeping car, the compartment for 8 *chevaux*, 40 *hommes*—all provide transport services with varying combinations of labour and capital.

When we say that the factors of production can be combined in different proportions we are really saying that they are substitutes for one another. We can produce the same quantity of product by using more capital and less labour (substituting capital for labour) or by using less capital and more labour (substituting labour for capital). The ease with which we can change the proportions by substituting one factor for another varies from industry to industry. In some industries substitution is practically impossible; the technique of the industry is inflexible and dictates the use of productive agents in a fixed, or almost fixed, proportion. In the building of brick cottages, for example, both the materials required and the number of bricklayers, plumbers, carpenters, slaters, etc., are practically fixed once the plans are drawn.[1] In most industries, however, technique is fairly elastic, and a factor which has become specially cheap can be substituted for factors which remain dear. In the steel industry, for example, steel scrap and pig-iron can be substituted for one another in the making of steel whenever one of them becomes relatively scarce and expensive.

### The law of diminishing returns

There are two general principles which govern the substitution of one factor for another. The first is that no one factor is a perfect substitute for another. This follows from the definition of a factor of production; if factors could be freely substituted for one another in all uses they would all belong to a single group of factors. The second principle, which is based on experience, is that substitution becomes progressively more difficult the more of one factor we try to substitute for another. We can easily do without a little of one factor and use a little of another instead; but we cannot easily do without a great deal of one factor and replace it by another. A small change in the pig-iron–scrap ratio makes little difference, but a large change creates great technical difficulties. The two principles, taken together, give us the "law" of diminishing returns to the factors of production. This is simply a statement that, sooner or later, other things remaining the same, the combination of an increasing number of units of one factor with a given number of units of other factors must lead to a less than proportionate increase in output. The total product increases, but it does not increase so rapidly as the variable factor. The reason for this is just that some factors are not increased at the same time as the variable factor, and that increased supplies of the variable factor cannot entirely make up for this deficiency unless the variable factor and the fixed factors are perfect substitutes for one another.

The law is illustrated in Table 12. The first three columns of the table are hypothetical and provide the data from which the last two columns are calculated. Column 4 is obtained by dividing the total product by the number of units of A in use. If column 4 is increasing as output increases, the increase in output is more than in proportion to the increase in A; and if column 4 is decreasing, the increase in output is less than in proportion to the increase in A. In the first stage we have increasing, and in the second decreasing, returns. A third stage is also possible, intermediate between these two, at which output

---

[1] Even here there are possibilities of variation, e.g., by substituting more skilled for less skilled men, or high quality for low quality materials.

increases exactly in proportion to the increase in A, so that for a time column 4 remains constant. At this stage we have constant returns.

According to the law of diminishing returns we must ultimately reach the stage at which output increases less rapidly than units of A. But is there any reason why we need pass through the earlier stages of increasing or constant returns? If, for example, we can produce 1,530 units of product with six units of A and ten of B, why isn't it possible to produce half as much (i.e., 765 units of product) with three units of A and five units of B, instead of the mere 600

TABLE 12

VARIATIONS IN FACTOR PROPORTIONS

| Units of A | Units of B | Units of product | Average product per unit of A | Average cost of production when A=£20, B=£10 |
|---|---|---|---|---|
| 1 | 10 | 50 | 50 | 2·40 |
| 2 | 10 | 200 | 100 | ·70 |
| 3 | 10 | 600 | 200 | ·27 |
| 4 | 10 | 960 | 240 | ·19 |
| 5 | 10 | 1,270 | 254 | ·16 |
| 6 | 10 | 1,530 | 255 | ·144 |
| 7 | 10 | 1,750 | 250 | ·137 |
| 8 | 10 | 1,920 | 240 | ·136 |
| 9 | 10 | 2,070 | 230 | ·135 |
| 10 | 10 | 2,200 | 220 | ·136 |

units which our table gives as the joint product of three units of A and ten units of B? Why can't we save five units of B and still turn out 165 units more? Isn't there an obvious waste in using *any* of the first five combinations, whatever the cost of the factors or the price of their product? Is there any reason, other than muddleheadedness, why these combinations should ever be adopted in the real world? The answer, to take an example we have just given, is that it may not be possible to use only five units of B, or find a market for 1,530 units of product. If B is indivisible (i.e., if it cannot be duplicated on a smaller scale so that a smaller number of units can always be taken if desired) it may be necessary to use one of the earlier combinations of A and B so as to produce a limited quantity of product; and, secondly, it may be necessary to limit output because the market is narrow. A small motor-factory, for example, may have half the capital of a large one and, although employing more than half as many men, may turn out less than half as many cars. It is not of much use to recommend the small factory to adopt the methods of the large one and turn itself into a kind of half-scale replica, for it is only factories which are of a certain minimum size that can avail themselves of the methods of the large factory. Nor is it worth while to recommend the small factory to double its output and become a whole-scale replica of the large factory, for the increased output may not find a market. In other words, where there are economies of scale and market resistance to expansion we will find increasing returns operating, and continuing to operate.

Suppose now that units of A cost £20 and units of B £10. The tendencies to increasing and decreasing return are then converted into tendencies to decreasing and increasing cost. The average cost of production falls until output is at 2,070 units and rises for larger outputs. It will be observed that the output at which average cost begins to increase is considerably greater than the output at which returns begin to diminish. This is due to the spreading of the fixed cost of £100's worth of B over each output. Cost per unit of A is at a minimum when the return per unit of A is at a maximum. But cost per unit of A *plus* B continues to fall for some time. If a large amount of capital has to be sunk in a railway, the total cost per passenger will go on falling long after each additional train has begun to carry a smaller and smaller number of extra passengers.

The calculations of Table 12 are intended to show how the substitution of one factor for another is, after a certain point, increasingly ineffective. It is assumed that only a strictly limited supply of one factor (B) is available, and that there is an unlimited supply of another factor (A). This assumption is obviously an extreme one. But if we remove it, and suppose instead that the supply of B is *more limited* than the supply of A, or that B is *relatively* scarcer than A, the principle illustrated in Table 12 is unaffected. As output expands there will be a shortage of both A and B, and the cost of both will increase. But since B will be relatively scarcer and more expensive than A, it will pay to use a larger proportion of A and to economise B. The change in the proportion of A to B, whatever the absolute amounts of A and B used, will bring the law of diminishing returns into play, exactly as in Table 12. The substitution of the relatively cheaper for the relatively dearer factor can keep down cost of production only within limits.

Thus if all the factors employed in an industry are equally available there will be no reason—apart from economies of scale—why one should be substituted for the other as output increases. The two will be combined in the proportion which makes costs a minimum, and if output has to be doubled, twice as much of each—again apart from economies of scale—will be used. If it is open to every industry, for example, to draw freely on land, labour and capital at current prices, each industry can double its output without increase in cost; there will simply be two factories for every one there was before. So long as there is no reason to economise one factor rather than another, and so long as both are available in abundance at a constant price, costs cannot rise. If there is a limited supply of both factors, costs will rise because the factors are costing more as the industry seeks to attract increased supplies of each of them. If the supply of one factor is more limited than the supply of the other, so that the only units of the first factor that can be recruited are costly or second-rate, while the second factor can still be obtained in comparative abundance, then there will be good reason to substitute the second factor for the first. If such substitution were impossible and the factors had to be combined in a fixed proportion, costs would rise steeply. If substitution were perfect, and the second factor obtainable without limit at a fixed price, costs would not rise at all. In practice, as we have seen, the law of diminishing returns makes substitution imperfect and costs rise none the less. Thus it is because industries are forced to make do with the factors of which they *can* make increased use, meeting a deficiency of other factors as best they can, that diminishing returns come into play. Using a larger proportion of the factor which can be most easily increased is simply a method of economising the other factors and avoiding the consequences of their scarcity.

### Increasing and diminishing returns

Economies of scale, and economies of scale alone, make costs fall as output increases in a given state of technical knowledge. The greater are economies of scale, the greater is the range of output over which costs will fall. If there were no economies of scale, increasing returns would disappear; and with increasing returns would disappear decreasing costs. Scarcity, combined with the law of diminishing returns, makes costs rise with output. Scarcity can be partially circumvented by substitution of one factor for another, but this substitution is limited by the tendency towards diminishing returns.

The laws of increasing and decreasing returns (and the corresponding laws of decreasing and increasing cost) are often cited as if they were in some way parallel to one another. But is it now clear that they are quite distinct. Scarcity, in which the law of decreasing returns originates, has no connection with economies of scale which give rise to increasing returns. Nor are the industries in which the two laws operate distinct from one another. Each industry has its bottlenecks—points at which the scarcity of some factor or factors presses heavily—and each industry has its economies of scale. In some industries economies of scale predominate and in others they are comparatively insignificant. In the first group costs will be falling, and in the second they will be rising, as output increases. But the laws of decreasing and increasing returns operate simultaneously in each; it is only *on balance* that we can draw a line of division between them.

It is often said, for example, that agriculture is subject to decreasing, and industry to increasing, returns. But agriculture is full of examples of economies of scale—through the use of the combine-harvester, tractors, milking machines, and so on. It happens that the scale of production at which these economies can be realised is very small, while the market for agricultural products is very large. It is rare, therefore, to find any branch of farming working under conditions of increasing return. Scarcity, on the other hand, makes itself felt in farming very markedly. There is a scarcity of fertile land; so that, if the output of all farm products has to be increased, farmers must either bring into cultivation sub-marginal land, or cultivate the existing area more intensively by applying to it an increased amount of labour and capital. The first expedient raises farming costs because sub-marginal land is inferior in fertility or in situation to the land already under cultivation. The second expedient raises farming costs because, if the proportion of labour and capital to land is increased, the tendency to diminishing returns comes into play. Each successive application of labour and capital, if the land has already been properly worked, yields a diminishing increment of product. If the output of only one farm product, e.g., wheat, has to be increased, scarcity will again force up costs. Land below the margin— this time the margin of transference —will have to be brought under wheat, and/or existing wheat land will have to be cultivated more intensively. The first expedient means paying a higher rent or renting inferior wheat land; the second brings decreasing returns into operation. If agricultural labour is also scarce, and the channels through which capital can be borrowed or credit obtained are narrow, then the rise in farming costs will be all the steeper.

In industry, on the other hand, the scale of production at which fresh economies cease to be made is enormous, and the market is comparatively narrow. Thus it is rare for an industry to be so placed that it could not more than double its output with the use of twice as much land, labour and capital. The average industry is producing under conditions of increasing return. The pressure of scarcity, too, is less severe. The capacity of the industry can be increased by building plant exactly similar to the plant already in use. More workers can be found and trained much more easily and quickly than agricultural workers. Capital can be obtained in almost unlimited quantities. Thus costs of production rise only when output has to be increased very hastily, and when scarcity, therefore, is at its greatest. In the long run, costs in industry generally fall when output is increased.

# CHAPTER 19

# SUPPLY: COST IN RELATION TO TIME

When there is a change in the conditions of demand or supply, the full effects of such a change are rarely felt immediately. Consumers may go on buying the same goods for some time after prices have risen and only gradually transfer their expenditure to other goods; producers may continue in business for years at prices which yield them a poor, or even a negative, return on their capital, and may only give up when their plant is completely worn out. Generally demand adjusts itself to changes in price much more rapidly than supply, and in the short run, therefore, dominates the course of prices; in the long run, however, supply becomes progressively more important as prices are pulled into line with cost.

A period sufficiently long to allow a full response of demand and supply to a change in prices is called "the long period." A period so short that there is no time for the "capacity" of an industry (its fixed plant and organisation) to alter appreciably is known as "the short period." But there are, of course, a whole series of periods, of increasing length, in which successively closer approximations are made to a full adjustment of demand and supply. This full adjustment, in which there is no further tendency for price to change, is described as "equilibrium." In the long period, therefore, price will always reach its equilibrium level. Equilibrium is something which never exists, but is always coming into existence; price never has time to adjust itself finally to one change in demand or supply before another change interrupts progress towards equilibrium. The fact that a position of long-period equilibrium is never reached in the real world does not mean that the analysis of the last few chapters (which is almost exclusively in terms of long-period equilibrium) is quite futile. There are always long-period tendencies at work in each successive short period through which we live; and long-period equilibrium is simply the logical conclusion of these tendencies—their end-product, other things remaining the same. Moreover, if we understand what governs prices in the long run, we shall find it comparatively easy to apply the same line of reasoning to shorter periods.

## The very short period

In the very short run—say, in the day's marketing—supply can be altered only by drawing on or adding to stocks. If the commodity is highly perishable there will be no stocks, and the influence of supply on price will be nil. In Covent Garden, for example, the supply of strawberries on sale every day will be fixed by the deliveries arriving in the morning, and will not respond to a rise or fall in prices during the day. The price of strawberries will be governed by the demand, in the sense that the price must fall to the level at which the whole supply will be bought. The demand is likely to be fairly elastic, since many buyers will be able to hold off until the following day if prices are abnormally high, and will be able to increase their purchases if prices are abnormally low. There will probably also be some minimum price at which sellers prefer to keep back their strawberries for disposal to jam manufacturers, and at this "reserve price" supply will become extremely elastic since there will be a very elastic limit to the surplus from one day's sales that can be made into jam.

A similar example, covering a longer period of time, might be taken from potato-growing, where no increase can be made to the supply for almost a year after the crop has been harvested. The price is driven to the level at which the fixed supply can be rationed out amongst consumers so as to leave no surplus unsold. But amongst those consumers are the potato-growers themselves. For if prices fall too low they will feed their potatoes to stock instead of selling them for human consumption. Like the strawberry growers, they have a reserve price at which they withhold supplies from the market and below which, therefore, the market price cannot fall. In exactly the same way the price of commodities which are not perishable and can be stored cannot, in the short period, fall below the price which holders of the commodity expect to receive if they refuse to sell until later. This anticipated price (less carrying costs such as storage and interest charges) is their reserve price at which, so to speak, they enter the market on their own account.

## The short period

In the short period, supply can be altered through a decision on the part of any firm either to make a marginal change in its output, or to discontinue production for the time being. The first decision will hinge on the relationship between marginal costs and revenue; the second on the relationship between total cost and revenue. But neither the marginal nor total cost of producing an article is the same in the short period as it is in the long. Suppose, for example, that I own a season ticket between Cambridge and London, and I stop to ask myself how much a journey to London is costing me. The answer, until the season ticket expires, is "nothing at all." I have paid in advance for as many

I*

journeys as I care to make. Suppose now that I am wondering whether I ought to renew my season ticket. Then the cost of a journey to London becomes something positive and calculable. It is equal to what I can save by not travelling. If I mean to make only a few journeys, for example, then the cost of each is clearly equal to the ordinary return fare. In the short period while my season ticket is unexpired, the cost of a journey is nil; in the long period, it may be as much as the ordinary return fare. In the same way the cost of using a piece of machinery, once it is installed, is often negligible, but the cost of using the machinery if it has to be hired every time it is used is by no means negligible.

The fact is that cost is not the same in the short period as it is in the long, because the alternatives open to us are not the same. In the long run we have the alternatives of *not* renewing our season tickets or the machinery which we have installed; in the short run, this alternative does not exist. A cost can only be a cost if it is something that can be avoided. But we cannot, in the short period, avoid the cost either of season tickets or of machinery; the cost of both has already been met, and since "bygones are forever bygones" we cannot avoid the cost *now*. If the machinery depreciates more rapidly when in use than when it is idle, the *extra* depreciation can be avoided by not using the machinery and does, therefore, constitute a true cost, even in the short period.

It follows from this that costs which are fixed in the short period, and do not vary with output, are not really short-period costs at all. For example, firms cannot, in the short period, avoid payment of rates and taxes or debenture interest. Nor can they alter their fixed plant and organisation and so avoid the cost of depreciation and obsolescence. These costs are fixed, whatever the level of output; they have to be met even if nothing is being produced. There is, so to speak, a cost of producing nothing. Now the cost of producing a given output is, as we have seen, what we could save by not producing it—what we could save by producing nothing. But the alternative of producing nothing may still involve us in expense. That expense, therefore, forms no part of the cost of what we do produce. It is only the additional *avoidable* outlay which is incurred that enters into the short-period cost of production.

## Overhead costs

The cost of producing nothing is, for all practical purposes, the same thing as "overhead" or "supplementary" cost.[1] Overhead costs, therefore, are fixed

---

[1] An alternative (and less novel) definition of overhead cost may be simpler to understand. Overhead cost can be taken to mean the difference between total cost and the cost of those factors of production (e.g., labour and materials) which vary with output in the short period. This alternative does not require any considerable modification of the statements made above.

independently of output and have, or should have, no bearing on the questions: What output, if any, is most profitable now? What is the highest price that I can charge and the lowest that I can accept? In the short period it will pay to produce goods if they make any contribution whatever to overhead costs and fetch little more than their prime or avoidable costs; and in deciding what price to charge or to accept for his goods, a manufacturer will be guided more by his idea of what the market will bear than by the allowance which he thinks he must make for overheads. The plea that he must cover his overheads may be useful in mollifying his customers, and the suggested allowance for overheads may enable him to judge what price he can safely charge without inviting fresh competition from new firms. But it will be information on *marginal* costs—the cost of a few units more or a few units less—rather than on *average* prime and overhead costs that will be of most service to him so long as he remains in production. The allocation of overhead costs between different units of output, is, from the economic point of view, an irrelevant piece of ritual. In the long run, of course, overhead costs must be covered or manufacturers will stop producing. But they need not be covered consistently. Normally, some surplus over prime or variable costs will be earned. Sometimes this surplus will rise above and sometimes fall below overhead costs. It will fluctuate with the state of demand, increasing when an active demand allows prices to be raised, and decreasing when demand falls away and prices have to be reduced. The course of prices will govern the allowance that can be made for overheads.

**The long period**

In the long run, however, the position is reversed—the allowance that has to be made for overheads must ultimately influence prices. How does this come about?

The answer is that in the long period overheads are true costs. Outlay on overheads can be avoided by going out of business, or by closing down plant, which is idle and expensive to maintain, or by failing to repair and renew buildings and plant. In the short period these alternatives do not exist. A business will be willing to spend money in order to remain a going concern producing nothing; it will be willing to meet the cost of producing nothing. It is only in the long run, when it has no incentive to remain a going concern, that it will prefer to produce nothing for nothing instead of at considerable expense. Similarly it will meet the cost of maintaining idle plant so long as there is a prospect that this cost of maintenance—not the original cost of the plant—will be recouped. The problem of replacements and renewals introduces even more elasticity for there will be some plant that falls due for renewal every year, perhaps even every month—and if prices are not high enough to justify renewal, output will immediately fall. What was a fixed cost in the lifetime of an old machine becomes a variable cost when the purchase of a new one is being considered, and all variable costs necessarily influence supply and price.[1]

## Marginal cost in short and long periods

We can now return to the two sets of decisions by which supply is altered in the short period. A marginal change in output may cost either more or less in the short period than in the long. A marginal reduction, for example, will save only the cost of labour and materials in the short period, while in the long period it will save part of the overhead cost of machinery and plant. On the other hand, a marginal expansion in output may, if the firm is working to capacity, be much more costly in the short period when there is no time to install additional machinery or train additional men, and the firm has to make shift by overdriving its machinery and overworking its employees. Especially if there has to be more overtime, with correspondingly high rates of pay, the short period cost of a marginal expansion in output may be far in excess of the cost of a similar expansion over a long period.

The complications introduced by time make the problem of pricing an exceptionally delicate one. A firm has to weigh cost now and in the future against revenue now and in the future, trying to ensure that no marginal change in output will yield it a greater profit now without damage to profits in the future. It must hesitate, for example, to refuse a rush order from an important customer even when marginal cost is high—higher than price—if it fears that refusal will prejudice its sales in future years. Equally it must abstain from methods of production which leave a balance of profit now only by ruining all chance of producing at a low cost in time to come.

## Shut-down costs

The second set of decisions—to shut down temporarily or open up again—depends upon the relationship between total cost and total revenue: in other words, if we confine ourselves to the decision to close down, upon how big a loss firms are making. But the *amount* of the loss will not be the sole factor. We have also to ask, "*In what sense* is a loss being made?" If, for example, the firm is making a loss on total costs (including overheads) it is not likely to stop producing. If it cannot cover its debenture interest it may, of course, be forced

---

[1] It follows that when we speak of overhead cost we ought to specify some period of time during which cost remains fixed. Overhead cost is the cost of producing nothing in some given interval of time and in a given state of expectation (e.g., about future costs and prices). This interval of time will generally be one in which replacements of plant are negligible.

into bankruptcy. But since a prime profit is being made (i.e., since the firm is making a profit over prime cost) it will generally pay the creditors to allow production to go on. It is better to have some return than none at all.

If a prime loss is being made, the action of the firm will depend upon three main factors:—its financial strength, the view which it takes of future prospects, and the cost of closing down temporarily and opening up again.

(1) The *ability* of a firm to make a prime loss will depend on its ability either to raise money on loan or to draw on reserves. No firm can go on disbursing more each week than it receives in the form of sales proceeds without running into debt.

(2) The *willingness* of a firm to incur debt (assuming that lenders can be found) will depend upon its faith in such a revival in demand as will allow the debt to be repaid. A loss on prime costs is a species of investment on which a return is expected at a later date when the firm hopes to profit from having maintained its plant and organisation in good condition.

(3) The *wisdom* of continuing to make a prime loss will depend upon the costliness of the most attractive alternative. It may be cheaper, for example, to shut down temporarily, putting the plant on a care and maintenance basis. But this is a course which firms are reluctant to take, since it may mean the loss of business connections, disorganisation of staff, and the dispersion of a reliable and carefully selected body of workers, trained in the ways of the firm. Frequently, therefore, firms prefer to work on a skeleton output in order to maintain contact with markets, staff and workpeople. Where shut-down and reopening costs, broadly defined, are high, firms will prefer to go on producing at correspondingly high prime losses.

### Marginal firms in the short period

In the short period, as in the long, there will be some firms that are marginal and others that are intra-marginal. Marginal firms will be on the verge of closing down or opening up, and a small change in price will be sufficient to turn the scale. The average short-period cost of such a firm can be calculated by deducting from its total costs the alternative cost of closing down and producing nothing and averaging the residue over the firm's output. Below this average cost, price will not fall. Monopolistic influences may, however, succeed in maintaining prices above the average short-period cost of even the least favourably situated firm.

### Summary

A change in price will have immediate and delayed reactions on supply. These reactions will be governed at each stage by the alternatives open to producers, and the range of alternatives will widen with the passage of time. Supply is more elastic the longer the period which we have in view.

This is particularly true of a *reduction* in supply. What is saved by contracting output in the short period is often small in comparison with what can ultimately be saved (e.g., by refraining from plant renewals). Especially when overheads are high, the adjustment of an industry to a *fall* in price is difficult and protracted. On the other hand, an industry generally attempts to expand its capacity quickly to meet a *rise* in price because short-period expedients for increasing output tend to be much more costly than the long-period expedient of installing more plant.

# CHAPTER 20

# INTER-RELATIONSHIPS OF SUPPLY AND DEMAND

The effect of a change in price is never confined to a single product; there are repercussions on the prices of other products, linked with the first either in supply or in demand. These repercussions can be classified under five headings:—

**1 Joint supply**—There are some commodities which can only be produced in association with other commodities; familiar examples, are wheat and straw, mutton and wool, gas and coke. These commodities are said to be in joint supply. Commodities are in joint supply whenever one commodity is a by-product of another, so that it is impossible to increase the supply of one without simultaneously increasing the supply of the other. If there is an increase in the demand for one joint product, therefore, the supply of *both* will increase, and, since there will be a larger supply of the second product to dispose of, its price will tend to fall. Similarly, a fall in the demand for one joint product will tend to increase the price of the other.

**2 Joint demand**—Some commodities are wanted in association with other commodities, and when the demand for one increases, the demand for the complementary commodity increases simultaneously. For example, there is a joint demand for tea and sugar, collars and ties, bacon and eggs, whisky and soda. If any one of these becomes cheaper because of an increase in the supply, both joint products will be in greater demand, and the price of the second, which is no more plentiful, will tend to rise. Similarly, if one joint product becomes scarcer, the price of the other will tend to fall.

**3 Composite supply**—Commodities in composite supply are substitutes for one another. Butter and margarine, for example, form a composite supply for the satisfaction of one want: tea, coffee, cocoa, etc., for the satisfaction of another. If, of two commodities in composite supply, one becomes cheaper, the demand for the substitute commodity will clearly be reduced, and its price will tend to fall, too.

**4  Composite demand**—Commodities are in composite demand when they are wanted for several different purposes. Electricity, for example, is in composite demand for lighting, heating and cooking; for electric razors, clocks and wireless sets; and for driving electric motors in many different industries. If more electricity is needed for lighting, there will be less available for heating and cooking; an increased demand in one use will put pressure on the supply in alternative uses, and prices will tend to rise all round. In the same way, engineering labour is in composite demand for all the industries in which it can be employed. If, then, more engineers are urgently needed in one set of industries (e.g., the motor vehicle industries), the scarcity of labour in these industries will communicate itself to all industries employing engineering workers and engineering wages will go up all round.

**5  Derived demand**—The demand for some commodities *derives from* the demand for other commodities. No one wants crude steel for its own sake; it is wanted for the manufacture of steel products. The demand for steel is a derived demand; yet from it, in turn, other demands derive—the demand for iron ore, coal, scrap iron and manganese. It is only when we reach the ultimate factors of production that the chain of derived demand comes to an end. At the other end of the chain are the final products of industry ready for sale to consumers. The demand for the services of the factors of production, therefore, is derived from the demand of the consumers of finished goods.

### Interconnections between demand and supply

These five relations sum up the inter-connections of different industries and different markets. One product is tied to others in the most unexpected ways, and without a vivid sense of these obscure ties we cannot lay claim to a real understanding of the theory of value. Consider, for example, the ramifications of a programme of rearmament. More steel has to be produced. Hence there will be a larger output of furnace slag—to take one by-product out of many—and the price of cement and of fertilisers, both of which can be made from slag, will tend to fall (joint supply). More munitions factories will have to be built (joint demand), and this may create a shortage of bricklayers, so upsetting the housing programmes of local authorities (composite demand) and forcing them to build timber and concrete houses (composite supply). At the same time rearmament will give a fillip to all the industries supplying raw materials for arms, from the producers of optical lenses for service binoculars to the makers of buttons for uniforms (derived demand). The reader will find it instructive to work out less obvious repercussions; to trace, for example, how recruiting and aerodrome construction create a shortage of agricultural labour, increase the demand for tractors and milking machines, and reduce the demand for horses and oats.

## The marginal cost of joint products

When two commodities are interdependent, on the side either of supply or of demand, the task of disentangling the cost and utility of one from the cost and utility of the other might appear to be almost impossible. We cannot produce wheat without straw; what, then, is the cost of the wheat and what the cost of the straw? If we know the joint cost of wheat and straw taken together, how are we to assign this cost between the two? This question can be answered satisfactorily only if we understand why it is ever asked. Information about the cost and utility of a commodity is of value only if it helps us to decide whether too much or too little of the commodity is being produced. That is, the information ought to bear on *marginal* units of the commodity and show whether there is a balance of gain or loss in producing these units. It is vital, therefore, for a firm to know the *marginal* cost of each of its products. But to divide up joint costs and distribute the total between each joint product is quite meaningless. The allocation of joint costs, while it may decorate a balance sheet and flatter the accountant's sense of propriety, serves no purpose whatever.

How, then, can we calculate the marginal cost of wheat? If wheat and straw are always yielded in a fixed ratio, so that we cannot increase the supply of one *at the expense of the other*, the answer is quite simple. The marginal cost of wheat is what can be saved by not growing a little of it, and this necessarily includes the cost of that inevitable concomitant of wheat-growing—straw. Similarly, the marginal cost of the straw includes the cost of the wheat that grows on it. The marginal cost of each is equal to the joint marginal cost of both. At the same time the marginal revenue of wheat will include the value of the straw which is produced simultaneously, while the marginal revenue of straw will include the value of the wheat which is produced simultaneously.

This may seem a very complicated way of explaining that the cost of wheat is neither separable nor different from the cost of straw. But observe how illuminating the explanation becomes if we *can* vary the proportion in which wheat and straw are grown—if, for example, we can grow wheat on a longer stalk or with a heavier ear. A marginal addition to the supply of wheat can then be made without sowing a larger acreage, for example, by sowing varieties of seed, or using types of fertilisers, or taking the kind of trouble over cultivation that will yield more wheat on a given weight of straw. There will be various marginal adjustments, that is, each of which will increase the yield of wheat without increasing the yield of straw proportionately—adjustments which, in other words, will substitute wheat for straw. Suppose that these adjustments are made in such a way as to yield the same quantity of straw as before and an additional bushel of wheat. Let us select that particular device by which this can be contrived at lowest cost. Then this lowest cost of producing an extra bushel of wheat gives us the marginal cost of wheat. When the marginal cost of wheat can be calculated in this way it is obviously quite distinct from the marginal cost of straw.

This is not a full solution to our problem. The price of wheat, even in the long run, may remain below marginal cost as calculated above. For although it may be *possible* to grow an additional bushel of wheat on the same quantity of straw, this may not be the most *profitable* expedient. It may be easier to grow a little more straw, and a good deal more wheat, setting the value of the additional straw against the increase in total costs. The price of wheat will then be governed by the rule that marginal cost tends to equal marginal revenue, the first including the cost of any additional straw and the second its value.

### Joint supply and composite demand

We have seen that since wheat and straw are joint products, an increase in the demand for one will tend to bring down the price of the other. But this conclusion was reached on the assumption that more wheat could not be produced without the simultaneous production of more straw. If the proportion between wheat and straw could be easily varied, the conclusion would be reversed, for it would be possible to grow more wheat by growing *less* straw and so making it dearer instead of cheaper. There would, in fact, be a *composite demand* for the wheat crop, and wheat and straw would be alternative rather than joint products. When two commodities are produced together, therefore, there are two aspects to the association. When there is great difficulty in varying the proportion in which they are produced, we say that they are in joint supply; when the proportion is easily varied, we say that there is a composite demand for the factors engaged in their production. If the demand for one commodity increases, the price of the other will rise or fall according as the aspect of composite demand or joint supply predominates. To put the same conclusion rather differently; the greater the ease with which the production of A can be abandoned in favour of the production of B—in technical terms, the greater the elasticity of substitution of A for B—the stronger will be the tendency for the prices of A and B to move in the same direction.

## Joint demand and composite supply

On the side of demand symmetrical conclusions apply. Goods in joint demand are bought in fairly constant proportions, while goods in composite supply, being substitutes for one another, are bought in highly variable proportions. If the aspect of joint demand predominates, an increase in the supply of A tends to raise the price of B; if there is more whisky to be had, we shall want more soda and probably have to pay more for it. On the other hand, if the aspect of composite supply predominates, an increase in the supply of A tends to reduce the price of B; if tea is more abundant, we shall be less anxious to buy coffee, and its price will fall. The greater the ease with which we can substitute one commodity for another—the greater the elasticity of substitution by consumers—the stronger will be the tendency for the prices of the two commodities to move in the same direction.

## Joint products from the point of view of the firm[1]

The practical implications of these ideas may be clearer if we apply them to the problems that face the individual firm. Suppose, for example, that some machines, or some generator of power, or some piece of floor space is contributing to the output of several commodities. Then it will be a waste of time to try to allocate to each commodity its share in the joint or "overhead" costs[2] of the machine, or the power plant, or the floor space. But it will be of the utmost importance to find what saving could be made on these overhead costs by reducing the output of any one commodity, and what additional outlay on overhead costs would be necessary in order to increase the output of that commodity. If there is no *measurable* saving or additional outlay attributable to individual commodities—if changes in overhead costs affect all commodities equally—then we must try to find out, on the assumption that overhead costs remain unchanged, what reduction in the output and sale of *other* goods is necessary in order to provide for an expansion in the output and sale of each individual commodity. For example, a shop which sells handbags and suitcases and has a fixed amount of floor space, may be able to estimate the loss in revenue from suitcases that will result from the stocking of more handbags and fewer suitcases. This loss in revenue can be regarded as the marginal cost of retailing handbags and should be weighed against the gain in revenue from the additional handbags that are sold. The problem of charging suitcases and handbags with their appropriate share of the cost of floor space (the rent of the shop) simply does not arise.

---

[1] Strictly speaking, joint products are products that must be produced simultaneously; the term is used here more elastically to cover products that are in fact produced together.

[2] Notice that in this context overhead costs are "costs common to a number of commodities," not "costs fixed over a period of time."

Handbags and suitcases are not only in joint supply, but also in joint demand —that is, many customers normally purchase both in the same shop. A shopkeeper who reduces the price of handbags, therefore, will not only increase his sales of handbags, but will also attact custom in other lines, such as suitcases, and the profit which he makes on his additional sales of suitcases will go to reduce the margin required to cover the cost of retailing handbags. If handbags are sold at a specially low price, the sacrifice of profit on handbags may really be a species of advertisement designed to increase profits from the sale of other merchandise.

This parallel with advertisement and selling costs suggests that the principles governing selling costs apply equally to joint products. As before, once we define marginal cost and marginal revenue broadly, the rule that they tend to equality with one another holds. The position of maximum profit, when several products are being produced or several markets supplied, will be one in which there is no commodity such that by producing more of it the additional net revenue exceeds the additional net cost. The net (marginal) revenue will include the rise in the proceeds of sale to the commodity, less the fall in returns from any commodity the output of which has had to be cut down, plus the rise in returns from any commodity which is in joint demand with the first. The net marginal cost will include net additional outlay plus any additional depreciation due to the expansion of output.

The same line of reasoning applies to the discontinuance or initiation of the production of some commodity in the long period. If there is a prospect of additional profit, taking into account all extra outlays and the balance of increase in receipts, then the commodity is *ipso facto* profitable. The problem of saddling the commodity with its "share" of overhead costs, which are perhaps unaffected by this new departure, does not arise.

When the question of renewal presents itself, the considerations on which a decision should be based are similar. A machine may be used in the manufacture of several commodities. The manufacturer will, therefore, have to sum the various reductions in his receipts which failure to renew will involve and weigh the total against the annual charge for upkeep, depreciation and interest on a new machine. If there is some other method of production which promises larger profits, or lower losses, then the machine will not be renewed.

The fundamental point is that costs must be approached from the point of view, first, of alternatives, and, secondly, of the margin. The changes which have to be analysed are generally marginal changes—repercussions of a suggested change must be worked out and the result compared with the existing position. The profitability of any output is thus purely relative. It may pay to make an apparent loss because an offsetting gain is being made, or is expected to be made, in consequence of the loss. To insist on making a profit everywhere may result in reducing profits all round.

## Price discrimination

The practice of price discrimination offers an excellent illustration of this truth. Discrimination may arise whenever the products of a firm are in composite demand by distinct groups of consumers, each group being made to pay a different price for exactly the same product or service. Before the war the Milk Marketing Board, for example, charged one price to consumers of liquid milk, and a range of much lower prices for milk to be used for manufacture into butter, cheese, milk powder, and other milk products. Now it can readily

|               | Price | Sales | Total Receipts | Average Cost |
|---------------|-------|-------|----------------|--------------|
| First Market  | £40   | 200   | £8,000         | £30 (200 units) |
| Second Market | £18   | 300   | £5,400         | £20 (500 units) |

be shown that if a firm which is in a position to discriminate insists on making a profit in each market, its total profits may be less than they would be if the firm were satisfied with an apparent "loss" in some of its markets. Suppose, for example, that the firm possesses semi-monopolistic powers in one market (e.g., the home market) and is open to severe competition in another (e.g., the export market) so that it is more reluctant to spoil the first market than the second. The price in the first market may be £40, and in the second £18, while sales are 200 in the first and 300 in the second.

Suppose also that the average cost of production of 200 units is £30, while the average cost of (200 + 300) units is £20. Then it might appear that every unit sold in the second market would lose the firm £(20—18) or £2. In fact, however, refusal to sell in the second market results in the loss of £5,400 in revenue, and saves only £(500 × 20)—(200 × 30) or £4,000 in cost. In other words, selling below (average) cost in the second market increases total profits by £1,400.

Once again, thinking in terms of marginal cost and revenue saves us from confused reasoning. The marginal cost of output will depend mainly on the total amount produced and will be more or less independent of variations in the proportion disposed of in any one market. Now it will pay the manufacturer to make marginal cost and marginal revenue equal in *each* market, and since the gap between marginal revenue and price will be least in the highly competitive export market, he will tend to charge a lower price there than in the home market. If demand in the export market is so elastic that his power to depress or raise prices is negligible, then he will expand his sales abroad until marginal cost is equal to the world price, and since marginal cost will remain below average cost so long as costs are falling, price will also be lower than average cost.

It should be observed that the incentive to discriminate originates not in unused capacity as is sometimes suggested, but in the imperfection of competition. If competition acted with equal force in all markets, manufacturers would charge the same price all round, whether their costs were rising or falling. If it were impossible to separate one market from another, the same would be true. Discrimination can only be resorted to whenever groups of consumers can be separated out by geographical area, or income, or membership of some society, or propensity to visit particular shopping centres, or to buy particular qualities of product. There must also be some barrier to movement from one group to another. For example, goods dumped abroad may, if the price disparity is excessive, be reimported and bring down prices at home. British motor cars, if there were no import restrictions, could not be sold at one price in France and another in Britain.

### Joint products from the point of view of society

From the social point of view, all products are, in the broad sense, in joint supply; the stream of goods and services that makes up the national output is the joint product of all our resources of land, labour and capital. From the social point of view, all products are also in joint demand; the stream of income that makes up the national income provides, when expended, the joint demand for the products and services of the factors of production. The national income is, in fact, simply the national output upside down, or looked at from the point of view of the consumer instead of the producer. What we produce flows into a reservoir in which are pooled the products of our neighbours. What we consume is drawn from the same reservoir, from the joint output of the community.

Thus whereas the individual firm, in balancing cost against price, can confine itself to the limited range of products which it manufactures, and whereas the individual consumer, in balancing price against utility, can confine himself to the limited range of products which he buys, calculations of *social* welfare must embrace *all* goods and services. In private accounting there are many repercussions of our decisions to buy or sell that we can, if we choose, neglect; but in social accounting, since all products are joint products, none of these repercussions—unless they are trifling—can be neglected. The producer of chemicals, whose waste gases pollute the atmosphere, does not reckon in pollution as part of his output. The consumer who burns raw coal in the domestic grate does not deduct the soot and dust which he creates from the utility of the fire. Private costs and private preferences are partial and incomplete. Our private interests and the interests of society do not coincide.

To these points we shall return in the next chapter when we consider whether prices in a capitalist society adequately reflect the wants of the community.

# CHAPTER 21

# SOCIAL ASPECTS OF PRICING

Now that we have seen how prices are fixed, it is time to turn to the more perplexing problem how prices should be fixed. This is a question which people ask for several quite different reasons. They may want to know on what basis to decide whether a price is fair or just; they may be thinking of the problems of a war-time government armed with powers to fix prices and ration goods; or they may have in mind a socialist economy in which prices are not governed by market forces but have somehow to be "planned." It is unlikely that these different sets of questions can be given a single set of answers. St. Thomas Aquinas and Stalin would hardly have seen eye to eye on the matter, and Lord Woolton, who was Minister of Food in war-time Britain, would have had good reasons for differing from them both.

A common sense answer to the question would be that prices should be equal to cost of production. But, as we have seen, cost is a rather ambiguous concept: different firms have different costs; their short-run costs are not necessarily equal to their long-run costs; and the distinction between cost and profit tends, on closer examination, to become a little blurred. On top of this, cost may vary with scale of production, so that average cost and marginal cost are not necessarily equal. The common sense answer, therefore, is not altogether satisfactory.

## Marginal cost pricing

Nevertheless, it is in line with the general thinking of economists on the subject. They would be inclined to take the price that would rule under conditions of perfect competition as a useful point of departure, recognising that this was not in all circumstances a satisfactory norm and that there might be good practical reasons for using some other basis of pricing. This would mean that prices ought, as a rule, to be equal to marginal cost of production. This formula would be justified by economists on the grounds that it would lead to an allocation of resources between different uses that was in keeping with the preferences of producers and consumers. Put briefly, the argument is that the price of a commodity measures the value that consumers set on an extra unit of it; its marginal cost measures the cost of producing such a unit. If price is above marginal cost, therefore, too little of the commodity is being produced. Equality between price and marginal cost secures the "right" balance between value and cost and the "right" output of the commodity.

To elaborate this argument at any length would take us too deeply into welfare economics, a disputed territory where even professional economists walk warily. But at the risk of confusing the reader, we may explain the gist of the matter as follows. Suppose that we need consider only two commodities A and B, that all resources are fully employed in the production of A and B and that a marginal shift of resources between A and B can take place freely and without any cost of transfer. Suppose also that the marginal costs of A and B are equal. If in those circumstances the price of A is above its marginal cost and the price of B is not, a transfer of resources from B to A would leave consumers better off without any injury to producers. By spending less on B, consumers would release resources that could produce just as much of A, for which they have to pay more than they do for B. They would therefore gain by an amount equal to the difference between the price and marginal cost of A. Similarly, if the price of A were below its marginal cost it would pay to transfer resources away from the production of A.

There are many services the output of which is not left to competition and which cannot be priced in this way. Even where competition does operate, an attempt to price on the basis of marginal cost would raise practical difficulties where costs fall with volume of output. In those cases, marginal cost would be below average cost and price would, therefore, also be below average cost; in other words, it would be necessary to run at a loss. This loss might be covered out of a subsidy from the state. There is nothing necessarily wrong about subsidising an industry; but if the practice were to become very common, one might well conclude that the idea of pricing on the basis of marginal cost needed some re-examination.

Few economists have ever contemplated that the idea should be applied rigorously and systematically in a capitalist economy. If the state took responsibility for fixing prices, and introduced a system of levies and subsidies in order to balance out the profits and losses that resulted, it is almost inconceivable that it could escape taking control of the operation of the industries affected. If some industries were obliged to make consistent losses because their prices were held down by the state and subsidies were given in compensation, it would be necessary to have some guarantee that the losses were not made an excuse for slackness and that the subsidies were not unnecessarily large. There would have to be frequent adjustments in the rates of levy and subsidy—deliberate adjustments which would meet with vigorous resistance from the industries affected. These difficulties might be overcome if the state had full and accurate knowledge of marginal costs in each industry; but it neither has nor could easily acquire such knowledge and any data that it collected would be open to conflicting interpretations.

The measurement of marginal cost is never a straightforward affair. There are ambiguities in the concept itself: it is relative to the period of time under discussion and the expectations that can reasonably be entertained about future developments. There are complications in its measurement whenever several commodities are produced in the same factory.[1] There are further complications when, as often happens, a firm does not produce the same thing continuously for more than a year—or, like the local cinema, for more than three nights running—and when its efficiency depends far more on its success in improving or varying its product than in producing any single product at minimum cost. In some industries a firm may spend £1 million in tooling-up and a few pence or shillings in meeting direct costs per unit, only to re-tool after a limited run. In many industries (e.g., publishing) the number of price quotations runs into thousands. Experience of price-control in war-time does not suggest that the magic of a single golden rule will suffice to dispel the practical problems of pricing and leave industrial efficiency unaffected.

Nevertheless there are circumstances in which it would be both practicable and desirable to give effect to the logic of the idea. Suppose that a bridge could be built that would cost nothing to maintain after erection. The marginal cost of using it is nil so that, on the principle of marginal cost pricing, no toll should be charged. This might mean that a great many people used the bridge who would not use it if a toll were charged; and the total gain to the users might well exceed the cost of erection. Whether it would be right to build the bridge at the expense of the general tax-payer for the benefit of a limited group of users is another matter; if this decision *were* taken, there would be everything to be said subsequently for allowing the bridge to be fully used. Another example would be that of railway-building in a country still relatively thinly populated, where the marginal cost of railway services would be low in comparison with their average cost. However railway charges were fixed, revenue might be insufficient to cover costs and the fear of making a loss would deter private interests from undertaking the building of the railway. The social importance of having an adequate railway might, however, induce the state to provide the capital and, once the railway was in operation, pricing on a marginal cost basis

---

[1] See above, pp. 275-7.

would yield greater social gains than attempts to base charges on average costs.

It is clear that in these two examples, the case for marginal cost pricing rests on the desirability of making full use of some indivisible lump of equipment; it is because the cost of using this equipment is spread over an increasing volume of output that the cost curve is downward sloping and marginal cost is below average cost. If is also clear that the key decision relates to the construction of the equipment in the first place rather than to its operation; it is the initial investment that needs to be subsidised. It would be possible to select other examples where the case for charging *more* than average cost rested on the undesirability of overloading existing fixed assets; if users were penalised by having to pay marginal cost, this would help to relieve a form of congestion. In such examples, it would again be the decision not to construct more of the fixed assets that was the critical one, since pricing on the basis of marginal cost would be a means of giving effect to this decision so as to minimise inconvenience to the consumer. Where there are no indivisible elements to give rise to unnecessary under-utilisation on the one hand, or congestion on the other, and where resources are mobile and freely variable, costs will be constant and marginal cost will not diverge from average cost. Once this point is grasped, it is much easier to see in what directions the principle of marginal cost pricing has a practical bearing; and there is less reason for supposing that at least the more glaring applications of the principle will escape notice and support.

It is conceivable, as some economists have argued, that the principle might be given wider application in a socialist economy and that it might even be made the basis on which the output of individual enterprises was planned. It is conceivable, that is to say, that countries dedicated to the planning of their economies because of distrust of the outcome of the uncontrolled operation of market forces might, in a fit of paradox, adopt the very principle to which those forces, carried to the limit of their own logic, would give effect. But if conceivable, it is, to say the least, unlikely. Countries that are attracted by the idea of planning do not usually begin by planning prices; they plan output. No doubt they discover in time that they cannot neglect market forces and that it helps if prices pull along with, and not against, output plans; just as countries that rely mainly on the price-mechanism discover, in moments of stress, that it may be necessary to take direct measures to control output rather than wait until prices have brought about the desired reactions. This is most obvious in war-time when the whole productive system has to be quickly re-oriented to serve a quite new purpose—that of winning the war. But it is also apparent in peacetime when any large structural change has to be brought about: for example, when it is necessary to effect large economies in important materials or a major change in the balance between imports and exports . At such times *current* costs (and prices closely related to them) are a poor guide to the direction that productive effort should take and some short-circuiting of market mechanisms by those who are planning or regulating production is plainly desirable.

### Discrimination

There are also circumstances in which it may be socially desirable to charge two or more prices for the same thing, so that cost of production is an inadequate guide. Price discrimination may be introduced, for example, in the interests of poor consumers or with a view to using up a temporary surplus. The first of those cases may be illustrated by the practice of giving milk free or on special terms to schoolchildren or of offering houses at low rents in slum clearance schemes. A case of the second type would be the distribution of surplus fruit, fish and other foodstuffs at low prices to consumers who were generally unable to purchase enough of them and who could be induced to consume more without upsetting the market. Similarly, isolated villages might be allowed to use the telephone at less than cost, and electricity might be installed in working-class houses at specially low rates. Discrimination, in short, can be used deliberately as an instrument of social policy so as to direct the demand of groups of consumers towards certain essential commodities or towards commodities especially subject to economies of scale.

### Some wider considerations

The principle that price should be based on marginal cost is intended to secure that the wants of consumers receive the fullest possible satisfaction—if we are willing to sacrifice a little of A for the sake of a little more of B produced at equal cost, then our preference will be met by an appropriate transfer of resources from the production of A to the production of B. But what if we want to sacrifice a little of A for the sake of something not on the market at all? We cannot give effect, as individual consumers, to a preference for a less varied and cheaper selection of goods; or for economic progress rather than economic security; or for an increased national debt rather than increased unemployment. We have freedom of choice, but only within the limits of existing market conditions. If we want to change market conditions we must associate with other like-minded consumers in bringing pressure on the government. Our preferences find expression, not in the market, but in Parliament. But they are none the less preferences of which account must be taken in deciding what is to be produced and how it is to be produced. Preferences backed by voting power can be just as important in arriving at a just price or an ideal output as preferences backed by purchasing power; and as the market contracts they become more important.

Nor is this a trifling difficulty. For the deepest wants of man have little to do with the scarcity which economic activity is primarily designed to combat. Man craves most of all a sense of purpose, a role in life and in society. Deny him that, make him feel of no consequence, and he will take revenge by over-turning any economic system, however well regulated. It is not enough to offer him value for his money in goods and services. He must have a place to match his sense of merit—something to admire and defend, entertainment and amusement, responsibility and initiative. Without these, goods and services are as dust and ashes, and any one output is as far from ideal as any other.

So long as we refuse to go behind man's wants to the inner motives which inspire them, the rules of pricing can be reduced to simple axioms. We can treat each want atomically as a demand for this or that service, and discuss choice as the balancing of one want against another. But immediately we begin to think of wants as fused by a sense of purpose, the tool of marginal analysis breaks in our hands. It is borne in on us that it is not just the surface wants that cry out for satisfaction, but the deeper urges which they often express. People buy goods not for their own sake so much as for what they symbolise. The African chief who, in fear of death at the hands of his tribe, seeks hair-dye of white travellers to prolong his youth and his rule: the *nouveau riche* who buys a country seat so as to impress his associates: the purchaser of cosmetics, parrots, or holy relics; all have resort to market agencies in order to satisfy wants that are denied satisfaction in other ways. And this is true not just of a few odd people or of a few odd purchases, but of practically everyone at some time and of the bulk of the purchases which most of us make at any time. We do not buy the cheapest article available and only those articles which are indispensable to living. We buy what appeals to our imagination under the pressure of social standards. In economic activity as in other spheres of life the motives which dominate us are rarely hunger and want in the narrow sense (except at a very low standard of living) but the desire for power, the desire to make others feel that power, to show off to and keep up with, our neighbours, to plan and build and dream. We seek distinction, for example, in our dress or in our profession; and power over others through our wealth or as their employers. To isolate individual buyers and sellers in some vacuum of choice, therefore, and discuss how industry can best maximise an ethereal utility is to misconceive the problem. We might as well discuss what combination of medicines will most promote health, with-out regard to the causes of ill-health or to the other remedies (fresh-air, exercise, good food, adequate clothing, and so on) that lie to hand. To substitute one assortment of goods and services for another may do far less for the people's welfare than the setting of new social standards or the direction of their energies into new and more acceptable channels.

Nor is this all. For the act of substitution of itself *changes* social standards and *creates* new demands. If, for example, we provide cheaper wireless sets we may reduce the demand for theatre seats and increase the demand for coal, since more people will wish to stay at home and listen in. Thus the balance between value and cost is upset and no one can say with assurance whether it is upset for better or for worse. We cannot assume, therefore, that if output is adjusted so as to keep prices in line with costs we are giving fuller satisfaction to the wants of consumers, for these wants are themselves affected by variations in output.

Again, many of our wants are shaped by the very system of production which exists to supply them. A man's habits of living and of expenditure depend partly upon the work which he is called upon to do. A worker in casual employment has a different scale of values from a worker in regular employment. A factory worker, a miner, an agricultural labourer, a stockbroker, and a doctor have each their own outlook and make their own peculiar purchases. By changing methods of production, therefore, we can simultaneously change the demand of consumers. If we provide well ventilated and clean factories we can create a demand for well ventilated and clean houses. If we cut down overtime we may be able to reduce the demand for medical services—or for whisky.

## Private and social values

In short, we cannot base prices solely on current market valuations because the money costs and values which find expression in the market are incomplete measures of social costs and values. Buying and selling go on against a social background from which we cannot abstract in estimating the value of what is bought or the cost of what is sold. Consider, for example, the building of a house. It costs, let us say, £4,000 and is valued at the same figure. But do we enter up in the cost the noise which the neighbours endure, the nuisance to passers-by from added traffic congestion, or the loss of amenities to other householders? Do we include in the value of the house its effect on our health and on the health of our children (matters of immediate interest to the community, which may have to support us if we fall ill, has to combat any infectious disease which we may help to spread, and is out of pocket on the cost of our education if we are unable to do regular work and to pay our taxes)? Do we include the effect which living in such a house has on our character and so on our work and friendships? Do we include the pleasure which other people derive from our garden? It is highly unlikely that we include any of these things. Yet they affect the cost and value of the house to the community just as surely as the cost in bricks and mortar and the number and size of the rooms.

Thus the machinery of the market—even when regulated so as to keep marginal utility and marginal cost equal to one another—is insufficient to make the output of each commodity ideal. We must supplement market competition, with its narrow perspective of self-interest, by some other kind of competition from which a broad judgment of social welfare will emerge. In democratic countries, this second kind of competition takes the form of competition for votes. It is the electorate which, in the last resort, has power to decide whether one industry is too small or another too large to be in the social interest.

### Private values and state intervention

A wider question remains. Is it right to take demand for granted and give it the fullest possible satisfaction, without first deciding whether or not it *ought* to be satisfied? Clearly, there is no ideal output of drugs. But what of hundreds of other commodities which consumers buy ill-advisedly or ignorantly? Is the consumer the best judge of his own interests when he buys patent medicines, or petrol, or electric fittings? Still more important, should the value which he sets on milk or on opera or on education be the sole criterion by which the output of these things should be determined? In general, it is wise to leave the consumer to learn from his own mistakes and not to dragoon him too insistently into paths of wisdom and virtue prepared by a very fallible government. But there are times when, in fixing prices, the State may properly disregard individual valuations as shortsighted, mistaken or wrong, deny access to certain commodities in the quantities which consumers would be willing to absorb, and offer other commodities in larger quantities, in more attractive surroundings or backed by more advertising pressure, than free competition would provide. If technical experts are practically unanimous in praising one commodity and in condemning another, the State will be justified in setting aside any contrary verdict by individual consumers. It will be right to encourage, or even to enforce consumption of the first, and to discourage or suppress the sale of the second. When informed opinion is seriously divided, however, or when important moral issues are involved, the State will be unwise to interfere unnecessarily with the free choice of consumers in order to impose upon them ideals which they do not share. To prohibit the drinking of methylated spirits is one thing; to prohibit the drinking of beer, quite another.

This is not, however, the end of the matter. The State's influence on prices extends far beyond a paternal anxiety to push the sale of milk and prohibit the sale of opium. The whole price system is honeycombed with the influence of the State, direct or indirect: a tax here, a subsidy there, the provision of facilities at one point, their denial at another. This influence is sometimes opportunist: it may reflect no more than the fact that it is easier to tax the smoker than the football pool enthusiast. Sometimes it expresses State policy towards a particular industry: the desire to encourage agriculture, for example. But to an increasing extent, it is the general economic policy of the State that guides its intervention: the objective of greater social equality may prompt it to subsidise foodstuffs or housing; the aim of full employment may induce it to control interest rates; the need to redress an adverse balance of payments may lead it to restrict the supply of imported goods of various kinds, with repercussions on their price. The action of the State is then based, not on any deliberate disregard of individual valuations of particular commodities or services, but on a positive policy related to those major objectives. Such action can only be satisfactorily judged, therefore, in relation to the State's objectives and policy. The issues involved will form the subject of Part VII.

# PART IV—THE DISTRIBUTION OF INCOME

CHAPTER 22

# THE DISTRIBUTION OF INCOME

The theory of distribution might be expected to deal with the reasons why some people are rich while others are poor, and whether there is any justification for these inequalities. Traditionally, however, economists have preferred to put the question in a different way. They have analysed the distribution of the national income, not between persons, but between the factors of production—land, labour and capital. They have set themselves to explain how rent, interest, profits and wages are fixed, leaving over for later study the resulting distribution of income between the owners of the factors of production. This procedure splits the problem of distribution into two parts. The first, which is an extension of the theory of value, analyses the forces governing the *prices* of the factors of production; it is a study of the tendencies of competition. The second, which involves research into the social structure of particular communities rather than the working out of economic principles, analyses the forces governing the *ownership* of the factors of production; it is mainly a study of the influence of inheritance and political power. Once we know what governs both the earnings and ownership of the factors of production, we know also what governs the distribution of income between persons and we can go on to discuss how far this inequality is either necessary or justifiable.

In this chapter we shall concentrate on the first problem. We shall assume, to begin with, conditions of perfect competition. We shall also assume conditions of full employment—meaning by this that the economic system is functioning so as to allow each factor as much employment as its owner wishes at the current rate of remuneration. By making these assumptions, and setting aside the influence of monopoly and unemployment, we are able to concentrate on a single issue: What are the tendencies of competition?

The price of any factor of production, like the price of a commodity, is governed by supply and demand. The scarcer the factor, the greater the demand for its services, the higher will be its earnings. The more abundant the factor, and the less urgently it is required, the lower will be its earnings.

K

But this does not take us very far. What is it that governs supply and demand?

## SUPPLY

In early theories of value no importance was attached to demand. The only lasting influence on price was that of supply—in other words, of cost of production. This was true not only of commodities but also of factors of production; and just as an exception was made in favour of "rare statues and pictures, scarce books and coins," where competition was powerless to increase the supply, so also an exception was made in favour of land, where again the supply could not be increased. The price of old masters depended solely on the demand: so also did the rent of land. But interest and profit, and above all wages, were governed by supply. The Subsistence Theory of Wages, for example—the so-called "Iron Law of Wages"—was simply a statement that the price of labour tended to be just sufficient to cover the cost of production of the labourer. Wages, it was thought, must oscillate round a level that was just high enough to afford the wage-earner a bare subsistence. Higher earnings would induce workers to have larger families, the labour market would become overstocked, and wages would be forced down again. Similarly, if wages fell below the level of subsistence, workers would die off and the birth-rate would fall until the ensuing shortage of labour raised wages again.

This gloomy theory rested largely on the work of Malthus who argued that the human race had the power—and the propensity—to multiply its numbers more rapidly than the means of subsistence, that population was in fact increasing, and that this increase would inevitably lead to pressure on the means of subsistence resulting in a high death-rate through famine, war and disease, unless mankind curbed its unruly instincts in later and less fertile marriages. The middle classes, convinced that the instincts of the poor could never be curbed, found Malthus's doctrines singularly soothing. If money given to the poor only encouraged them to multiply, then the money was far better in the pockets of the would-be philanthropists—and their numerous children. Those who, sharing Malthus's views, struggled to raise the standard of living of the workers, must have felt that they were building on sand and that no real advance could be made so long as the population kept on increasing. It is significant that the development of the public social services in Britain made little progress until the views of Malthus lost favour.

The experience of the nineteenth century proved that Malthus's fears, although not altogether groundless, were exaggerated. The population of England and Wales, it is true, increased fourfold. But instead of an accompanying fall in wages below the level of subsistence, wages too increased fourfold; and instead of a rise in the birth-rate to match the increasing prosperity of the working class, the birth-rate began to fall and kept on falling. Far from high wages increasing the "supply" of wage-earners, the reverse appeared to be true; the birth-rate was lowest in countries where wages were highest. Thus the Malthusian theory was turned upside-down. Measures to raise the standard of living of the poorer classes might relieve, not aggravate, the pressure of population.

The fact is that, although the growth of population does depend upon the level of wages, the connection is by no means a straight-forward one, and there are many other influences quite unconnected with wages. We may study these influences and try to forecast the future of population, and may study also how changes in population will react on wages. But this is a very different thing from laying it down that whatever happens to population, wages will tend to sink to the level of subsistence and that the demand for labour can, therefore, be neglected. A cost theory of wages along these lines must be ruled out.

### Real costs: efforts and sacrifices

Wages are not related very closely—at any rate in an industrialised community—to the cost of "producing" labourers (i.e., of rearing children). But what of the cost of inducing labourers to work, putting up with hardship and discomfort for long hours with short holidays? Can we not say that each hour of work costs the worker something in the effort which he expends and the sacrifices which he undergoes? For those efforts and sacrifices wages are presumably intended to compensate, and high wages, therefore—whatever their effects on population—may be expected to call forth a greater supply of work by disposing the worker to make greater efforts and greater sacrifices. We decide how much work we are willing to do by weighing the wage offered against the subjective "cost" of working; the wages must be high enough to overcome our disinclination to undertake disagreeable tasks. Indeed, we can go further. Provided we are free to choose which tasks we will do, the wage must be high enough to compensate us for the *most disagreeable* tasks. We balance the additional earnings which we can make against the additional hardship of working for one more hour, or at higher speed, or in less pleasant surroundings. It is the *marginal* disutility of work—the disagreeableness of those tasks which we are most tempted to decline—that governs the supply of labour.

This view of costs has two important disadvantages. In the first place, it suggests that a rise in wages will call forth greater effort from wage earners. But it often happens that a rise in wages, by making it easier for workers to reach their customary standard of living, induces them to work less energetically, or take longer holidays, or absent themselves more frequently from work. It is well known, also, that in times of trade depression when wages are falling, workers often respond by increasing their output, partly for fear of losing their jobs but partly also in an effort to maintain the old level of earnings. The more firmly workers cling to some fixed standard of living, the more likely it is that the supply of labour will move in the opposite direction to wages.

Secondly, the linking of wages with real costs suggests that wages are somehow *proportional* to real costs. But is would be ludicrous to suggest that the duties of a professor are ten times as disagreeable as those for a coal-miner or blast-furnaceman, or that his income is ten times greater than theirs because of the greater efforts and sacrifices which his training required. Earnings may be related, but are certainly not proportioned, to efforts and sacrifices. This is particularly obvious if we look at the earnings of the other two factors of production. The efforts and sacrifices for which labour is compensated are real enough. But in return for what efforts or sacrifices do we pay interest on capital or rent for land? The provision of land, as we have seen, involves no sacrifice because the land already exists and cannot go out of existence. The provision of capital does, however, involve a sacrifice since we can add to the stock only by saving, and saving means denying ourselves present enjoyments. It costs us something to refrain from spending money, and the interest which we earn on our savings can be regarded, therefore, as compensation for our self-denial. But no one would dream of suggesting that this self-denial is as great for the millionaire as it is for the wage-earner, although both are paid equally at the same rate of interest. In addition, the stock of capital that was accumulated by past generations requires no fresh sacrifice, although it continues to earn interest. Clearly, then, the payments which are made to the factors of production bear little relation to the sacrifices by which they are earned. Rent is earned without effort on the part of anyone, interest by dint of thrift or in virtue of inheritance, and wages by the sweat of the brow. The service sold by one man for a pound may cost him a far lighter sacrifice than the service sold by another man for a shilling.

### Supply price: costs as relinquished alternatives

Payments to the factors of production are made, not in compensation for sacrifices, but as inducements to effort. These payments—the prices of the factors—must be high enough to provide an adequate incentive to the owners of the factors to continue to supply them. Each factor must earn its "supply price" —the minimum price, expectation of which will just suffice to call forth the required amount of the factor—or its services will not be made available. This supply price will depend upon the pull of the alternatives open to the factor. If an hour of leisure is very attractive in comparison with an hour of work, then the supply price of labour will be correspondingly high. If we are little troubled by thoughts of a rainy day in the distant future, and weak against the fascinations of present enjoyments, then it will require a very high rate of interest to turn the scale in favour of thrift. Our time can be spent in work or in leisure, and our money can be spent or saved. The greater our preference for work, the lower will be the supply price of labour. The greater our preference for thrift, the lower will be the supply price of capital. The strength of our preference will make itself felt at the margin. The choice before us is one of a little more work or a little less, a little more spending or a little less. Thus it will be our marginal preference for work, as compared with leisure, which governs the supply of labour (in the sense of actual effort), and it will be our marginal preference for thrift which governs the supply of capital (in the sense of current savings).

The rate of wages and the rate of interest must be at least equal to the supply of labour and of capital, and these supply prices are governed by our marginal preference for work and for thrift. In other words, the rates of wages and of interest measure the attractiveness at the margin of the alternatives which we relinquish by working or by saving. The value of these alternatives is the true cost of working and saving.

### Supply price and transfer cost

This conception of cost as relinquished alternatives is one with which we have already met.[1] We saw how the cost of producing any commodity is equal to the value *for other purposes* of the factors engaged in producing it—what we called their transfer cost. Now "transfer cost" is just another name for "supply price." But whereas in the present chapter we have been discussing the supply price of labour and capital *for any purpose*, what we discussed previously was the supply price of labour and capital to some *particular industry*. There is a distinction between the question: What determines the total amount of labour and capital seeking employment? and the question: What determines how a given amount of labour and capital will be distributed between competing industries?

This distinction is of great importance when we come to consider the third factor of production—land. The supply price of land-in-general is zero. There is no alternative to using land except not using it, and since there is nothing to be gained by not using it, its supply price is zero. The entire earnings of land, in the economic sense, therefore, form a surplus above its supply-price and it is by analogy with land that any excess of earnings over transfer cost or supply price is called "rent." On the other hand, the supply price of land to any one branch of agriculture is by no means zero. If, for example, land can

---

[1] See above, pp. 256–7.

be used either for wheat growing or for barley growing, then the supply price of the land to either industry will be its value under the other crop. The cost of using the land for wheat growing, therefore, is quite different from the simple cost of using the land; the alternative to be overcome is the comparatively attractive one of using the land for barley growing, not the quite unattractive one of letting the land go out to cultivation.

### Rent and cost: an illustration

To illustrate this point in more detail it is necessary to elaborate the theory of economic rent. Economic rent is the payment made by a tenant for the use of land alone. The rent paid by a British farmer (contract rent) is generally greater than economic rent since it includes a payment for the use of buildings and fences and for other improvements such as clearing and ditching.

The essence of the theory of economic rent as it used to be stated—for example, by Ricardo—is that rent "does not and cannot enter in the least degree"[1] into price, but is itself governed by price. Clearly, this is true only if we are thinking of land-in-general. If it were possible to use land for a single purpose only, say for wheat growing, then the rent of land would have no influence upon the price of wheat. The supply price of land would be zero— that is, there would be no level of rent below which land would cease to be available for wheat growing. Rent, therefore, would be a surplus governed by the demand for wheat and the cost of cultivation. It would be high if wheat was fetching a high price, or if the cost of cultivation was low, so that there was competition for farms; and it would be low if an agricultural depression, by bringing down the price of wheat relatively to farming costs, made it difficult for farmers to carry on. If the price of wheat were high it would not be because high rents had to be paid. The reverse would be true; it would be because the price of wheat was high that high rents could be paid.

This proposition is most readily understood when it is related to the idea of the margin. The price of wheat will be equal, under perfect competition, to the marginal cost of growing wheat—in other words, to the cost of growing wheat on marginal land. If the price is higher, additional land will be brought under cultivation, and if it is lower, some land will fall out of cultivation. But marginal land pays no rent because the costs of working it are only just covered and rent, therefore, cannot form part of the cost of cultivation at the margin. It is this cost which tends to equal the price of wheat; rent, therefore, can have no influence on the price of wheat. Rent will be paid by intra-marginal pieces of land, on which the cost of cultivation is lower than at the margin, and since

---

[1] David Ricardo, *Principles of Political Economy* (Everyman Edition), pp. 40–41.

farmers are free to choose between marginal land and land of greater fertility or superior situation, the rent which they will offer for any piece of land will measure the differential advantage which it possesses over land at the margin. If the demand for wheat increases, forcing up the price and making it profitable to cultivate, at increasing cost, land which was previously sub-marginal, the differential advantage of a given piece of land over marginal land will automatically increase and the rent which is offered for it will increase correspondingly. But the rise in rent will be the consequence not the cause of the rise in wheat prices. The price of wheat would not be affected if farmers paid no rent whatever because the price is governed by the cost of cultivation on marginal land, which pays no rent.

The same conclusion holds of urban rents. Goods in Bond Street are dear not because the shops there pay high rents, but because customers are willing to pay high prices. These high prices increase the demand for shop sites in Bond Street, and so enable rents to be paid. Bond Street rents, in other words, reflect the differential advantages of sites in the centre of London over sites on the outskirts.

Suppose, however, that there are other crops than wheat and that Bond Street shops do not sell goods of the same kind. Then the supply price of land *for any one purpose* ceases to be zero. Land can be rented for wheat growing only if its use is denied to other crops, and the rent which it might yield under the most profitable of these other crops—the transfer cost of land—does enter into the cost and into the price of wheat. If this cost is not met, the land will cease to be available for wheat growing and will cross the margin of transference into the next most profitable use. Land on the margin of cultivation pays no rent; land on the margin of transference does pay rent. This rent enters into the cost of *particular* agricultural products because it enters into the cost of marginal producers; it is not a surplus over the cost of cultivation, but is itself part of the cost of cultivation, governing, not governed by, price.

The general level of rents, therefore, is governed by the demand for agricultural products as a whole and by the cost of cultivation at the margin; from the point of view of land-in-general, economic rent is a surplus, not a cost. The rent of a particular piece of ground depends, first upon the general level of rents, and secondly upon its differential advantages of fertility, situation, climate and so on, over other pieces of land; from the point of view of a single branch of agriculture, all or part of this rent is a cost, not a surplus.

## Demand

Given the supply of any factor of production, its earnings depend upon the demand for its services. Here the governing influence is productivity—the more productive a factor is, the greater will be the demand for it, and the higher it will be paid. Productivity might seem to imply the creation of something of real social value, but as we have seen, the term is used in economics in a much narrower sense to refer to the creation of utility. Society might be little the worse if expert manicurists and animal dentists were exterminated, and a great deal the worse if farmers and bricklayers disappeared. But manicurists may nevertheless be paid more than farmers because they are more "productive" —more productive in the sense that a greater value is set on their services by those who have plenty of money with which to back their valuations. If there were as many manicurists as farmers, however, it would be the farmers who were more productive. We would have more manicurists than we could possibly use, and they would require to offer their services for next to nothing. Just as the utility of a commodity declines the more we have of it, so the productivity of 'any factor of production declines the more of it we are already employing. There is a law of diminishing productivity parallel to the law of diminishing utility.

## Marginal productivity

It is, in fact, not simply the productivity of a factor that governs the price which we will offer for its services (our "demand price"). It is the productivity of the factor at the margin, or its marginal productivity. The earnings of any factor of production tend to be equal to the value of the marginal product of the factor. This may be defined as the value of the contribution to output made by that unit of the factor which is engaged in the least productive task.

Suppose, for example, that a farmer is hiring workers all of whom are of equal efficiency and all of whom, if competition is perfect, will have to be paid the same wage. It may be worth £8 a week to the farmer to have the services of one ploughman, £6 a week to have the services of a second, and £5 a week to have the services of a third. The second ploughman will not be so indispensable as the first: if, for example, the farmer has no difficulty in laying down part of his land to grass but wishes to keep some minimum area under the plough; or if there are enough odd jobs about the farm to keep one ploughman busy in slack times but hardly enough for two. Similarly, the work done by the third ploughman will be less vital to the farm as an enterprise than the work of the second ploughman. There may also be other workers on the farm— cattlemen, shepherds, etc.—who are entrusted with tasks of varying productivity but who are all on the same level of efficiency. If the wage at which agricultural workers can be hired is fixed, the farmer will add to the number of men whom he is employing until the addition to the produce of the farm made by the last or marginal man just balances his wages. To employ more men would mean a needless sacrifice of profit; to employ fewer would be to miss an opportunity of a further small profit. Thus the marginal man will earn a wage equal to the value of the tasks which he performs, and other workers, being of the same efficiency as the marginal worker, will be paid the same wage whatever the value of the tasks on which they are engaged. If the workers are all inter-changeable so that the farmer is quite indifferent which of them he employs, he will have no reason to pay a high wage to one man and a lower wage to another. He will pay all alike the value of the marginal product of agricultural labour.

What is true of one farm will be true of all. Each farmer will take on more men up to the point at which the marginal product of labour is equal to the wage that has to be paid. If, when all farmers are trying to do this, there is a shortage of labour, then farmers on whose land the marginal product of labour is above its wage will require to bid away workers from farms on which these workers are not being employed to the best advantage. This will force up wages; a variety of tasks which were previously undertaken by labour will cease to be worth while; the demand for labour will be reduced; and equilibrium between demand and supply will be restored at a higher level of wages and marginal productivity. On the other hand, if wages are so high that farmers do not find it profitable to employ all the workers who are looking for jobs in agriculture, it will be necessary for wages to fall, so extending the field of employment to include tasks which were previously sub-marginal, before the unemployed workers can find jobs.

The marginal product of labour may be greater on one farm than on another. While competition for workers is making itself felt, we may find a prosperous and expanding farm on which the marginal product of labour is above the level of wages, and a depressed and contracting farm on which the marginal product of labour is below the level of wages. The first farm will be trying to increase its staff, the second to diminish its staff. But if competition is effective we will not find the first farm paying high wages and the second low wages. The state of profits on any single farm will not, so long as labour can move freely from one farm to another, affect the terms on which that particular farm can hire its labour. Nor will wages be high or low on any single farm because the marginal product of labour *on that farm* is high or low. We must measure the marginal product of labour not on a farm which is more prosperous or more depressed than the general run of farms, but on a representative farm which will reflect the trend of farming. Such a farm will be in equilibrium when farming is in equilibrium, and will make excessive or inadequate profits according as the industry is progressing or depressed. The rate at which a representative farm hires its workers will be the rate which other farms also will require to pay. Agricultural wages are governed, on the side of demand, by the marginal product of labour on a representative farm. This conclusion applies not only to

K*

agriculture, but to all industries. For "farm" we can just as well read "firm." In each industry wages tend to equality with the marginal product of labour in a representative firm.

The line of reasoning which we have so far followed can readily be extended to cover the whole of industry. If there is free movement of labour between industries—and this is far less likely than free movement between firms—then the wages paid to labour of a given grade of skill and efficiency will be the same in each industry. The state of prosperity of an industry will not affect the terms on which it hires its workers. Those terms will be governed by the marginal productivity of labour in a representative industry which is sensitive to the dominant trends in employment, expanding or contracting as the general level of employment expands or contracts.

### Marginal productivity and substitution

The marginal productivity of a factor, like the marginal utility of a commodity, diminishes as it becomes more abundant. When we studied the demand for a commodity we found the idea of the margin bound up with that of substitution. In studying the demand for a factor of production we find this association repeated. The rate at which the marginal productivity of a factor diminishes depends upon what we might call its "substitutability"—that is, upon the ease with which additional units of the factor can be substituted for other factors. If two factors can be readily substituted for one another, the marginal productivity of either of them will diminish slowly, for there will be a large number of tasks performed by one factor which could be easily undertaken by the other if more of it were to become available. Now our ability to substitute one factor for another is limited by, and subject to, the law of diminishing returns. This law is little more than a statement that the substitution of one factor for another becomes progressively more difficult as the ratio of combination alters. It is a law, so to speak, of diminishing "substitutability." In the law of diminishing returns, therefore, we have one reason—a technical reason—why marginal productivity declines. Additional supplies of any factor can be absorbed into employment with increasing difficulty, because, in the extra uses to which the factor is put, it is a less and less effective substitute for the other (constant) factors. Its value in these extra uses—the value of its marginal product—diminishes, and the price which it can command falls correspondingly.

Diminishing marginal productivity can also be traced to the law of diminishing utility. If any factor is less scarce, its products will also be less scarce and, therefore, of less utility. They will fetch a lower price, and the factor which produces them will be forced to content itself with lower earnings. Here we have a second reason—a psychological one—why marginal productivity declines.

If the supply of any factor of production increases. therefore, there will be a double substitution—by producers, in conformity with the law of diminishing returns, and by consumers, in conformity with the law of diminishing utility. Suppose, for example, that more people want to find jobs in agriculture. Then increased competition will force down agricultural wages until farmers have an incentive to take on more men. This incentive will be twofold.

First, since labour is cheaper relatively to capital and land, it will pay, in the growing of any particular crop, to use more labour and less capital and land. Farmers who were forced by the high cost of labour to install milking machines, and to use tractors for ploughing, will now be able to go back to hand-milking and horse-ploughing. Where cultivation was extensive, so as to economise labour, it will become more intensive as the use of labour becomes less costly. Thus a given quantity of product will be raised by a larger number of men, working either with less capital or on a smaller area of land than before.

Secondly, the fall in agricultural wages will not affect all branches of agriculture equally. Wages are a much larger item in the cost of wheat than in the cost of wool, and they are a still larger item in the cost of vegetables. A fall in wages, therefore, will reduce the price of wheat relatively to the price of wool, and will reduce the price of vegetables even more. The greater the reduction in price, the greater will be the increase in demand; consumers will buy more of the relatively cheaper and fewer of the relatively dearer goods. There will be a great expansion in vegetable growing and those branches of agriculture which make most use of labour, and a comparatively slight expansion in sheep-farming and those branches of agriculture in which labour is least used. Consumers will substitute goods using much, for goods using little labour and the total demand for labour will, therefore, increase. The more readily consumers can adjust their budget so as to transfer demand from one group of goods to the other, when wage-costs are rising or falling; the more sensitive will be the demand for labour to a change in wages; the more elastic, in other words, will be the demand for labour.

### Elasticity of demand

The rate at which the marginal productivity of a factor diminishes as the supply of the factor increases is the same thing, if the factor always earns the value of its marginal product, as the elasticity of demand for the factor. Thus our conclusions as to diminishing marginal productivity can be easily re-stated in terms of elasticity—the elasticity of demand for any factor will be governed by the technical obstacles to substituting that factor for other factors of production, and by the psychological obstacles to substituting its products for their products. It will depend also upon the elasticity of supply of appropriate substitutes, both to producers and to consumers.

Although each factor of production can be substituted for the other factors at the margin, substitution cannot be carried so far that we can do without one factor altogether. It is difficult to imagine a type of production into which land, labour and capital do not all enter. Thus the factors are simultaneously in competition and in co-operation with one another; they are at once rival and complementary. This two-sided relationship, which arises because the factors are simultaneously in joint demand and in composite supply, raised problems similar to those touched on in Chapter 20. How, for example, will a change in the supply of one factor react on the earnings of the others?

Suppose, first of all, that there are only two factors of production—labour and property. Then an increase in the supply of one will necessarily raise the earnings of the other. If more workers have to be employed, the marginal productivity of labour will fall, and each worker, not just each additional worker, will earn a lower wage. Since the additional men employed will be contributing to the value of output at least as much as their wages, the residue of product after payment of wages to all workers, will be greater. This residue will be equal to the earnings of property. The return on property will necessarily increase. But the share of property in the total product may not increase. If the demand for labour is elastic, employers will spend more on labour as it becomes cheaper, so that a greater aggregate wage-bill will be distributed amongst the large number of workers. The aggregate earnings, both of labour and of property, will increase; and if the demand for labour is sufficiently elastic—in other words, if labour is easily substituted for property—the share of labour will increase. The wage-bill will form a higher proportion of the national income, although wages per man will, of course, be lower.

There is reason to believe that labour and property are not in fact easily substituted for one another. If we think of property as made up of machinery, this conclusion will seem very puzzling; machinery is constantly being substituted for labour, and if labour became cheaper instead of dearer the substitution might be reversed. But if we think of property as made up of dwelling-houses, power stations, railways, agricultural land, and so on, our difficulty will be to see how any kind of substitution of labour is possible: substitution has to be more roundabout—as, for example, scarcity of domestic servants induces us to move from an old house that needs a great many servants to run it, to an expensively fitted flat that needs very little domestic help. Since property of the second type predominates over property of the first type, labour and property are not very good substitutes for one another. They are more complementary than rival, and an increase in one, therefore, tends to diminish its share in the national income, and to increase the share of the other.[1]

When there are more factors than two, an increase in the supply of one factor may be of advantage to some and of disadvantage to others. If, for example, America were to admit a large number of Chinese immigrants, the wages of domestic servants, dock labourers, laundry workers, etc., would probably fall, while the middle classes would find themselves better off because they would be able to buy the services of Chinese workers more cheaply without suffering any loss of income either from property or from work. The immigrants would be almost entirely rival to the first group of workers, and almost entirely complementary to the second. There might also be an intermediate group of workers, such as farmers or semi-skilled factory workers who, on balance, would neither gain nor lose appreciably.

## Implications of the theory

The conclusions reached above are very far-reaching in their implications. For example, it will be in the interest of any group of people that workers in other trades should be as numerous and hard-working and efficient as possible, while other workers in their own trades, or in close competition with it, should be as few, as lazy and as inefficient as possible. The first condition will make for cheapness in what they buy and the second for dearness in what they sell. Again, it will be in the interest of the working-class that capitalists should accumulate property as rapidly as possible rather than dissipate their income in private extravagance, since as the stock of property increases the return on it will fall, the earnings of labour will rise, and the share of labour in the national income will very probably rise also.[2] On the other hand, it will be in the interest of the propertied classes if the population increases rapidly, if hours of work remain long, and if wage earners work hard and save little. It is clear that the analysis of this chapter provides a clue to many serious conflicts of interest between classes and countries.

## Marginal product and marginal net product

The marginal productivity theory, as stated so far, is based upon an assumption which we have not yet investigated. That assumption is that it is possible to *measure* the productivity of each factor of production. But if labour is always used in conjunction with capital and land, how are we to disentangle the peculiar

---

[1] Over the last hundred years, property has been increasing more rapidly than labour and yet the share of each in the national income before tax has been remarkably stable. Presumably invention has been maintaining the marginal productivity of property just sufficiently to offset the influence of its growing abundance.

[2] This will, however, depend on the rate of increase of population and the elasticity of demand for property.

contribution of labour from the joint product of all three? How much of the timber cut by a lumberman is to be "attributed" to his labour, how much to the capital sunk in his axe, and how much to the natural fertility of the soil? According to the marginal productivity theory, this question can be answered only by going to the margin and measuring the value of the timber cut by an additional lumberman. But if he has no axe he can cut no timber, and this productivity will be nil. If he *has* an axe, we have still to decide what *its* productivity is. We seem to be no further on. The theory of marginal productivity ceases to be applicable if an increased quantity of one factor can be used only in conjunction with a correspondingly increased quantity of the other factors. In other words, the theory presupposes that it is technically possible to vary the proportions in which the factors of production are combined.[1]

This is not a very extravagent assumption. If methods of production were dictated everywhere by technique, the task of the employer would be an easy one. No search after improved methods, no substitution of one factor for another in a ceaseless effort to keep down costs! Instead, the automatic adoption of routine technique, unchanged from boom to slump and back again! In fact, however, employers are not so fortunate. Technique is plastic and responsive to changes in the relative scarcity and price of the factors of production. Variation in "technical coefficients"—the ratios in which the factors of production are combined—can be made in three ways.

First, employers may use extra units of one factor with a constant quantity of the others by changing the form in which the other factors are provided. They may, for example, employ more lumbermen and cheaper axes so that everyone has an axe but not such a good one as before. In the average industrial concern, even a change of this kind would not be necessary; it would be sufficient to institute a night-shift with the existing plant.

Second, there are generally wide variations in technical methods between the firms in an industry, some firms relying on a lavish use of machinery and plant, and others on a lavish use of labour. These variations are possible because of differences in the scale of operations and in management. But if the cost of either labour or capital increases, some firms will suffer a disproportionate reduction in profits because of their dependence on the dearer factor; and these firms will tend to be squeezed out of production, while the firms which employ a larger proportion of the other factor will continue.

Third, the prosperity of different industries, equally with the prosperity of competing firms, depends upon the comparative cost of the preponderant factors of production. If the course of wages is upwards, the coal industry,

---

[1] For the similar problem of joint cost, see p. 273.

which employs a very high proportion of labour to capital, will be more embarrassed than the chemical industries in which capital preponderates. It is possible to vary the range of uses for labour while the supply of other factors remains constant by expanding one set of industries and contracting another.

Since these variations in technical coefficients do take place it is unnecessary to assume that employers can or should attempt to measure the marginal productivity of each factor. It will be sufficient if they measure something rather different—something which, in equilibrium, will be equal to marginal productivity. This alternative concept is marginal *net* productivity.

The marginal net product of any factor is the net value of the contribution to output made by a marginal unit of the factor when combined with the appropriate quantity of other factors; a "marginal unit" being *any* unit of the factor when engaged in the least productive use to which it is put; and "net value" being understood to mean the total value less the cost of extra units of the other factors. Thus the marginal net product of lumbermen will be the value of the timber cut by the marginal lumbermen, less the cost of his axe and the royalty on the timber. *Provided* these last items can be taken for granted and we already know how their price is determined, it will be enough to think in terms of marginal *net* product. The marginal net product of lumbermen will govern the demand for their services and will tend—given perfect competition —to be equal to their wage.

### Marginal productivity and surpluses

It might appear that if one factor of production earned no more than its value in a marginal use, other factors of production would necessarily reap a surplus income; or that, if all the factors of production earned the value of their marginal product and no more, their joint income would fall short of the value of their total product. We have already seen, however, that under perfect competition price is equal to average cost, including normal profit; there is therefore no surplus income accruing as profit to the entrepreneur. Price is also equal to marginal cost, and the value of a marginal addition to output is equal therefore to the joint earnings of marginal units of each of the factors, combined in the optimum ratio to one another. This is just another way of saying that each factor is paid the value of its marginal net product. But it implies the absence of any surplus. For since each unit of output has the same value and requires just as much effort to produce, and since units of the factors of production are paid alike, what is true at the margin is true of total output and total earnings. The social product is exhausted when each factor earns the value of its marginal net product, and in conditions of perfect competition this will be equal to the value of its marginal product.

## Long-run influences on earnings

In order to give concreteness to the general theory outlined above, we may try to list the various influences which, in the long run, will make for an increase in the earnings of one of the factors of production. For this purpose we may concentrate on labour. In what circumstances should we anticipate a general rise in wage-earnings?

(i) Labour may become scarcer. This will restrict the range of tasks on which labour can be employed, eliminate tasks of inferior productivity, and so raise the productivity of labour at the margin. Or at least this is what would happen given constant returns. But if it requires a large population to exploit advances in technique—if, for example, a railway system, hydro-electric power stations, and so on would not come into existence without it—then the answer is not quite so simple.

(ii) Land and capital may become less scarce or it may become possible to make more intensive use of the existing supply (e.g., by growing two crops where one was grown before or by running two shifts instead of one). This will reduce the marginal productivity of land and capital and induce employers to compete more eagerly for the limited supply of labour. There will be a larger *number* of tasks to be performed in conjunction with the additional supply of other factors, and it will be necessary, therefore, to reserve labour for the *kind of task* in which other factors cannot readily be substituted for it. The use of labour will be limited to tasks of higher productivity than before and the marginal productivity of labour will, therefore, increase. For example, if farmers suddenly found themselves with larger areas of land to cultivate, they would probably have to take men from work on the farm which just repaid itself and set them to plough the extra land. The work of ploughing being of greater productivity than the work from which the men were taken, farmers would be able to pay higher wages, and if they wished to retain the services of their workers in face of competition from other farmers, would be *forced* to pay higher wages.

(iii) Workers may work harder, or faster, or for longer hours than before. The supply of *work*, although not of *labour*, will increase; the range of tasks performed by labour will be extended, and the marginal productivity of work will be reduced. Workers will be paid less per unit of effort; but, if the demand for work is elastic, the total reward for effort (the wage-*bill*) will increase, and since this total has to be divided amongst a constant number of workers, wages also will increase. A greater disposition to effort will be to the advantage of the other factors of production in the same way as an increase in the number of workers. From the point of view of the other factors it makes little difference whether labour is more abundant or more hard-working; either change increases the supply of work. It is only from the point of view of labour that there is a difference. If there are more workers, each will be paid less; if everyone works harder, and the demand for work is elastic, each worker will be paid more. Conversely, if the demand for work is inelastic and there is a shortage of labour, workers will be able to earn higher wages by showing a greater disinclination to effort. The other factors of production will stand to lose from such a restriction of the supply of work just as they stand to lose by a reduction in the number of workers.

(iv) Workers may become more efficient, or better trained, or more skilful. Since these changes increase the productivity of labour, each of them will, in general, lead to a rise in wages. An increase in training or in skill will tend to raise wages, but an increase in efficiency may conceivably operate to reduce wages. Faster work, as we have seen, will reduce wages when the demand for effort is inelastic; and an increased speed of working is just as likely to result from greater efficiency as from greater application. Some *kinds* of increase in efficiency, however, are quite certain to raise wages. Greater efficiency in the use of property, for example, will reduce the number of breakages, fires, etc., and allow the supply of property to increase more rapidly. Greater efficiency in the use of loan-capital, by directing it into industries where it is less likely to be wasted, will have the same effect. Unless the property which is "salvaged" in this way is mainly of the type which is in close competition with labour (e.g., machinery), labour will necessarily gain from the greater abundance of property.

(v) The productivity of factors other than labour may increase; for example, new inventions may be made. How do inventions affect wages? Do they make for a rising standard of living for everyone, or do they lead to unemployment and low wages?

### Invention and wages

Inventions are generally "labour-saving"—that is, they generally economise labour more than they economise capital or land. The greater the economy of labour, the stronger will be the tendency to unemployment and lower wages. But an invention may be labour-saving and yet increase both employment and wages. The railway engine, for example, has probably done more to save human effort than any other single invention. Yet nothing did more to increase the volume of employment in the nineteenth century than railway-building, and nothing contributed more to the raising of the standard of life than cheap railway transport. Similarly, although labour-saving machinery tends to create unemployment and low wages in the industry into which it is introduced, workers in other industries may derive a more than counterbalancing advantage from the fall in costs and prices to which the invention leads. So far as can be judged from the history of labour-saving inventions, they have generally done much more to raise than to lower the general level of wages, both by improving the worker's standard of living and by making labour less irksome. But if they have been of advantage to labour, they have been of even greater advantage to capital, since they have increased the productivity of capital more than the productivity of labour, so tending to increase the *share* of the national income accruing to capital.[1] It should be observed, too, that labour-saving inventions are not of equal advantage or disadvantage to all classes of workers. An invention may, for example, be skill-saving or toil-saving. If the invention is skill-saving, and strikes at an established handicraft such as hand-loom weaving, the earnings of skilled workers as a body will tend to suffer. If, on the other hand, the invention is toil-saving, and like the mechanical navvy economises muscular effort, then it will be the earnings of unskilled workers that tend to be reduced. In either event, since greater mechanisation is involved, machine-operators are likely to benefit.

Some inventions are not labour-saving, but capital-saving or land-saving. Communication by wireless, for example, requires less capital than communication by telephone or by deep sea cable. In urban transport, the motor omnibus is less capitalistic than the Tube. Similarly a new fertiliser which increases the fertility of the soil economises land, while urban sites are economised by improvements in the construction of skyscrapers. These inventions, while they may increase the total earnings of capital and land, just as labour-saving inventions may increase real wages, will tend to reduce the *share* of capital and land in the national income. Possibly because it has been labour which, of all the factors of production, has risen most in price over the past two hundred years, most inventions have been labour-saving, while capital- and land-saving inventions have been less important. On the whole, therefore, invention has been of greater service to property than to labour, and has done more to raise the return on property than to raise wages.[2]

## MONOPOLY AND UNEMPLOYMENT

### Monopolistic influences on wages

We can now relax the drastic assumption of perfect competition which has

---

[1] If, for example, the national income is divided in the ratio of 55 : 45 between labour and capital, and labour saving inventions increase the national income by 20 per cent., the enlarged national income may be divided between labour and capital in the ratio of 60 : 60.

[2] It is perhaps unnecessary to point out that just as some workers gain while others lose by an invention, so some property-owners will gain while others lose. There is an obvious loss to those whose property becomes obsolete, and an equally obvious gain to those who own the invention or who use its products.

been made throughout this chapter. Employers do not bid for more labour, land and capital without regard to the effect of their bids on the price at which they hire the factors of production. They do not exclude, in deciding what to pay and whom to employ, everything except their immediate financial interest. And they are rarely able to strike bargains with individual wage-earners as to the rate of wages which they will pay. In most industries wages are fixed by a process of collective bargaining between employers' associations and trade unions; sometimes by direct negotiations, sometimes by arbitration after argument of the case by both sides before an independent chairman; sometimes by an intermediate procedure of conciliation and discussion between the parties to the dispute with an added representation of independent or semi-independent opinion.

Collective bargaining, whatever the form which it assumes, is bargaining in which monopoly power is exerted by both sides; competition continues to influence the outcome, but the full force of competition is not exerted. The maximum rate which employers will pay is governed by the range of alternative open to them; the minimum rate which the factors will accept is governed by the range of alternatives open to them. But the alternatives vary with the degree of competition. Under perfect competition no employer would offer a wage higher than the value of the marginal product of labour since, if wages exceed marginal productivity, the dismissal of workers would yield an increased profit; and no worker would accept less than the value of his marginal product since if this were refused him by one employer he could find work at a higher rate of wages elsewhere. Immediately collective bargaining takes the place of private bargaining between each worker and each employer, the alternatives are transformed. There is still a maximum which employers will offer—the loss which they would suffer through the withdrawal of labour.[1] There is also a minimum

---

[1] This will fall short of the value of the marginal product of labour for two reasons.

In the first place, employers are not disposing of their output in conditions of perfect competition. If they lose or dismiss a worker, they sacrifice, not the full value of labour's marginal product, in the sense of physical product multiplied by price, but only the marginal physical product multiplied by marginal revenue. The output of an additional worker may be worth £10 a week on the assumption that additional sales are effected at unchanged prices; but if prices have to be lowered, the net return to the employer will be less than £10. The more imperfect the market for a given product, therefore, the lower will be the demand price for labour in relation to its marginal productivity, and the more restricted will be the employment of labour.

In the second place, even if competition in goods were perfect, employers have an incentive to limit their demand price for labour whenever they feel that increased employment will involve them in paying higher wages. If the value of the marginal product of labour is £12 employers may continue to pay £10 and abstain from taking on more men because of the higher rate of wages that they would have to pay, not only to the extra men but also to those already in their employment. In limiting their demand for labour in this way, they may be influenced by custom and regard for other employers. They may, for example, limit their offers of wages to some customary or minimum rate, partly from self-interest but partly so as to stand well with their neighbours.

which workers will accept—what they could earn in another occupation less the cost of changing their occupation and the money-measure of their preference for their existing job over other work. But between the demand-price of employers and the supply-price of the workers there may be a wide range of indeterminacy, within which bargaining power has free play.

On the tactics of the trials of strength that occur in wage disputes something will be said in the next chapter. For the present, only the broad strategy is in question.

### Monopolistic influences on the earnings of capital

It is no more true of capital than of labour that its earnings are fixed by perfect competition. One business has easy access to capital because of the personal contacts of its directors, while another, almost equally credit-worthy, is forced to expand out of profits. Interlocking directorates, the ramifications of holding companies, customary association, and all the links, tangible and intangible, that bind one business to another serve to break up the capital market into semi-monopolistic groups. In countries with slender resources of capital a few financial institutions may be almost the sole channels through which domestic savings (and still more, borrowings from abroad) can flow into investment. These institutions will obviously be extremely powerful, and the terms upon which they lend are not likely to be those upon which the same supply of capital would be offered by a new banking house seeking only to cover its costs. In Great Britain the general abundance of capital limits the power of the banks and finance houses, but in backward countries the danger of monopolistic exploitation is a very real one.

### Unemployment

The fact of unemployment takes greatly from the value of the marginal productivity theory. For the theory assumes throughout that all of the factors of production will be absorbed into continuous full employment, and that rates of earnings must be such as to bring this about. If, in fact, earnings remain steady and it is employment that fluctuates, then the theory of marginal productivity misconceives the problem and we must try another line of approach.

Over very long periods there can be no doubt that rates of earnings serve to equilibrate the supply of, and demand for, the factors of production; and the assumption of no unemployment does not destroy the usefulness of the marginal productivity theory as a guide to the response of earnings to changes either in supply or in demand. But, in the short or fairly short period, fluctuations in employment, and the persistence of involuntary unemployment, must be accounted for, and their influence on the distribution of income incorporated in the general theory.

No attempt will be made at this stage to expand the theory of distribution to cover fluctuations in employment. But an illustration may be given of the way in which a too hasty application of the marginal productivity theory leads to a quite false deduction. It would seem to be an obvious corollary of the theory that a reduction in wage rates will produce an increase in employment. But this is true of a reduction in *real* wage rates. If money wages are reduced the cost of living will probably fall simultaneously, leaving real wages as they were. That is, it is a great deal more difficult than one might suppose to make real wage rates fall, and the apparently obvious cure for unemployment of cutting money wages may not achieve the intended result.

## Summary

The argument of this chapter has been conducted at a high level of abstraction from real life. But the problem of distribution is so complex that it must be approached in stages, and the first stage is to understand the tendency of competition. Setting aside the influence of monopoly and unemployment, we have seen that the distribution of the national income between the factors of production is governed by the relative scarcity of the factors and by their marginal productivity. The supply of labour and capital depends upon our marginal preference for work and thrift, while the supply of land is fixed by nature. The ratios in which the factors are combined are determined by employers, who give effect to the twin principles of substitution and diminishing marginal productivity, varying their demand for any one factor until its marginal productivity is equal to its price or earnings. The removal of the assumption of perfect competition introduces an element of indeterminacy. The earnings of a factor will lie between the lower limit set by the supply price of the factor and the upper limit set by its loss value to employers.

## CHAPTER 23

# WAGES

### 1  COMPETITIVE INFLUENCES

The theory of wages deals mainly with two questions—what determines the general level of wages and the share of labour in the national product? and why do wages differ in different places and occupations? An answer to the first question has already been given in the previous chapter. There it was assumed that all wage-earners were alike in efficiency, training and skill so that no employer would offer higher wages to one worker than to another. It was assumed also that all wage-earners were alike by temperament and taste, and that they worked under similar conditions in occupations and places that were equally agreeable or disagreeable, so that no worker would demand higher wages in one job than in another. On these assumptions we found that the tendency of competition was to make the general level of wages equal to the value of the marginal product of labour.

The second question arises as soon as we drop the assumptions. Wage-earners differ in efficiency, training and skill, and these differences are reflected in differences in wage rates. But even amongst workers of the same general calibre there are fairly large differences in wages. Why is this? Why is it that workers who are free to choose their occupation and place of work continue to accept low wages when they might move to better-paid jobs? Why do different industries and districts pay different rates of wages for the same grade of work?

**"Horizontal" differences in wages**

We may begin with differences that arise when workers are alike in skill, training and efficiency, taking a kind of horizontal cross-section of labour. One source of such differences is that wage rates are generally expressed in terms of the full-time weekly rate of wages—sometimes called "nominal wages." But the nominal wages payable in any occupation may be greater or less than the average income which workers in that occupation can normally expect to earn.

The cash wage may be supplemented by an allowance of free coal, or potatoes, or house-room, and these perquisites—which are of particular importance in the earnings of agricultural workers—obviously form part of the "real wages" payable to the worker. On the other hand, a deduction should be made from nominal wages in some occupations to cover any outlay on uniforms, overalls, travelling expenses, social display, etc., associated with the workers' duties. Nominal wages will also differ from real wages if overtime, short time or unemployment are normal features of an occupation. A bricklayer whose work is frequently interrupted by bad weather will not be so well off as a postman whose nominal wages are the same and who has the advantage of steady employment. As for unemployment, an occupation like shipbuilding which suffers from periodic slumps will require to offer fairly high nominal wages before the real wages obtainable in it over a period of years reach a moderate level. A final point of distinction is that whereas nominal wages are expressed in terms of money, real wages consist of the goods and services which this money will buy. Thus if we find a 'bus driver in London earning £20 a week and a 'bus driver in Glasgow earning only £15 a week we must not jump to the conclusion that wages are higher in London than in Glasgow, for it may cost £20 to buy in London what can be had in Glasgow for £15. Differences in nominal wage between occupations and places may be quite consistent, therefore, with equality of real wages.

**Net advantages**—Workers may accept comparatively low wages in one place or occupation because of some compensating advantage which they enjoy over places and occupations where wages are higher. There may be opportunities, for example, of alternative or supplementary employment either for the worker himself or for his family. A textile worker may prefer to accept low wages in Lancashire, where all his family can find employment, rather than move to a well-paid job in Lincoln or Shrewsbury, where his family might earn little or nothing. Similarly, a married man with a young family may hesitate to give up agricultural work because of the ease with which he can find work for his children on the land. If he happens to have a great deal of spare time every winter, and can use this spare time for toy-making, his income from this supplementary work will be an added inducement to remain in agriculture.

Opportunities of rapid promotion and prospects of spectacular earnings will also compensate for comparatively low initial earnings and this compensation will be greater than, on a strictly rational view, it should be. Since most of us have a good conceit of ourselves, and exaggerate our own chances of success, we allow ourselves to be unduly influenced by the *maximum* earnings of an occupation, and are not always deterred by low *average* earnings. The knowledge that the most eminent lawyers earn more than the most eminent doctors will have more weight with an ambitious young man than the knowledge that the average doctor earns more than the average lawyer.

Compensation for a comparatively low wage may also be found in various amenities which attach to the job and enhance its attractiveness—what might be called the "kudos other than cash"—which the worker enjoys. A man may prefer to seek employment in a poorly-paid job because the sacrifice in earnings is more than balanced by these non-pecuniary amenities. He may find the work more agreeable because it is carried on in the country, or in a well-ventilated factory, or with less danger to health. He may be attracted by the regularity and security of the job, or by the opportunities of leisure or absenteeism which it affords, or by the power and prestige attaching to it, or by the scope which it offers for the exercise of some special bent. On the other hand, he will avoid work which is exhausting (e.g., mining), or causes great discomfort (e.g., road-breaking), or endangers life (e.g., the work of the steeplejack, the sailor, etc.), or which is carried on in an unhealthy atmosphere (e.g., the roasting of copper ore, stoking, the manufacture of chemicals, etc.), or which is monotonous or excessively speeded up.

What determines the attractiveness of a trade, in other words, is not just the wage which it pays but its net advantages. Even when workers are alike in efficiency, and can move freely from one job to another, competition will not drive wages to the same level in all places and occupations. It will be the net advantages of each place and occupation that tend to equality. There are, however, a number of obstacles to the free movement of labour and hence to the equalisation of net advantages. These obstacles, and the resulting immobility of labour, provide a second reason for difference in wages between places and industries.

**Mobility and immobility**—When an industry becomes comparatively overcrowded, as coal-mining did after 1921, it is not possible for workers to transfer themselves immediately to other industries. Movement would mean the sacrifice of an acquired technique, and a long irksome period of re-training. The older the worker, the greater the difficulty. The older men are less adaptable, and have more at stake in the revival of the industry. In it their industrial experience has taken shape, and in it they become accustomed to ways of life which they are reluctant to abandon. They are the more willing to wait in the hope of re-employment because their chances of employment in other industries are small. Employers will hesitate to start them on comparatively unfamiliar work so long as there is an over-supply of younger workers in the same district. The burden of change, therefore, falls on these younger workers. The same is true of geographical movement. If there is a depression in one part of the country, it will be particularly difficult for the older workers to move in search of employment. They are tied by family responsibilities and by old associations. They may own their house and be forced to sell it at a bargain price. On the other hand, they may have great difficulty in renting or buying a house in districts where there is no lack of work. The mere cost of transferring a family from one district to another may be enough to deter a married man from moving to a better-paid job. The young worker, with no family and no property, will move much more readily.

Thus changes in the distribution of labour between places and occupations come about more through the action of young workers in moving where prospects are good than through transfers on the part of older workers out of contracting industries and localities. Young workers are not yet in a groove. They have fewer commitments and more enterprise, and do not need to overcome the inertia of an earlier choice. The higher the proportion of workers in the younger age-groups, therefore, the greater is likely to be the mobility of labour. Since the proportion has in fact been declining for over forty years, and will almost certainly continue to decline for some time, there are clearly strong forces at work making for a less mobile and less adaptable population.

Even the mobility of young workers, however, tends to be rather low. The range of occupations open to them, particularly in districts like South Wales, and towns like Bradford, is generally narrow, and the range of choice is often restricted by family circumstances. The need of working-class families for immediate income may force children into blind alley occupations. Or, by the force of example of parents and relatives, children may be induced to enter the industry with which their family is most familiar. This may, and does, happen even when the industry is in process of contraction and the older members of the family cannot find work in it. The tendency for boys to follow their fathers' footsteps is not due solely to bias towards the parental occupation, but quite as much to limited knowledge and limited contacts. Neither the boy nor his parents are likely to be so knowledgeable about alternative occupations, and the father may lack both the means and the influence to give the boy a start in some other industry. Juvenile labour, therefore, does not always flow to the points of scarcity, but tends to remain within grooves cut by family circumstances.

Immobility may result from the worker's disinclination to move—a disinclination originating in ignorance, uncertainty, poverty, family ties, or sheer inertia. But there are other, external, reasons for immobility; there may be impediments to the free movement of labour. A man cannot leave one country and enter another whenever he hears that wages are higher abroad; there are laws restricting immigration. Even within a country his movements may be restricted—an agricultural worker may require permission to take a job in industry, a teacher born in one county may be debarred from employment in other counties, or there may be discrimination by race, language or religion, limiting certain occupations to members of a single group. When such restrictions have not the force of law, prejudice, bias and custom may give rise to a boycott which is no less effective in limiting the field of employment. There are many occupations, for example, from which women have never been excluded by law, but in which, until recently, they rarely if ever found employment. This has partly been due to the pressure of trade unions and the rules of professional associations like the General Medical Council. These bodies, in an effort to increase their powers of monopoly, have not unnaturally sought to limit their numbers by erecting barriers against entry into their occupation or profession. Women—amongst others—have suffered since they have been forced to squeeze into occupations where entry is freer and which, as a result, are comparatively overcrowded. One reason, therefore, why women's earnings are lower than men's is just that they are not allowed to participate in the monopoly gains of "protected" industries, but have to crowd into the limited range of occupations which men have thought fit to surrender to them.

**Unfair wages**—Immobility of labour, whether due to disinclination to move or to artificial impediments to movement, creates disparity between the net advantages of different places and occupations. Labour of the same calibre will be paid higher wages or enjoy better conditions of work in one place or occupation than in another. A comparative surplus of labour in one trade will reduce its marginal productivity there, while a comparative shortage in another will raise the marginal productivity of labour there. Wages in the two trades will diverge and the divergence will continue until there is a movement of labour out of the first trade and into the second. If, for example, the demand for railway travel falls, then railwaymen will probably be paid lower wages than are paid in other industries. Railway work will be comparatively unattractive, but railwaymen may have to put up with the change in conditions because of their inability or reluctance to find work in other industries.

The net advantages of railway work will be less than the net advantages of other occupations employing workers of equal efficiency. This is sometimes expressed by saying that the wages of railwaymen will be "unfair," the term "unfair" being used to mean "less than can be earned with equal effort by similar workers in other industries." In this sense, the wages of agricultural workers before the war were "unfair." Agriculture was "overcrowded" in relation to the demand for agricultural products, foodstuffs had to be sold at low prices, and the incomes both of farmers and of agricultural labourers were depressed below the level which equal skill and effort would have procured in other industries. These low incomes, moreover, were earned by all farm workers, not just by those who were ultimately forced to give up farming. Thus the relative over-supply of farming labour exposed it to what was, in effect, exploitation by workers in other trades who got their food at abnormally low prices. The immobility of farm workers kept down their wages to an "unfair" level.

In the world of the future a high degree of labour mobility will be more than ever essential, partly to secure speed of adjustment to violent changes in technique and in the direction of trade, and partly because there will be in the labour market a higher proportion of older and less mobile workers. In the last thirty years innovations in methods of manufacture have been at a prodigious pace, which shows no sign of slackening; great industries have toppled headlong and younger industries have thrust their way upwards; and at the same time the age-distribution of the working population has been less and less favourable to the rapid displacement of old methods and industries by new. In the next thirty years these things will undoubtedly continue. The more we can increase mobility, therefore, the better.

The methods by which this can be done are well-known. They include the provision of fuller and more accurate information to workers in search of alternative employment, grants towards the cost of movement, and measures to improve or supplement training and educational facilities. A vocational advisory service, working in conjunction with the schools and the Labour Exchange, can help juvenile workers to choose from a wider variety of careers. The Labour Exchanges may also assist industrial mobility by giving more prominence or preferential treatment to vacancies in industries where there is a general shortage of labour. The Ministry of Labour has power to make payments of grants and allowances to meet the cost of removal from one district to another or of living away from home pending removal. It also runs a number of Government Training Centres which can concentrate their efforts on overcoming shortages of labour in particular trades or on helping unemployed or disabled workers to re-train for a new occupation.

High mobility and high employment go together. If there are plenty of jobs, people will change more readily from one job to another or from one district to another. With full employment the movement of labour between firms, and labour turnover in firms, is often embarrassingly high; the movement between industries and (if there is no housing shortage) districts, if not actually embarrassing, is normally much higher than in an industrial depression. On the other hand, it is a thankless task trying to increase mobility when there are no jobs to be had: men generally prefer to be unemployed where they are rather than volunteer for re-training or transfer without the certainty of getting and keeping a new job.

## "Vertical" differences in wages

So far, we have taken a kind of horizontal cross-section of labour and confined the discussion to workers of equal efficiency, training and skill. But when we think of differences in earnings we generally have in mind inequalities whose origin lies in "vertical" rather than in "horizontal" differences between workers. We think of lawyers and film-stars and company directors and compare their earnings with those of clerks and charwomen and navvies. We reflect that, far from these differences in earnings being compensated by differences in amenities, it seems to be the best-paid jobs that require least effort and afford most leisure. We may even ask ourselves why, if the jobs at the top are so attractive, so many people remain at the bottom. Three reasons suggest themselves— lack of ability, lack of training and lack of opportunity.

Differences between workers in natural ability are exactly like differences between pieces of land in natural fertility; just as the more fertile pieces of land command a premium over the less fertile, so the more able workers can obtain higher wages than the average. Indeed, economists often speak of a "rent of ability" when comparing the earnings of superior talent with the earnings of mediocrity, so extending to labour the conception of rent as a differential surplus. This surplus, like land rent, is determined solely by demand. It is not enough to have rare gifts, superior to the gifts of others, in order to earn an exceptionally large income. It is necessary also to have those particular gifts which are most in demand. Few artists have ever made a fortune, or even a decent livelihood; just as few landlords have ever made money by improving the landscape. The ability of a statesman, a social reformer, or a philosopher is far more poorly rewarded—except in prestige—than the ability to cheat and dissimulate and take advantage of the ignorance of others. The most "able" workers—like the most "fertile" pieces of land—are those who can provide the services for which people pay, not those who, on a moral or aesthetic judgment, are most deserving of reward.

Differences in training also produce differences in earnings. If a worker has to sink capital in a long and expensive education (e.g., at a university) or in acquiring skill (e.g., in an apprenticeship), he will expect to be recompensed by appointment to a post which is either more agreeable or better paid than the posts open to him without training. A barrister, for example, has to spend many years, during which he earns little or nothing, preparing for examinations which he may never pass, and waiting for briefs which he may never be given. He has to pay stiff fees to examining bodies and to professional associations, and may also have a premium to pay on apprenticeship. Only the prospect of a high income—in cash or in amenities—will induce him to make the necessary sacrifices; he will look to be compensated, in the course of his career, for all his outlay, and for the long period of waiting and uncertainty—to say nothing of the cost of midnight oil.

So far as the cost of training is part of the supply price of labour—that is, so far as higher earnings are a necessary inducement to training—the extra earnings of trained workers will contain no element of rent corresponding to the rent of superior ability. But if at any time there is a shortage of trained workers, and apprentices cannot be trained quickly to meet the demand, the limited supply of trained workers will be able to obtain abnormally high earnings. Their earnings, in the short period during which no more workers can be trained, will be governed solely by demand and will be swollen by an element of *quasi-rent*. Quasi-rent resembles rent in that it is a surplus over cost or supply price, but differs from rent in that it disappears in the long run when supply is given time to increase.[1] Compare, for example, the earnings of a professor of mathematics and those of a 'bus-driver. The professor can go on earning a high salary because few people are capable of expounding Einstein; but the 'bus-driver can rarely earn much more than an unskilled worker, since there are large numbers of unskilled workers who could fairly easily learn 'bus-driving. The high salary of the professor contains an element of rent—rent of ability. The 'bus-driver's wage, on the other hand, will contain an element of rent only if, during a temporary shortage of drivers, their wages have been increased. This element of rent will be transitory—a *quasi*-rent—since in course of time more trained 'bus-drivers will become available.

Inequality of earnings may also be due to inequality of opportunity. Workers are not equally lucky in meeting with opportunities of earning higher wages. In particular, they are not equally lucky in their choice of parents. Some people are given a better start in life than others because of the superiority of their parents in character, or in education, or in wealth. The children of rich parents, for example, enjoy a more expensive education and a wider cultural background, have more freedom in their choice of occupation and better guidance in choosing it, and have more opportunity of making valuable social contacts. Thus they start with a fairly large advantage in income-earning power, and are generally able, given moderate ability, to keep ahead in the high-income group. Social mobility, therefore, is generally low. A worker tends to stay in the class into which he was born.

Just as there are often artificial impediments to movement between places and occupations, so there are often artificial impediments to movement between social classes. Under the caste system, for example, social mobility is nil. In

---

[1] This use of the term "quasi-rent" is to be carefully distinguished from its use in the following chapter to mean "the earnings of an instrument of production." On this second definition, the rent of a house is a quasi-rent.

countries inhabited by different races the dominant race often monopolises positions of responsibility so that members of the subject-race cannot climb to a higher status. The effect of these restrictions is to shelter a privileged class of persons from competition and to swell their incomes with a surplus or rent, akin to the surplus profits of a monopolistic producer. A somewhat similar surplus emerges when social mobility is limited by inequality of opportunity rather than of privilege. The differential advantages of birth in a rich family are as substantial, if not as secure, as the differential advantages of birth in a superior caste. Advantages of either kind are the product of institutions devised by man—the institution of inheritance or of the caste system—and the surplus income or rent corresponding to these advantages is called, therefore, "institutional rent." Since human institutions can be modified by appropriate legislation (e.g., by laws abolishing caste or limiting bequest) this source of inequality can be reduced at will (i.e., at the will of those who command political power). But it can never be entirely eliminated. It is impossible to contrive that everyone shall have exactly equal opportunities. We cannot, for example, equalise the ability of parents to bring up children, although we can see to it that the children are given more or less equal opportunities of education in schools and universities. We can increase social mobility, but we cannot make it perfect.

## Summary

On a horizontal plane competition makes for equality of net advantages between places and occupations, while immobility—either geographical or occupational—limits the effectiveness of competition and preserves inequalities. Immobility may be reinforced by restrictions on movement which buttress the monopolistic advantages of particular groups of workers. On a vertical plane, competition tends to equate earnings from work with innate differences in efficiency (as assessed by employers or by consumers) or with differences in efficiency which are the product of education and training. Competition, however, takes place within an institutional framework which limits social mobility by creating inequalities of opportunity. These inequalities tend to restrict access to highly-paid occupations, which are recruited mainly from the well-to-do. Inequality of earnings from work, therefore, is partly due to immobility and partly to differences in efficiency. Hence if we wish to reduce inequality, we must either increase mobility or abandon efficiency as a criterion of reward.

### 2   BARGAINING INFLUENCES

The rate of wages in any industry, then, depends upon the competitive

pull which other industries are able to exert on its labour, upon the cost of
moving to the most attractive alternative industry, and upon the strength of
the workers' disinclination to move—that is, it depends upon the supply price
of labour to the industry. It goes without saying that the rate of wages depends
also upon the demand price of employers. For workers of given productivity
this will be governed by the price (or, under imperfect competition, by the
marginal revenue) of the product of the industry. In the short run, fluctuations
in wage-rates are closely linked with fluctuations in prices; the most powerful
force bringing about an increase or decrease in the rate of wages paid to any
group of workers is an increase or decrease in the price of the goods which they
make. In the long run, when there is time for a change in the relative attractiveness of an industry to cause workers to move from it or to it, it is the supply
price of labour that is the dominant factor; much as, in the long run, it is to
cost rather than marginal utility that prices respond.

The rate of wages in an industry depends also upon a third factor—the
strength of the organisations of workers and employers. In the trials of strength
to determine where, within the limits of indeterminacy, wage rates are to be
fixed, it is open to employers' associations to threaten to lock out their workers
and to trade unions to retaliate by the threat of a strike.

The tactical advantages of the two sides depend greatly on the state of trade.
If there is severe unemployment a trade union will be in a relatively weak position: it may be in low water financially through having to pay benefit to its
members; it may have less command over the loyalty of the workers, whether
members or non-members, since they will be more afraid of losing their jobs;
and if it adopts a truculent and uncompromising attitude, it may force some
firms to close down that might otherwise keep going. On the other hand, with
full employment there is a seller's market for labour and employers will be far
more willing to make concessions in order to maintain their output and so
profit from favourable market conditions. The trade unions will frequently
wait before submitting wage-demands until unemployment has fallen to a
relatively low level, when expanding economic activity is beginning to be
accompanied by rising costs. They will try by their intervention to cut down
the lag that often occurs in such circumstances between the rise in costs and prices
and the rise in money-wages.

Except in conditions of full employment the position of an Employers'
Association is generally a strong one. Where there are few masters and many
men it is easier for the masters to hold together than for the men; it is easier
for them to frame a common policy, and they can negotiate with more assurance
and authority. They have the advantages of education and influence; they can
put their case more skilfully before the public—or even before the men; and

they can, if they choose, bring pressure to obtain publicity of the right sort. Above all, they have greater reserves. In a depression, the prospect of closing down for a time while surplus stocks are disposed of, and the organisation and plant are overhauled, is not altogether unattractive. But for the worker his wage-earnings are normally his sole source of income, and strike pay out of the accumulated funds of his union is poor compensation. Thus it generally requires an angry resentment or an obstinate devotion to some cherished view of right and wrong to provoke the mass of wage-earners to a lengthy strike.[1]

In conditions of full employment, the boot is on the other foot. The employer is pressed by the government and the public to produce all he can and is practically powerless to declare a lock-out. He cannot count on replacing a worker if he dismisses one and cannot afford to have the bad reputation as an employer that he would acquire if he took up too unbending an attitude on wages.

The real strength of an employer's position is weakened by non-economic influences. Most employers have a pride in their business and are anxious to preserve good relations with their workers for the sake of the business. It would be a travesty of the facts to suggest that in the middle of a wage dispute employers pack their bags and go off for a round of golf by the seaside while their workers brood over an empty larder and their common wrongs. Employers may be under less compulsion to re-start, but are generally no less eager. Moreover, although it ought to be easy for them to make common cause, they have a way of falling out with one another and playing blackleg. Their calling puts a premium on masterfulness and private judgment and releases them from much of the discipline of joint effort; there are often some wayward spirits, therefore, who refuse to abide by their association's "official" plan of campaign.

### The economy of high wages

There are also economic factors disposing employers to pay higher rates of wages than they need. The economic interest of the employer is not in low wages but in low *wage-costs*. He pays a certain rate of money-wages and receives in exchange the services of his work-people. The more favourable the terms upon which he can hire these services, the greater will be his profits. This does not mean, however, that it will pay him to offer low rates of wages; low-paid labour is often the dearest labour.

First of all, low wages mean a low standard of living, and this in turn means

---

[1] Not that most strikes are about wages—far from it. Strikes because of working conditions, dismissals, allegations of victimisation, or to secure recognition for a Union, are much more frequent although generally less prolonged. There are also plenty of strikes for no reason at all except a deep feeling of frustration: violent outbursts of insubordination and disaffection.

a low standard of efficiency. Workers who are not properly fed and housed, or who are left with little leisure, are unlikely to reach the outputs of more highly-paid labour. They cannot stand up to the strain of modern industry so readily, or show the same initiative, or undertake as responsible work. When we find that workers in India and China are paid much less than British workers, therefore, we must not jump to the conclusion that wage-costs are correspondingly low, and that competition with such countries is impossible. The fact that India is still one of Britain's biggest markets suggests that low wages have their disadvantages. On the other hand, we must not jump to the topsy-turvy conclusion that India would compete more successfully if employers there were to grant immediate increases in wages. Workers do not begin to work harder whenever their wages go up. Their first reaction is often to relax and either work *less* hard, so as to keep their earnings at much the same level as before, or spend less carefully, using the rise in their pay haphazardly and without advantage to their efficiency. It is some time before higher wages seep through to raise the level of efficiency, and since employers can rarely afford to take the long view—they may lose their workers at any time to their competitors—they are unlikely to pay high wages with an eye solely to their workers' standard of living. Particularly if this standard is already high, any gain in efficiency will appear small and speculative while the cost of a rise in wages will be large and certain.

There are, however, two further motives which are likely to be stronger in their appeal to the self-interest of the employer. The first is that by paying high wages it may be possible to "cream" the labour market—that is, to attract workers of more than average efficiency. The second is that high wages may purchase the goodwill of a firm's employees, and create an atmosphere in which they are not deterred by suspicion and discontent from working wholeheartedly on behalf of the firm. Both of these motives, it will be observed may induce a firm to keep wages high in relation to its immediate competitors in the district from which its labour is drawn; neither motive is sufficient to ensure that wages will be high *throughout* an industry or district.

## Trade unions

The self-interest of employers is hardly the best guarantee of high wages. In order to secure improvements in their standard of living and conditions of employment, workers generally prefer to rely on their own organisations. The chief aim of these is to press for higher wages, shorter hours, and better working conditions. Sometimes trade unions have more militant objects, such as the overthrow of the capitalist system by direct action. But in Great Britain the trade unions show no revolutionary ardour.

L

This does not prevent the trade unions from exercising great political power. They have a profound influence on the thinking of both of the major political parties; their views largely inspire the programme of the Labour Party; many of their officials and members are Members of Parliament. The lack of any revolutionary ambitions has not prevented the trade unions from contributing powerfully over the past fifty years to something very like a social revolution.

One of the prime objects of trade unions has always been to give the worker a sense of status—the feeling that he is one of a body of workers organised to protect their rights and interests, not alone and defenceless against the whims of employers. Again, trade unions, by employing skilled negotiators, can put the workers' case with more finesse, confidence and knowledge and can take his part in the hundred and one day-to-day grievances on things not covered by any formal contract. This is not without its advantages to the employer also, for it creates a regular channel through which grumbles can reach him, and allows him to enter into agreements which are binding on all his workers.

From the point of view of the community, too, trade unions serve a useful purpose in preventing employers from resorting in bad times to the attractive device of cutting wages as a means of cutting costs; and in bringing pressure on employers to examine carefully fresh methods of economising labour. But the pressure of trade unions does not always make for increased efficiency. In the first place, when unions are organised on a craft (or occupational) rather than on an industrial basis, they are apt to have narrow demarcation rules and insist that given jobs should be done by members of their craft even when they involve little skill and could be done with much more convenience by other people. The cumulative effect of these rules in holding up urgent work and in perpetuating obsolete industrial practices is to cause a great deal of waste of time and labour contrary to the social interest, although very much to the monopoly advantage of the union. Rules limiting the number of learners and apprentices to be employed with each journeyman, or the number of women to each man, may have a similar effect. These rules are often no more than a safeguard against attempts by employers to get work done cheaply by learners who are not given an adequate training, and for whom no provision is made by the employer at the end of their time. But the tendency of such rules is plainly monopolistic and they are frequently pushed beyond the point at which they are in the social interest. Finally, if trade unions stick out for high wages over the whole field of industry, they may restrict the volume of employment exactly as a monopolist restricts his output of goods, and may achieve a high standard of living for those who continue in employment, quite as much at the expense of those who fail to get employment as at the expense of employers as a class.

## Limits to the bargaining power of trade unions

Fear of creating general unemployment will not deter a particular trade union from pressing for higher wages. Trade unions in expanding industries will not regard it as part of their duty to keep wages low so as to ensure the rapid absorption of unemployed labour from less fortunate industries. Nor will a trade union necessarily be deterred if, by raising wages, it also raises prices and helps inflation along. Unemployment and inflation may influence the trade unions as a body, and each of the unions may abide loyally by decisions taken jointly through the Trades Union Congress not to press wage claims at certain times. Such decisions apart, trade unions will be guided mainly by the tactical position at the moment within the industry or industries which they cover and will, as a rule, give weight to the groans or expostulations of the public only in so far as they tend to weaken that position.

There are three major limitations on the power of trade unions to secure a lasting increase in wages in a single industry:—

**(i) Elasticity of substitution**—The more readily employers can economise labour by using alternative methods of production, the more effective will be their resistance to claims for wage advances. The simplest expedient is to install more machinery; employers may re-vamp the layout of their plant so as to replace old-fashioned machines by more modern labour-saving types, or they may be induced, even in up-to-date plants, to turn over to more highly mechanised processes which were just not worth while when labour was cheaper. Either way, capital will be substituted for labour by a change in the proportion in which the two are used. The rate at which substitution proceeds—the rate at which the proportion of the two factors changes as their relative price changes —is called the elasticity of substitution; and the elasticity of substitution is the first damper on wages.

Substitution is not confined to the replacement of labour by capital; replacement of labour by labour, directly or indirectly, is quite as effective. If employers can find "blacklegs," or import labour from other areas, or get women or un-skilled workers to do what was previously done by skilled men, they need trouble themselves no further about substitution. Alternatively, they may replace workers in one occupation by workers in another. Rather than pay higher wages to ploughmen, for example, farmers will tend to substitute cattlemen and shepherds by putting more land under stock and less under crops. In the same way, if stonemasons extort a thumping increase in wages, and bricklayers and carpenters are paid at the same rates as before, builders will tend to put up more houses of brick or wood and fewer houses of stone.

(ii) **Elasticity of supply of alternative factors**—How far substitution can be pushed depends not only upon the ease with which technical changes can be made, but also upon the ease with which additional supplies of the substitute can be procured. In a boom or in war-time, manufacturers of machinery may be booked up for months ahead and practically all workers absorbed into employment. These are obviously favourable times for seeking wage advances. On the other hand, substitutes are in highly elastic supply during a depression and the bargaining power of trade unions is then at its lowest.

(iii) **Elasticity of demand**—Consumers as well as producers can indulge in substitution, and the measure of their ability to find substitutes is the elasticity of demand for the product of the industry. Where demand is elastic, employers have difficulty in passing on an increase in wage-costs to consumers and they tend, therefore, to offer more resistance to demands for higher wages. A case in point is provided by the export industries which supply a fiercely competitive market and in which, between the two wars, even the strongest unions were hard put to it to maintain wages while the trend of wages in other industries was upwards.

These limitations of the bargaining power of trade unions are, in effect, limitations on the demand price for labour and are tantamount, therefore, to a threat of unemployment in the particular industry if wages are pushed too high. Apart from this ultimate sanction, there is generally a good deal of "play" in wage-rates depending on the current fortunes of the industry. If, for example, profits are high, and employers enjoy monopolistic or semi-monopolistic advantages, labour may be able to obtain a share in the swag and secure rates of pay which are well above the general run of wages in other industries. The employers may even go out of their way to make concessions to their workers in order to disarm criticism of their monopoly. A different kind of blackmail may be practised by a small but truculent union in an occupation which forms an indispensable part of large enterprises (e.g., the printing of newspapers). Rather than have the whole of the work held up from time to time by demands for higher wages from a relatively insignificant number of workers, employers may seek to forestall these demands and treat the extra outlay in wages as a cost normal in their line of business.

### The State and wages

In the United Kingdom it has been usual for the State to try to stand aside from the process of collective bargaining. Governments have laid down from time to time what is legitimate and what is not in a trial of strength between workers and their employers—whether, for example, peaceful picketing or a general strike is legal. The State has also passed legislation on how trade union funds can be employed—whether, for example, members can be obliged to subscribe to levies in support of a political party. But in general it has not attempted to decide particular disputes not even to require that some particular machinery of negotiation be used.

To this an increasing number of qualifications are now necessary. Since 1909 the State has set up a number of Trade Boards, which were given extended powers and re-named Wages Councils in 1945, in industries where wages were unreasonably low or where the existing machinery of collective bargaining was inadequate. Separate legislation has led to the setting up of Wages Boards in agriculture and catering. The Wages Councils and Boards have power to fix minimum wages and other conditions of employment. In all, statutory wage-fixing arrangements cover almost one-third of total employment, although in some industries these arrangements overlap with voluntary collective bargaining.

Apart from statutory regulation of wages, the State may intervene in an industrial dispute either in order to arbitrate at the request of both parties or to bring conciliation machinery into play at the request of either party. Any industrial dispute likely to lead to a stoppage of work must be brought to the attention of the Ministry of Labour; and if the danger of a serious stoppage is great, the government is likely to take part in the subsequent negotiations. Moreover, where voluntary arrangements have been made for the submission of disputes to arbitration or conciliation, the members of the Tribunals or Committees that are looking into the dispute will be guided to some extent by any general declarations of policy that have been made by the government. Finally, apart from intervention in particular disputes, the government may join with employers' and trade union organisations in a general compact that wage adjustments should be limited as far as possible to cases complying with a set list of conditions (e.g., industries where there is a labour shortage). When this stage is reached, collective bargaining has become subordinate to the wages policy pursued by the government as part of its general economic policy. So far from leaving wages to be settled freely by negotiations between employers and employed, the State, in those conditions, is influencing both the size of the wage-bill and the changes in wage-differentials.

This is still some way off. So long as workers are free to strike and wage-disputes continue, the rulings of wages councils, arbitration tribunals, conciliation committees, and so on, are obeyed only if they are not felt to be manifestly unjust. The various tribunals and councils in their turn may accept or reject any guidance offered to them by the government. The central organisations of employers and employed—the T.U.C. and C.B.I.[1]—may reach general agreement with the government on wages policy without preventing individual unions or employers' associations—and still more individual workmen and employers—from taking a quite independent line. Shop stewards may pull in one direction while trade union officials are pulling in another, so that official strikes give way increasingly to unofficial ones. The more the trade unions are associated with the government and with the employers in formulating a common line of policy, the more they are put in the position of apologists of that policy, and the more they are obliged to check the very propensity of their members to demand a better bargain on which their strength has been built up. However strongly the government wishes to regulate wages, and however closely it carries the T.U.C. and C.B.I. with it, it must still have regard to the movement of opinion among the workers if it is not either to discredit the trade unions or to deny them the right to strike.

### Labour's share in economic progress

The average worker assumes that if an employer introduces new machinery in order to cut costs, some part of the saving should be passed on to his men. There is an appearance of common sense about this assumption; but there is really no reason why the men operating the new machines should profit from their introduction rather than the men who made them or the men who normally supply the raw materials that are processed by them. The fruits of economic progress should go to the mass of consumers through a reduction in prices, not to groups of producers who have a quite fortuitous association with the increase in productivity. The situation would be a different one if the new machines called for extra effort or skill, so that higher wages in relation to other types of employment were clearly merited. But if the work does not change, neither should the wages. Workers do not ask for extra pay when technical progress takes the form of a cheaper raw material, a more durable product, an entirely new process of manufacture, and so on. Why should improved machinery (which is a special case of technical progress) be treated differently?

The reasoning of the worker starts from the other end; from the high profits that may be made by the firm installing the machinery. Until competition is attracted, these profits represent a quasi-rent, something very like a monopoly profit. To squeeze higher wages out of a monopoly profit is just as legitimate as squeezing high prices out of the consumer. What other workers are earning

---

[1] Trades Union Congress and Confederation of British Industries.

is irrelevant; it is a question of sharing the pickings. Now if there is a genuine monopoly in the use of the new machinery, this is a sound enough view. But if not, the effect of putting up wages will be to delay and limit its use and prevent the consumer from deriving full advantage from better methods of production. Competition would spread the gains over the community; the worker, in trying to seize a share from his employer, is acting like a monopolist, narrowing the margin on which competition can work, and reducing the total gain to the community.

This reasoning might seem to imply that prices ought to fall steadily under the continuous pressure of technical improvements. If, for example, those improvements were equal to a saving in costs of 2 per cent.–3 per cent. per head per annum (which is a common estimate of the normal rate of increase in productivity), the cost of living would fall steadily and many of the problems associated with deflation would make themselves felt. But if, for one reason or another, wages were rising at 2 per cent.–3 per cent. per annum, prices would be kept constant; and if wages rose faster, prices would rise. Without making the general level of prices increase, it would be possible to leave room for an increase in money-wages in some industries (different industries, perhaps, every year). Technical improvements could be allowed to bring down the price of some goods; increased wages might raise the price of others; and the two (conceivably at least) might remain roughly in balance.

### What do wage disputes really settle?

If the workers in an industry secure an increase in their wages and do exactly the same work as before, who is it that surrenders the income that the workers gain? That someone must be worse off is plain; the national income is no greater, and one section of workers is receiving more. Who, then, is "squeezed"?

It is common to assume that the extra wages come out of profits and that it is the employers, therefore, who are the losers. But if employers can pass on the extra burden of cost in the form of higher prices, they can maintain their profits and it is then the consumer, not the employer, who is "squeezed." Now "the consumer," when we are dealing with any large industry, includes other groups of workers as well as those who spend out of profits or rent. The gains of one section of workers, therefore, are likely to be in part at least at the expense of other workers. If wages rise all round, the cost of living will also tend to rise, and the real income of labour may be no greater than before.

This is not simply an academic contingency but what commonly happens. Twice in war-time we have seen violent increases in wages and prices, and on both occasions the two have kept fairly closely in step with one another. It is true that this was at least as much because wages followed prices upwards as because prices responded to the upward trend in wages; but the fact is striking none the less. In the famous Blum experiment in France in 1936 it was only too obvious that the general rise in wages was the controlling factor in the corresponding rise in prices. The experience of the United States under the National Recovery Administration in 1933 points to the same conclusion.

If workers were unorganised and employers organised, wage disputes associated with the formation of trade unions might increase the share of labour in the national income. But if both sides are already highly organised, the chances of labour's gaining at the expense of capital through wage disputes are far less strong, except perhaps in the middle of an inflation, in which wages are lagging behind the rise in the cost of living. Wage disputes are more likely to settle the distribution of the wage-bill between one section of labour and another, or between one industry and another. As a rule an increase in wages in one industry represents a levy on other industries and on the general consumer. If consumers cannot stint their requirements of the goods made by the industry, they will have to meet the whole of the increase in wages in the form of higher prices. But if demand is elastic, some part of the burden will recoil on employers in reduced profits and on the workers in reduced employment.

Broadly speaking, therefore, wage disputes are disputes over *relative* rates of wages. They do not fix the return on capital. But if not, what does? To this question we must now turn.

# CHAPTER 24

# INTEREST AND PROFIT

## 1   INTEREST

Interest is the price paid for the hire of loan-capital; more briefly, it is the price of a loan. This price is usually expressed as an annual rate, calculated on the principal of the loan. If, for example, I borrow £100 for one year on impeccable security, I am likely to be asked to pay back £105 at the end of the year—that is, interest will be charged at the rate of 5 per cent. per annum. But why should I be asked to pay interest? What has my creditor done to earn his £5 in interest?

### THE SUPPLY OF CAPITAL

The immediate reason why interest is paid is that loan-capital is scarce. The amount of money which people are willing to lend every year falls far short of the amount which would be borrowed if no interest were charged. So it is necessary to ration the limited supply by putting a price on loans—that is, by charging interest on them. Only those borrowers who are willing to pay the current rate of interest will be able to obtain loans; those who cannot pay the price will be forced to go unsatisfied.

But why is loan-capital scarce? Why don't people lend more? There are three possible reasons:—

(a) Unless we are bankers, we cannot lend without going to the trouble of saving, and there is a limit to our willingness and ability to save. We can, however, lend to any single borrower without saving more; all we need do is to ask for repayment from some other borrower and lend the sum repaid.

(b) We cannot lend without denying ourselves the use of our own savings. If we save more, therefore, we do not necessarily lend more; we may, instead, apply our savings to increase our stock of goods. For example, we may buy machinery for use in our business; or make a speculative purchase of raw

L*

materials to guard against, or profit from, a rise in their price; or store food-stuffs in fear of war; or buy a house, or a motor-car, or some similar durable commodity. In other words, we may choose to lend to ourselves rather than to other people, and hold our savings in the form of *goods* rather than in the form of debt.

(*c*) We cannot lend without parting with our money for a period of time and leaving ourselves in a comparatively illiquid position during that time. Money is more convenient for many purposes than even the best of I.O.U.s, and be-cause of this greater convenience we are never willing to lend out all our money. In other words, we may prefer to keep part of our savings in the form of *money* rather than in the form of debt or durable goods.

## Savings

Of these three reasons we shall, for the present, disregard the last, and treat the second as a variant of the first. We shall assume, that is, that when people save more they will also lend more. On this assumption, the only possible reason for the scarcity of loan-capital is the scarcity of savings. Upon what, then, do savings depend?

(i) **The rate of interest**—It might be supposed that the supply of savings, like the supply of oranges, depended mainly on their price, i.e., on the rate of interest. It is generally agreed, however, that although the payment of interest does offer an inducement to thrift, this inducement is subordinate to others. A low price would make us give up orange-growing, but it might require a *negative* rate of interest to make us give up saving. If the price of oranges rises from 3d. to 4d. we can be quite certain that more oranges will be put on the market. But if the rate of interest rises from 3 per cent. to 4 per cent. we cannot be certain that savings will increase. A man who wishes to save just enough to yield him £300 a year in interest when he retires will save *less* at the higher rate; at 4 per cent. he will require to accumulate only £7,500, whereas at 3 per cent. he will need £10,000.

Similarly, life insurance companies may find that their premium income (which is a substantial part of the total savings of the community) is reduced rather than increased by a rise in interest rates. It is doubtful, however, whether many people have such rigid ideas about the future income at which they are aiming, and it is likely that, on balance, a rise in interest rates will increase savings.

At very low rates of interest there would probably be a heavy falling-off in savings, while at very high rates savings might be greatly stimulated. A rate of 2 per cent., for example, would tempt many people to consume their capital by purchasing an annuity instead of keeping their capital intact and trying to live on the interest.

On the other hand, rates of 8 or 10 per cent. would put such an enormous bounty on saving that many people would make sacrifices in their habitual standards of living in order to add to their future income. Within the range of interest rates which have been customary in the United Kingdom, however—from about 3 to about 6 per cent.—it is doubtful whether saving shows much elasticity.

The nominal rate of interest is not an accurate measure of the *effective* inducement to saving. First we must deduct from the nominal rate of interest any taxes payable by the lender. If there is an income tax of 5s. in the £1, I must pay this 5s. whether I spend the £1 or save it. But if I save it, I shall later be asked to pay income tax on the interest. When the nominal rate of interest is 4 per cent., therefore, the real rate to the saver is only 3 per cent. His choice lies between spending £100 this year and having £104 less £1 in tax next year. On each £100 saved he gains only £3. Secondly, we must make provision for changes in the value of money. If I expect prices to rise by 5 per cent. over the year, I shall make a bad bargain by lending money at 4 per cent., for £104 in a year's time will buy less than £100 does now. The *real* rate of interest will be *minus* 1 per cent. On the other hand, if I expect prices to fall by 5 per cent., and my expectations are well founded, the real rate of interest will be 4 plus 5, or 9 per cent. A given rate of interest, therefore, offers a greater incentive to saving in times of falling than in times of rising prices. If we wished the real rate of interest to remain constant, we should require to lower the nominal rate when prices were falling and raise it again when prices were rising. Strangely enough, this is exactly how the rate of interest does behave, although the changes in the rate of interest are generally small in comparison with the changes in the value of money. The reason for these sympathetic movements in interest rates and prices is not, as one might suppose, that more is saved when prices are falling, nor even that there is an increased pressure to lend, but rather that people are less willing to borrow. Their reluctance is to some extent a reflection of the fact that although the nominal rate is low the real rate (in relation to price trends) is high.

**(ii) Social institutions**—Savings depend upon the encouragement and reassurance offered to the saver by existing social arrangements and practices. If there are numerous outlets for savings, if lenders are brought readily into contact with borrowers, and if there is widespread approval of thrift as a civic virtue, the disposition to save will be immensely stronger than in communities where capital is little in demand, the capital market is inefficiently organised and the general temper of society is unfavourable to thrift. Saving is promoted also by a high code of business morality which gives savers confidence in the good faith of their debtors and permits loans to be made without undue fear of default; and by a tranquil and orderly social system which protects life and property and allows savers to reap the fruits of their thrift. Habits of saving, therefore, vary from one society to another. They were stronger under Queen Victoria than under Queen Elizabeth, and a great deal stronger than under Queen Boadicea. They are stronger in a stable capitalist society than in communities where the danger of repudiation or confiscation is serious, or where to possess capital is to court persecution or murder.

(iii) **Income**—Every increase in our income adds to our ability to save. Of course, we are unlikely to save the whole of the increase, for when we become richer we generally scale up our standard of living. But neither are we all likely to spend the whole of the increase. Some of us will add to our savings— especially at first, while our customary standard of living is still unadjusted to the change in our income. Experience suggests that this part is generally fairly large, and that we tend to save not only a larger sum of money but also a larger *proportion* of our income. Experience suggests also that if, instead of comparing the same person at two levels of income, we compare rich people and poor people, rich people as a class save a larger proportion of their income than poor people as a class, and that the richer the class, the higher is the proportion of income saved. It follows that a rich community saves a higher proportion of its income than a poor community, even when the poor community is exceedingly thrifty. The richer the community, the greater is the danger that saving will be carried to excess.

(iv) **Wealth**—Our ability to save depends also on our wealth. The more wealth we have, the greater is the income which it yields and the more readily, therefore, can we add to our accumulated wealth by further saving. Wealth grows like a snowball; as has often been remarked, it is easier to make the second million than the first hundred.

An increase in our wealth enables us to save more only if there is an accompanying increase in our income. An increase in wealth unaccompanied by any increase in income will dispose us to save *less* of our income, since the more wealth we have the weaker is the motive to further accumulation. If our holdings of Stock Exchange securities rise in price (as generally happens when interest rates fall) we are likely to have less hesitation in spending out of our current income; while, if we feel ourselves impoverished by a fall in security values, we may spend our income less freely. In the United States consumer-spending seems to be sensitive to any major fluctuation on Wall Street.

(v) **Thrift**—In a given order of society, at a given level of income, how much we save depends on the strength of the motives disposing us to thrift. These motives rarely induce us to make provision for savings by setting aside a definite sum; unless, of course, we are under contract to save—for example, by making repayment on a mortgage to a building society, or by paying an annual premium on our insurance policy. These payments apart, our expenditure is governed largely by the desire to maintain some customary standard of living. If our income is more than sufficient to maintain this standard, we save the surplus; if it is less than sufficient, we borrow the deficit (e.g., by running up debts to tradesmen or an overdraft at the bank) or live on our capital. In the short run, therefore, savings are a residue after meeting customary expenses. In the long run, however, people have standards of thrift as well as of expediture. If they find that they are saving consistently more than they wish, they will raise their standard of living. On the other hand, if they find that they are running into debt, or are saving less than they think desirable, they will try to economise and reduce their expediture. In the long run, savings cease to be residual and are fixed more and more deliberately.

Our standards of thrift vary with our preference for future as compared with present goods. If the rate of interest is 5 per cent., we can choose between £100 now and £105 next year. Those of us who are thrifty will have a comparatively strong preference for £105 next year. We may be uncertain of the future and anxious to provide for emergencies; or hopeful of achieving a greater measure of independence and a higher standard of living; or eager to have more capital at our disposal to expand our business and back speculative projects; or full of ambition to build up a fortune and acquire social status; or we may have more foresight or be more alive than others to future needs and future pleasures; or we may want to accumulate money for its own sake out of sheer miserliness.[1] Other people, less concerned for the future, or attaching less importance to the possession of wealth, will discount future goods more heavily and be more attracted by £100 now. Everyone, whatever his motives to thrift, will modify his preference for future goods the larger the proportion of his income which he saves until at the margin he is indifferent

---

[1] Charles Booth drew an interesting contrast between the motives to thrift in rich and poor: "With the working classes the object (of saving) is to render irregularity of income equal to the calls of a regular expenditure; with the rich this is reversed, and the aim is rather to make a comparatively fixed income meet the claims of a varying expenditure" (*Life and Labour in London*, Final Volume, p. 94).

whether his last pound is spent or left to accumulate interest—that is, until his marginal preference for future goods is measured by the rate of interest.

## Corporate saving

A large proportion of the savings of a modern industrial community are made by companies, not by individuals. Out of their total profits, companies distribute part in dividends and "plough back" the remainder into the business. This "ploughing back" of profits springs from much the same motives as induce individuals to save for speculative projects which they have in view. The chief motives are enterprise and prudence. A business which is making large profits will generally be tempted to expand further, and it will be much less troublesome to finance expansion out of profits than to make a new issue on the Stock Exchange, especially if a new issue requires government approval. Since directors are frequently given credit for rising dividends which are the product of reinvested profits rather than of increased efficiency, the allocation made to reserve may be more generous than enterprise alone would justify. A second slice of profits may be saved in order to provide the business with liquid reserves against such contingencies as increased competition, strikes, industrial depression, higher taxes and so on, or in order to equalise dividend payments over a period of years. Some profits may also be put to reserve to cover an increase in the replacement cost of plant above its original cost. But this is not really saving at all if it does no more than maintain capital intact; it represents a belated adjustment in the allowance for depreciation.

## Government saving

The government has also, on occasion, made an important contribution to the savings of the country. It may do so, for example, by accumulating a budget surplus, rates of tax being so fixed as to leave an excess of revenue over current outgoings. Included in government savings will be any expenditure out of revenue that adds to, or improves, the capital stock of the country, and any payments (e.g., in respect of war damage claims) that will be treated by the recipients as capital. Current revenue that is paid out of capital (e.g., death duties) should be excluded. Apart from the budget surplus of the central government, there may also be a surplus in the accounts of the local authorities or of various public bodies, including the boards of the nationalised industries.[1]

## The justification of interest

We have seen that, for a variety of reasons, savings are scarce and command a

---

[1] For statistics of Government saving in Britain in 1948, 1956 and 1964, see below, pp. 374, 379.

price which we call the rate of interest. But does this *justify* the payment of interest? Can we, for example, regard interest as compensation for the sacrifice involved in saving as we can regard wages as compensation for the irksomeness of work?

Like the earnings of any other factor of production, interest is both a price and a source of income. Regarded as a price, interest performs a useful social function by rationing out a limited supply of savings between competing borrowers. Even in a socialist community, this is a function which interest might continue to perform, for it would still be desirable to determine the priority of schemes calling for the use of capital and to eliminate those schemes which showed an insufficient return. If the return could be measured in money terms, the charging of a rate of interest would automatically secure this result, since it would give priority to schemes offering prospects of a higher return, and weed out schemes of lesser productivity. Regarded as a source of income, interest is less easy to justify. It is paid to some people rather than to others, because some people own loan-capital while others do not. If we wish to justify interest *payments*, therefore, we must first justify these differences in ownership. Secondly, we must show that without the offer of interest, capital would cease to be accumulated or cease to be lent. The first point raises issues too wide for treatment here.

The second point raises quite different issues. We know that it is only at the margin that the rate of interest has a decisive influence on thrift, and that the vast bulk of savings would continue to be supplied at lower rates. True, capitalists may *consume* part of their savings (or the savings of past generations) at low rates of interest, so that interest payments may be a bribe to dissuade them from this alternative. There is little doubt that capital consumption is in fact already being practised by the wealthy. It is arguable, however, that this arises mainly because of various disincentives to thrift, such as high death duties and high rates of income tax, which dispose many people to draw on their capital to maintain a customary standard of living but are unconnected with the rate of interest. It is also arguable that the real return to a wealthy person on a loan, given current rates of tax and an apparently chronic tendency for prices to rise, is negligible and perhaps even negative. However that may be, a more immediate danger would make itself felt before low rates of interest caused savings to dry up or the total stock of capital to be run down—the disinclination of capitalists to *lend*.

## Time-preference and liquidity-preference

This brings us to the second reason why loan-capital is scarce.[1] We have to overcome not only our reluctance to save, but also our reluctance to lend.

---

[1] See above, p. 330, para. (c).

Just as we may prefer present to future goods, and must be offered interest in order to overcome our "time-preference," so we may prefer money now to the promise of money at some future date, and require the offer of interest before we can overcome our "liquidity-preference." The phrase "liquidity-preference" sums up the various motives which prompt people to hold money rather than lend it at interest. The more we prefer money to I.O.U.s of any kind—i.e., the greater our liquidity-preference—the more difficult it will be to induce us to lend, and the higher, therefore, will be the rate of interest.

The conception of liquidity-preference is one which cannot easily be understood without some explanation of what money is and what it exists to do. This explanation we must postpone. We can, however, go part of the way towards an understanding of liquidity-preference by asking why this phrase is used to describe our demand for money. What is this mysterious thing "liquidity" and what connection has it with money? By "liquidity" is meant "power to convert into other commodities or into something which is generally acceptable in final settlement of a debt." Now money is of all things the most readily exchangeable into other commodities and the most generally acceptable in payment of a debt. Nothing is so easy to get rid of in all circumstances. Nothing, that is, is more liquid. Money, therefore, sets a standard of liquidity against which we can measure the liquidity of everything else. So the term "liquidity" comes to mean "power to convert into money." A preference for liquidity is a preference for money.

Consider, for example, the liquidity of bank advances. A banker who makes a loan to a merchant for the purpose of buying stocks of goods can rely on rapid and more or less automatic repayment, even in a crisis, because stocks are comparatively liquid; they can be readily converted into money so long as consumers go on buying, and will be converted automatically as the merchant disposes of them in the ordinary course of trade. Loans of this kind are liquid, therefore, because the stocks which provide security for the loan are liquid. On the other hand, an advance to a householder to enable him to buy his house will not be particularly liquid. The householder will not be put in possession of funds with which to repay the loan by merely living in the house. In a crisis he can pay off the loan in cash only out of his savings (which may be inadequate) or by fresh borrowing elsewhere (which will certainly be difficult) or by finding a buyer for the house (which may be even more difficult). The bank cannot be sure of immediate repayment—i.e., of converting the loan into money—and the loan, therefore, is illiquid.

### Differences in interest rates

Here we have one of the reasons why different rates of interest are charged on loans of different kinds. Loans are made for different periods of time. At one extreme, we have money deposited with a bank on current account; the money can be withdrawn without notice, so that the period for which it is lent to the bank is as short as depositors choose to make it. At the other extreme, we have bonds such as British Government Consols which the owners can never ask to have repaid; the holders of Consols have lent their money for an infinite period of time—although they can generally recover their money without difficulty whenever they need it by finding someone to take over the loan, i.e., to buy the bonds from them. Between these extremes there is a wide range of loans made for varying periods. The longer the period of the loan, the less liquid it will be, and the higher, generally speaking, will be the rate of interest payable. In normal circumstances, there will be a family of interest rates, increasing in magnitude from nil on bank deposits to a maximum on irredeemable bonds. A British Government loan maturing in forty years will normally require to be floated at a higher rate of interest than one maturing in twenty years and this in turn will carry a higher rate than Treasury Bills which mature in three months. In abnormal circumstances, however, rates of interest may be higher on short-term than on long-term loans. In a financial crisis, it may be impossible to borrow money on good security for three months at less than 6 per cent., while loans for three years are still being made at 4 per cent. This preference on the part of lenders for a less liquid and apparently less remunerative investment is puzzling. But it simply reflects a general expectation that when the crisis passes rates of interest will fall again, and that the fall will be heavier on short-term than on long-term rates. A comparatively small change in long-term rates is sufficient to compensate for a large but ephemeral change in short-term rates. All that is necessary, indeed, is that people should *believe* the change in short-run rates to be ephemeral; for this belief will rob high short-term rates of their attractiveness and leave the supply of long-term loans undisturbed at much the same price as before. Short-term rates, therefore, are much more variable than long-term rates. It requires a revolution in the outlook of lenders to produce a major change in long-term rates of interest; but short-term rates are extremely sensitive to the state of trade and of confidence.

A second reason for differences in interest rates is that all borrowers cannot offer equally good security. Where the risk of default is negligible—e.g., on British Government securities—loans will be made at rock-bottom rates. But whenever lenders feel doubtful of the borrower's honesty, or of his financial strength, they will be reluctant to lend, and will either refuse altogether or will insist on a higher rate of interest to cover the risk of default. They will charge a premium in excess of the rate payable by borrowers whose credit is irreproachable. This premium will vary with the standing of the borrower, his past record, and the pledges which he can offer as guarantees of ultimate repayment. It will vary, too, with the period for which loans are made, so that long-term loans are not only less liquid but also less secure.

Differences in interest rates may also be due to market imperfection. The capital market is made up of a great many sub-markets specialising in different kinds of loans and not always in close competition with one another. The banks cater for one kind of borrower, the building societies for another. The insurance companies cater for one kind of lender, the investment trusts for another. The market for short-term loans is cut off from the market for long-term loans. Thus borrowers and lenders, attached by habit or by ignorance to one sub-market, may raise or make loans on terms less favourable than the rates ruling in other sub-markets. Lenders, for example, may continue to make long-term loans at low rates of interest without giving adequate thought to the alternatives offered in the market for short-term loans; or they may put their money in a savings bank as a matter of course without considering the terms offered by building societies for deposits or by local authorities for short-term loans.[1] They may lend to business associates at less than the competitive rate so as to build up goodwill, or to friends at a nominal rate as an obligement. In the same way, borrowers may continue to raise capital through some customary channel at more than the market rate of interest. Market imperfection is greatest when the obstacles to competition are geographical. The rates payable in one country, or in one part of the country, are often higher than elsewhere because borrowers have access only to the local capital market, and have either no experience of borrowing in other markets or are not sufficiently well known to lenders outside their own district.

Finally, differences in marketability lead to differences in the interest payable on large and on small loans. A company which makes a small issue of bonds may have to pay a comparatively high rate of interest because, since trading in these bonds will be restricted, there will be greater difficulty in disposing of them at short notice when lenders wish to recover their money and also because, in a narrow market, the value of the bonds will tend to fluctuate more abruptly.

## The Demand for Capital

Since borrowers are willing to pay interest, it is to be presumed that loans render some service at least equal in value to the interest paid. What is this

---

[1] Between 1914 and 1918, for example, withdrawals from Savings Banks in Great Britain were comparatively trifling although much higher rates were obtainable on the loans issued during this period by the Government.

service? By what process does the £100 which I borrow this year become the £105 which I shall be asked to repay next year? Do loans, in some mysterious way, increase the product of industry, or is the additional £5 paid out of the profits of exploitation by robbing workers of the full value of their labour? Few questions in economics have given rise to so much controversy.

The most famous exponent of the exploitation argument was Karl Marx. According to Marx, the only productive agents are human labour and natural forces. Machines for example, are made by man from mineral deposits with the help of other machines; these machines in turn were made with the help of earlier machines. If we go back far enough to the first tools with which machines were made, these tools must have been the direct product of human labour. Machinery, therefore, is stored-up labour, and this past labour should be paid for at the same rate as present labour, without any addition of interest or profit. Capital is reducible to the labour and land which it embodies and renders no independent service. Nature, which partners labour in production, asks no compensation for its services. The full value of what is produced, therefore, is labour's by right; anything that goes in rent, interest or profit to the land-owner, or to the capitalist, is seized from labour by exploitation.

This is a plausible argument, and one with a strong emotional appeal. But there is a flaw in it; it overlooks the value of time. Now time is precisely the service which is rendered to producers and to consumers by capital. We recognise this clearly enough when we are given credit—that is, when a loan frees us from the necessity of making immediate payment. For the privilege of paying at some more convenient time, we are willing to allow interest to be added to our bill; in other words, we are willing to buy time. But this is far from being the only kind of transaction in which time is of value. In nearly all productive processes an interval of time must elapse between the work which we do and the consumption of the finished product. There is an interval between ploughing and sowing, between sowing and reaping, between reaping and milling, between milling and baking. There is an interval between the commencement and completion of a house, a ship, or a machine, and a still longer interval before the full value of such durable goods is exhausted in the shelter or transport or manu-factured goods which they yield over their years of service. Thus the efforts of a farmer or a builder bring in no immediate return; they fructify at some more or less distant date. It is necessary to *wait* for that fructification, and this waiting is possible only if someone saves. The farmer must support himself and his workers until his crop is sold, and if he is to obtain command of the necessary purchasing power he must either save himself—i.e., postpone consumption— or borrow from some other saver—i.e., induce someone else to postpone con-sumption. To the work done by the farmer, therefore, there must be added the waiting done by the saver. Waiting is just as indispensable a constituent of production as working. Capital, which is the product of waiting, is as much a factor of production as labour, by which working is undertaken. To put the point another way; capital cannot be reduced entirely to past labour. For combined with the past labour which is stored up in machinery and other capital goods is the waiting that must be done before that labour repays itself.

The longer the interval of time between effort and return—what is sometimes called the "period of production"—the more effectively we can work. Suppose, for example, that Robinson Crusoe (whom no one can exploit) goes fishing. The most primitive method which he can use is to catch fish with his hands, as boys do. Then he may use a more roundabout method—carve a spear, or take a day off to make a rod and tackle and look for bait. Instead of spending all his time fishing, he now divides up his time between making fishing gear and using it. Later, he may use still more roundabout methods, building a boat and making nets for himself before resuming his fishing. Each change of method involves the use of an increasing amount of capital—first a spear, then a rod, then a boat and nets. Thus an increasing amount of capital is the product of an increasing amount of waiting; Crusoe's exertions in building the boat for example, add nothing to this catch until the boat is ready for the water. But these exertions will *ultimately* increase his catch by far more than he could ever have caught by more primitive methods in the time which he gave to the work of construction. He is more than compensated for this work because of the technical superiority of roundabout or capitalistic methods of fishing. But he can only use such methods if he is able to wait for the greater reward that boat-building will ultimately bring him. If, in a less deserted island, he could borrow enough to pay for a boat, he would be able to transfer the burden of waiting to other shoulders by the offer of interest; and this interest would come out of the increased catch which he could make with the help of the boat.

This illustration can readily be generalised. Most commodities can be produced by a variety of methods, some requiring a great deal of capital, some comparatively little. Producers can use first very primitive methods with easily constructed tools; then more elaborate methods with simple types of machinery; then power-driven machinery in expensive factory buildings. At each stage, output per man increases—not simply per man operating the machinery, but output per worker, including engineers, bricklayers, and all who build and repair the factory equipment. Although output per head is greater, the product is not available for consumption until a longer period of time has elapsed. The work which is done (e.g., by engineers) is directed to the satisfaction of wants that are increasingly remote as the period of production is extended. There is more "jam to-morrow," but only if we are willing to wait until to-morrow. On the one hand, therefore, the use of capital increases the time-interval between taking the first steps in production (e.g., making tools) and turning out the finished goods, and so permits of the introduction of more efficient methods. On the other hand, since these methods, far from increasing current output, are made possible only by the withdrawal of resources from meeting immediate wants—as one withdraws eggs for incubation—they cannot be adopted without sacrifice—the sacrifice involved in waiting or saving. Borrowers are willing to pay interest because of the technical advantages of lengthy and roundabout methods of production; they are forced to pay interest because the burden of saving which the community is willing to carry is a limited one.

Capital is required, then, because production takes time; by taking advantage of more roundabout techniques of production, a given number of men can produce more than twice as much at the end of two years as they can produce at the end of one, but they have to be maintained out of savings during the extra year. Capital may be required also for other reasons. First of all, goods may grow in value over time, without any additional expediture of effort. Given time, the forces of nature will cause wine to mature and trees to grow, unassisted by man. The function of capital here is not to allow of the introduction of a more roundabout process, but to allow us to wait while nature does its work; the technique is of nature's devising, not man's. Secondly, capital may enable goods to be transferred from a time of plenty to a time of scarcity, or from a time when they are little in demand to a time when the need for them is comparatively great. Potatoes are plentiful in September and scarce in April; the capitalist, therefore, by buying potatoes in September, and *waiting* until April, renders a service exactly similar to the services of traders in buying potatoes in *places* where they are abundant and carrying them to *places* where they are scarce. The greater scarcity of potatoes in April will raise their price and leave the capitalist with a profit, part of which is really interest on his capital.

Thirdly, capital may allow us to enter into immediate possession of goods which we urgently need. Not having sufficient capital ourselves, we borrow from other people and pay them a premium in interest for taking over from us the burden of waiting. The man who buys goods on the instalment system, the spendthrift who runs into debt, and the government which raises a war loan, share a common preference for present rather than future goods. They are disposed to dis-save, not to save; to anticipate their future income instead of trying to add to it. Each of them is using up saving, and none of them—apart, possibly, from the man who buys on the instalment system—is adding to the capital stock of the community as a whole. Nevertheless the loan of capital is of as real service to them as loans made for other purposes, and the interest paid is in recognition of this service.

## The marginal productivity of capital

Capital, then, does render a service to those who borrow it; it *is* productive. Its productivity falls, however, as the supply increases; capital, like the other factors of production, is subject to diminishing marginal productivity, other things remaining equal. Each fresh extension of the period of production, for example, yields a diminishing increment of product. When capital is scarce, only those time-consuming methods of production which promise great ultimate gain can be adopted; when more capital becomes available it is possible to use methods which repay themselves less handsomely. With a little capital we can generate electricity from coal and obtain all the advantages of electric over labour power; with more capital we may reduce the cost of electricity by the construction of dams and of hydro-electric power stations. With a little capital we can buy a second-hand motor-car; with twice as much capital we can buy either a new car or a higher-powered second-hand car. For the additional outlay we enjoy added comfort or speed. But we probably rate this added pleasure below the pleasure provided by our original investment; our enjoyment is not increased in proportion to the cost of the car. This tendency to diminishing productivity is almost universal. With more capital a merchant can keep a larger stock on hand, or a wider variety of goods; a manufacturer can use machines of better quality or more capitalistic techniques. But the additional capital yields a smaller return than the existing stock.

The productivity of capital, in this context, means the productivity of *loan*-capital, i.e., the productivity of the things which can be bought out of a loan. The marginal product of capital is the additional return, after allowing for depreciation, which the borrower expects to obtain through the *use* of an additional unit of loan-capital. The marginal productivity of capital varies, therefore, not only with the annual return expected on capital equipment, but also with the cost of such equipment. If, as capital accumulates, machinery becomes more costly in relation to the price of its product, the marginal productivity of capital will fall, both because the uses to which the additional machinery can be put will be less urgent, and because a greater investment of capital will be necessary for the purchase of the machinery.

In many uses to which capital is put its productivity is not easily measured. Who can say, for example, whether houses are more productive than roads, or roads than battleships? The measuring-rod of money can be applied to houses to give the annual return on the capital invested, but roads and battleships yield no monetary return. Are we to say, therefore, that houses alone are productive? Clearly, this would be absurd. What we must say is that productivity is measured by the borrower himself—sometimes, when he is producing goods for sale, with an eye to the judgments of productivity expressed by consumers in the prices which they pay; and sometimes, when he is meeting his own immediate wants, on the basis of his private judgment of how these wants can best be met. A business man's judgment of productivity rests on his expectations of profit—which is measurable; a government's judgment rests on its conception of the needs of the community—which may not be measurable.

The marginal productivity of capital governs the rate of interest which borrowers are prepared to pay. Producers, for example, will put capital to uses in which the prospective return becomes progressively smaller as more and more capital is applied. Under perfect competition, they will increase their borrowings until, on a further loan, the prospective return over the period of the loan is a trifle less than the interest payable on it—that is, until the marginal productivity of capital and the rate of interest are equal. The return which producers balance against the interest cost of a loan is generally obtained through the conversion of the loan into concrete capital assets. Since the contribution made by these assets to the value of output extends into the future over the period of their life, the gross return in not certain, but must be estimated by producers on the basis of their experience of the past and their anticipations of the future; it is a *prospective* return. Since, secondly, capital assets depreciate over their life, provision must be made out of the gross return for the probable cost of depreciation; it is the *net* return which is balanced against the interest charge. Thirdly, the return will vary according to the period for which the loan is made. Producers can generally turn long-term loans to better account than short-term loans, and will generally be willing, therefore, to offer comparatively high rates of interest for long-term loans. For some purposes, however, they will prefer to borrow for short periods even at high rates; for instance, to finance a temporary, or a seasonal, increase in the stocks of raw materials or of finished goods which they wish to carry, or to tide over a trade depression, or to provide themselves with liquid funds for emergency payments. The rate of interest on loans for any given period of time will tend to be equal to the marginal productivity of capital invested for that period of time.

When competition is not perfect, the marginal productivity of capital will exceed the rate of interest for two reasons. If there is imperfect competition in the market for loans, borrowers may find it impossible to obtain command of additional capital except by paying successively higher rates as their borrowings increase. They will tend, therefore, to restrict their borrowings since each additional loan, while adding to the value of output, not only adds to their costs the interest charge on the new loan, but also increases the interest charge on previous loans.[1] If there is imperfect competition in the market for goods, borrowers, as we have seen, will restrict output so as to keep up prices, and in restricting output will also restrict their borrowings. They will set against the value of the goods produced from additional capital, the fall in the value of the goods produced by the existing stock of capital. Thus the *net* return to a marginal application of capital will fall below the marginal productivity of capital because the consequent increase in sales will drive down prices.

## Changes in marginal productivity

The demand for capital will increase or diminish whenever there is a rise or fall in the marginal productivity of capital. A rise may occur as a result of invention; for example, the invention of new means of transport (the railway and the steamship in the nineteenth century, the motor-car and the aeroplane in the twentieth), or of communications (by cable, telephone or wireless); or of new sources of power (steam, electricity, petrol and oil). Secondly, the marginal productivity of capital will be increased by anything which makes concrete capital scarce relatively to the other factors of production—the destruction of property on a large scale in an earthquake or a war; an increase in population; an increase in the efficiency of labour; the discovery of new natural resources—minerals, oils, etc.—and the settlement of new and undeveloped countries. Thirdly, the marginal productivity of capital will be increased by anything which disposes people to anticipate their income and consume the savings of others; governments, for example, may borrow heavily to finance preparations for war and the conduct of the war itself. Fourthly, the marginal productivity of capital will be increased by a change in tastes from goods which require a low proportion to goods which require a high proportion of capital in their manufacture; for example, people may spend more on rent and move to larger houses, which require the investment of a great deal of capital; and spend correspondingly less on drink into which capital does not enter so largely. *Any* change in demand, indeed, will be likely to raise the marginal productivity of capital. For it will be necessary to provide more of one commodity and less of another; and since the machinery and plant used in the manufacture of the second commodity is unlikely to be adaptable for the manufacture of the first, more machinery and plant will have to be constructed if the output of the first commodity is to be increased. The demand for capital, therefore, will increase and the increase will be all the greater if a comparatively high proportion of

---

[1] This assumes that they pay the same rate of interest on all their borrowings. If they can discriminate between one lender and another, they will continue to borrow until the rate of interest *on the last loan* made to them is equal to the marginal productivity of capital.

capital to labour is used in the manufacture of the first commodity. Fifthly, the marginal productivity of capital will be increased by anything inducing business men to take a more optimistic view of the future. If, for example, producers are in a more optimistic frame of mind, they will entertain more favourable expectations of profit; this will raise the prospective return on capital and stimulate borrowing. An important influence making for optimism is past experience of a steadily expanding market. The marginal productivity of capital is higher in a world of expanding population and trade than in a world where population is tending to become stationary and trade restrictions accumulate. It is higher not only because business men tend to be more adventurous, but also because, whatever their mood, they can justifiably look forward to an expanding return from year to year.

## The mobility of capital

The savings of the past have already been invested; they are fixed in the stock of concrete capital which society has accumulated. The savings of the present are still free and undecided in their use; they are available for financing additions to the stock of capital in those industries and districts where the demand for capital is most urgent. If the demand for capital increases in any one use, therefore, it is mainly out of "free" capital that this demand is met. The rate of interest tends to be forced up, choking off demand elsewhere, and diverting savings to the expanding industry or district from other industries and districts in which these savings would normally have been invested. Just as the mobility of labour is greatest amongst new entrants, so the mobility of capital is greatest when capital is still free. But fixed capital, too, may be transferred from one use to another. If the production of one commodity is discontinued, the buildings and machinery used in its manufacture may be adapted for use in the production of some other commodity. The same plant may turn out a variety of products any one of which may be substituted for the others without dislocation; shop space may be used for the retailing of a variable range of goods; a dismantled ship may supply a hotel with furniture and panelling, a coal-mine with machinery, and a steelworks with scrap. Thus one industry may decline and others take its place without drawing extensively on free capital. A third element of mobility arises through the conversion of fixed into free capital. As fixed capital wears out, a sum of money is set aside annually to provide for its ultimate replacement. These sums we may call "depreciation funds," since they are supposed to provide for current depreciation. Now depreciation funds are really free capital. They can, if their owners so choose, be reinvested in *other* kinds of property—in other industries and districts—which are yielding a high return, instead of being applied automatically to the replacement of property which may be yielding a comparatively low return. There is no *necessity* to replace property as it wears out and so preserve unchanged the physical stock of capital. Indeed, it is very unusual for the new property to be precisely similar to the old; when plant is replaced an improved model is generally introduced. But it *is* rather unusual for the owners of depreciation funds to withdraw them from a comparatively unprofitable business and invest them in some other business which offers a better return. From motives of optimism or of pride in his business, the company director—and still more, the individual *entrepreneur* —will continue to renew buildings and plant in spite of the attractiveness of competing opportunities of investment. Thus although in an industrialised community depreciation funds are usually about equal in amount to current savings, it is savings which make the greater contribution to capital mobility. It is not so much through the leakage of capital out of declining into expanding industries as through the diversion of savings into expanding industries that adaptation to changes in the demand for capital is secured.

## THE RATE OF INTEREST

So far we have made no attempt to formulate with any precision the forces controlling interest rates. At one time interest rates have been made to depend upon the state of liquidity-preference of the public; their role has been to equalise the advantages of holding money and loans. At another time, attention has been focussed on the supply of loanable funds and the demand for their use, and the role of interest rates has been to preserve equality between the two. The first explanation is in terms of the existing *stock* of loans, the second in terms of the *flow* of loanable funds. But what appear to be two distinct and conflicting explanations are really different versions of the same explanation.

According to the liquidity-preference version the public must choose between holding its wealth in the form either of loans or of money, or of other assets.[1] Given the supply of money and of loans, the demand for each must be such as to absorb this supply. The price of loans in terms of money, therefore, will vary until the public has no incentive to change from loans to money or from money to loans. But the price of loans is simply another expression for the rate of interest. The rate of interest, therefore, is governed by the demand for money relatively to loans (liquidity-preference) and by the supply of money relatively to loans. The rate of interest will change for one of three reasons—a change in liquidity-preference, a change in the supply of money, and a change in the supply of loans. Now of these three reasons the last is equivalent to a change

---

[1] Other assets are ignored here for the sake of simplicity.

in the demand for loanable funds while the first two are equivalent to a change in the supply of loanable funds. Suppose, for example, that there is an increase in the marginal productivity of capital. Then more will be borrowed and the rate of interest will rise—from one point of view, because the consequent addition to the existing stock of loans forces down their price in terms of money; from the other point of view, because increased borrowing puts greater pressure on the public's willingness to lend and hence on the supply of loanable funds. Or suppose that there is an increase in the supply of money. The increase, which may be made through inflation of the currency by the government or through the grant of additional credit by the banks, will add to the supply of loanable funds and reduce their price; alternatively, it will add to the stock of money, and diminish the price at which people are willing to purchase liquidity. From either point of view, the increase in the supply of money will operate to depress interest rates. Finally, a change in liquidity-preference clearly implies a change in the public's willingness to lend. If people are less anxious to hold their wealth in monetary form they will be more willing to lend it. The supply of loanable funds, therefore, will increase whenever there is a reduction in liquidity-preference.

Although there is a close connection between the amount which the community succeeds in saving and the supply of loanable funds, this does not mean that increased thrift necessarily increases the supply of loanable funds and so reduces the rate of interest. For increased thrift does not necessarily or automatically increase the amount saved by a community, although it does necessarily increase the amount saved by any one person. It is within the power of one man to add to his savings by increased thrift. But it is not within his power to add to the total savings of the community. His decision to save more may cause someone else to save less. If, for example, he spends less on bread, the baker will make a lower profit and will have less income out of which to save. If the baker tries to save as much as before, he in turn will spend less and reduce the profits of some other tradesman. And so it may go on, with each man trying to save as much as before and in doing so reducing his neighbour's income. An excess of thrift does not of itself increase the amount saved or the supply of loanable funds; it may, instead, make for industrial depression and unemployment. Only when additional thrift is compensated by additional loan-expenditure is there a net increase in savings. For then the income of the community is undisturbed; some people lose because the savers spend less, while others gain as the borrowers spend more.

The fact is that the amount which the community saves does not depend upon conscious decisions taken in advance by the savers. For savers cannot, in advance, decide what their incomes will be; and savings, as we have seen, depend upon income. We may plan what we mean to save, but since we do not know what others are planning or what the future holds for us, our realised and our anticipated incomes may differ; some part of what we save will be undesigned. On the other hand, nothing of what we *lend* is undesigned; we can plan at any moment how much of our wealth we will lend and how much we will retain in the form of money and other assets. Thus we can draw a supply curve of loanable funds, showing how much we will lend at any given rate of interest. We can also draw a supply curve of planned savings to show how much we will plan to save at any given rate of interest. But we cannot draw a supply curve of amounts actually *saved* for a supply curve is the expression of an attitude towards the future, not a statement about the past.

Here, for the time being, with many puzzling questions unresolved, we must leave the theory of interest. Later, when we come to discuss economic fluctuations, we shall return to the subject.

## 2  PROFIT

Profit, as generally understood, is the difference between the total expenses incurred in producing or acquiring a commodity and the total revenue accruing from its sale. This difference may be expressed as a return on *capital*, the total profit over a year being related to the amount of capital employed; alternatively, profit may be expressed as the proportion by which the price per unit sold exceeds its cost, i.e., as a rate on turnover. A village chemist, for example, may be able to make a very large profit on turnover and only a moderate return on his capital; whereas a firm of wholesalers may make a comparatively trifling margin of profit on turnover, and yet obtain an abnormally high return on its capital. Profit on turnover is of no significance in the theory of distribution. It is profit *as a source of income* that we are studying, and since income is a flow measurable over time, profit can form part of income only if it, too, is measured over time instead of being expressed as a ratio on individual transactions. We shall confine ourselves, therefore, to profit as a return on capital.[1]

### Gross and net profit

Profit as defined above is described by economists as *gross* profit, because it may include some items which are not really profit at all. The first of these is earnings of management. A joint-stock company includes in its expenses (and

---

[1] Profit on turnover can be derived from profit on capital by dividing by the rate of turnover of capital. If, for example, capital is turned over twice annually and annual profits are 6 per cent., then the rate of profit on turnover is obviously 3 per cent.

so excludes from profits) the salaries of those who undertake the work of management. But in businesses which are managed by their owner (e.g., farms, shops, etc.) the same kind of work is done without expense, and profits are swollen therefore, by the value of this work. The true or *net* profit can be arrived at only after deduction of the expense to which the owners of such businesses would be put if they had to hire the services of a manager; or, alternatively, after deduction of the salary which the owners might obtain by doing equal work for a joint-stock company.[1] Secondly, gross profit may include what ought properly to appear under the heading of interest. A business which uses borrowed capital counts the interest on this capital as an expense and excludes it from profit. Other businesses, using their own capital, include in profit the whole return on their capital. The proper procedure, if we wish to isolate net profit, is to deduct from the gross return on capital the interest which might have been earned by lending that capital on good security. A third item which ought properly to be excluded is the rent of land or buildings owned by the firm. A farmer, for example, might fail to reckon the rentable value of his land as a business expense in arriving at his profit on the year's working.[2]

## Distinguishing features of profit

Profit differs from other kinds of income in three ways. First, it may be negative. Neither wages, rent nor interest are ever likely to be negative, but every year there are some firms which make a loss and there are few firms which do not make a loss at some time or another. Some economists even take the view that, taking into account business failures, net profits are, on the average, negative—that is, that those who expose their capital to the uncertainties of business could earn a higher return, on the average, by lending out their money at interest. The statistical evidence, which is not very adequate, suggests that this view is too extravagant. But there can be no doubt that the *average* net profit which is earned in business (after deducting all losses and making provision for interest on capital) is comparatively small, and that it is greatly

---

[1] Strictly speaking, a rather larger deduction should be made. It costs something to bring capital and business ability together, so that an important advantage is lost by any business man who lends out his capital and hires himself to a joint-stock company for a salary. This advantage, which is similar to the advantage of favourably situated land, gives rise to an element of rent which should be included in earnings of management rather than in net profit.

[2] The distinction between gross and net profit is by no means an academic one. When, for example, a tax is levied on profits, the usual basis of assessment is gross profit. This obviously discrimates against businesses managed by their owners or employing their owners' capital. There is also, as we shall see, discrimination against young, enterprising and growing firms in comparison with old and established ones. A tax on *excess* profit—i.e., on profit in excess of some "fair" or "normal" return—may also involve discrimination against firms which are making a high *gross* profit and only a normal *net* profit.

exaggerated by those who think too exclusively of a few exceptional gains. Secondly, profit fluctuates more than any other kind of income. Between boom and slump there is comparatively little change in wage-rates (or even in wage-incomes), in interest-rates (the change in long-term rates is generally trifling), or in rents; the brunt of the change falls on profit. Profit responds immediately to a change in price; other incomes are adjusted more slowly and less violently. Thirdly—and this is the crucial distinction—profit is not, like other kinds of income, a contractual and certain income, agreed on in advance, but an uncertain residue determined by the luck of events. A man's wage, for example, is predetermined and certain in amount; but the income of his employer is not. The man is paid now for goods produced in anticipation of future demand; and, since the future can never be foreseen with certainty, the goods which the employer obtains for a given wage-payment are of uncertain value. If eventually the price which the goods realise exceeds the cost incurred in their production, the employer will make a profit; if the selling-price turns out to be lower than the cost which he has incurred, he will make a loss. But he does not, and cannot, know in advance that he will be able to make a profit. He *expects* to make a profit, but he may be unlucky.

### The origin of profit

Thus profit originates in uncertainty. That uncertainty arises out of the responsibilities of ownership in a world of change and imperfect foresight. If everything could be reduced to routine, or if the future could be exactly predicted, there would be no uncertainty, no need to take chances, and no profit in the strict sense.[1] But in the world as we know it, there *is* uncertainty, the burden of which is all the greater because of our intricate economic system with its intense specialisation and its production for markets distant in time and space. The burden of uncertainty is one which *someone* must bear. To induce property owners to assume the burden of uncertainty the lure of profits is required; they will not run the risk of loss except in the hope of eventual gain.[2] There may be some people with such a liking for uncertainty that even the prospect of loss would not deter them from indulging their adventurousness; but most people take chances less from love of gambling for its own sake than from hope of making a profit if they are lucky. It does not follow from this that profit must

---

[1] There would, however, be *monopoly* profits. As to these, see pp. 251–253.

[2] The burden of uncertainty is borne mainly, but not exclusively by property-owners. An important part is borne by labour, since workers run the risk of injury, ill-health, or unemployment. The burden on labour, however, has been relieved by schemes of social insurance and by State expenditure on the social services. Part of the burden on capital has also been transferred to the State, since it may be induced to offer special assistance to industries undergoing a severe depression and so relieve their owners of some of the risk of financial loss. In addition, the State assumes the burden of uncertainty for all property in its ownership.

be on the average a positive quantity. But it does follow that some people must make a profit and others a loss; there must be a prospect of profit which more than compensates for the risk of loss.

## Profit and cost

People will take chances, therefore, only if they judge the chances to be in their favour—that is, only if they expect to make a profit. Before they will invest their capital in any industry they must have a sufficiently strong expectation of profit to overcome their fear of loss. This prospective profit is a cost exactly like wages, interest and rent. It is a necessary inducement without which adequate supplies of capital would not be obtainable. Prospective profit, therefore, enters into the supply-price of finished goods; the price anticipated must be high enough to cover wages and interest charges and leave a margin which is considered adequate by business men to cover the various contingencies to which they are exposed. This margin will be larger for some business men than for others; those who are temperamentally cautious and averse to the assumption of risk will work to a larger margin than those who are more confident and venturesome. Those who take a gloomy view of the probable trend of prices will hesitate to take risks which seem moderate to more optimistic competitors. Thus there are marginal risk-takers, just as there are marginal savers and marginal workers; and it is the marginal risk-takers to whom expected prices must offer an adequate prospect of profit.

Although prospective profit enters into cost, realised profit does not. It is the reward for successful risk-taking and is a surplus governed by, not governing, price. At the same time, since men's expectations are generally grounded on their experience, prospective profit and realised profit are likely to move together. In the long run, if an industry consistently fails to yield a profit, business men will give up expecting it to yield one. By influencing expectations, therefore, and so controlling prospective profit, realised profit in the long run enters indirectly into price.

Realised profit is partly the result of luck, partly the result of good judgment —since some people take foolish risks—and partly the result of the skilful avoidance or elimination of unnecessary risks—i.e., of outstanding organising ability. But if anyone shows evidence of good judgment and is right oftener than other people, the return which he obtains on his capital is not all pure profit but a combination of profit and earnings of management. For a man of sound judgment can hire his services for a salary to people who have no faith in their own judgment or who recognise their own capacity. In the same way if one man is more skilful than his fellows in *avoiding* or *eliminating* risks because of his superior powers of organisation he will earn a higher profit which reflects, not better luck, but greater talent. Once the return to superior organising ability, like the return to superior judgment, has been transferred to earnings of management we are left with a residue of pure profit which is the net return to uncertainty-bearing and is governed solely by luck.

## Profit and business fluctuations

The most important single influence on realised profit is the level of economic activity. If business is brisk and firms are operating at or near capacity, their average costs are likely to be not far from the minimum, while their sales are not far from the maximum. This conjunction generally causes profits to rise steeply, particularly if prices simultaneously begin to increase ahead of costs. On the other hand, at a low level of activity, with heavy standing charges and falling prices, profits tend to disappear and be replaced by losses. For industry as a whole, the same conclusions hold good. Aggregate profits move sharply up and down with boom and slump, inflation and deflation.

While an explanation of fluctuations in profit is necessarily wrapped up in the general theory of business fluctuations, the reasons why profit is higher in one industry than in another and why, over a long period, profits rise or fall, do not hinge entirely on such a theory and can be put quite simply. In what follows it will be assumed that we can disregard fluctuations in the total volume of economic activity but not fluctuations in particular sectors of activity.

## Variations in profit between industries

The tendency of competition is to make profits highest in those trades in which the burden of uncertainty is felt to be heaviest. Profits are likely to be high in industries in which methods of production are constantly changing, so that there is need for continuous adaptation of technique—in industries supplying luxury products the demand for which fluctuates rapidly; in industries which are still too young for their prospects to be judged with assurance; in industries in which a long interval elapses between investment and return of capital; in industries in which the labour and capital employed must be more or less irrevocably committed to narrowly specialised tasks; and in industries exposed to specific risks the incidence of which is uncertain—agriculture, for example, with its dependence on weather conditions, or brewing, with the threat of prohibition or of higher duties hanging over it. There is no tendency towards equality of profits, but only towards such rates of profit as equalise differences in the degree of uncertainty felt by investors in different industries.

## Monopoly profit

Just as an element of rent may be included in wages or in interest, so profit may be maintained above the level which is necessary to induce capitalists to bear uncertainty. This surplus profit arises in trades into which entry is not free and in businesses which enjoy some monopolistic advantage over their rivals. The general level of profit may also be maintained at an artificially high level if there are any restrictions on new businesses in general, or any unnecessary impediments to the acquisition of command over capital by enterprising men.

## The general level of profit

When there is great uncertainty the normal rate of profit tends to be high. In forecasting the future, people will leave themselves a wide margin of error, and in normal circumstances this will be reflected in a correspondingly high margin of realised profit *on the average*. For *individual* risk-takers, however, profit will range between a very large positive and a very large negative quantity; in a new industry, for example, some firms generally earn enormous profits while others lose their capital altogether. When uncertainty is comparatively negligible, the average margin of prospective, and of realised, profit will be correspondingly small and profit will range within fairly narrow limits; businesses supplying some staple article of clothing or of diet, for example, can generally predict their future profit with much more assurance than firms of shipbuilders and steelmakers. The correspondence between degree of uncertainty and prospective profit—and *a fortiori* between uncertainty and realised profit—is by no means perfect. Many people are more attracted by a spectacular chance of sudden fortune than by humdrum risks which are not likely to cause heavy loss and are equally unlikely to bring great gain; some outsiders, so to speak, are always more heavily backed than they should be. Thus profit is often highest in trades where risks are moderate—neither so negligible as to make risk-bearing almost superfluous, nor so enormous as to attract the incautious and the speculative. It was neither the railways nor the gold-mining industry which earned the highest profits in the late nineteenth century; it is neither the plastics nor the film industry nowadays.

The degree of uncertainty, and hence the rate of profit, will be higher the greater the rate of social change and the greater the degree of immobility of productive resources. The more rapidly change takes place, the more difficult and dangerous is the task of predicting the future and of undertaking the adjustment of resources to future wants. Whether that adjustment is planned by the State or undertaken by private enterprise a larger margin of profit will require to be added to present costs to provide for the uncertainties of the future. The task of adjusting resources to wants will be greatly complicated if these resources are specialised and immobile; for once they are committed to one use it will be difficult to adapt them for other purposes when new information or

M

discoveries call for a change of plans. If resources are immobile the burden of uncertainty in deciding their use is heavy, and any acceleration of social change, by dictating more frequent and more drastic readjustment of resources to wants, will aggravate the burden. The risk of loss through sinking capital in forms no longer required is increased, and to overcome this increased risk of loss there will require to be a correspondingly higher expectation of profit.

### Profits and development

The rate of profit, therefore, is intimately connected with what we have called "development".[1] A business contributes to development by pioneering new methods and new products. If its innovations are successful it reaps a profit; if it is unfortunate or injudicious it loses its capital. Because development means change, it creates uncertainty; and because development means increased efficiency it creates a prospect of profit. Development, therefore, is one of the chief forces maintaining the rate of profit and is itself one of the chief sources out of which profit is paid.

---

[1] See above, p. 67.

# PART V—INCOME, EMPLOYMENT AND MONEY

CHAPTER 25

# THE NATIONAL INCOME

In earlier parts of this book we have begged a great many questions by taking for granted the total output and income of the community. We have discussed relative prices and relative shares without much thought of the general level of prices, the size of the national income, the volume of employment, and all the other aggregates which, from now on, will be in the forefront.

## The national income

One of the most important of these aggregates is the national income. It is not a new conception: the first great work by an economist, written nearly two hundred years ago, was called *The Wealth of Nations*, or, as we might now say, "national incomes." But at that stage the conception was a rather vague one, not even defined much less quantified. Indeed, it is only since the beginning of this century that systematic attempts have been made to measure the national income of any country and the changes in it from year to year, although there are isolated estimates of considerable ingenuity going back as far as the seventeenth century.

The use of the term "national income" is apt to suggest some association with the revenue of the government. It is important to guard against any confusion of this kind: the national income relates to the total income of the members of a community not to that part of it which passes in rates and taxes to public authorities. The significance of the national income lies precisely in the fact that it is a measure of the economic well-being of the community. Just as a private person is keenly interested in anything that would increase his income, so the economist is interested in changes that are calculated to increase the national income.

The mere fact that the national income is increasing is not proof, however, that the country is better off. The increase may be due to inflation and may simply reflect a fall in the value of the units of money in which the national income is measured. Or it may be due to the growth of population and be

355

accompanied by an increase in the number of people who have to be maintained out of the larger output. In war-time the national income may be swollen in ways that represent an actual sacrifice in living standards: partly at the expense of leisure (there is more overtime); partly at the expense of health (people work harder); partly at the expense of personal freedom (more people work for a wage or salary instead of on their own); and partly at the expense of enjoyment (many people are obliged to work in surroundings which they dislike). Changes in the distribution of the national income have also to be considered; it is possible to have more riches and more poverty simultaneously. The national income may grow larger and at the same time fluctuate more widely between boom and slump; its stability is a circumstance that ranks in importance with its size. Again, the national income may expand over a period at the cost of a later generation through neglect to maintain the existing stock of wealth; it is always possible to have jam today by opening tomorrow's jam-pots. These considerations, however, do not detract from the importance of the national income; they point to the need to study not only the increase in the national income but also the circumstances of the increase.

### Income, output and expenditure

The national income can be looked at in any one of three ways: as the national income, measured by adding up everybody's income; as the national output, measured by adding up everybody's output—the value of the goods that people are paid to produce and the services that they render; or as the national expenditure, measured by adding up the value of all the things that people buy. More formal definitions can be given of each of these. The national output of a country, for example, is defined as the aggregate joint product of its resources of labour, land and capital over any given period (generally a year) or as the money value of the goods and services which flow into being during that period and which are customarily exchanged for money.

It is not immediately obvious that there is any equality between income and output or between both and expenditure. We know that our personal income and expenditure are only too apt to diverge from one another and we have generally very little notion how anyone can measure our output. Why should things be so different at the national level? That there is *some* connection between the three is, of course, incontestable: we all recognise, in a general way, that the standard of living (income) and production (output) are inter-connected, and that, in the last resort, income controls expenditure. But are they necessarily equal?

First of all, the reader should be on his guard against analogies between his personal economic problem and the problem of social economy. For example, if his income falls he knows that he must cut his expenditure too. He may therefore urge in the middle of a slump that, since the country is poorer, the government should cut its coat according to its cloth and retrench on public expenditure. But this would hardly make sense since its immediate effect is to throw more people out of jobs and make matters worse.

Secondly, the equality of income and output is much easier to grasp if we abstract from a number of complications such as those introduced by foreign trade, and by saving and capital accumulation. If there were no foreign trade (as is true of the world as a whole) and if there were no saving or dis-saving, what was earned would automatically be spent, so that total income and expenditure would necessarily be equal; and what was spent would equal the value of what was produced, so that total expenditure and output would necessarily be equal. There would be a circular flow of expenditure and income, the expenditure providing the sales proceeds of current output and the source from which wages, salaries and other incomes were paid: while these incomes in turn would form the source of the expenditure. The flow of goods and services into production would coincide with the flow of goods and services into consumption and form the national income of the community.

### Saving and dis-saving

This remains true if we relax the assumption that there is no saving or dis-saving. It makes no difference to the conclusion if one person saves and another dis-saves: if, for example, someone buys a refrigerator on hire purchase and

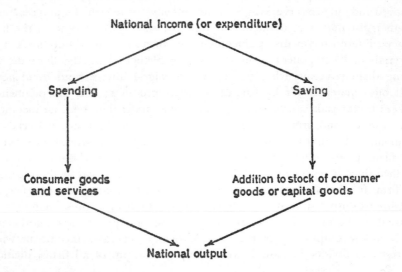

someone saves what is needed in order to finance the transaction, the circular flow of income and expenditure is not interrupted. We need only assume that there is no *net* saving and no accumulation or decumulation of stocks of goods flowing into consumption. Even this assumption, as further reflection will show, is not necessary. If people choose to save, and if their savings are matched by an equivalent addition to stocks, either of consumer goods or of capital goods, the stream of income and output splits into two separate flows but the two remain equal to one another, as illustrated on page 357.

What if savings are not matched in this way? We shall dodge this question for the time being as it leads straight into the theory of income determination. From the point of view of definition (as opposed to causation), so long as we are looking backwards after the event, we are bound to find income and output equal whatever happens to savings. What the community *succeeds* in saving is measured by the addition to its stock of assets, whatever may have been the intention of the savers: total savings, in the sense of the difference between yesterday's income and yesterday's spending, cannot but be equal to the increment in the assets of the community, although it may not be immediately obvious why this should be so.

### Income and output in the individual firm

It is perhaps easier to see why the net value of output and income must be equal by thinking in terms of a single firm instead of a whole community. What a firm receives from sales every year must be distributed in wages, or in payments of interest and dividends, or in buying raw materials and components, or it must be saved and put to reserve. Wages become income to the firm's employees; profits whether distributed in dividends or put to reserve, are income to the firm's owners; interest payments are income to the firm's creditors. Purchases of raw materials and components generate income further along the line; the firm selling them pays out what it receives in wages, interest and dividends or itself buys materials for incorporation in its products; and the payments it makes for materials can be traced further back until they become income for other workers and property-owners. Since what is paid for raw materials and components does not form part of the income of those who work for or own the first firm, it can be left out of account; it is also no part of the net output of the firm since it represents work done elsewhere. If we treat as the income of the firm its sales proceeds less the cost of bought-in materials and parts, and measure its output in terms of value added by the firm to those materials and parts, then the firm's income and output must be equal to one another: the whole of the output of the firm automatically generates income in wages, interest and dividends. Now if we add up the output of all firms, including one-man businesses and work done in the public sector, we get the national output, and if we add up their income (including both owners and employees) we get the national income. It is true of the country, just as it is true of a firm, that what is distributed in income to the factors of production is equal to the value of what the factors co-operate to produce.

It follows from this that we cannot increase the national income without simultaneously increasing the national output. Before we can consume more there must be more to consume. The suggestion which is sometimes made that we should be better off if purchasing power were to be increased is true only if the increase in purchasing power is accompanied by an increase in production, and this increase will be possible only if some productive resources are either not being used to the best advantage or are not being used at all (that is, are unemployed). An increase in the employment or in the productivity of labour, for example, will certainly increase the national income; but an increase in wages may not. Higher wages will give wage-earners more purchasing power. But other people—for instance, those who pay wages—may have correspondingly less; or, if they are able to pass on the rise in wage-costs to the consumer in the form of higher prices, the increased purchasing power of the community may be absorbed in paying higher prices for the same quantity of goods and services. *Real* incomes will then be no greater than before, and the community, will be no better off.

## Some fundamental equations

We can express the relationship between income, output and expenditure in the form of an equation. Following the notation usual in economic textbooks:

$$Y = O = D \qquad \qquad \ldots\ldots(1)$$

where Y is national income, O is national output and D is national expenditure. The use of the symbol D reminds us that expenditure forms the effective demand for what is produced. By virtue of equation (1), effective demand is equal to income (or purchasing power) as well as to output. But nothing in equation (1) tells us what causal connection to expect between Y, O and D, or what causes any of these quantities to be what they are. It is merely an accounting relationship, like the relationship between the takings and outgoings of a firm.

We may also write:

$$Y = C + S \qquad \qquad \ldots\ldots(2)$$

where C stands for consumption and S for savings. This tells us that income is either spent or saved. The parallel relationship on the side of output can be written:

$$O = C + I \qquad \dots (3)$$

where C represents sales to final consumers and I represents additions to the stock of assets, including stocks of consumer goods. The symbol I stands for investment, not in the sense of financial investment or the purchase of financial assets, but capital formation in the sense of outlay on new assets (allowing for depreciation of existing assets).

We can then deduce that

$$S = I \qquad \dots (4)$$

recognising, however, that this equality between savings and investment rests on arbitrary definitions of the variables involved and that on other, quite legitimate, definitions, the two things could diverge from one another.

These equations serve a number of purposes. They form the starting point of further analysis, to which we shall come in Chapter 26, of what it is that governs the level of economic activity. At the same time, as we shall see below, they help us to arrange our information about what is happening to income and output in the form of a set of national accounts. They also enable us to make more reliable estimates of national income and other economic aggregates; it is to this problem of estimation that we now turn.

## Methods of estimating national income

It follows from equation (1) that we can estimate national income in any one of three ways: from the side of income or output or expenditure. This means that we may start with statistical data about people's incomes—based, for example, on the returns they make to the Inland Revenue authorities—or with production figures obtained from various trades and services, or with figures of retail sales and other data relating to expenditure. In the same way, savings and investment can be measured either in terms of equation (2) as the difference between income and consumption, or in terms of equation (3) as the output of capital goods, or as the capital expenditure of the ultimate purchasers of capital goods. The available statistical data for any one of these quantities may be of doubtful reliability, or be incomplete and omit some items that form part of the total; but by taking bearings from different starting-points, it is possible to plot the point of intersection with some confidence.

When these alternative methods are used, it goes without saying that the definitions used must be mutually consistent. For example, the goods and services that enter into income and those that enter into output should be governed by the same conventions. We cannot include an item in income and simultaneously exclude it from output. If some people rent their house and others are owner-occupiers, we may be obliged to impute a value to the income of the latter from their property (as the tax-gatherer habitually does) but in doing so we must enter this imputed income on the side of output as well.

There are several important practical and conceptual problems that confront the statistician who tries to measure the size of the national income.

**(a) Changes over time in services included**—The national income, viewed from the side of production, consists of a flow of services, which are the subject of a money payment. But services that are rendered free in one generation may have to be paid for by a later generation, so that the "coverage" of the national income does not remain constant. Various services formerly rendered at home have been taken over progressively by canteens, restaurants, laundries, market-gardens, and so on, and are included in the national income at cost although they may not correspond to any greater amount of work done or any real improvement in the standard of living.

**(b) Depreciation and keeping capital intact**—Some of the services that enter into production and income are current services and some are past services embodied in fixed assets. The value of current services is thus a gross total out of which provision has to be made for putting back into the stock of capital the equivalent of what has been drawn from it. But how are we to decide what is equivalent? What provision for depreciation will serve to maintain capital intact? These are questions to which there is no simple answer. It is not enough merely to look at the financial provision that is made in accordance with accounting conventions, because these conventions are based on convenience rather than logic and may yield results that are quite obviously wrong. For example, if prices double and depreciation continues to be reckoned on the original cost of a machine, the sum of the financial allowances made for depreciation will be insufficient to meet the cost of replacement. What most statisticians do is to assume that all assets have a fixed life and that they are used up at a steady rate over that period; but even this is no more than an approximation based on an arbitrary and often unrealistic assumption.

**(c) Cost elements in income**—Some of the services rendered in a community enter directly into consumption and others are purely instrumental, in the sense that they allow other services to be performed. For example, if towns increase in size, more effort goes to transporting people to their work but this extra effort represents a cost of urban living, not an addition to net

M*

incomes. People have to spend more on fares and although there is a corresponding increase in the value of transport services, this increased flow of
services signifies a diminished, not an increased, flow of income since people
have the inconvenience of a longer journey to work. The same kind of situation
arises when people are involved in heavier expenditure (e.g., on uniforms, or
meals) by virtue of their employment. This extra expenditure is not part of their
income but is a cost and must be deducted from the total payments made to
them.

These may seem examples of a rather unusual situation; but a little reflection
will show that the instrumental, or cost, element in income is really quite large.
A good deal of the average man's income goes in ways which he thinks will
help to maintain his earning-power. The manual worker's beefsteak, the doctor's Cadillac, and even the teacher's holiday abroad have an instrumental aspect,
however much they enter simultaneously into income. Where both aspects are
present, we may treat services as part of final income; but where consumers
make payments that add nothing to their welfare and are the price of what
they are enabled to earn, such payments should be excluded from income.

**(d) Transfer payments**—The operations of government give rise to a
danger of duplication. People pay money to the government while other people
receive money from it and both sets of payments are liable to be included in
estimates of the national income. The sums received by private persons in
national insurance benefits, national assistance, family allowances, interest on
the national debt, and so on, are undoubtedly part of their income. But they
are paid out of the incomes of other persons who make national insurance
contributions or pay taxes. They are *transferred* from the one set of incomes to
the other set without any service being rendered in exchange. Since the same
income cannot be earned twice, it should not be counted twice. In estimating
the national income, therefore, we must deduct from the total of individual
incomes any sums received from the State by way of benefit, pension or grant,
or as interest on the national debt. On the other hand, we do not deduct payments made by the State for current services (e.g., the income of policemen)
since these add to the flow of goods and services which form the real income of
the country.

These and other problems of estimation and interpretation will be clearer
to the reader once he has read the Appendix to this Chapter. There he will
find a simplified version of the national accounts published for the United
Kingdom. Some readers will find these accounts useful in bringing out the inter-
relationship between the constituent elements in national income while others
will be inclined to pass on hastily because of a constitutional inability to look at

statistical tables without a swimming of the head. Since the tables are some-what complicated and the commentary on the tables is somewhat technical, both the tables and the commentary have been detached from the rest of the chapter and put in an Appendix where they can be easily by-passed by anyone who is prone to statistical amnesia.

## Social accounting

The national income is the basis of what is often described as "social accounting." Just as a firm can draw up a balance sheet, or a profit and loss account, so it is possible to draw up a series of statements for the country as a whole, using the same principles of double-entry book-keeping, every receipt by one account appearing also as a payment out of another account. These statements may try to reconcile, for example, an estimate of total personal income, as received in the form of wages, salaries, dividends, interest, rent, etc., with a separate estimate of total personal expenditure and savings, based on figures showing total purchases of food, clothing, furniture, etc. Another statement may show how the various sums which people save, including the savings of businesses and of public authorities, are balanced by the additions that are made to the real assets of the country in the form of new buildings, machinery, and so on. Yet another may set out the transactions with foreign countries, showing imports and other transactions involving payments on one side and exports and other transactions involving receipts on the other.

These statements or accounts provide a check on one another since the figures used in one set of accounts must be consistent with the figures used in the others and since they are estimated independently from different sources. Thus they narrow down the element of uncertainty unavoidable in estimates of this kind; and when they have been prepared over a series of years for the same constituent items they acquire an increasing reliability if it becomes apparent that the figures not only fit together and add up properly but also show trends that are in conformity with the expectations of common sense and ordinary observation.

The primary purpose of a set of national accounts is to anatomise the economy: to show in the form of a statistical skeleton the bare bones of its structure. The accounts serve to indicate how the structure is changing, particularly over the long run. They can also be valuable in diagnosing short-term threats to the balance and momentum of the economy; but for this purpose they are not the only nor indeed the best clue to what is going on. The Bank of England is likely to learn a great deal faster from a movement of its gold reserves what changes are in progress in the balance of payments than by waiting for the publication of a White Paper giving a full statement of all the items (imports, exports, and the rest) on both sides of the account. Inflation will generally show itself in the movement of prices long before the national accounts provide confirmation. But the national accounts give a more systematic view of the working of the whole economy than do other indices, such as unemployment or the cost of living, and allow any fresh change to be assessed against a wider background of information.

A rational and self-consistent view of the past is a great help to a sound judgment of the future. The national accounts, by throwing light on what has happened and is happening, can serve as an instrument in planning the future. Even the Budget, which has come to be regarded by the government as the pivot of economic policy, is now fitted into the national accounts, the government seeking to adjust its revenue and expenditure—and the excess of the one over the other—to its expectations of the broad changes over the coming year in the national income, and its main constituents.

Estimates of the national income and of its constituent elements, therefore, serve a wide variety of purposes. They show how incomes are earned and on what they are spent. They show the distribution of income between classes. They can be used to measure the prosperity of one country compared with another, or the prosperity of the same country at different stages in its history. They provide an index of economic activity and an instrument of economic planning.

# THE NATIONAL ACCOUNTS

The national accounts of the United Kingdom are published annually in a Blue Book on *National Income and Expenditure* and quarterly estimates of the national income appear in the *Monthly Digest of Statistics*. Most other industrial countries also publish national accounts on an annual basis.

In Tables 13–19 the national accounts for the United Kingdom are shown in simplified form together with the figures for 1948, 1956 and 1964. We shall first comment on the Tables without much regard to the figures in order to bring out the inter-relationship between the items included. Then we can concentrate on the figures to see what can be deduced from them.

**National income**

In Table 13 income is shown under three headings; income from employment, income from property and income from abroad. The first of these includes wages and salaries, the pay in money or in kind of the Armed Forces, and the earnings of small (unincorporated) businesses, farmers and professional persons; these items appear in more detail in Table 15. The second and third items both represent income from property and consist mainly of payments of rent, interest and dividends. Net income from abroad is shown separately so as to distinguish income produced from domestic assets from net earnings on investments abroad; while the second item includes the return on capital assets located and owned in the United Kingdom, the third item is the balance between the return on assets located abroad and owned in Britain and the corresponding payments made to foreigners on their holdings of assets in Britain.

The total obtained by adding up these three items is adjusted for:

(a) windfall changes in the value of stocks due to price fluctuations ("stock appreciation") and

(b) the depreciation or "using up" of capital assets that has to be made good before arriving at true net income (sometimes called "capital consumption").

The first of these adjustments is important only when the value of money is changing. A general rise in prices over the year will leave an unchanged quantity of goods commanding a higher money value at the end than at the beginning of the year, but this inflation of values will not represent any accumulation of real assets or form any part of the year's income. If businesses always valued their stocks at fixed prices, no adjustment would be necessary, since income from property (including company profits) would not be swollen by any appreciation in stocks; in fact, however, under current accounting conventions, so long as stocks are being turned over every few months and valued at cost, or at market value, their value is bound to change with the price at which they are acquired and may diverge sharply from the initial valuation of the same quantity of goods. When prices are rising, as in recent years, a deduction has to be made from profits (included in "income from property"), and when prices are falling, as in pre-war years, the opposite correction is necessary since accounting profits then understate the true contribution to income.

Whether we make the second adjustment or not depends upon whether we wish to measure national income net or gross of depreciation. The difference between the two represents the sum that should be set aside out of the gross return on capital in order to keep capital intact: for example, the financial provision that has to be made by businesses out of their total profits for the maintenance and renewal of existing assets. It may seem surprising that any importance should attach to the gross total. Yet in many countries it is this total ("gross national product") rather than the net total that is given prominence, and for some years no official figures of net income were published by the British government, the Blue Book figures relating exclusively to gross national product. The reason for this is that it must always be a matter of debate what financial provision should be made in order to maintain capital intact, particularly since the value of fixed assets is affected not only by wear and tear but also by obsolescence, business sentiment, and changes in the value of money. It is only by making some rather arbitrary assumptions, such as that all assets will have a fixed life and yield their value at a steady rate throughout that life, that the statisticians have been able to arrive at estimates of capital consumption. On the other hand, it is a simpler affair to obtain figures of gross income and output. For this purpose it is necessary only to know the value of *new* fixed assets created without troubling about depreciation on existing assets.

## National expenditure

This is more apparent when we turn to the other side of the balance sheet in Table 13. The third item given there is called "gross investment at home," and represents outlay on new fixed assets, together with the value of any increment that has taken place in the physical quantity of goods in stock or in progress. While there may be some ambiguity as to what constitutes a fixed asset, the measurement of gross investment in this sense is not attended by all the difficulties of definition and identification that surround the idea of depreciation. Not that the use of gross rather than net figures disposes of the difficulties: it merely avoids them and leaves a total which diverges by an unstated amount from national income. This divergence will consist principally of the depreciation and obsolescence of existing fixed assets; but it will also be affected by any element of betterment resulting from repairs to those assets if this is not already set against wear and tear and obsolescence.

Investment in new assets represents an actual outlay and so forms part of the effective demand that guides the flow of economic activity. Expenditure on goods and services by private consumers and by the government and other public authorities is clearly in the same category. Some allowance has also to be made for demand from abroad for British goods and services. Strictly speaking, this should be represented by a figure for exports (the first item on the credit side of Table 19) and in some accounts, this figure is introduced, with imports added to the other side of the account. If this were done, Table 13 would then show, on the right-hand side, the calls made on available resources through the demands of private consumers, public consumers, and foreign consumers, or through capital outlay, while on the left-hand side would appear the sources from which these calls were met. This form of account is frequently used but in Table 13 we include only the balance between exports and imports, or (what comes to the same thing) the net addition made to foreign assets out of current income. This, together with the first three items, and a small item for remittances abroad, adds up to gross national expenditure.

In order to hitch this on to national income we have two adjustments to make. The first has already been explained: we must make an allowance for depreciation of domestic assets. We need not, however, make any deduction for stock appreciation; the figures for gross investment already exclude this, since only the value of the physical change in stocks, not the full change in the value of stocks, however arising, is included. The second adjustment is a puzzling one: it is necessary to deduct indirect taxes and add back subsidies. This is done in order to avoid double-counting. The figures of expenditure on goods and services include taxes which are paid to the public authorities and used by them to finance the provision of services such as education. If we count in both the expenditure of private consumers on beer and tobacco at full market value and expenditure by the public authorities out of those taxes on the salaries of school teachers, we are obviously counting the same thing twice. We ought to measure the purchases of the public at the prices that would rule in the absence of indirect taxes and, by a simple extension of the argument, in the absence of

## TABLE 13

### INCOME ACCOUNT OF THE UNITED KINGDOM, 1948–64     £m.

| National Income | 1948 | 1956 | 1964 | National Expenditure | 1948 | 1956 | 1964 |
|---|---|---|---|---|---|---|---|
| 1. Income from employment (Table 15,6) ... | 8111 | 13994 | 21914 | 10. Expenditure by private consumers (Table 15,10) ... | 8615 | 13829 | 21334 |
| 2. Income from property (Table 15,7 + Table 17,7 and 8 + Table 18,4 less 7b − Table 19,9 less 2) ... ... | 2444 | 4230 | 7140 | 11. Expenditure on goods and services by public authorities (Table 18,6) ... ... | 1756 | 3433 | 5411 |
| 3. Less stock appreciation (Table 14,6) ... | −325 | −208 | −315 | 12. Gross investment at home (Table 14,9 and 10) ... | 1597 | 3354 | 6328 |
| 4. Residual error (Table 14,5) ... ... | 61 | 178 | −234 | 13. Less depreciation of domestic assets (Table 14,13) | −848 | −1584 | −2454 |
| 5. Gross domestic product ... ... | 10291 | 18194 | 28505 | 14. Grants, remittances and other net transfers abroad (Table 19,4 and 5) ... ... | 67 | 60 | 186 |
| 6. Net property income from abroad (Table 19, 9 and 10 less Table 19,2 and 3) ... ... | 235 | 227 | 405 | 15. Net addition to foreign assets out of current income (Table 19,6 − Table 19,11) ... ... ... | −70 | 209 | −412 |
| 7. Gross national product ... ... | 10526 | 18421 | 28910 | 16. National expenditure at market prices ... ... | 11117 | 19301 | 30389 |
| 8. Less depreciation of domestic assets (Table 14,13) ... ... | −848 | −1584 | −2458 | 17. Indirect taxes less subsidies (Table 18,2) ... ... ... | 1439 | 2464 | 3937 |
| 9. National income ... | 9678 | 16837 | 26452 | 18. National expenditure at factor cost ... ... ... | 9678 | 16837 | 26452 |

subsidies. What this comes to is that we should deduct from aggregate outlay or expenditure the indirect taxes (including rates) levied by the public authorities and add in any government subsidies designed to keep down the cost of living. If we do this, we are measuring the actual incomes of the factors of production generated by expenditure, free from what the government keeps back for its own use. Hence the use of the phrase "at factor cost" after the words "national expenditure."

### Residual errors

Anyone coming fresh to national accounts of this kind is always baffled to find two apparently different sets of figures adding up to the same total. There are two reasons for surprise: first, that there should be any *presumption* of equality between the totals and second, that the imperfect statistics from which Table 13 is built up should yield such exact agreement. The second cause for surprise is entirely reasonable: if each figure were independently estimated there would be quite a considerable margin of error in the aggregates. In practice, however, either one figure is obtained residually after all the others have been estimated, or some of the more doubtful figures are scaled up or down until the totals match, or the account is balanced through the inclusion on one side of the account of a "residual error." The procedure varies from country to country and even from Table to Table. In Table 13 a small "residual error" is shown on the left-hand side, and it re-appears in Table 14. In spite of the inclusion of a balancing item of this kind, it would be unwise to assume that all the other figures have been estimated directly and independently of one another and that their reliability can be taken for granted. Some are comparatively firm figures and others are extremely shaky; when any conclusions are drawn from the tables, this variability in the quality of the estimates should be remembered, and an effort made to discover which are firm and which are not.

### Equality of income and expenditure

The presumption of equality is a different matter, since it rests on logic, not on imperfect statistical data. One man's expenditure is another man's income; so that if total expenditure is added up it yields total income simultaneously. Where expenditure is on the purchase of an existing asset such as a house no income is generated; but the transaction, being a swap, is also excluded from expenditure on goods and services flowing into production, and so is ignored in Table 13. If one man buys the house, another must sell it; if we include the purchases we must also include the sales and if we add in the one and deduct the other the two will necessarily cancel out. If, on the other hand, a man has a house built for himself, or by purchasing a new issue of shares, finances industrial expansion, his expenditure goes directly or indirectly on new assets and on the productive services of those who build the house or manufacture industrial equipment. This expenditure is therefore included in Table 13 together with the income which it generates.

### Savings and investment

When we turn to Table 14 we have moved from equation (1) on page 359 to equation (4)—the equality between savings and investment. On the left-hand side of Table 14 are listed the main sources of savings and on the right-hand side the uses to which they are put. Savings are made by persons (who here include farmers, shopkeepers and other unincorporated businesses), by joint-stock companies and by the public authorities. The savings of joint-stock companies take the form of profits not distributed to their shareholders and either ploughed back into the business or appropriated to reserve; the savings of public authorities are made either through a budget surplus or through the receipt of gifts and grants from abroad. The distribution of the total between private persons, businesses, and public authorities is a little arbitrary. A shop-keeper would find it hard to say what he was saving in his private capacity and what he was saving in his business capacity. He might also be hard put to it to know how to treat the taxes that he would have to pay later on the income he was currently earning and might treat them as a deduction from his savings because they represented eventual liabilities; they would then be savings of the public authorities although not yet paid over to the authorities. The author-ities, in their turn might decide that, in any calculation of public saving, pay-ments of estate duty should be deducted from the budget surplus because such payments are better treated as a receipt of capital rather than as current income; this would make public saving lower and private saving higher. Sometimes it is convenient to show separately some of the items that are most difficult to classify; the fourth item on the left of Table 14 shows additions to tax reserves by persons and companies, an item which might be included either under public or private saving.

TABLE 14

CAPITAL ACCOUNT OF THE UNITED KINGDOM, 1948–64          £m.

| Saving | 1948 | 1956 | 1964 | Investment | 1948 | 1956 | 1964 |
|---|---|---|---|---|---|---|---|
| 1. Persons (Table 15, 11) | 36 | 825 | 1841 | 9. Gross domestic fixed capital formation (Part of Table 13, 12) ... ... | 1422 | 2096 | 5802 |
| 2. Companies and public corporations (Table 17, 8) | 1031 | 2083 | 3536 | | | | |
| 3. Public authorities:— | | | | 10. Value of physical increase in stocks (Part of Table 13, 12) ... ... ... | 175 | 258 | 526 |
| (a) Budget surpluses (Table 18, 9) ... ... | 582 | 538 | 854 | | | | |
| (b) Capital grants and receipts from abroad (Table 19, 11) ... | 234 | — | — | 11. Net investment abroad (Table 19, 6) ... ... | 164 | 209 | −412 |
| 4. Additions to tax reserves (Part of Table 15, 12 and Table 17, 7) ... ... | 142 | 147 | 234 | 12. Gross investment ... | 1761 | 3563 | 5916 |
| 5. Residual error (Table 13, 4) | 61 | 178 | −234 | 13. Less depreciation of do-mestic assets (Table 13, 8) | −848 | −1584 | −2458 |
| 6. Less stock appreciation (Table 13, 3) ... ... | −325 | −208 | −315 | | | | |
| 7. Less depreciation of do-mestic assets (Table 13, 8) | −848 | −1584 | −2458 | | | | |
| 8. Net saving ... ... | 913 | 1979 | 3458 | 14. Net investment... ... | 913 | 1979 | 3458 |

The first two items on the other side of Table 14 add up to "gross investment at home" as shown in Table 13. The third item, "net investment abroad" differs somewhat from the corresponding item in Table 13 "net addition to foreign assets out of current income." The reason for this difference lies partly in the receipt of Marshall Aid and other capital grants from abroad and partly in the settlement of government debts, sales of surplus war stores held abroad, and similar transactions of a capital nature. These capital receipts made it possible to add to investments abroad in years such as 1948 when no addition was possible out of current income. The figures for item 15 in Table 13 are thus equal to the difference between items 11 and 3b in Table 14.

## Personal income

In Table 15 we move from national income to a slightly narrower concept— that of total personal income. This excludes income retained by joint-stock companies and not distributed to their shareholders and it also differs from national income because of the operations of the public authorities. The figures of income under the first five headings yield the total shown in Table 13 for income from employment. This total includes payments made by employers on behalf of their employees either as national insurance contributions or in superannuation premiums, contributions to private pension schemes, and so on. The remaining items of income represent payments to individuals of rent,

TABLE 15

PERSONAL INCOME ACCOUNT OF THE UNITED KINGDOM, 1948–64 £m.

| Income | 1948 | 1956 | 1964 | Expenditure | 1948 | 1956 | 1964 |
|---|---|---|---|---|---|---|---|
| *Income from employment* <br> 1. Wages and salaries (incl. pay of Armed Forces) | 6428 | 11511 | 18120 | 10. Consumers' expenditure (Table 13, 10) ... ... | 8615 | 13829 | 21334 |
| | | | | 11. Saving[1] (Table 14, 1) ... | 36 | 825 | 1841 |
| 2. Employers contributions to national insurance, pension schemes, etc. | 357 | 745 | 1457 | 12. Taxes on income, incl. additions to tax reserves | 1001 | 1480 | 2752 |
| *Income from self-employment* <br> 3. Professional persons ... | 209 | 271 | 405 | 13. National insurance contributions (Table 18, 3) | 335 | 642 | 1444 |
| 4. Farmers ... ... | 307 | 429 | 562 | 14. Net remittances abroad (Table 19, 4) ... ... | 26 | 18 | 23 |
| 5. Other unincorporated businesses ... ... | 810 | 1038 | 1370 | | | | |
| 6. Total income from employment (Table 14, 1) | 8111 | 13994 | 21914 | | | | |
| 7. Rent, interest and dividends (Table 13, 2 and 6 less Table 17, 7 and 8 plus Table 18, 7b less 4 plus Table 19, 3 less 10) ... | 1197 | 1607 | 3118 | | | | |
| 8. National insurance benefits and grants from public authorities (Table 18, 7a) ... ... ... | 705 | 1193 | 2362 | | | | |
| | | | | 15. Gross personal expenditure ... ... ... | 10013 | 16794 | 27394 |
| 9. Gross personal income | 10013 | 16794 | 27394 | | | | |

[1] Before providing for depreciation and stock appreciation

interest and dividends and receipts by individuals of various social service benefits paid for by the State either out of taxation or from national insurance contributions. These contributions appear on the other side of the balance sheet along with the other uses to which consumers put their incomes. Their expenditure on consumer goods and services, which is naturally by far the largest of such uses, has already appeared in Table 13; their saving, which comes next in the list, has already appeared in Table 14; the remaining items represent payments of rates and taxes, national insurance contributions, and net remittances abroad (e.g., by immigrants).

When we try to relate personal income to national income, as in Table 16, we find that an important point of difference arises from the "transfer payments" which we discussed above.[1] A second and larger difference—at least in the United Kingdom—lies in the undistributed income of companies and public corporations. This undistributed income is larger than the company savings shown in Table 14 because it includes what is paid in taxation to the State or held against future tax liabilities. It does not, however, include taxes and dividend payments that are deducted at source: such taxes are included under "taxes on income" in Table 15, and the figures of income from "rent dividends and interest" on the left of Table 15 are reckoned before payment of income tax.

TABLE 16

RECONCILIATION BETWEEN NATIONAL INCOME AND PERSONAL INCOME ACCOUNTS     £m.

| | 1948 | 1956 | 1964 |
|---|---|---|---|
| 1. Gross personal income (Table 15, 9) ... ... ... ... ... | 10013 | 16794 | 27394 |
| 2. *Less* transfer payments | | | |
| (a) National insurance benefits and grants to persons by public authorities (Table 18, 7a) ... ... ... ... ... ... | −705 | −1193 | −2362 |
| (b) Payments of debt interest by public authorities (Table 18, 7b) ... | −575 | −918 | −1387 |
| 3. *Plus* income from property of public authorities (Table 18, 4)... ... | +275 | +654 | +1267 |
| 4. *Plus* undistributed income of companies and public corporations (Table 17, 7 and 8) ... ... ... ... ... ... ... ... | +1777 | +3104 | +4535 |
| 5. *Plus* taxes paid by non-residents less taxes paid abroad by U.K. residents (Table 19, 10 less 3) ... ... ... ... ... ... | +5 | +10 | +12 |
| 6. *Less* stock appreciation (Table 13, 3) ... ... ... ... ... | −325 | −208 | −315 |
| 7. Residual error (Table 13, 4) ... ... ... ... ... ... | +61 | +178 | −234 |
| 8. Gross national product (Table 13, 7) ... ... ... ... ... | 10526 | 18421 | 28910 |

A third, and much smaller difference is the return obtained by public authorities in rent, interest or profit on the capital assets which they own or

[1] Above, p. 362.

operate. This return includes, for example, the earnings of the Post Office, harbour and dock authorities, public transport undertakings, and so on. It also includes interest payments made by public corporations to the central government on money advanced to them. Earnings under this heading are analogous to those included in the undistributed income of companies and need no further comment.

If we deduct transfer payments and add the income from property of the public authorities and the undistributed income of companies we obtain a total which, subject to residual errors, is equal to the aggregate of the first two and the sixth items in Table 13. After adjusting for stock appreciation, as in Table 13, this gives us the gross national product, or, after a further adjustment for depreciation of fixed assets, the national income.

## The company sector

It is sometimes convenient to sub-divide the private sector of the economy into various sub-sectors such as private households, unincorporated businesses and companies. The division between the first two is not an easy one to make and in Table 13 both are grouped together. The remainder of the private sector—the company sector—is easier to treat separately and an account showing the income of this sector and its allocation is given in Table 17. Following customary practice, this account includes the nationalised industries, although they obviously form part of the public not the private sector.

TABLE 17

APPROPRIATION ACCOUNT OF UNITED KINGDOM COMPANIES AND PUBLIC CORPORATIONS, 1948–64                                                    £m.

| Income | 1948 | 1956 | 1964 | Allocation of income | 1948 | 1956 | 1964 |
|---|---|---|---|---|---|---|---|
| 1. Gross trading profits in U.K. ... ... ... | 1910 | 3283 | 5460 | 5. Dividend and interest payments[1] ... ... | 683 | 1160 | 2503 |
| 2. Gross profits earned abroad ... ... ... | 471 | 828 | 1245 | 6. Taxes and profits re-mitted abroad ... | 222 | 444 | 681 |
| 3. Non-trading income ... | 301 | 597 | 1014 | 7. Tax payments in U.K., incl. additions to tax reserves ... ... | 746 | 1021 | 999 |
| | | | | 8. Retained income ... | 1031 | 2083 | 3536 |
| 4. Total ... ... ... | 2682 | 4708 | 7179 | 9. Total ... ... ... | 2682 | 4708 | 7719 |

[1] Before deduction of income tax and including payments to charities

The first two items on the income side form part of the total shown in Table 13 for income from property and so also does rent from property owned by companies, which is included in the third item, non-trading income. The remainder of this third item consists largely of interest on holdings of government securities and is not included in the national income since it represents a transfer payment. Company income goes either in dividends and interest, or in taxes and tax reserves or is appropriated to reserve, i.e., is saved. The two latter amounts re-appear in Table 16 as the undistributed income of public companies. Payments of dividend and interest are included in the figures of rent, dividends and interest received by persons given in Table 15.

## The public sector

Table 18 shows the revenue account of the public sector of the British economy. It is arrived at by combining the figures of revenue and expenditure for the central government with those for the local authorities, but excludes the nationalised industries which have been classed in Table 17 with joint-stock companies. On the revenue side come taxes on income, whether paid by persons or by companies; then indirect taxes less subsidies; then national insurance contributions; and finally, income from property. All of these items have appeared in earlier tables. On the side of expenditure come items which have also appeared already: expenditure on goods and services; transfer payments; and the residue, which represents the savings of the public authorities out of revenue. Thus every item on both sides can be extracted from other tables and the two sides add up to totals that are exactly equal.

TABLE 18

REVENUE ACCOUNTS OF UNITED KINGDOM PUBLIC AUTHORITIES (INCLUDING NATIONAL INSURANCE FUNDS), 1948–64                                                   £m.

| Revenue | 1948 | 1956 | 1964 | Expenditure | 1948 | 1956 | 1964 |
|---------|------|------|------|-------------|------|------|------|
| 1. Taxes on income ... | 1610 | 2364 | 3529 | 6. Expenditure on goods and services ... ... | 1756 | 3433 | 5411 |
| 2. Indirect taxes *less* subsidies ... ... ... | 1439 | 2464 | 3937 | 7. Transfer payments (a) National insurance benefits and grants to persons ... ... | 705 | 1193 | 2362 |
| 3. National Insurance contributions ... ... | 335 | 642 | 1444 | (b) Debt interest ... | 575 | 918 | 1387 |
| 4. Income from property | 275 | 654 | 1267 | 8. Net grants paid abroad | 41 | 42 | 163 |
| | | | | 9. Budget surpluses ... | 582 | 538 | 854 |
| 5. Total ... ... ... | 3659 | 6124 | 10177 | 10. Total ... ... ... | 3659 | 6124 | 10177 |

TABLE 19

TRANSACTIONS OF THE U.K. WITH THE REST OF THE WORLD, 1948–64       £m.

| U.K. debits | 1948 | 1956 | 1964 | U.K. credits | 1948 | 1956 | 1964 |
|---|---|---|---|---|---|---|---|
| 1. Purchases from abroad of goods and services ... | 2434 | 4556 | 6721 | 8. Sales abroad of goods and services ... ... | 2196 | 4598 | 6090 |
| 2. Property income paid abroad (net of tax) ... | 130 | 352 | 473 | 9. Property income received from abroad (net of tax) ... ... ... | 360 | 569 | 866 |
| 3. Taxes paid abroad by U.K. residents on property income ... ... | 5 | 8 | 8 | 10. U.K. taxes paid by non-residents on portfolio income ... ... ... | 10 | 18 | 20 |
| 4. Net remittances abroad by persons ... ... | 26 | 18 | 23 | 11. Grants from overseas governments and net capital receipts of U.K. government from abroad ... ... | 234 | — | — |
| 5. Net grants by U.K. government to persons and governments abroad ... | 41 | 42 | 163 | | | | |
| 6. Net investment abroad | 164 | 209 | −412 | | | | |
| 7. Total debits ... ... | 2800 | 5185 | 6976 | 12. Total credits ... ... | 2800 | 5185 | 6976 |

## Transactions with other countries

This leaves Table 19, which summarises transactions with other countries. Payments to foreign countries are shown on the left-hand side and receipts from foreign countries on the right-hand side. The purchases and sales, which are by far the largest items, do not consist exclusively of imports and exports as shown in the Trade Returns but includes shipping earnings, tourist disbursements, and various other so-called "invisible" items (i.e., services as distinct from commodities; there is no official record of services since they are not the subject of customs declarations). Income from property in the form of interest, dividends, or retained profits has already appeared in Table 13 on a net basis but in Table 19 the outgoings and receipts are shown separately. Apart from various small items, such as remittances abroad, and an item for capital grants and receipts which is also, in most years, small or negligible, the balance consists of net investment abroad. The figure for this item is perhaps the most important in the table. It is the difference between the addition to British investments abroad and the additions made by foreigners to their investments in Britain, and is thus a measure of the net improvement during the year in Britain's creditor position.

## Some deductions from the figures

Let us now turn to the figures in the tables. We cannot linger over them too long since an adequate commentary would require a book to itself: the figures provide a fairly adequate agenda for a discussion of the economic and financial history of the United Kingdom since the war. Such a discussion would be out of place here; but it is not out of place to emphasise that one of the prime objects of such tables is to furnish the agenda for a stock-taking of the national economy. They bring together some of the key quantities in terms of which we can begin to understand what is happening and round which we can organise our thoughts about what is likely to happen in future. This will become clearer in Chapter 26 when we try to pinpoint the sources of instability in economic activity.

At first sight Table 13 appears to depict an extraordinary growth in prosperity, with the national income rising nearly threefold in less than twenty years. If the reader suspects that there is a catch somewhere, he is quite right. A great deal of the increase is merely a reflection of the change in the value of money since the war: roughly speaking, prices rose by about 50 per cent. between 1948 and 1956 and about half as fast over the next eight years. By 1964 the pound had lost more than half the value it had at the end of the war and over two-thirds of the value it had before the war. In real terms, therefore, the increase in output and income was a great deal less than threefold. Over the first eight years it was probably about 25 per cent. and over the second eight years rather more, between 25 and 30 per cent.

Table 13 brings out the high proportion of income that comes from employment. If we look at the left-hand side of the Table and ignore everything except the first item and the total at the end, we can see that about five-sixths of the national income in the post-war period has come from employment as distinct from property. This is a distinctly higher ratio than in pre-war years and the change would be even more pronounced if incomes were measured net of tax. It is true that *gross* income from property in the United Kingdom came to over £7,000m. in 1964 and that the return on overseas investments (net of foreign, but not British, taxes) brought the total up to nearly £8,000m. But this total is inflated by the amount needed to cover depreciation of fixed assets as well as the smaller amount represented by stock appreciation. The gross total falls to a little over £5,000m. once these amounts have been deducted, as compared with just under £22,000m. for income from employment.

The picture becomes clearer when we turn to the personal income account in Table 15. Property income reaching individuals in the form of rent, interest and dividends was about £3,100m. in 1964—a long way short of total property income, some of which accrues to public bodies (e.g. as rent on houses owned by local authorities) while still more is retained by joint-stock companies and nationalised industries to meet tax liabilities or finance expansion of their activities. Of total personal income before tax, including pensions, national insurance benefits, etc., only 11 per cent. came from property in 1964— slightly less than in 1948 and far less than in 1938 when the ratio was over 22 per cent. These ratios would be diminished still further if income were measured net of tax as the income freely disposable by individual earners. In 1964 20 per cent of personal income from property and from self-employment (added together) was taken in direct tax; for wages and salaries the ratio was about 9 per cent.

On the side of expenditure, the most important item is obviously spending by private consumers. This accounted in 1964 for just over 70 per cent. of total national expenditure, measured for this purpose—as it obviously should be—at market prices. Gross investment accounted for a further 21 per cent. (compared with only 14.4 per cent. in 1948) but if depreciation is deducted so as to yield an estimate of net investment this comes down to 12.7 per cent. This in turn is rather higher than the ratio for net saving because there was a large external deficit in 1964 which helped to finance the domestic investment undertaken in that year.

Although gross investment was the most rapidly growing item on the expenditure side of the account, expenditure by public authorities did not lag far behind and by 1964 it represented over a quarter of expenditure by private consumers compared with just over a sixth in 1938. The figures in Table 13 do not, of course, refer to the *total* expenditure of public authorities (as Table 18 brings out) since they omit all transfer payments. They are a measure of the importance of public authorities as employers of labour and other real resources rather than of their importance in financial terms. The revenue available to the public authorities (including national insurance contributions, rates collected by the local authorities, etc.) amounted in 1964 to over £10,000m. and represented nearly 40 per cent. of the national income. But their expenditure on goods and services was not much over half their total revenue and represented about a fifth of the national income or, to take a more meaningful ratio, 18 per cent. of national expenditure at market prices.

When we turn to Table 14 we find on the right-hand side fuller details of the changes in investment that have been taking place. Investment in fixed assets has increased both in the absolute sense and in comparison with national income and output. Measured net of depreciation the increase has been from about £575m. in 1948 to about £3,350m. in 1964. Since fixed assets rose in price by 60–65 per cent. during this period, the growth in net investment was not so rapid as this might suggest; but it is probably not far out to put the rate of accumulation of fixed assets in 1964 at about three and a half times the rate in 1948.

On the other hand, where there was some net addition to foreign investments in 1948 and 1956 the balance ran the other way in 1964 when it was necessary to borrow heavily abroad. In each of the years shown—and indeed in almost every year since the war—there was a small accumulation of stocks sufficient to maintain a fairly steady ratio of stocks to current output of approximately 40 per cent.

The sources from which investment was financed are shown on the left-hand side of Table 14. The relative importance of persons, companies and public authorities is, however, distorted by the use of gross rather than net figures of saving, since most of the assets subject to appreciation and depreciation are in the company sector. If the figures for 1964 were adjusted so as to leave out stock appreciation and depreciation of fixed assets under each heading, the first three items would become £1,250m., £1,700m. and £500m. respectively and this is a fairer indication of the relative contribution made by each sector to total savings. The public authorities were the most important source of net saving in 1948 and, although budget surpluses in monetary terms were larger in 1964, their role was by then much more limited. On the other hand, personal saving (including saving by shopkeepers, farmers and other unincorporated businesses) was negative in the early post-war years and grew strongly thereafter. Quite a high proportion of the increase in consumers' real incomes over the period was devoted to additional savings. For companies and corporations it is usually not a bad rule of thumb to treat half their gross investment in fixed assets as replacement; and this works out fairly well in 1964 since gross investment in this sector was just over £3,400m. while of total retained income £1,580m. is estimated to have represented capital consumption.

This brings us to Table 17 which shows how the total income of British companies and public corporations was made up and how it was allocated. The profits shown under the first heading are the major component in the figure given in Table 13 for income from property in the United Kingdom, most of the remainder coming under the head of income from public property in Table 18, or under that part of item 3 in Table 17 that consists of rent. The rise in gross trading profits was fairly closely in step with the rise in national income although it seems to have lagged behind the growth in corporate assets, so that the return on capital was probably less in 1964 than in 1948. Gross profits earned abroad, the second major component of company income, grew at about the same rate as other trading profits. A good chunk of these profits—over a third—goes in tax to foreign governments so that the *net* contribution of profits remitted from abroad to total company revenue is not quite as large as the gross figure indicates. There is also a slice of the profits made by foreign-owned companies operating in Britain that has to be transferred to shareholders abroad. This is included under item 6 in Table 17 and it is increasing comparatively rapidly.

The low proportion of company income paid out in dividends and interest may be thought surprising. The pre-war ratio appears to have been around 60 per cent. but after the war it was much lower. In 1948 it was slightly above, and in 1956 slightly below, 25 per cent. By 1964, partly because of various changes in taxation and an actual reduction in the amount paid in tax or appropriated against tax liabilities, the ratio had climbed to over 30 per cent. Company savings, or retained income, on the other hand, have come to be a much higher proportion of total income than in pre-war days. In 1938 they were about 30 per cent; in 1964 they were not far short of half. The change would be even more striking if retained income were measured net of depreciation and compared with outgoings in dividends and interest.

Table 18 does not point to any marked expansion in the role of public authorities since 1948: total revenue bore roughly the same relationship to national income in 1964 as in 1948. But this partly reflects the big increase that had already taken place in the decade or so before 1948. Within the total, some important changes were in progress, notably the rapid growth in national insurance contributions and benefits and in property income accruing to local authorities. The budget surpluses shown in Table 18 do not purport to be cash surpluses such as many people take to be the sign of a genuine surplus but represent the net addition that the budgets of central and local authorities permitted either to physical assets in public ownership or to financial assets through redemption of debt, loans to nationalised industries, and so on. The outcome of these surpluses, which continued throughout the years from 1948 to 1964, was inevitably to improve the future flow of revenue except to the extent that the assets acquired proved worthless (e.g. debts due from nationalised industries that had to be written off) or brought in no public revenue (e.g. roads) or where the surplus was used to make a capital grant (e.g. to a colonial territory) or to build up external reserves.

The final table, although showing the main items that go to make up the balance of payments is not well devised to show how this changed over the post-war years or how the changes affected the rest of the British economy. What does emerge is that exports and imports of goods and services were by far the biggest items (goods accounted for about three-quarters and services for about one-quarter of the total in 1964); that they increased at about the same rate; that an excess of imports was largely offset by an excess of property income receipts over payments; and that net investment abroad can swing from a positive to a negative quantity. But the significance of such swings is not very obvious from the Table and further discussion must wait until Chapter 32.

# CHAPTER 26

# FLUCTUATIONS IN THE NATIONAL INCOME

The national income fluctuates, sometimes violently and with terrible consequences for large groups of people. Between 1929 and 1932 the national income of the United States fell, in money terms, by over 50 per cent. and the wage- and salary-bill by 40 per cent.; between 1938 and 1942 national income doubled and wages and salaries almost doubled. In real terms the fluctuations were rather less severe because prices fell in the first of those periods and rose in the second; but even in real terms the changes in the level of economic activity were enormous.

## UNEMPLOYMENT

These changes were not due to some temporary aberration in productivity such as a fluctuation in harvest yields but reflected a failure to make full and continuous use of the productive resources available. This failure was most conspicuous in relation to man-power. The outstanding feature of the periodic slumps of pre-war years was the waste of productive power in unemployment that accompanied them. The loss due to unemployment in the United States in the thirties was at least as great as the loss suffered in war-time through the absence of millions of men in the armed services and the diversion of man-power to the production of munitions. In Britain the loss in income in the decade before the war through failure to find a use for the energies of the unemployed can be put at not less than 10 per cent.

The evil of unemployment is not to be measured in purely economic terms any more than is the cost of making war. It was the unemployment of one German industrial worker in three in 1933, as much as any other single thing, that gave Hitler his chance of power. The social strain of intense and protracted unemployment could overturn any economic system. Even in personal terms, unemployment cannot be equated with mere loss of income. A long spell of unemployment ruins a man's self-respect by depriving him of an honourable opportunity of earning a living; it creates a sense of frustration and finally of usefulness; it saps his powers of concentration and his capacity for normal enjoyments; it makes for tension within the family and within the community; and it leaves men apathetic to ordinary social activities and duties, or ready to lend a willing ear to violent expedients for regaining status and a sense of purpose.

The worker's attitude to his job is also perverted. He goes in fear of losing it and yet in fear of excelling in it: he can neither afford to be conspicuously inefficient nor to be conspicuously efficient. "So long as there is a scramble for jobs, it is idle to deplore the inevitable growth of jealous restrictions, of demarcations, or organised or voluntary limitations of output, of resistance to technical advance. . . . Failure to use our productive powers is the source of an interminable succession of evils."[1]

### Voluntary unemployment

Not all unemployment is avoidable: some, for example, is voluntary. In Great Britain a married man with a large family may actually find himself out of pocket if he accepts employment and is frequently only a few shillings to the good for a hard week's work. These facts cannot be disregarded. But there is no reason to believe that voluntary unemployment accounts for more than a small proportion of total unemployment. The larger problem is one of the involuntary unemployment of workers who, however willing, are unable to find work at current wage rates.

### Frictional unemployment

Even in war-time, when the demand for labour is intense, unemployment never entirely disappears. A residue remains which, in more normal circumstances, may reach quite considerable dimensions. This residue includes, first of all, seasonal unemployment. There are few industries in which it is possible to maintain steady employment all the year round; either there are seasonal peaks in demand (e.g., in the manufacture of umbrellas, toys and motor-cars), or weather conditions hold up work at certain seasons of the year (e.g., in agriculture and building). These seasonal irregularities do not necessarily create unemployment. Sometimes it is possible without excessive inconvenience, to make use of the services of married women in peaks periods, or to provide off-peak employment for regular workers by dovetailing one kind of work with another (e.g., by making straw hats and bowler hats in the same works). Some workers, too—the salaried staff, for example—may be able to cope with

---

[1] Lord Beveridge, *Full Employment in a Free Society*, p. 248.

seasonal pressure by working harder, slacking off again once the rush is over—a practice of particular importance in peasant communities where the problem of seasonal unemployment tends to be transformed into one of *under*-employment during the winter months.

Unemployment also arises in industries in which demand fluctuates erratically. A dock labourer, for example, may work at high pressure for a few hours or a few days when a large number of ships put in, and find himself unemployed for the rest of the week when the berths are empty. Anyone who is engaged in repair work, or in making goods influenced by fashion, is likely to have a similar experience. Bad organisation, accident and failure of supplies may also lead to unemployment.

It is common, too, for some days or even weeks of unemployment to elapse between the conclusion of one job and the discovery of another. There may be vacancies in plenty in other places and industries, but none of them, given human immobility, quite suitable. However well-organised the labour market, therefore, and however keen the demand for labour, some unemployment will persist.

### Structural unemployment

Hardly less avoidable than frictional unemployment, and sometimes classified with it, is unemployment caused by changes in the structure of industry: by changes in industrial organisation and technique, by the decline of major industries, and by the migration of industry from one region to another. All of these played an important part in the unemployment problem which Britain and other countries had to face in the 'twenties and 'thirties. Technical progress was extremely rapid and displaced workers who could not always be re-absorbed in other industries. Schemes of industrial reconstruction, designed to eliminate surplus capacity and to concentrate output in fewer and larger plants, led to wholesale dismissals from the works which were shut down. Important war industries, such as iron and steel, engineering and shipbuilding, had to make a swift change-over to a peace-time basis in competition with the over-expanded war industries of other countries. The export industries, cut off from their markets by four years of war, found that native industries had grown up there in the meantime, and, protected by high tariffs, showed no signs of disappearing. Above all, the new and growing industries, such as motor-car manufacturing instead of expanding alongside the older and declining industries and absorbing unemployed workers in the vicinity of their homes, grew up in the very parts of the country where there was least unemployment, and created a major problem of labour transference from contracting to expanding areas. No group of workers suffered more from these changes than the coalminers. Employment fell from 1,212,000 in June 1923, to 638,000 in June 1932, and since mobility was low in comparison with other industries, and opportunities of alternative employment rare, a serious problem of long-term unemployment came into existence in the mining areas. Of 325,000 workers who had been continuously unemployed for over a year in June, 1936, no less than 81,000 were miners, and many more must have had only occasional spells of employment during the year.

Structural unemployment of this kind represents the "hard core" of unemployment. It is not intermittent like other types of unemployment, but results from a permanent change in opportunities of employment to which workers have to adjust themselves. Men engaged in work of one kind or in one place find themselves shut out from their customary employment and forced to change their occupation or domicile. The more immobile they are, and the greater the structural change in progress, the greater is the resulting unemployment. In pre-war Britain, the changed balance between export and home markets, between capital and consumption goods, and between north and south, put a heavy strain on the adaptability of industry. Structural unemployment, therefore, was unusually high.

## Full employment

When people talk of "full employment," therefore, they do not mean that no one is out of a job. In almost any circumstances, some unemployment will persist and is really unavoidable. How much is unavoidable depends on all the things that have just been discussed: on whether big structural changes are going on, whether demand in export markets is fickle or failing, whether labour is mobile, and so on.

At the end of the war Lord Beveridge suggested that it might be possible to maintain an average unemployment rate of 3 per cent., this figure being made up of 1 per cent. to cover seasonal unemployment, 1 per cent. as a "margin for change of employment incidental to progress," and 1 per cent. to provide for fluctuations in overseas demand.[1] How do these figures compare with past experience? Between 1946 and 1966 the unemployment rate in Britain was comparatively steady between 1 and 3 per cent.; before the war, the rate was many times higher, averaging 14 per cent. between 1921 and 1939; further back still, in the fifty or sixty years before the first world war, the average was probably slightly under 5 per cent., and in many years the rate was much higher.[2] No one would regard the rate of unemployment between the wars

---

[1] Lord Beveridge, op. cit., p. 128.
[2] These figures are not strictly comparable. A much larger number of workers are now included in the national insurance scheme than were included in the pre-war unemployment insurance scheme. The nineteenth century figures refer only to members of a small group of trade unions

as anything but intolerably high; even in Victorian times the record was far from one of continuous full employment on any definition. The post-war record, however, is so much lower that it is natural to hesitate before accepting it as a new norm.

Even when unemployment remains constant the identity of those who are unemployed does not; there is no "standing army" of the unemployed. The vast majority of those who are unemployed on any given date have been in work at some time within the preceding year and will be in work again at some time in the succeeding year. But when unemployment is on the pre-war scale the normal lag between losing one job and finding another is greatly increased. In 1936 one man in four of those registered as unemployed had been idle for at least twelve months.

### Fluctuations in unemployment

The fluctuations that have taken place in the last forty years are illustrated in Diagram 11. In the nineteen twenties unemployment was almost continuously in excess of 1 million and in the following decade it hardly ever fell below 1·5 million. It melted away in the first two years of the war and was latterly under 100,000. Once the war was over and the special compulsions of war-time were relaxed, unemployment increased slightly, oscillating in the succeeding years between 250,000 and 500,000.

### The consequences of full employment

Full employment, however defined, means a fundamental change in the position of the worker. Before the war, perhaps one worker in two had learnt what it was to be out of work at some time or another, not because of a personal failing, but because there were not enough jobs to go round. Whether he was in work depended on his luck as well as on his free choice. He was in a buyers' market for labour, in which employers could choose their men, but workers were not so free to choose their employers. The threat of unemployment, therefore, could be used like a whip to make a worker conform to the standards of his place of employment. With full employment, all this is changed: the buyers' market for labour becomes a sellers' market. Where the master was in a position to say: "If you don't want the job, there are plenty of others who do," the man can now say: "If you don't want to employ me, there are plenty of others who will." In terms of labour relations this means that new ways of preserving industrial discipline have to be worked out. Secondly, since labour is scarce, new methods of production become worth while in order to economise it (for example, the greater use of mechanical appliances). Most important of all, the bargaining position of labour is strongly reinforced so that trade unions are put in a favourable position to force up wages and—if full employment continues—keep forcing them up. Since each fresh increase tends also to raise prices, this can easily precipitate a general inflation. If full employment brings

DIAGRAM 11

UNEMPLOYMENT IN THE UNITED KINGDOM, 1922–59

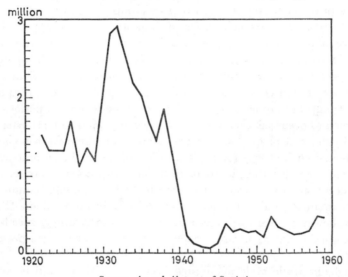

*Source: Annual Abstract of Statistics*

on continuous inflation because the advantages of a sellers' market are abused, there may be nothing for it but to retreat from full employment or to put an end to collective bargaining and hand over wage-fixing to a statutory body.

## The causes of unemployment

If we are to learn how to maintain full employment we shall do well to study the causes of unemployment in the past. Many of the same forces are still at work but the momentum that they can develop can only be gauged by looking at past events when they were allowed to get out of control. Full employment is far from being so normal that we can take it for granted or assume that unemployment is easily mastered, given the will.

### THE TRADE CYCLE

Nowadays it is natural to think of fluctuations in economic activity primarily in terms of changes in the level of employment and unemployment. When

N

economists first began to study those fluctuations, however, there were no official figures of employment and output and it was the movement of prices, which could be more readily measured, on which they concentrated their attention. In looking at price indices, economists became aware of a more or less regular alternation between boom and slump and gave to this phenomenon the name "trade cycle." The oscillations that took place were not confined to individual prices or particular industries or groups of industry, although some parts of the economy were more affected than others. It was apparent that the *general* level of prices and of economic activity was alternately raised and lowered over a period varying in length from six to ten years, all, or nearly all, industries being simultaneously prosperous or depressed. In periods when the long-term trend in prices was downwards—for example between 1874 and 1896 —the cycle appeared to lengthen and become more severe; in periods of rising prices—such as occurred after 1896—the cycle appeared to be shorter and less violent. In the first of the two periods referred to, there were booms in the United Kingdom in 1873, 1882–3 and 1890 while in the second period the booms were closer together, in 1900, 1907 and 1913. Booms in other countries did not occur in exactly those years; trade cycles, although common to all industrial countries, did not synchronise perfectly in all of them. Differences in timing, however, steadily diminished and it was increasingly rare for one of the leading industrial countries to experience a different cyclical pattern from the others.

Although the trade cycle manifested itself in a periodic and fairly regular fluctuation in prices it was primarily a cycle in activity, whether measured by employment or output. It also showed up in many other economic and social phenomena: profits, for example, and wages; exports and imports; the birthrate, drunkenness and crime. A common cyclical pattern stamped itself on many things between which there was obviously little direct connection— the classical example is the marriage-rate and the consumption of beer—suggesting causal relationships where none existed.

### The cycle and economic growth

The beginnings of the trade cycle seem to lie in the late eighteenth century in that period of quickening economic growth which we now call the industrial revolution. Whether it goes further back it is difficult to say because the statistical data for earlier periods is inadequate; but many economists would now be inclined to suspect that it is not altogether accidental that cyclical fluctuations and more rapid growth make their appearance together. There are grounds for thinking that cycles are a feature of growing economies and that the causes which produce both the cycles and the upward trend round which fluctuations occur lie deep in the economic system that took shape during the industrial revolution.

Whether the trade cycle is now a thing of the past is more debatable. In the United States there has been a check to economic activity about every four years since the war—in 1949, 1953-4 and 1957-8—and this check has been communicated in varying degrees to other countries. A four-year cycle is in accordance with American experience over the past century although not with British and continental experience. Between the two world wars there were turning-points in the United States and in the United Kingdom in 1920, 1929 and 1937 but it is difficult to regard the two latter years as booms and the intervening slump was of quite unprecedented severity. The instability of the pre-war period seems to have been due to special circumstances calling for a rather different explanation from the Victorian cycle; and the comparative stability of the post-war period equally requires a special explanation.

### The cumulative process

The main characteristic of the trade cycle is that in the upswing there is a *cumulative* expansion and in the downswing a *cumulative* contraction. Everything seems to work in favour of an indefinite continuation of either movement. Yet this is not what happens: the process of expansion seems to carry within itself the seeds of the ensuing depression just as the process of contraction seems to contain the seeds of revival. The upward movement ultimately loses momentum like a pendulum, reaches the high point of the swing and then passes, almost imperceptibly at first, into a movement in the reverse direction. What is it that arrests and reverses the movement of activity? Is it inevitable that the boom should break or that the slump should end? Is there some intrinsic instability in the economic system that makes it impossible for production to remain balanced at a high level?

These are questions to which we shall return presently. But we must first look at the process of cumulative expansion and contraction to see how it operates.

An essential element in the process derives from the simple fact that one man's expenditure is another man's income. Suppose that, at the bottom of a depression something happens to increase effective demand for goods and services. It may be that consumers spontaneously begin to spend more, or, more probably, that larger orders are placed with manufacturers in order to re-build stocks or to renew or extend capital equipment. To fill these orders manufacturers will have to engage more workers and the newly-employed workers will spend more freely out of their increased incomes. This will cause further orders to be placed to replace the goods that have now found a market and these extra orders will give a fresh stimulus to production. As fast as more goods are despatched for sale to new consumers, more income will be generated and out of the additional income more goods will be bought. If production is shrinking, the reverse process will operate, every reduction in output and employment limiting the market for the goods produced and setting off a fresh contraction in output.

## The multiplier and the accelerator

This kind of instability is the basis of an important economic concept—the *multiplier*. We shall try to give precision to this concept later but the essence of the idea is that, the more people spend out of any increase in their income the more any initial change in spending is multiplied in its repercussions on the level of income of the community. A second concept—that of the *accelerator*—can be illustrated from another source of instability which is superimposed on the first. If business men find their market reviving, they may decide to place orders that are larger than the sales they have just made and are related instead to the *rate of increase* of those sales. For example, they may try to build up stocks in the expectation that sales will go on increasing or to add to their capacity so as to be ready to meet the level of sales which, given the current trend, they expect to make at some later date. On the other hand, when the trend in sales is downwards they may think it unwise to place orders that match current sales and may cut their orders so as to take account of the trend. Similarly they may postpone additions to capacity or even the renewal of some of their equipment because the trend in sales leads them to take a pessimistic view of the future level of demand. Action of this kind represents a change in what the economist calls *investment intentions* (plans to add to stocks or to fixed capital) and accelerates the impact on output and employment of a given change in effective demand.

## Prices in the trade cycle

A further source of instability lies in the movement of prices. When recovery from a depression begins, there is usually ample unused capacity and costs remain more or less constant. As output nears the limits of industrial capacity, however, prices begin to rise. Raw materials rise fastest and earliest because the supply is highly inelastic in the short period, while the demand, in view of the comparative insignificance in total costs of many raw materials, is generally also inelastic. As time goes on, something of a scramble for raw materials may develop, since producers will wish to ensure fulfilment of contracts into which they have entered. The rise in prices is by no means confined to raw materials: it is common to all industries in which an increasing demand pushes against a relatively fixed supply. Whenever a "bottleneck" appears, and the scarcity of some key type of equipment, labour or raw material limits output, price is forced upwards. Confronted with a rising cost of living, and strengthened by the decline in unemployment which accompanies trade revival, wage-earners begin to claim wage-advances, and these, when granted, drive costs and prices still higher. The rise in prices, especially if it outstrips the rise in costs, inflates profits and disposes business men, unless they have reason to expect the trend in prices to be arrested, to take a more optimistic view of the future. To the incentive to expansion that comes from an increased volume of sales is added an additional incentive because of the more favourable terms on which those sales are made, and the expectation that future prices will remain favourable in relation to current costs. When prices are falling, on the other hand, costs are likely to be sticky and the contraction that begins with a falling turnover is reinforced by falling profits and profit expectations.

### The role of the banks

There are several other features of the trade cycle on which economists have laid stress. One is the role of the banking system. The fluctuations between boom and slump have often been aggravated by the creation of bank credit in the boom and restriction of credit in the slump. How much importance should be attached to changes in the money supply is by no means clear. Some economists take the view that unless the banks help to finance the expansion in activity by creating more credit it will never get very far; others are inclined to doubt whether the banks do more than add fuel to the fire. There is perhaps more agreement about the influence of the banks on the turning-points in the cycle. A rise in interest rates in the later stages has at times been the means of breaking the boom by creating a liquidity scare: that is, by making business men alarmed that they might not have enough cash to meet their forward commitments. Such a rise in interest rates may occur if the boom gives rise to an unfavourable balance of payments and by producing a drain of gold to other countries and a fall in the gold reserves causes the monetary authorities to restrict credit in self-defence.

### Competitive over-investment

Some explanations of the trade cycle—though these explanations would not be regarded nowadays as very adequate—have laid stress on the competitive character of production under capitalism. Capital may be invested in competing projects, each begun in ignorance of the others, and each doomed to disappointment when the others come into production. Each firm independently hopes to profit from an abnormally active demand by expanding its capacity, but the aggregate expansion is more than sufficient to meet market requirements, so that each miscalculates by taking no account of the actions of its rivals. The miscalculation first engenders a state of boom while capacity is being built and is then succeeded by a slump once the results of the miscalculation become apparent.

## Business confidence

This line of thought is frequently coupled with emphasis on another and slightly different feature of the cycle: the tendency for business confidence to fluctuate and to acquire a more or less independent influence on the level of activity. Confidence is high in the boom and spreads from one set of industries to another, to some extent quite rationally since turnover is expanding and profits are growing. There are, however, many business decisions that relate to a fairly distant future and have to be taken on a balance of probabilities that is impossible to strike by any process of logic. Such decisions are leaps in the dark, acts of faith, expressions of animal spirits or of desperation. They commonly reflect the prevailing mood, and this mood, alternating between incautious optimism and timid pessimism, can contribute powerfully to cyclical fluctuations even if it does not itself produce them.

Of these two lines of thought the first is little more than an example of the way in which the accelerator might operate: it involves the same kind of exaggerated response to a change in the level of demand. In industries where there are a large number of competing firms it has obviously some real substance; what is more doubtful is how it applies to the more typical industry where the number of firms is comparatively small and each has a shrewd idea both of the course of total demand and of the plans of its competitors for expanding capacity.

The second suggestion is also of limited force. When a crowd collects there is usually something for it to stare at; although the more people are there already, the easier it is to attract others. In the same way, when a mood of optimism grows, there are usually some real grounds for it, although once it begins to spread it quickly gathers force. The prevailing mood, whether it is one of optimism or of pessimism, tends to contribute to its own justification. If it is one of optimism, enterprise is encouraged, employment increases and the prosperity to which people looked forward comes into existence; if it is one of pessimism, enterprise is discouraged, unemployment increases and the community is plunged into the depression which was so widely anticipated. But these changes of mood are unlikely to be spontaneous over the whole field of industry. Behind them we are fairly sure to find some real change—possibly in the world of politics, but more usually in the profit situation—and it is in this change, and not in a change of mood, that upswing and downswing originate.

## SUPPLY AND DEMAND IN THE TRADE CYCLE

### (1) Supply

It would now be generally agreed that the trade cycle has to be explained in terms of fluctuations in effective *demand* and that, although changes in the conditions of *supply* are not without influence on the course and timing of the cycle, they occupy a subordinate place in any theory that tries to account for the cyclical shape of economic fluctuations. Nevertheless, some of the early theories of the cycle were couched in terms of supply rather than demand and many popular explanations of unemployment continue to lay stress on supply factors.

**Over-production**—At one time, for example, it was common to talk about slumps as if they were due to periodic over-production. This seems a very odd way of looking at the matter: so long as many of our wants go unsatisfied a *general* over-production of goods is impossible. If there is a surplus of unsaleable goods it must be because there is a deficiency of effective demand, not because there are more goods than people want to buy. If this deficiency were to disappear—as happens in a boom—it would soon become apparent that too little was being produced, not too much. There may, however, be genuine over-production of particular commodities and a corresponding under-production of other commodities. Output, that is, may be lop-sided, so that workers remain unemployed in some industries while there is a labour shortage in others. Such structural unemployment always seems larger in a depression than it really is. For workers do not move in search of employment when there is unemployment wherever they go; they move only when there are vacancies to move to. Thus as trade revives, mobility increases, and adjustments which were hopeless within the rigid framework of depression are made with comparative ease in the more expansive atmosphere of a boom. Moreover, since it is generally the most depressed industries which recover most ground as trade improves, the need for adjustment is diminished simultaneously with the difficulties of making it; outputs which seemed lop-sided in the depression become normal in the ensuing boom.

**Sunspots**—Another theory laying stress on supply factors is the well-known sunspots theory put forward by W. S. Jevons a hundred years ago. Jevons traced cyclical fluctuations in trade to a cycle in harvest yields of approximately the same length, and this in turn he found to be correlated with the appearance of spots on the face of the sun. This theory was not quite so crazy as it sounds since it is arguable that sunspots have some connection with weather conditions, the weather governs harvest yields, and harvest yields react on industrial prosperity. Most economists would concede that harvest fluctuations can play an important part in the trade cycle; but they would regard these fluctuations as affecting the *timing* of revival and recession rather than as causing the cycle itself. They would also point out that bumper crops tend to bring prices down while the characteristic feature of price changes in the trade cycle is that prices and output rise and fall together. It is this fact that makes it difficult to take very seriously attempts to base an explanation of the cycle on changes on the side of supply.

### (2) Demand

When, however, we try to base an explanation on demand factors, we encounter a number of intellectual stumbling-blocks. For a long time, economists were greatly influenced by what is often referred to as Say's Law, after its supposed author, the French economist J. B. Say. According to Say's Law, production creates its own demand and there can never, therefore, be a general deficiency of demand for whatever is produced. Of course, there can be a deficiency of demand for particular things: for the goods produced by a single firm, or a single industry, or a single area. But if so, there will be a corresponding excess of demand for the goods produced by other firms, industries or areas. Production means paying people for what they produce and the income distributed for productive services must be exactly equal to the value added to the materials on which they work.

Now this is a line of thought which we have already pursued in Chapter 25, where we saw that it justified us in treating national income and national output as equal to one another. But we also saw that there were some difficulties once we took account of the fact that people may save part of their income and withhold it from the stream of effective demand. We implied that similar difficulties might arise because of some lack of balance between government revenue and government expenditure or between total imports and total exports. These difficulties, coupled with the fact that production does fluctuate, are bound to make one a little suspicious of the universality of Say's Law; the circular flow of income and expenditure obviously can be broken and the instability of both income and expenditure suggest strongly that it is in fact broken.

**The significance of investment**—Our suspicions are heightened when we discover that fluctuations have always been much more pronounced in industries making capital goods than in industries making consumer goods. A depression hits industries like shipbuilding and steel-making much harder than industries like transport and distribution. Roughly speaking, the more durable the product, the greater the fluctuations in output. This strongly suggests that an explanation of the cycle must be closely linked with the process by which savings are absorbed and the stock of capital grows. When we follow this clue our attention becomes concentrated on the process of saving and capital accumulation.

**Savings and investment**—In a community where people lend their savings to others, there are two independent sets of decisions about savings that have to be taken by different people and that need not synchronise exactly with one another. One set of decisions concerns saving and spending, and is taken by consumers; the other set concerns investment or loan-expenditure,[1] and is taken by manufacturers, public utilities, local and central government authorities, etc. The first set of decisions involves the release of real resources, including labour, from meeting the immediate requirements of the savers; the second set of decisions involves the employment of real resources (including labour) on works of capital construction. There is no automatic machinery for marrying these decisions to one another so as to see to it that the resources released by the savers are absorbed by capital expenditure.

Habits of saving, as we have seen, are not subject to violent change; saving is generally a residue after customary needs have been met, and varies mainly with income. Changes in thrift are gradual; but if incomes change, the first effect is usually on savings rather than on consumption. A person whose income is suddenly doubled will save the greater part of the increase. Later, he will adjust his customary standard of living; but the average man will end up by saving rather more than before.

So long as the national income is fairly constant, therefore, no large changes in effective demand are to be expected on the side of private saving. Expenditure on consumers' goods will be relatively stable, but will increase as income increases: not quite so fast and not quite to the full extent. Investment, on the other hand, is inherently unstable. This is so for a variety of reasons.

**The instability of investment**—First, capital expenditure is *postponable*, whereas expenditure on goods for current consumption cannot easily be cut

---

[1] It should be clearly understood that in this context "investment" means, not the purchase of a piece of paper (whether bond, stock, share, mortgage or the like), but capital expenditure on some instrument of production (e.g., the manufacture of machinery, the construction of roads, bridges, houses, etc., afforestation and so forth).

down or expanded. A farmer who wants to replace his horse by a tractor can delay buying the tractor; but he cannot delay feeding oats to his horse.

Secondly, the requirements for which capital expenditure provides are less calculable because more distant in time than current requirements. The longer the period in view the more difficult it is to predict changes in demand, in the cost of operating or renewing plant, in the rate of interest, in technique, and so on. The longer the period for which capital has to be sunk, therefore, the more responsive is capital expenditure to the changing expectations of business men about the future. A spirit of caution will bring about a sharp fall in investment; if the uncertainty passes, there will be an equally sharp rise in order to make up lost ground.

The same reasoning applies whether capital goods take a long time to manufacture or whether their length of useful life is so great that a long interval must elapse before their original cost is recovered. Railway-building in the nineteenth century proceeded by fits and starts partly because railways last such a long time. No one could hope to pass judgment with any degree of confidence on their profitability in fifty, or even twenty years' time; and the pace of construction tended to fluctuate, therefore, with the whims and moods of investors, played upon on the one hand by a few dominating personalities amongst the contractors, and on the other by changes in the current fortunes of existing railways. These fluctuations in railway-building were aggravated by the time which it took to promote and build a railway. Several years might elapse between the initial flotation on the Stock Exchange and the completion of the first stretch of line. This stretch generally involved the sinking of a large indivisible amount of capital which could not be cut without abandonment of the scheme as a whole. Once a start had been made on any important project, such as a trans-continental railway in Canada or the U.S.A., or a trans-alpine railway between France and Italy, the project had to be pushed on with even when it proved much more costly or less remunerative than had been expected. More and more capital was sunk in order to get some return on what had already been spent, with the natural result that investors were doubly shy of similar large-scale projects for some time to come.

This lumpiness of some types of investment is a third factor making for instability. The original decision to build, once taken, is irreversible, and investors are committed to the completion or abandonment of the project. Since they cannot readily cut their losses and cannot be certain to what scale of investment they are committed, they require all the more exuberance to be willing to finance the scheme. In practice, this means that it is easiest to obtain financial support near the top of the boom, although costs are rising and a break in prices is not far distant. The commencement of large schemes of capital expenditure at such times intensifies the boom; and the poor return which they earn in the ensuing slump keeps investment low and impedes recovery.

**The accelerator again**—A fourth cause of instability lies in the fact that the demand for capital goods derives from the demand for consumable goods, Suppose that sales of motor-cars amount to one million per annum and that 10 per cent. of the plant is renewed every year. Then if sales go up by 20 per cent. to 1·2 million, and if the extra plant to make additional cars has to be installed within the year, the total amount of plant to be built will be thrice as much as in previous years; instead of the normal 10 per cent. for renewals, it will be necessary to provide an extra 20 per cent. to meet the expansion in demand. The fluctuation in employment will obviously be much larger in the firms making machinery for motor-car manufacture than in the motor-car industry. The increase in the first will be 200 per cent.; in the second, only 20 per cent.

This last point may be put in a slightly different way by saying that the demand for consumption goods is at bottom a replacement demand, since a stream of these goods is constantly moving towards points of sale to replace the goods which are being consumed. The demand for capital goods, however, is at bottom an extension demand, designed to provide further supplies of consumable goods at some future date. The demand for consumable goods is largely governed by custom and habit which exercise a stabilising influence; but the demand for capital goods is governed to a large extent by *changes* in the demand for consumable goods, and these changes are magnified out of all proportion in their repercussions on investment.

To say this is merely to repeat, in a different form, what was said earlier about the "accelerator." This concept was illustrated above in terms of new orders and current sales; but as the motor-car example shows, the orders that show the working of the principle most strikingly are those for capital equipment. As capacity working is approached these orders increase more rapidly than consumer demand for motor-cars: investment accelerates in relation to consumption.

## INTEREST RATES

### The rate of interest as a balancing factor

At this point, we encounter a fresh stumbling-block. Is investment free to be as unstable as all this implies? Is it not in fact tied by the need to finance capital expenditure and so, in the end, by the flow of current savings? Where does the money come from to make possible a sudden increase in investment if savings are stable? And if investment drops, what happens to the savings that are no longer absorbed? A generation ago many economists would have found these difficult questions to answer. Some of them, indeed, might have been inclined to say that the forces governing savings and the forces governing investment would normally be held in balance by the rate of interest, just as supply and demand are held in balance by any other price. We know that capital expenditure—and perhaps also thrift, although this is more doubtful— responds to changes in interest rates. There may be disagreement as to how much or how quickly it responds, or why it responds; but everyone would agree that an increase in interest rates would exert some effect, sooner or later, on investment and help to keep it in check if for any reason it became unusually attractive. May it not be, then, that the rate of interest, like the price of a commodity, rations the available supply of savings so as to keep the effective demand within the limits of the supply?

In the light of the facts we have already adduced about the behaviour of savings and investment, this plainly will not do. The analogy with the operations of supply and demand must be a false one: if it held good, and the economic system was so self-adjusting that all savings were automatically absorbed into investment at an appropriate rate of interest, there could be no lack of balance between thrift on the one side and investment on the other. A change in investment opportunities would either elicit an immediate (and fortuitous) response in savings or be offset by a change in interest rates sufficient to prevent the very fluctuations in investment for which we have to account.

### The natural rate of interest

The next stage in economic sophistication was to introduce the banking system into the argument. The banks, it was pointed out, can create credit and *supplement* the supply of savings; or contract credit and reduce the flow of funds into investment. The rate of interest may be held down below its "natural" level by the first process or sustained above its "natural" level by the second.

The Swedish economist Knut Wicksell developed a theory of the trade cycle following out this line of thought and concentrating on the failure of the rate of interest, because of monetary influences, to maintain an even balance between savings and investment. His ideas were carried further by later Swedish economists, notably Ohlin and Myrdal, and similar ideas were evolved in Cambridge, starting with Alfred Marshall and continuing through the work of Sir Ralph Hawtrey, Sir Dennis Robertson and Lord Keynes. It is impossible to do justice here to the contribution made by each of these economists or to show in what respects they differed from one another. We shall confine ourselves to an exposition of some of the main ideas that emerged from their work and are still accepted as a starting-point in more recent explanations of the cycle.

### The Keynesian theory of interest rates

For the past thirty years economists have engaged in controversy about what determines rates of interest and what influence they have on economic activity. It would probably now be admitted that this concentration on interest rates, while justified on other grounds, tended to convey an exaggerated impression of their true importance in relation to fluctuations in output and to the measures by which the violence of those fluctuations could be reduced. This impression derives largely from the way in which Lord Keynes, who took a leading part in the controversy, gave the rate of interest a central place in his *General Theory of Employment, Interest and Money*, appearing to imply that it occupied an equally important strategic position in the regulation of production and employment. The real significance of Keynes' theory of interest rates in this context, however, was essentially negative: he wanted to demonstrate that the rate of interest was *not* governed by savings and investment, that it responded to forces largely or entirely *independent* of savings and investment, and that it was possible to have large fluctuations in investment matched by corresponding fluctuations in savings *without* any appreciable change in the rate of interest. The positive part of what he had to say related to the mechanism by which investment and savings were kept in step with one another, and this is a great deal easier to understand than what he had to say about interest rates. As we shall see, it is fluctuations in income rather than in the rate of interest that operate to bring savings and investment together: if investment falls and people are no less thrifty than before, their incomes will be cut by unemployment and trade depression until they *have* to save less.

### Liquidity-preference

Keynes' view of interest rates was that they are not determined by savings and investment or by the supply of, and demand for, loanable funds: they are the price of liquidity. The complex of interest rates, he argued, is governed by the state of liquidity-preference.[1] Interest rates will be lower, therefore, the larger the supply and the smaller the demand for money; and those rates of interest will be most responsive to changes in the supply of money which are paid on short-dated, highly liquid securities.

The supply of money is within the control of the banking system; by a suitable credit policy, therefore, pressure can be brought to bear to increase

---

[1] See above, pp. 335–6, 346–8.

or reduce interest rates. This pressure is not likely, however, to be effective of itself in bringing about a parallel change in long-term rates of interest. Investors must first be convinced that cheap money has come to stay.[1] If they believe that a fall in short-term rates is "unnatural" and due to an "unsound" policy which will later be reversed, their reaction may be perverse: they may give expression to an increased preference for cash by offering lower prices for bonds and forcing up long-term interest rates. Long-term rates reflect long-term views. They are influenced more by propaganda than by open-market operations. Moreover, they are less vulnerable to pressure in a downwards than in an upwards direction. The insensitivity of long-term rates cannot be overcome by reducing short-term rates indefinitely (certainly not below zero); but it can be overcome by an indefinite increase in short-term rates. Even more important in setting a lower limit to long-term rates is the part played by uncertainty about the future of interest rates, and the consequent danger of capital depreciation. The lower the rate of interest, the higher is the price of bonds, and the smaller is the annual yield in relation to the risk of capital depreciation through an unforeseen recovery in interest rates. If the entire weight of the banking system is behind efforts to reduce interest rates in a slump, they may still fail. And historically, the banking system has often sought to restrict credit at such times and to expand it in times of boom.

The Keynesian theory of interest rates directs our attention to two determinants of interest rates: the supply of money and the demand for money. It might equally direct our attention to the supply of debt and the demand for debt; but since liquidity-preference embraces both money and debt, we can ignore the fourth of these variables. No one would quarrel with the emphasis which the theory lays on the supply of money: an increase in the supply of money would usually, in the absence of any other changes, push down interest rates. There might be agreement also that changes in outstanding debt—for example, the replacement of long-dated by short-dated debt—would react on the structure of interest rates. As to liquidity-preference, no one can take issue with the proposition that if the market is free to switch from one form of debt (including money) to another, the price of each debt must be such as to ensure that it finds a holder; this means that the complex of prices of debts—or, what comes to the same thing, the complex of interest rates—must be equal to the liquidity-preference of marginal holders. The same could be said of any commodity market where people go on holding a stock rather than sell for cash; but no one tries to argue that the price of wool or rubber is governed by liquidity-preference to the exclusion of the forces of supply and demand. Does the intro-

---

[1] See above, p. 337.

duction of the idea of liquidity-preference mean that there is no room for thrift and capital productivity to influence interest rates? At times Keynes appeared to be arguing that it did. In a slump, or when the rate of interest is down to rock-bottom, savings may in fact have no influence on interest rates; but when there is full employment, the traditional view comes into its own that a high rate of savings helps to keep down the rate of interest while high productivity of capital helps to push it up.

We shall defer a fuller discussion of interest rates until we have explained how the monetary system works and what determines the supply of, and demand for, money. We shall assume that, although movements in interest rates may aggravate (or moderate) cyclical fluctuations, they are not the source of the cyclical pattern or at least that the cycle could continue even if interest rates were held constant.

### Saving and investment ex post and ex ante

Let us now try to put together a little more formally the elements round which economists build their theories of economic fluctuations. We begin with the equations set out in Chapter 25:

$$Y = C + S \qquad \dots (2)$$

$$O = C + I \qquad \dots (3)$$

$$S = I \qquad \dots (4)$$

In these equations we are measuring income (Y) output (O) savings (S) and investment (I), *after the event*, and defining them in such a way that savings and investment *must* be equal to one another. There are many other possible definitions where this equality would not hold: for example, we might define savings as the difference between last week's income and this week's expenditure rather than as the difference between this week's income and this week's expenditure. On the definitions we are using, any money that we mean to spend remains part of our savings until we actually spend it; on other definitions, this would not be so.

While savings and investment are equal (on our definitions) *ex post*, they are not equal *ex ante*. Or, to re-state the matter in plain English instead of the jargon introduced by the Swedish economists, while past savings and past investment cannot be different from one another, planned savings and planned investment may differ. One set of people may be planning to save more than another set of people are planning to borrow from them for purposes of investment. When this happens, neither group will be conscious that anything is amiss. Each saver will accumulate his savings in cash or he will buy securities or put his money into savings certificates or whatever investment he favours, without knowing what is happening to total savings and without any need to interest himself in the statistics of savings. Exactly the same applies to investment: each decision to spend on capital account is taken on its merits, generally in ignorance of the movement of total capital expenditure throughout the country. How then can it subsequently appear that, looking backwards, savings and investment remain equal?

The answer is implicit in our earlier discussion of "the multiplier." If one man saves more, he withholds effective demand and releases productive resources. If some one else invests in additional capital assets (whether fixed assets, working capital or stocks) this absorbs the productive resources released; if no one does so, the productive resources are wasted and remain idle. In concrete terms, this means that men are thrown out of work and lose most of their current income. At this stage the extra savings will either be balanced by additions to the stock of goods because the drop in purchasing power deprives them of their customary retail market; or, if sales are maintained because the unemployed men draw on their savings or are paid unemployment benefit out of the national insurance fund, the extra savings by one group of people are offset by negative savings on the part of the unemployed or through the insurance fund. In the first case, investment is increased to the level of planned savings as a result of some unplanned investment in stocks; in the second case, savings are held to the level of planned investment because of some unplanned dis-saving. The system works so as to make one man's plans thwart the plans of another.

The first stage is obviously not the end of the story. If unsold stocks begin to pile up, replacement orders will fall off and producers will make arrangements to cut down output, for example by reducing their labour force. The resulting fall in incomes reacts on consumer demand and is multiplied in the way we have already described; but it also reacts on savings, and each successive fall in income makes the rate of saving lower than before. This reaction on savings, if producers' investment intentions are unaltered, ultimately restores equilibrium: not in the sense that it makes savings equal to investment (because that will be true throughout) but in the sense that the downward movement in incomes is halted and savings and investment are fully adjusted to the level of income. As the economy retreats to this reduced level of income, the additional savings which started things off are offset either by unplanned investment in stocks (which producers will try to bring to an end by reducing their intake from new production) or by dis-saving (which consumers will also try to stop by spending less on consumption goods). A full adjustment comes about only when producers and distributors have no incentive to make further changes in the orders they place and when consumers have no incentive to change their current expenditure on goods and services.

### Thrift is negative

Thus although it is open to each of us to decide how much of our income we wish to save, our joint decisions do not determine how much in the aggregate the community saves. So long as investment remains constant, savings must remain constant. All that the public can do is *spend* more or less: alter what Lord Keynes calls their "propensity to consume" or (looked at the other way round) their state of thriftiness. This is not the same as *saving* more or less. For the act of spending affects other people's incomes and *their* savings. Greater thriftiness, if not accompanied by greater investment, merely impoverishes the community; the increase in thrift is offset by a reduction in income, and the resources which are released by the thrifty are left idle for lack of investment. All that thrift can accomplish is negative if there is no machinery by which acts of thrift are translated into acts of investment.

The fact that our exposition has been in terms of a rise in savings should not make the reader jump to the conclusion that the mischief usually lies on the side of thrift. It is in fact rare for there to be a sudden change in thrift and, as we have already emphasised, it is investment, not thrift, that is the unstable element in the economy. A fall in investment has effects exactly parallel to those ascribed above to a rise in savings. Similarly a rise in investment and an increase in consumer spending have parallel effects in the opposite direction.

### The effects of a building boom

Suppose, for example, that investment increases because of a great rehousing campaign. It will then be necessary to employ more workers in the building industry and in all the ancillary industries—the timber and furniture trades, brick-making, the iron and steel industries and so on—which provide materials and fittings for houses. Earnings in these industries will increase by the amount of the additional investment. As earnings increase, so will expenditure. The spendings of those who benefit directly will create secondary employment in other industries—the clothing trades, for example—and these industries in turn will have more to spend. The increase in income to which the original investment gave rise, will be multiplied as prosperity spreads. Savings and investment will be equal at each stage. But this equality will be achieved in the early stages (a) because consumers have not had time to spend their increased earnings and are holding more cash than they intend to; and (b) because there will be some *dis*investment in stocks of consumable goods which

manufacturers will wish to replace once they have taken on more workers. Full
equilibrium is not reached until consumers have adjusted their habits of spending and manufacturers have adjusted their output. When equilibrium is reached,
incomes will be so much higher than before that the increased scale of investment is matched by a correspondingly increased rate of saving. Investment
generates the savings out of which it is financed.

### Investment and savings with full employment

To those who think of savings as an indispensable preliminary to investment (as it is for each of us), this may appear to put the cart before the horse.
Before we, as a community, can save, we must invest; and if we do invest, this
of itself will create the necessary savings. These seem paradoxical conclusions.
Do they apply in all circumstances? Are we to deduce that we can increase
the national income indefinitely by the simple device of steadily expanding
investment?

The answer is that, in *money* terms, we can; but in *real* terms, obviously not.
It is only in a situation in which there are still unemployed resources to be
brought into use that further investment will increase *real* income. Once investment passes the rate which would sustain full employment, inflation results.
The extra investment is financed by credit creation; workers who would otherwise find employment in making consumable goods are attracted into the
constructional trades by the offer of higher money wages and are paid from
advances made by the banks. The new money created in this way is saved in the
sense that at any moment in time somebody owns it and has not yet spent it;
but it is not saved in the sense that its owner intend to invest it rather than part
with it in exchange for consumable goods. Total money incomes are inflated
by the extra bank credits; and total savings are equally inflated, but only
momentarily. Sooner or later the additional purchasing power will be spent.
But the output of consumable goods will have reached the limit of expansion
and will be threatening to contract because of the diversion of labour to the
production of capital goods. The output of consumable goods, therefore, will
fall short of the quantity which the public wishes to buy at current prices with
the purchasing power at their command. In the scramble for these goods, prices
will be forced upwards; wages will follow: it will be necessary, in order to maintain the scale of real investment, to have recourse to the banks for additional
credits out of which to meet the increased cost of capital goods; and these additional credits will give a fresh impetus to inflation.

The situation, in short, becomes one in which producers of capital goods
and consumable goods are in active competition with one another for command over real resources, and their joint demand is greater than can be met

from the resources available. The result of their tug-of-war is to bid up the prices both of the factors of production and of finished goods, the makers of capital goods sustaining their demand through the creation of additional bank credits, and the makers of consumable goods sustaining their demand because these credits ultimately swell their takings.

It is when we approach a situation of this kind that savings begin to fulfil their true function of releasing resources for employment in works of capital construction. *Then* investment can increase without provoking inflation, only if the demand for consumable goods is held in check by fresh saving. At this stage, too, the rate of interest does begin to operate to keep savings and investment in step. For if the banks, taking fright at the prospect of inflation, refuse to create additional credit, it will be partly by raising interest rates that they seek to ration credit amongst competing claimants. Each successful project of investment that elbows its way forward to receive the financial backing of the banks or of private investors will simultaneously oust some other project which does not offer a large enough prospective return to cover the interest payable. Investment can generally be kept within limits in spite of a rise in the marginal productivity of capital if the rate of interest is allowed to rise simultaneously.

### Investment in a boom

Even if long-term rates of interest were completely under control, this of itself would not ensure stability of employment. The quality as well as the volume of investment changes in the transition from slump to boom and projects are financed which, looked at with due prudence, cannot hope to give a return equal to the current rate of interest. If the rate of interest is increased to meet a multiplication of such projects, the effect may be only to assist them in supplanting other more worth-while projects. In due course when the misdirection of investment becomes apparent, it may be too late to check the set-back in investment by anything short of a nil or negative rate of interest; for the projects which were shelved will take some time to revive, and the immediate effect of the crash in speculative investment will be to create an atmosphere most unfavourable to further investment, however attractive in normal circumstances.

### Economic instability and foreign trade

Fluctuations in economic activity have so far been explained in terms of a closed community, not in terms of a single country engaging in trade with other countries. But it not infrequently happens that unemployment originates in a country's export industries through a failure of demand abroad; the cause of unemployment then lies outside the country and not in some maladjustment within it. Indeed, for most industrial countries other than the United States, the main practical problem is how to guard against the instability of foreign markets and prevent the infection of unemployment spreading to their own. It is only when foreign trade occupies a quite subordinate place in a country's economy, or when, as with the United States, a country possesses sufficient economic strength to draw world markets along with it, that it can disregard changes in economic activity and in demand in other countries.

There are few countries where this is so evident as in the United Kingdom. In the nineteenth century it was the common experience that the export industries were the first to feel the effects of a slump and the first to show signs of a recovery. This was not in conflict with the theory that fluctuations in investment are the main source of instability in employment. On the contrary, it was precisely because investment by Britain *in countries overseas* developed a cyclical pattern that exports to those and other countries fluctuated cyclically. If British capital was used to speed up the economic development of, say, Canada, by financing railway construction, new opportunities of employment were created there, the income of the country increased and the demand for goods of all kinds was swollen. Part of this demand overflowed on to imports, and British goods—locomotives, textiles, etc.—found a market either in Canada itself or in other countries which profited from the stimulus of expanding activity in Canada. Nor was this the end of the story. For the prosperity of the British export industries gave a fillip to shipbuilding and set off a boom in the home market. Even when Britain occupied a dominant economic position, therefore, she was highly sensitive to changes occurring abroad, and the level of employment that she experienced was closely dependent on the prosperity of foreign markets.

After the first world war this dependence was painfully evident. In the middle twenties the volume of exports remained far below the level that had been reached in 1913 and the export industries underwent a corresponding contraction, leaving heavy localised unemployment in the areas that had specialised in the manufacture of exports.[1] Then came the slump that began in 1929; in three years total employment in the export trades fell by nearly one million.[2] In a single year (1931) the fall was probably not far short of half a million. The unemployment of those years was obviously dominated by international factors. The slump of 1929–32 was one of unusual severity; but later experience

---

[1] The volume of exports in 1924 was about 25 per cent. below the volume in 1913. If, as has been estimated by Dr. E. C. Snow, the total man-power employed in exporting in 1924 was 2·4 million the consequential reduction in employment may have been of the order of 800,000.

[2] E. A. G. Robinson: "Sir William Beveridge and Full Employment," *Economic Journal*, April 1945, p. 73.

showed that it was by no means exceptional in the speed with which it affected British exports. In the brief recession of 1938, for example, the volume of exports fell by one-eighth in a year, or the equivalent of over 200,000 workers.

It is this kind of catastrophe with which a British government aiming at full employment has to reckon. There are various measures by which the worst effects might be mitigated.[1] But it would be foolish to pretend that any action taken by a single government could prevent serious dislocation and distress in the face of a sudden slump in exports. Effective action must be international.

## THE MULTIPLIER AND THE ACCELERATOR

### (1) The multiplier

The ideas so far developed are more helpful in explaining changes in the level of activity than in demonstrating why these changes should assume a cyclical pattern. They emphasis the instability of investment, but seem to assume a succession of discontinuous changes in investment (to which income and savings have to adjust themselves) not the kind of see-saw movement that actually occurs. This is not altogether surprising: for the ideas are largely those of Keynes, and the problem uppermost in his mind was not the trade cycle but prolonged unemployment. He wanted to show that the economy might get stuck in a position of less than full employment without any automatic tendency to further expansion: it might simply stagnate because the opportunities for the fruitful use of capital were insufficient to absorb the savings that people would like to make under conditions of full employment. This is not a problem that has been prominent over the past twenty years: the more pressing need has been to encourage thrift and overcome a general shortage of capital, not to prevent savings from running to waste in unemployment. In the meantime economists have taken Keynes' ideas further and used them to provide a more satisfactory theory of economic instability and the trade cycle.

In doing this, they have continued to make use of the concept of "the multiplier" to which we have already referred. Let us assume that people save a fixed proportion of their income, say 10 per cent. so that if their income increases they will save 10 per cent of the increase. Then if there is a discontinuous rise in investment (such as we assumed on p. 401), and this generates additional income and additional savings along the lines already discussed, we know that the increase in savings will at each stage be exactly equal to one-tenth of the increase in income; and this will also be true at the end of the process when income, savings and investment are again in equilibrium. The expansion in

---

[1] See pp. 591–92, 594–95.

income will be ten times the expansion in savings and therefore ten times the expansion in investment. An increase in investment by £1m. will generate an extra £10m. in income: it will be multiplied tenfold. The multiplier is thus the reciprocal of the ratio of savings to income.

**Ambiguities in the multiplier**—This is to put things crudely and leave out many important complications. First of all, there is the obvious fact that the process by which income expands takes time: the successive rounds of expenditure go on indefinitely, with income approaching the equilibrium level asymptotically. We can deal with this either by arguing as we have done above, that it also takes time for investment to increase because there is a kind of backlash effect on stocks, or by showing that the first few rounds of expenditure are enough to bring income near to the equilibrium level. Next, there is a question of fact: do people save a constant proportion of their income? To this there can be only one answer: whatever may be true of the whole community in the long run, individuals do not save a fixed proportion of any increment in their incomes. The most that one can say with confidence is that they are unlikely to increase their expenditure by the full amount of the increment in income, and this is all that Keynes took for granted in his own exposition of the multiplier.

**The consumption function**—Keynes started from what he called "the consumption function": that is the functional relationship between income and consumption. We can represent this by the equation:

$$C = f(Y)$$

This function represents "the propensity to consume" and shows how consumption increases as income increases. In Diagram 12 we show how this function becomes a straight line through the origin if savings form a fixed proportion of income. In this case the proportion of income spent on consumption ("the average propensity to consume") is exactly equal to the proportion of an increment in income that is spent on consumption ("the marginal propensity to consume").[1] Normally, however, we should expect the marginal propensity

---

[1] If k represents the fraction of income that is saved, we have:
$$C = (1 - k)Y$$

The average propensity to consume $= \dfrac{C}{Y} = 1 - k$

The marginal propensity to consume $= \dfrac{\delta C}{\delta Y} = 1 - k$

The multiplier $= \dfrac{\delta Y}{\delta Y - \delta C} = \dfrac{1}{1 - (1 - k)} = \dfrac{1}{k}$

DIAGRAM 12

CONSUMPTION FUNCTION WITH CONSTANT SAVINGS RATIO

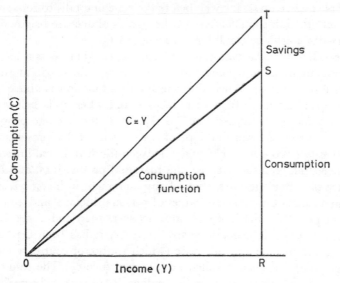

DIAGRAM 13

CONSUMPTION FUNCTION WITH RISING SAVINGS RATIO

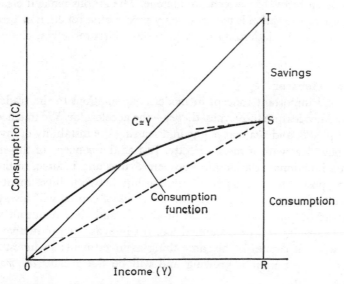

to consume to be lower than the average on the grounds that rich people tend to save a higher proportion of their income than poor people. We should also expect people to give up saving well before their income falls to zero so that the consumption function should intersect the Y axis above the origin. We show a function satisfying these conditions in Diagram 13.

The line OT in this Diagram (and in Diagram 12) represents a level of consumption exactly equal to income and passes through the origin at an angle of 45 degrees to the X axis. When the consumption function is above this line, people are spending more than their income and when it is below they are saving. The slope of the dotted line OS represents the average propensity to consume at income OR and the slope of the tangent at S represents the marginal propensity to consume. The angle between the two dotted lines measures the divergence between the average and marginal propensities, and illustrates how a more than average proportion of any increment in income is saved.

Diagram 14 plots the observed values of personal income and consumption (at constant prices) in the United States between 1929 and 1958. Instead of plotting consumption in absolute terms, however, it has been expressed as a ratio of personal income and this ratio (which is also, of course, a measure of the savings ratio) has been graphed against real income. The result is not a single function but three, one corresponding to pre-war observations, one to wartime when savings were abnormally high, and one to post-war conditions, in which, in spite of the great increase in real income, personal consumption has never fallen below 92 per cent. of income. The graphs make it clear that in any one year consumption is not an exactly predictable function of income and that the functional relationship may, in certain circumstances, change rather abruptly.

## (2) The accelerator

The second important concept in modern explanations of the trade cycle is one that did not feature in Keynes' theory—the accelerator. We touched on this concept at p. 388, and again at p. 395 in discussing the instability of investment; we must now deal with it more directly. Just as the concept of the multiplier hinges on a functional relationship between savings and income, so that of the accelerator postulates a functional relationship between investment and *the rate of growth* of income. It assumes that the stock of capital will always be adjusted to the output that has to be produced, and that if output expands, productive capacity will be expanded too. An increase in productive capacity or in the stock of capital is the same thing as investment: so investment will take place where output is growing and will be the greater *the more rapidly* output is growing.

DIAGRAM 14

CONSUMPTION FUNCTIONS FOR UNITED STATES, 1929–58

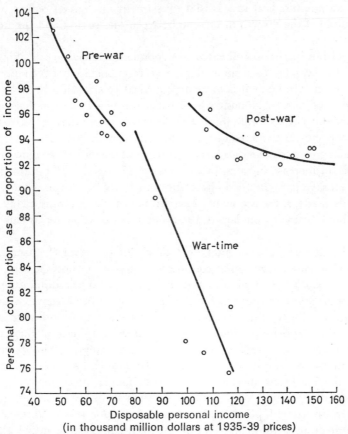

Sources: 1929–52—*Historical Statistics of the United States, 1789–1945*, Tables A 117, A 142, A 143;
1952–58—*Statistical Abstract of the United States*, 1956, Table 353; 1959, Table 395.

If we write K for the stock of capital, and v for the ratio of capital to output we have:

$$K = vO$$

$$= vY \qquad\qquad ....(1)$$

$$\text{and } I_t = K_t - K_{t-1}$$

$$= v(Y_t - Y_{t-1}) \qquad\qquad ....(2)$$

where the suffix t denotes a period of time, so that $I_t$ is investment during a period $t$ and and $I_{t-1}$ is investment during the preceding period, and so on. What equation (2) says is that investment in a given period will be a fixed multiple of the growth in income between one period and the next.

**Ambiguities in the accelerator**—A moment's reflection will show that it is just as extravagant to assume this fixed relationship between investment and changes in income as it is to assume a fixed relationship between savings and the level of income. Nobody who is conscious of all the complex influences on investment decisions would think it realistic to suppose that they are designed to bring capacity instantaneously into accord with the current level of sales. We may all agree that, *taking the long view*, the most powerful incentive to expand capacity is an increase in sales, just as, *taking the long view*, the most powerful influence on savings is the level of income. But in the short run when decisions are actually made, there are many other influences at work and many reasons why we should expect time-lags in the adjustment of capacity to current output.

There is, for example, a good deal of elasticity about "capacity." It is possible to increase output quite considerably above the normal level without enlarging the stock of capital, although in course of time continuous operation without a normal margin of spare capacity will drive producers to order more equipment. Similarly, there is no difficulty about under-utilising capacity and when this happens producers need not necessarily cancel their plans of expansion even if they are free to do so. It is increasingly common for manufacturers to frame long-term investment programmes, to which they try to adhere in the face of unexpected changes in demand; the accelerator principle is obviously inapplicable to investment by such firms. Even in firms that do revise their investment plans when sales and output take unforeseen turns, the adjustment may be delayed until the trend in sales is unmistakable or until it is possible to obtain additional plant or until outstanding arrangements for expansion have been completed. There is nothing instantaneous about the reaction.

There is one further qualification. While income can drop very sharply, the stock of capital cannot contract rapidly: a limit is set by the rate of depreciation and obsolescence. Although investment can be negative—when no new capital assets are constructed and the existing assets continue to wear out— it cannot be so negative that capacity falls at the same pace as output does in a severe slump.

**An unstable model**—Let us put these qualifications on one side for a moment and assume that both the accelerator and the multiplier operate in their full vigour. Then we have two equations:

$$I_t = kY_t$$

$$I_t = v(Y_t - Y_{t-1})$$

Investment is simultaneously a function of income (the multiplier relationship) and of the rate of change of income (the accelerator relationship). This makes the system highly unstable: an increase in investment not only pushes up output and income (see above p. 401) but investment is in turn increased in order to allow the stock of capital to keep step with output. There would seem no limit to the thrust upwards or downwards that a combination of these forces would exert on the economy. But there is a lower limit to investment, even if a negative one, and this sets a lower limit to income provided savings ever become negative. Once income has sunk to this lower limit and output has "bumped along the bottom" for a time, the normal ratio of capital to output is gradually restored by a fall in the stock of capital, and an incentive to add to the stock begins to emerge. Investment becomes positive again. As soon as it does, the multiplier gets to work and the accelerator joins in. Output is driven up from the floor to the ceiling—a ceiling set by full employment. When the ceiling is reached income ceases to grow (or grows very slowly) and investment, which varies with the rate of growth of income, falls back towards zero. This check to investment is multiplied in its effect on income and a cumulative contraction sets in.

In a model of this kind, fluctuations would be cyclical and very violent— far more violent than in the real world since in every slump net investment would plunge below zero. A more realistic model would, therefore, have to introduce some of the damping factors and lags that help to keep investment steady in relation to output changes and maintain it, except on rare occasions like the slump of the early thirties, above the level of capital consumption.

There is a great deal in this brief summary that one might elaborate or qualify and there are many learned works in which the reader will find ample elaboration and qualification. But there is neither room nor necessity for them here, and many of the more important points are implicit in what we have already said.[1] The ideas of the multiplier and the accelerator are fascinating to the mathematician who can produce cycles from them with the dexterity that others show in producing rabbits out of hats. To the layman, less impressed

---

[1] For a useful outline see R. C. O. Mathews, *The Trade Cycle* (Cambridge, 1959).

by constants which turn out on examination not to be constants at all, and more troubled by the lack of empirical evidence for a relationship like the accelerator, it is enough that the ideas provide a clue to an understanding of the instability of the economy. The models of the mathematicians may not explain everything; but they show us where to begin in interpreting economic fluctuations.

# CHAPTER 27

# FLUCTUATIONS IN THE VALUE OF MONEY

In the previous chapter we have discussed fluctuations in income and output without paying much regard to the fluctuations in prices which accompany them. In this chapter we turn our attention to the price level and to those general movements in prices upwards or downwards that either coincide with boom and slump or take place over longer periods of time.

When such general movements in prices occur they automatically involve changes in the value of money. If we say that prices have doubled we are implying that money has lost half its value: each unit of money will go only half as far. We can either look at the change in terms of the price level or turn it round the other way and put it in terms of the value of money.

## The importance of monetary stability

There are serious inconveniences in using money that fluctuates in value. Such fluctuations may be unavoidable or may result from policies that are desirable on other grounds; they may benefit particular groups in the community and even serve, for a time, as a stimulant to total production. But if a reasonable measure of stability in the value of money is not preserved, the whole basis on which economic activity rests is threatened. It is in monetary units that we plan our expenditure, comparing the values of alternative purchases. It is in monetary units that our incomes and expenditure are measured and in monetary units, therefore, that we strike a balance between them, planning how much to spend and how much to save. It is in monetary units also that producers compare the relative costliness of different factors of production, planning methods of production which will substitute relatively cheap for relatively dear factors.

Finally it is in monetary units that producers plan their future volume of output, forming their expectations of profit by comparison of present with prospective money-prices. It is of enormous importance, therefore, that monetary units should be as stable in value as possible. Without reasonably stable units in which to plan, we cannot hope to plan accurately.

Even comparatively small fluctuations in the value of money may create a state of uncertainty damaging to sound enterprise. Our forecasts of the future may be thrown into confusion because the monetary units in which these forecasts are expressed change unexpectedly in value. Producers are likely to find, when the value on money falls—and when prices, therefore, go up—that they have made a larger profit than they expected. When the value of money rises —that is, when prices fall—they are likely to make equally unexpected losses. Neither the profits nor the losses can be foreseen so long as changes in the value of money are unforeseen. Fluctuations in the value of money, therefore, create additional uncertainty and make the already difficult task of planning still more difficult. If such fluctuations could be avoided, so that we were able to plan with a stable and dependable measuring rod, economic activity would be steadier and more wholesome.

### When prices change fastest

The fact that money does change in value is familiar enough, especially after two world wars. In most countries prices have ambled steadily upwards for the better part of thirty years or broken into a gallop during the war and its aftermath. The days of falling prices between 1920 and 1932 have not yet altogether faded from memory, although the mere supposition that prices might once again come tumbling down begins to look almost extravagant. The pace of inflation has varied from country to country. Nowhere has it quite equalled the fine careless rapture of the pengö as it whizzed across the financial sky in 1946, multiplying itself 300,000 million million million million times. On the other hand, there was hardly a country in which the cost of living in 1960 was less than double what it was before the war.

In comparison with nineteenth century experience, this instability was abnormal. In Britain, for example, the maximum fluctuation in the value of money, one way or the other, was probably not more than 20 or 30 per cent. in the ninety years before 1914. Prices fell steadily, but very gradually, from the end of the Napoleonic Wars until 1896, with a short interval of rising prices in the fifties and sixties. After 1896 prices began to rise again, but until 1914 the rise was no more rapid than the previous fall. What produced rapid inflation, in 1914 as in 1939, was war; the changes in the value of money in peace-time were all within limits that now seem relatively narrow.

When the pace of change is relatively slow, the movement is not so easy to observe and, as some prices may be rising while others are falling, it may be difficult to say whether, on the average, prices are going up or coming down. We may rely on personal impressions and point to a number of particular changes in price as indications of the general trend. But it is obviously desirable to have a more exact measure, and this is provided by what are known as "index numbers," which are indices of the average changes in price. The method by which index numbers are constructed is explained in an Appendix to this chapter.

Index numbers measure changes in the value of money for particular purposes or to particular groups of people; but money has a different value for different purposes and for different people. An index number of the cost of living, such as is discussed in the Appendix, aims at measuring changes in the value of money used by a typical consumer for the purchase of finished goods; or, to look at things the other way round, in the price level of goods and services sold to consumers. But money is used in order to buy other kinds of goods —raw materials, semi-finished goods, machinery, exports, imports, stock exchange securities, and so on—and its purchasing power over these goods may change in a different direction or to a different degree from its purchasing power over finished goods. Instead of a single price level—the price level of finished goods or the retail price level—there is a whole host of price levels corresponding to the different groups of things that we can buy for money: for example, the wholesale price level, the export price level, the price level of capital goods, the price level of bonds, the wage level and so on. A separate index number can be calculated to measure changes in each price level, and the method of constructing these indices is exactly the same as that used in constructing a cost-of-living index number.

Different price-levels do not move exactly in parallel with one another and this is one reason why changes in the value of money are so important. A general movement of prices up or down causes some prices to run ahead of others: wholesale prices, for example, outstrip retail prices, and wages and other costs may lag behind both. Normal profit margins and price relationships are upset, and strains and stresses are set up in the price structure. The pressure on productive activity at various points can be gauged by the use of price indices to measure the spread between price levels. By comparing any two indices we can see where normal price margins have been disturbed, and on what scale the disturbance has been. A comparison of indices of export and import prices, for example, shows whether a country is obtaining imports more cheaply in terms of the exports which it sends in payment. Similarly, a comparison of indices for farm products and manufactured articles, shows how much more heavily a fall in price bears on farmers than on the rest of the community. Index numbers of prices sum up the changes that re-orientate business activity;

they make it easier to interpret these changes intelligently and to control them.

## The Consequences of Changes in the Value of Money

Because different price levels do not move together, a change in the value of money is accompanied by windfall gains and losses to particular classes in the community. Some people find that the goods they buy are rising faster in price than the goods they sell; others find that their money incomes do not change, or change slowly, when the value of money changes. The shifts in purchasing power that result can generate social discontent on a formidable scale. Their impact on the distribution and production of wealth is also far-reaching.

### Effects on distribution

Incomes, as we saw in Chapter 24, are either fixed by contract or variable with market prices. The income of labour, supposing no change in employment, is fixed by a number of wage bargains, the majority of which can only be revised slowly and after much bickering. Income from loan capital is fixed for periods varying with the duration of the loan. Income from ownership of land and of dwelling-houses is also slow to change, either because rents are fixed for a number of years ahead or because custom inhibits the raising of rents to existing tenants. Profit, on the other hand, is free to vary as prices move up or down.

There is, first of all, a transfer of wealth from creditors to debtors if prices rise, and from debtors to creditors if prices fall: when debts can be discharged in money that has fallen in value, the real burden of debt is diminished, while if money has risen in value, the real burden of debt is increased. By far the largest debtor in the community is the government; inflation is therefore not without its attractions to governments that have debt obligations. No one supposes that the great inflation in every major country over the past quarter of a century can be attributed to a deliberate effort to lighten these obligations. Nevertheless the gain to governments and the corresponding injury to their creditors, the unfortunate holders of public debt, has been one of the outstanding consequences of the inflation. In the United Kingdom, for example, although the net debt of public authorities to all private creditors increased nearly fourfold between 1935 and 1960, the national income, mainly because of inflation, rose even faster and the service of the debt, after the most costly war in history, was a smaller element in the budget than before the outbreak of war.

In the private sector the largest debtors are financial institutions like insurance companies and commercial banks; and as they are creditors at the same time, they have losses to set off against their gains when the value of money falls. This is true also, although to a much smaller extent, of industrial and commercial undertakings: in so far as they work with borrowed capital they are clearly beneficiaries of a fall in the value of money; but part or all of this advantage may be offset if they simultaneously hold large liquid reserves which depreciate in value in a period of inflation. Among private persons, the rentier whose money is invested in fixed interest securities, is bound to suffer an uncovenanted loss as prices rise and the real value of his income falls, because he is helpless to protect himself by seeking a revised loan contract. Other private persons, who have a mortgage on their house, stand to gain. With persons as with businesses, inflation operates in favour of the *net* debtor and deflation in favour of the *net* creditor: there is a transfer of real income to or from those whose debts exceed their holdings of other people's debts, including the debt of public authorities (i.e., government securities) insurance companies (i.e., insurance policies), building societies (i.e., deposits with those societies) and banks (i.e., bank deposits).

A second transfer of income results from the lag of some prices behind others; this type of transfer, unlike the first, does not survive a change in the value of money but continues only so long as the change is in progress. Landlords, for example, may be in a weak position to put up the rent of land or buildings when other prices are rising but find it comparatively easy to resist a fall in rents when other prices are falling. Wages may lag behind the prices of finished goods because it takes time for workers to bring pressure to bear on their employers for an increase in good times, and employers find it difficult or impossible to cut wages in bad times. Either lag confers a bounty on one party at the expense of another: on landlord or tenant, employer or wage-earner. While there is plenty of evidence for transfers between landlords and tenants occasioned by inflation or deflation, it is much more difficult to find satisfactory evidence for transfers between employers and wage-earners that can be attributed to monetary factors. The strongest evidence relates to periods of heavy government spending in war-time; at other times it would seem that profit margins are comparatively steady and that, whether because of the competition of employers for labour or because of the pressure of trade unions, wages do not lag much behind prices during an inflation, while the steadiness of wages prevents a sharp fall in the price of manufactured goods during a deflation. Primary produce, on the other hand, fluctuates widely in price and is usually relatively dear in a period of inflation and relatively cheap in a period of deflation. There is, therefore, some transfer of income to and from primary producers as prices fluctuate—a transfer which has very important consequences for countries that depend heavily on the export of primary produce.

o

## Effects on production

While rising prices may do comparatively little to widen profit-margins, they usually increase turnover both in real terms and still more in money terms. This raises profits and stimulates production. But since production cannot expand beyond the limit set by full employment of labour, the stimulus is felt only in the early stages of an inflation when productive resources are still idle. Thereafter, moderate inflation is likely to maintain output at a higher level than steady or gradually falling prices. This effect, however, is not altogether certain. Easy profits relax the pressure on employers to maintain efficiency at its highest pitch; it is not when trade is most active that the greatest advances in technique and organisation are made. If prices rise very rapidly, there will be no further gain in employment (there may even be a fall) and a considerable drop in productivity.

Falling prices, unless accompanied by falling costs of production, mean falling profits and unemployment. Producers are unable to cover their costs and try to protect themselves by curtailing output. Part of the burden is thus passed on to the wage-earner, who loses his job or is put on short-time. A smaller quantity of goods is produced so that the national output is diminished. Deflation, therefore, is generally more creative of social distress than all but the most rapid inflation. If inflation tends to wipe out savings and inflict hardship on special classes, deflation can be far more disastrous in causing unemployment amongst those whose resistance to it is the weakest, in driving businesses into unmerited bankruptcy, and in impoverishing the community by throwing productive resources into needless idleness.

Why do changes in the price level and in the value of money take place? Sometimes, when prices are rising rapidly, people blame "profiteers." But this is to confuse cause and effect. It is not because producers have become greedier that they charge higher prices; it is because prices are higher that producers are able to earn abnormally large profits. This is obvious enough when prices *fall*; low profits are the consequence, not the cause, of low prices. A less simple-minded explanation is that goods become dearer because they are scarcer. In war-time, for example, imports of foodstuffs are cut off, and fewer workers are available for ordinary industrial employment; so prices rise. Even this explanation, however, is not very satisfactory. Prices are just as likely to rise because there is more money to spend as because there are fewer goods on which to spend it.

## THE QUANTITY THEORY OF MONEY

This provides the starting-point for an analysis of inflation and deflation which makes both processes turn on the supply of money. What has become known as the Quantity Theory of Money is based on the simple fact that, like the value of everything else, the value of money depends upon how much there is of it. This is a truth which we recognise every time we use the word "inflation." Most of us (including the Oxford Dictionary) are not quite sure whether we mean by inflation a rise in prices or an increase in the quantity of money; and we could hardly be in doubt unless we recognised that these two things were somehow connected with one another.

According to the Quantity Theory the value of money is governed by two flows—the flow of money on to the market for goods, and the flow of goods coming forward for sale against money. The larger the flow of money and the smaller the flow of goods, the higher will be the price level and the lower the value of money. Now the flow of money, which is simply our money outlay or expenditure, depends upon how many units of money we have, and the rapidity with which this money circulates. The flow of goods depends upon the volume of current production, and upon changes in stocks of finished goods. There are three possible reasons, therefore, why the price level may change between one year and another—first, because of a change in the quantity of money in our possession; second, because of a change in the velocity of circulation of the stock of money; and third, because of a change in the volume of output or of stocks. The first change is on the side of supply; the second and third are on the side of demand. If money circulates less rapidly, this must be because we are turning over our stock of it more slowly and are using more of it *in relation to* the money transactions in which we engage; the demand for money rises. If the volume of output increases, more goods have to be exchanged; there is more work for money to do, and again the demand for money rises. This increase in demand has exactly the same effect as a reduction in supply in raising the value of money (or in bringing down prices). If demand remains constant—if money circulates with a constant velocity against a constant volume of goods—the price level will vary with, and in direct proportion to, the quantity of money.

The Quantity Theory is sometimes thrown into the form of an equation. If for the supply of money we write M; for the velocity of circulation, or average number of times a unit of money is spent, we write V; for the volume of transactions or of goods exchanged we write T; and for the price level we write P— then it is easy to show that:—

$$MV = PT.$$

For MV is our money outlay. If, at any given time, everyone has £20 in his possession (M) and if every £1 is spent ten times on the average (V) during a

period of, say, one year, then the average man's money outlay in the year is
£200 (MV). PT, being the quantity of goods sold, multiplied by their price, is
the value of sales. But sales and purchases must be equal: the value of what is
sold to us (PT) is equal to what we have to pay (MV).

The equation can be re-written so as to read:—

$$P = \frac{MV}{T}$$

and this formula, which we owe to Professor Irving Fisher, is generally referred
to as the Fisher formula.

This formula has the appearance of being very precise and definite. But
when we come to interpret it, difficulties arise. First of all, the symbols are
ambiguous. Take P, for example. There is no price level to which P *must* refer;
there are, as we have seen, many sectional price levels, depending upon the
particular group of commodities which money is used to buy. We might try to
make P refer to the price level of *all* commodities and transactions. But this
"general price level" would be a hotch-potch of no real interest. We cannot
average, in any way that makes sense, movements in wholesale and retail prices,
and in the prices of raw materials, Stock Exchange securities, old houses and
motor-cars, skilled and unskilled labour, and all the other goods and services
on which money is expended. What we can do—and what we should do—is
to make P refer unambiguously to the price level of finished goods—the goods
on which, as consumers, we spend our income. T, M and V can then be defined
correspondingly. T will include sales of finished goods only; it will not include
sales of raw materials, semi-finished goods, Stock Exchange securities, etc. M
will include money held by income-receivers with a view to disbursement on
goods and services; it will not include money held for business purposes or
hoarded as an investment. V will be the velocity of circulation, not of all units
of money, but of those units only which we include in M. On this definition,
V is equal to the number of times that a unit of money held by income-receivers
circulates from hand to hand in the course of a year, and it is referred to, therefore, as the *income*-velocity of circulation.

The dependence of the price level on the quantity of money is clearly less
direct than the simplicity of the Fisher formula might seem to suggest. It is not
the *total* amount of money (in coin, notes and bank deposits), nor the activity
of this total that exerts pressure on the price level, but the amount and activity
of a portion only of the money supply. How great this portion is and what
changes take place in its size from time to time it is not easy, in the absence of
reliable data, to say. We certainly cannot assume that every increase in the

total money supply increases M proportionately. It may well be that a large increase in the money supply adds little or nothing to the amount of money in circulation against finished goods and is simply hoarded by consumers in preference to alternative investments. In times of trade depression, indeed, this reaction to an increase in the money supply is typical rather than exceptional; the increase tends to be absorbed by investors and by business men who are anxious to improve their liquidity. Thus the change in the price level is by no means in proportion to the change in the total quantity of money.

A second difficulty in interpreting the Fisher formula is that while it tells us that P is *equal* to $\frac{MV}{T}$ it does not tell us what causal connection there is between M, V, T and P. If we were to re-write the formula to read $M = \frac{PT}{V}$ we might be tempted to deduce that P, T and V summed up the forces governing M. But we should be hopelessly wrong. For we know that M is determined by the banking system and by the government—that is, by forces which do not appear in the formula at all. Similarly V, although it is equal to $\frac{PT}{M}$, is determined primarily by the monetary habits of consumers; and T, although it is equal to $\frac{MV}{P}$, depends mainly upon producers' expectations of profit. An algebraic formula, therefore, is a very different thing from a statement of causal connection. The Fisher formula gives us no more reason for supposing that P depends upon M, or V, or T, than for supposing (what is by no means impossible) that M and V and T depend upon P.

Nevertheless the Quantity Theory does postulate a causal connection between the variables in the formula. The whole point of the theory is that an increase in M *causes* an increase in P—that an increase in the money supply tends to spend itself in driving up the cost of living rather than in making us better off by causing more goods to be produced. If there is no such connection of cause and effect—if it is the level of output and not of prices which rises when more money is created—then the Quality Theory is misleading and mischievous. For nothing is easier than to increase the quantity of money, and it would be criminal folly to allow a mistaken theory to deter us from so inviting a remedy for human poverty. Hence it is important to consider, in the light of experience, what effects—on the price level, on trade, and on the velocity of circulation—an increase in the money supply is likely to have. When we go to the facts, what causal connections between M, V, P and T do we observe?

Broadly speaking, the generalisation made in the Quantity Theory is vindicated by experience—a persistent increase in the quantity of money does tend to raise prices and lower the value of money. Not only so, but there is no other force which, in the course of human history, has made so strongly for a fall in the value of money. Any sudden fall, such as takes place in war-time, or any prolonged fall, such as took place in the sixteenth and seventeenth centuries, is almost invariably to be traced to inflation of the money supply. In looking for the main causes of rising and falling prices, therefore, we are right in singling out changes in the quantity of money for special emphasis; and we are right in stressing that an increase in the money supply, if too large or too long-continued, brings no lasting benefit in increased output and simply raises the price of what is already being produced. But we must not push these conclusions too far. There are times when quite large changes take place in the price level without any accompanying change in the quantity of money; and there are times when an increase in the quantity of money helps to stabilise or to expand the output of industry.

In the swing from industrial depression to industrial prosperity and back again prices generally rise and fall. The money supply *may* undergo similar changes, the banks lending more money in the upswing and contracting credit in the slump. But even if the money supply were to remain constant throughout, booms and slumps would not disappear. Here, therefore, changes in the money supply are only one of the factors bringing about price fluctuations. In time of industrial depression, moreover, it ceases to be true that an increase in the money supply is of no real advantage to society. The first effect of creating and spending more money in a slump is to generate a demand for goods which were previously unsaleable and to bring back into employment workers who were previously unemployed. So long as there are still large numbers of men out of work, and large stocks of raw materials available, there is no reason to expect a rise in prices. The burden of adjustment to the increase in M falls on T, not on P. There is an increase in the supply of goods to match the increase in the supply of money and with these additional goods a higher standard of living can be maintained.

Suppose, however, that money continues to be created and spent until a shortage of raw materials or of labour develops. We then enter upon a period of real inflation to which the Quantity Theory can be applied in its full rigour. A mounting stream of money expenditure, fed by additions to the money supply, meets a constant stream of goods. Prices begin to rise, and the rise is soon accelerated by an increase in the velocity of circulation. Finding that money is losing its purchasing power, consumers hasten to exchange it for goods; they buy clothes, furniture, jewels—anything that can be relied upon to keep its value. These purchases force up prices still further, and the rise in prices, in a kind of vicious spiral, causes money to circulate faster than ever.

The rise in prices reacts also on the supply of money. A government which resorts to inflation as the easiest method of balancing its budget soon finds that while most of its expenses move upwards with the price-level (interest payments apart) tax receipts lag behind. The more notes it prints one year, the more notes it needs the next. Once well started on the path of inflation governments have every inducement to continue along it. The same is true when inflation is initiated, not by the government, but by the banking system. By granting credit too freely the banks can add just as effectively to the money supply as the government when it prints too many notes; and just as rising prices put pressure on the government to issue still more notes, so also pressure is put on the banks to grant still more credit. Rising prices mean easy profits; one need only borrow money and use it either to buy or to manufacture stocks of goods, selling them at the higher prices which they can be relied upon to fetch so long as the upward movement continues. The banks, therefore, are besieged with borrowers; some who are in search of a speculative profit, and some who, at the higher level of prices, cannot obtain enough working capital for their business unless they are given a proportionately higher loan. The more credit is created, the more rapidly do prices rise, and the more urgent is the clamour for still more credit. It is a familiar paradox that money is never so scarce as when it is most abundant.[1]

$P = \dfrac{MV}{T}$ is not the only formula in terms of which we can represent the forces governing the price level. From some points of view it is not even the best formula. Its advantages are that it concentrates our attention on the force which, historically, has dominated the course of prices; that it hangs out a warning against the fatal expedient of inflation by reminding us that money loses its value whenever we make it too plentiful; and that when we are making broad comparisons between price levels in different years, it is a useful pointer to the forces underlying the change from one price level to the other. Its weakness is that it does not provide us with an adequate picture of the *process* of change. We can see in a general way that changes in the quantity of money will work through to the price level; but if we want to make a closer study of the machinery of change we find ourselves beginning to discuss wage rates, interest rates, expectations of profit, and other variables which find no place in the formula. We can still construe everything—with some difficulty—in terms of the formula; but only when we have worked out, by another route, what is

---

[1] The Reichsbank, at the height of the German inflation, apologised for its inability to meet the demand for notes, and hoped that, by increasing output to a trillion marks per week, it would catch up with the demand.

happening. We do not learn from the formula; we read into it what we have already discovered.

Those economists who take a kindlier view of the Quantity Theory usually dwell on two circumstances. The first is that it serves as a reminder to the monetary authorities, who control the supply of money, that they have at their disposal an instrument for operating on the price level and maintaining stability in the value of money. They may decide not to make use of it: in war-time, because they have no alternative ready source of finance; in peace-time, because they shrink from the consequences (e.g., in higher interestrates) of limiting the supply of money. But they cannot escape implication in any inflation that results. Secondly, there is merit in citing the Quantity Theory in circumstances like those following a war, when the supply of money and other liquid assets has been greatly expanded while the price level has undergone relatively little change: unless steps are taken to remove the excessive liquidity, the chances are that prices will rise progressively until the supply of money has regained its normal relationship to the value of monetary transactions.

## AN ALTERNATIVE APPROACH

The Quantity Theory, in its simplest form, seems a natural application of the theory of value—the greater the supply of money, the less its value. But what from one point of view is a change in the value of money, is from another point of view a change in the price level of commodities. Now a change in the price level of commodities can come about only through a mass of change in the prices of particular commodities. And if we ask of the theory of value why the price of any *particular* commodity should change we receive an answer which has apparently no connection whatever with the explanation given by the Quantity Theory why prices in general should change. We learn that the price of a commodity will rise if there is an increase in the demand for it or an increase in its cost of production. Corresponding to this distinction there are two possible ways in which inflation may come about: there may be a demand inflation caused by pressure of demand or a cost inflation in which the pressure is exercised on the side of costs. The first type of inflation can be represented by a movement of the demand schedule for goods and services and the second type by a movement of the supply schedule.

This antithesis may suggest that it is easy to tell which type of inflation is in progress. It usually happens, however, that once inflation starts, both sets of forces come into operation. If demand increases and output responds, the time comes when labour and materials become scarce, higher wages have to be paid, and the cost-curve of a representative producer shifts upwards. If, on the other hand, the initial push comes from the side of costs—for example, because trade unions press successfully for higher wages—consumers may become alarmed by the prospect of having to pay still more at a later date and they will then increase their immediate purchases. When we are dealing with the total output of the community, and not with the output of a single firm, we are apt to find a hen-and-egg relationship between demand and supply and to be uncertain where to put the responsibility for a continuing inflation in prices and costs.

Let us for the moment put aside the possibility of a spontaneous movement in costs and see how a demand inflation operates. We have already explained how economic fluctuations normally reflect changes in effective demand and that these changes are tied up with the process of saving and investment. The theory of inflation should follow from this explanation since fluctuations in prices are normally associated with fluctuations in the level of economic activity and it would be surprising if the two kinds of fluctuation had different explanations. It is one of the defects of the Quantity Theory that it seems to offer just such a different explanation, unconnected with savings and investment. Effective demand, in the Fisher formula, is represented by MV; but this is broken up into M and V, not into the two principal constituents of demand, outlay on consumable goods and outlay on capital goods. The Quantity Theory stresses the influence of M and V separately on the price-level: it suggests that, if people spend more, it must be because more money has been created or because the existing stock circulates more rapidly; and it implies that—at any rate in the long run—the second possibility can be largely disregarded. All this may be perfectly sound, but it does not link up very easily with the modern theory of fluctuations in economic activity.

This theory, as we have seen in Chapter 26, treats investment as the driving force behind effective demand. Expenditure on consumable goods is a thing of custom and habit, ruled by familiar standards, and altered only when incomes alter or when the incentives to thrift gain or lose in strength. On the other hand, expenditure on capital goods, whether by producers or consumers, proceeds by fits and starts; it is not tied, like purchases of food and clothing, to present needs of a constant urgency, but is sensitive to changing expectations about the future. The instability of investment is the greater, the longer the period for which capital has to be sunk and the more difficult it is to estimate the prospective return on new assets over the course of their life. Investment is unstable because the marginal efficiency of capital is unstable; but it can be stabilised in various ways and one of those ways is by making access to finance easier or more difficult.

It is at this point that the money supply enters. An increase in the money

O*

supply affects financial conditions by reducing interest rates and making it easier to obtain credit; it tends, therefore, to encourage investment and to promote an expansion in effective demand. This increase in demand, in due course, drives up prices. There is thus a real connection between money and prices through interest rates and investment, and no necessary connection between the Quantity Theory and the modern approach to monetary problems. But the links in the chain of connection are hidden from us in the Fisher formula.

### How demand inflation develops

As effective demand increases—whether because of easier financial conditions or for other reasons—it pushes up output and employment. Sooner or later this brings into play the general tendency, when industry is straining to meet demand, for marginal costs to rise with output. No such rise need occur at low levels of output when capacity is under-utilised and there is still a great deal of unemployment. But as trade revives, raw materials and primary products begin to recover in price; most of these products are in relatively inelastic supply, except from stock, and only the existence of unusually large stocks in a slump serves to dampen the reaction in prices when demand accelerates.

At first, any rise in prices is likely to be very gradual, the advantage of a larger turnover offsetting the upward trend in the cost of raw materials. As output expands, however, the cost curve begins to turn more sharply upwards. Workers of less than average efficiency are taken on, old and obsolete machinery is brought into use, organisation becomes slacker, and employers resort to a variety of makeshift devices for increasing output such as working overtime and running machinery beyond its normal capacity. Labour turnover and absenteeism increase, and a labour force of carefully selected workers begins to lose its cohesion and team spirit. Shortages of raw materials and bottlenecks in plant capacity and labour skills make it necessary to improvise alternative techniques. In short, firms lack the elbow room in materials, plant and labour that are necessary to smooth, continuous working. They are also under less pressure to quote fine prices and to keep their costs within a fixed limit. Costs and the margin of profit tend to rise. To set against this, there are some large economies: less time and effort are spent in selling and in the changes in style, finish, pattern and so on by which customers have usually to be attracted; new machinery and new methods of production can be introduced at a faster rate because firms are more disposed to experiment and workers have less reason to object, and also because firms have the means to finance improvements requiring a large outlay; workers may also be more willing to relax restrictive practices such as ca' canny if they can be convinced that their jobs are not in danger. Allowing all this, there nevertheless comes a point at which the tendency of a sellers' market to raise costs and prices asserts itself.

Although we are excluding in this chapter nearly all the complications introduced by foreign trade, we cannot disregard the way in which foreign trade acts as a kind of safety valve to inflation. As effective demand increases, some of the additional purchasing power flows towards imported goods or towards goods capable of export; this flow is the greater, the more rapidly bottlenecks develop in domestic supplies since imports make it possible to by-pass the bottlenecks and the capacity of exporters may also relieve the pressure of domestic demand. Relief obtained in this way exacts its own price in the form of an unfavourable balance of payments; if the unfavourable balance continues long enough or reaches large proportions, it will drain away the country's reserves of gold and foreign exchange and precipitate a financial crisis. Thus, while foreign trade may act at first as a safety valve to inflation it becomes in time a fire-alarm. It is very often the effect of inflation on the balance of payments that obliges a government to take drastic action to check it; economists who dislike inflation are not ill-content therefore to see their country faced with a recurring problem of balancing its international accounts.

The process of inflation which we have described so far is not necessarily self-reinforcing. It postulates a once-for-all rise in prices corresponding to the expansion in output and the rise in costs due to that expansion: in terms of cost curves, a movement along the cost curve of total output, away from the origin and upwards by an amount governed by the shape of the cost curve. We show in Diagram 15 what the cost curve of output might be expected to look like: roughly parallel to the X axis at low levels of output and roughly parallel to the Y axis once full employment is approached. If output never got beyond OP prices would remain comparatively steady: but if output were pushed up to OQ the price level would rise sharply in about the same ratio as QC bears to PB.

Now at some point between P and Q (and perhaps even below P) the rise in prices may provoke a movement upwards of the entire cost curve. Labour is likely to be increasingly restive if wage-rates remain constant while the cost of living rises with each expansion in output. There will be wage-demands on two grounds. The first and more obvious is that a sellers' market for labour is developing: workers will be in a position to ask for and obtain an increase in wages; and if the shortage of labour is acute, they may not even have to ask, since employers will be competing actively for additional workers and will not find it easy to discriminate in favour of the *newest* members of their staff. The second and less obvious reason is that workers who are receiving an unchanged rate of pay and are faced with a higher cost of living feel that they are worse off while their employers, who see profits are rising, are better off. The only way open to workers to redress the balance is to demand higher money wages; at least, that is how matters look to the workers, however much economists may try to demonstrate that the rise in wages will merely be passed on in higher prices and reproduce the previous distribution.

DIAGRAM 15

COST CURVE OF TOTAL OUTPUT

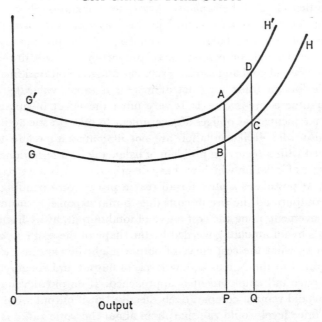

Once wages start to move upwards, the cost curve moves with it (e.g., from the position GH to the position G'H'), and so also does the demand curve since the increased earnings of wage-earners flow back in increased expenditure. Prices are likely to rise in about the same proportion as costs; that is, in the ratio of QD to QC. The rise in prices for the first time becomes dissociated from the expansion in output and the rise in marginal costs that accompanies it; inflation becomes self-reinforcing. Each fresh rise in prices provokes renewed demands for wage increases; and these, if granted, raise costs and prices still further.

It might seem as if successive increases in wages and prices could follow one another without limit. But a persistent rise in prices or in wages is possible only if the money supply keeps in step. A rise in wages increases the demand for money; the worker, having earned more money in wages, tends to keep a larger stock of it by him or at the bank; and the employer, having more money to pay in wages, requires to hold a larger balance to cover his wage bill. The consequent rise in prices works in the same direction; since goods are dearer, people need more ready money in order to make their usual purchases, and business men, if they wish to lay in stocks or to engage in dealings of any kind, find it equally necessary to keep a larger bank balance. If the money supply were to be kept constant in face of this increased demand for money, interest rates would be forced up, there would be a set-back in trade, and prices would come tumbling down, dragging wages after them. Other things remaining the same, an increase in the money supply is indispensable to a persistent increase in wages and prices. Here again we link up with the Quantity Theory: an increase in the supply of money has no obvious direct influence on wages; but it does *permit* an increase in wages (and so in prices) however initiated, and is a *prerequisite* of a continuing upward movement.

### Cost inflation

We may now turn back to the second type of inflation which we put aside for the time being.[1] How real is the danger that cost inflation may develop independently of any pressure of demand? This is not an easy question to answer. The danger cannot be assessed in purely economic terms since it depends on the strength and structure of workers' and employers' organisations, their mood and outlook, the leadership they enjoy, the political background, and so on. The wage-demands that are put forward; the size, timing, generality and vehemence of such demands; the readiness with which they are conceded— none of these is narrowly determined by the state of the labour market. Even if they were, this would not dispose of the danger of cost inflation and make it a mere facet of a process governed by the rising pressure of demand.

There are several different questions which we must distinguish. First of all, is there a determinate point on the cost curve at which cost inflation is unleashed? We assumed earlier that there was some such point; but this is obviously an over-simplification. There are likely to be some industries in which wages are already moving upwards well below full employment in the economy as a whole; and employment may either expand over a wide tract of the curve without much acceleration of this movement, or, at other times, a sharp and widespread increase in wages may occur at a much earlier stage. Moreover, we cannot realistically treat employment as changing discontinuously from one level to another, and prices as changing simultaneously in step with marginal

---

[1] See above, p. 425.

costs; we have to take account of the *rate* at which the change takes place, the expectations that develop of *further* changes, the *continuous* advance and retreat of economic activity, that prevent output and prices from settling at any given level. The movement of wage-rates may be very different at the same level of output if the tempo of expansion and the attitudes that accompany it are different. We have also to be on our guard against the convenient assumption that full employment and the virtual disappearance of unemployment are the same thing: employment in Britain grew between 1949 and 1957 by 1½ million workers while the number of unemployed workers remained unchanged at 250,000 and the population of working age rose comparatively slowly. An acute shortage of labour may draw more workers into the labour market, given the time necessary for the creation of new industrial capacity. The *shape* of the cost curve may be altering while output is in course of expansion.

Thus if we ask whether there is some critical level of employment at which cost inflation will occur, and the growth in wage-rates will exceed the normal rate of improvement in productivity, we are unlikely to find such a level from simple observation. We may, nonetheless, find that cost inflation is unlikely to take place below a certain level of employment and unlikely to be avoided above some higher level, and regard the intervening belt of employment as an area of indeterminacy. Even this conclusion may not be open to us. It may happen, for example, that after years of continuing inflation, workers become conditioned to expect a periodic round of wage increases and are prepared to strike in support of fresh wage claims although output may have been stationary for a long time or is actually contracting. In such circumstances the resulting inflation cannot be ascribed to any current change in effective demand and is undeniably cost inflation.

The experience of the late fifties suggests that a situation of this kind is by no means altogether imaginary and that when demand inflation has spent itself cost inflation may take over. It can do so only if employers do not lay off workers when money wage-rates are pushed up and if higher prices do not deter consumers from spending as freely as before. These assumptions may be reasonable in a closed economic system; but in one that is open to foreign competition, cost inflation will begin to meet with increasing resistance, not least because of public alarm at the consequences, and is likely to be slowed down unless fed by a fresh inflation of demand.

A second question we have to ask is whether costs are ever jolted upwards in circumstances free from any recent experience of inflation. Three examples may be given of such circumstances. First of all, there have been times when, in the middle of a slump, efforts were made to raise the wages or reduce the hours of wage-earners. Money wage-rates were increased by nearly 30 per cent.

under the so-called "Blum experiment" in France in 1936–37 and the effect was to raise the cost of living in almost the same proportion without any perceptible change in output. Similarly under the National Recovery Administration in 1933, efforts were made to increase the earnings of American farmers and workers and succeeded in raising costs simultaneously.

A second type of inflationary jolt may be given by a rise in the cost of imported foodstuffs and materials. Prices in any one country answer to the tug of world prices: this tug may make itself felt in an industrial country like the United Kingdom through a jerk upwards or downwards in the price of imported goods while in primary producing countries the more powerful influence is on the price of exports. A world inflation is likely to spread from one industrial country to another, therefore, through cost inflation. After the outbreak of war in Korea, for example, the cost of British imports rose by nearly 50 per cent. in two years, and this increase was inevitably reflected in a steep rise in costs of production and in the cost of living. In some countries the same kind of influence can be exerted by harvest failures and other sudden changes in the supply of important domestic foodstuffs or materials. When the cost of living is increased by changes of this kind the rise is generally carried further through the efforts of wage-earners to restore the real value of their pay: one kind of cost inflation sets off another.

A third type of jolt may be given by depreciation of the exchange rate. As we shall see in Chapter 33, the main effects of depreciation on prices are a sharp increase in the cost of imported goods, coupled with a parallel increase in export prices. It closely resembles, therefore, the second type of cost inflation, discussed in the preceding paragraph, and requires no further discussion at this point.

## Suppressed inflation

Inflationary tendencies generally show themselves when the flow of consumers' expenditure is in excess of the flow of goods for sale. But this excess may fail to produce a rise in prices. Manufacturers and retailers may prefer to sell off their stocks and ration their customers, letting then queue up or offering them a quota of their requirements. They may do this voluntarily, rather than put up prices to protect their stocks, because they do not wish to lay themselves open to the charge of profiteering. They may also do it at the request or behest of the government. If their goods are subject to price-control, for example, producers have no option but to put them on sale within the limits of price fixed by the authorities, even if this leaves a balance of unsatisfied demand. Controls may also be introduced to lop off part of the demand and suppress it by a system of rationing, allocation or licensing. Rationing is the system usually adopted for limiting the demand for food and clothing; it is designed to let everyone have a fair share, in conditions of shortage, at a price lower than unrationed demand would result in. Allocation does the same thing for raw materials and licensing for a number of transactions such as new building.

These controls do not purge inflation from the system by restoring a balance between what consumers would like to spend and the flow of goods available for purchase. They merely dam up demand at particular points and leave the surplus free to swirl past at points where there are no controls. If people have money to spare and coal is rationed, they can burn electricity instead; the shortage of coal will be relieved at the cost of a shortage of power. If people cannot buy enough meat on the ration they will, if they have money to spare, buy unrationed foods—cooked meats, poultry, fancy cheeses, and so on—at several times the value of the meat ration. This diversion of demand must lead to a corresponding diversion of effort in order to satisfy it; and the net result may be wasteful both in man-power and in foreign exchange.

Although controls suppress rather than extinguish inflation, they may take much of the sting out of it if they are used to meet an emergency and not kept indefinitely. There are usually substantial stocks that can be drawn down for some time before shop-shortages result; the shop-shortages, if fairly widespread, may induce people to save their money rather than spend it frivolously; and for those who insist on spending it, stiff taxes on tobacco, beer, and other uncontrolled articles may help them to get rid of their money without diversion of men and materials from other tasks. The surplus purchasing power can then leak through into savings or into taxes, so that an uneasy equilibrium is preserved between consumers' expenditure and the supply of consumable goods, without a really serious rise in prices. At the same time action can be taken to prevent inflation from bursting through in higher wage-costs—a danger second only to that of an inflated money-demand. The government may either "freeze" money-wages, making it illegal to strike for higher pay, or it may "freeze" the cost of living by food subsidies, rent restriction acts, etc., and then get the trade unions to agree not to press for higher wages so long as prices remain steady. Even if no open agreement is reached, provided prices are kept down by the controls (reinforced by a moderate subsidy on essential foodstuffs) the Trade Union Cerberus is unlikely to bark very loudly.

In the long-run, however, the weaknesses of such a position become increasingly apparent. Since there is inflation and shortage (whether prices rise or not), producers are under constant pressure to supply more goods and workers are daily exhorted to bestir themselves and turn out the goods. "Productivity" is the great battle-cry; but with practically everyone in work it might equally well be "output." With the usual perversity of human nature, it is precisely in those conditions that the workers begin to agitate for shorter hours, longer holidays, and smaller stints. This is not altogether surprising. Controls and shop-shortages imply that everyone is free to earn money—indeed is encouraged to do so—but that the spending of it is a difficult and irksome business. Either another currency—the ration coupon—is circulating alongside it and taking from its value or the goods that are most needed are not to be bought at all because they are not in stock. As the consumer soon learns, prices do not tell the whole story about the cost of living.

The first adverse result of suppressing inflation, therefore, is a loss of incentive because additional money-earnings become less attractive. A second drawback is that it perverts the normal pattern of demand, reducing the fraction of consumers' expenditure that goes on rationed goods and increasing the fraction that goes on unrationed goods. Consumers may spend more on football pools, beer and tobacco, and less on bread and cheese. This change on the side of demand necessarily communicates itself to the distribution of man-power between one industry and another and creates an additional demand for labour in luxury industries that are free from control. The vicious circle will be completed if this labour would otherwise have entered one of the industries making rationed goods and so have relieved the labour shortage in that industry. Consumers will then find that their own purchases are preventing them from getting what they most want.

Other disadvantages lie in the amount of man-power that becomes tied up in administering the controls (although this is generally exaggerated), in the vested interests that grow up behind the shelter of the controls, and in the world of spivs and black markets that comes into existence alongside legitimate trade. A major drawback is the inelasticity that results from the abandonment of the price-mechanism as one commodity after another comes under control. The shock tactics of limiting demand in particular sectors of the economy are indispensable in war-time and may also be of great value in some circumstances in peace-time. But if the disease is an excess of *total* demand, the treatment must be calculated to limit *total* demand and not just to prevent the symptoms from showing themselves in higher prices for particular products. Otherwise the inflationary fever will remain to waste and weaken the whole system; and prices will drift away from the relationships proper to a satisfactory matching of the wants of consumers and the efforts of producers.

## APPENDIX TO CHAPTER 27

# INDEX NUMBERS

The first step in constructing an index number of prices is to obtain quotations of the market prices of a representative selection of commodities in the years which we wish to compare. We then choose some year as a basis of comparison and relate prices in every other year to prices in this base year. Suppose, for example, that the price of a loaf is 8d., 6d., 7d. and 9d. in Years I, II, III and IV, and that we have decided to use Year I as our base year. Then we represent the price of a loaf in Year I by the number 100, and the price in Years II, III and IV can then be represented by the numbers 75, 87·5 and 112·5. These numbers are known as price-relatives. The prices of other commodities can be dealt with in the same way, each being expressed in terms of price-relatives. The convenience of these price-relatives is obvious; they allow us to read off at once the percentage change in price since the base year so that we know exactly in what proportion the price has risen or fallen. Once we have a complete series of price-relatives for each commodity, we can calculate the average change in prices by adding together the price-relatives for each year and dividing by the number of commodities.[1] If we were dealing with only five commodities—say, bread, butter, milk, eggs and potatoes—we might construct a table like Table 20 on page 435.

The numbers 100, 90, 114·5 and 109·5 are index numbers of the cost of living in Years I, II, III and IV, and they tell us in what proportion prices have risen or fallen since the base year (Year I). In Year II prices were 10 per cent. lower, in Year III 14·5 per cent. higher, and in Year IV 9·5 per cent. higher than in Year I. A corresponding but opposite change has taken place in the value of money; in Year II, for example, it had 100/90 or 111 per cent. of its purchasing power in Year I.

---

[1] Sometimes the price-relatives instead of being added are multiplied together. If there are $n$ commodities, the $n$th root of the product is then taken. This gives us the Geometric Mean as opposed to the Arithmetic Mean, or simple average, obtained by adding the price-relatives together and dividing by $n$.

TABLE 20

PRICE-RELATIVES

|  | Year I | Year II | Year III | Year IV |
|---|---|---|---|---|
| Bread .. .. .. | 100 | 75 | 87·5 | 112·5 |
| Butter .. .. .. | 100 | 90 | 95 | 105 |
| Milk .. .. .. | 100 | 105 | 110 | 120 |
| Eggs .. .. .. | 100 | 110 | 80 | 90 |
| Potatoes .. .. .. | 100 | 70 | 200 | 120 |
| Total .. .. | 500 | 450 | 572·5 | 547·5 |
| Average .. .. | 100 | 90 | 114·5 | 109·5 |

This was the procedure by which the earliest index numbers were calculated. It was not, however, altogether satisfactory. The most obvious objection was that it attached equal importance to each commodity included; equal weight was given to a large change in the price of bread and a large change in the price of chocolate. But it is obvious that even a comparatively small change in the price of bread affects the cost of living much more than a very large change in the price of chocolate. We must find some way, therefore, of giving due weight to each change in price when we are constructing index numbers.

**Weighting**

This is done by taking a "weighted" instead of a simple average of price-relatives. Suppose, for example, that the relative importance of the five commodities in Table 20 can be represented by the numbers 10, 3, 4, 1 and 2 respectively. Then these numbers are called "weights." They are multiplied by the appropriate price-relatives, and an average is struck by dividing the total for each year by the sum of the weights instead of, as in Table 11, by the number of commodities.

The result of this procedure, as is illustrated in Table 21, is to show a fall in prices between Year I and Year II of 15·5 per cent. compared with a fall of only 10 per cent. by the earlier method. The weighted index number has fallen further than the unweighted, because the heaviest fall in prices has taken place in the commodities entering most largely into consumption (e.g., bread). It will be observed that the last two columns of Table 21 are headed Expenditure-Relatives. The reason for this is that if the figures in column 4 represent our expenditure on each commodity in Year I, our bill for the same commodities at the prices ruling in Year II is exactly represented by the figures in column 5. The weights, it will be remembered, correspond to the relative

TABLE 21

WEIGHTING

| | Price-Relatives | | Weight | Expenditure-Relatives (Price-Relatives × Weight) | |
|---|---|---|---|---|---|
| | Year I | Year II | | Year I | Year II |
| Bread.. .. | 100 | 75 | 10 | 1,000 | 750 |
| Butter .. | 100 | 90 | 3 | 300 | 270 |
| Milk .. .. | 100 | 105 | 4 | 400 | 420 |
| Eggs .. .. | 100 | 100 | 1 | 100 | 110 |
| Potatoes .. | 100 | 70 | 2 | 200 | 140 |
| Total .. | 500 | 450 | 20 | 2,000 | 1,690 |
| Average .. | 100 | 90 | — | 100 | 84·5 |

importance of each commodity; in other words, to the proportion between our expenditure on each commodity and our total expenditure on all commodities taken together. If we give bread as large a weight as all the remaining commodities taken together, this *means* that half of our total expenditure goes on bread; of 2,000 units of purchasing power we expend 1,000 on bread. A fall in the price of bread by 25 per cent. will cut our bread bill by 25 per cent. We require only 750 units of purchasing power to buy what previously cost 1,000 units. Similarly with butter, milk, eggs and potatoes. At the level of prices ruling in Year II we can make the same purchases with 1,690 units of purchasing power as we made in Year I with 2,000 units. The purchasing power of money has increased in the ratio 2,000:1,690, and the cost of living has fallen in the ratio 1,690:2,000. What we are really doing, therefore, when we weight an index number of the cost of living by the method used in Table 12 is to calculate the cost in successive years of a constant bundle of commodities—the bundle on which a typical family may be supposed to spend its income. If prices fall by 10 per cent. then this bundle will cost 10 per cent. less; if prices rise by 10 per cent., then it will cost 10 per cent. more to maintain the old standard of living. By watching how the cost changes from year to year, we can measure changes in the price-level and in the value of money.

But how do we decide which commodities to include in the standard bundle and how much of each to include? How, in other words, do we arrive at the proper *weights*? The answer is: from family budgets. We require to gather from a large number of families particulars of how they spend their income. We can then calculate the proportion of their income which people spend *on the average* on each commodity. This information, together with price-quotations from different parts of the country for each commodity, is all that we need in order to construct an index number of the cost of living.

## Difficulties in the construction of index numbers

If all prices moved together, there would be no need to construct index numbers; the change in any one price would measure the change in the average level of prices. But prices do not move together. Some rise more than others in a general upward movement; some may even fall while the others are rising. The core of our problem, therefore, is to average one change against another. But—and here we come to the first, and major, difficulty—everyone is not affected in the same way by any given change in price. A rise in the price of Rolls-Royce cars, for example, means a higher cost of living to one group of people but leaves others unaffected. A rise in the price of bread raises the cost of living far more to a poor man than to a rich man. Different people spend money on different things and buy different amounts of the same things. Thus the weights appropriate to one man's expenditure may be quite inappropriate to another man's expenditure. For no two persons or families will the weights be exactly the same; strictly speaking, therefore, we ought to calculate a separate index number of the cost of living for everyone, since, because of differences in taste and in income, in size of family and in place of residence, the bundle of goods which each of us consumes differs from the standard bundle consumed by that compromise—the average family. In practice, it is found to be unnecessary to construct a large number of index numbers; even with quite different weights from those used at present much the same results are obtained. It is highly desirable, nevertheless, that we should at least have separate indices for people in different income groups. An index which is intended to measure changes in the working class cost of living may be seriously misleading if it is taken as a measure of changes in the value of middle and upper class incomes. At a higher standard of living, a much higher proportion of income is spent on direct services—the services, for example, of doctors, lawyers, teachers, waiters, gardeners, etc.—and these services are naturally given much less weight in an index intended to apply to working class standards than they would be in an index designed to represent changes in the purchasing power of money to the well-to-do.

## Changes in purchases

A second difficulty is that people buy different things at different times. New tastes and habits of mind develop and we vary our customary purchases. New goods come into use and a place has to be found for them in our budget. One commodity becomes relatively dear and another relatively cheap, and we adapt our consumption to take advantage of the change in relative prices. Some services (e.g., education) are taken over and provided free by the State so that they drop out of our budget; for others (e.g., insurance) we are forced by law to make provision. Thus the bundle of goods which we purchase in Year II differs from the bundle which we purchased in Year I. Exact comparison, therefore, between the purchasing power of money in Years I and II becomes impossible. For we can make such comparisons only when money is used to make the same purchases in both years.[1] Suppose, for example, that we calculate the cost in Year II of the purchases which we made in Year I and then, reversing the procedure, calculate the cost in Year I of the purchases which we made in Year II.[2] There is no guarantee that these two calculations would yield the same result; the change in the cost of living measured *backwards* may be quite different from the change measured *forwards*. Nor is there any reason why we should rule out one calculation as less true than the other; both can claim to measure the "true" change in the purchasing power of money, according as we look backwards or forwards. The wisest course is probably to average the results of both calculations, without speculating too deeply on the precise meaning of the average obtained.

The practical importance of the difficulty raised by changes in purchases is generally small in the short run and increasingly great as time wears on. The main items of expenditure in our budget change little from year to year, and the other items play only a subordinate part in causing changes in the cost of living. The introduction of new commodities is hardly rapid enough to have much effect on the cost of living within a short space of time. Even the consumer's efforts to cut down expenditure on relatively dear commodities and to increase his purchases on relatively cheap ones (e.g., the regular oscillation between butter and margarine as the gap in price widens and narrows) is rarely on a sufficient scale to cause any serious error in our calculations. But when we take a longer view, the problem is by no means a trivial one. He would be a bold man who undertook to compare the value of the £1 in 1066 with its present value.

---

[1] This is not altogether correct. If I know that £300 in Year I would have left me as well off as £400 in Year II then I am justified in saying that (for me) money has lost a quarter of its purchasing power. I am justified in saying so even although my purchases in Year I with £300 might have been quite different from my purchases in Year II with £400. But since the comparison is in part a subjective one I have no means of proving to the satisfaction of other people that money has lost a quarter of its purchasing power; and they are at liberty to point out that, while my judgment may be sound given my present tastes and values, I might have expressed a different judgment in Year I, with the tastes and values that I had then.

[2] Neither calculation can be exact. Some goods available in Year II were not available in Year I, while other goods, available in Year I, will not be available in Year II.

## Chain indices

It might be thought that changes in purchases could be satisfactorily represented by changes in the weights used in the construction of index numbers. We might revise the weights every year in accordance with observed changes in consumption and link prices in each year with prices in the succeeding year. The series of links might then be formed into a chain by letting 100 represent the price level in some base year and attaching each link—each successive change in prices—in turn. Such a chain index number, however, would disregard rather than solve our problem. It would be based on the assumption than changes in purchases in adjacent years were negligible. But it is precisely these changes which we wish to take into account. If we give up using butter when margarine comes on the market, an index of the cost of living ought to reflect the advantage to us of the new and cheaper substitute. But all that a chain index does is to attach more and more importance to changes in the price of margarine as our consumption of it increases. This is an advantage on the more usual procedure of assuming that we eat just as much butter as before. But in the long run it is little more satisfactory. The cumulative advantages which we derive from the new commodities introduced year by year are equally disregarded.

## Practical difficulties

There are also a number of practical difficulties in the construction of index numbers. First, we must be careful in our choice of a base year. A year should be chosen in which prices are in a fairly normal relationship to one another, and in which our expenditure is distributed between each commodity in a fairly normal way, thus providing a satisfactory base from which to measure off changes in prices and weights which are in keeping with our normal consumption. Sometimes the average of a series of years is chosen as a base, and this has the advantage that the resulting index cannot be biased by the peculiarities of any single year. Secondly, we must exercise great care in making comparisons between different prices, since these prices may be paid for goods or services which do not remain constant from year to year. We may be given goods of better quality; for example, the butter which town workers buy nowadays is greatly superior to the butter on sale half a century ago. Or we may be given better service—as when bottled milk from disease-free herds is delivered on our doorstep. Or we may be given better terms of credit as a result of the growth of banking facilities. Even in the short run what are really changes in price may be disguised as changes in quality or in service; for example, shopkeepers who are in the habit of issuing price lists will find it convenient to charge a constant price and provide goods of better or inferior quality as wholesale prices vary.

Thus the extraction of price-relatives from a mass of information about prices is no easy task. Unless we are deliberately setting out to "cook" our index numbers, we must make sure that all price quotations are strictly comparable.

## Other index numbers

Money, as we have seen, has a different purchasing power for different people. It has also a different purchasing power for different purposes. We have been assuming up till now that the only purpose for which money is used is the purchase of finished goods, and we have been trying to devise a method of measuring changes in the purchasing power of money to consumers of finished goods. But money is used also to buy other kinds of goods—raw materials, semi-finished goods, machinery, exports, imports and so on—and its purchasing power over these goods may change in a different direction or to a different degree from its purchasing power over finished goods. To look at things the other way round, instead of one price level—the price level of finished goods or the retail price level—there are a large number of price levels corresponding to the different groups of things that we can buy for money. There is the wholesale price level, the export price level, the price level of capital goods, the price level of bonds, the wage level, and a whole host of other price levels. A separate index number can be calculated to measure changes in each price level, and the method of constructing these indices is exactly the same as that used in constructing a cost-of-living index number.

# CHAPTER 28

# THE DEMAND FOR MONEY

In the preceding chapters we have taken for granted some understanding of the place that money occupies in the modern world: what money is and what it does; what governs monetary habits; how control is exercised over the supply. By jumping ahead in this way we were able to see how monetary influences affect production by making access to finance easy or difficult: the supply of money reacts on interest rates which in turn react on investment and so on effective demand. We must now turn back to examine the role of money more clearly.

## A definition of money

What distinguishes money from other commodities is its acceptability, or—to use a term introduced in Chapter 24—its liquidity. Money is anything which, by custom or law, is generally acceptable without question in payment for goods and services or in final settlement of a debt. We accept other commodities for their own sake because we wish to consume them; if we do not wish to consume them, we have to go to the trouble of finding a buyer for them. Money, on the other hand, we accept not necessarily for its own sake, but because we know that other people will accept it; we know that there is never any trouble in finding a "buyer" for money—people will take it in exchange for goods of any kind at almost any time. We can never be stranded with money as we can be stranded with other commodities. The man who has just lost his return ticket, for example, will have much less difficulty in inducing the ticket collector to accept a pound note than to accept a book which originally cost £1. The pound note gives him a claim to any goods that he may care to buy; it gives him freedom of choice and security in emergencies. But the book is of use to him only amongst people who know its value and wish to possess it. The pound note is liquid; the book is not.

Money performs four distinct services: it is a medium of exchange, a store of value, a measure of value and a standard of deferred payments. Let us take each of these in turn.

## Money as a medium of exchange

Men will specialise, as we saw in Chapter 6, only if the limited range of goods which they produce can be exchanged quickly and conveniently for the much wider variety of goods which they wish to consume. But exchange is quick and convenient only if some commodity is singled out as the standard medium of exchange—that is, as money. The alternative of direct barter leads to endless delays and inconvenience. First, there has to be what is called "a double coincidence of wants." The man who wishes to exchange his pig for a gramophone must not only find a buyer for his pig, he must find a buyer with a gramophone to sell. Secondly, the gramophone must be such a good one that he is willing to give his pig for it, and the owner of the gramophone must think highly enough of the pig to be willing to take it in exchange. It is impossible to sell part of the pig or part of the gramophone; both must be offered as indivisible units. Similar difficulties arise when services have to be bartered; the carpenter, the lecturer and the dentist, for example, are likely to have the greatest difficulty in striking satisfactory bargains. The use of money overcomes these difficulties. It allows specialists to obtain for their products or services general purchasing power. Any kind of product or service can be sold for money, and the money so obtained can be used in payment for other products and services. There is an automatic coincidence of wants since everyone wants money; and there is automatic divisibility of the means of payment since monetary units can be made as small as we wish.

The use of money, therefore, arises out of the inconvenience of direct barter in a community of specialists. A good monetary system, by facilitating exchange between producers allows them to carry specialisation further, just as a good transport system, by facilitating exchange between different regions and countries, extends the area of dealings and promotes regional specialisation.

## Money as a store of value

It is a short step from using money as a means of payment to holding money in reserve against *future* payments. Some of these payments may have to be made in the very near future—when we go shopping, for example. We do not wish to be without money when we board an omnibus, or when we see a bargain in a shop window, or when someone calls to collect the rent. Other payments may be more distant. There will be various bills to be met; or we may be saving up in order to buy a motor-car or a house. In addition to the payments which we already contemplate there will be some against which we must guard but which cannot be foreseen—payments due to unexpected illness, or to sudden requests for money from relatives, or to miscalculation of the patience of our creditors. We will generally keep a margin of cash in excess of prospective payments in order to provide for these unforeseen contingencies. Again, since it is in money that our incomes are paid, we may not trouble, because of the expense or inconvenience involved, to invest what we feel to be surplus to our requirements. Or we may decide to hold a store of money in preference to alternative investments, such as bonds, shares or property, because we do not feel confident in the stability of the value of these investments or because we take the view that their value will fall. From all these motives we try to keep by us a stock of money as a reserve of liquid purchasing power. We want money to hold, not just for paying away immediately.

### Money as a measure of value

Money is not only the *thing* with which we pay for goods and services; it is also the *scale* in which we measure their value. Money provides a scale of pounds, shillings and pence by which we can make comparisons of value, just as a thermometer provides a scale of degrees centigrade by which we can make comparisons of temperature. Even if we had to resort to barter some such scale would be indispensable. We could not possibly carry in our minds a complete catalogue of exchange-values, expressing the value of each commodity in terms of a different amount of every other commodity. We should want some common denominator of exchange-values and this common denominator would be money. It would not be money proper—the thing which we exchange. It would be money-of-account—the abstract unit in which price-quotations are made and in which debts are expressed. In Great Britain the pound note is money proper, while the pound sterling is the money-of-account. No one has ever seen a pound sterling—any more than anyone has ever seen a degree centigrade or a mile or any other unit of measurement. What we do see, from time to time, are Bank of England pound notes, with which undertakings to pay one pound sterling may be discharged. The pound sterling does not exist; it is an instrument of thought to assist us in making comparisons of value. The pound note, on the other hand, does exist; it is a piece of paper, fairly constant in value, and generally acceptable in payment for goods priced at one pound sterling. The pound sterling is very ancient; it goes back to Charlemagne. The Bank of England one pound note, on the other hand, dates only from 1928. Thus a new kind of money-proper may come into use without any change in the money-of account. In the German inflation of 1922–23, the reverse took place. Because of the rapid and incalculable depreciation of the mark, which sometimes lost half of its value over the week-end, contracts were entered into in terms of the United States dollar, the Swiss franc, or commodities like coal and oil, but payment was ultimately made in marks at whatever value they had sunk to. The mark continued to fulfil its function as money-proper, but ceased—in some transactions at any rate—to be the money-of-account.

As a measure of value money makes possible a system of prices. Exchange-values, instead of varying between one transaction and another, become co-ordinated and regularised into market prices. A "market" for each commodity comes into existence and the gain from sales and purchases becomes more calculable. The existence of the market, and the greater calculability which it permits, encourage increased trading, and with this increased trading goes increased specialisation. Once again the use of money lies at the root of specialised production.

## Money as a standard of deferred payments

Besides being the unit in which we measure prices (present payments), money is also the unit in which we measure debts (future or *deferred* payments). A debt is an undertaking to pay something—usually money—at some future time; and what has to be paid is measured in terms of some standard unit—the money-of-account. In Britain, for example, contracts of debt are expressed in terms of the pound sterling, but what is actually paid is hard cash—either banknotes or a cheque.

Just as dealings in commodities would be exceedingly complicated without a measure of value, so borrowing and lending would be exceedingly complicated without a unit for the measurement of debts. Instead of borrowing general purchasing power and buying with it such goods as we required, we should be forced to hire or rent the desired selection of goods, returning them (or similar goods) at the end of some agreed period, together with an additional payment of goods as rent. We should be unable to reduce the goods borrowed to a common measure and make repayment in *other* goods of equal value or in a single generally acceptable commodity. It would be impossible also to set debts to a given value against credits to the same value and so to cancel out payments between different traders. Every transaction would stand by itself. Dealings in debts—the work of the Stock Exchange, the insurance companies, building societies, commercial banks and other financial intermediaries—would cease.

By providing a unit in which debts can be measured, money makes borrowing and lending enormously easier. A capital market can come into existence in which debts are traded just as goods are traded in commodity markets. With the capital market come large-scale production and increased specialisation. Here, therefore, is yet another link between money and specialisation.

## The demand for money

Because money acts as a medium of exchange and a store of value, there is a demand for it for its own sake. People want to hold a stock of money just as they want a stock of clothes; they carry about with them or hold at the bank a quantity of purchasing power on which they do not, as a rule, earn interest but which offers them the compensating advantage of liquidity. The sum of the individual money balances held must be such as to add up to the total supply since all the money in the country must obviously be *somewhere*: and if more money is put into circulation, *somebody* must add to his stock of purchasing power. If the supply of money is unchanged and one group of people want more of it, they can only acquire it by persuading another group of people to run down their money balances, for example in exchange for stock exchange securities; ownership of the existing supply of money is then redistributed. The total stock that people hold has a purchasing power that can be represented as a fraction of the national income or as sufficient to buy, say, K units of goods. If the demand for money balances were to increase, this would show itself in a rise in the ratio of the money supply to the national income and in the quantity of goods (K) that total money balances would purchase.

The demand for money, measured in this way, is simply the inverse of the velocity of circulation (V) which we discussed in Chapter 27. If we start from the formula $MV = PT$ and write $V = \dfrac{PT}{M}$ then, on one set of definitions at least, we can identify PT with national income and V becomes the ratio of the national income to the money supply while K, as just defined, is the ratio of the money supply to the national income. An increase in the demand for money can be thought of, therefore, either as a fall in V or a rise in K.

Whoever holds money must presumably have some motive for doing so, since he could, if he chose, earn interest by lending it. What are the motives which prompt people to hold money? Upon what, in other words, does K depend?

There are, broadly speaking, three sets of motives:—

**I  The receipts and payments motive**—First, we may hold money in order to bridge over the gap between the time when we receive money and the time when we pay it away. We receive our incomes in the form of money, as wages, salary payments, dividends, and so on, and pay them away in exchange for goods and services of all kinds. If receipts and payments were simultaneous— if, for example, we ran up accounts and paid them off as our income reached us—we should require very little money. But if we are paid only once a quarter, and have payments to make at a steady rate, we shall be left at the beginning of the quarter with a large cash balance which gradually diminishes until it is replenished at the next pay-day. If we are paid weekly, our income will reach us in smaller lumps and we are not likely to hold so large a balance. The time intervals which separate income payments, therefore, have an important influence on the amount of money which the community normally holds. The same is true of the time intervals which separate payments for goods and services. If income tax, for example, is paid half-yearly it will be necessary to build up a cash balance every six months so as to be able to pay the tax, whereas a tax payable weekly would not add very appreciably to the normal stock of money held by the taxpayer.

The gap between receipts and payments is not enough of itself to prompt consumers to hold money. The gap must also be so short that it is not worth the consumer's while to lend his spare cash and earn interest on it. If the interest which he could earn is small (e.g., on deposit account with a bank), the mere trouble of arranging a loan may be counted too great in comparison; and even if the interest is appreciable (e.g., on industrial debentures) the cost of making the loan (commissions on sale and purchase) may cancel most of the prospective gain.

It should also be kept in mind that the payments against which the consumer holds money include payments for investments which he proposes to make later. A man may resist the temptation to lend, even temporarily, the small sum which he has accumulated, because he hopes shortly to have enough for a larger and more profitable investment.

The same time intervals between receipts and payments which induce consumers to hold a stock of money exist in business. Business men, too, therefore, hold money balances to provide for any large payments which are in prospect or as the residue of receipts not yet expended. Indeed, in an industrial community, the balances held for business purposes may be just as large as the balances held by consumers against future payments. The cash requirements of business will vary with trade activity, rising in a boom and falling in a slump. In a boom, when higher profits are being made, larger balances will be required to provide for increased dividend disbursements, and to finance extensions to buildings and plant. Other payments and receipts will also be higher in value, partly because of expanding trade, partly because of rising prices, so that, if the time intervals between receipts and payments remain as before, businesses will find themselves holding, or requiring to hold, more money. In a slump, all these tendencies will be reversed, and businesses will hold reduced money balances. Consumers respond to fluctuations in trade in the same way. The higher their income, the more money they will hold, and the higher prices are, the more money they will require to hold in order to make their normal purchases. When trade is good, and incomes and prices are rising, consumers will increase their stock of money; and in a depression, with incomes and prices falling, they will diminish it. Thus the strength of the first motive to hold money depends mainly upon the level of incomes and prices, and upon the normal time intervals between receipts and payments.

2 **The speculative motive**—The second motive is an expectation that prices will fall. This expectation will lead people to hold money instead of using it to buy goods which they hope to obtain later at lower prices. If the expectation is sufficiently widespread it will *cause* prices to fall and so produce its own justification. But the expectation cannot be universal or prices will fall at once into line with the general market expectation; for consumers will not pay prices which they think too high, and producers, sharing the general opinion, will have no motive to hold out for existing prices. The fall in prices will remove the divergence between fact and expectation, and unless *some* consumers expect a further fall, the second motive to hold money will disappear. In other words, the second motive presupposes divisions of opinion on the future trend of prices. One group of people satisfied with existing prices, continues to buy. Others, anticipating a fall, reduce their purchases and add to their bank balances instead. But prices at any given moment are always low enough to clear the market of all goods offered for sale, an addition to stock being regarded as a purchase by the holder.

When prices begin to rise, and are commonly expected to rise further, the second motive to hold money is transformed into a motive to get rid of it. No one wants to hold money, a depreciating asset, longer than is necessary, and it is passed on hastily like a bad penny. In a major inflation, people keep by them just enough money to meet day-to-day expenses and do all they can to reduce the normal intervals between receipts and payments. Thus the store of real purchasing power which they hold in the form of money (K) falls heavily. At the end of October, 1923, the note issue in Germany had increased 400 millionfold in comparison with 1913; but in spite of this enormous inflation, which raised the printing of notes to the status of a major industry, the real purchasing power of the note issue in terms of gold was less than a fortieth of the purchasing power of the pre-war note issue.

3 **The precautionary motive**—The third and final motive to hold money springs from uncertainty. We can never be quite certain in what payments the future will involve us, nor what receipts we shall ultimately obtain. Lacking certainty, we arm ourselves with money against emergencies—against calamities like illness and death, and the expense to which they put us; against sudden calls on our charity; against opportunities of purchase on favourable terms; against delays guessed at or unforeseen in the receipt of income. The

money that we hold gives us security; it makes us *liquid*. The motives to liquidity are particularly strong when it is the price of securities about which we are uncertain. Even if we do not expect that security prices will fall—that is, even when the second motive to hold money is absent—we may have too little confidence in our judgment to come in and buy. We may prefer to hold a large part of our wealth in monetary form until the future course of prices is less in doubt.

### Hoarding

A demand for money from the second or third motive is primarily a demand for money to hoard. We want the money, not for some specific purpose but as a safeguard or as the best investment open to us. For the time being we want to keep it idle. To suggest therefore—as is so often done—that there is something heinous about "piling up idle deposits in the banks" is to misunderstand completely the functions of money. It is the business of bank deposits—other than those held from the first motive—to be idle. Nor does it lie within the power of the general public to alter the total volume of bank deposits, except by devious ways such as stuffing their pockets with notes; the level of bank deposits depends upon the policy of the monetary authorities. Nor, in point of fact, are bank deposits at an abnormally high level in the years of depression when "idle deposits" are most lamented; they are generally *below* the level reached in more prosperous years. What is true, and what does lend colour to the complaints, is that a larger proportion of bank deposits is hoarded in a depression— that is, is held exclusively from the second and third motives. But the remedy lies not so much with the public as with the banking system, which, by creating more money, can satisfy the increased desire for liquidity. The public might, of course, spend more, and give money more work to do, but this would change, not their aggregate bank balances, but their savings.

### Liquidity and interest rates

The increased "hoarding" that takes place in a depression shows itself, as a rule, in an increase in K—the ratio of the money supply to the national income. An increase in K is also likely to occur in war-time: in the years 1940–47, for example, the supply of money grew faster than the national income because of heavy government borrowing on short-term (which inflated the money supply) and the exercise of controls over various types of expenditure (which checked the inflation of incomes). People built up large liquid balances which they could not spend at once but which they intended to use once the war was over. The war-time rise in K was followed by a gradual decline as people brought their money balances into closer relationship with their more normal requirements. These movements are illustrated in Diagram 16 which shows the ratio of the net deposits of the London clearing banks to the British national income in the years 1919–58. It will be seen that there are three peaks in K, one after each of the two world wars and one at the bottom of the depression in 1933.

DIAGRAM 16

THE SUPPLY OF MONEY AND THE RATE OF INTEREST

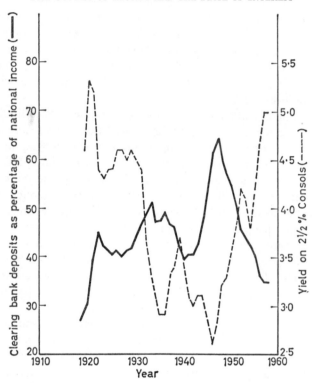

*Source:* F. W. Paish, "Gilt-edged and the Money Supply," *The Banker,* January 1959, p. 18.

Diagram 16 also shows the fluctuations over the same period in the long-term rate of interest as measured by the yield on Consols. The rate of interest appears to have varied inversely with K as if the fluctuations in the one have an important influence on the other.

There are two possible lines of explanation of this phenomenon, one in terms of the speculative motive, one in terms of the precautionary. We have already seen that the speculative motive results in efforts to economise money balances when they are expected to depreciate. The same expectation of

P

inflation will also make people avoid fixed interest securities since a constant money return will represent a diminishing yield in terms of future prices; this loss of favour sends down the price of fixed interest securities and raises the rate of interest. As K falls, the rate of interest rises.

The first line of explanation is thus in terms of a diminishing demand, under inflationary conditions, for money and bonds. It lays stress on the effects of a general loss of confidence in the future value of money but does not presuppose any exact correspondence from year to year between changes in interest rates and in the real value of money balances. What happens in any one year will depend on the way in which the authorities try to stem inflation. There may well be some recovery in the gilt-edged market while prices go on rising and the money supply undergoes little change, so that, for the time being, interest rates and K both increase.

The second line of explanation is in terms of the motives to liquidity which, as we saw in Chapter 24, are linked with interest rates. Our demand for money is a function of our preference for it in comparison with less liquid alternatives such as Consols. If we are anxious to remain liquid we are prepared to sacrifice the interest that we might earn by buying Consols and the more anxious we are the more interest we will forego. In a period when the money-supply is not expanding as fast as the national income, there is less money in relation to the work it has to do, people are less liquid, and they are less willing therefore to lend money or buy government securities and run down their cash balances. In other words, interest rates rise as a reflection of a higher liquidity-preference. Conversely, if interest rates rise, the cost of remaining liquid rises too and some people will be tempted to lend their money or exchange it for fixed interest securities.[1]

At this point we rejoin the main stream of argument. The demand for money, together with the supply, helps to determine the complex of interest rates and through interest rates the level of economic activity. An increase in the demand for money acts as a brake on investment while a decrease makes investment easier and cheaper to finance.

---

[1] This second line of explanation can be modified so as to make the argument turn on the behaviour of short-term interest rates. These reflect monetary policy and at the same time re-act on long-term rates. A restrictive monetary policy will operate to reduce the money supply in relation to national income, will involve high short-term interest rates, and will produce a sympathetic rise in long-term rates.

# CHAPTER 29

# THE SUPPLY OF MONEY

In the course of human history, many different things have served as money. In early times various commodities were used: either common articles of trade like tobacco, skins, salt, etc., or, among pastoral tribes, animals such as cattle, sheep or goats. The precious metals had many advantages over these kinds of money in durability, divisibility, portability and so on, and they were also remarkably stable in value because the existing stock did not alter quickly. Once they came to be coined, the convenience of using the precious metals as money was greatly reinforced and they acquired an almost unchallenged prestige, circulating all over Europe for more than a thousand years with little competition from other kinds of money.

**Paper money**

Coins are now used only for petty cash transactions. In larger payments their place has been taken by banknotes, and in still larger payments by cheques. The use of banknotes in Britain goes back to the seventeenth century, when the landowners began to keep their cash with the goldsmiths, partly out of concern for its safety (as in the Civil War), partly for the sake of the interest offered on deposits. A certificate, or a number of certificates, to the value of the sum deposited was issued by the goldsmiths and these certificates entitled the depositors to withdraw their cash and valuables whenever they wished. Like modern banknotes the certificates were promises to pay on demand; unlike modern banknotes they were receipts made out to a named person and payable only to him or to his order. Gradually, however, banknotes came to be made out to bearer, so that they no longer required endorsement and could pass freely from hand to hand. By the time when, in 1729, printed notes made their appearance it had become the common practice to have notes made out to a named payee or bearer, and by the end of the century notes payable simply to bearer had begun to circulate.

The receipts issued by the goldsmiths represented real value; hence banknotes are sometimes spoken of as "representative money." But there was no necessary equivalence in value between the notes in circulation and the gold and other valuables stored with the goldsmith bankers. For the goldsmiths, finding that their depositors did not all withdraw their funds at the same time, were able to lend out some of the gold deposited in their custody, or to make loans with notes against which they held no reserve of gold. They could *create* paper money and lend it without preliminary thrift. Modern banks also, like the goldsmiths, issue notes in excess of their gold holdings; part of the note issue, in Britain and elsewhere, is "fiduciary"—based on public confidence, not on a gold backing. But it does not rest with modern banks, as it rested with the goldsmith, to determine how large this fiduciary issue shall be. The law lays down strict limits—sometimes, as in Britain, a fixed *total*; sometimes, as in the United States, a fixed *multiple* of the gold held by the note-issuing banks.

### Limitations on the note issue

The notes issued by the goldsmiths were redeemable in gold on demand, and this limited the size of issue which they could prudently make. Their promises to pay enjoyed more confidence and were more freely accepted than other men's only so long as their credit was above suspicion: that is, so long as they were thought to be in a position to honour their promises. This meant that they had to keep substantial reserves and to be in a position to call in their loans in an emergency.

The notes now in circulation in the United Kingdom, however, are not redeemable in gold. Apart from the notes issued by the Scottish and Irish banks, the only notes in use are those issued by the Bank of England and these notes are legal tender: that is, they must be accepted when offered in payment for goods or in settlement of a debt. They are not linked, either in practice or by statute, with the gold reserves of the Bank—which are virtually nil— nor of the country—which have been held since 1939 in an account known as the Exchange Equalisation Account. The maximum note issue is fixed by the government and changes several times a year.

### Bank money

Many people think of money as currency (i.e., notes and coin). But there is another kind of money of far greater importance as a means of payment— bank-money. Unlike currency, bank-money, or money deposited with a bank, is not a commodity. There are, it is true, ultra-cautious depositors who make periodic visits to their bank to see for themselves that their money is still there, and who are handed banknotes (a commodity) by the teller. But the banknotes which they inspect are not the same thing as their bank account. Banknotes are oblong pieces of paper decorated with a promise to pay whereas a bank account is an entry in a ledger. This entry gives us the right to ask the bank for a specified amount of currency—a right which, if we make all our payments by cheque, we shall never use. The entry also gives us the right—if our balance is held on "current account"—to draw cheques directing the bank to transfer money from our account to some other person's account. So long as the bank remains solvent and our cheques continue to be accepted freely, we can use our bank balances almost as effectively as notes to make a purchase or to settle a debt. In times of crisis the risk of banking failures may cause people to insist on payment in notes; notes, being legal tender, are absolutely liquid, but a bank account may be frozen if the bank is unable to meet its obligations. In normal times the difference in acceptability or liquidity is small; we may even prefer payment by cheque to payment in banknotes.

Cheques themselves are not money: they are devices for transferring the ownership of bank-money from one person to another. But chequable bank deposits, or current accounts, can normally be classed as money. So also may other bank deposits—deposit and savings accounts. Unlike current accounts, these cannot be drawn on at any moment; the depositor requires to give notice of his intention to draw on them and they are less liquid, therefore, than current accounts. But they are so much more liquid than other assets, and are so commonly classed with current accounts when we are mentally contrasting money with alternative investments, that any sharp line of division between current and other accounts would be false to the facts.

## Money and other liquid assets

If we include savings accounts in money where are we to stop? Is money lent to a savings bank, money? Or money invested in bills of exchange? Or money used for the purchase of Consols? For an answer to these questions we must go back to our definition. Money, we said, was anything generally acceptable without question in payment for goods and services or in final settlement of a debt. Now acceptability is a matter of degree.

Unless something is much more acceptable than all possible substitutes, we cannot draw a hard and fast line between what is money and what is not. All we can do is to arrange things in order of liquidity and stop at the first big gap that we come to. We might think that bills of exchange and Consols could be ruled out because they are debts, not money. But some kinds of money are simply debts. Pound notes, for example, are promises to pay—acknowledgments of debt; current accounts are debts due to us by our bank. Pound notes, it might also be suggested, are a perpetual debt; the Bank of England is never likely to be asked to redeem its promises. But the same is true of Consols; they, too, are a perpetual debt unlikely ever to be redeemed. What then is the difference? Is it that Consols bear interest while money does not? Not at all; interest-bearing notes were used as money for over a century. The only ultimate difference is one of degree. Consols are a less liquid asset than money; they are not so generally acceptable as a means of payment. Similarly, bills of exchange and savings bank deposits should be excluded; they stand on the other side of the gap that separates money from less liquid assests.

The convenience of using bank-money is so great we could almost manage without currency altogether, receiving our incomes by cheque and paying them away by cheque. No money would ever change hands; we should simply instruct our bankers to reduce our balance and increase our creditor's balance correspondingly. Money would consist entirely of claims on the banks, transferable by cheque, and all payments would be made by appropriate entries in bank ledgers. From this day of universal reckoning in bank ledgers we are still, however, some distance away. We do not all go shopping with cheque-books, and we are not all successful in running up bills (to be settled later by cheque) with tradesmen, landlords and others. We pay for most of our smaller purchases in cash. Hence we still need currency. But currency plays a minor part in modern business. A century ago, it was spoken of as "the small change of credit." To-day, with the rapid growth of banking and the cheque-system, the predominance of bank-money is even more marked. At the end of 1965 the British public held nearly four times as much on deposit with the commercial banks as it held in notes and coin.

## BANK-MONEY and CREDIT CREATION

If most of the money in use is bank-money, the supply of money must depend upon how bank-money is created. Indeed, we can leave coin and notes entirely out of account because the supply is expanded nowadays to keep pace with the demand. If anyone is short of change he can draw on his bank balance for the coin or notes that he needs; the output of coin from the Mint and of notes from the Bank of England's printing press is governed by the public's desire to hold money in this form rather than in the form of bank-money. If a member of the public wants more bank-money, on the other hand, he cannot, as a rule force the banks to create more of it. He can, it is true, pay more notes across the counter and so increase his own bank balance. But this will not necessarily add to the total of all bank balances since some other person may be withdrawing notes and running down his bank balance; only if there is a *general* reduction (or increase) in the total of notes in circulation can the public act on the supply of bank-money. Such a reduction, in point of fact, is rarely accompanied by an expansion in bank balances; more commonly the note issue and bank deposits contract (or expand) together. Presumably, therefore, a change in the supply of money is initiated, not by the public but by the banks.

We start, therefore, from a paradox. Everyone is free to decide for himself how much money he will keep on deposit with the banks; but the public as a body has little or no influence on the total volume of bank deposits. To understand how this can be so we must look at the way in which the banks conduct their business.

## Manufacturing money

The primary function of banks, which is to mobilise savings, has become entangled with a second, and quite distinct, function—that of creating the means of payment. Ever since the introduction of banknotes, banks have been able to *manufacture* money. At first they did this by issuing notes in excess of the valuables deposited with them. By increasing their loans they could put more notes into circulation, the loan being drawn upon and paid away in banknotes. Similarly, by calling in their loans (that is, by "restricting credit") they could reduce the notes in circulation and hence the supply of money. At this stage in the evolution of banking, the notes put into circulation were limited only by the reserves which the issuing banks thought fit to keep. If, for example, they held rigorously to a reserve ratio of 20 per cent. (i.e., if they held £20 in gold against every £100 in notes), they issued notes to the value of five times their gold reserve. Whenever an additional deposit was made with them, they could lend five times the value of the new deposit and so add four times its value to the amount of money in circulation. A withdrawal of deposits reacted automatically to reduce the note-issue in the same proportion by forcing the banks to call for repayment of their loans.

When gold disappears from circulation, and the issue of notes is limited or taken over by the government, the power of the banks to create money does not by any means come to an end. Just as they were once able to vary their note issue by increasing or diminishing their loans, so the banks can now vary their deposits by exactly the same technique. By lending more freely they can *create* deposits, and by restricting credit they can extinguish them.

The mechanism by which they do this depends upon the reserves which they hold against their deposit liabilities and the ratios which they maintain between reserves and deposits. Suppose, for example, that it is regarded as good banking practice to keep a cash reserve of 10 per cent. against deposit liabilities, and that this ratio is adhered to by every bank. Then total deposits will necessarily be equal to ten times the cash reserves of the banks as a group, and a change in the money supply will come about whenever these cash reserves are expanded or contracted. In a monetary system of this kind, the money supply will be a function of what is usually called "the cash base."

## The cash base

Let us make the simplifying assumption that cash reserves consist entirely of till-money, and that till-money consists entirely of notes. Let us also assume —it is not a very extravagant assumption—that the public wants to divide its money in a fixed ratio—say 5:1—between bank deposits and notes. Finally, let us assume—again without much departure from fact—that the government has an exclusive right to issue notes. Then the supply of money will expand whenever the government puts more notes into circulation (e.g., to pay for the construction of new roads): at first by the amount of the additional notes but eventually by much more. The initial increase in notes will exceed what the public wants to hold at the current level of income and some of the notes will be deposited with the banks, where they will swell the cash reserves. This will dispose the banks to lend more freely (or to add to their investments) and as a result of their loans (or purchases of securities) bank deposits will expand. The process of expansion will continue until the banks are obliged to limit their lending by the insufficiency of their reserves. Once the additional notes have been absorbed and there is no scope for further creation of credit without infringing the normal reserve ratio of the banks, the public will again be holding five times as much bank-money as notes and the total supply of money will have expanded by much more than the initial injection of additional notes: on the particular assumptions that we have made, by four times as much.[1]

## Credit creation and bank profits

This brief description of credit creation may suggest that banking is a highly profitable pursuit since banks can literally make money out of nothing. In fact, however, it is by no means inevitable that banks will make higher profits when the money supply is expanding than when it is contracting. When a bank "creates money" it adds simultaneously to its assets (loans and investments) and to its liabilities (deposits, i.e., bank-money); whether it makes a higher profit depends upon what inflation does to the return on its assets and the interest it has to pay on its deposits, not just upon what inflation does to the

---

[1] Let B = bank deposits, N = notes held by the public, T = notes held by the banks. Then B = 5 N, B = 10T, so that N = 2T.

Of the increase in notes (X), two-thirds will ultimately be retained by the public and one-third will be held by the banks as till-money, providing backing for a tenfold expansion in deposits.

The increase in the money-supply will eventually be $\frac{2}{3} X + \frac{10}{3} X = 4X$,

or four times the initial expansion in the note issue.

magnitudes on each side of the balance-sheet. It is not unknown, for example, for interest rates to increase during a period of inflation and for this increase to cause a serious depreciation in the value of the gilt-edged securities that form a large proportion of bank assets. At the same time, the changes in interest rates may be more pronounced on the liabilities side than on the side of bank assets, though this is not likely to happen except in rather special circumstances.

### Banks and other financial institutions

There is, however, a more fundamental misunderstanding about the role of the banks in credit creation. Banks are financial institutions, in many ways like other financial institutions. They are dealers in financial assets—loans and debts—borrowing from some people and lending to others, hiring money and hiring it out again. This is what all financial institutions do: building societies, insurance companies, investment trusts, discount houses, finance houses, and so on, all raise money and lend or invest it. There are, of course, differences between these institutions in the sources of their funds and in the purposes to which they are applied. There are also differences between banks: some draw their funds mainly from their shareholders, others mainly from depositors; some lend mainly to industry, others mainly to public bodies, including the central government; some deal in short loans, borrowing and lending for short periods, while others deal in long-term loans, borrowing and lending for comparatively long periods. But all banks, and all financial institutions have this in common: that by incurring fresh liabilities they can acquire additional assets. A building society can take steps to attract larger deposits and lend the proceeds on mortgage to householders; an investment trust can raise money on the stock exchange and invest it in securities. The distinguishing feature of a bank, or at least of a deposit bank accepting money on deposit from the public, lies in the character of the liabilities it creates. These liabilities, unlike deposits with a building society, shares in an investment trust, insurance policies, etc., are themselves money: not just something capable of being turned into money, or forming security for a loan of money, but money-at-the-bank.

It follows from this that banks are not alone in their power to create credit if by credit we mean liquid assets. The liabilities of most financial institutions are relatively liquid in the sense that they can be readily disposed of at little cost and without much sacrifice of their face value. They differ from money, but the difference is a matter of degree. If the liabilities of financial institutions other than deposit banks are increased, the money supply remains unaffected but something happens that is very much akin to an increase in the money supply: the economy becomes more liquid and less in need of bank-money. If people have more on deposit with the building societies, or hold more savings

P*

certificates or bigger insurance policies, they have less motive for holding a large balance at the bank; their need for liquidity is satisfied in other ways. Now all financial institutions are in competition with one another for money and the banks are not immune from this competition; they may lose ground to savings banks, building societies, and other competitors. If this happens, the place of the banks in the whole financial structure will alter and so will the place of bank-money in relation to other kinds of liquid asset. The changes taking place in the supply of money will then be a very misleading guide to the changes taking place in general liquidity and it is the latter that are significant in the management of the economy. Changes in the supply of money are no more than a means of acting on liquidity; and deposit banks are only one group of financial institutions capable of generating additional liquidity.

Moreover if we look at the process of credit creation through the eyes of an individual bank, its behaviour does not seem very different from that of other financial institutions. It balances its books just as they do, entertaining fresh applications for loans or buying additional securities only if there is a surplus above normal reserve requirements. If it decides to hold a rather larger or rather smaller reserve against its liabilities, it is again making a decision that other financial institutions may take when they think it prudent to increase their liquid reserves or are content with a narrower margin in hand. A bank can no more afford to increase its liabilities without regard to its reputation than can any other financial institution.

We must not push these arguments too far. While it is true that other institutions create credit, and that a great deal of credit is given by one business to another or by one person to another without the intervention of any institution, the banks occupy a central position in the creation of credit and liquidity. They do so for three reasons. First of all, banks as a group usually have command over much larger resources than other financial institutions. In the United Kingdom, for example, the assets of the commercial banks in 1965 were about £10,000m. while the building societies had assets of £5,000m., the discount houses of £1,300m. and the investment trusts of £3,000m. Only the insurance companies and pension funds, with a total of some £14,000m., rivalled the commercial banks in the size of their assets, but insurance policies lie far apart from bank-money in point of liquidity. This illustrates the second reason for the key position of the banks: their liabilities are more liquid—generally much more liquid—than those of other financial institutions. While bank-money is not the sole source of liquidity it is a much more satisfactory source than most other liquid assets. Thirdly, the banks offer a relatively convenient instrument of control over general liquidity: if the authorities can control the supply of bank-money, they have a very powerful lever for controlling general liquidity.

## Bank-money and the cash base

This brings us back to the main issue which we set out to discuss: what determines the supply of money? We have seen that the general public has only a very limited influence, exercised through a switch between notes and bank deposits; that individual banks have little power to initiate a change except by altering their customary reserve-ratio; but that, if the cash base changes, the banking system will expand or contract credit proportionately. This seems to make everything turn on the size of the cash base and directs attention to the factors operating upon it. In the example which we took, the cash base consisted entirely of notes in the till, and these notes were the residue of the total issue after providing for the requirements of the public. The money supply depended on the size of the note issue, the state of preference of the public for notes in relation to bank deposits, and the reserve ratio maintained by the banks.

In one respect this example was a highly artificial one: it made no reference to any central bank such as now exists in most countries —for example, the Bank of England in the United Kingdom or the Federal Reserve Board in the United States—yet it usually rests with the central bank, in association with the government, to regulate the supply of money. The real power to create or contract credit is exercised, as a rule, by the monetary authorities, a term which is used to cover the central bank (if there is one) and any agencies or departments of government (such as the Ministry of Finance or the Treasury) that exercise control over monetary policy. The powers and techniques used by the monetary authorities to control the money supply vary from one country to another, and the relationship between the central bank and the government also varies. The position in the United Kingdom is discussed more fully in Chapter 30 on British Financial Institutions: what is said below is intended to be of general application. In order to avoid a detailed description of banking institutions, however, the argument is set out in terms of central banking operations and the monetary authorities are identified, for simplicity, with the central bank. The central bank is assumed to control, with the concurrence of the government, the size of the cash base and hence, given fixed reserve-ratios, the total volume of credit.

Where there is a central bank, the commercial banks normally keep part of their reserves in the form of a balance with the central bank. They may be required to do so by law or by a convention that has the force of law. But there is also an obvious convenience to the commercial banks in the centralisation of their reserves; if they all hold balances with the central bank, they can settle surpluses and deficits at the clearing by a simple book entry, the banks with a deficit making a transfer from their balances to the banks with a surplus. From the point of view of the central bank, the advantage of centralisation is the power which it confers over the cash base: it puts the central bank in the same relationship to the commercial banks as the commercial banks occupy in relation to the public. The public holds money on deposit with the commercial banks which in turn hold money on deposit with the central bank. Just as the commercial banks can create deposits with themselves, so also can the central bank. It may lend directly to the commercial banks (although this never happens in the United Kingdom), or it may lend indirectly (as when it helps out the discount market at the same time as the commercial banks are withdrawing funds from the discount market), or it may buy government securities, paying with a cheque drawn on itself. If it chooses the third course, and resorts to "open market operations," the cheque will be paid into a commercial bank by the seller of the securities and the proceeds credited to him. This bank in turn will be credited by the central bank with an increase in its balance there. The action of the central bank causes the public to switch from government securities to money and to hold additional deposits with a commercial bank; simultaneously it adds to the cash reserves of the commercial bank and puts it in a position to initiate a cumulative expansion of credit of the same type as would result from an increase in the note issue.

If the central bank wants to initiate a contraction of credit, it reduces its lending or sells securities. This forces the commercial banks to part with some of their reserves either in repayment of loans or in settlement, on behalf of their customers, of the securities which they have purchased. The loss of reserves, in the form of balances with the central bank, sets in motion a general contraction of credit as the commercial banks try to restore their reserve-ratios.

In what has been said so far, no reference has been made to till-money which was treated earlier as the entire cash reserve of a commercial bank. In practice, cash reserves are made up partly of till-money, and partly of balances with the central bank; sometimes they also include balances with other banks and gold. In most countries the variable element in reserves consists of balances with the central bank and no real violence to the facts is involved in concentrating exclusively on this; but in some countries, particularly those where there is no central bank, the situation is rather more complicated.

### Methods of credit control

Even where such complications can be disregarded, the central bank does not rely exclusively on open-market operations and variations in its loans to commercial banks in order to control credit. It may operate directly on the commercial banks by varying the reserve-ratios which they are asked or required to maintain; this has the same effect on the banks as a change in the size of their reserves without the embarrassments that sometimes accompany open market operations (e.g., if the central bank wants to sell government securities it has to find buyers for them and the presence in the market of a large seller may be discouraging to possible buyers). The central bank may also operate through interest rates: it may, for example, raise its lending rates, rather than simply restrict its loans, and take what action it can to force a general increase in rates. Any restriction of credit is likely to involve a rise in interest rates but there is a choice between raising the cost of credit so as to limit the demand and reducing the supply of credit, knowing that this will raise the cost. A third weapon which the central bank may use is selective credit control: it may require a limitation by the commercial banks of lending for some purposes which are deemed to be of low priority, or it may make borrowing for those purposes more difficult or more onerous. An example of such action is an increase in the margin which purchasers of stock exchange securities have to provide from their own resources when seeking bank accommodation for the remainder. Similarly, importers may be asked to make cash deposits before being granted permission to import some types of commodity, these deposits increasing the cost or difficulty of financing the transaction. Credit control of this kind, while qualitative in form, has a quantitative effect and it may be this effect which the authorities most desire.

## PECULIARITIES OF THE BRITISH SYSTEM

In the United Kingdom, there is an unusual relationship between the central bank and the commercial banks since there are no direct dealings between the two. Instead, the discount market as explained in Chapter 30 acts as a buffer. This in itself makes the British system unique. But there is a further point of difference: the cash reserves of the British commercial banks are not nowadays the pivot of the monetary system and are dictated by, instead of dictating, the supply of money. It is true that they form a steady 8 per cent of total deposit liabilities; but this is not because deposits move up and down in step with reserves. What happens is that the Bank of England takes action to maintain reserves at 8 per cent. of the pre-determined level of deposits.

It might seem that this would oblige us to start all over again in a search for the factors governing the supply of money in the United Kingdom. Fortunately, this is not necessary; much of what has been said still applies. The main difference arises because the reserves which govern the behaviour of the British banks embrace a wider range of assets than cash in hand and balances with the Bank of England; they extend to all "quick" assets, including loans at call, bills of exchange and, above all, Treasury Bills. The British banks maintain a fairly constant proportion of 28 per cent between their "quick" or liquid assets and their deposit liabilities. They do so not altogether from choice—although, historically, it was common for the proportion to be in the neighbourhood of 30 per cent.—but because to allow the proportion to fall below 28 per cent. would be to invite the displeasure of the Bank of England. The reason why the British banks need not attach special importance to their cash reserves is that they can without difficulty turn their other liquid assets into cash and that when they try to do so they can count on the complaisance or active co-operation of the Bank of England. There is no point in their keeping more than the fixed minimum of 8 per cent. in cash since this yields no return to them and they can use the remaining 20 per cent. in interest-earning assets which simultaneously provide a liquid reserve that can be readily converted into cash.

### The liquid assets base

From the point of view of the monetary authorities, what this means is that they no longer seek to operate on the cash base, in the narrow sense of bankers' balances at the Bank of England, but aim instead at regulating the supply of liquid assets available to the banks. In practice this amounts to regulating the banks' holdings of Treasury Bills, which usually represent 90 day loans to the British government. If the banks are deprived of some of these assets they are obliged to restrict their loans or investments in the same way as they would be if their behaviour was governed by their cash ratio and they lost cash. It is not quite so easy, however, to operate on the liquid assets of the banks as to operate on their cash. If a central bank wants to cut down the cash base it can pursue open market operations and sell either short-dated or long-dated government securities ("bills" or "bonds") at its own choice. But if it wants to reduce the liquid assets ratio it must either prevail on the central government to issue fewer bills or take action to re-distribute outstanding bills between the banks and the public.

The first course of action is not easy because the government's borrowing requirements are usually highly inelastic. All that the central bank can hope to do is to get the government to borrow less on short-term and more on long-term; alternatively, it can sell long-dated securities to the public and withdraw short-dated securities, so leaving fewer bills for the banks to acquire. This alternative is sometimes referred to as "funding" although this was not the original meaning of the term.[1] "Funding" compresses the liquidity of the banks (and generally of other financial institutions as well) and sets in motion a

---

[1] "Funding" used to mean the consolidation of national debt by the issue of "funded" debt (i.e., long-dated, or undated, government securities) in place of "floating" debt (i.e., Treasury Bills, Ways and Means Advances, and so on). The term has now come to mean an extension in the maturity of government debt, generally involving a reduction in the issue of Treasury Bills.

deflation of the money supply. But although it is easier to change the composition of the national debt by funding than to reduce it by refraining from borrowing, there are often technical obstacles to large-scale operations in the market for long-term securities that make a central bank shy away from this course of action.

The second possibility—that of redistributing existing liquid assets between the banks and the public—also has its difficulties. The normal method of doing so is to put up interest rates on Treasury Bills and make them a more attractive investment. This can be done by raising Bank Rate,[1] and so stiffening the terms on which the discount market can obtain cash, in the last resort, from the Bank of England. A rise in Bank Rate produces a sympathetic (but not necessarily equal) rise in the rate of discount on bills held in the market and on other rates of interest that are traditionally associated with Bank Rate. But the greater returns on Treasury Bills that this involves will only bring in non-bank purchasers if people (including foreigners) are accustomed to thinking of Treasury Bills as a possible investment for their money and if the banks do not hit back by offering correspondingly higher rates on their deposits so that no one thinks it worth while to switch. In some countries both these conditions are fulfilled: there is an active market in Treasury Bills, and the rates of interest that commercial banks offer are either not directly related to the Treasury Bill rate or are subject to control by the central bank itself. In the United Kingdom, however, the first condition is only imperfectly fulfilled (non-bank holdings of Treasury Bills are comparatively small and have been tending to decline) and the second condition is often not fulfilled at all because the market rate on Treasury Bills and the rate on deposit accounts both move with Bank Rate.

### Direct operation on the banks

In the British monetary system, therefore, the supply of money is neither so closely related to the size of the cash reserves of the banks nor so immediately under the control of the monetary authorities as our previous argument implied. But this is not the end of the matter; for, once again, the authorities can make use of more direct instruments of control. They can, for example, deprive the banks of some of their liquid assets by bringing pressure on them to exchange Treasury Bills for short-dated bonds which do not rank for inclusion in their

---

[1] Bank Rate is the minimum rate at which the Bank of England, acting as lender of last resort, will discount first-class bills or make advances to a discount house against eligible paper (see below, pp. 486–7). Bank Rate governs the movement of market rates of discount, although these usually remain below Bank Rate by a margin which fluctuates but is rarely large except in a depression. Bank Rate also, by custom, governs the movement of many administered interest rates, such as the rates on commercial bank deposits and advances.

liquid reserves; on two occasions in the early fifties such a conversion operation took place. They can require the banks to make "special deposits" with the Bank of England over and above their normal cash holdings and so freeze some of the banks' liquid assets. Alternatively they may, in future, take advantage of a recommendation by the Radcliffe Committee and vary the liquidity requirement; this would operate in very much the same way as would a variation in the cash ratio in a system where cash rather than liquid assets were the pivot. Finally, the monetary authorities may limit bank *lending*, for example, by putting a ceiling on bank advances. They are likely to do this in order to make it more difficult to obtain command over money rather than with a view to limiting its supply; but a check to expansion in one of the main assets of the banks (their loans to customers) may simultaneously check expansion in their liabilities, especially if the principal alternative outlet for their funds, namely government securities, happens to look unattractive because they are falling in price.

## Wider Relevance of the British System

This discussion of control over the money supply in the United Kingdom is of more relevance to the situation in other countries than has so far been implied. Without entering into too great detail, let us examine three points of similarity.

### Monetary policy and debt management

First of all, there is a close interconnection between the money supply and the national debt or, at the level of policy, between control over the money supply and the management of the national debt. This is true everywhere and not just in the United Kingdom. Where the monetary authorities act on the cash ratio, they normally make use of open market operations and these are operations involving the buying or selling of government debt obligations. Where the monetary authorities, as in the United Kingdom, act on the liquidity ratio they are likely to do so by trying to vary the maturity of the outstanding debt, and are again involved in operations in government securities. This is not a matter of accident but is inevitable wherever there is a large public debt; indeed, there are countries such as Western Germany where the monetary authorities have been positively embarrased by the absence of a sufficiently large volume of government debt in which to operate.

Why is it inevitable? The answer lies in the relationship between money and debt. Money when it consists of bank notes is usually itself a form of government debt; with the advantage from the government's point of view that it need never be redeemed. When it consists of bank-money, the debt is a private liability of the banks (unless they happen to be publicly owned); but since a large proportion of the assets of the banks, in the United Kingdom and elsewhere, consists of government securities, the private liability is half-way to becoming a public one. If we look at the whole range of liquid assets, and not just at that end of the spectrum which is so liquid that we accept it as money, we find that by far the largest block consists of government debt, varying in maturity from Treasury Bills, with only a week or less to run, to long-dated and irredeemable securities. The amount of government debt held by the British public, excluding the banks, is far in excess of their holdings of private debt, especially debt in which there is an active market, and is about twice as large as their holdings of notes and bank-money. The main alternatives open to anyone seeking liquidity, therefore, lie between money and government debt and the choice ultimately made is governed by the importance attached to complete liquidity (or liquidity preference) on the one hand and the terms on which money and debt can be exchanged (in other words by the rate of interest) on the other. The monetary authorities in seeking to control the supply of money not only find it impossible to ignore other forms of debt but are inevitably preoccupied with them, and particularly with the national debt as the nearest available substitute for money.

### The money supply and liquidity

But, secondly, this pre-occupation is really not with money and debt as such but with the general state of liquidity and the terms on which is is possible to contract new debts. The more our account of the British monetary system proceeded, the more apparent it must have been that the supply of money is, in a sense, a side-issue: a by-product of the actions of the monetary authorities, not the real criterion of action. The money supply matters in any economic system only to the extent that it reacts on effective demand and this reaction takes place mainly through an easing or tightening of access to liquid resources. The reaction may involve an expansion or contraction of the money supply and generally does; but there may be several different ways of acting on the liquidity of the economy, and varying the money supply may not be the most effective of these different expedients. It may be more important to operate on interest rates, for example, and try to alter the whole structure of interest rates, not merely to change the level of short-term rates.

This is a controversial issue which cannot be taken much further here. Some economists take the view that central banking policy should be directed towards maintaining or altering the complex of interest rates, and that the money supply should be adjusted to suit this complex; others argue that the monetary authorities should content themselves with expanding or contracting the credit base, leaving this to work its way through to the supply of money and to market rates of interest. The weight of opinion in the United Kingdom lies more in the direction of the first view, with some reservations about the wisdom of attempting to shape too deliberately the pattern of long-term rates. One reason for the prevalence of this view may lie in the combination of duties discharged by the Bank of England, which is not only in a position to dictate short-term interest rates because of the swamping of the money market with government paper, but can also exert strong pressure on long-term rates because of its responsibilities in the management of the national debt. In the United States, where the Federal Reserve Board has no such responsibilities and the system of debt management is different, the monetary authorities have not the same freedom of action in varying the maturity distribution of government debt.

### Variations in reserve requirements

There is a third way in which British monetary arrangements are of general interest. It is not only in the United Kingdom that cash reserve ratios have lost some of their former importance and central banks have been obliged to freeze some of the excessive liquidity in the system. In a number of other countries, especially during and after the war, the central bank instituted a system of "special deposits" or increased reserve requirements in order to limit the creation of credit. Sometimes this excessive liquidity originated in heavy government spending, so that the banks were really being obliged to make a forced loan to the government; sometimes it had its origin in a favourable balance of payments with other countries and the monetary authorities were seeking to prevent this from correcting itself by generating inflation through the banking system. Whatever prompted the freezing of reserves, the effect was to put pressure on the banks to lend less freely and to prevent a sharp increase in the supply of money and credit.

### INTERNATIONAL INFLUENCES ON THE MONEY SUPPLY

Money is no more immune from international influence than any other aspect of economic life. So far we have disregarded this influence and we shall defer a full discussion of it until Chapter 32; but it may be useful to indicate briefly how it makes itself felt.

Just as a commercial bank has to be ready to settle any deficit at the clearing by drawing on its cash reserves, so the central bank of a country has to be in a position to settle an external deficit in the balance of payments by drawing on its reserves of foreign exchange. The parallel is not complete because the central bank may make use of exchange control to ration the supply of foreign exchange between importers and preserve a balance between what is paid in by exporters and what is taken out by importers without allowing its reserve to be drawn upon; or it may stand aside from the market in foreign exchange and let fluctuations in the rate of exchange take the strain, hoping that private financiers will help to balance supply and demand without too violent a movement in the rate. But if it wants to peg the rate of exchange at a fixed parity and to allow free dealings at that rate, it has no alternative but to come forward when necessary and either release enough foreign exchange to bridge a deficit in the balance of payments or absorb enough to clear a surplus. For this purpose, it has to maintain a reserve of internationally acceptable currency.

### Foreign exchange reserves

This reserve may take one of three forms. It may consist of gold, which has long been the most acceptable means of international payment; it may consist of some currency such as sterling or dollars which is extensively used in international commerce and can be expected to remain relatively stable in value; or, finally, it may consist of deposits with some international banking organisation or an automatic line of credit from such an organisation. In practice, gold forms much the largest element in international reserves, amounting in 1964 to $40,800m. for all countries outside the Soviet bloc. About two-fifths of this total, however, was held by one country, the United States, and when the U.S. gold holding is deducted from the total nearly half the remainder ($24,500m. compared with $25,300m.) took the form of dollars, sterling and other national currencies, or liabilities of international institutions like the International Monetary Fund. These liabilities, although relatively small, seem destined to play an increasingly important part in the settlement of international accounts.

If a drain of gold and foreign exchange takes place, the automatic effect is a reduction in the money supply since those who make payments abroad with the gold and foreign exchange acquire it by drawing on their bank accounts and so extinguish deposits to an equivalent value. The central bank may then, if it chooses, offset this reduction by open market operations; or it may, in alarm at the loss of reserves, reinforce the reduction in the money supply by setting in motion a further restriction of credit. Here, therefore, is a second point at which the reactions of commercial banks to a loss of cash reserves finds no parallel in the reactions of a central bank. Commercial banks hold to a more or less steady reserve ratio and are very unlikely to meet a fall in their reserves by an expansion of credit. A central bank, unless required to do so by legislation, has normally no fixed ratio by which to regulate its behaviour and unless it has some reason for anxiety about the absolute level of its reserves is under no compulsion to contract credit when a deficit occurs. What it decides to do depends upon its diagnosis of the reasons for the deficit and upon other elements in the situation that make it appropriate or inappropriate to bring monetary weapons into play.

CHAPTER 30

# BRITISH FINANCIAL INSTITUTIONS

We now turn to examine in more detail the financial institutions of a single country, the United Kingdom, and to the way in which these institutions affect the flow of funds into investment in real assets. We shall draw attention as we go along to any marked peculiarities of British institutions and refer from time to time to the institutions of other countries, particularly the United States.

We have already seen that from the point of view of anyone wishing to hold his savings in liquid form, there are a number of alternative types of investment, varying in liquidity and competitive with one another. From the point of view of anyone wishing to obtain command over liquid resources, the various financial institutions, such as banks, insurance companies and investment trusts, again provide a series of alternatives. There is a capital market in which financial institutions compete for funds and through which they make funds available. The market is not perfect because lenders prefer to make use of customary channels, and borrowers, as the Radcliffe Committee remarked, "do not turn readily or without difficulty to alternative sources of finance. There are, as it were, faults in the structure of the market which are difficult to cross, partly because of ignorance, custom or prejudice, and partly because of the greater inconvenience or cost of using a different type of financial institution." But there is nonetheless "an underlying unity in the market for loanable funds."[1]

The truth of this may be checked by reflecting on the way in which the head of a small business obtains his capital. If he needs more he may, and usually does, draw more heavily on his own savings, ploughing back a larger portion of his profits, realising some of his investments or drawing on his bank balance. He may also go to his bank for a bigger overdraft, mortgage his house or borrow money on his insurance policy, buy some equipment on hire purchase, take fuller advantage of credit from his suppliers or put off paying his bills, or try

---

[1] *Report of the Committee on the Working of the Monetary System* (Cmnd. 827) para. 319.

to raise money from an institution that specialises in advancing long-term capital to small businesses with good prospects of expansion. There is hardly a single type of financial institution that he may not conceivably approach.

### Self-finance

Table 22 shows the flow of credit through the main channels of investment in the years 1952–58. It excludes, however, the most important single source of capital—self-finance: just as the private householder relies heavily on his own savings when he buys capital equipment such as a motor-car, a washing machine, or a bedroom suite, so the average business usually turns first to appropriations from profit as a source of capital. There are no figures for all British businesses, but if we take companies alone and exclude companies in insurance, banking and finance, the total appropriation that they made to reserves in 1955–57 averaged over £1,500m.—much more than any of the figures in Table 22. A large part of this sum went to the renewal of capital assets and is not strictly comparable, therefore, with the other figures; but even if company saving were taken net of depreciation it would still stand out as by far the largest source of funds for new investment in real assets.

### The new issue market

For public companies the next most important source was the new issue market. Issues of stocks and shares through the new issue market cannot be made by private companies since the flotation, unless it takes the form of a private "placing" of shares with no provision for their subsequent sale to the public, has to be accompanied by an application to the Stock Exchange for permission to deal and no dealings in the shares of private companies can take place on the Stock Exchange. Issues by public companies in the middle fifties averaged about £200m. and this may have financed about 30 per cent. of net new investment by those companies.[1] Most of the capital raised in this way was in issues of over £1m. but issues down to £250,000 are not uncommon and a number of smaller issues for sums as low as £50,000 have been made. These smaller issues are rarely accompanied by a prospectus, as this method of issue would be too expensive, and are usually "placed" with an insurance company or other institutional investor. Since these investors are usually not prepared to take more than a limited share of a company's capital, it may safely be assumed that even the smallest issues are likely to be in companies with a total

---

[1] In the years 1949–53 the proportion was 28 per cent. (*Studies in Company Finance*, ed. B. Tew and R. F. Henderson, (Cambridge 1959) p. 65).

TABLE 22

FLOW OF CREDIT THROUGH MAIN CHANNELS IN THE UNITED KINGDOM 1952–58

| | Annual average (£m.) | | |
|---|---|---|---|
| | 1952–54 | 1955–57 | 1958 |
| *Mainly to private sector* | | | |
| 1. New capital issues by U.K. public companies .. .. .. .. | 151 | 245 | 195 |
| 2. Bank advances (excluding advances to nationalised industries): | | | |
| (a) London clearing banks .. | —37 | 12 | 353 |
| (b) Scottish banks .. .. .. | 2 | —3 | 29 |
| 3. Commercial bills .. .. .. | —7 | 40 | —40 |
| 4. Mortgages by insurance companies established in Great Britain .. | 39 | 77 | 65 |
| 5. Changes in trade credit received by quoted companies .. .. .. | 82 | 188 | — |
| 6. Hire purchase debt on business purchases .. .. .. .. | — | 2 | 25 |
| 7. Lending to persons for house purchase: | | | |
| (a) London clearing banks (also included in items 2 and 10) .. | —3 | —5 | 22 |
| (b) Building societies (net advances) .. .. .. .. | 139 | 153 | 143 |
| (c) Insurance company mortgages (also included in item 4) .. | | (47) | (40) |
| (d) Local authorities .. .. | 23 | 45 | 20 |
| 8. Loans on policies and personal security by insurance companies in Great Britain .. .. .. | 5 | 7 | 7 |
| 9. Hire purchase debt on consumers' purchases .. .. .. .. | — | 3 | 98 |
| 10. Personal and professional bank advances by members of the British Bankers Association (partly included in item 2) .. .. .. | —17 | —22 | 90 |
| *Overseas* | | | |
| 11. New capital issues for overseas .. | 63 | 61 | 74 |
| *Public sector* | | | |
| 12. Treasury Bills .. .. .. | 225 | 4 | 46 |
| 13. Gilt-edged securities for cash .. | 292 | 56 | 101 |
| 14. Local authority mortgages, etc. .. | 129 | 243 | 376 |

*Source: Report of Committee on Working of Monetary System,* Table 21.

capital of £250,000 or more. The facilities of the new issue market are almost entirely confined, therefore, to the larger public companies.

## Trade credit

Next in order of importance, but for very different purposes, is trade credit. Most businesses have at any one time large amounts outstanding to their credit for goods supplied and at the same time owe large amounts for goods they have received. The credit which they give and take is one of the leading causes of fluctuation in their liquidity and in their need of funds, and these fluctuations may, and do, give rise to insolvency. The figures shown in Table 22 relate only to credit received, without offsetting credit given, and to public companies whose shares are quoted on the Stock Exchange, not to all businesses. If all businesses were included, the *net* change in trade credit from year to year would no doubt be much smaller but it would not fall to zero because a large amount of credit is given by exporters to their foreign customers and by retailers and others to private persons.

## Personal credit

Some of the credit received by private persons appears under items 7–10 in Table 22. Their largest borrowings are for house purchase and for this purpose they may go to their building society, their insurance company, their local authority, or their bank; building societies are by far the chief source of finance. Durable consumers' goods bought on hire purchase absorb a further large amount of credit: these sales are mainly financed by specialised institutions, the finance houses, which in turn raise the necessary funds from the banks and from deposits made by private persons, or, more commonly, by businesses with cash to spare for a limited period.

The remaining items in Table 22, apart from items 2 and 3 to which we return below, relate either to new issues on the Stock Exchange for overseas borrowers or to the net absorption by the market of Treasury Bills, local authority mortgages, or government securities. The new issues shown do not represent the total flow of credit overseas since there is in addition a large-scale reinvestment of profits by British companies operating abroad and an annual increment in the total amount of credit due to British exporters from foreign customers. The absorption of government paper shown in Table 22 is also incomplete since the government raises money through the sale of savings certificates and in other ways not included in the total.

Table 22 is thus rather fragmentary and conveys only a limited picture of the functioning of the capital market. It also fails to bring out the place in the market of the main financial intermediaries through which a large part of the flow of credit is channelled. The relative importance of these institutions is more apparent from Table 23.

## BRITISH BANKS

Since the banks are a most important group of financial institutions we deal with them first and in some detail. In Britain as in other countries there are several different types of bank and it is not easy to know where to draw the line between what is and what is not a bank. For example, some of the smaller finance houses call themselves "industrial bankers" although not generally regarded as forming part of the banking community; on the other hand, the old-established "merchant banks" of the City of London are usually referred to as "accepting houses" although no one would dispute that they are banks.

We shall not discuss the various British *savings* banks, such as the Post Office Savings Bank and the Trustee Savings Bank, which invest their funds exclusively or almost exclusively in government securities. We shall also make no reference to *mortgage* banks, which play an important part in some countries in providing capital on mortgage for real estate: in Britain somewhat similar functions are performed in relation to housing finance by the building societies, which we discuss in a different context, and in relation to farming by the Agricultural Mortgage Corporation and the Scottish Agricultural Securities Corporation, which make loans to farmers for periods of up to sixty years at fixed rates of interest. Finally, we shall make no specific reference to *development* banks, the main business of which is to finance new enterprise by providing long-term capital: the nearest approach to institutions of this kind are the Commonwealth Development Finance Co., which is engaged in financing long-term development in the Commonwealth, the Finance Corporation for Industry, which has financed a number of major industrial projects in post-war Britain, and the Industrial and Commercial Finance Corporation which lends to, or invests in, smaller British concerns in amounts up to £200,000. We shall concentrate on the deposit banks, which conform more closely to the average man's conception of a bank and transact most of the ordinary banking business of the country.

### The clearing banks

The banking business of England and Wales is largely in the hands of five banks, Barclays, Lloyds, the Midland, the National Provincial and the Westminster (the "Big Five"), which together with six smaller banks enjoy clearing facilities through the London Clearing House. The eleven clearing banks had total assets at the end of 1964 of over £9,000m. and of this total six-sevenths were

TABLE 23

ASSETS OF SELECTED BRITISH FINANCIAL INSTITUTIONS[a]

$£m.$

|  | 1938 | 1958 End of year (or nearest available date) | 1964 |
|---|---|---|---|
| 1. London clearing banks .. .. | 2,320 | 7,302 | 9,241 |
| 2. Scottish banks .. .. .. | 380 | 933 | 1,093 |
| 3. Northern Irish banks .. .. | 56 | 153 | 197 |
| 4. C.W.S. and S.C.W.S. banks .. | 113 | 196 | 187 |
| 5. Overseas and foreign banks .. | — | 1,071 | 4,048[b] |
| 6. Accepting houses .. .. .. | — | 257 | 1,080 |
| 7. Discount houses .. .. .. | — | 1,053 | 1,283 |
| 8. Post Office Savings Bank .. .. | 530 | 1,646 | 1,814 |
| 9. Trustee Savings Banks | | | |
|     Ordinary departments .. | 151 | 815 | 999 |
|     Special investment departments | 103 | 341 | 882 |
| 10. Building societies .. .. .. | 759 | 2,633 | 4,888 |
| 11. Hire purchase finance companies | — | 280 | 990 |
| 12. Life assurance companies ⎫ | 1,745 | 5,990 | 8,143 |
| 13. Other insurance companies ⎭ | | | 989 |
| 14. Superannuation funds .. .. | — | 2,500 | 5,007 |
| 15. Investment trusts[c] .. .. | 311 | 832 | 2,917 |
| 16. Unit trusts .. .. .. | 80 | 90 | 406 |
| 17. Friendly societies .. ,.. .. | 152 | 238 | 280 |
| 18. Industrial and provident societies | 361 | 942 | 1,228 |
| 19. Collecting societies .. .. | 89 | 305 | 407 |
| 20. Special finance agencies[d] .. | 10 | 120 | 280 |
| Grand Total .. .. .. | — | 27,697 | 46,359 |

[a] The basis of valuation is book or nominal value or cost except for the assets of investment and unit trusts, the bulk of the superannuation funds, and securities held by the special invest-ment departments of the Trustee savings banks which are at market value.
[b] Including £921m. for banks not reporting in 1958.
[c] The figures for 1938 and 1958 relate to 1939 and 1959 respectively.
[d] Finance Corporation for Industry, Industrial and Commercial Finance Corporation and Agricultural Mortgage Corporation.

*Source: Financial Statistics*, October 1965.

---

the assets of the "Big Five." All of the "Big Five" have branches throughout England and Wales but two of the smaller banks (Glyn Mills and Coutts) are confined to London and one (Williams Deacon's) is predominantly a Lancashire bank; of the other three clearing banks, two (Martin's and the

District) operate mainly in the north and the other (the National) is an Irish bank although it has branches in England and Wales.

## Other banks

There are in addition a number of small banks, of which the C.W.S. Bank is the largest, which do not have access to the London Clearing House, a group of merchant banks to which we refer below, and some 75 banks, operating mainly abroad or as exchange dealers, but with offices in London. Most of these "overseas and foreign banks" (as they are described in Table 23) are British companies like Barclays Bank, D.C.O. or the Bank of London and South America, with their head office in London and their branches in other countries. The deposit liabilities of such banks are mainly to non-residents, and although their total assets have been growing rapidly and were not far short of £4,000m. at the end of 1964, the accounts of residents in the United Kingdom were not much in excess of £500m.

Of the five Scottish banks, two are wholly owned by members of the "Big Five," and another of the "Big Five," has a minority interest in a third. The Royal Bank of Scotland, on the other hand, owns two of the English clearing banks (Glyn Mills and Williams Deacon's). The fifth of the Scottish banks, the Bank of Scotland, has no affiliation with any of the English banks.

## American banks

The banking system of the United Kingdom is in striking contrast to that of the United States. There are some 14,000 American banks, of which 9,000, chartered under Federal law, are National Banks and 5,000, authorised under the law of one of the 50 States, are called State Banks. Whereas in Britain the two largest banks have over 2,000 branches each, in the United States the *total* number of branches does not exceed 4,000, most of these being sub-offices in the home town.[1] This difference arises because American legislation is dominated by fear of a banking monopoly—a "Money Trust"—and either prohibits branch-banking (as in many of the States) or submits it to stringent limitations. While the British system puts a small number of very strong banks in a semi-monopolistic position, the American system runs the risk of extensive bank failures. Between 1921 and 1933 no less than 10,000 American banks closed their doors. The events of those years are not likely to repeat themselves,

---

[1] In Chicago, for example, there is no branch-banking at all and there are only two banking offices in the whole of the central part of the city. On the other hand, in California branch-banking is allowed anywhere in the State; and in New York there are a number of very large branch banks with offices in various parts of the town. (R. S. Sayers, *American Banking System*, pp. 21–23).

and the system is now far more capable of weathering a financial crisis; but the risk of bank failures is still far greater than in Britain.[1]

## BANK LIABILITIES

### Deposits

The resources of the British banks are drawn mainly from depositors. (See Table 24). The banks continue to attach importance to the total of their capital, reserves and undivided profits, no doubt because the value of their assets fluctuates and might fall below their deposit liabilities. They are likely, therefore, to go on raising capital from shareholders; but for all practical purposes we can ignore this quaint piece of ritual and treat bank liabilities as co-extensive with deposits. We may also ignore, among the deposit liabilities, the so-called "other accounts" which consist partly of hidden reserves and partly of the "float" of cheques drawn by the customers of one bank on the customers of other banks and in course of collection from them. These form no part of the net deposit liabilities of the banks to their customers at any point in time.

Nearly two-thirds of bank deposits in England and Wales and rather less than half in Scotland are on current account: these earn no interest, are withdrawable on demand and can be drawn upon by cheque. The remaining deposits are held on deposit account: these earn a rate of interest which is usually 2 per cent. under Bank Rate, can be withdrawn only at seven days' notice and are not directly chequable. In practice, banks are usually prepared to allow money to be transferred from time to time from deposit to current account without notice but subject to loss of interest, so that deposit accounts are not appreciably less liquid than current accounts. The distinction between current and deposit accounts is not unlike the distinction in other countries such as the United States between "demand" and "time" deposits; but in those countries there is usually more competition and more variety in the terms on which deposits are accepted and a wide range of periods of notice and rates of interest is offered.

In the United Kingdom the rates paid on deposit accounts and the periods of notice are fixed by agreement among the banks, which compete with one another only in the services they offer. Some of these services are advisory and book-keeping: the banks are willing, for example, to act as trustees, to collect dividends, and to execute wills. Their principal services to

---

[1] America is the only country of importance in which there is no developed system of branch banking. In France, for example, there are four large deposit banks with the head offices in Paris and branches all over the country. In Germany, up to the war, there were three (although now the number of banks runs into hundreds).

their customers, however, consist in facilities for making payment by cheque or standing order and for borrowing from time to time on overdraft. These facilities attach to the current rather than the deposit accounts of their customers whose deposit accounts are merely a convenient reserve of liquidity supplementing their slightly more liquid chequable deposits.

TABLE 24

LONDON CLEARING BANKS: LIABILITIES AND ASSETS, 17TH MARCH, 1965

| | | £million | Per cent of deposits |
|---|---|---|---|
| *Liabilities* | | | |
| Total deposits .. .. .. .. | | 8,722 | 100·00 |
| Current accounts .. .. .. | 4,800 | | 55·0 |
| Deposit accounts .. .. .. | 3,155 | | 36·2 |
| Other accounts .. .. .. | 767 | | 8·8 |
| Capital paid up and reserve funds .. | | 511 | 5·9 |
| Total liabilities .. .. .. .. | | 9,234 | |
| *Assets* | | | |
| Total liquid assets .. .. .. | | 2,571 | 29·5 |
| Cash in hand .. .. .. .. | 433 | | 5·0 |
| Balances with Bank of England .. | 290 | | 3·3 |
| Money at call and short notice .. | 846 | | 9·7 |
| U.K. Treasury Bills .. .. .. | 559 | | 6·4 |
| Other bills and re-financeable credits.. | 443 | | 5·1 |
| Advances to customers and other accounts | | 4,854 | 55·6 |
| Investments at book value .. .. | | 1,048 | 12·0 |
| Balances with other banks and items in tranist .. .. .. .. .. | | 501 | 5·7 |
| Bank premises, investments in affiliated companies etc. .. .. .. | | 260 | 2·9 |
| Total .. .. .. .. .. | | 9,234 | |

BANK ASSETS

**Advances**

The principal use to which the British banks like to put their funds is in advances to customers and these are also the most profitable of bank assets. A small proportion of these advances consists of fixed loans but by far the greater part of them are made on overdraft. Borrowers on overdraft are allowed to withdraw money up to an agreed limit and are charged interest on the outstanding balance at a rate that is normally 1 per cent. over Bank Rate, with a minimum of 5 per cent. The security for the advance varies with the customer: the most usual collateral consists of stock exchange securities but advances are also made against life insurance policies, commodities, personal guarantees or the unsupported credit of the borrower.

From the point of view of the average borrower a bank overdraft is usually much the most convenient and generally also the cheapest source of credit. His financial position can be more readily explained to his bank manager than to other institutions with which he has less frequent and intimate contacts and he can either make repayments or add to his outstanding debt, within the agreed limits, without any need for renegotiation of the loan. The most important drawback, if he is faced not with a seasonal but with a continuing need for credit, is that bank overdrafts are reviewed annually so that he may be called upon to reduce his overdraft at an awkward moment. Banks do, however, lend for periods much longer than a year—for example, for the purchase of a farm or a house or to finance an extension of plant—and although they are rarely willing to make the loan formally one extending over several years, they may give an informal undertaking not to call for repayment so long as they are satisfied that they hold adequate collateral or can count on the gradual elimination of the overdraft out of current earnings.

## Term loans

In other countries, notably the United States, there has been a growth in what are called "term" loans—fixed loans for a definite term of years, rarely extending beyond ten—and this practice may also develop in the United Kingdom. It has the virtue of certainty and allows the borrower to make firm plans for the use of the borrowed money; but it may involve him in higher rates of interest, and offer less flexibility in repayment. The borrower may also be confident that a less formal arrangement, renewed from year to year, will not lead to any embarrassment so long as his affairs are in good order, since the banks do not like to abuse their dominant position and have every incentive to keep the good will of their customers. For this reason the banks like to maintain their other assets in a sufficiently liquid form to be able to refrain from calling in their loans and to meet any unexpected increase in the use made of overdraft facilities or in the pressure to expand them.

In principle the British banks do not like to lock up their money in long-term investments. They are particularly averse to investments that involve them in exercising control over the management of industrial and commercial undertakings although their directors may themselves also sit on the boards of such undertakings. This attitude derives partly from the relative importance of deposits as a source of their funds and partly from the comparative ease with which industrial expansion could be financed in England in the formative years of banking development. In some of the continental countries where the capital market was less highly developed, the links between banking and industry were closer from the start because the finance which the banks were able to mobilise was indispensable to some of the larger and more capital-intensive projects upon which industrialisation depended.

## Self-liquidating advances

The general preference of the British banks is for advances which help to tide over a temporary shortage of funds. The shortage may be a seasonal one as in agriculture where the farmer is faced at harvest-time with a heavy outlay in wages which he will recover only when his crop is sold. In the same way merchants may make use of their overdraft facilities as stocks rise to a temporary peak and make repayment as they sell off the surplus and let their stocks run down again to a normal level. An industrialist may deal with a temporary divergence between outgoings and receipts in the same way and so also may a private consumer faced with large demands for payment of income tax. Bank advances can thus be turned over from one use to another, relieving financial pressure in a succession of different parts of the economy. There is a continuous process of repayment and renewal of bank indebtedness as each transaction is brought to a close and succeeded by others.

Not all bank advances, however, conform to this self-liquidating pattern. Many businesses maintain a substantial overdraft throughout the year and would be highly embarrassed if obliged to repay the entire amount within twelve months. There are also various forms of medium financing in which the banks now engage: they provide credit to exporters for periods of up to five years against guarantees from the Export Credits Guarantee Department; they have made loans for a term of years for purposes such as tanker construction; they are shareholders in the Industrial and Commerical Finance Corporation, which makes long-term investments in industry, and they own or control most of the larger hire-purchase finance houses; they have also begun to make personal loans for the purchase of motor-cars and other durable goods by consumers; and they have long made a practice of lending to farmers and householders for the purchase of farms and house property. Their preference for short-term, self-liquidating advances is not allowed, therefore, to govern their lending policy to the exclusion of medium and longer-term loans.

This preference originated in the days when a small bank might have to meet a sudden run on its deposits and had to be ready to turn its assets quickly into cash. Even in those days the banks by no means confined their lending to short-term requirements and often participated in investment in railways and similar enterprises. In present circumstances, the chances that a bank's deposits will suddenly melt away can be regarded as negligible and the only justification for preferring short-term to long-term advances is that it is easier for a bank manager to assess the credit-worthiness of a customer over a limited period than to gauge his long-term prospects.[1]

### Limits to bank advances

There is a limit to the proportion of a bank's assets which it can safely employ in advances to customers. Whether they are self-liquidating or not, bank advances are not a particularly liquid asset. They cannot be sold because there is no market in them; an advance involves a personal assessment of the borrower's credit—of the security which he offers, of his character and ability, and of the prospects of his business—and the bank manager's assessment is not one that other people unacquainted with the borrower could make with the same confidence. There are also difficulties in the way of contracting bank advances either by refusing to renew loans or by calling them in. The denial of overdraft facilities is a very personal transaction, unlike the sale of Treasury Bills or gilt-edged securities on the market to the most willing buyer. It may mean the loss of a customer; it may even push a customer into bankruptcy; and it is quite likely, if too sudden and pressing, to force the borrower to realise some of his assets at far below their true value. Thus if a bank finds it necessary to contract credit, it is likely to play for time by selling off investments rather than reduce its advances too rapidly. Similarly, if a bank finds itself accumulating large surplus funds it will generally invest them in government securities, rather than relax too far the standards of security which it requires from borrowers.

The London Clearing Banks would probably be willing to see their advances reaches between 55 and 60 per cent. of their deposit liabilities. In 1929 the proportion reached 56 per cent.; but in the ensuing slump the proportion fell steeply, falling below 40 per cent. in 1933. The banks maintained their overdraft rate at 5 per cent. even when long-term rates were below 3 per cent. and short-term rates so low that it was actually cheaper to borrow money for

---

[1] "The great majority of overdraft agreements made by the banks must be based, at least in large part, on the judgment of branch managers, and these managers may reasonably be expected to assess the capacity of a borrower to repay in a short time, though they could have no assurance in estimating long-term profitability. English bankers have therefore traditionally regarded, and continue to regard, themselves as properly engaged in financing working capital, particularly of the 'seed-time to harvest' kind, 'bridging transactions', and (within cautious limits) the temporary financing of fixed capital developments pending the raising of long-term finance through other channels. Thus the lending banker does not directly promote the purchase of real resources, but stands ready to help with temporary finance the business man who embarks on the 'real' transactions." (*Report of the Committee on the Working of the Monetary System*, para. 136).

three months than to print it. As a result of this policy many businesses paid off their outstanding bank loans out of capital borrowed on long-term on the Stock Exchange, or financed themselves out of their own reserves without recourse to the banks, or borrowed at low rates outside the banking system altogether. The growing importance of holding companies worked in the same direction, for the debts of one company in the group could be financed out of the credit balance of another. At the outbreak of war in 1939 bank advances were still only 40 per cent. of deposits.

During the war the downward trend in the ratio was resumed. The banks were under pressure to lend to the government rather than to the private sector, while firms engaged on government contracts were able to obtain much of the finance they needed from progress payments without resort to the banks. By the autumn of 1945 bank advances were down to 15 per cent. of deposits— far below what the banks regarded as desirable or normal. Throughout the post-war period they remained under-lent, largely because business had accu-mulated large liquid reserves during the war and was not able to make use of the surplus very rapidly so long as investment was limited by various controls and by shortages of materials and equipment. Apart from any falling-off in demand, bank advances were subject to regulation, formal or informal, by the government. The banks were invited to refrain from lending for speculative purposes and to give preference to borrowers with export contracts. They were also called upon in 1955 to make a "positive and significant reduction" in the levels of their advances, and in 1956 were summoned to a meeting with the Chancellor of the Exchequer to be told that "the contraction of credit should be resolutely pursued." Thus the recovery of bank advances was limited first by a system of qualitative regulation of credit facilities in accordance with government requests and latterly by a general freeze which made it necessary to ration credit within a fixed ceiling. It was only after 1958 that the banks were free to take full advantage of their opportunities of lending, trying out new types of loan and entering lines of business such as hire purchase finance which they would have been debarred from entering earlier. At the end of 1964, after a remarkable upswing that raised advances by the Clearing Banks to twice their end-1958 level, a fresh credit squeeze began. Although the ratio of advances to deposits was by then over 50 per cent., the banks did not appear to regard this as excessive, or feel obliged, on grounds of liquidity, to refrain from in-creasing their lending. For a generation the level of advances in Britain has been controlled by factors other than the liquidity of the banks.

Bank credit forms a more important element in the calculations of small borrowers than large. It is true that the accounts of public companies do not show much variation between small and large companies in the ratio of bank

Q

credit to total net assets; it is also remarkable that this ratio averages, for all quoted companies, no more than 4 per cent.—a reminder of the limited role of bank credit in industrial finance.[1] But the indebtedness of a company to its banker, as shown in its balance sheet, does not measure the degree of its dependence on bank credit when it is in difficulties or is trying to expand.[2] Large public companies, and even smaller ones, have a much wider array of alternative sources of finance than small private businesses, which would normally turn first to their banker for additional credit.

The bulk of the advances made by the banks, measured in value, are, however, for large amounts. Of the total outstanding at the end of 1958 one-fifth was for sums in excess of £1m., and two-thirds for sums in excess of £10,000 although all but 2 per cent. of the borrowers had advances under £10,000. (See Table 25).

TABLE 25

LONDON CLEARING BANKS: ADVANCES BY SIZE, 1958

|  | Number % | Value % |
|---|---|---|
| Under £10,000     .. | 98·07 | 33·2 |
| £10,000–£100,000..     .. | 1·75 | 22·9 |
| £100,000–£1m.   ..     .. | 0·165 | 23·0 |
| Over £1m.     ..     .. | 0·015 | 20·8 |
|  | 100·0 | 100·0 |

*Source:* Evidence given to Committee on the Working of the Monetary System.

### Investments

The investments of the banks are nowadays almost exclusively in British Government securities. They are more liquid than advances, in the sense that they can be realised at short notice, but less liquid than other bank assets because, since they are long-term investments, realisation may involve a capital

---

[1] B. Tew and R. F. Henderson, *op. cit.*, pp. 80–82.
[2] Of those public companies that had a bank overdraft in the years 1949–53, nearly two-thirds of the smallest size-group had *large* overdrafts compared with only about one-quarter of the companies in the largest size-group. Most large companies, run an overdraft but only a minority of small ones; this minority, however, borrows more heavily. (B. Tew and R. F. Henderson, *loc. cit.*)

loss. In the nineteenth century, before the days of Treasury Bills, a bank would have regarded its holdings of government securities as perhaps the most liquid assets in its portfolio. They had a wide market at a very stable value and a large block could be sold in a short time at a price known in advance. Even discounted bills, although superficially far more liquid, were in practice less so. They were invariably held to maturity because to put them on the market, with a bank's name on them, might give rise to undesirable speculation as to the bank's reason for selling them. Today the situation has changed. Once customers' requirements for loans and investments have been met, the main choice no longer lies between short-term commercial paper and long-term government securities. The supply of commercial paper is much more limited; and the money market deals principally in short-term government paper—Treasury Bills and short bonds with less than five years to run to maturity—which was of negligible importance until the first world war brought into existence a large floating debt.

The banks are amply provided, therefore, with short-term investments which are extremely liquid and which they need have no hesitation in selling. At the same time, long-term government securities have lost much of their attraction. They are not stable in value, but have fallen progressively ever since the war, the fall being heaviest in the longer-dated and irredeemable issues. In the nineteenth century, the banks found it particularly convenient to hold Consols; but they would now regard Consols, because they are irredeemable, as a most inappropriate and illiquid investment. Of their total holdings of government securities about half consist of short bonds. These are more stable in value but not always easy to sell in large blocks because the banks between them hold such a large proportion of the outstanding issues. In 1957 they held, together with the discount houses, over half the total amount in the hands of the public.[1]

The banks regard their investments as a residual use of funds so long as advances are below the level at which they would consider themselves fully lent. On the one hand, they might be prepared to let advances rise to perhaps 60 per cent. of deposit liabilities; on the other, they have to hold about 30 per cent. in reserves and liquid assets of various kinds. This means that they could let their investments fall to around 10 per cent. of deposits before limiting their total advances in the interests of liquidity.[2] In practice, they might go further

---

[1] *Report of the Committee on the Working of the Monetary System*, p. 198. For longer-dated government securities the corresponding proportion was a little over one-fifth.

[2] This assumes a rough equality between the total of advances, investments and liquid assets and total deposit liabilities. In practice, this equality is by no means exact because there are other assets and liabilities in a bank's balance-sheet (e.g., its capital, the "float" of cheques in course of collection, bank premises, etc.).

if they had strong reasons for wanting to sell government securities or they might stop short through reluctance to incur losses on such sales. More probably, they would not be left entirely free to choose the precise distribution of their assets between advances (which are mainly to the private sector) and investments (which are almost entirely loans to the public sector) but would be given strong hints by the monetary authorities as to the policy they should pursue, or obliged to comply with the wishes of the authorities through one or other of the devices discussed in Chapter 29.

Historically, the proportion of investments to deposits has fluctuated widely. In the late twenties, when bank advances were unusually high in relation to deposits, investments were correspondingly low: for the clearing banks, the proportion of investments to deposits was about one-seventh. This proportion doubled in the slump of the early thirties, the banks increasing their investments as their customers paid off more and more of their overdrafts. The higher proportion was maintained in the war and fell only gradually once the war was over. Indeed, it was not until the ending of the credit squeeze of 1955–58, and the sharp increase in advances that succeeded it, that the banks were able to bring their asset ratios within reach of traditional "norms." Between the end of 1958 and the middle of 1965 their investment ratio fell from nearly 30 per cent. to under 12 per cent.

**Liquid assets**

The liquid assets of the clearing banks include the first five items shown in Table 24. Taken together they form a proportion of total deposits which fluctuates seasonally and reaches a minimum in March when the banks' holdings of Treasury Bills—the largest of the five items—are reduced by the usual seasonal reduction in government borrowing. The seasonal minimum since 1963 has been 28 per cent., but at other times of year the proportion is a good deal higher and even in March it is not always allowed to fall to 28 per cent.

The clearing banks used to treat cash in hand and balances at the Bank of England as their first line of reserve, and it was this cash reserve rather than total liquid assets that was significant for monetary policy. Today, however, the proportion of cash to deposits is held almost rigidly at 8 per cent.; and the action which the banks take in order to restore the proportion when it is disturbed has ceased, for technical reasons, to be of major importance. They need only exchange one liquid asset for another, and so long as their total liquid assets are unaffected, the money supply will be unchanged.

The next item, money at call and short notice, is of about the same order of magnitude. Most of this money is lent on a day-to-day basis to the discount market, which in turn lends most of it to the government by holding Treasury Bills or short-dated government bonds.[1] The special significance of call-money in the British monetary system will become apparent when we deal with the discount houses.

Finally, the banks are large holders of Treasury Bills and, to a much smaller extent, of commercial bills. Treasury Bills are government securities with a maturity that is usually of 91 days and occasionally of 63 days. They are issued by tender every week, allotment being made to the highest bidder, and as the price at which they are sold is below their face or redemption value, the difference, or discount, provides a return to the holder and is the effective yield on the bill. The practice of the clearing banks is not to tender their own account (although they do so for customers) but to acquire bills by purchase from the discount market. It is also the practice of the banks so to arrange their portfolio that some bills mature every week or even every day.

The supply of Treasury Bills varies with the fiscal requirements of the government and its success in selling longer-term securities to the public. If more Treasury Bills are issued and taken up by the banks and the discount market, the liquid assets of the banks are augmented either directly through their purchases of bills or indirectly through increased loans to the discount market. The credit base is thus enlarged and the money supply is free to grow correspondingly.

## OTHER FINANCIAL INSTITUTIONS

### Bills of exchange

We have referred above to the commercial bills held by the clearing banks and we shall find that these bills are also of some importance in the operations of the discount market and the accepting houses. The legal definition of a bill of exchange is that it is "an unconditional order in writing, addressed by one person to another, signed by the person giving it, requiring the person to whom it is addressed to pay on demand or at a fixed or determinable future time a sum certain in money to or to the order of a specified person or to bearer." The person to whom it is addressed "accepts" the bill by signing it, usually on the understanding that the drawer will put him in funds by the date the bill falls due and pay him a commission for acceptance. This commission is in recognition of the added marketability that the bill enjoys when it carries the name of an acceptor of undoubted credit-worthiness. Most bills are drawn

---

[1] At the end of 1964 the London clearing banks had lent £882 m. at call or short notice, of which the discount market had borrowed £705 m.

for a period of three months and are a means of obtaining credit for that period, the bill being sold, or "discounted," after acceptance so as to enable the drawer to obtain payment at once. Other bills ("sight drafts") are payable on presentation and are primarily a means of settlement of international transactions.

Although some bills continue to be used to finance purchases from another part of the country ("inland bills"), most bills arise in connection with imports and exports. An importer of wool, for example, may pay with a bill of exchange drawn on his bank or on one of the London acceptance houses: the exporter will turn the bill over to his bank (together with various other documents) and ask to have it discounted in London after acceptance. The bill is purchased on the strength of the acceptor's standing in the market and the exporter is paid from the proceeds while the importer obtains credit from the holder of the bill. By the time the bill falls due, the importer will have sold his wool and be able to send the acceptance house the funds necessary for paying the bill.

The importance of the London bill in the nineteenth century was that it helped to finance the large volume of trade between London and the rest of the world and was a means by which other countries were able to borrow at short term in London. There is still a close connection between the volume of bills drawn and the volume of British trade; but the London discount market is no longer a channel through which credit flows in large net amounts to other countries. At the same time, bills of exchange have grown more slowly than Treasury Bills, which now account for the larger part of the business of the discount market.

### Discount houses

One of the unique features of the British monetary system is the discount market. This consists of twelve large discount houses and about the same number of smaller firms which are not members of the Discount Market Association and are mainly engaged in other, more specialised, activities. The assets of the larger houses are of the order of £1,000m., of which all but about one-tenth consists of Treasury Bills and gilt-edged securities. To finance these holdings, the market operates largely on borrowed funds, nearly all supplied by the banks, including overseas and foreign banks; in view of the fluctuations in their cash position it is a convenience to the banks to be able to employ a temporary surplus of cash in this way by lending it on a day-to-day basis to the discount market.

The special importance of the discount market arises because it is through the market that the Bank of England acts in its capacity of "lender of last resort." If there is a shortage of funds, and rates of interest are being pressed up against Bank Rate, it is the discount houses which are able to go to the Bank of England and borrow against eligible paper.[1] The commercial banks are not able to do so but can transfer any squeeze on their own cash position to the discount market by reducing their loans to it. The market thus acts as a buffer between the central bank and the commercial banks. This had its convenience in circumstances when the central bank was content to exercise pressure almost exclusively through the bill market and when it was anxious to keep its distance from the market, as a lender of last resort, rather than operate continuously in it. The arrangement is less satisfactory in present circumstances when monetary policy involves a much closer co-ordination between the operations of the central bank and those of the commercial banks.

Because of its position as the most sensitive element in the bill market, it is in the discount market that any pressure on funds first makes itself felt. This pressure is reflected in the movement of short-term interest rates and the market occupies a strategic place, therefore, in the determination of those rates. If the Bank of England makes open market sales of securities, the immediate effect is to reduce the cash reserves of the commercial banks, force them to replenish their cash at the expense of the discount market and oblige the market in turn to come to the Bank for assistance. This enables the Bank to make its rate effective; if the discount houses are forced into the Bank on relatively onerous terms,[2] they inevitably stiffen the rates at which they themselves are prepared to tender for Treasury Bills. The same effect can be (and is) obtained by simply increasing the size of the weekly tender, since this amounts to putting more bills on the market, so producing a fall in their price and a corresponding rise in the rate of discount. If Bank Rate is increased, a further impulse is given to the rise in bill rates from the side of costs, since the commercial banks will raise their loan rates to the discount market, and this will increase the minimum rate at which bill-brokers can afford to trade. Even if Bank Rate does not increase, but the market merely expects an increase, the expectation will be sufficient to cause a precautionary rise in discount rates. New bills acquired at current prices will not mature for three months and any rise in interest rates over that period would involve a fall in their value; any strong expectation of such a rise, therefore, makes the market reluctant to tender except at a rate which is sufficiently high to discount the danger of a further increase.

---

[1] Eligible paper consists either of Treasury Bills or gilt-edged securities with less than five years to run ("short bonds") or of first-class commercial bills that satisfy certain conditions laid down by the Bank of England. In other money markets, the central bank is usually prepared to rediscount bills but in Britain it rarely does so.

[2] The discount houses have to borrow at Bank Rate (and for a minimum of seven days) whereas the money lent to them by the commercial banks (on a day-to-day basis) bears a rate 1 to $1\frac{3}{4}$ per cent. below Bank Rate.

In the last thirty years a major change has taken place in the relations between the Bank of England and the discount market. An understanding now exists that the discount houses will always "cover the tender" for Treasury Bills by a syndicated bid while the Bank of England will ensure that the market has adequate funds for this purpose. This means that the Bank is less of a "lender of last resort" and that the market is much more frequently "in the Bank"; it also means that the power of the Bank to control the movement of interest rates is exercised more directly, whether by "smoothing" purchases and sales of bills or by regulation of the tender issue of Treasury Bills.

In comparison with other countries, however, it is one of the features of the British system that the market does not expect to draw its resources to any appreciable extent from the central bank. It is the regular practice elsewhere, but not in Britain, for the commercial banks to obtain funds by rediscounting bills, promissory notes and other "eligible paper" from the central bank, and it is largely through its control over the supply of such funds that the central bank exerts its influence on the money supply.

### Accepting houses

Among the financial institutions which accept bills of exchange are the accepting houses. These are sometimes referred to as "merchant bankers" and most of them were originally merchant houses engaged in trade before specialising in financial operations. Their standing as traders made it advantageous to have their name on a bill, so that from accepting their own bills they were induced in course of time to accept bills for others. There are eighteen members of the Accepting Houses Committee and between them, they accept 20–25 per cent. of all bills outstanding. Their name on a bill, together with one other British name, makes it a Bank bill, eligible for discount at the Bank of England, and ensures that the drawer will be able to discount it on the most favourable possible terms.

In addition to their acceptance business, all of the accepting houses do ordinary banking business on behalf of their customers. This largely arises out of their accepting and other business and is ancillary to it. Their deposits, for example, are drawn largely from foreign banks and companies or from long-established domestic customers. These deposits, as was apparent in 1957, are highly volatile and make it necessary to hold large liquid assets. A high proportion of these in recent years has taken the form of short loans to local authorities.

Apart from merchanting, foreign exchange and other business, the accepting houses also act as investment advisers and as issuing houses. They are by no means the only issuing houses but include many of the largest.

## Issuing houses

The function of an issuing house is to sponsor and guarantee a new issue rather than to find the money out of its own resources. The issuing house first discusses the terms of the issue with its client and satisfies itself that the amount sought is reasonable and likely to be forthcoming on terms acceptable to the borrower. Since its own reputation is involved in the making of the issue, the issuing house has to study both the financial needs of its client and the general economic outlook with a view to choosing the best method of raising fresh capital and the best time at which to go to the market. This expert examination assists the borrower in getting satisfactory terms and at the same time gives the investor confidence that the issue is a well-considered one and made under reputable auspices.

Once the issuing house has agreed to make the issue it makes itself responsible for the underwriting and sets about arranging the sub-underwriting with insurance companies, investment trusts and other institutional investors.[1] It also prepares the prospectus, draws up the advertisements that are required, and carries out all the necessary negotiations with the Stock Exchange authorities. If it is desired to save the cost of a prospectus issue, the issuing house may "place" the issue privately with financial institutions.

Not all issues in Britain are made by issuing houses. For example, the large issues by the British government and by the nationalised industries make no use of the services of an issuing house and are handled directly by the Bank of England. The main clients of the issuing houses are public companies and local authorities. But even public companies may dispense with an issuing house and use an issuing broker, who does not have the same close and continuous contacts with his clients. About 40 per cent. by value of the money raised in Britain by public companies since the war has been raised by issuing brokers rather than by issuing houses.

## Insurance companies and pension funds

The importance of the insurance companies and pension funds in the British capital market can be judged from the rate at which their assets are increasing—over £1,100m. per annum. This increase reflects both the saving undertaken by individual policy-holders and the spread of group schemes designed to provide pensions for the employees of business firms and other corporate bodies. The amounts saved in this way may be abnormally high because the population is still in the process of "ageing" (in the sense that the proportion of the population in the higher age-groups is steadily increasing) and pension rights are

---

[1] An underwriter guarantees, for a commission, to take up any part of a new issue for which the public fails to subscribe at the price of the issue.

Q*

therefore accumulating at a faster rate than they are being drawn upon. This enables the insurance companies to add to their funds out of current premium income and so to make provision for the pensions they will eventually have to pay. On the other hand, the fact that inflation tends to diminish the real value of an insurance policy that is fixed in money terms may be to some extent a deterrent to this form of private saving.

The life insurance companies invest their funds almost exclusively on long term. At the end of the war an abnormally high proportion of their assets took the form of gilt-edged securities, as they had been under pressure to support the market for government bonds and so assist the government's borrowing operations. In post-war condition, government bonds were a relatively unattractive investment because of the steady fall in the price of fixed interest securities, and equities were correspondingly attractive, all the more because of the temporary distortion of the insurance companies' asset structure. A large proportion of the current accretion to their funds was therefore invested in equities, the proportion varying from company to company and from year to year. The pension funds have shown similar investment preferences. In 1963–64 half the value of the net new assets acquired was represented by equities.

The insurance companies and pension funds are also large lenders to local authorities, usually for periods of ten years or longer. Another substantial proportion of their funds is invested in company debentures. The remainder of their assets are distributed between preference shares, real property, mortgages (especially mortgages on offices, shops, flats and similar blocks of property) and—to a diminishing extent—Commonwealth and foreign government securities.

The insurance companies are interested only in the return which they obtain on their investments, not in the control or management of the companies whose securities they acquire. They prefer to limit their stake in any one company so as to avoid having to exercise such control as well as to ensure the marketability of their holding.

Because they are such large buyers of securities, the insurance companies are an important element in the new issue market. They engage in underwriting and are likely to do at least half the underwriting of a new issue. This activity, combined with their purchases of stocks and shares, contributes towards the finance of British industry by making it easier to raise capital on the Stock Exchange.

### Investment trusts

An investment trust invests the money entrusted to it by shareholders (or borrowed on debenture) in a diversified range of securities so as to obtain for them a higher or more secure return than they could obtain through individual investment. The portfolio of the investment trust may be varied at the discretion of the management—as in the older type of "managed" trusts—or it may be restricted to a list of securities set out in the trust deed—as is usual with "unit" trusts. The subscriber to a unit trust does not buy shares in a limited liability company but is issued with a certificate at a price that reflects the market value of the underlying securities held by the trust, and can sell the certificate back to the managers at a price that is calculated in the same way but leaves a margin for operating expenses. Additional certificates can be sold by the management whenever there is a demand for them, without the need to issue a special prospectus or, indeed, make any announcement.[1]

In Britain the managed trusts held assets with a market value in 1965 of about £3,000m. Until the late fifties unit trusts were not much in the public eye but a large number of issues were made in the next few years and by 1964 their assets had passed £400m. Even this total did not quite restore them to the relative position which they held in the market in the late thirties and it fell far short of the corresponding total for the American "mutual funds" which are the Transatlantic equivalent of unit trusts. In March 1959 the assets of the mutual funds were already over £5,000m. and were increasingly rapidly.

The early success of British investment trusts was attributable to the skill of their managements. This was particularly evidenced in the investments which they made in other countries, about whose affairs they were more knowledgeable than the average private investor. Their later popularity owes more to the continuance of inflation. Nearly the whole of their portfolio is in equities and it is the conviction that a diversified holding of ordinary shares is the best hedge against inflation that has created so ready a market for unit trust certificates.

Like insurance companies investment trusts act as underwriters and like them do not usually seek to exercise control over the companies in which they invest. Some investment trusts, however, have links with companies specialising in the finance of promising small businesses which they intend later to float on the Stock Exchange, and some trusts also make investments in the unquoted securities of smaller companies. The total amount of money provided to industry in these ways is relatively small and not comparable with the substantial holdings of the investment trusts in freely marketed industrial securities.

## Building societies

The building societies are keen competitors for small savings, which they

---

[1] For this reason, unit trusts are sometimes referred to as "open-end" trusts.

apply mainly to the finance of house-ownership. The money deposited with them amounted at the end of 1964 to some £5,000m., held in over four million names. Most of this represented "shares" rather than deposits; but shares in a building society are in practice almost indistinguishable from deposits in spite of the formal requirement to give one month's notice (or longer) of withdrawal. There is usually a steady inflow of new funds which is supplemented by repayments by borrowers, and these funds are used to make loans on a first mortgage within the United Kingdom. Over two million property-owners have building society mortgages which they are in process of paying off over a period of years; most mortgages are for periods of twenty years or more, but because borrowers are able to accelerate the rate of repayment the average period for which mortgages are outstanding is well under twenty years. The vast majority of the borrowers are private house-owners and it has been estimated that the societies provide finance for about two-thirds of private house-building. Some of the societies lend to builders as well as to house-owners and a few of them have also engaged in the finance of commercial property development, not always with satisfactory results.

The rates of interest payable to their shareholders and depositors is governed by the competition which the societies have to meet. They generally defer an increase until they find the inflow of funds affected by the offer of more attractive terms by local authorities or by other institutions such as the Trustee Savings Banks or the hire purchase finance companies. If, on the other hand, the inflow is becoming embarrassingly large, they may limit the amount which they are prepared to receive annually from any one person. The lag in their borrowing rates is paralleled by a lag in their lending rates. These are not fixed for the entire period of a mortgage, as are other long-term rates, but can be revised upwards or downwards with market conditions; the societies are not in so vulnerable a position, therefore, as one might expect from the liquidity of their liabilities and the illiquidity of their assets. They are naturally reluctant, however, to make frequent changes in mortgage rates and if faced with a shrinkage of funds are inclined to limit their lending by introducing more stringent conditions rather than make immediate adjustments in the rates at which they borrow and lend.

### Hire-purchase finance houses

Instalment credit or hire-purchase finance is mainly of importance in the United Kingdom in the sale of durable consumers' goods. The total amount of credit outstanding in 1965 was about £1,200m. of which nearly half had been advanced for the purchase of motor-cars and commercial vehicles, and about a quarter for furniture, most of the remainder being for electrical equipment of all kinds, such as radio and television sets, washing machines and so on. Comparatively little hire-purchase credit is used in Britain for purchases of business equipment, the total amount, inclusive of motor vehicles of all kinds, being of the order of £150m. There is evidence, however, that hire-purchase credit is extensively used for the purchase of vehicles, plant and machinery by small and growing firms.

A large part of this credit is provided directly by retailers and dealers but the bulk of it comes from a specialised group of institutions—the hire-purchase finance houses. There are a very large number of those institutions, most of them relatively small; of the larger ones which are members of the Finance Houses Association, the majority are linked with, or controlled by, one of the clearing banks. These larger finance houses draw their funds partly from their own capital, partly from the commercial banks, and partly from unsecured deposits by business concerns and others. They usually prefer to rely on the banks for most of the necessary money but if there are impediments to this form of borrowing they can attract more money from other sources by the offer of relatively high interest rates. This power to generate additional hire-purchase credit at a time when the monetary authorities are applying a "squeeze" to the banks and other financial institutions gives rise to some uneasiness, since it is felt to be unfair that one set of institutions which competes for deposits should be free from restrictions to which another set of institutions (e.g., the banks) is subject. It is, however, arguable that the more satisfactory way of controlling hire-purchase credit is by operating on the demand for it rather than on the supply. Regulations governing down-payments and maximum periods of repayment are perhaps easier to apply to the comparatively limited range of transactions that involve the use of hire-purchase credit.

## THE BANK OF ENGLAND

We come finally to the most important of British financial institutions, the Bank of England. It is not possible to give more than the briefest account of its work, but something has already been said in Chapter 29 and in the discussion, earlier in this Chapter, of the banks and the discount market.

The Bank of England is first and foremost a central bank whose prime responsibility is to put into effect the monetary policy of the country. As is true of nearly every other central bank, the Bank is publicly owned and acts as the government's bank. But it was a central bank long before it was nationalised and for many years it has acted in close consultation with government departments, especially the Treasury. For the policy which it pursues, the government takes ultimate responsibility; but it is inevitable that in the formulation of that policy the Bank should play a leading part. In giving effect to the policy, the Bank is brought into contact at many points with the entire financial community and enters also into close association with the financial institutions of other countries and with various international financial institutions.

In its domestic business, the Bank acts as financial agent to the government, managing the note issue and the national debt and supervising the issue of all government loans. It is the government's banker, keeping both the central account of the government—the Exchequer Account—and a number of other official accounts. It also provides the government with expert financial advice both on the technical problems of day-to-day monetary operations and on the longer-term issues that arise in connection with those operations.

In its external business, the Bank stands equally close to the government. It manages the Exchange Equalisation Account, engaging in dealings in foreign exchange so as to hold the rate of exchange within the limits accepted by the United Kingdom as a member of the International Monetary Fund; it may also conduct both spot and forward transactions, at its discretion. The regulations governing foreign exchange control are administered by the Bank, the policy governing this control being agreed between the Bank and the Treasury. The Bank also has extensive dealings with the central banks of other countries and with international financial institutions of which the United Kingdom is a member, such as the International Monetary Fund and the Bank for International Settlements. These dealings embrace both actual operations such as the purchase and sale of gold and the management of the sterling holdings of sterling area countries, and the exchange of information and discussion of financial and trade policy.

In addition to its relations with governments and government agencies, the Bank exercises great influence over the operations of British financial institutions. It holds the cash reserves, other than till-money, of the clearing banks and provides them with the kind of facilities in making payment to one another that an ordinary bank customer enjoys from the use of his bank account. There is also frequent and regular contact on monetary operations and policy between the Bank and representatives of the clearing banks, and the Bank is the normal channel of communication between the Treasury and the clearing banks. It acts as banker to the discount houses, which have to maintain working balances with it and are dependent in their operations on the power which they enjoy to obtain cash from the Bank by borrowing against eligible collateral. It is also in close touch with the acceptance houses in order to satisfy itself as to their liquidity.

The contacts of the Bank with other financial institutions are not simply of the banker-customer type nor confined to an exchange of views or an exposition of government policy. They arise to a much greater extent because of the involvement of the Bank in actual dealings in the bill market and in the gilt-edged market. Through its command of the issue of Treasury Bills it is by far the largest operator in the money market and through its command of new issues of government bonds it is by far the largest operator in the gilt-edged market. Its operations are not confined to sales since it can, if it chooses, buy bills, and it regularly engages, for technical reasons, in large-scale switching operations in bonds. We have already seen (pp. 464–5) the close connection that exists between monetary policy and debt management; this connection finds expression in the United Kingdom in the combination of functions which makes the Bank of England manage the public debt as well as carry out all the other duties of a central bank.

### The Federal Reserve Board

In this the situation in the United Kingdom differs from that in the United States where the functions are divided between the Treasury on the one hand and the Federal Reserve Board on the other. There is also a different relationship between the commercial banks and the central monetary authorities. There is no American bank corresponding to the Bank of England. Instead, there are twelve Federal Reserve Banks, one in each of the twelve Federal Reserve districts and a Board of Governors of the Federal Reserve System sitting in Washington. The Federal Reserve Board acts as a central bank but it does not have the same range of executive responsibilities as the Bank of England and is much more of a policy-shaping body.

The Federal Reserve Banks act as bankers' banks for their members who include most, but by no means all, of the commercial banks. They hold the cash reserves of the member banks, rediscount bills for them and lend to them, provide them with clearing facilities, and act as a link between their members and the Board of Governors in Washington. They also issue about two-thirds of the total note circulation of the United States. The powers of the Board of Governors were originally supervisory but were greatly strengthened in 1935. They can prescribe the minimum reserve ratio to be preserved between the cash deposits of member banks at the Reserve Banks and customers' deposits at the member banks; they can fix maximum rates of interest on deposits, whether with member banks or non-member banks; and they have final authority over discount and other interest rates charged by the Reserve Banks. A separate body, although all the Governors are members—the Federal Open Market Committee—controls purchases of government securities by the Reserve Banks. The Federal Advisory Council, which is composed of twelve representatives of the member banks, advises the Board of Governors on the views of member-bankers. Lastly, there is the U.S. Treasury itself, sometimes in sharp conflict with the Federal Reserve System, and armed with ample powers (particularly over gold and foreign exchange) to interfere with its operation if it wishes to do so.

# PART VI—INTERNATIONAL TRADE AND FINANCE

CHAPTER 31

# INTERNATIONAL TRADE

### Trade and specialisation

There is no fundamental cleavage between one kind of trade and another. All trade, whether between persons, towns, regions, or countries, originates in specialisation, and, whatever form specialisation assumes, the principles governing it are the same. A person, by specialising and exchanging, supplements his natural or acquired gifts out of the comparative proficiencies of his neighbours; in the same way, a region by trading with other regions, supplements the resources with which it is most poorly supplied out of the comparative abundance of these resources elsewhere. The individual specialist, in order to make the best use of his limited time and energy, concentrates on a narrow range of tasks, relinquishing to others work which he could readily undertake himself; similarly, a region, in order to make the best use of its limited productive resources, specialises in the industries in which its comparative advantages are greatest and sacrifices other industries, in whole or in part, to competition from outside. It makes little difference whether the boundaries of the region are those of a county or of a country; the broad principles are the same whatever the frontiers across which trade flows.

### International and domestic trade

Regarded as the outcome of geographical specialisation, trade between countries is of no more interest than trade between other areas. Whatever the unit of area, much the same problems present themselves and much the same principles can be applied.

It makes little difference whether we ask of a country or of a county why it does not pursue a policy of self-sufficiency, why it carries on this industry rather than that, and why it is a prosperous area when others are not. Indeed, there is a positive advantage in framing such questions in terms of local rather than of national units. For nothing makes so strongly against clear thinking about trade as the belief that international and domestic trade are fundamentally

497

different from one another, and that, while it is natural and desirable to interfere with the one, it is equally unnatural and undesirable to interfere with the
other. If we were to make a habit of recasting every argument about international trade in terms of inter-county trade we should be imposed upon far less
readily by the gross and mischievous fallacies which colour popular economics.
We should see the inconsistency of the American who supports tariffs on imports from low-wage countries, such as Japan, but never thinks of duties on
imports from low-wage States within the Union, such as Tennessee. We should
see that an unfavourable balance of payments between South Wales or the
Highlands and the rest of Britain has much the same significance as an unfavourable balance between Britain and other countries. And we should realise that,
from the economic point of view, political boundaries are quite arbitrary; that
much the same principles apply to trade between Berlin and Vienna when they
are in different countries as when they are in the same country; that there was
no major change in Ireland's trade when the north was severed from the south,
nor in Britain's when England and Scotland were joined.

### Do we need a separate theory of international trade?

In spite of the fundamental resemblance between international and domestic
trade there are also points of difference. But for these points of difference a
separate theory of international trade would be unnecessary, since it would be
nothing more than a simple application of the general theory of localisation.
It would be sufficient to discuss (as we have already discussed in Chapter 7)
what industries tend to settle in an area with given productive resources and on
what scale these industries will be carried on. But countries are more than geographical areas; they are areas with economic systems of their own, cut off
by political frontiers from the economic systems of their neighbours. They have,
as a rule, their own currency and their own banking system. Their commodity markets are hedged about with customs duties and customs officers.
Their capital-market is partially insulated from other capital-markets by restrictions on the export of capital and by the reluctance of investors to entrust
their capital to distant enterprises and foreign governments. Their labour
market is protected against immigration by visa restrictions and quota regulations as well as by the ordinary deterrents to long-distance migration such as
ignorance of opportunities, travel expenses and language difficulties. Above all,
each country has its own government, controlling trade on a national scale
from the standpoint of national interests. We need a separate theory of international trade, therefore, both to take account of the comparative immobility
of productive resources between one country and another, and in order to
furnish general principles of national policy as a guide to action. First we,

require to adapt the general theory of trade to the facts of immobility; and, second, we require to re-state it in terms of national units—the units of control.

## The implications of immobility

Since the factors of production cannot move freely between one country and another, they are often forced to remain in countries where their productivity is comparatively low, and where, in consequence, they are comparatively poorly paid. Workers who could obtain high wages if admitted to the United States or to Great Britain continue to accept much lower wages in Italy and Japan. Capital which, if invested in India or Poland, might show a high return, continues to be lent at much lower rates to American and British enterprises. Moreover, since resources are not used where their productivity is highest, goods are not produced where costs are lowest. They are certainly produced where *money* costs are lowest, but not where costs are lowest in terms of real resources or of the efforts and sacrifices which go to production. It is far cheaper, in terms of human effort, to grow wheat in Canada than in India. But Indian farmers continue to grow wheat in competition with Canadian farmers. Whatever they grow, their efforts are less amply rewarded than they would be in Canada. So they choose crops which, although not better suited to India than to other countries, are better suited to it than other crops. They choose crops in which, although they may be at an absolute disadvantage in comparison with other countries, they are nevertheless at a *comparative* advantage relatively to other crops. The real cost of growing such crops is higher than elsewhere, but the money cost is lower because a given amount of effort on the part of an Indian worker earns less than the same amount of effort by foreign workers of equal efficiency.

## Absolute and comparative advantages

To illustrate this distinction more fully, let us suppose that there are only two countries, Anywhere and Nowhere, that each produces only two commodities, sugar and salt, and that the only factor of production in either country is labour (land being free and of uniform quality). Let us also suppose that Anywhere is better suited to the production of sugar and Nowhere better suited to the production of salt. For example, let:—

10 days' labour in Anywhere produce 100 units of sugar.

| 10 | ,, | ,, | ,, | ,, | 80 | ,, | salt. |
| 10 | ,, | ,, | Nowhere | ,, | 50 | ,, | sugar. |
| 10 | ,, | ,, | ,, | ,, | 200 | ,, | salt. |

Before trade begins, sugar in Anywhere will sell at four-fifths of the price of salt, while in Nowhere it will fetch four times the price of salt. There will be an obvious advantage to both countries, therefore, if Anywhere exports sugar in exchange for salt at any price within these limits. What price will actually be established will depend upon the strength of the demand for sugar and salt in the two countries. Let us suppose that, the cost of transport being negligible, the price in both countries settles down after the opening of trade at two units of salt per unit of sugar. Then Anywhere, by exporting 100 units of sugar will obtain in return 200 units of salt; so that, by 10 days' labour in sugar production, it saves 25 days' labour in the production of salt. Similarly, by exporting 200 units of salt, which it took ten days to produce, Nowhere obtains 100 units of sugar which it would have taken 20 days to produce; 20 days' labour in the two countries produce as much salt and sugar as formerly required 45 days' labour.

In this example, Anywhere has an absolute and also a comparative advantage in the production of sugar, while Nowhere has an absolute and also a comparative advantage in the production of salt. But suppose that 10 days' labour in Nowhere produce, not 200, but only 50 units of salt. Then Anywhere will have an absolute advantage in the production both of sugar and of salt. It will still be worth its while, however, to trade with Nowhere, for Nowhere retains its comparative advantage in the production of salt; it can produce as many units of salt as of sugar per day's labour, whereas Anywhere can produce only four-fifths as much. At any price between four-fifths and one, both countries will gain from trade. Suppose, for example, that the terms of trade fixed by the joint demand of both countries for sugar and salt are 10 units of sugar for nine units of salt. By expending 10 days' labour in the production of sugar and exporting it in exchange for salt, Anywhere can obtain in return 90 units of salt which would otherwise have taken $11\frac{1}{4}$ days to produce. Similarly, instead of spending 10 days' labour in producing 50 units of sugar, Nowhere can obtain just as much by trade through nine days' labour in salt production. The only real difference from the first example—apart from the smaller gain from trade—is that the lower productivity of labour in both industries in Nowhere reduces wages there below the level in Anywhere. In our first example, wages must be exactly equal in both countries since 100 units of sugar (produced by 10 days' labour in Anywhere) are assumed to be equal in value to 200 units of salt (produced by 10 days' labour in Nowhere). Given terms of trade more favourable to sugar, however, wages will be higher in Anywhere, and given terms more favourable to salt, they will be higher in Nowhere. In the second example, it is easy to calculate that wages in Anywhere will be nine-fifth times wages in Nowhere. Here again, however, relative wage-rates depend upon the terms of trade between sugar and salt, and may lie anywhere between ten-fifths and eight-fifths.

## Incomplete specialisation

There is no suggestion in this argument that a country gains only through the import of goods which it cannot produce for itself. We have explicitly assumed that sugar and salt can be produced both in Anywhere and in Nowhere, and have tried to show that each gains from a policy of specialisation. The logical conclusion of our argument would, in fact, be complete specialisation, Anywhere giving up salt production and Nowhere sugar production. But specialisation is usually limited by forces of which we have taken no account. Both industries, for example, may be subject to increasing marginal costs, so that it is not worth while to expand sugar production in Anywhere beyond a certain point, while it is worth while to continue salt production on a modest scale. To push sugar production further would raise costs excessively, while the cost of producing salt can be kept down so long as the output is low. Transport costs between Anywhere and Nowhere also limit specialisation by adding to the cost, and therefore taking from the profit, of exchanging salt and sugar. It may happen also that Anywhere cannot spare enough sugar, after meeting all its own requirements, to meet the needs of Nowhere. Or some of the sugar produced in Nowhere may be of a special quality which enables it to find a market in the teeth of competition from Anywhere. In the real world, at all events, specialisation is far from complete. In addition to its export industries, each country has industries which compete with imports, and industries which, like building, transport and distribution, supply a sheltered local market, neither exporting nor competing with imports.

## Extension of the argument to more commodities than two

The general lines of reasoning given above can be extended to any number of commodities and to any number of countries. Each country can arrange its products in descending order of comparative advantage—those which it is particular well suited to produce coming at the head of the list and being exported; those which it cannot so easily produce coming at the bottom and being imported. Where the line of division between exports and imports is drawn depends upon the country's terms of trade—that is, upon the price which it obtains for its exports in relation to the price which it pays for its imports. The more favourable its terms of trade, the less will the country require to export in payment for a given quantity of imports; while a deterioration in its terms of trade will force it to export a larger quantity and a wider range of goods. The line of division between exports and imports, therefore, is not fixed, but moves up or down as the terms of trade move in favour of, or against, the country.

### The significance of the terms of trade

A change in the terms on which a country trades with the rest of the world has repercussions of enormous importance upon its whole economic life. If, for example, its exports fall in price, without any accompanying fall in their real cost of production, the gain which the country derives from trade, and with it the general level of incomes, is automatically reduced. If 100 units of sugar, instead of buying 200 units of salt, buy only 100 units, then wages in Anywhere will fall by 50 per cent. In the same way, if Australian wool and wheat fetch lower prices on the world market, Australian farmers will earn lower incomes and pay lower wages; and since incomes and wages in one industry cannot get far out of line with incomes and wages in other industries, the fall in agriculture will initiate a general reduction. If there are other industries in which Australia enjoys a comparative advantage not much inferior to her comparative advantage in wool and wheat, then these industries will come forward as wages fall and will supplement Australian exports. If there are no such industries, if Australia has a very marked comparative advantage in wool and wheat only, and if both of these commodities are in inelastic demand by the rest of the world,[1] then Australia will be particularly vulnerable to an adverse movement in its terms of trade. It will gain enormously from trade so long as wool and wheat prices are high, and lose proportionately when wool and wheat prices fall. A particularly striking example is that of Chile, which was extremely dependent upon its exports of nitre and suffered heavily when artificial nitrates came on the market. The "resourcefulness of supply"—to use a phrase of Marshall's— was low and the vulnerability of Chilean trade was correspondingly high.

Changes in Britain's terms of trade amount, broadly speaking, to changes in the price of manufactured goods relatively to the price of foodstuffs and raw materials. Such changes have been on a large scale, both in the long period and in the short. Within the limits of the trade cycle, for example, the terms of trade tend to move in Britain's favour during the slump and against her during the boom, since the price of foodstuffs and of raw materials oscillates more violently than the price of manufactured goods. Thus she is protected from some of the worst consequences of the slump by a fall in the price of her imports, while her prosperity in the boom is moderated by a rise in their price. In the long period she has had the benefit of steadily improving terms of trade—an improvement which has done a great deal to raise the standard of living in Britain. The revolution in transport and the opening up of distant countries (which Victorian capital financed) have enabled her to acquire much larger quantities of foodstuffs and materials from abroad on terms far better than her

---

[1] Notice the qualification; "by the rest of the world." The demand for wheat is highly inelastic but the demand for *Australian* wheat is not.

own labour could have supplied them and indeed at much less cost in man-hours per unit of imports than a hundred years ago.

One consequence of the change in her terms of trade has been the eclipse of British agriculture. She imports food because she is at a comparative disadvantage in producing it; the cheaper food becomes, the greater is this comparative disadvantage. By employing workers to make manufactured exports she can obtain in return far more food than the same men could produce on British farms. She can afford also to pay them higher wages. By taking men from the land she takes them from an occupation where their productivity is low, and by putting them in industry she puts them in occupations where their productivity is comparatively high. It was by getting workers off the land that the Victorians were able to raise the standard of living. Had they failed to develop new outlets for labour in industry, the law of diminishing returns would soon have made havoc of Victorian "progress."

### Extension of the argument to more countries than two

The fact that there are several countries, not just two, introduces no important complications. From the point of view of each country the rest of the world is a unit which, for trading purposes, can legitimately be regarded as a single country. It is only when governments begin to manoeuvre for bargaining power, or to force trade into the channels of a preconceived policy, that we need to take account of third parties. A policy of Imperial Preference, for example, involves discrimination between empire and foreign countries with a view to fostering trade within the empire. In the same way, a trade agreement may aim at extending trade between the signatories at the expense of other countries. Trade becomes canalised between two countries instead of being carried on, on equal terms, between every trading country. The markets of one country are tied to the export industries of another, while third parties are excluded from markets which they formerly supplied. International trade, as private bargaining between traders gives way to direct bargaining between governments, has to be thought of more and more in terms of international diplomacy—not as a series of bargains struck by free and impersonal competition between traders, but as a struggle for economic power between rival governments. Trade has not, however, gone so far along this road that the principles of comparative advantage are no longer applicable. Nor, since the principles of government bargaining are a perpetual mystery, are there any other principles to put in their place.

### Trade is multilaterial

Although the division of the rest of the world into separate countries works no great change in the principles of international trade, it does create much misunderstanding. People speak as if it were necessary or fair that each country should buy from us as much as we buy from it. But clearly, all that is necessary is that our *total* exports should be as great as our *total* imports—apart from international borrowing or lending. We can have an unfavourable balance with one country so long as we have a favourable balance with some other country. We can go on buying eggs from Denmark, for example, so long as we sell machinery to South Africa. For the South Africans can pay for our eggs by sending oranges to Denmark; or payment may be even more round-about, South African oranges being sold to France, and French wines going to Denmark in payment. Trade is not bilateral; it is multilateral. A coalminer who buys bread does not insist that the baker must buy his coal, nor does the baker try to pay his rent in bread. In the same way, there is no reason why a country should bully each of its neighbours into buying from it as much as they sell to it; it would generally do much better to give thanks for receiving so much at so little cost.[1]

## An Alternative Approach

Our exposition so far has been based on the traditional assumption that there is only one factor of production in each country. This assumption is convenient and illuminating, since it simplifies the reasoning and leads to conclusions of great practical value. But it is also unrealistic and leaves us rather in the dark as to the *origin* of a comparative advantage. It is worth while, therefore, to turn back a little and follow a different track, attaching due importance to the existence of a multiplicity of factors and sub-factors of production.

### International trade and diversity of resources

International trade, like other kinds of trade, originates in the scarcity and diversity of productive resources. The resources of each country are limited, and they differ from the resources of other countries. By trading, therefore, a country enlarges the range of its resources, drawing on the bounty of other countries instead of contenting itself with home-produced articles. By refusing to trade and seeking after self-sufficiency it denies itself access to resources which are relatively scarce—or cannot be found at all—within its borders; it deliberately restricts its "Lebensraum" or "living-room." That this is so of raw

---

[1] *Cf.* Hume: "And no doubt had the Heptarchy persisted in England, the legislature of each state had been continually alarmed by the fear of a wrong balance; and as it is probable that the mutual hatred of these states would have been extremely violent on account of their close neighbourhood, they would have loaded and oppressed all commerce by a jealous and superfluous caution." (Essay on the Balance of Trade.)

materials is generally agreed; everyone sees the advantage of importing essential raw materials. But what is true of natural resources is equally true of labour and of capital. If one country is well endowed with skilled labour, while in another skilled labour is relatively scarce and unskilled labour plentiful, then it will be to the mutual advantage of both countries if the first sells commodities embodying much skilled labour in return for commodities embodying much unskilled labour. Similarly, countries in which capital is scarce relatively to labour can trade profitably with countries in which labour is scarce relatively to capital. It is differences in *relative* scarcity which gives rise to trade, and these differences are by no means confined to raw materials.

Consider, for example, the international trade of Great Britain. Britain is a thickly populated country with abundant skilled labour and capital and comparatively little fertile land. Britain, therefore, finds it worth while—enormously worth while—to specialise in the production of manufactured articles which make full use of its skill and capital, and to leave food production to countries like Canada, Australia and Argentine in which land is abundant and industrial skill and experience relatively scarce. By exporting machinery, high-quality manufactured articles, and the services of its banking houses, insurance companies and mercantile marine, it receives in return foodstuffs which it could not produce at comparable cost on its own soil. Not that agriculture in Britain or industry in Australia is wiped out. Distance affords adequate protection to perishable and bulky products, such as milk and vegetables, and gives partial protection to others, such as fresh meat. In the same way, many of the lighter industries in Australia are sufficiently insulated by distance from foreign competition to thrive naturally, without protection from the State. But it is not only distance which enables British agriculture to survive. There is also an adaptation of farming methods to the comparative scarcity of land. Since land is scarce relatively to labour and capital, it is also relatively dear. There is every incentive, therefore, to economise land and use a high proportion of labour and capital per acre; in other words, to farm intensively. In Canada and Australia, on the other hand, land is relatively abundant and therefore relatively cheap. As a result, farming is extensive, with a low output per acre and a high output per man.

It must not be supposed, however, that Britain's trade is simply a bartering of manufactured goods for foodstuffs. She has always had an extensive trade with other manufacturing countries such as Germany and the Unites States. For many years she has imported more from the United States than from any other country, and has found in the United States one of her most important markets. In 1913 she imported more from Germany than from any other country except India, and sold to Germany twice as much as she sold to

Australia. Part of this trade with other manufacturing countries is in raw materials—cotton imported from the United States, coal exported to Germany. But a large proportion is in finished goods in the manufacture of which one country or another is particularly proficient. No manufacturing country has workers of optimum skill in all industries; some countries excel in the manufacture of chemicals, some in textiles, some in glassware, some in engineering and shipbuilding. Thus within the range of skills at each country's command there are, so to speak, interstices into which trade fits the special skills of other countries. It is not only in the relative scarcity of land, labour and capital that countries differ, but in the relative scarcity of types of land, types of labour and types of capital equipment. These differences, equally with the broader differences, give rise to trade of mutual advantage to both parties.

To summarise the argument so far. Wherever some factor or sub-factor of production is relatively abundant, it is also relatively cheap. Goods into the manufacture of which that factor or sub-factor enters largely will also be relatively cheap, especially as methods of production will be adapted so as to make extensive use of the cheap factor. On the other hand, goods into the manufacture of which other and relatively scarce factors enter largely will be relatively dear. There will be a tendency, therefore, for the first set of goods to be exported and for the second set to be imported. The resulting exchange of goods will be of advantage because the imports relieve the pressure on the supply of relatively scarce factors, while the exports will provide a vent for the relatively abundant factor.

This argument can now be amplified. First, it should be observed that it is based upon differences in the comparative cost of the factors of production in the trading countries. If the absolute cost of each factor is the same in all countries, the incentive to trade disappears. For the object of trade is to take advantage of the *comparative* cheapness of commodities in other countries; and if the factors of production are everywhere paid alike, costs of production will be the same everywhere and no commodity will be cheaper in one country than in another. If, for example, there is only one factor of production, labour, which is equally efficient and equally versatile in every country, then no worker will have any reason for trading with other workers either in his own country or abroad. It is only when workers differ from one another, or (what comes to much the same) when there are several factors of production available in different proportions in different places, that trade is worth while. For then there are differences in the relative costs of the factors of production, and differences in the relative prices of their products. Some goods are relatively cheap in one country and some relatively cheap in others, so that there is an all-round advantage in exchanging one set of goods for the other. The volume of trade increases until—setting aside transport costs—prices are brought into line in all countries.

But the earnings of the factors of production are not brought into line. Trade does not make wages equal in all countries, nor interest rates, nor rents. In India, for example, labour continues to earn low wages (even in relation to its low efficiency) because of its abundance relatively to the capital and natural resources of the country. In Britain, capital continues to earn a comparatively low return because there is much more of it per worker than in most other countries. In the leading manufacturing countries, labour earns comparatively high wages because it is skilled and plentifully supplied with capital in a world in which skill and capital are relatively scarce. If the factors of production moved freely from one country to another, these differences could not persist. Workers would emigrate from countries in which wages were low to countries in which wages were high, and capital would flow out to countries, in which it is relatively scarce, until the return to labour and capital was equal all over the globe. Since international mobility is low, these movements do not in fact take place. Each country continues to have a relative abundance of some factors and a relative scarcity of others, so that the first factors earn less than elsewhere and the second factors more.

Although trade does not equalise the earnings of the factors of production in different countries, it does tend to level out differences. In the absence of trade, there would be a greater superfluity of labour and a greater scarcity of capital than ever; wages would fall still lower and interest rates rise still higher. Trade has the effect of bringing wages nearer to the level in other countries. The pace is set by the export industries which, having the advantage of cheap unskilled labour, are able to undersell competitors abroad and, by drawing more and more workers from domestic industries, lever up wages all round. This process could be seen at work quite clearly in pre-war Japan where the demand for exports created a corresponding demand for labour in the export industries and brought wages nearer to the level in foreign countries. The movement of goods between countries is, in fact, a substitute for the movement of factors of production. Instead of making use of Japanese labour by allowing it to immigrate, people make use of it at long range by buying its products. Thus they admit it to competition with their own labour only under the handicap of distance. In the same way, unable to borrow British capital for their own industries, other countries can make use of it indirectly by buying British exports in the manufacture of which a great deal of capital has been used. Wages in Japan are raised—although not as much as they would be by direct emigration; and the return on British capital is maintained—although not perhaps so successfully as it would be by investment abroad.

The illogicality of refusing to trade with a country because its wage-rates are low should now be plain. By such a refusal we merely force the country to pay still lower wages; we *intensify* the comparative superfluity of labour in the country by cutting off one source of demand. If there were too many workers in the mining industry and their wages were correspondingly low, we should be doing their cause little good if we stopped buying coal in protest against their low wages; exactly the same is true of workers in foreign industries. Nor are we doing ourselves a service. We do not "protect our standard of living"; we lower it. If a foreign country finds itself able to supply us with iron ore at less than the cost of mining it at home, there is no reason in the world why we should refuse to import it unless our ironminers can find no alternative employment or unless ironmining is an industry which we are determined, in the national interests, to preserve. In exactly the same way, if cheap textile products are offered to us— whether they are made by high-paid or low-paid workers makes not one jot of difference—there is no reason in the world why we should exclude them from our markets unless our textile workers cannot hope to be re-employed in other industries. The question is not really one of low wages in foreign countries at all; it is one of potential unemployment at home. Whatever the reason why cheap imports are offered to us, we cannot exclude them just because they are cheap ( or we should never import anything); nor can we exclude them because some particular factor of production—whether labour, land or capital—is underpaid by our standards; our objection must be rooted in the domestic economic position, in some disadvantage to us (such as unemployment) which outweighs the immediate advantage of cheapness.

It is worth adding, finally, that it is not always certain that Britain would gain through a rise in wages in countries like Japan. If Japanese workers spend little on imports, while Japanese manufacturers use a large proportion of their profits for the purchase of machinery and other capital goods from abroad, then a change in the distribution of income in favour of labour may have even larger repercussions on the market for imports in Japan than on Japan's power to compete in foreign markets. If the Japanese market is more valuable to Great Britain than the markets in which she has to face competition from Japanese exporters, then she may lose rather than gain from a rise in wages in Japan.

It must not be inferred from this argument that every increase in competition from abroad is to Britain's interest. Whether she gains or loses depends upon the kind of resources brought into competition with hers. Some of her resources—skilled labour, for example—are relatively scarce in other parts of the world and relatively plentiful in Britain. Thus their earnings are high, and will remain high so long as foreigners wish to make use of their services. But if these scarce factors become more plentiful elsewhere—if foreigners acquire skill, accumulate capital, or discover new deposits of coal—our comparative advantage in having large supplies—of skill, capital or coal—is immediately reduced. On the other hand, if the resources in which Britain is most deficient become more plentiful elsewhere—if more territory is opened up, or better methods of farming are introduced—Britain will be able to trade more advantageously. An increase in foreign competition, therefore, is to our interest when it is in commodities which, because of our comparative deficiency in the necessary resources, we are relatively ill-adapted to produce. An increase in foreign competition is contrary to our interest when it is in commodities which, because of our comparative wealth in the necessary resources, we are particularly well-suited to produce. But since we are generally powerless to prevent such increased competition, we must just make the best of it. The competition is felt, as a rule, not in our home market but in our export markets where we have no control; and if it does begin to reach the home market, we should only make matters worse by shutting it out.

It is clear that different sections of the community are differently affected by foreign competition. Those factors of production which are relatively plentiful gain most, since it is their products to which a larger market is opened; those factors which are relatively scarce gain least, or lose absolutely, by being brought into competition with the comparative surplus available in other countries. British capitalists, for example, gain enormously from foreign trade; British landowners would gain even more enormously if foreign trade were suddenly to become impossible. The advantage of foreign trade to the community as a whole, however, is unmistakable. It can be measured in terms of the loss which the country would suffer if it had to exist exclusively on home-produced goods—that is, by the loss inflicted through the diversion of productive resources from the manufacture of exports to the manufacture of substitutes for imports. For most countries, this loss would be very considerable, and the gain which they derive from trade is correspondingly great—so great, one may safely conclude, that it will be rare for a section of the community not to participate in it. Landlords who have been cited as losing from foreign trade, are in a highly exceptional position. For agricultural land is not only indispensable to the economic life of every community, but is strictly limited in supply; so that any thickly-populated country which tries to be self-supporting is at the mercy of its landlords, and is forced to pay higher rents than under free competition with foreign agriculture. Unskilled labour is a more typical example. Unskilled workers in Britain share in the advantages of international trade equally with skilled workers. For although in comparison with other countries they are relatively scarce—and might seem to be threatened, therefore, by foreign competition—they would cease to be so scarce if trade with other countries stopped and the demand for skilled export workers vanished. The export trades widen the market for skill and draw off workers who would otherwise compete with unskilled labour. At the same time, the cheap imported foodstuffs which her exports procure lower the cost of living for everyone, and particularly for those who, like unskilled workers, spend a large proportion of their income on food. Not all countries are so dependent on foreign trade as Great Britain. But the rule would appear to be generally applicable—that while some sectional gains from foreign trade are greater than others, sectional losses are rare.

### Implications of the theory

It is not surprising that many people should deduce from the theory of comparative costs the wisdom of a policy of free trade, just as many people deduced from the marginal theory of value the wisdom of a policy of laissez-faire. The more one understands the working of market forces the more alive one becomes to their effectiveness in allocating resources and promoting a useful division of labour. But just as there are many reasons why the State finds it necessary to control the forces operating in the domestic market so there are many reasons why it cannot leave international trade unregulated.

First of all, the fact that an international division of labour is obviously sensible does not imply that a single country would be sensible to trade freely with other countries. It might derive advantages from restrictions that were disadvantageous from the point of view of the international community. If other countries had high tariffs, it might decide to have a tariff too, purely for bargaining purposes and with every intention of making concessions in return for tariff reductions on its principal exports. It might also impose tariffs that forced other countries to accept less favourable terms of trade; it could do so if other countries had an inelastic demand for its goods or if they had an inelastic supply of the goods which it imported from them. If it supplied the world with goods unobtainable elsewhere, it might exploit its advantage by export levies designed to raise their price on world markets; similarly, if it were almost the sole market for some commodities, it might tax them heavily and oblige foreign suppliers to accept lower prices.

Again, it might, by protecting industries in which there were important advantages in producing on a large scale, steal a march on the corresponding industries in other countries and establish itself as a low-cost producer, supplying a protected home market and under-cutting foreign producers in other markets. It could do this the more readily because protection would allow it to charge lower prices abroad without fear that the goods would be shipped back again to the domestic market; that is, it could "dump" or discriminate if necessary. More usually, since open dumping gives rise to protest and retaliatory legislation, it could absorb some of the costs of developing foreign markets and charge a price which did not fully cover these additional costs.

Specialisation, moreover, tends to be on the basis of existing skills and market opportunities; it is governed by today's comparative costs, not tomorrow's. But in an economy in process of development, it may be desirable to anticipate later changes and to build up industries for which the long-term prospects are good even although, in the short-run, they are unable to cover their costs. Where we are dealing with marginal changes within an existing framework, the price-mechanism is a fairly reliable means of bringing them about; when an economy is undergoing the great structural upheavals associated with industrialisation, it is not nearly so satisfactory. It allows individual producers and consumers to make their choices without looking too far ahead or taking into account the total effect of what they do. If, however, the principal object of economic policy is to transform the economy and to make it grow faster, the long view may differ widely from the short and the outcome of individual decisions may run counter to collective needs.

The force of this argument was recognised long ago when the champions of free trade themselves advanced the "infant industry" argument for a tariff: the argument that an industry might have to be nurtured for a time by protection before it was sufficiently established to stand on its own feet. Nowadays the scope of the argument has widened and it is applied to the economy as a whole: not in the sense that anyone suggests protection for every economic activity—since that would be self-defeating, protection for any one activity reducing the advantages enjoyed by all the others—but rather in the sense that economic development is no longer regarded as best accomplished by competitive forces and without active encouragement by the State. Where economists differ is on the form that such encouragement might usefully take and on the extent to which it need involve restrictions on trade with other countries.

Finally, the theory of comparative costs assumes a relatively stable world in which a country can disregard the changes in progress abroad and the large fluctuations that occur in foreign markets. But as we have seen (pp. 403–5) these fluctuations may be large and sudden. In an industrial country they result in widespread unemployment, and in primary producing countries in large swings in prices and incomes. This instability is extremely costly and detracts from the advantages that foreign trade offers to a single country. It is often to protect themselves against instability in foreign markets that countries impose restrictions on trade. They may try to make themselves less vulnerable by developing a wider range of exports or by building up domestic industries so as to reduce their dependence on imports. They may also try to safeguard themselves by entering into long-term agreements with other countries, by forming a trading bloc, or by joining regional and international organisations in which the members pledge themselves to offer one another mutual support.

The theory of international trade, therefore, cannot be an adequate guide to policy if it abstracts from the forces of dynamic change inside and outside a country and limits itself to an exposition of the tendencies of free competition. Nevertheless an understanding of those tendencies, with which this chapter has been mainly concerned, is indispensable in any approach to problems of commercial policy.

# CHAPTER 32

# THE BALANCE OF PAYMENTS

Payments between countries generally differ from domestic payments in that they involve the exchange of one kind of money for another. Each country has its own money, which is not freely accepted abroad, but must be changed into foreign money at a rate which may be either fixed or variable. The rate of exchange, whether fixed or variable, is a price; and, like any other price, must be such as to balance supply and demand. At any given rate, sales of foreign exchange must be equal to purchases; the payments made by foreign countries must be equal to the payments made to them. If the balance of payments is tipped against a country, there will be increased pressure to buy foreign exchange, and, if the rate of exchange is free to vary, the price of foreign moneys will rise—that is, the currency of the country will depreciate. If the balance of payments is favourable to the country, there will be increased pressure to sell foreign exchange, and this pressure will tend to raise the value of the country's currency; or, in other words, cause it to appreciate.

This idea of a balance of payments which may be either favourable or unfavourable is fundamental to the whole theory of foreign exchange and requires careful explanation. Strictly speaking, since payments on both sides of the account must balance in the sense that sales and purchases are necessarily equal, they can never be out of balance in the sense that there is a deficit on all items taken together. A deficit, or unfavourable balance, must relate to a partial balance leaving out some item or items; for example, any sales of gold from the reserve of the central bank which may preserve equilibrium in the foreign exchange market for the time being but cannot continue indefinitely.

The expression "balance of payments" is in fact used in several different ways, depending upon what is left out as a residual or balancing item: and the more one examines different usages the more apparent it becomes that what matters is *how* a balance is preserved rather than the size of the deficit or surplus on any particular definition.

R

There are three balances in common use that merit explanation:—[1]

**(i) The balance of trade**—In speaking of an unfavourable balance of payments we may have in mind an excess of imports of merchandise over exports. Since details of these imports and exports are published monthly, and since merchandise forms a large proportion of total trade, this "balance of trade" figures very prominently in most popular discussions. But that it is of limited importance is clear from the fact that Britain had an unfavourable balance of merchandise trade for over a hundred years without any unfortunate consequences.

**(ii) The balance of payments on current (or income) account**—In addition to merchandise exports and imports there are various "invisible" exports and imports whose value is not officially recorded although estimates are made. For example, large sums are earned every year by the British mercantile marine in carrying goods and passengers from one foreign country to another, or between British and foreign ports. The Board of Trade records the value of British exports "f.o.b." (free on board—that is, at the port of embarkation), and the value of British imports "c.i.f." (cost, insurance, freight—that is, at the port of landing). Thus its returns exaggerate the adverse balance by leaving shipping earnings out of account. Since foreigners require to make additional payments to cover sea transport charges on exports carried in British vessels, and since Britain is spared from making payments to foreigners to cover sea transport charges on imports carried in British vessels, the earnings of British ships in carrying goods to and from Britain go to reduce any visible adverse balance of trade. Further deductions must be made in respect of the fares of foreign passengers in British ships, transport of goods between foreign ports, and disbursements of foreign ships and sailors in British ports. On the other hand, disbursements by British ships in foreign ports (for example, for fuel or in payment of port dues) add to any unfavourable balance.

A second "invisible" item is interest and profit on foreign investments. Interest and profits represent a kind of "invisible" export; they can be regarded as payments for the hire of British capital just as freight payments are payments for the hire of British ships. Similarly, interest payments on capital invested in Britain are "invisible" imports. Before the war about a quarter of Britain's net imports came in payment for past investments of capital in foreign countries. The disposal of foreign investments during the war and the debts then incurred greatly reduced the size of net earningss under this heading, the average in the

---

[1] The reader will find it helpful to refer back at this point to Table 19 in Chapter 25, Appendix on *The National Accounts*.

years 1956–58 being only £235 million compared with imports in the same years of nearly £3,500 million. The loss of investment income was one of the main causes of Britain's post-war balance of payments difficulties.

To these two items may be added a large number of others. There are, for example, disbursements by British tourists abroad, remittances to friends and relatives in other countries, grants to colonial governments, and so on. Against these payments must be set similar payments due to Britain by foreign countries, including the commissions earned on her marine underwriting, insurance and acceptance business, etc.

Once all these items have been included we reach a quite different balance, representing the difference between the value of goods and services currently produced in Britain and sold abroad, and the value of foreign goods and services bought from abroad. This balance is usually called "the balance of payments on income account." It was consistently favourable to Britain all through the second half of the nineteenth century and did not become unfavourable (apart from the war years 1914–18) until 1931. Thereafter the balance on income account was not markedly favourable or unfavourable, but oscillated between small positive and small negative quantities until the outbreak of war in 1939. During the war it was increasingly in deficit, and the deficit continued into the post-war years. By the middle of 1948 equilibrium had been restored and in 1950 there was, for the first time for many years, a substantial surplus. Apart from a large deficit in 1951 and a smaller one in 1955, a surplus continued to be earned throughout the fifties. In 1960, however, the current account was again in deficit and after an improvement over the next three years it was in heavy deficit in 1964–65.

**(iii) The balance on current and long-term capital account**—The balance of payments on income account is of limited significance. It provides a measure of the addition that a country is making to its net overseas assets (including its reserves of gold and foreign exchange): for if it is selling more goods and services to foreign countries than it buys from them it can lend or invest the difference. Indeed, the only way in which the account can be equated is by a capital transaction that offsets the current account surplus; or rather, the net outcome of all the capital transactions must exactly offset the net outcome of all the current transactions. Now it may be a matter for disquiet if the balance on current account is in deficit and the country is having to borrow abroad; but there is nothing necessarily undesirable or "unfavourable" in such a state of affairs. Suppose, for example, that a country is engaged in building a new railway system and that its own savings are inadequate to finance the work. By borrowing from other countries it can make purchases of railway equipment abroad and pay for these purchases not by equal exports, but out of the borrowed funds. In the same way, if Britain has an unfavourable balance on income account, this may simply reflect unusually active investment at home; she may be drawing on her accumulated foreign investments in order to finance a building boom or the construction of atomic power stations. A country can choose between investing its savings at home or abroad. The more it inclines to home investment the less favourable will be its balance of payments as measured by the difference between exports and imports; for it will have less resources to spare for the manufacture of exports and it will be more anxious to draw on the resources of other countries by importing from them.

Although there is nothing necessarily unfavourable about a negative (or "passive") balance of payments which is covered by *long-term* borrowing abroad, a negative balance which is met either by short-term, "makeshift," borrowing, or by exports of gold, is quite another matter. Long-term borrowing designed to finance the construction of capital assets can go on with impunity for very long periods. But short-term foreign loans are generally obtained only if there are good prospects that the loans can be repaid. A country can borrow on short-term to tide over a temporary deficit in its balance of payments; but it cannot continue to add to its short-term borrowings without simultaneously taking measures to correct the unfavourable balance. Similarly, it can finance a deficit in its balance of payments by the sale of gold; but, since its stock of gold is limited, the loss of gold cannot go on indefinitely. Short-term borrowing and gold exports, therefore, are palliatives which, so long as they continue, keep the rate of exchange from depreciating, just as the sale of goods from stock keeps their price from rising when demand increases. Both expedients are danger signals as well as palliatives. They indicate that, unless action is taken to correct the unfavourable balance and so reverse the inward flow of credits or the outward flow of gold, depreciation is inevitable.

Considerations of this kind direct our attention to a different balance, sometimes referred to as the "basic" balance, which adds together the balance on current account and the net balance on long-term capital account. The latter includes direct investment inwards and outwards by business undertakings as well as portfolio movements involving the sale or purchase of bonds and stock exchange securities. This balance on current and long-term capital account is necessarily equal in magnitude to the balance of all other transactions, since total sales and total purchases of foreign exchange must be equal to one another. In the British accounts, this residue is called "the balance on monetary transactions" and consists of the gain or loss in reserves plus the net transfer of funds on short-term capital account.

Even this, however, may not be the significant balance if what we are trying to isolate is some measure of external disequilibrium: the amount of accommodating finance that bridges what would otherwise be a deficit in the balance of payments. Movements of short-term funds *may* represent flows of "hot" money of a purely temporary kind, liable to sudden reversals. But they may also reflect longer-term influences that make it convenient to accumulate funds or obtain finance in some particular centre such as London or New York. It would be going too far, therefore, to regard a net inflow of short-term funds as a temporary substitute for a run-down in the reserves: the net inflow may be as stable an element in the balance of payments as any other and just as capable of exerting an independent influence on the level at which balance is achieved. There is in fact no single, precise way of measuring the size of an external deficit in the sense used above of an almost passive response to the difference between the other "active" items.

For this reason there is also no universally agreed convention observed by all countries. The United Kingdom, for example, measures its surplus or deficit in terms of the balance on current and long-term capital account. On the other hand, the United States follows a practice that makes its deficit larger than on this definition by the amount of any net outflow of U.S. private short-term capital. It does not, however, set against this outflow the net inflow of short-term capital from abroad on the grounds that such an inflow gives rise to liquid liabilities to foreigners and is better regarded as a way of financing a deficit than as a straightforward capital receipt. This treatment is open to the objection that it is asymmetrical and that if every country adopted it they might all find themselves in deficit simultaneously. The Bernstein Committee, reporting on this in 1965, suggested the inclusion of all short-term capital flows, inwards and outwards, in the American balance of payments, subject to one exception: inflows from abroad representing an increase in liabilities to foreign central banks and other monetary authorities and hence in the reserve assets (in the form of dollar holdings) of those authorities.[1]

## THE GOLD STANDARD

Conditions under which countries rely mainly on gold as a means of settling surpluses or deficits with one another are the hallmark of the gold standard. These conditions might obtain even if there were no central bank so long as there was some means of converting currency freely into gold and shipping it abroad in settlement of debts. But there is a second and perhaps more important charac-

---

[1] *The Balance of Payments Statistics of the United States.* Report to the Bureau of the Budget, April 1965.

teristic of the gold standard: convertibility of currency into gold *on fixed terms*. It is this characteristic that explains the use of the word "standard": gold acts as the standard of value in the sense that its price is fixed in terms of the unit of account, e.g., the pound sterling.

If gold coins are in circulation and all other kinds of money, such as bank notes, are promises to pay gold then free convertibility into gold at a fixed price is automatically secured. Even if, as in Britain between 1925 and 1931, there is no gold currency but only a law instructing the central bank to purchase all gold offered to it at a fixed price, and to sell gold bullion at a slightly higher price, the condition is still fulfilled. It is also fulfilled if the central bank is instructed to buy and sell at fixed prices not gold, but the money of some other gold standard country; for this money is itself convertible into gold at a fixed price. The first kind of standard was the one generally adopted up till 1914; the second, the gold bullion standard, came into use after the war of 1914–18; while the third, the gold exchange standard, was adopted by countries like India which could not afford a full gold standard, preferring instead to link their currencies with sterling, and so, indirectly with gold.

The gold standard is a means of preserving constant, or almost constant, exchange rates between different countries. If the United States and Great Britain are both on the gold standard, the dollar and sterling prices of gold will both be fixed, and the terms on which pounds and dollars exchange will, therefore, also be fixed. Suppose, for example, that the mint price of gold in New York is $35 an ounce and in London £7 an ounce. Then the mint par of exchange will be $5 to the £1. It will be foolish for an American to offer more than $5 for £1 since by buying gold and shipping it to London he can obtain pounds at this rate. On the other hand, no American will sell pounds for less than $5, since by buying gold in London and bringing it to New York he can convert his sterling balances into dollars at this rate. But the shipping of gold in either direction puts him to some expense, and various obstacles may be put in his way by central banks which do not like to lose gold too easily. If he can buy pounds on the market for foreign exchange, therefore, he will be willing to pay rather more than $5 to save himself trouble and expense, and if he has pounds to sell he will be willing to accept rather less than $5 for the same reason. Thus the gold standard does not entirely eliminate variations in exchange rates; but it sets narrow limits to them. For each country there will be a maximum price of foreign exchange above which gold begins to flow out ("gold export point") and a minimum price below which gold begins to flow in ("gold import point").

The gold standard provides a common medium of exchange, with which, in the last resort, international payments can be made. But only in the last resort. Importers do not normally send gold in payment for the goods which they import; nor do exporters fetch the same gold back again in payment for the goods which they export. Instead, importers procure from exporters the foreign exchange which they require and so save the double cost of transport of gold. So long as the balance of payments is in equilibrium, and total exports are equal to total imports, there is no need for gold to move at all. It is only when imports and exports get out of line with one another that some residual transfer of gold is necessary in order to balance the two. Gold will flow in when exporters have more foreign exchange than importers will buy (so that its price drops to gold import point) and will flow out when the supply of foreign exchange is insufficient to meet the demand (so that its price rises to gold export point). The gold is purchased by, or obtained from, the central bank which, since it is its duty to keep the price of gold constant, must hold a substantial stock of it, adding to the stock or drawing on it whenever the balance of payments is favourable or unfavourable.

If a country is on the gold standard the central bank must do more than hold a stock of gold and relieve any pressure on the exchanges by appropriate purchases and sales. It must also be able to safeguard its stock by taking action to check any drain of gold. To some extent it can rely on the flow of gold to reverse itself automatically, but a large flow one way or the other will call for active intervention by the central bank.

### Reserves

When there is a deficit in the balance of payments two problems arise. The first is to settle the deficit and the second is to get rid of it. The second problem is discussed in the next chapter. The settlement of the deficit, except in so far as short-term borrowing takes place, must be in some internationally acceptable means of payment. The most obvious example of such a medium is gold; but there are various currencies, notably the pound and the dollar, that are used internationally and it is likely that in course of time balances held with some international body such as the International Monetary Fund will be of increasing importance. Whatever the means of settlement between countries, they are usually held by the central bank and constitute its reserves of foreign exchange. The purpose of these reserves is to provide ammunition against an unfavourable balance of payments and allow time for corrective action to take effect. Since reserves represent an investment of capital that could be used for other purposes there is a limit to the amount that countries are prepared to accumulate, particularly if, like gold, it brings no revenue.

In Britain most of the reserves are held in gold although there is also a working balance of dollars; in present-day conditions the normal method of settlement is in dollars and when the Bank of England intervenes in the market the currency which it buys or offers for sale is the dollar. The reserves are held in an Exchange Equalisation Account set up in 1932 after Britain left the gold standard. This is managed by the Bank of England on behalf of the Treasury, and is financed by the issue of Treasury Bills. During periods when the balance of payments is in favour of Britain, the Account adds to its stock of gold and foreign exchange, issuing more Treasury Bills in order to raise the sterling necessary for its purchases; when the balance of payments is unfavourable, it sells gold and foreign exchange for sterling and pays off a corresponding portion of its sterling debt.

The object of the Account in the thirties was not, as at present, to maintain a fixed rate of exchange; it could use its discretion in allowing the rate to depreciate or appreciate. Its aim was to reduce fluctuations in the rate by supplementing the supply of foreign exchange when there was a danger of depreciation and by making purchases of foreign exchange when the pound was appreciating. When there was a persistent movement against sterling the Account was powerless to control it since its holdings of foreign exchange were limited. It had to content itself with preventing fluctuations due to speculation, and to keep them from affecting trade and credit without trying to prevent fluctuations attributable to more fundamental "real" causes.

The system in use was thus intermediate between one of fixed exchanges and one of freely fluctuating rates. The range of variations in exchange rates was steadily narrowed in each successive year from 1933 onwards. From the outbreak of war until the devaluation of 1949 the pound-dollar exchange rate was held constant at $4·02=£1; after devaluation, the rate remained fixed at $2·80=£1. In this respect, therefore, the post-war system represented a return to pre-1931 conditions, although in many other respects it differed widely from it.

## Sterling balances

Because the dollar and sterling are both used as international currencies the reserve position of the United States and the United Kingdom is more complicated than that of other countries. The reserves of sterling area countries,[1] for example, are largely held in sterling and can be drawn upon, like any other reserves, to meet an external deficit. The fact that the sterling area countries trade extensively with one another makes this a convenient arrangement since intra-area deficits and surpluses can be cleared in sterling without any need to use gold for the purpose. But if a deficit arises in trade with countries outside

[1] See below, pp. 542–543.

the sterling area it has to be settled in gold or in some currency acceptable to the country that is in surplus. The settlement is made out of the central reserves of the sterling area, i.e., out of the gold and foreign exchange held in the Exchange Equalisation Account, the sterling area country that is in deficit paying in sterling from the balances that it holds in London while the Bank of England automatically makes available the necessary foreign exchange in return. The United Kingdom acts as banker for the other members of the system; and the sterling balances which to them are reserves of foreign exchange are to the United Kingdom sterling liabilities approaching in character negative reserves.

## International liquidity

If international reserves consisted exclusively of gold this would obviously create a danger of excess or shortage in relation to the scale of international trade and payments. The stock of gold increases slowly in comparison with the growth of the world economy and this could give rise to a powerful deflationary drag on monetary policy if it created widespread anxieties in the leading countries about the adequacy of their reserves. Just as no one would wish to tie the growth of the domestic money supply to the amount of gold mined every year, so it would be unfortunate if the growth of international means of payment were to be governed by the same irrelevant factor.

The fact that reserves have in fact grown rapidly since the war is due to special circumstances. In the early post-war years when the United States was in overwhelming surplus it did not drain every other country of its gold reserves but tried to reduce the imbalance between North America and the rest of the world through the Marshall Plan. Then in the early fifties the American balance of payments moved into deficit and it continued in deficit throughout the rest of the fifties and into the sixties.

This meant:

(i) that the major deficit calling for the use of reserves fell on a country amply supplied with them;

(ii) that so far as the deficit was met in gold, the rest of the world was able to increase its monetary holdings of gold at a much more rapid rate than would have been possible from newly mined gold alone;

(iii) that so far as the deficit was not settled in gold, the rest of the world was able to acquire an equally acceptable means of international payment in the form of dollars.

But it is obvious that none of these favourable circumstances can continue indefinitely. The U.S. cannot remain in deficit much longer; if it did, it would begin to run out of gold; and even if it could meet the deficit in dollars, the

R*

willingness of central banks to accumulate the currency of a country in chronic deficit is not unlimited.

There is, therefore, a dilemma. The longer the U.S. deficit continues, the greater the danger that one international asset, the dollar, comes to be distrusted and exchanged for another, gold, which may rise in value if the American deficit ends in devaluation. The possibility of such a switch limits the extent to which it is possible to supplement the gold reserves of the world through the use of international currencies such as the dollar or the pound. If, to take the other horn of the dilemma, the U.S. deficit comes to an end, and still more if it is succeeded by a surplus, the main source of additional international liquidity in the post-war world will dry up.

It would take us too far to discuss in any detail how this dilemma might be resolved.[1] But a number of possibilities exist.

First of all, international reserves could be increased very easily if the price of gold were raised. It would need no more than a decision on the part of the United States for the world price to be doubled; what keeps the price at its present level is the willingness of the United States to sell gold to other central banks at $35 an ounce. But apart from any political objections to increasing the price—and the countries producing gold or holding their reserves in gold rather than foreign exchange might not see these in the same light as their less fortunate neighbours—there is the awkward fact that if action is taken to increase liquidity in this way the expectation will be created of further revaluations of gold later on. This may make countries reluctant to hold their reserves in some other form that would not benefit from a rise in the price of gold. Even if there were not a flight from the dollar or from sterling into gold there would certainly be more difficulty in paving the way for the supercession of gold by some more elastic international asset, which many people would think highly desirable.

A second possibility that has been canvassed is the creation of a new asset, Collective Reserve Units or C.R.U's, by a group of countries each of which puts up some of its own currency and receives in return a corresponding issue of C.R.U's. It would be able to use these units in making settlements with other members of the group and would bind itself at the same time to accept units tendered to it by other members when they were in deficit. This way of creating new international liquidity is not unlike the issue of additional currency notes by a national government against a fiduciary backing of its own securities. It allows the participants to share the advantages of international money

---

[1] A useful summary is given in the Ossola Report on the Creation of Reserve Assets (1965).

creation—advantages at present monopolised by the United States and the United Kingdom when other countries add to their dollar or sterling reserves; and it spares them the need to devote real resources to this purpose either by mining gold or by making exports in payment for it. The snags in the scheme become apparent once it is necessary to settle who is to take part, how much is to be issued, and how the total is to be divided between the participants. If the scheme is exclusive the countries that are left out will complain; if every country is included the scheme will be difficult to manage. Most versions of the scheme are drawn up on an exclusive basis with participation limited to the ten or a dozen major countries. If it were proposed to open it to all members —over 100—of the International Monetary Fund it would probably be simpler to adapt the Fund in the kind of way suggested below.

It is unlikely that the scheme could be brought into operation initially on a large scale, so that it would have to be operated for a long time side-by-side with the use of international currencies. But this raises fresh difficulties since the greater the variety of ways in which international reserves can be held the greater the danger that some will come to be ranked below the others, held reluctantly, and got rid of at the first opportunity. The business of arranging from time to time for a fresh issue and settling its amount also presents a problem although not one peculiar to the C.R.U. type of scheme. Agreement would be necessary on the criteria by which the total issue could be allocated to member countries and in particular on what link, if any, there should be between a country's entitlement and its existing gold reserves. If, as in some versions, this link was a close one and the share-out was in proportion to gold holdings, the scheme would be little more than a rather devious way of raising the price of gold in favour of the countries taking part.

A third way of increasing international liquidity would be to give countries greater borrowing rights as members of the International Monetary Fund. While it is not quite so convenient to have larger overdraft facilities as to have more cash in the bank, both serve much the same purpose in helping to tide over pressure on liquidity. Borrowing rights are sometimes described as "conditional reserves" (because there are usually pre-conditions to any loans) as distinct from "owned reserves"; but in practice the distinction can become rather a fine one. If, for example, the I.M.F. allows a country to borrow up to 25 per cent. of its quota without question and does not set limits to the period over which it must be repaid, it is hard to distinguish such borrowing rights from ordinary reserve assets. The more freely countries could make use of their borrowing rights the more liquid they would be. But freer access by borrowers would only be possible if there were simultaneously a greater willingness on the part of creditor countries to allow themselves to be drawn upon by the I.M.F.

If, for example, they were prepared to regard a claim on the I.M.F. as part of their reserves and could use such a claim in due course to settle a deficit with other member countries, this would be a great step forwards towards a more satisfactory system of international payments.

Finally, we must not overlook the connection between the need for international reserves and the ease with which countries are able to get back into balance. If the process of adjustment to an external deficit is hard and prolonged, countries will have more need of reserves than when they are confident that they will be able to get rid of a deficit quickly. The next chapter discusses how adjustment takes place and what can be done to bring it about.

# CHAPTER 33

# THE MECHANISM OF INTERNATIONAL ADJUSTMENT

## Pressures on the balance of payments

The balance of payments may become unfavourable because of pressures on it from inside or outside the country. We have already seen how it can act as a safety valve to domestic inflationary pressure until the resulting loss of foreign exchange obliges the monetary authorities to take corrective action.[1] We have also seen that inflation in the outside world may put strains and stresses on trade and payments and tug at the prices of goods entering into international trade.[2] It drives up the price of imported goods, including foodstuffs and raw materials and spreads to domestic costs of production as money-wages chase the cost of living upwards, so that both material and wage costs are inflated. Just as inflation spreads from one part of a country to another, so it can very easily spread from one country to another.

Deflation abroad is equally contagious. If purchasing power collapses in overseas markets, the export trades begin to suffer from unemployment; at the same time imports may be swollen by distress sales of goods that have fallen disastrously in price and cannot find a market elsewhere; the balance of trade will become unfavourable and the central bank will find its reserves oozing away to cover the deficit. Few countries are strong enough to preserve internal financial stability if world markets are slumping.

A country may decide to concentrate either on internal balance or external balance. Short of complete autarchy—the abandonment of all trade—it cannot afford to neglect either; but it may give preference to the one over the other. If it tries at all costs to maintain a fixed rate of exchange and free convertibility of its currency into other currencies—the two main features of the gold standard—it has come down heavily on the side of external balance: it is prepared to let its prices follow world prices, come what may. If, on the other hand,

---

[1] Above, p. 427.　　　　　　　　　　[2] Above, p. 431.

it allows exchange rates to fluctuate freely and tries to keep domestic prices steady, it is plumping for internal rather than external balance: it is hoping to be able to insulate itself from movements in world prices by letting the rate of exchange take the shock. It may go further and bring all transactions in foreign currencies under exchange control, seeking to manipulate payments and receipts by requisitioning (in return for its sterling equivalent) the foreign exchange earned by exporters and rationing the foreign exchange required by importers; this will hedge foreign trade and payments around with difficulties and complications but will give the monetary authorities more latitude in dealing with domestic financial problems.

It might seem from this that the choice lay between a high volume of trade and a smaller one: and that some countries deliberately restricted their trade for the sake of greater domestic stability. There are no doubt countries that are faced with such a choice. It is also true that, whatever is decided, the decision will be influenced by the risk of a contraction in trade. But the real choice relates, not to the volume of trade, but to the *method* by which an adverse balance of payments is eliminated—by forcing prices and incomes into line with prices and incomes elsewhere, by allowing exchange rates to fluctuate or by direct action on payments and receipts.

### The mechanism of adjustment in the balance of payments

Pressure on the exchanges may arise for one of three reasons:

(i) it may be due to a larger volume of purchases of imports or sales of exports;

(ii) there may be a change in the terms on which imports and exports are exchanged (i.e., in the terms of trade) and therefore in the average price of imports in relation to the average price of exports;

(iii) even when current transactions are stable in value, there may be a transfer of capital across the exchanges because of heavier borrowing from, or lending to, foreigners.

Pressure due to these factors may be to some extent self-correcting.

Suppose, for example, that there is a boom in exports and that foreigners are buying a larger volume or paying higher prices for British goods. This increase in demand operates like any other increase in demand to raise British incomes and there is a multiplier effect exactly like the effect that we analysed in Chapter 26 in relation to an increase in investment. Just as the investment multiplier is limited because some of the extra income is saved, so the export multiplier is limited because some of the extra income is spent on imports. The people who find jobs in the export industries spend more out of the higher incomes they earn; this creates more jobs for other people in the home market;

these newly-employed workers are also able to spend more; and so the process goes on. But at each stage in the cumulative process of expansion there is, so to speak, a leak of purchasing power to expenditure on imports without any subsequent return flow of demand unless the country supplying the imports is in the habit of using additional income to make purchases from Britain.

If the British authorities were prepared to allow the whole process of adjustment to operate through employment and incomes, the increase in exports would eventually be counterbalanced, at a higher level of incomes, by a corresponding increase in imports, just as an increase in investment is counterbalanced by an increase in savings.

That this is not an altogether fanciful account of the way in which adjustment can take place is obvious from the experience of primary producing countries. It is not uncommon for the exports of those countries to fluctuate violently and for those fluctuations to be accompanied by equally violent fluctuations in imports. There may not even be any perceptible lag in imports behind exports; for if it is plain that export prices are rising sharply, importers will know that their customers are having a good year and will take action at once to stock up with suitable commodities. It happens that in many primary producing countries there is a high income-elasticity of demand for imported manufactures (i.e., a high proportion of any increase in income is spent on those imports) and this speeds up the process of adjustment. Where the appetite for imports is less easily stimulated (or inhibited) the flow of expenditure is concentrated on the domestic market; but since, as a rule, output in primary producing countries is highly inelastic, the immediate effect is a sharp, all-round inflation of prices. This inflation accomplishes what the increase in incomes by itself failed to accomplish: it makes imports seem relatively cheap and attractive and widens the market for them. In the end, therefore, the same adjustment takes place but at a higher level of money incomes.

In a manufacturing country this kind of automatic adjustment would operate through swings in employment rather than in price. If, for example, exports fell off, this would first be reflected in unemployment in the export industries and the depression in the export industries would then be communicated to other industries as the volume of demand contracted. The resulting depression would reduce the current off-take of imported materials and would also react on the demand for imported foodstuffs and finished goods of all kinds. In the absence of government action, this process would continue until the deficit in the balance of payments disappeared.

A movement of capital can also be self-correcting but in a rather different way. It might result, for example, from a decision to build new fixed assets abroad rather than at home, although such decisions are rare and not typical of the normal decisions that lead to an export of capital. The fall in British investment would release resources in Britain while the rise in investment abroad might increase the demand for exports of capital goods from Britain, so that a shift in the employment of British resources into the export trades earned the foreign exchange necessary to accomplish the financial transfer of capital.

This kind of situation was more likely to arise half a century ago when the United Kingdom was both the major exporter of capital and the chief supplier of most of the capital-importing countries. But even at that time, the mechanism of adjustment was usually a great deal more complicated. The main effect of an increase in the export of capital was to make it more difficult to finance investment in Britain, so that it helped to depress the level of domestic investment. At the same time, foreign countries tended to borrow from Britain at a time when British exports were high, so that the pressure on the export trades compensated for the lack of pressure on the building industry. This made it possible to transfer capital without giving rise to recurrent crises in the balance of payments; but there was nothing in the nature of things that made this inevitable.

A transfer of capital might be self-correcting in its effects on the balance of payments if it caused interest rates to rise in the lending country and fall in the borrowing country. These movements in interest rates would tend to check capital formation in the one and stimulate it in the other. Changes in the rate of capital formation, as we saw in Chapter 26, are intimately connected with changes in the level of effective demand and employment. The lending country would experience a depression which checked its demand for imports while the borrowing country would undergo an expansion in activity which rein-forced its demand for imports. If the two countries traded with one another, as is likely, the whole of the adjustment would not fall on their imports but would also affect their exports to one another (or to third countries) and this change in their exports would moderate the fluctuation in employment necessary to restore equilibrium.

So far we have left out of account the monetary effects of a change in the balance of payments and any action that the monetary authorities may take to speed up or delay the process of adjustment. These effects differ according as dealings in foreign exchange are free or restricted, at a fixed rate or at a fluctuating rate. We may begin by taking the case where dealings are free and at a fixed par of exchange. Since the fixed par is usually defined in terms of the price of gold, or of some currency convertible into gold, this case is for all practical purposes that of the gold standard.

### The mechanism of adjustment under gold standard conditions

It will simplify matters if we identify gold standard conditions with those ruling in Britain in the period before 1914, without taking into account modifications introduced since that time and neglecting differences in the practice of other countries. Most of those modifications and differences relate to the precise part played by gold movements in the mechanism of adjustment.

First of all, the excess of payments has to be financed. Under the conditions which we are assuming it was financed, once the gold export point was reached, by purchases of gold from the Bank of England. Those purchases were paid for in the ordinary way by cheques on a commercial bank and the Bank of England, on receipt of the cheques, debited them against the bankers' balances which it held. This had two consequences. The first was a contraction in total bank deposits and so in the supply of money. The second was a fall in the cash reserves of the commercial banks and in their reserve-ratios. Unless the Bank of England took action to restore bankers' balances by open market operations, therefore, a contraction of credit ensued exactly like the contraction that would follow the sale of government securities by the Bank of England. The commercial banks were forced to call in their loans to the discount market and reinforce the immediate fall in their deposit liabilities caused by the purchases of gold by a further reduction through credit restriction. This made money "tight" and brought about a rise in interest rates.

The earliest and largest increase was in discount rates, since it was the money market which felt the immediate impact of credit restriction. The higher rates of discount made London a less attractive source of short-term credit and reduced the flow of bills sent for discount on the London market. To a lesser extent it also increased the demand for sterling funds in order to take advantage of the higher return obtainable in London. The combined effect of a reduced demand for foreign exchange and an increased demand for pounds was to move the rate of exchange away from gold export point and to bring to a stop the outward flow of gold.

If the deficit in the balance of payments was a temporary one—due, for example, to seasonal pressure—this effect was adequate to correct it. If the deficit arose because the level of costs and prices in Britain was rising relatively to costs and prices elsewhere, or because the pressure of demand was becoming excessive, the rise in interest rates might be sufficient either to moderate the pressure or give time for the divergence in prices and costs to correct itself. But if the source of disequilibrium was more deep-seated, the effect of higher interest rates on the flow of international credit could only be a stop-gap. So long as foreign borrowing was curtailed or foreign balances continued to be attracted to London,[1] imports could remain in excess of exports without any movements of gold. But immediately no further change in the flow of credit took place, gold exports had to be resumed. Or if, for any reason, the deficit had made foreigners fear devaluation—as in those days never happened—and a flow of "hot" money out of sterling had begun, the pressure on sterling would have been greatly aggravated. A continuing deficit could be cured only by a fall in imports or a rise in exports.

To this cure the rise in interest rates and the restriction of credit contributed. They operated in the same direction as the automatic influences on employment and incomes which we discussed above and were not easy to distinguish from these influences. Dear money discouraged investment and limited demand so that there was an incentive to ship to foreign markets goods that could not be sold at home. At the same time, the fall in incomes that accompanied the lower level of investment reduced the demand for imports of all kinds. By depressing economic activity, it was possible to bring imports and exports back into balance with one another.

Eventually, yet another effect might make itself felt. The depression in activity tended to drive down the level of costs and make Britain a relatively cheap market from which to buy and a difficult market in which to compete. This fall in costs might arise simply from lower profit margins or from a closer attention to more economical methods of production by manufacturers facing keener competition; or there might, in conditions of intense depression, be reductions in wages forced on workers under pressure of unemployment. Whatever the cause, lower costs would allow exports to rise, drive down imports and reverse the unfavourable trend in the balance of payments.

So long as a country remains on the gold standard, therefore, equilibrium in its balance of payments tends to be maintained by a number of different forces some of which come into play automatically while others are released by monetary forces. The monetary forces operate through interest rates, first on the flow of credit to or from the country, then on the level of economic activity, and finally on the level of costs and prices. This is true, whether, as we have supposed, the disequilibrium expresses itself in a deficit or takes the form of a surplus: a fall in interest rates sets off changes that are similar, but in the reverse direction, to those set off by a rise in interest rates.

The extent to which monetary forces are brought into operation depends

---

[1] There was, of course, no *physical* movement of foreign money into London. All that happened was that foreigners bought pounds and sold foreign money in exchange: this foreign money was then used in payment for excess imports. In the same way, when we talk of money leaving the country, no money (except gold) moves: it is its ownership, not its situation, that changes. Some people sell pounds (which other people buy) in return for foreign moneys.

upon the policy of the central bank and on the urgency with which it seeks to wipe out a deficit or surplus. The forces arresting a loss of gold, for example, may be slow in gathering strength, while the effect on the bank's reserves are immediate and serious. If the gold reserve is already small, and little in excess of the minimum legal requirements of the bank, there is a danger of panic. Foreigners, afraid that the country may be forced to devalue, and that gold or foreign exchange will then be obtainable only at a much higher price, rush to withdraw their balances, and by increasing the pressure on the bank's gold stock, add to the very danger which alarms them. The bank, therefore, may be forced to take drastic action in self-defence. Alternatively, if it has reason to believe that the loss of gold is temporary and that no tightening of credit is necessary in order to secure its return, it may seek to counteract and alleviate the direct impact on the money-supply of the loss of gold.

This it can do by open market operations. By buying government securities it can prevent a contraction of credit just as, by selling them, it can reinforce it. Whatever assets the central bank acquires—government securities, gold, Treasury Bills—it creates deposits with itself (generally in favour of the commercial banks), broadens the base of credit, and gives the whole monetary system an inflationary impetus; whatever assets it sells, and whatever loans it calls in, it cancels deposits with itself, narrows the base of credit, and applies deflationary pressure to the commercial banks. The purchase of one asset is equal and opposite in its effects to the sale of another. A loss of gold, therefore, can be offset by the purchase of government securities; an inflow of gold can be offset (or sterilised) by the sale of government securities. By keeping its total assets constant the central bank can insulate the whole credit system from the effects of gold movements; but only so long as it still has gold to sell when the flow is outwards or government securities to sell when the flow is inwards.

The gold standard leaves some scope, therefore, for monetary management. There is still need for discretion and judgment in deciding what action to take when gold is flowing in or out. The central bank has to decide whether to offset or reinforce the movement; it has to reconcile, as best it can, the credit requirements of domestic industry with the state of the foreign exchanges; it has also to avoid unnecessary embarrassment to other central banks and seek their co-operation in its own policies. But the need to preserve a fixed par of exchange sets narrow limits to management of the currency, and may face the central bank with many unpleasant dilemmas. In some circumstances, as we have seen, it may even be obliged to acquiesce in severe credit restriction that can only result—and is intended to result—in a deflation of output and incomes.

If a country has to impoverish itself by restricting output and incomes so as to remain on the gold standard, it is hardly likely to feel much enthusiasm for the gold standard. It is even less likely to accept a standard that obliges it to bring its costs into line with those of other countries by periodic cuts in money wages since downward adjustments in wage-rates are notoriously difficult to bring about. On the other hand, there are undoubtedly great conveniences to a trading country in a stable and fixed rate of exchange. It is natural to ask, therefore, whether some relaxation of gold standard conditions might not allow adjustment to take place at less cost and with less harshness and without sacrificing the advantages of a stable exchange rate. One such relaxation—if it may be so described—is to be ready, in appropriate circumstances, to change the par value of the currency. It would be a mistake for any country to do this often, but if the alternative is to try to bring about a sharp adjustment in domestic prices and incomes, devaluation (or, on very rare occasions, revaluation upwards) is likely to be preferable.

## Devaluation

Devaluation means the adoption of a new and lower parity of exchange; the price of gold in terms of the currency is increased and the value of the currency, therefore, in terms either of gold or of other currencies is reduced. The effect of devaluation is, as a rule, to wipe out the unfavourable balance and to convert it ultimately into a favourable balance. Suppose, for example, that the pound falls in value from $3 to $2. Then British exports to the United States which were previously sold at $3 can now be sold at $2 without any reduction in the number of pounds received by the exporter. By quoting the same price in terms of sterling, therefore, British exporters will be able to undersell their foreign competitors; this will give a fillip to exports and reduce the unfavourable trade balance. On the other hand, if exporters quote the same price in terms of dollars, they will still sell as large a quantity of goods as before and the sterling value of exports will again increase. Similarly, imports into Britain will require to be sold at prices 50 per cent. higher if the proceeds in terms of dollars are to be maintained; for each pound will now fetch only two instead of three dollars. The rise in the price of imports will cause a reduction in the volume of purchases and also, if the demand is elastic, a reduction in the value of imports. This will reinforce the improvement in the balance of trade and relieve the pressure against sterling. When imports consist very largely of foodstuffs and raw materials, however, they will be in inelastic demand and devaluation, far from reducing their value, will actually increase it. In such circumstances devaluation may be comparatively ineffective as a means of correcting an unfavourable balance;[1] it is even conceivable that devaluation might aggravate

---

[1] See below, pp. 537–538.

the unfavourable balance. In practice, a country's demand for imports and the foreign demand for its exports rarely fail to be elastic enough to produce a contraction in imports and an expansion in exports. Devaluation turns the balance of payments in its favour and relieves the pressure on its exchanges.

Devaluation can hardly be a recurring expedient. If a country devalues its currency every time it suffers from an unfavourable balance, it will destroy the confidence of traders and speculators in the fixity of its exchange rate and lead them to expect further depreciation. Without that confidence, half the value of the gold standard in facilitating international trade and investment is lost; the country has moved half-way from a system of fixed to a system of free exchanges.

## The mechanism of adjustment with fluctuating exchange rates

Let us now suppose that there is no Exchange Equalisation Fund and that the authorities allow the ordinary forces of the exchange market—the pressures to buy and sell foreign exchange—to govern exchange rates. Where will the exchange rate settle? Will it really settle at all, even within wide limits? And how will exchange fluctuations help an adverse balance of payments to correct itself?

For an answer to the first of these questions—what determines the normal equilibrium rate of exchange—we must study the country's balance of short-term indebtedness. If the country is losing gold or is selling foreign balances or is being forced to borrow on short-term in order to finance its imports, then its exchange is overvalued and is likely to depreciate. But if the country is gaining gold or accumulating large balances of foreign exchange, because it is not importing on the same scale as it is exporting, then its currency is under-valued and is likely to appreciate. It is not necessarily true, however, that the equilibrium rate of exchange is one at which no change in the country's short-term indebtedness will be taking place. The country may be a centre in which there is an increasing and natural tendency for the short-term funds of other countries to find investment. Or the country may be trying to make a gradual addition to its holdings of gold and foreign exchange in order to safeguard itself against the effects of violent fluctuations in its exports.

## Purchasing power parity

A rather different, and more easily applicable, test of equilibrium in the rate of exchange has been put forward in the "purchasing power parity" theory.[1]

---

[1] The "purchasing power parity" theory is generally associated with the name of Professor Gustav Cassel, but the gist of the theory was put forward a century earlier during the controversies over the Bullion Report of 1810.

It has been suggested that exchange rates tend to be pulled into line with their "purchasing power parities." Sometimes this is taken to mean that if £1 has the same purchasing power in Britain as $2·8 in America, then the equilibrium rate of exchange is £1 = $2·8. Sometimes with more justification, the theory is modified so as to refer, not to a comparison between the purchasing power of the pound and the dollar at any particular time, but to a comparison between the *changes* in their purchasing power since some base date. If, for example, the purchasing power of the pound has been halved while the purchasing power of the dollar has been doubled, then, it is argued, the dollar will tend to exchange for four times as many pounds as before. In other words, changes in the external value of a currency (its value in exchange for other currencies) tend to reflect changes in its internal value (its purchasing power over commodities).

The first version of the theory is clearly untenable. Every tourist knows that it is cheaper to live in some countries than in others and that, since prices are higher in America than in Britain, he can buy more with £1 than with the $2·8 for which it exchanges. Some prices, the prices of traded goods, must be more or less in line in both countries; but other prices—fares, hotel charges, lawyers' fees, etc.—need not correspond because there is no way by which people living in one country can take advantage of cheap services provided in another. The second version of the theory is more reasonable. It is clear that if prices rise in any country (so that its currency loses purchasing power) there will be a strong tendency for exports to diminish and for imports to increase; the balance of payments will become unfavourable, and exchange depreciation will result. There is a presumption, therefore, that changes in purchasing power will be followed by similar changes in exchange rates. But this presumption must not be interpreted too rigorously; the changes in purchasing power and in exchange rates need not be in exact accordance with one another.

If we take the price of any staple traded commodity, such as wheat, we are likely to find that, converting at current rates of exchange, this price is the same in all countries, allowance being made for transport costs and tariff barriers. So long as the rate of exchange is $4 = £1, wheat selling at a dollar a bushel in Chicago will sell at rather more than 5s. a bushel in Liverpool. If the Liverpool price rises, more wheat will be shipped until the local scarcity disappears. In the same way a fall in the Liverpool price will reduce imports until parity with the Chicago price is re-established. Or if the rate of exchange depreciates to $3 = £1, the Liverpool price—failing any change in price in Chicago—will be marked up automatically by 1s. 8d. a bushel. What is true of wheat is true also of other traded goods. Prices in each country must conform to one another at current exchange rates whatever these rates happen to be. Thus it is useless to compare changes in the purchasing powers of two currencies over *traded* goods as a test of equilibrium. For unless freights or tariffs have altered,[1] these changes in purchasing power *must* be equal whether exchange rates are in equilibrium or not. It is the prices of traded goods which are pulled into line with exchange rates rather than exchange rates which are pulled into line with the prices of traded goods.

When we turn to domestic goods—that is, goods which do not enter into international trade, such as house-room, milk, services of all kinds—we find nothing to couple their prices in one country rapidly and automatically with prices in other countries. If, for example, domestic goods double in price in Britain and remain unchanged in the United States there is no obvious reason why the sterling-dollar exchange rate should immediately fall by 50 per cent. Purchasing power parities measured in terms of domestic goods, therefore, may certainly diverge from exchange parities. But can the divergence *continue*? Is the divergence a measure of disequilibrium in exchange rates and a safe basis on which to forecast their future course?

It should be noted, first of all, that the divergence can equally well be expressed as a divergence between the price-levels of domestic and traded goods. The link between exchange rates and the price-level of traded goods must also bind the general price-level unless domestic goods fail to keep in line with traded goods. If the price-level of domestic goods lags behind the price-level of traded goods, the purchasing power of the currency will also lag behind movements in exchange rates. And if equilibrium requires an equal change in purchasing power and in exchange rates, it must also require, therefore, an equal change in the price-levels of domestic and of trade goods.

Now there are strong forces linking together these two price-levels. If either group of commodities becomes dearer, the most likely cause is a rise in the cost of wages and materials which, if it is at all great, is fairly certain to spread to the other group of commodities. A persistent rise in wages in the export industries, for example, will soon lead to a sympathetic rise in wages in allied industries supplying the home market. First of all, domestic workers in the same craft will share in the rise, then workers in the same grade of labour, and finally workers of greater or inferior skill. Similarly, with raw materials. A rise in the price of steel affects ship plates for export equally with girders for offices and shops at home. Prices are stitched by competition into a fabric which resists distortion. Pressure at one point is felt on all sides, and, although the fabric may give for a time, the old price relationships are soon restored.

It is to this inertia of the price structure that we must turn if we wish to justify

---

[1] A rise in British tariffs or in freight charges on British imports will increase the margin between the price of traded goods in Britain and abroad. Prices will tend to rise in Britain, but since purchases from, and payments to, foreigners will fall, the balance of payments will be more favourable and the rate of exchange, instead of depreciating will probably appreciate. Thus purchasing power and exchange parities will diverge from one another.

the purchasing power parity theory. If the prices of traded and non-traded goods keep in step, so also will exchange rates and purchasing power parities. But we must be careful not to exaggerate the stability of the price structure. Dissimilar changes in the level of output, the unequal incidence of invention, the immobility of labour, and the imperfections of competition make for irregular movements in wages and in prices in different industries, and even in large groups of industries. The experience of the so-called "sheltered" industries—those which supply the domestic market and are immune from foreign competition—need not parallel the experience of the "unsheltered" industries—those which produce traded goods and are, therefore, in competition with foreign industries. Indeed, it is not unusual for the fortunes of these industries to be widely different. Now if, as may happen, costs in the sheltered industries increase, while costs in the unsheltered industries do not, the country's competing power *vis-à-vis* other countries will be practically unchanged and exchange rates will not be much affected. But the level of prices will be higher and the purchasing power of the currency will be correspondlingly lower. The test of purchasing power parity will have broken down.

A similar breakdown takes place whenever there is a change in a country's terms of trade. Suppose, for example, that of two countries each consumes equal amounts of its own and of the other country's goods. A fall in the price of one country's exports will then affect prices (but not incomes) similarly in both countries, and will at the same time cause a depreciation in the rate of exchange parallel to the fall in export prices. That is, the rate of exchange will alter without any similar alteration in purchasing power parity.

A divergence between the rate of exchange and purchasing power parity may also arise because of international capital movements. If a country is lending large sums abroad, or if speculators are transferring balances to other financial centres, heavy sales will be made of the country's currency and its value will depreciate. But prices—at any rate, domestic prices—will not be directly affected by these transfers of capital, and the depreciation in exchange rates will not be accompanied by an equal fall in the purchasing power of the currency.

Once the appropriate qualifications have been made, the purchasing power parity theory loses much of its precision. It is an unsatisfactory short-period theory because it makes no provision for the influence of speculation, capital movements, and so on; and it is an unsatisfactory long-period theory, because it fails to take account of the fact that wages and prices in different groups of industries do not move together.

### The dynamics of fluctuating exchanges

The popularity of the purchasing power parity theory after the first world war was largely due to the emphasis which it laid on inflation as a source of exchange depreciation. It suggested that the proper way to bring that depreciation to a halt was to restrict credit inside the country: this would stop the rise in prices, stabilise the purchasing power of the currency and arrest the depreciation. This point of view was a useful corrective to the tendency of governments to look on an adverse balance of payments as an Act of God and to believe that their domestic financial policy had no connection with any unfavourable movements in exchange rates. A budget deficit, in circumstances of full employment, can be (and almost always is) highly inflationary; and inflation soon reacts on the balance of payments and the rate of exchange. In real terms, if the government sucks away productive resources by over-spending its income, somebody else has to go short; either the export industries find difficulty in obtaining men and materials at wages and prices that allow them to compete, or additional imports are drawn in from abroad to relieve the shortage of goods. Either way, the balance of payments will soon show a deficit. The ensuing depreciation normally has a therapeutic effect since it restores the competitive position of the export trades and diverts demand from imports by making them dearer. But if the government goes on over-spending, prices will go on increasing and the process of squeezing out exports and sucking in more imports will be resumed. Indeed it is just for this reason that in a galloping inflation the exchange rate falls faster than prices rise: because speculators will have no confidence that prices have reached a ceiling and will only be willing to buy the currency at a discount on its purchasing power parity.

## Cumulative movements in exchange rates

Although a fall in the rate of exchange generally serves to improve a country's balance of payments, there are circumstances in which it may actually aggravate an existing deficit. Suppose, for example, that the country's exports are in inelastic demand in foreign markets and that they are also in inelastic supply. These conditions will apply if the country has a limited range of exports, consisting largely of staple products, and if it is the principal supplier of those products. Obvious examples are Australia and Malaya, the former being heavily dependent on exports of wool and wheat, the latter on exports of rubber and tin. A fall in the rate of exchange will automatically reduce the price of exports in terms of foreign currencies, while the volume of exports will show little response either because of difficulties in expanding the supply or because of the inelasticity of demand in world markets. The net result, therefore, will be a reduction in the amount earned in foreign exchange. If there is a similar inelasticity on the side of imports—for example, because they consist largely of foodstuffs—a fall in the rates of exchange may do little to diminish their volume and their cost in terms of foreign currencies. The excess of imports over exports will then be higher than before. Moreover, since imported goods will rise in price in terms of the local currency there will be a strong tendency towards a general inflation of prices and a strain throughout the whole financial system. Inflation rebounds on the balance of payments even if there is considerable elasticity on the side both of exports and imports; but if the elasticities are low, the rebound will be tremendous. A cumulative process of exchange depreciation and internal inflation may be started off, the balance of payments getting steadily worse, not better.

For a fall in the rate of exchange to add to an already adverse balance is rare, except where the elasticities involved are abnormally low. Even when the balance of payments is slow in swinging round, speculative forces generally come into play at an early stage and these forces help to sustain the rate of exchange by a transfer of funds into the depreciating currency as soon as it appears to be undervalued. Not all economists, however, would agree with this judgment; and there have been a number of elaborate calculations purporting to show that, in international trade, the elasticities involved are often surprisingly low.

Whatever the truth of the matter, there is no doubt that most countries are afraid that *in their case* the elasticities will be low and are full of good reasons for not allowing their currency to depreciate in spite of a persistently unfavourable balance of payments. They have the same reluctance about a voluntary depreciation as a monopolist has about cutting his price. A country that lowers its rate of exchange is deliberately accepting less favourable terms of trade, since import prices in the country's currency will rise relatively to export prices. It may feel, therefore, that it would have to make a large concession (for example, in additional exports) for a small gain in its balance of payments. For this reason, and also for reasons of prestige, few countries devalue except from sheer necessity. On the other hand, few carry this reasoning to the point of deliberately *raising* their rate of exchange.

### The dollar shortage

Since the war there has been one notable example of an adverse balance that exchange depreciation might well have aggravated: the adverse balance of the rest of the world with the United States. There was good reason to suppose that, in the immediate post-war years, a general devaluation of currencies against the dollar would not have induced the United States to buy a substantially larger volume of imports; that it would take time before the rest of the world could muster its export potential and surmount the high American tariff wall; and that it would be extremely difficult for Europe in particular to cut her purchases in North America of the foodstuffs, materials and equipment that were unprocurable elsewhere and indispensable to the reconstruction of a disorganised and devastated continent. If the rest of the world had tried to balance dollar receipts and payments by making dollars dearer, they might have become still scarcer. More than this: if the major trading countries had succeeded in balancing their dollar accounts by direct cuts in imports from North America, some of them would have suffered severe dislocation and unemployment through lack of essential raw materials, and all of them would have perceptibly delayed their economic recovery. No doubt a more severe financial policy would have helped; once budget deficits were brought under control and interest rates allowed to rise, it did help. But it required dollar loans and dollar grants to balance the international accounts without a quite disproportionate loss of output and income in the recipient countries.

The shortage of dollars in the immediate post-war years was more than a shortage of a particular currency: it was also a shortage of capital. Without external aid Europe could not have met so successfully the double strain of restoring pre-war standards of living and replenishing or rehabilitating her pre-war capital stock. With external aid she was able to supplement her own resources out of the margin of productive power that America alone could spare. With those additional resources put at her disposal by Marshall Aid she was able to accelerate the work of reconstruction. Marshall Aid was, in effect, a grant of capital at a time when local savings were insufficient to sustain reconstruction on the scale required. But it was in some ways a coincidence that the capital was supplied by the country from which imports were most urgently required. It just happened that the things that Europe most needed for recovery were imported foodstuffs, raw materials and equipment and that, for all practical purposes, these could come from no other country but America. America happened to have both the specific commodities required and the margin of productive power from which to make a grant of capital.

The dollar shortage, therefore, was to some extent a reflection of the shortage of resources in Europe, and would have been mitigated by aid to Europe whatever the country providing it. But to some extent also the dollar shortage existed independently of the shortage of capital. There was a problem of making sufficient sales to the United States, over her tariff and in competition with her great industries, to balance what the world was likely to buy from the United States at current rates of exchange, and perhaps also at substantially different ones. Europe could not be sure of increasing her dollar earnings whatever the pressure she put on her exporters or the favours and advantages that she granted them. There was no sign that America would spend much more on European goods once Europe had no lack of goods to sell; nor that American imports from elsewhere would increase sufficiently to offer other countries a chance of earning a surplus of dollars. There could be no guarantee that a large and costly depreciation in terms of the dollar would wipe out the gap in the dollar balance of payments. This gap depended quite as much on American policy as on the policy of other countries.

### Exchange control

When a country is unwilling to allow market forces to operate unchecked on its rate of exchange, or fears that market forces will not operate to restore equilibrium in its balance of payments, it can institute a system of exchange control. The banks will then be allowed to supply foreign exchange only to make payments approved by the government while all receipts in foreign currencies will have to be handed over to the banks. A system of exchange control has been in force in Britain since the outbreak of war in 1939 and was put on a statutory basis by the Exchange Control Act, 1947.

The mere canalising of receipts and payments through a control would make little difference if there were not a simultaneous limitation on the transactions permitted by the government. The first such limitation is on capital movements. Loans to foreign countries, purchases of securities from foreigners, even transfers of money by emigrants, come under strict control. There may also be limitations on current transactions. The machinery of import licensing imposes a ceiling on imports of particular goods, or fixes quotas for imports of the goods from each country. Tourists may be given a ration of foreign currency which they must not exceed. Various other transactions involving payment in foreign currencies can be made illegal or subject to licence.

Because exchange control is more mysterious or more remote than other types of control many people are disposed to accept it as more effective. But it is subject to the same limitations. There is the same scope for administrative muddle; there are black markets in foreign exchange as in commodities; there are flights of capital even when capital movements are forbidden. It only requires a minor delay on the part of exporters in surrendering foreign exchange and a minor scurry on the part of importers to meet their obligations in foreign exchange to create a disconcerting divergence between the excess of exports over imports and the excess of receipts over payments. The terms of credit which importers enjoy or for which exporters are asked depend upon the confidence of foreigners in the currency: if their confidence is shaken, the terms of payment will move against the country and the balance of payments will reflect this move without any transgression of the law or any change in imports and exports. Speculative movements of funds may have been driven out of the door; but they have a way of coming in again at the window.

## Hard and soft currencies

When exchange control is instituted, the monetary authorities soon find that they are accumulating some currencies and running short of others. If they are free to set a surplus against a deficit because currencies are freely convertible, this makes no difference. But if other currencies are not freely convertible, the surplus of "soft" currencies will not help to finance imports for which payment has to be made in "hard" currencies. Transactions in hard currencies are therefore subjected to more severe restrictions than transactions in soft currencies and countries try to regulate their trade so as not to be left with deficits that have to be settled in hard currencies. If for "hard currencies" we read "gold and dollars"[1] this means that imports costing dollars are limited more strictly than other imports, that exports to dollar markets are boosted by administrative pressure or by special inducements, and that efforts are made to develop new sources of supply for goods that would otherwise have to be bought for dollars. In other words, there is discrimination against "dollar" goods and in favour of "non-dollar" goods. This discrimination obliges consumers to content themselves with goods bought with soft currencies even when they are of inferior quality, more costly, or less to the taste of consumers. It serves to improve the dollar balance of payments and so to make the dollar softer, while heavier purchases from other countries in replacement of dollar imports make the soft currencies harder.

Discrimination is not directed exclusively against the countries that use the hardest of hard currencies. It extends also to countries which insist that any excess of payments due to them should be settled in "gold and dollars." If Britain finds that she is paying gold to Belgium, for example, she may try to put a stop to those payments by restricting imports from Belgium so as to get nearer to an exact balance of payments and receipts. Alternatively, she may invite Belgium to accept settlement of the difference in sterling or at least to allow the deficit to reach an agreed figure before gold becomes payable.

## Bilateralism

Once discrimination becomes the order of the day, the pattern of international trade is inevitably distorted. Goods are bought which in other circumstances would not be bought and goods cannot be bought which, with multilateral trading arrangements, would be much in demand. Trade tends to be governed by bilateral bargains between pairs of countries in which each country undertakes to supply the other with a quota of goods that are not easily obtainable

---

[1] Gold, because it is convertible into any currency; dollars, because in conditions of dollar shortage, the dollar became the hardest currency.

elsewhere and to admit a quota of goods to which it would otherwise deny a market. These bargains are so regulated as to limit the difference between exports and imports and the amount of gold and other hard currencies needed in settlement. The result is a general pressure to economise in the use of hard currencies.

The pressure is not equally severe on all countries since some are likely to have a traditional (or "structural") deficit in their trade with the "dollar" countries and to be in great need of earning "dollars" by multilateral trade with third countries; while others may have a traditional surplus and have "dollars" to spare. Denmark, for example, would be much more embarrassed if no one would pay her dollars (with which to buy feeding-stuffs from overseas) than would Switzerland (which has a large dollar income from her investments in the United States). The United Kingdom might also be in a rather awkward position if she had to rule out any possibility of buying in North America more than she could pay for out of her current earnings from exports to North America, without drawing on supplementary earnings through trade with other countries.

Bilaterism involves a contraction in the area of competition. Imports from some countries are admitted but not from others. Quotas can be adjusted arbitrarily to suit a particular commercial agreement or because some currency has changed from "hard" to "soft" or vice versa. The home producer, therefore, is protected from the competition of hard currency products; and even his soft currency competitors cannot build up an undisturbed market connection that puts them on a footing of equality. Exporters may have to face not only import restrictions imposed abroad but export licensing restrictions at home, and they, too, feel the disturbance of normal commercial links. There is, therefore, a real danger of a general inflation of costs and a loss of productive efficiency.

Added to this, discrimination as such is not a healthy feature of international trade. It can easily generate bad blood between one country and another, invites retaliation, and imports into commercial dealings between nations political considerations that do not make for stability. Although commercial discrimination is a powerful weapon in an emergency, therefore, and can help to cure an otherwise unmanageable deficit or surplus in one country's balance of payments, it is not a weapon to be used lightly so long as there is a reasonable prospect of avoiding a general lack of balance and of maintaining a steady expansion on a multilateral basis.

### The sterling area

The rigours of bilateralism were softened in the United Kingdom by the special arrangements under which other countries, mainly members of the

Commonwealth, were grouped with Britain in the sterling area. The main feature of the sterling area is that members are prepared to accept sterling freely and to settle any deficits with one another in this currency. The members other than Britain hold only limited reserves of gold and convertible currencies (other than sterling) and pool their earnings of those currencies, accepting sterling in return and enjoying free access to the central reserves of the area when they have payments to make across the exchanges. These arrangements, which are of long standing and grew out of trading and banking relationships in the nineteenth century, were not formalised until exchange control was introduced in 1939 and it became necessary to designate the countries—the "scheduled territories"—between which payments could be made freely and without exchange control. A common barrier of controls was erected round the countries of the sterling area: not so that each administered an identical set of regulations but rather so that each adapted to its own local situation a common policy of limiting transactions involving an outlay in gold, dollars, and other hard currencies. This barrier has since crumbled with every step taken towards free convertibility of sterling into other currencies; but so long as it existed, it made subject to discrimination trade with countries that insisted on payment in hard currencies. Within the sterling area, however, multilateral trading arrangements were preserved and in trade agreements with other countries sterling remained fully expendable within any part of the sterling area. As the trade of the sterling area is a large fraction of total world trade, this meant that the scope for multilateral trade remained substantial even in the worst days of bilateralism.

## The European Payments Union

An important step away from bilateral trading arrangements was taken in 1950 with the setting up of a European Payments Union (E.P.U.) under the Organisation for European Economic Co-operation (O.E.E.C.). This enabled the members of the O.E.E.C. (the Western European countries which joined in the Marshall Plan) to set off their surpluses and deficits in trade with one another and left each of them to settle only its *total* surplus or deficit in such trade. The first slice of any such deficit was covered by a credit from the E.P.U. Later slices had to be covered by an increasing proportion of gold and a diminishing proportion of credit. The total amount of credit that a country could obtain from the E.P.U. was fixed, except by special arrangement with the Managing Board, and was determined by the country's quota in the Union.

These arrangements made it largely a matter of indifference whether payments had to be made in the currency of one member country or in that of another, and went a long way, therefore, towards removing any incentive to treat one European currency as harder than another. They also removed most of the justification for discriminating against other member countries. The payments arrangements were therefore coupled with an agreement to refrain from discrimination in intra-European trade and to "liberalise" (that is, to free from import licensing restrictions) a large proportion—initially, 60 per cent.— of all imports from other member countries. Although non-European members of the sterling area were not included in the O.E.E.C. group of countries, and did not benefit under the agreement on commercial policy, the fact that sterling was one of the currencies coming within the settlements made in E.P.U. greatly extended the scope of these settlements since all sterling transactions, and not just those with the United Kingdom, were brought to account.

The E.P.U., therefore, represented a move towards a wider area of multilateral trade and towards the restoration of gold settlements of deficits in the balance of payments; and a move away from bilateralism and discrimination. It brought a large proportion of world trade into a single payments system, mobilised a large pool of credit to cover temporary deficits, and provided incentives to relax trade restrictions instead of tightening them. In doing this, it left each country with a good deal of elbow-room. If any member found itself running into deficit at an alarming rate, it was free to suspend measures for the liberalisation of its trade (that is, to withdraw the relaxations of import restrictions) provided it did not discriminate between one member and another; if any member was in chronic surplus with the Union, the E.P.U. could waive the rule of non-discrimination and empower other members to limit their imports from the creditor. While many countries availed themselves of the first of those provisions, the second was never in fact brought into operation.

When the E.P.U. came to an end in December 1958 and was replaced by the European Monetary Agreement, all the members except three (Greece, Turkey and Iceland) restored the external convertibility of their currencies for non-resident holders: that is, any foreigner was free to ask for payment in a currency of his own choosing. This removed any logical basis for continuing discrimination on balance of payments grounds against other countries, since if it was possible to pay a non-American in dollars for goods obtained outside the United States there could be no valid reason for withholding permission to buy the same goods in the United States and pay an American for them in dollars. It was, however, some time before convertibility of European currencies was followed by the abandonment of discrimination against "dollar imports."

The credit which members of the E.P.U. extended to one another automatically is available to a much smaller extent and on much stricter conditions under the European Monetary Agreement. The capital which can be called upon is $600m. and this can be used, at the discretion of the O.E.C.D. (as the

O.E.E.C. has now become), to help members to survive temporary balance of payments difficulties without reimposing trade restrictions. The Agreement also provides a general framework within which European governments can co-operate in framing their monetary policies. In addition, there is, and has been throughout the post-war period, a regular exchange of views between the central banks of the leading European countries at the monthly meetings of the Bank for International Settlements in Basle.

## The International Monetary Fund

The liquidation of the European Payments Union makes it all the more necessary that international monetary co-operation should be secured through the organisation that was created for that purpose—the International Monetary Fund (I.M.F.). The I.M.F. is world-wide in scope, its members including the United States, the United Kingdom, and all the countries of the British Commonwealth except New Zealand. This very universality, while a source of strength in normal conditions, was in some ways a source of weakness in the post-war years when it proved easier to organise monetary reconstruction on a regional basis. The Fund was suspicious of arrangements like the E.P.U. and the sterling area that put discrimination on an organised footing, and seemed to many people to be so busy pursuing a set of ideal conditions that it overlooked what was really feasible. There was never any doubt, however, that in the long run, a world-wide organisation was indispensable and that once the immediate post-war difficulties had been overcome, it would have an increasingly important part to play.

The I.M.F. was planned at Bretton Woods in 1944 and was brought into existence after the war "to assist in the establishment of a multilateral system of payments in respect of current transactions between members and in the elimination of foreign exchange restrictions which hamper the growth of world trade." The principal aim of the Fund, like that of the gold standard, is to secure a general convertibility of currencies as stable rates of exchange; unlike the gold standard, it tries to combine with this aim the preservation of internal economic balance and a high and stable level of activity in the member countries. It is possible, however, to accept convertibility, fixed exchanges and internal balance as objectives of policy without specifying in what sequence each should be approached, in what order of priority they should be ranked, or by what means they should be achieved. In practice, the Fund laid emphasis on the early declaration of fixed parities of exchange and the early removal of exchange restrictions, without contributing a great deal during the critical post-war period towards establishing conditions in which these things were appropriate.

The emphasis on fixed rates of exchange was in reaction against the

S

experience of the thirties and designed to prevent competitive depreciations. Every member was required to keep its rate of exchange within a margin of 1 per cent. of the gold parity declared to the Fund and to consult the Fund before changing this parity. Such changes were allowable in principle if the country was in a state of "fundamental disequilibrium" (presumably when it had a chronic deficit—or surplus—in its balance of payments). The British depreciation of 1949, however, was decided upon without any real consultation with the Fund (although it was delayed so that the Fund could be informed); other countries have adopted multiple exchange rates or fluctuating exchange rates without prior consultation with the Fund. Thus the general principle that rates should only be varied (by more than 10 per cent.) after consultation and with the concurrence of the Fund is largely a dead letter.

Convertibility of currencies was supposed to be achieved by the end of a short transition period. A distinction was drawn between capital transactions which could continue to be restricted and current transactions which could be restricted only during the transition period. This distinction arose largely out of the "hot money" movements of the thirties—movements which were patently de-stabilising in their effects. The distinction, although clear in principle, was much more difficult to apply in practice since capital movements could take place through the medium of current transactions and were correspondingly difficult to control in the absence of a simultaneous control over current transactions. For many years, however, the distinction had little practical importance since both types of transaction were controlled and the transition stretched out indefinitely. The premature efforts of the United Kingdom to introduce convertibility in 1947, under the Washington Loan Agreement of the previous year, scotched any further attempts for a long time and although exchange restrictions were relaxed in the middle fifties, it was not until the end of the decade that a decisive step towards external convertibility was taken.

The Fund also tries to help its members in various ways to reconcile internal and external balance. This it can do in two ways: by penalising countries that remain persistently in surplus and by giving credit to countries in temporary deficit. It can, for example, declare a general scarcity of a currency if the country concerned is draining away other countries' reserves and throwing them out of balance; it can also declare a currency scarce on the more technical grounds that its own holdings of the currency have been exhausted through loans to its members. In fact, the Fund has never declared any currency scarce on either ground and it is highly unlikely that it ever will. It has relied instead on the advance of credits to its members.

These credits take the form of purchases from the Fund's pool of foreign currencies, to which all members have contributed. The amount contributed to this pool by each country (and its voting rights in the Fund) is governed by its quota, one quarter of the quota being payable in gold or dollars and the rest in its own currency. Each country can withdraw up to the first quarter more or less without question, but drawings in excess of this have to be justified by progressively stricter criteria and the maximum that can be drawn, with the Fund's agreement, is 125 per cent. of the country's quota. The credits are re-payable in gold or convertible currencies and bear charges that become in-creasingly onerous the larger the amount outstanding and the longer the period for which they are outstanding.

The lending operations of the Fund, after an initial period of activity, came almost to a standstill during the period of Marshall Aid and remained relatively small until the Suez Crisis in 1956, when the United Kingdom was allowed to draw $561m. and given a stand-by credit of $739m., equal to the whole of the remainder of its quota. From 1956 onwards, however, the Fund pursued a more active policy and in 1959, for the first time since the war, it increased members' quotas by 50 per cent, in order to obtain additional resources. A further increase by 25 per cent. was voted in 1964.

In the early post-war period, the difficulties of monetary reconstruction were bigger and more enduring than the Fund could have hoped to overcome, even if it had been trying to do the right things. To re-establish world trade on a multilateral basis, free from exchange restrictions, needed more time, more resources and more deviousness than had been imagined. Once this aim had been achieved, there was a chance that I.M.F. might come into its own; but it was still possible to doubt whether the resources at its disposal were adequate to maintain international equilibrium. There seemed room for further develop-ment of the Fund into something more closely resembling an international central bank, accepting deposits from the central banks of member countries and encouraging them to pool their reserves rather than hold them in gold and foreign currencies.

CHAPTER 34

# RISE AND DECLINE OF LAISSEZ-FAIRE

A century ago there was a general bias against interference by the State in the conduct of industry. The business of government was to preserve law and order, to defend the country from invasion, and, when opportunity arose, to extend the boundaries of empire. The business of industry was to make things cheaply. Interference by industry in politics was fatal to good government, and interference by the State in industry was fatal to efficient production. Business influences, it was argued, are apt to corrupt politics; and political influences are apt to corrupt business. The wisest course for a government to follow was to pursue a policy of laissez-faire; to abstain from a blundering intervention and leave industry to its own devices.

The movement in favour of laissez-faire drew strength from two more or less distinct groups. There were those who disliked government interference on principle, because it limited the freedom of action of the individual; and there were those who disliked such interference as they encountered in practice, because they felt it to be foolish or unjust. The first group appealed to the natural rights of the individual; the second, to their business experience. Both groups—philosophers and business men—were united in opposition to authoritarianism. They challenged "the right divine of kings to govern wrong" because of a common dislike of bureaucratic restrictions on freedom of opinion and of enterprise.[1] Not that these early "liberals," having taken to the path of individualism, had any clear idea where it led. The business men fought hardest—often from motives of self-interest—against particular restrictions which they found irksome or costly; but they were often disposed to put other restrictions—

---

[1] Thus it was not accident that religious toleration and laissez-faire grew up side by side. For both were rooted in the experience and outlook of a rising social class, concerned to get on and impatient of authority. In economics, this class demanded free trade in goods and the suppression of privileged monopolies; in religion, it demanded free trade in opinions and the suppression of religious discrimination. Competition in industry would eradicate inefficiency; competition in ideas would eradicate untruth.

no less intolerant and monopolistic—in their place. The philosophers fought against encroachments by the State on individual liberty; but they defended rights of property which could be as real a menace to the liberty of the unpropertied as any governmental despotism. Moreover, although both groups were united in condemning State interference as *undesirable,* it was not until laissez-faire found a third group of supporters—the economists—that interference came to be thought of as *unnecessary.* It was the economists who, by making the virtues of laissez-faire intelligible in a synthesis of principle and experience, paved the way for the final triumph of the policy.

### Economic arguments against government intervention

The case for laissez-faire was largely a demonstration of the superiority of the market over government regulation and control as an instrument of economic co-ordination. The market—so ran the argument—allowed producers and consumers to associate freely, on an impersonal basis, without the need to consult any interests but their own. There was no need for bargaining or negotiation; in a perfect market the price did not respond to the pressure of individual buyers or sellers, but only to the total pressure of all buyers and sellers, and was automatically such as to allow all who were prepared to do business to transact all the business they wanted at the market price. The weighing up of alternatives, the acceptance or rejection of offers for sale or purchase, the initiative in seeking improved ways of producing or in meeting wants in a more economical way, were left to producers and consumers who could be supposed to have an unrivalled knowledge of their own affairs. There was no need for argument or compulsion before a price moved up or down, a new technique of manufacture was adopted, or greater economy in a scarce product was practised: the silent pressure of the market settled prices, forced the inefficient out of business and steered the limited incomes of consumers away from expensive towards other, less costly, products. If a producer wanted to make things differently from his competitors he was free to do so and, if successful, might see them all obliged to follow suit, not from rivalry, but in self-preservation. If a consumer wanted to indulge some personal idiosyncrasy he, too, could do so without permit, licence or extra coupons. Individual preferences were given the maximum scope; innovation and capital accumulation were given the maximum encouragement. The cost of living was kept down because the inefficient went out of business and because, thanks to free trade, the maximum advantage could be taken of the willingness of foreigners to offer goods that could only be made at high cost in return for goods that could be made comparatively cheaply.

Thus whatever might be true of distribution—and it was arguable that, under perfect competition, everyone earned his deserts in the value of his contribution to output—the market was an admirable and automatic technique for controlling production. It was unnecessary for the government to regulate and plan industry because prices already balanced supply and demand, cost and utility; the price mechanism was an adequate substitute for planning.[1] It was also unwise for the government to intervene; governments were incapable of improving upon the delicate machinery of the market, and were likely, by their intervention, to throw the machinery out of gear, or to impose the dead hand of routine, or to act as the puppets of "sinister interests." By devolving the tasks of enterprise upon the business community, they could enlist stronger motives and more intimate knowledge in the planning of industrial output. And that output, produced at the lowest possible cost, would conform to the free choice of consumers as expressed in their purchases, not to some ideal imposed by an authoritarian government.

The case for laissez-faire was a strong one; it was realistic in its appeal to experience, and idealistic in its appeal to individualism. Historically, too, laissez-faire was a highly successful, if unnecessarily harsh, policy; the material progress made in the nineteenth century was immense, and it would be foolish to belittle it. But the policy had its drawbacks. and the arguments on which it rested, their flaws.

### The long-term trend towards regulation and control

Laissez-faire was a dogma rather than a fact: the State never yielded entirely to the general bias against intervention in industry. In particular, it showed more reluctance to leave domestic trade uncontrolled than to adopt free trade in international economic relations. The subsequent extension of government control, however, particularly over the last fifty years, represents something of a revolution in economic policy and it is no longer possible to treat such control as exceptional and running counter to the general temper of the age.

The decline of laissez-faire and the corresponding rise of government control, although gaining momentum after the first world war, date from an earlier period. There had been intervention against the abuse of monopoly power: railway, gas and electric power companies, for example, were not free to fix their charges, and were subject to various restrictions over dividends, new construction, and other matters. There had been intervention in sectors of the economy of critical importance to policy; the Bank Charter Act of 1844, for example, was designed to prevent the financial system from getting out of order.

---

[1] For a development of this line of thought, see pp. 186–188, 557–558.

There had been intervention also because the market ignored fundamental wants or was incapable of bringing them satisfaction. Public health legislation provides many examples: infectious diseases, like cholera, could not be got rid of by competition in any form but could be got rid of by better sanitation, and this involved common arrangements on behalf of all citizens, independently of their power to contribute to the cost. Ignorance was potentially as great a danger as disease; common arrangements had, therefore, to be made for the schooling of the population at the State's expense. Roads, public parks and libraries met other, communal, wants. In course of time the vast machinery of the social services was built up to meet common dangers, provide common enjoyment, and succour those who fell below a common minimum standard.

With all this there went a decline in the philosophy of individualism and an increased stress, partly under the influence of German writers and statesmen, first, on social ties and secondly, on the State as the means by which those ties could be preserved and fostered. It was realised that the State had a positive part to play in creating a social framework and in keeping enterprise in check where it might otherwise do injury to the common weal. This change in outlook contributed to the growth of free secondary education, the introduction of insurance against unemployment, old age pensions and other social services: these services were recognised as needs of a thriving community for which it was the responsibility of the State to cater. Direct restrictions on freedom of enterprise also increased. The State defined more narrowly the terms on which business of any kind could be carried on (e.g., in the Factory, Truck, and Marketing Acts). It legislated on maximum hours of work and gave Trade Boards power to fix minimum wages. But at this stage the State rarely sought to *replace* the market; it preferred to re-shape market conditions, retaining the motive force of competition through the price-mechanism and redirecting it into channels where it would serve the public interest, not clash with it. This meant a recognition that private enterprise did not uniformly promote the public interest; but it also meant a reliance on private enterprise within the leading-strings of legislation. The Bank Charter Act, for example, was not directed against the automatic operation of the money-market and intended as a preliminary to a managed monetary system; its object was rather to make the financial system function *more* automatically, but function in the right way. To prohibit the employment of women in coal-mines did not affect the ownership and control of the mines but merely ruled out one technique of operation. A protective tariff tilted market conditions more in favour of the industry protected without altering the basis of competition within the industry. The State could both limit the range of permissible activities and encourage desirable activities within that range without violence to the price-mechanism or serious limitations on enterprise.

Once the path of control and regulation had begun to be trodden, however, it was difficult to halt. The very idea of social control, in an age of science, had attractions that would have puzzled an earlier generation. The fascination of a system that worked automatically to the advantage both of individual and society gave way to the fascination of a system in which everything was planned in advance by a conscious effort. Those who had been taught to accept the verdict of the market on their services as a thing unalterable, saw the market itself under control. They began to learn that appeal could be made to the State, and that the decision of the State could be swayed in ways that did not operate through the market: by propaganda, by influence with a political party, by obstinacy in a national emergency. There was also less distrust of the government machine: the civil service had ceased to be corrupt, lazy and arbitrary and was capable of assuming wider duties whereas a century earlier its inefficiency and corruption argued powerfully for a limitation of its responsibilities.

### The justification of an active economic policy

Government intervention has developed piece-meal, each measure being adopted on its merits and only rarely in order to give effect to some theory of economic organisation. No-one can claim to have foreseen, much less planned, the present blend of private enterprise and State control, although a mixed system of some sort has long been recognised as desirable and indeed inevitable. The growth of State intervention has to be explained and justified, therefore, at least as much in terms of the practical reasons that have brought it about as in terms of the theoretical arguments by which it can be justified. It is important to distinguish these two lines of approach. It would be quite wrong to suppose that the transformation of capitalism into a controlled economy has resulted primarily from a demonstration of its theoretical imperfections; it has resulted far more from everyday necessities. It would also be wrong to suppose that theories of State intervention are always based on a faithful rendering of the kinds of intervention that are in fact practised, of the motives that govern them and the success that they achieve.

### War and State intervention

The practical reasons for State intervention include the upheavals of two world wars and the various legacies that these wars have left. A modern war cannot be fought by relying on the price-mechanism to mobilise resources effectively; if the economic system has to be geared to winning the war, and not to giving the consumer the highest possible standard of living, some conscious re-direction of resources is necessary, and this re-direction can be undertaken only by the State, since it is the State that is responsible for the waging of the war. The price-mechanism can play an important part in procuring the necessary re-distribution of resources; the movement of workers into the munitions trades, for example, can be accelerated by the offer of higher wages, and changes in the pattern of production can be facilitated by corresponding changes in the pattern of prices. But when the sudden and intense scarcities of war-time have to be met, it is impossible to rely exclusively on price adjustments: prices would swing too violently, and might get out of control altogether, instead of guiding demand and supply gently towards a new equilibrium. To speed up responses on the side both of supply and demand, compulsion in various forms has to be used; to ensure that the responses are in the right direction and fit into a general economic strategy, the State has to embark on comprehensive planning of production and consumption.

The reasons for intervention do not end when war ends. There is, first, the psychology of the matter. What can be done in war-time can be done in peace-time: all kinds of inhibitions about the functions of the State have been removed by experience of prolonged State intervention in the course of two world wars. To finance a war, the State is obliged to tax the rich; to prevent disaffection, it has to aim at the maintenance of a minimum standard of living for everyone. Why, then should it not turn its weight as powerfully in peace-time in favour of the masses and against the wealthy? The spectacle of easy riches made by profiteering or on the black market weakens respect for private property as an institution. The moral objection to the use of the State to make transfers of income from one set of people to another is deprived of much of its force. The eyes of the disadvantaged have been opened to their power to insist on such transfers; and once a power has been seen to be used, it is not lightly relinquished.

War also brings uncertainty. It heightens the sense of vulnerability and moves the government to treat a fresh outbreak of hostilities as a real contingency that cannot be neglected in the formulation of economic policy. Peace in 1910 was a tangible thing with every appearance of longevity; forty years later it was no longer so. With two world wars behind it, and the wide gulf between a free market economy and a cold war economy before it, no government could lightly decide to leap the gulf, dismantle all controls, and proclaim as normal, conditions of peace, security and freedom of enterprise which recent history showed to be anything but normal. Nineteenth-century governments had no conception of the controls appropriate to modern war and would have seen no use for them anyhow. Twentieth-century governments, having exercised those powers, found some of them readily adaptable to a cold war economy.

S*

It was not only that governments felt the need to take a firmer grip of their economy from motives of defence. The unsettling effects of war struck directly at the price mechanism. The security of person and property, established norms of conduct, and widening opportunities for exchange, out of which the price-mechanism developed, are not things that flourish with general uncertainty and unquiet times. The need is then for conscious direction of affairs, for leadership and control, not for reliance on mechanisms that have a way of getting out of order when the strain on them is too great.

**Unemployment**—The unemployment of the inter-war period also made for more intervention once the war was over. If governments could get rid of unemployment in war-time, it was all the more intolerable in peace-time. Many governments pledged themselves in Article 55 of the United Nations Charter to maintain full employment and this implied a commitment to plan and control their economy in one way or another.

**Foreign trade**—The changes in progress before and during the war in international trade and payments were at least as important as war and unemployment in promoting government intervention in post-war Britain. The deficit in the balance of payments, the shortages of key materials and foodstuffs imported from abroad, and above all the dollar shortage, led the government to a wide range of restrictions and controls.

### Planning for faster growth

Throughout the world, there has been a growing disinclination to leave it to market forces to govern the rate of economic growth. Market forces may be a useful instrument in allocating productive resources to the best advantage; but they do not automatically secure steady employment for the totality of available resources or swell the total as effectively as government policies aimed specifically at more rapid growth. If governments attach special importance to economic growth, and rank it ahead of other social objectives, it is in their power to force the pace by an increased investment in resources in the form either of productive assets or a better trained labour force. In engaging in such investment, they have to weigh up the immediate sacrifice which it imposes on the community against the future increase in income which it makes possible; and this in turn, if done with deliberation, is likely to involve the preparation of some kind of economic plan. Once a country regards the rate of growth as something over which it can exercise at least a limited degree of control, and seeks to reorient its policies with a view to faster growth it is well on the way to accepting the need for economic planning in some form.

But there are many different forms of planning—for example, *à la Russe* and *à la Francaise*. A plan is, in the end, no more than a self-consistent set of policies directed towards some stated objective. Countries that would readily admit to planning in this sense might deny strongly that they were planning in some other sense (Planning with a capital "P", as they might express it). The subject is one of sufficient importance to warrant a Chapter to itself.

# CHAPTER 35

# ECONOMIC PLANNING

All of us plan. Consumers have to decide what to do with their incomes; producers have to make a whole series of decisions on what to produce, and how, and where. These decisions add up to a plan. It is no use objecting that most of the decisions are taken at random, that they are not properly co-ordinated, that they are improvisations, not plans. The same objections could be urged against almost any form of economic planning that ever has existed or could exist in this wayward and uncertain world of ours. Naturally some of us are better planners than others: more alive to the future, to the necessity of posing alternatives and choosing between them, to the advantages of working to a programme or within a budget. Some of us have more of the self-control that is required in order to pursue a consistent line of action, derived from some fixed objective or some firm expectation of future events. But if things go wrong, if we have to change our objective or our expectation, we are just as likely as the average muddle-headed improviser to be branded as a "bad" planner.

The State also plans; and as the State, as George Unwin once pointed out, is "a collection of baldheaded men sitting in government offices," its plans are subject to much the same limitations as those of private citizens. It can try to foresee the future and shape its course accordingly; indeed, if it purports to have an economic policy at all, it *must* do so. But if it entertains any perfectionist notions that it can "dominate the future" by a blue-print and give up hum-drum improvisation, then either it is heading for trouble, or its citizens are heading for some dragooning and unpleasantness. A large organisation tends to be in more of a muddle than a small one; and the State, as the largest organisation in the country is bound to have its share of muddle.

The plans of the State arise partly because it has a revenue to raise, expenses to meet and property to administer; in short, because it has a budget. But in addition the State is responsible for the economic life of the country: it is pledged to maintain full employment; it must try to secure the most effective use of all available resources; it must ensure that adequate provision is made for the future through additions to the stock of capital; it has to give effect, as best it can, to the demand for social justice. Any one of these objectives may involve a great deal of government intervention, and if this intervention is to be successful, the various "controls" that the government employs must be co-ordinated, i.e., planned.

### Alternative systems of economic planning

In framing its plans the government may follow one or other of two courses. It may allow consumer spending to influence what is to be produced without itself planning production; or it may leave the consumer free to spend his money as he chooses, but only on such products as it allows to reach the market. The first alternative is the one adopted under a system of private enterprise, which confers on a great many individual producers the power to decide how the factors of production shall be employed, but submits these producers simultaneously to the compulsions of the market and the need to find willing buyers at prices to cover their costs. The second alternative involves comprehensive economic planning by the State and the setting of production targets that may bear little or no relation to current market shortages or surpluses.

There is a sharp antithesis between the two systems because the one is organised round market forces and prices and works through incentives of profit and loss, while the other sets out to organise production and supply by administrative decision. In a sense, the one system is the individual consumer writ large while the other is the individual firm writ large. In the one, planning is geared to demand, to the price mechanism, to discovering what consumers want most and letting them have it provided they can pay the price; there is a corresponding emphasis on selling and marketing—an emphasis which offends those critics of market forces who distrust the consumer's power to make sensible decisions under sales pressure. Under the other system, planning is looked at with the eye of a producer—one might almost say an engineer—aiming at an ever-expanding output and not much concerned about the demand for it; the task that is set each unit of production is not how to find a market for the goods that it can produce but how it can carry out its part of the plan, almost irrespective of the level of costs or profits; and the detachment of the plan from any necessary link with the spending of consumers gives to it a dictatorial character, quite apart from any drastic sanctions by which its fulfilment may be secured.

This sharp antithesis is often less acute in practice than it seems in theory. Under a system of private enterprise, there is already a large public sector in which the State is directly responsible for the planning of production and investment. Through taxation, moreover, it can abstract purchasing power from private consumers and apply it to purposes of which they or rather the electorate, may only vaguely approve when they come to vote at the next election. It may also "rig" market forces by taxes, subsidies, tariffs, and so on, in order to check some outputs and encourage others, until the result is almost indistinguishable from that obtained by central planning of production. In the last resort, it is because the consumer is also an elector rather than because of any difference in the role of the price mechanism that the two systems remain quite distinct.

Similarly, if one looks carefully at a centrally planned economy one finds that market forces are by no means disregarded and that individual producing units are not simply given a plan and told to carry it out; consumers' wants do influence production and producers still have to sell, if not their output, their view of what the plan for their factory should be. Just because an economic system is centrally planned, we need not assume that it does not respond to consumer values and that the consumer has to take whatever he is given; planners do not always dictate but try also to foresee what consumers will buy. Equally it would be unrealistic to assume that all economic decisions are taken administratively and that what goes on among producers in a centrally planned system does not have a great deal in common with what happens under private enterprise; the plan may reflect what producers are doing and will continue to do in response to prices, costs and market opportunities rather than represent a set of marching orders imposed from outside.

### Incentives and compulsion

In war-time the government is able to make many of its plans effective by compulsion and direction. It conscripts men for the Armed Services, it directs workers into jobs which they would not otherwise select, it introduces an array of prohibitions and licences all backed by the force of law in Statutory Rules and Orders. Yet it does not neglect the use of economic incentives. In civil industry men continue to be paid wages related to the value of the work they do; goods continue to be made for sale and to be sold at prices intended to yield a profit. The market continues to function, within narrower limits and subject to more controls, as an agency for co-ordinating the wants of consumers and the resources available for their satisfaction. Even when the government has complete power over the allocation of raw materials it charges a price for them and generally relates this price to its costs; it uses the market even when it is also using compulsion.

In peace-time, reliance on compulsion is unpopular and the government's plans necessarily rest far more heavily on price incentives. The government may, for example, decide to spend more heavily so as to put more purchasing power in the hands of consumers. No one is compelled to respond, but if there is more money to be had there are likely to be plenty of takers. Compulsion enters as soon as the government brings the other side of its budget into play and imposes fresh taxes: the payment of taxes *is* compulsory. Not, perhaps, in the same sense as direction of labour is compulsory: it is possible to avoid income tax by abandoning any attempt to earn an income above the tax exemption limit, and no one need pay tax on a commodity like tobacco as long as it is possible to exist without smoking.

The British government has not been in the habit of stopping short at the use of price incentives and taxation as its only weapon for securing the fulfilment of its plans. It has rationed consumers, maintained a strict control over imports, allocated raw materials, licensed new building, and prevented workers in industries like agriculture and coal-mining from leaving the industry. All of these involve a partial supersession of the price-mechanism, due to a disinclination to rely on prices to bring about the changes desired. Very often, the controls have been used on the grounds of "shortage": that is, because it was felt that a rise in price might do very little to speed up an increase in supply and/or might have to be undesirably large to restrict demand to the extent necessary. As the "shortages" were mastered, the controls were abandoned. Whatever the reason for them, controls spell compulsion. If meat is rationed, it means that no one is allowed to buy more than the ration; if imports are licensed, it means that no one is permitted to import more than the government has decided; and so on.

The mere fact of compulsion need not make us shiver; all law involves compulsion. Moreover, in a democracy compulsion cannot be arbitrary: plans do not pass into law and are not framed by a government unless they would be likely to command a wide measure of approval. But the more extensive the field of economic planning, the greater the temptation to resort to compulsion and either short-circuit or by-pass the market with its free association, freedom of choice and interplay of incentives.

### Central economic planning

The case for central economic planning of production rather than planning through the central budget is strongest when it is desired to bring about large or sudden changes in the structure of the economy. The price-mechanism, while a valuable instrument for securing marginal adjustments, is comparatively ineffective when the pattern of supply and demand has to be radically or quickly transformed. If the priorities of consumers change abruptly, existing prices will not serve as a guide to the re-allocation of resources that is called for; and if market forces are allowed free play, they may effect the necessary changes too slowly and only after violent fluctuations in prices and production.

The larger the adjustments to be made and the lower the elasticities of demand and supply the greater is this danger. A sharp rise in prices may set in motion forces that will ultimately cause a bigger adjustment in output than is desired while in the short run the adjustment may be much too small. In those circumstances, the swing in prices is liable to thwart the very approach to a new equilibrium of supply and demand which it is its function to promote.

This type of situation is most apparent in war-time when central economic planning is fostered by an independent set of circumstances. It is not merely that priorities suddenly change but that the priorities of civilian consumers are subordinated to a new objective to which only the government can give effect— the objective of winning the war. A single consumer, the government, may be employing half the total resources of the country directly and be willingly accorded a prior claim on any resources that will assist the war effort. The more whole-hearted this effort, the more the government is obliged to plan production in conformity with a single set of priorities laid down by itself for the effective conduct of the war.[1]

### Planning in under-developed countries

The same kind of situation arises where the economic effort of the community is directed, not so much towards satisfying the conflicting wants of a multitude of consumers as towards accomplishing some over-riding task such as industrialisation. This task imposes priorities of its own which it may be difficult to reconcile with consumer preferences through ordinary market mechanisms. Direct controls may be necessary in order to speed up industrial growth and assist the coordination of economic activity. These controls short-circuit the price-mechanism so as to bring outputs directly into line with the plans of the authorities. Elasticity is obtained, not through spontaneous reactions to price changes, but through administrative measures and compulsions: where the government wants output to expand, it can transfer resources from other, less urgent uses, and where it is not prepared to allow output to expand, it can throttle down demand through rationing and allocation arrangements.

The idea of central economic planning has a particular attraction for under-developed countries. There are several reasons for this:

(i) In terms of the argument set out above, it is in these countries that large and rapid changes in the structure of the economy are most commonly required;

(ii) Market forces in many under-developed countries work less powerfully than they do in industrial countries; elasticities are lower and the adjustments to price changes are less calculable and continuous.

---

[1] Cf. E. Devons, "Economic Planning in War and Peace," *The Manchester School*, January 1948.

(iii) When development takes place, it is more difficult to isolate the change taking place within a single firm from the changes occurring outside it than it usually is in an industrial country. One firm's actions overflow more readily so as to affect other firms. Any new departure in technique may have cumulative effects; any fresh investment may make it significantly easier for existing enterprises to expand; any training of one firm's labour may improve the prospects of attracting other firms. It is more difficult, therefore, to leave development to a number of independent enterprises and more tempting to the government to take in hand a co-ordinated programme of development.

(iv) Governments that are anxious to speed up industrialisation find it useful to dramatise the process. The preparation of a plan has dramatic appeal. Central economic planning for industrialisation usually goes with heavy capital expenditure financed to some extent out of taxation. The government has to show the taxpayer why it needs more money and a plan at least allows it to hold before the taxpayer the prospect of jam tomorrow while the tax-collector gets on with the job of collecting jam today. It can also be argued that one of the main needs in an under-developed country is to extend the time horizon and bring home to the average man the social importance of providing for posterity. This a plan helps to do when less drastic action might fail.

### The technique of planning

There are four principal aspects of any plan. First there are the objectives which the plan is designed to fulfil. Next there is the time horizon by which it is bounded. Thirdly a plan has to be based on an appreciation of the existing situation and the way in which it is likely to develop. Finally a plan should set forth the measures by which it is intended to take a grip of the situation forecast and mould it so as to realise the stated objectives.

There are many possible objectives of economic planning. They are different in war and in peace, in an industrialised and pre-industrial country, in circumstances of hyper-inflation and of slump. But as a rule the two principal objectives are stability on the one hand (including external stability) and growth on the other. The first of these is normally a short-term objective since stability, if achieved, is continuous from one year to the next. The second is necessarily a longer-term objective since economic growth is a fairly gradual process. While the time horizon for a stabilisation plan is unlikely to be much above a year, the time horizon for a plan of economic development is likely to be at least three years and may be anything up to seven or ten.

Short-term economic planning is discussed in the next chapter under the heading of "Employment Policy". The stability at which it aims is stability in the pressure on economic resources or, what comes to much the same thing, continuous full employment. It does not aim at stability in the level of economic activity, for there is an underlying upward trend in any progressive economy either because its resources in manpower and capital are expanding or because productivity is steadily rising. This underlying trend means that more can be produced each year without any change in the intensity of employment of available resources.

Short-term planning is based on short-term forecasting. This is a highly skilled activity involving an assessment of the existing economic situation and the changes to be expected in the main elements in effective demand over the coming year or so. The diagnosis of current trends is inevitably complicated by deficiencies in the statistical material, which may not be very up-to-date, is bound to be subject to seasonal and other influences, and usually presents an incomplete and rather self-contradictory picture of what is happening. Separate forecasts have to be prepared of the rate of investment, both public and private; the level of exports; and public expenditure on goods and services as indicated by the budgets of the central government and local authorities. These can be regarded as the major (more or less autonomous) influences on the level of output and income. But the forecast must also embrace the other elements in final demand: the flow of consumer spending and the rate of stockbuilding. The first must be consistent with a plausible view of the probable course of personal saving; and the second should tally with previous experience in similar circumstances and reflect the degree to which the stock-output ratio diverges from the normal.[1]

The forecast, once prepared, allows the government to judge whether effective demand is mounting in relation to current output and creating inflationary pressure, with its accompanying shortages and bottlenecks, or whether effective demand is lagging behind and likely to yield a lower level of employment and income. It is then possible for the government to devise measures, whether budgetary, monetary or administrative, to adjust the pressure of demand and keep it within acceptable limits. The fact that the measures, in Britain at least, are rarely described as a plan and more commonly as a budget or a "package" should not conceal the identity between the procedure followed and the procedure characteristic of planning. Indeed, it is hardly too much to say that what really matters in planning is not the periodic preparation of something that can be described as a plan but the continuous practice of forecasting and

---

[1] For a fuller description of the techniques of short-term economic forecasting see *Techniques of Economic Forecasting* (ed. C. W. McMahon, OECD, Paris 1965); and "Short-term Economic Forecasting in the United Kingdom," *Economic Trends*, August 1964.

standing ready to take any necessary measures to secure the major objectives of policy.

## Development programmes

Longer-term planning usually aims at accelerating economic growth, although it is only comparatively recently that the two ideas have become closely associated with one another and the extent to which planning does or can accelerate growth remains highly controversial.

There is not much doubt about the desirability of planning public expenditure. Where the expenditure is such that it can be varied at short notice the annual budget is an adequate instrument for this purpose. But most public expenditure is not of this kind and represents a continuing commitment over several years ahead. Expenditure on education and health, for example, cannot be quickly expanded or reduced except within comparatively narrow limits. Similarly defence expenditure, generally the biggest single item, does not lend itself to variations up or down at short notice. To make appreciable changes in expenditure of this kind requires major decisions of policy that are slow to affect the flow of expenditure on current output. Given this inflexibility of public expenditure from year to year, it is obviously necessary to relate decisions about its scale and composition not to the situation expected over the next twelve months but to an assessment stretching over a much longer period. It makes more sense to have a programme or plan of expenditure covering a number of years and registering the commitments that the government has already entered into or expects to have to shoulder during that time. Such a plan not only allows of a more rational allocation of funds between different public services but also makes for consistency between the different schemes being financed: for example, between the plans for school-building and the plans for teacher-training. On the other hand, the plan cannot be a completely firm one unless it is intended that public expenditure should contract out of any adjustments that the government is obliged to make in the management of the economy from year to year.

From planning public expenditure it is a fairly short step to planning the public sector as a whole. The central government, the local authorities, and the industries in public ownership are more likely to keep in step with one another if they are working to a common plan. But—and this can be a very material qualification—the more agencies have to be co-ordinated and the more diverse their functions, the greater the danger that the effort of planning and co-ordination will lead to over-centralisation and secure consistency at the expense of initiative and enterprise. Where this happens, growth may be jeopardized instead of being promoted. The art of successful planning is to achieve the right balance between centralisation and decentralisation.

This becomes a point of major importance when planning extends to the whole economy and embraces the private as well as the public sector. The place of the private sector in most long-term plans tends to be highly ambiguous. The public sector, in principle at least, (in practice, things are by no means quite so simple), can be made to conform to the plan. But there can be no guarantee that the private sector will do what the plan postulates. Exports, which come almost entirely from the private sector, may not grow at the rate required. The public may not save as much as the plan assumes. One industry may expand too fast and another too slow. The success of the plan may turn on a big increase in industrial investment and private industry may hang back.

This last possibility is perhaps the most awkward of all. The nub of a development plan is generally the investment programme. But most of the public investment undertaken is not directly productive and helps to accelerate growth only by providing an infra-structure for industrial expansion. The plan may take for granted a concomitant increase in private industrial investment. But no-one can be sure in advance that it will take place; and the funds which were assumed to flow into industrial investment may flow instead into property development or out of the country.

The government is by no means powerless in relation to the private sector. It can try to make its plans effective by a whole series of controls—import controls, rationing, building licensing, and so on. It can also offer various incentives to industry such as tax concessions, cheap credit, or output subsidies. It may also find industry anxious to be co-operative, happy to share in the preparation of the plan, and willing of its own accord to work for the implementation of the constituent parts of the plan. But when all is said and done, a plan for the private sector has a different significance from a plan for the public sector; and the more rigorously the government tries to control the private sector, or the more eagerly the private sector tries to transform itself into a quasi-public sector, the greater the danger referred to above of over-centralisation and a loss of managerial drive.

A long-term plan, like plans to keep the economy in balance, rests on a good deal of economic forecasting. But since the object of a long-term plan is usually to bring about important changes in the economy, not just to preserve balance, the forecasts are dependent on policy decisions. The outcome is a series of programmes reflecting the decisions which, taken together, make up the plan.

The function of a programme is to summarise policy, to register both expectations and decisions, to set out what is likely to be the course of events *taking into account* the action that the government has set or will set on foot. A programme mingles in one set of figures the government's view of what it would like to happen with its consciousness that its powers to influence what will happen are limited. An export programme, for example, might show a rise of only 10 per cent. over the next year, although the government would welcome an increase of 20 per cent. and would be prepared to take all necessary measures to facilitate the larger increase. The rise of 10 per cent. would then reflect the government's assessment of the outcome of the efforts of traders to export, aided or bullied by all the expedients that the government was proposing or had already devised. The programme would be a recognition of the difficulties of bringing about as large and as rapid an increase in exports as the government would like to plan. An export programme constructed on this basis would be quite different from an export *target*. The "target" might be no more than a calculation of the increase in exports necessary to wipe out a current adverse balance of payments without any indication of the measures by which the increase was to be accomplished, the speed at which it was likely to take place, or the reactions on other sectors of the economy through the employment of additional resources on exports.

The preparation of a development plan is symptomatic of a transformation in the attitude of the State to economic activity. The State is engaged in shaping economic activity, not just in regulating it. It is no longer, for example, in the position of taking the size and distribution of the national income for granted and adjusting its own plans to autonomous changes in the national income. It is itself one of the determinants. The size of the national income, indeed, is one of the first items that the State attempts to plan. The full employment of the country's resources, their allocation between competing claimants, their productivity however allocated, are all objects of State planning and policy. The distribution of the national income is also the subject of direct government decision. It is not merely that 30 per cent. of the national income passes through the hands of the government and that some redistribution of income inevitably takes place in the process. It is also that the government sometimes operates directly on incomes, freezing wages and dividends or entering into something like a compact with trade unionists and employers as to the changes in existing rates of pay that can be treated as compatible with public policy.

# CHAPTER 36

# PROBLEMS OF ECONOMIC POLICY

The central problems with which economic policy has to grapple have already been outlined in Chapter 2. If we may take them in the reverse order in which they were listed there, the two most important problems are to ensure continuous and at the same time steady growth in income per head. This calls for full and stable employment of the country's man-power, an enlargement of its stock of productive assets, and a progressive improvement in productivity. A third problem is to take full advantage of trade with other countries and obtain a better return from productive effort without paying too high a price in instability of employment. In the next place, producers have to be given reliable indicators of the most economical use of resources and incentives to respond to those indicators, whenever there are alternative methods of combining different resources for a given purpose. This problem embraces that of ensuring that new and better techniques will be sought out, experimented with, and widely applied. Fifthly, there are the problems associated with inequality of income and opportunity: the need to relieve poverty and insecurity and to prevent the abuse of economic power. Finally, the problems associated with choice of the right technology run into a rather different, but allied, set of problems associated with the allocation of resources between different uses.

On the one hand, these problems present themselves in terms of industrial organisation: for example, there are the dangers of slackness and inefficiency arising from monopoly and of duplication of effort arising from competition. On the other hand, the problems concern the effectiveness of prices as instruments of allocation: market forces direct resources into channels cut by prices but they may act slowly and harshly in conditions of structural change when an accelerated response, or one that tempered scarcity or over-production, might be brought about by direct controls.

Some of these problems have already been discussed in earlier chapters; a full discussion of them all would take at least another volume. We may,

however, pick out for further comment three of the most important: those relating to inequality, inefficiency and instability.

## INEQUALITY AND SOCIAL WELFARE

If every man is free to earn what he can, in a world which offers large profits to the enterprising and the fortunate, it is to be expected that some people
will earn much more than others. These inequalities, especially when they are
clearly due to luck or inheritance, and when the many still go in fear of unemployment and poverty, arouse envy and resentment; in a democratic community, where everyone is equal in voting power, it is felt to be inconsistent
to permit wide differences in purchasing power.

Before the war the top 5 per cent. of income-earners in Great Britain received
about 29 per cent. of personal incomes before tax and about 25 per cent. after
tax. By 1957 these proportions had fallen to 18 per cent. and 14 per cent. For
the top 1 per cent. of income-earners the fall was steeper; their share, both
before and after tax, was more than halved and in 1957 came to 5 per cent.
after tax.[1]

The distribution of income, therefore, has been changing comparatively
rapidly. The main reason for this is the diminution in the post-war period in the
relative size of income from capital, which forms a large element in the higher
incomes.[2] Before the war investment income came to nearly 60 per cent. of the
taxable income of the top 1 per cent. and in 1954–55 still formed nearly 40
per cent.; on the other hand, for at least half the population investment income
is a negligible item in income. This suggests that inequality of income is to a
considerable extent the outcome of inequality in the distribution of capital
and of the inheritance of property by which this inequality is perpetuated.
Capital is, in fact, much more unequally distributed than income: before the
war, three-fifths of the wealth of the country was estimated to be in the hands
of the 1 per cent. of the population who owned at least £10,000.[3]

Inequalities in the distribution of wealth are to some extent no more than a

---

[1] These figures and those in the following paragraph are taken from H. F. Lydall, "The Long-
term Trend in the Size Distribution of Income." *Journal of the Royal Statistical Society*, Vol. 122,
Part 1, 1959. As Mr. Lydall explains, there were four main reasons for the change in distribution
before tax. The first of these was the increasing tendency for married women to go out to work;
since the Inland Revenue authorities treat a married man's income as including that of his wife
this did not add to the number of "income-earners" but made a larger proportionate addition
to the lower than to the higher incomes. Three other factors operated to reduce investment
income, which is one of the principal sources of income inequality; rent control reduced
income from house-property; higher taxation of company profits and higher appropriations to
reserve reduced dividends; and inflation reduced the real value of fixed interest payments.

[2] For the statistics of rent, dividends and interest in 1948, 1956 and 1964 see above p. 371.

[3] G. W. Daniels and H. Campion, *Distribution of the National Capital*, (Manchester, 1936).

reflection of inequalities between old and young. Property accumulates in the hands of the old, while the young own little or nothing. Before the war there were three times as many men between 25 and 55 as there were over 55; but, of those dying in 1938, the older men owned more than ten times as much as the younger. The figures for women show an even greater concentration of wealth in the higher age groups: of the women who died in 1938 and left estates of from £10,000–£50,000, for example, 60 per cent. were over 75 and less than 2 per cent. under 45.[1]

There has been a gradual change in the distribution of wealth over the past generation. Between 1913 and 1947 the number of persons leaving £1,000–£5,000 at death increased sixfold while the number of persons leaving over £100,000 increased only threefold, in spite of the large rise in the value of property.[2] Most of this change took place in the period after 1939. It was not, measured against the shape of the pyramid of wealth, a dramatic change; 1 per cent. of the adult population still owns about half the privately owned wealth of the country. But it was a pointer to larger changes still in progress. The effect of high estate duties is not reflected in the size of estates passing at death until, on the death of the heir, the same estate comes up for assessment a second time; on the average this happens once every thirty years.

There is nothing abnormal about inequality of income or wealth; all social systems permit some measure of inequality, and in many of them inequality has been greater or harder to justify or has taken far more pernicious forms. But in a democracy the complete equality of voters cannot in the long run be consistent with extreme inequality of consumers. This is not a matter of moral rights and equity. It is a simple corollary from the proposition that voting power outweighs purchasing power. Once the mass of the people want economic equality, the only real issue is how to secure it, or at least to remove gross inequality, without serious injury to economic growth and without sacrificing some other social objective such as justice or freedom.

Reducing inequality is a task that occupies the State in a variety of ways. Taxation can limit the growth of large fortunes and the net income drawn from them; subsidised social services can raise the real income of the poor by reducing the cost of things of special importance in their budget or by assuring them of services that they could not otherwise afford. The danger of excessive concentration of control in private hands can be met by increased public control or by public ownership (i.e., by nationalisation).

---

[1] These figures are calculated fron tables in: Kathleen M. Langley, "The Distribution of Capital in Private Hands in 1936–38 and 1946–47," *Bulletin of the Oxford Institute of Statistics*, December 1950.
[2] Kathleen M. Langley, *op. cit.*

## Progressive taxation

The first method by which the State can make its influence felt in checking inequality is by taxation. It can play Robin Hood by taking from the rich and giving to the poor. By heavy death duties the State can prevent the passing of large estates intact to private persons by the accident of birth or favour; by steeply progressive rates of taxation (that is, rates which are higher, the richer the taxpayer) it can keep earnings, after payment of tax, within relatively narrow limits; by creating a system of social services, it can guarantee a minimum standard of living. All this within a social framework in which the flexibility of private enterprise can still, in great measure, be preserved. It is just such a compromise that is in process of being worked out in Great Britain.

This "compromise" involved a revolution in the theory of taxation. In 1900 a progressive income tax was still something of a novelty, and to suggest that it might be used deliberately to procure greater equality of income amounted almost to economic heresy. Economists defended progressive taxation on other grounds. They cited the rather oracular pronouncement of Adam Smith that people "ought to contribute towards the support of the government, as nearly as possible in proportion to their respective abilities," and undertook to prove that ability to pay increased more than in proportion to income. Or they put forward an "equality of sacrifice" theory and engaged in philosophic discussions on the rate at which the income tax would require to increase as income increased in order to involve rich and poor in an equal measure of sacrifice.

Whether their slogan was "ability to pay" or "equality of sacrifice," economists found arguments to justify progressive taxation. But they did not regard it as part of a comprehensive policy for checking the growth of large fortunes and financing a system of social services. The theory of progressive taxation was rather like that of discriminating monopoly—mathematical rather than ethical. The question posed was: Given the revenue to be raised and the number and relative incomes of the taxpayers, how much should each pay in tax? But there is, of course, a more fundamental question to which this leads: What incomes should people be left with after the State has raised and spent its revenue?

Our answer to this question depends upon the importance which we attach to ability and need as alternative principles of distribution. Men are both producers and consumers; and the distribution of income which spurs them to the greatest effort as producers may be grossly unfair when we look at the needs which have to be met out of the unequal earnings. But whether rewards should be related to ability and effort or to human needs, neither principle can justify the prevailing extremes of poverty and wealth. Rewards are obviously not in accord with needs. Neither are they proportioned uniformly to ability and effort. They depend also upon the wealth or opportunities bequeathed by one's parents; the efforts which are rewarded do not always confer a benefit on society, but may be directed to anti-social ends; and it is highly unlikely that the highest incomes are a necessary spur to the efforts and sacrifices for which these incomes are paid. It is possible, therefore, for a progressive income tax simultaneously to bring income and need, and income and effort, closer together. Moreover, the incentive that controls effort is frequently gross, not net, income; we are often content with the shadow of purchasing power while the government makes off with the substance. Hence taxation may go very far towards lining up income and needs without doing damage to the relationship between income and effort.

But not indefinitely far. There are limits to the usefulness of taxation as a means of redistributing income. In the first place, a high rate of tax affects people's inclination to work, and hence the supply of labour. Since the highest rate of tax is paid on marginal earnings, there is a natural temptation to work less hard, do less overtime, retire earlier from business. A skilled workman or professional man who is paying income tax at 10s. in the £1 on part of his earnings will naturally reflect that every £1 that he is offered for overtime work is worth only 10s. net of tax. If there is a fixed net income which he is determined to earn, he will have to work all the harder because of the tax which he has to pay. But he will generally be inclined to react the other way and sacrifice the 10s. for the sake of some leisure. After all, it is because he is fairly well off that he is liable to income tax at so high a rate; and since he is well off he is likely to be less rigid in his idea of the income that he wants to earn.

High taxation reacts on savings in a similar way. It reduces the surplus out of which people save; and it penalises saving more than expenditure, since the income set aside to be saved is taxed at the time, and when dividends are paid on the capital sum they, too, are taxed. On the other hand, when people are determined to make provision for a given *net* income from investments at some future time, the higher the rate of tax the more they will be forced to set aside. It is not a *necessary* consequence of high taxation, therefore, that it should reduce private savings; but we are pretty safe in concluding that in practice it does, on balance, have this effect.

This is of special importance when we are thinking of business profits. The traditional method of financing extensions to a successful small business is out of profit; but if a large part of the profit is drained away in tax, growth is retarded and the attractiveness of founding a small business is greatly reduced. One effect of a high income tax, therefore, is to fortify established businesses against competition from young and expanding rivals.

An additional reason why this tends to come about is that high taxation penalises risk-bearing. What was previously an even chance is now more likely to be a loss since tax is deducted from any profit earned, but no compensating refund is made for a loss. If, for example, there was formerly an equal chance of a profit of 10 per cent. or a loss of 2 per cent., the effect of an income tax of 10s. in the £1 is to turn this into an equal chance of a net profit of 5 per cent. or a net loss of 2 per cent.—obviously a much less attractive proposition. The established concern, whose risks are limited, gains once again by comparison with the young and struggling firm pioneering products or methods which have yet to be tested.

These limitations to taxation are obviously elastic and can be largely offset by other measures. If private savings diminish, the State can use public funds for capital construction. If the enterprise of young firms is checked, the State can foster new methods of industrial finance designed to put capital at the disposal of new and expanding businesses.

Whatever the theory of the matter, Britain has moved, within fifty years, from a state of things in which the largest incomes did not pay more than about 5 per cent. in tax and the lowest incomes paid at least as much, to one in which the largest incomes pay up to 90 per cent. in tax and the lowest incomes receive much more from State subsidies and services than is taken in tax. This change has been associated with the change in the electorate from the middle-class monopoly of the nineteenth century to the universal suffrage of the twentieth; and it has been greatly accelerated by the three costly wars which have been waged since the century began. It has been brought about, not by Socialist governments pledged to "soak the rich," but mainly by Conservative and Coalition governments in need of enormous revenues and anxious not to antagonise the wage-earner.

## The social services

The State is concerned not only to prevent the accumulation of economic power in private hands, but also to get rid of poverty by establishing a minimum standard of living for all citizens. This it tries to accomplish by means of what have come to be called "the social services": free education and health services; retirement and widows' pensions; social insurance against unemployment and sickness; family allowances and child welfare services; national assistance to those in need; and a host of other services, the aim of which is by no means simply to relieve poverty.

Expenditure on the social services has increased rapidly since the beginning of the century. The total rose from about £1 per head of population in 1900 to £10 per head of population in 1939 and approximately £80 per head in 1963. Even if the rise in prices and in the real income of the country over the past sixty years is taken into account, it is a phenomenal expansion; whereas in 1900 the social services absorbed one-fiftieth of the national income, in 1963 the proportion had grown to over one-sixth.

TABLE 26

CURRENT EXPENDITURE ON SOCIAL SERVICES BY BRITISH PUBLIC AUTHORITIES

£m.

|  | 1900 | 1946 | 1963 |
|---|---|---|---|
| Education and child care  ..    .. | 20 | 203 | 1,094 |
| Health services  ..    ..    ..    .. | 2 | 92 | 964 |
| Nutrition services ..    ..    ..    .. | — | 44 | 107 |
| Family allowances    ..    ..    .. | — | 20 | 145 |
| Pensions (incl. war pensions)    .. | — | 232 | 1,135 |
| Other national insurance (incl. administrative costs)  ..    ..    ..    .. | — | 73 | 390 |
| National assistance (incl. local welfare services) ..    ..    ..    ..    .. | 12 | 94 | 252 |
| Housing subsidies ..    ..    ..    .. | 1 | 45 | 137 |
|  | 35 | 803 | 4,224 |
| Subsidies to food and agriculture    .. | — | 286 | 306 |

Source: National Income and Expenditure, 1964.

The entire cost of these services is not borne by the general taxpayer. Part is met from contributions by those who benefit from the expenditure. National insurance contributions, for example, cover most of the current outlay on pensions, sickness and unemployment benefit. The net transfer of income to those who use the social services—mainly wage-earners—through State expenditure on the social services falls short, therefore, of the gross outlay. But the social services do undoubtedly make an addition to working class income which is large, if difficult to quantify; and this addition is mainly at the taxpayers' expense even though the benefits are open to all.

The social services are exceptionally cheap to administer where, as with insurance, pensions and family allowances, the size of the service is an advantage, the conditions of benefit are relatively easy to define, and the work of administration consists largely of simple book-keeping. The social services are more difficult to administer where, as with the national health service, there are personal relations (between doctors and patients), business relations (between government and doctors) and administrative relations (between one hospital and another) all mixed up with one another.

The great merit of the social services is that everyone is treated alike on a basis of need. On the one hand, benefit is drawn as of right without the stigma or humiliation of charity; the State lays down the terms upon which the service is made available, and so long as those terms are complied with, anyone may apply. On the other hand, society has the satisfaction of ensuring that minimum needs are covered and that, while gross incomes may be fixed in relation to productivity rather than need, in the final outcome the social services restore the balance sufficiently to give everyone a minimum of the essentials of life and liberty.

### The limits of redistribution

The changes that have already been brought about by State action are striking. A calculation by Mr. Seers suggests that the total effect of income-tax and price changes over the decade 1938–48 was to transfer about £1,000 million (at 1948 prices) from the top sixth of the United Kingdom to the other five-sixths of the population, cutting the real value of the purchasing power in the hands of the top sixth by some 30 per cent. and increasing the purchasing power in the hands of the rest of the population by about 25 per cent.[1] The increase in expenditure on the social services over the same period must have added considerably to these figures. The effect, moreover, is cumulative—particularly the effect of high estate duties—so that it is not yet fully visible.

The changes in progress rest above all on one thing: the willingness of people to pay their taxes. If people sought to evade taxation on a large scale—as happens in some other countries—the system would be in serious danger of breaking down. The British social system is pre-eminently a system for honest taxpayers. There are other dangers. One is that the tax system should become unintelligible (as the income tax is already) and ill-devised, so that the raising of revenue causes needless dislocation, destroys valuable incentives and penalises innovation (on which, more than anything, the industrial future of Britain depends). Another is that in an excess of zeal for equality, the tax base is kept too narrow and an increasing load heaped upon the superstructure. There is a limit to what taxation can squeeze out of the higher incomes, especially if lower incomes do not suffer the same "squeeze."

However much can be done by levelling, moreover, it is only by an increase in the total national income that the *average* standard of living can be improved. An extra 1 per cent. per annum in the rate of growth of the national income would soon contribute more to working-class incomes than a once-for-all

---

[1] Dudley Seers, "The Levelling of Incomes." *Bulletin of the Oxford Institute of Statistics*, October, 1950. These figures take account of the effect of food subsidies, rent control, etc., on the cost of living of both groups.

redistribution in their favour of the whole of the sum paid to private persons in rent, dividends and interest, which, as we saw in Chapter 25 is no more than 11 per cent. of the national income.

## CONTROL OF INDUSTRY

The relationship between the State and industry rests partly on expediency, partly on broad issues of principle. Of the issues of principle the one which has given rise to most controversy (except, perhaps, amongst economists, who have rarely worked themselves into much of a passion over it) is nationalisation.

### Nationalisation

The case for nationalising an industry can be rested either on the local circumstances of the industry or on the more universal grounds of social philosophy. Until some years ago the arguments commonly advanced fell mainly under the second heading. It seemed natural to many people that if private enterprise was unsuccessful or unjust as an economic system, the State should step in and run industry instead. This would have meant wholesale nationalisation, not selective nationalisation of particular industries.

There was a good deal of black and white in the background to this point of view and not much grey. It implied, for example, a sharp antithesis between full State ownership and control and private enterprise without government control; it dwelt on the defects of the one without developing any theory of how the other could function or the difficulties that it would be likely to encounter. It assumed that there was no other way of remedying the defects of the capital system: of maintaining full employment, reducing social inequality, and controlling monopoly. It was sometimes linked with the idea of confiscation as a means of "soaking the rich"; this put the stress on the *ownership* of capital. At other times it was linked with the idea of workers' control and syndicalism—of handing over each industry to the men engaged in it; this put the stress on the *control* of capital. Other ideas were also associated: the idea that the State should have more control over the economic system and be able to plan it without having to face the opposition of existing owners or alternatively allowing them uncovenanted benefits in order to have its way; the idea that it was less degrading for men to work in the service of the State than for the private profit of the capitalist; and so on.

There is no doubt that although some of these ideas are now less fashionable, they are still widely entertained. Nationalisation enjoys the backing of egalitarian sentiment even when full compensation is paid; the fact that it does nothing to promote social equality is submerged by the memory that it was once advocated on those grounds. Politicians still talk of "citadels of power" when they already exercise at least as much control over an industry as they can hope for after nationalisation. Workers still assume that they will enjoy more say in the running of a nationalised industry even when it is operated on commercial lines with instructions from the State to cover its costs (including interest charges).[1] But opinion lags a long way behind recent developments. The fact is that the State could bring about nearly all the changes in industry that it could desire by using the powers that it already possesses or could readily assume. Nationalisation *en masse* is largely an irrelevant issue; the real issue is what the State would like industry to do and what controls are necessary for that purpose.

When we come down from the high plane of social philosophy to the selection of particular industries as candidates for nationalisation, the problem becomes one of deciding what degree of control over an industry is necessary in the public interest and what form it should take. There are some industries where a strong case can be made. It can be argued, for example, that the British coal industry was in need of the kind of jolt given to it by the *act* of nationalisation and that, in private hands, there would have been insufficient investment of capital to maintain efficiency, or bad labour relations at a time when these could not be afforded. It can be argued also that it was right to nationalise the railways because the State makes great use of them in emergency, cannot afford to see their rolling stock and other equipment deteriorate, and might wish to sink money in fresh capital expenditure on them in times of slump when private companies might be hesitant about their future. Nationalisation of some industries, that is, can be defended on strategic grounds; or as relieving a long-standing antagonism between employers and employed; or as giving the State more room for manoeuvre in controlling capital expenditure. It may also be the most appropriate way of ensuring a continuous and efficient service or of ensuring that where powers of monopoly exist, these are not abused. Monopoly, however, takes many forms and so do the best ways of dealing with it.

## Control of monopoly

The importance of monopolistic elements in modern industry has repeatedly been emphasised. On the one hand, the imperfection of the market results in duplication of services and of plant, the insulation of inefficient firms from competitive pressure, and the excessive multiplication of brands and types of product. On the other hand, the increasing scale of enterprise leaves a few giant

---

[1] This feeling is well illustrated by the Durham miner who complained bitterly that what he wanted was "nationalisation and no more State interference," and the Scottish miner who told a fellow citizen that the mines "are no yours, they're oors."

concerns to divide the market, with no guarantee to consumers either that the monopolists are really efficient or that the benefit of reductions in costs will ever be passed on. The State has thus a double motive for intervening. It can hope to organise industry more efficiently than private enterprise, and it can ensure that the spoils of monopoly are not left in private hands. The wastes of imperfect competition can be eliminated by extensive rationalisation—by shutting down redundant plant, standardising output, and concentrating production in the most efficient firms. The extortions of monopoly can be prevented by setting up public corporations, aiming, not at maximum profits, but at efficient public service.

Public corporations are not likely to improve efficiency except where there are large economies of scale and where their market coincides with some convenient administrative unit. Where there are strong economic forces—the need for energetic and resourceful management, for instance—making against large-scale enterprise, or where, as commonly happens, the optimum unit lies midway in scope between the central government and a local authority, a public corporation is beset with difficulties from which private enterprise is likely to be free. Prices may still be reduced, especially if the danger of monopolistic exploitation is serious, but the gain to consumers will accrue out of the excessive profits of the monopolist, not from the greater efficiency of the public corporation. To enjoy the best of both worlds, it might be easier to leave the monopolist, with his more flexible organisation, in control of production, and, at the same time, to fix maximum prices for his output.[1]

Where a private monopoly is replaced by a department of State or by a municipality, the gain is still more dubious. Democratic governments and their officials are constantly under the necessity of explaining and defending their decisions. But sound practical judgments are not always easy to explain; they may be intuitive and incapable of exposition in a speech or on paper. A glib memorandum, therefore, tends to carry more weight than the unsupported wisdom of men of affairs.[2] At the same time, speed of decision is sacrificed to quality of decision. The need for a policy that can be publicly defended inculcates an excessive caution. Large risks, however justifiable, must result in occasional failures which can be seized upon by political opponents to discredit a democratic government.

---

[1] For a full discussion, see A. C. Pigou, *Economics of Welfare* (4th edition), pp. 336 *et seq.*
[2] Compare Hawtrey, *The Economic Problem*, p. 339: "To express in language even the decision itself is an effort: to express the grounds on which it is taken would often be a formidable exercise in both psychology and literary composition. . . . There is a tendency for any official hierarchy to be limited to those decisions that can be readily communicated in language from one functionary to another." (Quoted by Pigou, *op. cit.*, p. 388).

When a government ceases to be democratic or where, as in war-time, it has a single aim to which everything is subordinated, many of the above considerations lose much of their force. The achievements of dictatorships or of war-time governments cannot be readily compared with those either of private enterprise (competitive or monopolistic) or of democratic governments; for the sacrifices to which people will submit, or which they willingly accept, under a dictatorship or in war-time are immensely greater than those which a democracy would contemplate in peace-time. The task of economic organisation, for example, is enormously simplified by the sweeping aside of vested interests and the suppression of internal conflicts. A dictatorship can plunder whatever classes can be represented as enemies of the people, can conscript labour whenever it sees fit, and can, by suitable propaganda, represent as a resounding success what in a democracy would be denounced as a shocking muddle or a costly failure. In any discussion of government operation of industry, therefore, we must be on our guard against arguments based upon experience in other countries or in war-time.

If we think it unwise of a democratic government to try to operate more than a limited sector of industry (including the public utilities and other activities that are peculiarly subject to monopoly), we are left with the alternative of regulation and control. The State may try in various ways to limit the exercise of monopoly powers: by making restrictive agreements illegal, by taking powers to break up large units in order to restore competition, by supporting consumers' organisations that can set a counter-vailing power against the monopolists'. A programme of this kind must be based on a clear definition of the practices that are to be regarded as anti-social, and there must be provision for investigation of monopolistic behaviour, and powers to enforce decisions. It is not enough to set up a statutory body like the Monopolies Commission and leave it to rely on mobilising public opinion against the grosser abuses of monopoly power.

There are other ways in which the State could check the arbitrary exercise of monopoly powers. It could become a shareholder in the larger business units, not so as to participate in the profits but to rid them of monopoly elements. It could take powers to nominate one or more directors to the boards of public companies. It could threaten to enter into direct competition with monopolistic units.

There is a danger that in concentrating on ways of curbing monopoly a greater danger may be overlooked. The prime need is to make competition work where there is scope for it and to make it work so as to raise productivity. There is no great virtue in competition if it does not improve industrial efficiency. But in some of the most competitive industries such as agriculture it is doubtful whether improvements in technique are brought about as effectively

T

by competition as in other ways. Extension services which convey to the farmer the fruits of research and experiment may make him aware of ways of reducing his costs of which competition would leave him in ignorance. In other words, it may be more important to encourage technical progress than to introduce more competition. Competition is not an infallible instrument for generating technical progress, although it is more likely than monopoly to work in favour of technical progress and this is, or should be, the main plank in an anti-monopoly campaign.

## EMPLOYMENT POLICY

Large-scale unemployment usually arises because of a deficiency of effective demand. Now there is never any difficulty about increasing effective demand; it is all too easy. It can be done by increasing government spending or by giving consumers additional purchasing power or by the freer creation of credit. But after generations of combat against the extravagance of governments, against "boondoggling" to catch the favour of particular groups of consumers (and electors) and against reckless bank lending and unsound finance, it is the very ease with which the thing can be done that makes for doubts and hesitations. The beatitudes of full employment look suspiciously like the deadly sins of inflation. How far inflation can be held at arm's length while effective demand is regulated in the interests of full employment will be discussed presently. First, however, the technique of regulating demand calls for some explanation.

## 1  Budgetary policy

The most important instrument that the government can use to regulate demand and employment is the budget. This was not the official view a short time ago. In 1929 Sir Winston Churchill as Chancellor of the Exchequer gave it as "the orthodox Treasury dogma steadfastly held" that "very little additional employment and no permanent additional employment can, in fact, and as a general rule, be created by State borrowing and State expenditure." The "dogma," however, was without foundation in theory, and the experience of the war and post-war years has destroyed any foundation in fact.

But the budget can only exercise a significant influence on employment if the government is prepared to vary its expenditure and its revenue and to allow the two to diverge from one another. If the State aims consistently at a balanced budget and is not prepared to borrow (even to cover capital expenditure), or at other times to accumulate a surplus, then the direct impact of the budget on effective demand will be neutral. The State will merely be taking money from one pocket and putting it in another. If employment is low, the financial policy required from the State must be one calculated to raise demand, either by increased public expenditure or by remission of taxation, that is, by deliberately unbalancing the budget. In terms of the general theory of employment outlined in Chapter 26, if employment were higher, incomes would be higher and private savings would increase: provision must be made, therefore, either to harness the additional savings to finance more investment, or to offset them by deliberate dis-saving on the part of the State, instead of letting them run to waste in unemployment. If no one else is prepared to borrow and spend on the scale necessary, it is the State that must do so, and the addition that it will have to make to the National Debt in the process reflects the excess of savings which the State has to absorb. In times when the pressure of effective demand is excessive, all this has to be put into reverse. The need then is for a budget surplus (i.e., for government saving) to withdraw purchasing power from the public and keep demand in check. The State can apply the surplus to a reduction of debt. But there can be no guarantee that circumstances will allow surpluses and deficits to be exactly matched; the National Debt may have to be increased progressively.

In a community where the national income is steadily increasing this is not necessarily much of a stumbling-block. The interest that has to be paid on the additional debt will to some extent be balanced by additional tax revenue as the secular rise in productivity raises the taxable capacity of the country and the revenue from existing taxes (e.g., on income). If very large additions to the National Debt were in question, such as are made in war-time, the financial problem would sooner or later become acute. But as a rule, the net additions required are likely to be relatively modest. Moreover, if no action were taken to maintain effective demand, and large-scale unemployment resulted, the State would find its budget becoming unbalanced in another way: it would have to meet additional expenditure on unemployment benefit and allowances while tax revenue would fall off as incomes dwindled. It is obviously better to run into debt in order to keep people in jobs and create a larger flow of wealth than to run into debt with nothing better to show than high unemployment percentages.

**Consumption versus investment**—The State has the choice of trying to increase consumption or trying to increase investment. The former is likely to be the more expensive. If the State merely remits taxation, as is often proposed, taxpayers may save a large part of what is remitted instead of spending it all, so that a larger remission of taxation is needed in order to bring about a given rise in consumption. If, on the other hand, the State increases the capital expenditure under its control, it not only increases effective demand *pro rata* but brings into existence useful assets in the form of roads, houses, etc., which remain to enrich the country and to contribute, directly or indirectly, towards the debt charges that the State has incurred.

This is not, by itself, a decisive argument in favour of more investment rather than more consumption in times of trade depression. It is easier and quicker to remit taxation than to organise a programme of public works. Other ways of increasing consumption or investment have also to be considered. Larger family allowances may be granted and food subsidies increased or the rates of contribution to national insurance may be reduced. Credit facilities or grants may be devised to enable purchases to be made in particular directions and help to reduce unemployment more quickly and effectively in the industries or districts where it is concentrated. There may also be indications that the depression is due to a temporary exhaustion of the major investment opportunities so that an increase in investment by the State would prolong an excess of investment in relation to consumption. In adjusting its budget, therefore, the State must try to balance the claims of investment and consumption and make the best use it can of the instruments at its disposal for influencing them both.

Budget surpluses and deficits, however, are not always ruled by economic theory, least of all when the theory is a trifle oracular and leaves actual diagnosis and prescription to be fought out in the Treasuries and Parliaments of the world. It requires strong political leadership to budget for a surplus—it may even, in some countries with a federal constitution, be unconstitutional. Budget deficits, when a country is in economic difficulties already, are open to misinterpretation by those unacquainted with latter-day economic orthodoxy. There is, above all, the problem of deciding, *in practice*, whether the time has come to change from a surplus to a deficit or vice versa and by what measures the change should be brought about. These difficulties are not, however, peculiar to budgetary measures for dealing with unemployment. On the contrary, they affect every possible variety of technique, so long as the authorities have constantly to face a fresh situation and are responsive to public opinion.[1]

## 2 Control of investment

If fluctuations in employment are chiefly due to fluctuations in investment, the most obvious way of stabilising employment is to stabilise investment. This can be attempted in a number of ways. The first method is by a monetary policy designed to bring down interest rates in the slump and raise them in the boom; in this way industry will be offered an inducement to increase capital

---

[1] In monetary and public works policy, for example, there is a similar heavy dependence on political judgment and leadership. In both, it is much easier to bring pressure to bear in favour of an expansion than in favour of a contraction.

expenditure at times when it is low and to restrict it when it is excessive. The second method is by regulating investments by public authorities so as to offset fluctuations in the capital outlay of private firms and households. The third method is by direct control over investment, the State sanctioning no more in total than can be financed without inflation and making arrangements to enable an immediate acceleration of the work in hand if necessary. Let us take these three methods in turn:

(i) **Monetary policy and interest rates**—Until comparatively recently, the State did not attempt to influence long-term rates of interest except indirectly through Bank Rate policy. Changes in Bank Rate, however, generally affect only short-term rates of interest, and even a very large change in short-term rates will be ineffective in producing a comparable change in long-term rates, particularly if there is a general belief that the change in short-term rates is temporary and that it will be reversed within a few years or even a few months. In the boom, a slight rise in short-term rates may take effect because business men interpret it as a signal of the central bank's intentions and know that it can be followed up, if necessary, by a much larger rise. But in the slump, there is a clear limit to the reduction in short-term rates which the central bank can bring about, and an equally marked limit, therefore, to the effectiveness of monetary policy. The water of cheap money may be spread as abundantly as we choose but industry may disdain it. Indeed, the water may be so shallow that industry would have the greatest difficulty in drinking. Low short-term rates are not likely by themselves to encourage additional borrowing since the demand for short-term capital does not greatly depend upon its price. Credit policy in a slump, therefore, is not a very effective instrument in promoting recovery, except over a period of years or in conjunction with other measures.

More direct methods of controlling long-term rates of interest and investment have been developed. The State can bring pressure on the banking system to buy or sell government securities. It also has control over large extra-budgetary funds such as those administered through the National Debt Commissioners, national insurance funds, and so on; by varying the securities in which these funds are invested (for example, by switching from short-dated to long-dated securities) it can change the structure of interest rates. The same kind of operation is involved in funding or unfunding by the Bank of England. It is usual in such operations for the government broker to be instructed to deal at the going rate. If the government chose, it might deliberately raise or lower gilt-edged prices and so force long-term rates of interest down or up; but it could do so only within fairly narrow limits so long as there was a free market in bonds.

The government is far from being in a position to dictate what large-term rates should be.[1]

Post-war experience bears out this conclusion. For a time, a policy of ultra-cheap money was pursued, and the government, quite indefensibly, exerted direct pressure to reduce long-term rates of interest. But it was plain that, in the conditions of post-war years, the rate of interest appropriate to the current shortage of capital could hardly be less than before the war. Bond-holders formed their own judgment of the rate that would rule in the absence of inflation, given the low level of private savings and the high yield on new investment, and the government was unable to maintain the lower long-term rates at which it aimed. Even with a large budget surplus to reinforce private savings, and strict control over the major avenues of capital expenditure (amounting to investment rationing), the government had to bow to the pressure of the market and allow long-term rates to rise.

**(ii) A public works policy**—It is important to distinguish between a public works policy and a programme of relief works. The latter is designed to *create* work, the former to *re-phase* schemes which the government would wish to carry out anyhow, delaying them from boom to slump or accelerating them in a slump. In practice, the distinction is less clear since chronic unemployment may induce a government to expand its programme of construction beyond what it would otherwise have envisaged. In principle, however, the aim of the policy is to time the government's public works programme (covering public utilities, housing, roads, afforestation, etc.) so that more of it is undertaken in the slump and less in the boom. Vacancies are thus created for men in their ordinary employment at the usual rate of wages just when unemployment is most severe.

The objections that used to be urged against such a policy were mainly financial. It was said that the schemes would be needlessly expensive. If the policy operated as intended, however, it would actually save money: so far from raising costs a policy of transference of public works from boom to slump would avoid the high costs of constructional work at the peak of the boom and effect economies at the lower prices ruling in the slump. It was also argued that savings were insufficient in a slump to finance large schemes of public works. But this is to confuse cause and effect. Savings are low in a slump because income is low; and income is low because investment is low. If investment is increased, therefore, income will rise simultaneously, and the savings necessary to finance the new investment will be forthcoming out of the rise in income.

---

[1] See above, p. 398.

The real difficulties are not financial. They are, first of all, diagnostic. Can we rely upon governments to decide on the right moment to put into operation schemes of public works prepared beforehand? May they not be tempted to continue a programme of construction into the boom, through failure to read the signs of a slump to come? Or even to accelerate their programme when prosperity and budget surpluses spread a mood of optimism? May they not, by premature expansion of investment at the first signs of recession, simply restore and intensify boom conditions? Or, in a depression, may they not confuse with normal cyclical unemployment, unemployment which is due to structural changes in industry or to transcyclical shifts in the location of industry, and apply a remedy which, while appropriate to the one, is not necessarily appropriate to the other?

These difficulties extend to all efforts by the government to influence the level of investment or, indeed, of effective demand. But they are aggravated in the case of most forms of public investment by an inevitable lag between the original diagnosis and the time when a decision to check or supplement the flow of work takes effect. Although minor changes can be made fairly quickly, the slowing down of major projects without undue waste or the starting of new ones ahead of earlier plans does not usually offer much scope for variations in investment over the first twelve months or more.

Apart from organisational difficulties, public investment does not lend itself to quick changes. Some kinds of construction simply cannot be postponed (for example, the building of warships or the replacement of condemned bridges); others can be postponed only at the risk of a public outcry (slum clearance, for example); others, again, must, once commenced, be carried through to completion, boom or no boom (major schemes of road improvement, bridge building, the construction of docks, harbours, electric power stations, and so on). Moreover, it is not always easy for a local authority or a central government to foresee its requirements over the next five or ten years, since new duties may be imposed upon it, new types of equipment may become available, and changes may take place in the size and kind of population for which it has to provide. Plans prepared in advance, therefore, may prove to be in need of complete revision just when the government is urging that such plans should be implemented at once.

It is possible also that a policy of public works may fail in its object because its effects are discounted by private enterprise. If business men look on public works as a kind of pick-me-up, creating an "artificial" and temporary prosperity, they will be deterred by fear of the ensuing "headache" from reacting with the same vigour that a so-called "genuine" and spontaneous revival would produce. They will be induced to withhold from the private investment which should replace public works, and which public works are intended to underpin, through fear of a fresh collapse of industrial activity immediately the props which support it are withdrawn. Such perversity, however, is to be expected only in special circumstances—when government policy is half-hearted or does not command the confidence of business men; and when the marginal productivity of capital is so low that the scope for profitable investment by private enterprise is seriously limited in relation to potential savings.

**(iii) Direct control of investment**[1]—Investment may also be regulated by an annual investment "programme" in which the government seeks to plan capital expenditure, keeping it within the limits that the country's savings can support and approving, delaying or rejecting particular projects or groups of projects. This requires an elaborate apparatus of control over the various categories of capital expenditure, a stream of applicants for licenses to engage in such expenditure, and innumerable rulings by the authorities on the priorities to be observed. The control may reach the point—as in Britain immediately after the war—of requiring a licence for the expenditure of as little as £10 on redecorating a house; or it may be limited to large projects of, say, £1 million and over. But whatever the degree of detail, the decisions that are taken are necessarily rather arbitrary and are not left to the discretion of the persons making the investment.

Since a large part of the capital assets of the country are owned by the government and perhaps as much as 40 per cent. of new investment is on government account, it would be necessary in almost any circumstances to prepare some kind of review of projected capital expenditure, whether investment in the private sector was controlled or not. New housing, schools, hospitals, power stations, steelworks, coal mines, aircraft, roads and railways are all in one way or another responsive to government policy; and that policy cannot avoid taking account of the pressure of requirements in the private sector on the building and engineering resources of the country. It might do so by trying to give those requirements full satisfaction and varying government investment to match. But since requirements in the public sector may be just as urgent as those in the private sector, the State is almost inevitably drawn into measures of direct control.

If the State uses direct control it is at once faced with three major difficulties. The first is to ensure that the control is effective. If, for example, too many

---

[1] Although the discussion that follows is in terms of investment by producers it should be remembered that investment in durable goods by consumers can also be made subject to control by the regulation of hire-purchase credit. This control, particularly the regulation of down-payments and rates of repayment, can be highly effective, but it bears on a limited range of industries and may have more serious effects on their efficient operation than comparable fluctuations in the industries making producers' goods.

building licences are issued in relation either to the available building labour, or constructional steel, or timber, the licences will cease to be the limiting factor in investment and the schemes that are able to proceed will be those that get command of enough of the scarce factor (whatever it is) not those that the authorities have adjudged the most urgent. More serious, a great deal of work may be begun and then be held up for lack of men and materials, so leaving all the capital in the work in progress idle at a time when capital itself is unusually scarce. Both of these difficulties will tend to disappear if building materials are not subject to allocation and control at a fixed price but go to the highest bidder or if there is no shortage of them to hold up building work. But so long as there is a maladjustment between licences and real resources there is bound to be confusion and waste.

The second difficulty is that it is much easier to sanction a large scheme than a small. Repairs and alterations to the country's 14 million houses employ about one man in five in the building industry; the building of 200,000 new houses a year employs about the same number of men. But there is no comparison between the amount of administrative time needed to issue houseowners with licenses for maintenance work and to sanction the erection of 200,000 new houses mainly by local authorities. Nor is it a matter only of administrative time and convenience. There is the additional difficulty of forecasting what capital extensions the manufacturers in this or that industry will wish to make and of giving as much weight to their as yet unformulated programme as to the carefully prepared and documented plans of a nationalised industry such as coal-mining or steel. A small pottery may find itself without a building licence because the country's resources are already committed to the construction of a power station included in the programme submitted some years previously by the Electricity Council. The larger programmes submitted have generally the advantage of being more rounded, and of catering for some basic and easily indentifiable need; and they are more spectacular.

Finally, the control is almost inevitably exercised to curtail investment, not to boost it when it is flagging. It works when the danger is inflation but cannot work when the danger is deflation. In a slump there is little or nothing for the control to do except relax and withdraw. It is extremely difficult to keep the control in being against a future boom, and just as difficult to dismantle it and re-erect it all over again when inflation returns.

Some provision can, however, be made for accelerating investment when necessary. A mere relaxation of the control, reducing the queue of unsatisfied applicants, might be sufficient in a moderate recession. The housing programme could be increased by allowing construction to begin earlier on some schemes. The nationalised industries and public utilities could be encouraged to advance

T*

their projects by, say, six months. Many large industrial concerns might be prepared to do the same. Such arrangements could only be made, however, if cut-and-dried schemes had already been prepared and could be speeded up immediately more liberal licensing arrangements were announced. This would not mean that plans were prepared for adoption at some indefinite date and held in cold storage until that date but that one year's programme of capital expenditure would draw on schemes that would otherwise have been included in the following year's programme.

### Conflicting objectives in employment policy

Assuming that the State is able to regulate the pressure of demand to its liking, it has still to reconcile a number of conflicting objectives in the policy which it pursues:

(i) First of all, it has to reconcile full employment with a reasonable degree of stability in the value of money;

(ii) it has to reconcile both of those objectives with a sufficiently high level of investment to allow the economy to take full advantage of the opportunities of growth and development that are open to it;

(iii) it has to balance its international accounts or leave a margin in them that satisfies other objectives such as the need to allow for some growth in reserves of foreign exchange or the desire to contribute to the development of other countries by grants, loans or investments;

(iv) in order to achieve these objectives, it has to prevent the emergence in particular industries or districts of local surpluses and bottlenecks that interfere with the smooth expansion of production and the continued stability of prices.

### (i) Price stability

We have already analysed in some detail the threat to price stability of a rising pressure of demand in conditions approaching full employment.[1] Even in the absence of trade union pressure, costs become inflated at high levels of turnover; and the inflation is likely to gather force as high profits, a rising cost of living, and shortage of labour unite to strengthen the claim of trade unions for higher wages.

Beyond a certain point it is impossible to run the economy at higher pressure without sacrificing stability in prices and the value of money. This does not mean, however, that there is a straight choice between full employment (however defined) and avoidance of inflation (however defined). The alternatives are by no means so clear-cut.

---

[1] Above pp. 426 *et seq.*

First of all, it is a mistake to assume that inflation can continue indefinitely without beginning to disorganise production and reduce the level of employment. The pace of inflation can be held in check and its more damaging effects avoided so long as there is a widespread feeling that it will either come to an end or be brought to an end and can be treated as a temporary affair, not a settled feature of economic life. Once the conviction becomes rooted that it will neither end nor be stopped, and economic calculations begin to treat the future value of money as a variable rather than a fixed quantity, inflation speeds up and what was previously a stimulant becomes a poison. To hold money that is losing its value becomes a luxury and to lend money for repayment in the distant future an act of folly. Unless the rate of interest climbs to extraordinary levels or loans are made in some alternative unit of account, the capital market will cease to function. At the same time production becomes geared, not to the current relationships between prices and costs, but to expectations of the rate at which each will change. Speculation becomes an everyday necessity, and earnings a function of success in guessing the course of prices rather than of making what people want.

No doubt inflation can creep a long way before it begins to gallop; there is no reason for alarm if the pressure of demand becomes relatively intense for short spells of time. But if the pressure is maintained consistently over a long period, the long run effects of such pressure will be on a quite different scale from those that are visible when it is intermittent.

Secondly, the danger of inflation is not a simple function of the pressure of demand but is often more closely related to the rate at which demand is increasing. A slow increase in the level of activity may permit a progressive expansion in employment without inflation when a sharp increase from the same starting-point would make prices rise alarmingly.

Finally, a rise in costs and prices may be held in check in various ways by government action. While some upward drift in workers' earnings and in the cost of materials takes place under the pressure of demand, it is usually when wage-rates and prices begin to chase one another upwards that the danger of inflation becomes acute. If it were possible, therefore, to peg wage-rates, or at least rates in the more important industries, the chances of preserving reasonable stability of prices would be greatly improved. Such a proposal, however, is difficult to reconcile with free collective bargaining between employers and employed. Quite apart from this, it is doubtful whether pegging is practicable for any length of time except in war-time or a similar emergency.

## (ii) Rapid growth and high investment

Given the level of demand necessary to preserve full employment, it is necessary to preserve a balance between the main components of total expenditure and particularly between that part of the total which is designed to provide for current requirements and that part which adds to the productive assets of the community. It is not easy to judge at any time what contribution would be made to the more rapid growth of output if a larger proportion of current income were saved and invested in real assets but where there is clear evidence of a shortage in the sense that this contribution would be perceptible, the State has a responsibility to encourage a high level of investment. This means that it may have to offer tax and other inducements to private industry or prod the nationalised industries to increase the size of their investment programmes. Very often it means no more than that policy should be directed to ensuring that savings are adequate to finance the desired volume of investment—for example, by running a large budget surplus—or that it should be willing to permit borrowing abroad or, if necessary, borrow itself.

The problem is not just one of seeing to it that total investment is high but rather of ensuring that it is high in those sectors of the economy where it is essential to rapid development. It is a mistake, therefore, to treat the problem purely in terms of budget surpluses, foreign borrowing, and so on; encouragement may have to be given to particular forms of investment while others are delayed or discouraged. Policy will also differ according as the areas of heavy investment lie in the public or in the private sector of the economy. In some countries an active investment policy automatically involves the government in raising additional capital, and this may pose awkward financial problems that would take quite a different shape if the capital were being raised by private concerns.

The government, for example, would have to raise the money by the issue of bonds at fixed rates of interest while private industry would be likely to rely mainly on issues of equities. Similarly, in an under-developed country, high investment in the public sector may be particularly urgent in order to improve the transport system and lay the foundation for later development: such investment, in view of the absence of an organised capital market, would be far more likely to lead to foreign borrowing than an equal amount of private investment in, say, commercial property.

**Growth and stagnation**—When the economy is buoyant and markets have been expanding steadily over a long period, it is perhaps natural to assume that there must always be a shortage of capital and that the State should throw its influence on the side of an increase in investment in order to encourage still more rapid growth. But might it not happen in a rich community, given a long interval of peace, that it was impossible to take advantage of the community's thrift and that consumption rather than investment required a special stimulus?

This was a possibility that looked real enough in the thirties when it seemed as if there were few openings for fruitful investment and the very riches that disposed a country to save were proving its undoing in unemployment. In the conditions of that time people were driven to think in terms of a campaign to discourage private saving. Such a campaign is never likely to be very successful. People do not save out of sheer miserliness; they have generally solid reasons grounded on self-interest. For one thing, savings are a ladder—a method of rising to a higher social class; this was perhaps why the Victorians, who respected success, commended thrift. So long as social mobility depends upon saving, habits of thrift are not likely to yield to propaganda.

But savings and investment are no longer matters for private persons only. The State can exercise a major influence on both. If the public is too thrifty the State can be "unthrifty" and let the National Debt take up the public's savings. Similarly with investment. An even larger proportion of investment is undertaken by the State or by bodies prompted or controlled by the State. Thus it is by administrative decision rather than by reference exclusively to interest rates and prospective yields that investment is coming to be determined. This of itself helps to stabilise investment. But it also puts on the State an added responsibility for judging what level of investment is socially desirable in order to maintain stability and at the same time promote further growth.

#### (iii) Preservation of equilibrium in the balance of payments

Some of the most acute dilemmas of policy arise in trying to reconcile the requirements of the domestic situation with the need to maintain external balance. There are three contingencies against which it is particularly necessary to provide: in each case a disturbance in the balance of payments poses a threat to domestic stability. First of all, the country's competitive position may be weakened in relation to that of other countries so that at the current rate of exchange, exports fail to keep pace with imports. Secondly, a sharp recession abroad may reduce the market for exports and throw men out of work, first in the export trades and later in other industries. Thirdly, a movement of capital may drain away the country's reserves without any simultaneous change in the domestic market.

**(a) A decline in competitive power**—The first situation is one that should normally be dealt with by depreciating the currency and holding money incomes steady. Depreciation will help to restore the country's competitive position whether it is deteriorating because of a more rapid increase in prices than in other countries, or because of a less rapid increase in productivity. The fall in the rate of exchange will tend to make exports cheaper abroad and imports dearer at home and so help to bring the two into balance. Since the cost of living will have risen while money-incomes have not, the level of real income will be somewhat reduced (relatively at least to the normal upward trend—it may be sufficient to mark time for a year). If the country seeks to avoid this reduction in real income, depreciation will bring only transitory advantages: money-incomes, including wages, will follow prices up and the competitive advantage of a lower rate of exchange will be wiped out.

The first type of situation may arise, not because of a divergence in costs and prices from costs and prices in other countries, but because of an increase in income and employment. The rate of exchange that keeps exports and imports in balance when unemployment is at 10 per cent. is not likely to be the rate appropriate to conditions of full employment. Even if costs are comparable with costs elsewhere, it may be necessary to make imports less attractive and to give exports an additional stimulus, in order to prevent the increased purchasing power of the home market from flowing too heavily towards imported goods or goods that might be exported.

If a country is unwilling to depreciate under pressure of a persistently adverse balance, it has three possible courses of action. The first is to abandon the struggle to maintain full employment and deflate. This will allow it to bring its accounts into balance at a lower level of activity, with less income, lower imports and more unemployment. This is a desperate solution: but if countries are not prepared in an emergency to accept some check to the growth of real income— such as tends to follow depreciation and an adverse movement in the terms of trade—it is what may easily happen. The second course of action is to live on its reserves and on foreign borrowings in the hope that, given time, the balance of payments will begin to pull round (for example, because the policy of of maintaining full employment bears fruit in increased efficiency). This course is only possible, however, if reserves are large and the country's credit sound. A third line of action is to limit imports by quotas or "quantitative restrictions." These restrictions, so long as they do not react on exports, will reduce the payments to be made to other countries without any need to alter the relative price of imports and exports. The government simply decides that the country can no longer afford to buy certain things (or more than a certain amount of them) and takes steps to prevent them from entering the country. There are important disadvantages to this way of putting things right. It inflicts an arbitrary injury on the trade of other countries and may provoke retaliation. It is obviously not very appropriate if the root of the trouble is that the country's prices are getting steadily out of line with prices abroad, so that more and more imports would have to be restricted or banned in an effort to make ends meet. It does, however, provide a powerful instrument to reinforce either or both of the first two courses of action.

**(b) A decline in demand abroad**—The first type of situation is dangerous because of the financial pressure which it exerts; the second type of situation does not merely threaten unemployment but causes it.[1] Workers lose their jobs in the export industries and if no action is taken unemployment will spread to industries making for the home market. The action that the State can take depends first on the state of its reserves. If it has large reserves it can ignore the loss of foreign exchange as its exports fall, and create additional purchasing power without fear that this will aggravate an already serious balance of payments problem. If it has only moderate or low reserves it will not be able to pursue an expansionist policy without first restricting imports. The quickest way of restricting imports is by quantitative limitation. In a major depression this is one of the weapons that the State will almost inevitably use, but it is a weapon to be used with care. If every country uses quantitative restrictions, each will merely add to the others' difficulties; but if the restrictions are concentrated on imports from countries with a large favourable balance (while other countries are exempt) this will help to bring creditors and debtors more quickly into balance and allow the debtors to maintain trade with one another instead of being obliged to make cuts over the whole of their trade. Such discrimination against the countries with a credit balance, however, is not likely to be welcomed in those countries, especially if they are already wrestling with unemployment problems of their own. It will be desirable to have their agreement to such discrimination on the grounds that, since they are free from balance of payments anxieties, they are in the best position to pursue an expansionist policy. By pressing on with such a policy, they can give international trade an upward thrust that will help to remove the grounds for discrimination against them.

The scope for quantitative limitations depend upon the structure of a country's imports and the controls over consumption that it already uses or could institute. It is not necessarily sufficient, for example, to stop importing luxuries, for these may be a small fraction of the total or obtained from countries that would have no option but to retaliate if their markets were cut off. It may be necessary to limit imports of foodstuffs and ration them; or to allocate imported raw materials. A further problem arises from the supposed temporary character of the slump in exports. Quantitative restrictions are protective and, like tariffs,

---

[1] On the importance of this type of situation see above, pp. 404–5.

are easier to impose than to remove. When the slump ends, an assortment of new industries may have come into being under cover of arrangements originally designed to effect an emergency cut in imports. Fresh arrangements (e.g., higher tariffs) may confirm these industries in the protection they enjoy, and as they are not likely to be export industries, international trade will undergo an enduring contraction.

**(c) An outflow of capital**—There may be an outflow of short or long-term capital, involving a transfer from sterling (to take the example of Britain) to other currencies. The outflow may be due to distrust of sterling or it may be due to higher rates of interest or higher yields on investment abroad. Where the cause is lack of confidence a rise in interest rates will help to check the outflow only to the extent that higher interest rates are interpreted as a demonstration that the authorities will take decisive action to maintain the value of the currency. Where the cause is a disparity in the return on capital, however, a rise in interest rates can remove the disparity and stop the outflow. The disadvantage of such a remedy is that it condemns the monetary authorities to aligning their rates with rates in foreign money markets when credit conditions in Britain may make it appropriate to pursue a different policy. There may be good reasons for not making money dearer in Britain when rates are rising abroad.

It might seem that an easier solution would be to control capital movements. In fact, however, control is by no means easy. Quite apart from any evasion of regulations, there is always a large volume of commercial credit outstanding in favour of exporters or due by importers, and if there is any distrust of sterling or large differential in interest rates between London and other centres there is no obstacle to an acceleration of payments in one direction and a delay of payments in the other ("leads and lags") so as to increase the net credit due in foreign currencies.[1] This increase represents a net loss to the reserves since more foreign exchange has to be paid out and less is paid in. There is presumably some limit to a shift of commercial credit of this kind but it can be sufficiently large to alarm other holders of sterling and start off a withdrawal of banking and other funds held in London.

While there are various technical devices by which credit policy can be to some extent insulated from credit policy in the other leading financial centres, the fact remains that so long as there is any freedom of movement of international

---

[1] British importers will make payments more promptly in sterling because they expect foreign currencies to become dearer and exporters will delay bringing back earnings of foreign exchange for the same reason. An interest differential exercises a similar effect by bringing more bills for discount to the London market and inducing holders of London funds to move them elsewhere.

credit and capital, a persistent movement in interest rates in one centre restricts the freedom of action of the authorities in other centres, particularly if they maintain fixed rates of exchange. The simplest method by which they could add to the latitude they enjoy in credit policy would be to widen slightly the present narrow margin between buying and selling rates for foreign exchange.[1]

**The need for international action**—All this is on the assumption that each country has to act on its own and that the risks of trade depression are as great as ever in spite of pledges, plans, and controls. If the major countries can take joint action, however, their problems can be greatly eased. Two or three countries have it in their power, by maintaining stability in their own economy, to make full employment an attainable goal for most of the others; if the big countries fail, the others will almost certainly fail, too. It may be, as a group of international economists have suggested, that each country should be made to pay some penalty if it fails to maintain a steady level of activity; and that if it reduces its imports below some datum line it should make a loan (through the I.M.F.) to the countries that find themselves in balance of payments difficulties in consequence.[2] It may be simpler to offer I.M.F. credits to deficit countries that are hit by a world slump and to permit discrimination on an organised basis against countries that run large and persistent surpluses. The efforts of international agencies and concerted action by the leading countries can do more to remove the danger of unemployment than the single-handed efforts of each.

### (iv) Avoidance of bottlenecks

The greater the pressure of demand, the greater the danger that it will bear unevenly on the available resources and create acute shortages in some directions while there are still surpluses in others. In such a situation, there may be demands for higher wages based on the shortage of labour in some areas and industries while localised unemployment persists in others. There are likely also to be sharp increases in the prices of some products which may threaten

---

[1] The present margin in sterling-dollar rates is 2·78–2·82. Suppose that the margin were doubled and that rates in the United States were 1 per cent. higher than in the United Kingdom. A transfer of funds could be made unattractive by letting the pound depreciate. When the rate fell to 2·77, i.e., 1 per cent. below par, the loss of interest would be balanced by the prospect of subsequent appreciation. In practice, what would govern the movement of funds would be the forward, not the spot, rate for sterling; it would require a margin of 1 per cent. between the spot and forward rates to offset (mathematically) the difference in interest rates. Without pursuing all the complications that the suggestion involves, we need only observe that the wider the margin between buying and selling rates, the larger the possible forward premium over the spot rate.

[2] *National and International Measures for Full Employment* (United Nations, 1950).

the stability of prices generally. To allow demand to increase further would be to intensify the lack of balance in the economy without initially absorbing the surpluses. What is required in such circumstances is action to divert demand away from the bottlenecks to products for which there is still some unused capacity and to districts in which there are pockets of unemployed labour.

Such action is not easy; and without some leverage from the price-mechanism it is likely to be futile. A rise in prices where there is a bottleneck helps to divert the demand of consumers to substitute products and a rise in costs in districts where labour is scarce helps to direct orders more quickly to other districts. It is a mistake, therefore, to try to prevent *any* response of this kind in relative prices. But there is little to be gained and a great deal to be lost if the swing in prices and costs is violent. If the lack of balance seems unlikely to be enduring, the government, being itself a large consumer, may be able to switch some of its orders so as to relieve the pressure or it may allow or encourage additional imports for the same purpose. If the lack of balance appears to be more deep-rooted, it can offer financial and other inducements to firms that are prepared to create capacity in the appropriate areas and industries. In dealing with localised unemployment it can offer to build factories on behalf of firms willing to establish themselves in the areas affected and limit factory-building else-where. In the same way, it can try to alleviate industrial bottlenecks by en-couraging or subsidising expansions in capacity. But no *quick* results can gener-ally be hoped for from intervention along any of these lines and the total result, even in the long run, is often disappointing.

**Localised unemployment due to a fall in exports**—The heaviest unemployment that Britain has suffered in the past half century has been concentrated in her export industries. Had those industries been diffused over different parts of the country and made use of a wide range of skill and technical experience, much of this unemployment might have been made to yield to a gen-eral increase in the level of demand accompanied by restrictions on imports. Some exporting firms would have been able to bid for home market orders in place of exports orders and some workers would have moved to local firms making for the home market. In fact, however, the export industries were highly localised and highly specialised, and this reduced the effectiveness of a general increase in demand. To take an extreme case: it was of little help to unemployed ship-building workers in Glasgow, if people spent their extra earnings on beer, or, for that matter, on imported meat. There is a further dilemma. If the State decides that shipbuilding workers *must* be found employment in some other industry, it may incur the cost of re-training, moving and perhaps re-housing them (or of building new factories in the Glasgow district) only to find a little later that the shipbuilding industry is short of labour and that, with valuable export orders accumulating it cannot carry them out.

There is no simple way out of this dilemma. Something might be done to offset a temporary decline in exports by placing larger government contracts in the exporting areas; but it is not easy to delay or accelerate the placing of a large contract or to find another supplier who can meet the exact specifications. Something might also be done by adapting the government's investment programme to provide more work in the export areas and the export industries. The main firms in those industries might be assisted to develop some ancillary technique capable of expansion if the primary activity of the firm were depressed. When exports fell off, working hours might be reduced in selected industries, the cost of the reduction being shared between worker, employer and State; this would help to keep the existing labour force together and avoid unemployment. Finally, measures could be taken to improve labour mobility by more extensive facilities for re-training and transfer. It is difficult to predict what success such action might have. But if, by additional public expenditure, vacancies were created at some points in the economy it should at least prove easier to make the necessary adjustments than it was when the export industries and other industries moved downwards together into a depression.

# SOURCES OF BRITISH ECONOMIC STATISTICS

For long runs of annual statistics readers should consult:

*Abstract of Historical Statistics*, by B. R. Mitchell and Phyllis Deane. Cambridge University Press, 1962. 52s. 6d.

*The British Economy. Key Statistics 1900–1964*. Times Publishing Co. 6s.

Of these the first covers a much longer period than the second; similar volumes of *Historical Statistics* have been issued for a number of other countries such as the U.S.A. and Canada. *Key Statistics 1900–1964* contains a large number of leading series of statistics in common use. These series are kept up-to-date in the *London and Cambridge Economic Bulletin* published quarterly in *The Times*.

For more recent years the most comprehensive annual and monthly series of official statistics appear in:

*Annual Abstract of Statistics*

*Monthly Digest of Statistics*

The national accounts for the United Kingdom are published in:

*National Income and Expenditure* (usually referred to as the Blue Book and issued in the autumn).

*Preliminary Estimates of National Income and Balance of Payments* (a Red—or Pink—Book which like the Blue Book usually covers a span of about a decade).

*Economic Trends* (monthly)

The last of these gives the latest available *quarterly* national accounts (which also appear in the *Monthly Digest of Statistics*) together with a commentary. An official commentary, not on the statistics, but on the economic changes in progress, is published annually just before the Budget in:

*Economic Report*

Unofficial and less inhibited commentaries are included in two important quarterly publications:

The *Economic Review* of the National Institute of Economic and Social Research

*London and Cambridge Economic Bulletin*

Among other official and semi-official sources of British economic statistics, the following are important for financial, regional and man-power data:

*Financial Statistics* (monthly)

*Bank of England Statistical Summary* (quarterly)

*Abstract of Regional Statistics* (annual)

*Statistics on Incomes, Prices, Employment and Production* (quarterly)

For international statistics the most useful sources are:

*United Nations Statistical Year Book*

*United Nations Monthly Bulletin of Statistics*

*O.E.C.D. General Statistical Bulletin*

# INDEX

© 

BUTTERWORTH & CO. (PUBLISHERS) LTD.
1966

Printed in Great Britain by
Page Bros. (Norwich) Ltd., Norwich